PROFESSIONAL PERSONAL SELLING

PROFESSIONAL
PERSONAL SELLING

Rolph Anderson

Drexel University

PRENTICE HALL
Englewood Cliffs, New Jersey 07632

Library of Congress Cataloging-in-Publication Data

Anderson, Rolph E.
    Professional personal selling / Rolph Anderson.
        p.   cm.
    Includes bibliographical references and indexes.
    ISBN 0-13-725615-9
    1. Selling.   2. Sales personnel.   I. Title.
HF5438.25.A525   1991
658.8'5—dc20   90-47134
                                                  CIP

*For her lifelong inspiration, this book is
dedicated to my mother, Susanna James
Anderson, and to my talented and
understanding spouse, Sallie, and our two
delightful children, Rachel and Stuart.*

Editorial/production supervision: Eleanor Perz
Cover design and interior design: Aurora Graphics
Cover photo: The Image Bank
Photo editor: Rona Tuccillo
Photo research: Teri Stratford
Page layout: Karen Noferi
Manufacturing buyers: Trudy Pisciotti/Bob Anderson

© 1991 by Prentice-Hall, Inc.
A Division of Simon & Schuster
Englewood Cliffs, New Jersey 07632

Printed in the United States of America
10   9   8   7   6   5   4   3   2   1

ISBN 0-13-725615-9

Prentice-Hall International (UK) Limited, *London*

Prentice-Hall of Australia Pty. Limited, *Sydney*

Prentice-Hall Canada Inc., *Toronto*

Prentice-Hall Hispanoamericana, S.A., *Mexico*

Prentice-Hall of India Private Limited, *New Delhi*

Prentice-Hall of Japan, Inc., *Tokyo*

Prentice-Hall of Southeast Asia Pte. Ltd., *Singapore*

Editora Prentice-Hall do Brasil, Ltda., *Rio de Janeiro*

Brief Contents

Contents

Chapter 7
Communicating With Customers 196

PART THREE
PREPARING FOR SUCCESS IN PERSONAL SELLING

Chapter 8
Personal Preparation for Sales Success 236

Chapter 9
Understanding the Company, Products, Competition, and Markets 268

PART FOUR
THE PROFESSIONAL SELLING PROCESS

Chapter 10
Prospecting and Qualifying Prospects 300

Chapter 13
Negotiating Sales Resistance and Objections 408

Chapter 14
Confirming and Closing the Sale 446

CONTENTS

Preface

A TEXTBOOK FOR A NEW GENERATION
OF PROFESSIONAL SALESPEOPLE

Personal selling is changing dramatically! Revolutionary developments in communications and computer technology, rising customer expectations for product quality and services, the influx of women and minorities into selling and sales management, expanding use of direct marketing methods to sell to consumers, microsegmentation of multicultural markets in the United States, intense foreign competition, and the globalization of markets are bringing about remarkable changes in the ways that professional salespeople do their jobs—and the ways that they and other people perceive personal selling.

To enable salespeople of today and tomorrow deal successfully with these extraordinary developments, a fresh approach is needed for the study of personal selling. Sales theory and training in college and university classrooms are right now being raised to a level that corresponds with the high standards that today's well-educated and highly motivated professionals aspire to. *Professional Personal Selling* seeks to aid the college instructor in achieving this goal.

WHAT IS PROFESSIONAL ABOUT
PROFESSIONAL PERSONAL SELLING?

Some old stereotypes die hard, and perhaps none harder than the stereotype of the manipulative, back-slapping salesman trying to pull the wool over yet another customer's eyes. Vestiges of this stereotype persist even today, mostly in the attitudes and jokes of people who have never met or do not adequately understand the work of professional sales representatives. College instructors who regularly teach a selling course have long been aware that their institutions often view personal selling courses as little more than vocational training for jobs in door-to-door, retail, or other types of direct-to-consumer selling. Unfortunately, even the majority of the textbooks at their disposal reflect this bias—even though direct marketing methods like telemarketing, automatic vending, direct mail, and television home shopping have all but completely replaced many forms of basic consumer selling. These instructors realize that young men and women graduating from two-year and four-year colleges are not likely to start their sales careers in jobs like this.

Professional Personal Selling speaks to a generation of students who will most likely represent organizations that sell to other organizations. *Organizational selling,* which involves "field" selling to commercial firms, nonprofits, and government agencies, requires salespeople who are not only smart and well educated, but also well trained in specialized product areas. These salespeople are sales and marketing experts, businesspeople who manage a part of their company's business in the field and keep abreast of the latest developments for the products and services not only in their own companies but in their industries in general. This is what we mean by *professional.*

In line with the reality of today's sales environment, every chapter of *Professional Personal Selling* provides special pedagogical features to illustrate modern sales practices and techniques. Chapter-opening profiles of successful salespeople and the "Company Highlight," "Selling in Action," and "What Would You Do?" boxes bring the exciting world of professional personal selling into the classroom. The end of each chapter also features comprehensive review and study materials, as well as two well-written, thought-provoking cases.

THE MANY ROLES OF PROFESSIONAL SALESPEOPLE

Now more then ever, companies big and small make it their first priority to recruit, train, and generously compensate a field sales force consisting of professional businesspeople with broad knowledge and diverse capabilities in their chosen industries. The typical professional salesperson today acts as a *field marketing manager* who sells and markets the company's product in the field while managing a vital segment of the company's business. The professional salesperson uses the latest communications and computer technology simultaneously to coordinate and integrate field selling activities with headquarters marketing efforts and to improve effectiveness and efficiency in serving customers in long-run buyer-seller partnerships.

Professional Personal Selling seeks to increase student interest in sales careers by realistically depicting the many roles that professional salespeople play as the most visible representatives of their companies to customer companies.

As field marketing managers, today's sales representatives are *team coordinators* of company specialists from engineering, operations, inventory control, transportation, finance, accounting, and customer services who work together to solve customer problems.

They are *revenue generators* for their organizations, maintaining that critical frontline, face-to-face contact with prospects and customers—where the seller organization's fate is ultimately decided.

They are *sales forecasters,* helping their sales managers estimate future sales and set sales quotas in their assigned territories. Continuously seeking out market opportunities, they are sensitive to unsatisfied or even unrecognized customer needs calling for new products or services and innovative marketing mixes.

They are *market researchers* who understand and utilize industrial information and market research findings to improve their sales presentations and better satisfy present and potential customers.

They are *intelligence gatherers*—the "eyes and ears" of their companies in the field—who are alert and diligent in providing feedback information from their territories to headquarters marketing for new-product development and strategic planning purposes.

They are *scarce product allocators* who seek to be perceived by customers as efficient and fair in allocating products and services that are in short supply.

And perhaps most important, today's professional salespeople are *customer service representatives* whose companies often expect them to be advocates for their customers. Before making an approach, they carefully discover each prospect's unique needs and concerns and work toward not only what's best for their own companies, but what's best for their customers' companies, too.

THE BOOK'S FEATURES, ADVANTAGES, AND BENEFITS

Professional Personal Selling offers students and instructors of personal selling many specific features, advantages, and benefits, including:

- The most colorful, creative format and design layout of any personal selling textbook currently available.
- "Real world" applications of the latest communications and computer technology to personal selling (every chapter, especially Chapters 2 and 7).
- Clear, early focus on ethical issues and decision making for the professional salesperson (Chapter 3).
- Strong emphasis on integration of field sales and headquarters marketing activities (especially Chapter 4).
- Insightful coverage of the buying process and purchase decision influences for both consumers and organizations (Chapters 5 and 6).
- Thorough treatment of how to develop effective communication skills and negotiate "win–win" agreements (Chapter 7).
- Explanations of the special challenges and opportunities in international personal selling (Chapters 2 and 13).
- An inspirational chapter on self-evaluation and personal preparation for success in personal selling (Chapter 8).
- Exciting analysis of the Selling Process as it needs to be understood in today's business environment (Chapters 11–15).
- Chapter-opening profiles and helpful advice from contemporary salespeople (every chapter).
- Intriguing explanations of progressive company selling concepts, strategies, and practices that will awaken students to the exciting possibilities of a sales management or marketing career beginning with personal selling (Chapters 1 and 9).
- The latest techniques for managing the sales territory (Chapter 16) and the sales force (Chapter 17).
- Two interesting and challenging cases after each chapter to stimulate student thinking and understanding of major concepts in modern personal selling.
- Comprehensive chapter-end materials (summaries, review questions, topics for thought and class discussion, projects for personal growth, key terms, and cases).
- Running key terms and chapter-end and book-end glossaries.
- Complete set of ancillary teaching materials for instructors, including a comprehensive *Instructor's Manual* with detailed chapter outlines and full-color transparencies from both the text and outside sources.

- Comprehensive test bank of 50 multiple-choice questions, 25 true–false, and 10 essay questions per chapter plus many term paper project suggestions.
- ABC videos featuring topics relevant to personal selling.
- *The New York Times* A Contemporary View program.
- Lively and clear writing style blending the latest findings from research and "real world" practice.
- A special appendix titled "Starting Your Professional Personal Selling Career" that shows students how to use the professional personal selling process to sell their services to potential employers.

A Contemporary View of Sales Marketing

The New York Times and *Prentice Hall* are sponsoring A Contemporary View, a program designed to enhance student access to current information of relevance in the classroom.

Through this program, the core subject matter provided in the text is supplemented by a collection of time-sensitive articles from one of the world's most distinguished newspapers, *The New York Times*. These articles demonstrate the vital, ongoing connection between what is learned in the classroom and what is happening in the world around us.

So that students can enjoy the wealth of information in *The New York Times* daily, a reduced subscription rate is available. For information, call toll-free: 1-800-631-1222.

Prentice Hall and *The New York Times* are proud to co-sponsor A Contemporary View. We hope it will make the reading of both textbooks and newspapers a more dynamic, involving process.

ABOUT THE AUTHOR

Rolph Anderson is professor and head of the Department of Marketing at Drexel University. He earned his Ph.D. from the University of Florida, and his M.B.A. and B.A. degrees from Michigan State University. Dr. Anderson's research has been widely published in the major professional journals in his field, and he received the 1988 Mu Kappa Tau award for the best paper published in the *Journal of Personal Selling and Sales Management.* He is the co-author of six textbooks, including: *Multivariate Data Analysis,* Second Edition, *Professional Sales Management,* and *Professional Personal Selling.* He is also a member of several editorial boards, including the *Journal of Personal Selling and Sales Management* and the *Journal of Marketing Channels.* Professor Anderson has served several professional organizations as an officer: President, Southeast Institute for Decision Sciences; Secretary, Academy of Marketing Science; Board of Directors and Vice-President for Programming, American Marketing Association (Philadelphia Chapter); and Co-Chairperson, Sixty-First American Marketing Association Conference. Prior to entering academia, he worked for three Fortune 500 companies, and in his last position was New Product Development Manager for the Quaker Oats Company. Married and the father of two children, Dr. Anderson is listed in *Who's Who in America*.

ACKNOWLEDGEMENTS

Writing a college textbook is a long-term team effort that depends on contributions from a great many talented people. First, I am deeply grateful for the valuable comments and suggestions of these reviewers: Gordon Badovick, University of Wisconsin/Oshkosh; Michael Cicero, Highline Community College; Lucette Comer, Florida International University; Kenneth A. East, Delaware Technical and Community College; Joan K. Hall, Macomb Community College; Carol Harvey, Assumption College; and Delbert A. Shepard, University of Northern Iowa.

James T. Strong of the University of Akron, Paul F. Christ of Delaware Valley College, and Lisa Houde of Drexel University deserve special recognition for writing several excellent case studies and chapter-end questions. I would also like to thank Khalid Dubas of St. John's University, Dominic Nucera of IBM Corporation, Bert Brodo of the University of Pennsylvania, Ralph Day of Day & Gibeon Consulting Services, and Russell Lavery, Norman Leebron, Lawrence Colfer, David Hawsey, Diane Mollenkopf, Anurag Hingarani, Rajiv Mehta, and Mary Rhein, all of Drexel University, for their insights about this text. Paul E. Dascher, dean of Drexel's College of Business and Administration, provided generous support and encouragement.

Fresh, "real-world" materials for *Professional Personal Selling* were provided by many companies, and the following deserve special mention: Chemineer, Inc., Colgate-Palmolive Company, Dale Carnegie & Associates, Inc., The Dun & Bradstreet Corporation, E.I. du Pont de Nemours & Company, Eastman Kodak Company, Hewlett-Packard Company, NCR Corporation, NYNEX Company, Pierangeli Group, Inc., Rohm and Haas Company, ROLM Company, and Thomas Publishing Company.

Finally, I want to express my deep appreciation to the talented Prentice Hall team who helped bring *Professional Personal Selling* into being, especially Thom Moore (College Editorial Development) who read every word of the manuscript and made countless suggestions for the book's improvement. Invaluable support and guidance were provided by Chris Treiber, Dennis Hogan, and Chris's assistant, Dina Vaz (College Editorial). Eleanor Perz and Jeanne Hoeting (College Production), Lorinda Morris-Nantz, Teri Stratford, and Rona Tuccillo (Photo Research), Janet Schmid and Dawn Stanley (Design and Art), and Trudy Pisciotti and Bob Anderson (Manufacturing) were wonderfully thorough and painstaking despite a tight schedule. I have never worked with more talented, enthusiastic, and professional people.

R.A.

Chapter 1

Professional Selling

Everyone lives by selling something.

ROBERT LOUIS STEVENSON

"MOST of my curriculum in college was chemistry-related. I did, however, obtain a concentration in management, which proved valuable for my transition to sales," says Kathleen Herron, a sales representative for Rohm and Haas, the well-known chemical company based in Philadelphia. Like many industrial sales reps who started out with their companies as researchers, engineers, or technicians, Kathleen responded to an internal company posting for a sales position. "Having started out in Rohm and Haas Research, I felt sales was the best bet for launching a career in the 'business' end of the company."

Although she felt comfortable in her new position after only about six months, Kathleen's sales training lasted a full two years. She continues: "This included hands-on experience in marketing, research, and manufacturing. Time was also allocated for travel with experienced sales reps. Training time can vary, since it depends on the availability of territories." Kathleen quickly learned that Rohm and Haas sales are neither immediate nor one-shot deals. "We have long-standing relationships with our customers. In fact, most of my accounts are on contract. We are constantly servicing them with technical, safety, and handling information and presentations. Our customer service people work closely with our customers to provide quality shipments of product."

When we asked Kathleen about her sales presentation style, she stressed the importance of taking some time immediately before a sales call to review information about the prospect or customer—buyer and manager names, company purchase history and procedures, and her own objectives for the call—and then getting right to the point in the sales call: "I always try to spend 15 to 30 minutes before each sales call to review exactly what I want to achieve in that sales call. I've found that carefully choosing (and thus limiting) my objectives helps me have a more successful call. A clear, concise presentation style works best for me, and I always try to accommodate the customer's agenda."

Profile

Kathleen Herron

Kathleen is not interested in selling as a lifelong career, but is excited about the opportunity that a sales position offers to gain broad experience for future career goals. "Typically, at Rohm and Haas, people move in and out of different positions in the business units (sales, purchasing, marketing, production/operations, and so on.) There are a variety of career paths available to salespeople at Rohm and Haas, including marketing, purchasing, and sales management. It is also possible to achieve management levels staying in sales. I have been in sales two years. I expect next year either to move to a higher-level territory or to move back to our corporate office as a marketing specialist. I expect to have a management-level position in nine years."

Like her company, Kathleen Herron has a philosophy of gradual, steady growth and improvement. She readily admits that sales has occasional moments of frustration. "However, when things do work out in Rohm and Haas's favor, it's a really great feeling. You get a sense of accomplishment, and it certainly boosts your confidence. In sales, confidence is everything!" ■

After reading this chapter, you should understand:

- How yesterday's salesperson and today's professional salesperson differ

- What roles professional salespeople play in providing customer satisfaction within the framework of the marketing concept

- Many of the opportunities and advantages offered by a professional sales career

- The multiple career paths branching out from an initial job in personal selling

✻ Look up Marketing concept.

PROFESSIONAL PERSONAL SELLING: A NEW LOOK

One of the most exciting, rewarding, and dynamic of all possible careers is professional personal selling. It's also one of the most misunderstood, overlooked, and underrated career fields. What thoughts come to mind when you hear the term *salesperson*? Do you think of fast-talking caricatures in comic strips like "Blondie" or carnival pitchmen saying "Because I like ya . . . tell ya what I'm gonna do" or perhaps pathetic Willy Loman in Arthur Miller's play *Death of a Salesman*? Do you think of door-to-door salespeople with their foot in the door spouting spiels about encyclopedias or cosmetics? If these are your images of the salesperson, you're in for a real surprise as you learn about the exciting career opportunities and challenges in professional selling today.

Myth of the Born Salesperson

Yesterday's smiling, back-slapping, dirty-joke-telling salesmen (yes, they were mostly men) who sold on personal magnetism have all but disappeared. No longer can the bubbly personality armed with a quick wit and a few clever sales techniques make a successful career in sales. Pushiness, brashness, and puffery have given way to polished, well-trained professionalism that recognizes that today's customer wants to deal with salespeople who are honest, trustworthy, competent, and service-oriented. Most of today's sales practitioners and scholars view personal selling as either an art or a discipline to be learned. Most realistically, personal selling is a mixture of art and discipline. Some observers, however, express strong opinions one way or another about the nature of personal selling. Steve Bostic, former chief executive officer of American Photo Group, which topped the 1987 INC. 500 for growth, going from sales of $149,000 to $78 million in five years, says:

> Some people have more natural ability than others, but selling is not an art. It's a discipline. There's a specific selling process you have to go through, and anyone can learn it. It involves taking all the different steps, reducing them to a checklist, and then executing them one by one. There's no magic to it, and you don't need a lot of natural talent. What you need is a disciplined, organized approach to selling. If

Lee J. Cobb helped immortalize the character of the unhappy travelling salesman Willy Loman in Arthur Miller's Pulitzer prize-winning play *Death of a Salesman* (1949).

2

you have that, you'll outperform the great salesperson who doesn't understand the process every time. Selling can definitely be learned.[1]

Who Sells?

SELLING The use of persuasive communication to negotiate mutually beneficial agreements.

Selling, whether one considers it an art or a discipline, involves the use of persuasive communication to negotiate mutually beneficial agreements. It is at the heart of nearly all our relationships with other people. Although we concentrate on commercial selling situations in this book, the concepts and techniques we discuss apply to negotiating agreements in all areas of life, including business, school, social, and family relationships. The thing being sold may be a product, a service, an idea, an opinion, or a special point of view. As a youngster, you may have sold your lawn mowing services to neighbors or you may have sold candy to raise money for a school activity. Today you may be working part-time as a shoe salesperson or a real estate representative. Or you may be trying to cajole your parents into letting you go to Florida during the spring break. Perhaps you're attempting to convince one of your friends to loan you $50 for the upcoming weekend. Maybe you're trying to sell your boss on giving you a raise or a few days off. You may be struggling to induce that special person in your math class to go out with you. In all of these situations, you're using your knowledge of people and their needs to negotiate an agreement or commitment through persuasive communication. In other words, you're selling!

Selling Is Universal

Learning selling principles will improve anyone's chances for success in virtually any field.[2] It's been said that "All professionals must be good salespeople, and all good salespeople must be professional."

More than 11 million Americans sell to business organizations and consumers. (Even this huge number is understated because virtually every occupation involves an element of personal selling.) Professional selling ranges from the retail salesperson selling televisions in a department store to the industrial sales representative selling photocopiers to manufacturers to the stockbroker selling mutual funds to individual investors. We will focus on those professional sales representatives who consider personal selling either a lifelong career or a vital experience leading to a management career.

A Great Place to Start

Among entry-level positions, sales is one of the most open to college graduates. About 15 percent of all college graduates start out in selling jobs. At some companies sales experience is a prerequisite for advancement into managerial ranks. Many chief executive officers of Fortune 500 corporations began their careers as sales representatives. Billionaire H. Ross Perot, a former top salesman for IBM who became CEO of Electronic Data Systems, says: "I sold Christmas cards and garden seeds in Texarkana, Texas. At the age of 12, I peddled newspapers in a

---

[1]"Thriving on Order," *INC.*, December 1989, p. 49.
[2]John T. Molloy, *Molloy's Live for Success* (New York: Bantam Books, 1983), p. 87.

poor section of town filled with flophouses. I never thought of doing anything besides selling."[3]

Sales is a great place to start for almost any managerial career. When recently promoted executives were surveyed about which entry field they would choose if they had to start over, their most frequent response was "sales and marketing."[4]

Let's take a look at how personal selling became such an integral part of American business.

PERSONAL SELLING: YESTERDAY AND TODAY

A famous poster from the John Hancock Mutual Life Insurance Company describes the early American salesman this way:

> He came on muleback, dodging Indians as he went, with a pack full of better living and a tongue full of charms. For he was the great American salesman, and no man ever had a better thing to sell.
>
> He came by rickety wagon, one jump behind the pioneers, carrying axes for the farmer, fancy dress goods for his wife, and encyclopedias for the farmer's ambitious boy. For he was the great practical democrat, spreader of good things among more and more people.
>
> He came by upper berth and dusty black coupe, selling tractors and radios, iceboxes and movies, health and leisure, ambition and fulfillment. For he was America's emissary of abundance, Mr. High-Standard-of-Living in person.
>
> He rang a billion doorbells and enriched a billion lives. Without him, there'd be no American ships at sea, no busy factories, no 60 million jobs. For the great American salesman is the great American civilizer, and everywhere he goes he leaves people better off.[5]

Selling in Early America

YANKEE PEDDLER
Colonial American salesman who picked up goods from English merchants and colonial manufacturers and transported them throughout the colonies for sale to settlers.

During colonial times, **Yankee peddlers** were used by English merchants and small manufacturers along the East Coast to sell goods in the American colonies. These peddlers picked up goods from English ships, then lugged them on horseback or in backpacks across the wilderness. After crude trails were laid out, the peddlers drove carts and horse-drawn wagons filled with such frontier family essentials as weapons, nails, needles and pins, dishes, cloth, and patent medicines. These dauntless peddlers usually began their travels in early spring and did not return home until late summer. As the colonists moved westward, the Yankee peddlers set up trading posts and general stores—the first retail stores—in settlements with large populations.

In the early 1800s, manufacturers and wholesalers hired investigators to collect overdue bills from customers and verify creditworthiness. These **credit**

---

[3]Stephanie Bernardo, Elizabeth Meryman, Hanna Rubin, and Judith D. Schwartz, "Superstars of Selling," *Success*" November 1984, pp. 34–35.

[4]Floyd A. Bond, Herbert W. Hildebrand, Edwin L. Miller, and Alfred W. Swinyard, *The Newly Promoted Executive: A Study in Corporate Leadership, 1981–1982* (Ann Arbor, Mich.; University of Michigan, Division of Research, Graduate School of Business Administration, 1982), p. 14.

[5]John Hancock Mutual Life Insurance Company poster.

CREDIT INVESTIGATOR
Early-nineteenth-century
investigator hired by
manufacturers and
wholesalers to collect
overdue bills from
customers and verify
creditworthiness; often
also sold goods.

**GREETERS AND
DRUMMERS**
Early-nineteenth-century
salespeople hired by
suppliers to meet and
entertain retail merchants;
worked on commission.

investigators often sold goods en route to their destinations. Eventually, bill collection and credit investigation were taken over by financial agencies and the credit investigators were retained for selling only.

Also in the early 1800s, retail merchants began to visit large East Coast wholesalers about twice a year to select from the latest merchandise. The wholesale suppliers hired **greeters and drummers**—so called because they banged on drums—to meet and entertain these visiting retailers and introduce them to the suppliers. Today we still speak of "drumming up business." Instead of paying the greeters and drummers a set fee, the suppliers gave them a portion of the profit from each transaction, a practice that resembled today's payment of sales commissions. After 1860, railroad transportation and the telegraph opened up travel and communication with the West, and traveling salesmen (called "commercial travelers") helped nurture economic development and improve standards of living all across the country.

Evolution of Personal Selling Approaches

Selling approaches in the United States have evolved through at least four general eras of business philosophy: the *Pioneer Era,* the *Production Era,* the *Sales Era,* and the *Marketing Era.* Although these eras are only approximate and overlap, it is worthwhile to think about business philosophy in terms of eras in order to better understand the development of selling in North America.

Pioneer Era, 1650–1800
In pioneering days, products were scarce and people had to barter and trade to get the necessities of life such as salt, nails, tools, and cloth. This era was dominated by traders and merchants who ventured across the wilds of the New World to sell their wares. Traveling salespeople in pioneer days were welcome and often invited to stay overnight with the families to whom they sold, for they carried interesting news from other parts of the country. The legendary Johnny Appleseed was one of these early peddlers who trudged across the country by foot and horseback selling pots and pans (though he seems to have found time to plant apple trees wherever he went).

Production Era, 1800–1900
As the Industrial Revolution spread from England to the United States, more efficient production methods enabled American manufacturers to dramatically increase their output of exciting high-quality goods to satisfy burgeoning demand. It seemed there were always plenty of people to buy whatever could be produced. Contemporary economic theories stated confidently that supply created its own demand.[6] Or, as Ralph Waldo Emerson put it: "If a man can . . . make a better mousetrap than his neighbor, though he builds his house in the woods the world will make a beaten path to his door."[7] Selling skills were apparently superfluous in this era. All manufacturers needed to do was make their goods available to the people who wanted them.

[6]The French economist Jean-Baptist Say (1767–1832) is most identified with this concept of supply creating its own demand; he called it the "Law of Markets."
[7]John Bartlett, *Bartlett's Familiar Quotations,* 15th ed. (New York: Little, Brown, 1980), footnote 1, column 1, p. 496. Attributed to Emerson (in a lecture) by Sarah S. B. Yule and Mary S. Keene, *Borrowings* (1889).

Sales Era, 1900–1950

After the Industrial Revolution, most products were no longer scarce, and the Sales Era began. From 1870 to 1900, the number of traveling salespeople in the United States grew from 7,000 to 93,000. Because competition for customers increased accordingly, salespeople invented various selling strategies. Their initial approach might be called **social selling** because personality and social skills were thought to be essential to successful selling. Extroverted salespeople resembling Professor Harold Hill, the title character in the Broadway musical *The Music Man,* traveled their territories by train or automobile, using their flamboyant personalities, persuasive skills, and personal contacts to make sales. A less flamboyant fictional representative of the type is Willy Loman, who was convinced that you had to be well liked to be successful. A smile and a shoeshine were all he needed.

After World War I, salespeople began using a strategy that emphasized *explaining product functions and features* to potential customers, though customers were still responsible for relating these features and benefits to their own particular needs. The prevalent view in the field was that products would sell themselves if their features were accurately communicated. This was an updated version of the old production-oriented belief that somebody would buy whatever could be produced.

Another Sales Era strategy stressed programmed (canned) sales messages and sales formulas. Even today some novices memorize a sales pitch before calling on prospects. It is true that canned sales presentations or "structured company-prepared-and-planned presentations" can be very effective, but only if used as an overall guide rather than a rigid program to be followed.[8]

Marketing Era, 1950–Present

After World War II, U. S. manufacturers quickly converted their factories from producing military weapons and supplies to producing consumer goods for the vast pent-up American demand. Supply soon exceeded demand and sellers had to compete for customers' dollars. Instead of relying on the old product orientation of "we can sell what we make," business executives began to recognize that success depended on profitably satisfying the diverse needs and wants of customers. The new philosophy was "we'll make what we can sell." Thus began the Marketing Era, with its emphasis on customer needs and customer satisfaction.

SOCIAL SELLING The use of personality and social skills to sell products.

A famous picture of a well-known stereotype: Otto Hagel took this photograph of a Fuller Brush salesman in 1938. By that year, there were 4500 Fuller Brush men making 35 million door-to-door sales calls a year.

CONSULTATIVE SELLING AND THE MARKETING CONCEPT

In the Marketing Era, business shifted its orientation from production and selling to *identifying and solving customer problems*. The practical application to professional selling of this new orientation led to the development of a selling approach called *consultative selling.*

[8]Marvin A. Jolson, "The Underestimated Potential of the Canned Sales Presentation," *Journal of Marketing,* January 1975, pp. 75–78; Marvin A. Jolson, "Canned Adaptiveness: A New Direction for Modern Salesmanship," *Business Horizons,* January–February 1989, pp. 7–12.

Company Highlight

Quaker Chemical's Sales Engineers

Each year at least a dozen sales engineers earn more money than Peter Benoliel, CEO of Quaker Chemical Corporation in Conshohocken, Pennsylvania, which makes industrial cleaners, additives, and lubricants. Although Quaker Chemical's sales engineers are paid modest base salaries, their major compensation comes from commissions on the products they sell. There's no limit to what they can earn, claims Benoliel, who came up through sales and engineering himself. Benoliel feels that the success of his organization depends heavily on the sales team's technical expertise. Quaker Chemical salespeople are trained to be consulting engineers and problem solvers who address their customers' total operational process. Some Quaker salespeople succeed so well that customers' plant managers call them the people who know the most about their plants' operation.

In locating a customer's problem and explaining how Quaker can solve it, the salesperson must often suggest the development of an entirely new product or system of products.

The consultative salesperson tries to understand and help solve customer problems.

Consultative Selling

CONSULTATIVE SELLING
Selling through
understanding and helping
to solve customer
problems.

In **consultative selling,** the salesperson tries to understand and help solve customer problems, even if the solution sometimes does not include the purchase of the salesperson's products. Xerox's Sales Training School teaches consultative selling in order to build customer confidence in the motives and technical knowledge of Xerox's salespeople. Xerox sales representatives in both organizational and consumer markets employ the consultative approach. Sales engineers with the Quaker Chemical Corporation have also found success using the consultative approach, as the Company Highlight illustrates.

The Marketing Concept in Professional Selling

MARKETING CONCEPT
Business philosophy that
holds that achieving
organizational goals
depends on determining
the needs and wants of
target markets and
satisfying them more
effectively than
competitors.

Though it has great usefulness for professional salespeople, consultative selling is only one of many approaches and ideas that have grown out of a complete business philosophy known as the **marketing concept.** According to Kotler and Armstrong, "The marketing concept holds that achieving organizational goals depends on determining the needs and wants of target markets and delivering the desired satisfactions more effectively and efficiently than competitors."[9]

Organizations that adhere to this philosophy know that successful implementation requires that not only its sales force but also its entire administrative and sales support staff be oriented to customer satisfaction. In fact, a company-wide customer orientation is needed, as described by Frank "Buck" Rodgers, former marketing vice president for IBM and author of *The IBM Way:*

> At IBM, everybody sells! . . . Every employee has been trained to think that the customer comes first—everybody from the CEO, to the people in finance, to the receptionists, to those who work in manufacturing. . . . "IBM doesn't sell products. It sells solutions." . . . An IBM marketing rep's success depends totally on his ability to understand a prospect's business so well that he can identify and analyze its problems and then come up with a solution that makes sense to the customer.[10]

Development of the marketing concept has changed the focus of professional personal selling from a short-run emphasis on the needs of sellers to a long-run emphasis on the needs of customers. Contrasts between yesterday's salesperson and today's professional salesperson are summarized in Table 1-1.

What Is a Customer?

A customer may have many names: client, account, patron, patient, parishioner, student, fan, or voter. Whatever the name used, every organization thrives, survives, or dies on the basis of how well it satisfies its customers. L. L. Bean of Freeport, Maine, one of the country's most successful mail-order houses, defines the meaning of customer in its classic poster.

---

[9]Philip Kotler and Gary Armstrong, *Principles of Marketing* (Englewood Cliffs, N.J.: Prentice Hall, 1989), p. 14.

[10]F.G. "Buck" Rodgers, *The IBM Way: Insights into the World's Most Successful Marketing Organization* (New York: Harper & Row, 1985).

TABLE 1-1   Contrasting Yesterday's and Today's Salespeople

YESTERDAY'S SALESPERSON	TODAY'S PROFESSIONAL SALESPERSON
■ Product-oriented	■ Customer-oriented
■ Tries to create customer needs	■ Tries to discover customer needs
■ Makes sales pitches	■ Listens to and communicates with customers
■ Thinks in terms of manipulative selling techniques	■ Thinks in terms of helping and serving customers
■ Goal is to make immediate sales	■ Goal is to develop long-term relationships
■ Disappears once the sale is made	■ Follows up with customers to provide service and ensure satisfaction
■ Works alone and has little interest in understanding customer problems	■ Usually works as member of a team of specialists
■ Doesn't use new technology or understand how it can help him or his customers	■ Uses the latest computer and communications technology to serve customers

Customer Categories

There are two basic categories of customers or markets: consumers and organizations. Consumer markets consist of individuals who purchase goods and services for their own personal consumption. Organizational markets break down into two groups: profit-oriented and nonprofit organizations. Included in these groups are three types of markets: producers, resellers, and governments.

The producer market (also called the industrial market) includes individuals and organizations that purchase goods and services for the production of additional goods and services to sell, rent, or supply. For example, General Motors may purchase sheet steel from USX and automobile tires from Goodyear to manufacture its Buick Regal automobile for sale to its dealer customers. An example of a nonprofit producer market is a Methodist church that buys a Hammond organ to "produce" music at Sunday services.

The reseller market includes individuals and organizations that purchase goods to resell, rent, or conduct their own business operations. Resellers are "middlemen" who facilitate the flow of goods from producers to ultimate users and consumers. Three common types of resellers are industrial distributors,

---

WHAT IS A CUSTOMER

■ A Customer is the most important person ever in this office . . . in person or by mail.

■ A Customer is not dependent on us . . . we are dependent on him.

■ A Customer is not an interruption of our work . . . he is the purpose of it. We are not doing a favor by serving him . . . he is doing us a favor by giving us the opportunity to do so.

■ A Customer is not someone to argue or match wits with. Nobody ever won an argument with a Customer.

■ A Customer is a person who brings us his wants. It is our job to handle them profitably to him and ourselves.

Source: Poster of L. L. Bean, Inc., Freeport, Me.

wholesalers, and retailers. Each has its own category of customers: *Industrial distributors* sell primarily to manufacturers or producers of goods and services, *wholesalers* sell to retailers, and *retailers* sell to consumers. For example, a large wholesaler may buy Godiva chocolates from the Campbell Soup Company (a producer) to sell to Bloomingdale's (a retailer) for sale to shoppers in its department stores. A public library may become a nonprofit reseller by purchasing a Xerox copier to provide better services to its patrons.

Finally, the government market includes all local, state, and federal governmental units that purchase or rent products and services to carry out the functions of government. At the national level, the Defense Supply Agency (DSA) buys for all the armed services, while the General Services Administration (GSA) buys for the civilian branches and agencies of the federal government.

In order to sell successfully to consumers or organizations, sales representatives must understand how these markets buy. We provide in-depth discussions of consumer market behavior in Chapter 5 and of organizational buying behavior in Chapter 6.

What Is a Product?

PRODUCT Anything that is offered to a market to satisfy customer needs and wants, including tangible products and intangible services.

A **product** may be defined as anything that is offered to a market to satisfy customer needs and wants. It can be a *tangible product* like a television or an *intangible service* like professional advice from an estate planner. Note, though, that this distinction between tangible products and intangible services is not very precise because nearly all products have intangible aspects and all services have tangible aspects. A television usually comes with a warranty and may include a guarantee of service. Professional advice may include a detailed written financial analysis and an investment plan.

In buying products, customers are looking for *benefits or solutions to their problems.* They are not looking for razors and computer laser printers, but "clean shaves" and "attractive financial reports." Salespeople can never assume that the most obvious or functional benefit is the one that the customer is seeking. A friend of mine once owned ten wristwatches, none of which ever showed the correct time. She was simply more interested in a watch's benefit as an ornament than as a timepiece and had selected these watches to match various outfits she owned. The maker of Swatches recognized that many people were interested in this combination of customer benefits and profitably sold stylish, multicolored plastic watches.

CORE PRODUCT What the customer actually seeks in terms of a problem-solving benefit.

TANGIBLE PRODUCT Combination of a core product and product characteristics.

AUGMENTED PRODUCT The complete product package: the core product plus product characteristics plus supplemental benefits and services.

What a customer actually seeks in terms of a problem-solving benefit we call the **core product.** For example, a man may want something to quickly remove his overnight beard growth each morning. It takes product characteristics such as features, styling, quality level, packaging, and a brand name to turn this core product into something tangible such as a Gillette razor. We call this combination of a core product and product characteristics the **tangible product.** Many customers want additional tangible and intangible benefits like credit, repair service, and a warranty. We call the complete product package, made up of the core product, product characteristics, and supplemental benefits and services, the **augmented product,** as shown in Figure 1-1.

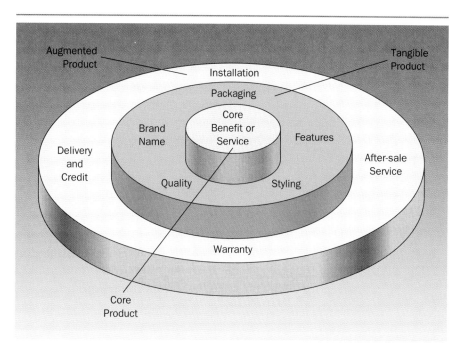

Figure 1-1 Core, Tangible, and Augmented Product
Source: Philip Kotler, _Marketing Management_ (Englewood Cliffs, N.J.: Prentice Hall, 1988), p. 446.

Let's see how a traditional product, the automobile, and a routine service, the haircut, both display the features of a core, tangible, and augmented product.

Automobile. One day, a customer walks into the showroom of a Chevrolet dealership with one thought in mind: I need an automobile for transportation. At first, the customer is concerned primarily with core product function and wants to learn only about the transportation capabilities of the various models. Then the customer decides that she wants something more than just good transportation. She is drawn toward a Corvette because of its sleek lines, sporty image, powerful engine, and the rich smell of the interior—in short, because of the tangible product of the Corvette. In addition to these product characteristics, the customer becomes interested in the Chevrolet dealer's offer of fast delivery, special financing, repair service, and warranty terms. Finally, this customer decides to buy the Corvette because of its complete, augmented product.

Haircut. Years ago, a haircut would have been called a simple "service." But now we know that actually cutting the hair is only one aspect of the haircut product. Although the core product is the haircut itself, the tangible product is the haircut combined with the hair stylist's special techniques of cutting and styling the hair, his business location, and his shops layout and artistic design. The augmented product might include the hair stylist's offer of two free "touch-up" appointments and a money-back guarantee if not completely satisfied.

As you can see, tangible and intangible benefits and services blend together to form every product. We will therefore use the term _product_ to refer to both products _and_ services.

DIVERSE ROLES OF THE PROFESSIONAL SALESPERSON

As products became more technical, competition more intense, buyers more sophisticated, and purchase decisions more shared (by several family members in households and by levels of managers and technical experts in organizations), personal selling grew in complexity. Behind the basic job of the professional salesperson today are a great many different types of selling roles, tasks, and responsibilities.

What Does a Professional Salesperson Do?

Though there are many different types of sales situations, every sales situation has the same seven basic stages. In order of completion, they are: (1) prospecting and qualifying, (2) planning the sales call (the preapproach), (3) approaching the prospect, (4) making the sales presentation and demonstration, (5) negotiating resistance or objections, (6) confirming and closing the sale, (7) following up and servicing the account.

We feel that the seven stages of the professional personal selling process are best depicted as a continous cycle or wheel of overlapping stages revolving around prospects and customers, as shown in Figure 1-2. Notice that once the Wheel of Professional Personal Selling is set in motion, it continues to revolve from one stage to the next. Using this depiction, it is easy to see that stage 7 is not the "end" of the sales cycle, but rather a new beginning, for the salesperson's follow-up and service activities generate repeat sales and purchases of new products as the customer's needs change over time. As you examine Figure 1-2, keep in mind that the *center* of the wheel is its most important part. Without prospects and customers, the wheel would have nothing to revolve around! Since each of the seven steps is discussed in depth in later chapters, we will provide only a brief overview of them here.

Prospecting and Qualifying
In order to increase or even maintain sales volume, salespeople must unceasingly search for new customers, for old customers are continually lost through death, bankruptcy, relocation, or switching to another supplier. Potential new customers are called prospects. Most salespeople spend more time on prospecting than on any other selling activity. Prospecting requires salespeople to obtain leads. A lead is basically the name and address or telephone number of a person or organization that may have a need for the company's product or service. Before a lead may be considered a genuine prospect, it must be qualified in terms of *need or want, money to buy, authority to buy,* and *eligibility to buy.*

Planning the Sales Call (the Preapproach)
In the preapproach stage, the salesperson obtains detailed information about the prospective buyer and the buying situation, and then develops a strategy for ensuring a favorable reception. Some valuable information can be found through general sources such as trade associations, chambers of commerce, credit bureaus, mailing-list companies, government and public libraries, and investment firms. Salespeople may also make a fact-finding preliminary call at the prospect's business site.

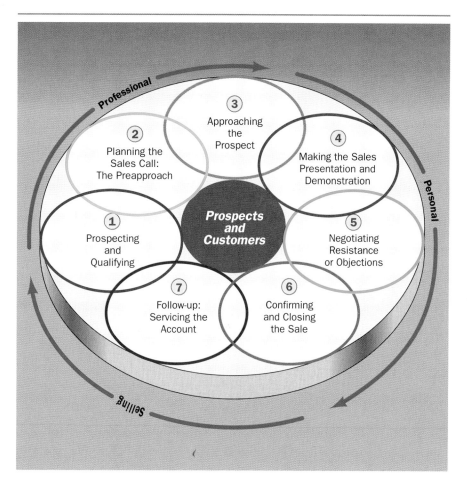

Figure 1-2 The Wheel of Professional Personal Selling

Approaching the Prospect

The approach is the stage in which the salesperson makes his or her vital first impression. Methods range from the mutual-acquaintance or reference approach to the free-gift or sample approach. The salesperson must learn to tailor the approach to suit the prospect.

Making the Sales Presentation and Demonstration

The sales presentation is the persuasive communication that is the heart of the selling process. Success at this stage demands careful planning of strategies and tactics, then rehearsal of the likely interactions between buyer and seller. Like the approach, the sales presentation must be tailored to the prospect and the selling situation. A practical sales presentation combined with a convincing product demonstration can favorably enhance the outcome of most sales calls.

Negotiating Resistance or Objections

A salesperson should not be discouraged by prospect resistance or objections. These are often positive signs of interest and involvement. Objections may be oblique requests for more information so that the prospect can justify a purchase decision.

Confirming and Closing the Sale

In order to increase their *hit ratio,* or sales per call, salespeople must become skillful closers. The close is the crowning achievement of the sales process, the moment the salesperson has been working so hard to get to, when the customer buys or agrees to order the product. Unfortunately, new salespeople are often shy about asking for the order. While no closing question is more decisive than "Will you give me the order?", it need not be that blatant. And there is no absolutely perfect moment to close the sale. The close may happen at any time during the sales process—in the first five minutes of the first sales call, or in the last few seconds of the tenth sales call.

Following Up and Servicing the Account

As we noted earlier, it is far easier to keep present customers satisfied than to search out and win over new customers. That is why, after making a sale, top-performing salespeople keep in close contact with the customer to handle any complaints and to provide customer service such as installation, repair, and credit approvals. Follow-up calls can also lead to sales of ancillary items or new products.

Selling Roles Vary Across Organizations

Retailers, wholesalers, industrial distributors, manufacturers, service firms, and nonprofit organizations are some examples of employers who need salespeople. Each of these organizations employs different types of salespeople for different selling roles. For example, the role of an IBM marketing representative who calls on large manufacturers to sell complex mainframe computers is quite different from that of the Procter & Gamble salesperson who sells laundry soap to wholesalers. Similarly, the Merrill Lynch stockbroker who sells common stock to small investors has different tasks and responsibilities from the salesperson who sells furniture to shoppers at Sears. If a customer's organization has a large and intricate structure, several salespeople from the same firm may be required to sell to various levels within that organization. Out of necessity, smaller firms often train their salespeople to handle a broad range of customers and customer needs. Factors that influence the numbers and kinds of salespeople a firm will hire include:

- ■ Size and characteristics of potential buyers
- ■ Price and complexity of products
- ■ Types and number of distribution channels
- ■ Level of marketing and technical support required

Response selling usually requires the salesperson simply to respond to customer requests.

Selling Roles

Selling can be divided into three basic roles: (1) order taking, (2) order supporting, and (3) order getting. These can be seen in a continuum of sales jobs ranging in complexity from mere response selling to the highly creative selling necessary to obtain new business, as follows:

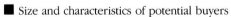

- Order Taking
    - Response selling
        - —Inside order taker
        - —Outside order taker
- Order Supporting
    - Missionary selling
- Order Getting
    - Trade selling
    - Technical selling
    - Creative selling

Response selling requires the salesperson simply to respond to customer requests. Response salespersons are either inside order takers, like retail clerks in department stores, or outside order takers, like truck driver–salespeople who travel a regular route to replenish inventories for customers such as retail grocery stores.

Missionary selling calls upon the salesperson to educate, build goodwill, and provide services to customers. The missionary salesperson is not permitted to take orders from customers directly, but he or she does furnish information about products to middlemen, who in turn recommend or sell the products to their own customers. For example, the drug "detail person" introduces physicians to new drugs and other pharmaceutical products in the hope that the physicians will prescribe these products for their patients. Distilleries, pharmaceutical houses, food manufacturers, and transportation firms commonly employ missionary salespeople to help their wholesale and retail customers sell to their own customers.

Merck & Company of Rahway, New Jersey, recently boosted its total sales staff by 36 percent because of the increasing number of new drug products they are introducing. "Doctors wouldn't know what to do with new drugs if they weren't detailed," says a manager for Scott-Levin Associates, health-care consultants of

The drug "detail person" is a type of missionary salesperson.

Field service is more important in trade selling than in response selling.

Newtown, Pennsylvania. With the outpouring of new drugs, a substantial increase is predicted in the number of missionary calls on physicians by drug company salespeople.[11]

Trade selling, like response selling, also requires the salesperson to respond to customer requests. Field service, however, is more important in trade selling. It consists largely of expediting orders, taking reorders, restocking shelves, setting up displays, providing in-store demonstrations, and distributing samples to store customers. Trade sellers are usually discouraged from hard selling to customers.

Technical selling requires a technically trained salesperson, often called a "sales engineer," to help customers solve their problems. Technical selling resembles professional consulting and is common in such industries as steel, chemicals, heavy machinery, and computers. A sales engineer typically helps customers understand the proper use of complex products, system design, and product installation and maintenance procedures.

Creative selling calls upon the salesperson to stimulate demand among present and potential new customers for a product. Creative selling includes *sales development* and *sales maintenance.* Sales development attempts to generate new customers. Sales maintenance tries to ensure a continuous flow of sales from present customers. If required to do both tasks, most salespeople tend to spend more time on maintenance work because the development of new prospects takes more time and may be less rewarding in the short run.

Although we have talked about selling roles as if each role had a definite set of tasks, it is important to realize that every selling job may contain all three roles: order taking, order supporting, and order getting. A retail salesperson who is dealing with a demanding and indecisive customer might give an elaborate product presentation and "get" an order. And some kinds of missionary salespeople actually "take" orders (a publisher's book representative, for example, may write out and deliver a professor's textbook order to the bookstore manager). No matter what the selling role, however, the bottom-line goal of all selling is to get the order. And *that* usually involves a certain amount of creativity.

Let's turn our attention to some specific sales careers, focusing on those types of salespeople who are engaged in creative selling.

A salesperson who does technical selling is often called a "sales engineer."

[11]*The Wall Street Journal*, July 20, 1989, p. 1.

Creative selling calls upon the salesperson to stimulate demand among present and potential new customers.

Types of Creative Salespeople

Sales & Marketing Management magazine lists five types of salespeople who do creative selling.[12]

1. *Account representative:* Calls on a large number of already established customers in industries such as food, textiles, apparel, and wholesaling.

2. *Detail salesperson:* Promotes and introduces products instead of soliciting orders directly. This type of salesperson is mainly involved in missionary selling.

3. *Sales engineer:* Normally trained in science or engineering, **sales engineers** possess the expertise to discuss technical aspects of products with customers in industries such as chemicals, machinery, and heavy equipment.

4. *Industrial products salesperson (nontechnical):* Sells *tangible* products, such as packaging materials and office equipment that do not require a high level of technical expertise, to organizational purchasers.

5. *Service salesperson:* Sells *intangible* products (i.e., services) like estate planning, accounting, consulting, or radio, television, and newspaper advertising space to businesses, nonprofit organizations, and consumers.

To this list from *Sales & Marketing Management* we add two more categories of creative salespeople.

6. *Self-employed salesperson:* An independent businessperson with special market experience and expertise who sells his or her own products or those of various organizations. An example of the self-employed salesperson is the *manufacturers' agent* (also called *manufacturers' rep*) who earns commissions by selling the products of several noncompeting manufacturers. Manufacturer's agents normally represent small manufacturers, but sometimes large companies like Quaker Oats use them to supplement their regular sales force in order to achieve specific goals such as increasing call frequencies on supermarkets.

[12]*Sales & Marketing Management*, February 25, 1986, p. 24.

7. *Counselor salesperson:* Usually holds a special license and develops a close, counselorlike relationship with clients on important financial matters.

Here's a brief look at three kinds of counselor salespeople:

■ *Real estate agents and brokers* are independent businesspeople who sell real estate or rent and manage properties. Most real estate agents show and sell residential property to people looking for homes, but those who work with large firms may specialize in commercial real estate.

■ *Stock and bond brokers* execute "buy" or "sell" orders for clients through securities markets like the New York and American Stock Exchanges. Securities salespeople also provide their clients with financial information and counseling.

■ *Insurance agents and brokers* help individuals or companies plan for and protect their financial security through the purchase of insurance for their life, home, car, or business. Agents sell the insurance policies of one company, whereas brokers are independent businesspeople who sell the insurance policies of several companies. These counselor salespeople can earn professional designations such as Chartered Life Underwriter (CLU), Chartered Financial Consultant (CFC), or Chartered Property Casualty Underwriter (CPCU).

The Selling in Action box shows how one highly successful counselor salesperson works.

PROFESSIONAL PERSONAL SELLING AS A CAREER

What Does a Sales Career Offer You?

A sales career offers many benefits, not least of which is its initial availability to just about anyone who is interested in a career rather than just a job. In the United States, over one million new or experienced salespeople will be needed annually for the remainder of this century. Let's take a look at some of the benefits you can expect to share in once you have started a career in professional selling.

Financial Rewards
Salespeople are among the best paid people in business. As shown in Table 1-2, the average top-level sales representative in consumer products earns over $63,000 a year and enjoys a travel and entertainment allowance of over $13,000. Sales trainees average $28,455 in industrial products. There are almost no limitations in sales other than the salesperson's drive and ability. More people in sales than in any other profession earn over $100,000 yearly;[13] a few actually earn more than $1 million. Unlike most jobs, which offer a small annual raise that is often based on a boss's subjective performance evaluation, the sales profession offers commissions, bonuses, and sales contest money and prizes in addition to a regular salary. Commissions are paid promptly on the size or profitability of an order; bonuses are awarded when salespeople exceed their annual sales quotas; and winners of sales contests may receive all kinds of booty (sailboats, exotic vacations, and entertainment packages) as well as prize money. People who are

---

[13]Beth Brophy and Gordon Witkin, "Ordinary Millionaires," *U.S. News and World Report,* January 13, 1984, pp. 43–52.

Selling in Action

Superstar Counselor Salesperson

Richard F. Greene of Merrill Lynch earns several million dollars every year while spending only one-third of his time selling to clients. Most of the rest of his time is spent scouting for new investments for his 200 active accounts. Using an unusually low-key approach, he is highly successful in making cold calls. For example, after reading a newspaper about the new head of marketing of a local company, Greene called the man to say: "Hello, I'm Dick Greene and I'm from Merrill Lynch in Boston. I know that you are the senior vice president of sales at your company, which means to me you're probably the best salesman at the firm. I think I'm the best salesman at Merrill Lynch. If you have an interest in the stock or bond market or are already in it, would you meet with me?" Arranging a breakfast meeting at a plush hotel, Greene doesn't talk much but actively listens. He says: "I don't go to

the meeting with something to sell. I want information about his risk profile so I can do the job right for him." With natural instincts on human psychology, Greene believes: "If you talk, you'll like me. If I talk, I'll like you—but if I do the talking, my business will not be served. Now, this fellow is the same as everyone else. His kids don't listen to him. His wife doesn't listen to him—and he doesn't listen to her. When he goes to parties the person he's talking to is looking over his shoulder to see what else is going on in the room. Then, all of a sudden, he goes to breakfast with me. He starts to answer a question. And he doesn't get interrupted."

Before breakfast is over, Greene has won another customer.

Source: Monci Jo Williams, "America's Best Salesmen," *Fortune,* October 26, 1987, pp. 122–134.

TABLE 1-2   Salesperson Compensation

	EARNINGS	TRAVEL & ENTERTAINMENT EXPENSES
Sales Trainees		
Consumer products	$23,297	$5,600
Industrial products	$28,455	$8,574
Service products	$22,506	$4,944
Middle-Level Salespeople		
Consumer products	$37,882	$10,255
Industrial products	$39,614	$11,889
Service products	$42,968	$6,654
Top-Level Salespeople		
Consumer products	$63,355	$13,189
Industrial products	$54,573	$13,978
Service products	$56,764	$7,665
Sales Supervisors		
Consumer products	$59,130	$12,784
Industrial products	$64,808	$19,670
Service products	$62,754	$11,385

Source: "1990 Survey of Selling Costs," *Sales & Marketing Management,* February 26, 1990, p. 75.

used to the idea of being paid a regular salary may not like the idea of being paid partially in commissions, but they shouldn't worry. Salespeople paid solely on commissions earn the most money.

Nonfinancial Rewards

Beyond financial rewards, most sales careers offer a high degree of "visibility." Top-performing salespeople are in-house celebrities known to the CEO and virtually everyone else in the company. Senior managers often give personal recognition to their best salespeople by interacting with them during special celebrations, vacation trips, or leadership seminars. At Paychex, Inc., a payroll-processing company with sales over $100 million a year, the top ten salespeople are invited to spend a day discussing organizational issues with the CEO. At one meeting, the top ten salespeople drafted a new compensation plan for the entire sales force.[14]

Perquisites

In addition to potentially high earnings, sales positions usually include certain perquisites, or "perks." Expense account benefits, for example, permit many sales reps to enjoy the "good life" while doing business with customers. Dinners at fine restaurants, tickets to ball games and concerts, and health club memberships are some examples of legitimate business entertainment. Many companies do everything they can to honor and reward salespeople, as shown in Table 1-3. At MacKay Envelope, the parking place just outside the door of the main office is not for the CEO, but for the "Salesperson of the Month." More than other employees, salespeople benefit from company-sponsored travel, training, and social events, and their spouses are more likely to be invited to company-sponsored events. Some companies buy their salespeople memberships in country clubs and social organizations so they can cultivate prospective customers, and

[14]Robert A. Mamis, "Manage Your Sales Force," *INC.*, January 1990, p. 122.

TABLE 1-3   Perks and Incentives Offered to Field Salespeople

TYPE OF PERK	INDUSTRY (% OFFERING)				
	Manufacturing	*Wholesaling*	*Retail*	*Finance*	*Service*
Entertainment expense account	60	63	53	41	54
Telephone credit card	52	43	37	24	38
Company car	46	32	32	24	23
Incentive travel	45	56	43	50	55
Company credit card	38	20	11	31	28
Merchandise	36	59	43	25	39
Frequent flyer program	28	15	16	10	21
Paid leave	25	13	29	25	35
Paid parking	16	18	11	28	29
Discounts on products	10	27	32	17	15
Car phone	13	12	5	7	11
Low-interest loans	7	7	11	14	10
Personal computer for home use	5	2	5	7	9
Health club membership	4	0	5	3	6
Country club membership	4	1	0	3	2

Source: National Institute of Business Management; 1988 Sales Compensation Survey, *Sales & Marketing Management*, February 20, 1989, pp. 24, 26.

many companies provide their salespeople with a new automobile every two or three years. On top of all this, Uncle Sam grants tax write-offs for home office expenses, allowing salespeople to live even better than their incomes suggest.

Always in Demand

Despite the many opportunities and high compensation in selling, there always seems to be a shortage of qualified salespeople. For example, when IBM announced that it would have to lay off 12,000 employees by the end of 1987, it simultaneously reassigned 3,000 people to its sales force. Mobility is higher for salespeople than for most professionals because selling skills are highly transferable to other products and virtually every organization needs quality salespeople. As the generators of cash—the lifeblood of any organization—salespeople are among the first to be hired and the last to be fired. Opportunities in various sales fields to the year 2000 are excellent, as shown in Table 1-4.

Opportunities for people entering sales careers are even better than indicated in Table 1-4 because across all industries there is a turnover of nearly 20 percent among salespeople.[15] Turnover is so high partly because sales managers must often hire marginal people. Many talented people never consider a sales career because they have negative ideas about selling, such as:

- Most salespeople are dishonest and unethical.
- All sales jobs require overnight traveling.
- Most sales jobs involve door-to-door selling.
- Most customers treat salespeople with contempt.
- Few salespeople hold college degrees.
- Salespeople must push unneeded products on people.
- Most salespeople suffer humiliating personal rejection.

Although these exaggerated negatives stem from outmoded tales about traveling and door-to-door salespeople, they are so widely held that many potentially successful salespeople fail to even consider sales as a career. It must be admitted that some sales jobs *do* require regular travel away from home, long working hours, continual pressure to achieve, dealing with difficult customers, frequent

[15]*Sales & Marketing Management*, February 20, 1989, p. 22.

TABLE 1-4   Opportunities in Different Sales Occupations, 1986–2000

SALES OCCUPATION	ESTIMATED EMPLOYMENT, 1986	% CHANGE IN EMPLOYMENT, 1986–2000	INCREASE IN EMPLOYMENT, 1986–2000
Insurance sales	463,000	22%	102,000
Manufacturer sales	543,000	3	18,000
Real estate agents and brokers	376,000	44	166,000
Retail trade sales	4,266,000	32	1,345,000
Securities sales	197,000	42	82,000
Travel agents	105,000	46	49,000
Services sales	419,000	56	237,000
Wholesale trade sales	1,217,000	33	405,000

Source: Occupational Outlook Quarterly, Spring 1988.

rejection, and constant self-management. On the other hand, these same drawbacks apply to many if not most other jobs.

Job Freedom and Independence

Most salespeople are like entrepreneurs or independent businesspeople in that they largely manage themselves. They set their own working hours and develop unique personal styles, yet still enjoy the security of working for an organization that provides medical coverage, vacation pay, and retirement benefits. Compared to the cost of starting one's own business, a sales career offers tremendous leverage on a small monetary investment. For example, a franchise may require an initial investment of $200,000 or more and provide an annual return of less than $50,000, even after several years of very long days. A salesperson may spend $1,500 on clothing and a nice briefcase and earn $50,000 in bonuses alone in one year of selling.

Salespeople seldom have a supervisor looking over their shoulders or timing their coffee breaks. In fact, if they do an outstanding job, they become something like talented professional baseball or basketball players whose worth to the organization is often greater than that of their coaches. Top salespeople, like top athletes, are not likely to suffer from unfair or capricious actions on the part of a sales manager who doesn't like them. Still, salespeople cannot afford to goof off. While job freedom and control are what attract many people to sales, there is always pressure, even if only self-imposed, to make a sales quota and earn higher commissions, bonuses, and other incentives. Being one's own boss sometimes means working for the most demanding person of all.

Adventure and Satisfaction

Selling is adventurous because it constantly challenges you to grow personally and professionally. It can be an invigorating experience to deal every day with people from diverse backgrounds and frames of reference. Many nonselling jobs are so narrowly defined and routine that they seldom present employees with a challenge and may actually limit their personal and professional growth. The only limits on creativity and growth in selling are self-imposed ones.

Selling can also give you more personal satisfaction than most jobs because the essence of the job is helping others to solve their problems and achieve their goals. The better salespeople are at their jobs, the more benefits they provide to others—their customers, company, family, even their country's economy. And for this they are well paid.

Objective Performance Evaluation

A salesperson who shows ability will be spotted quickly. In many fields, the seniority system or office politics seems to determine how much pay an employee receives. This is not the case in sales. Sales performance is highly visible and quantifiable. The salesperson is generally rewarded in relation to his or her sales productivity. In fact, if the salesperson works strictly on commissions, earnings are directly proportionate to sales. Few jobs offer such objective performance appraisals.

Careers for Different Types of Individuals

No single background, cultural heritage, ethnic group, sex, age, or personality assures success in selling to diverse customer types. On the contrary, studies have found that the effectiveness of a salesperson is related to the degree of similarity between the customer and salesperson. One classic study by Evans concluded:

> The more alike the salesperson and prospect are, the greater the likelihood for a sale. This is true for physical characteristics (age, height), other objective factors (income, religion, and education) and variables that may be related to personality factors (smoking, politics). It is also important to note that the *perceived* similarity for religion and politics is higher and of more importance than the *true* similarity.[16]

Accepting this logical research finding, many sales managers try to match their salespeople and customers. Women and minorities, for instance, are the best sales reps to call upon customers who are women and minorities, particularly when they are similar in other characteristics relevant to the buying situation, like product usage or lifestyle.

Contribution to Society

Salespeople make many valuable contributions to society. They improve the quality of people's lives by identifying their needs and wants, helping to solve their problems, adding value to products and services, and introducing new products. By generating income for their companies, salespeople provide jobs for millions of other people. With intensifying worldwide competition, the success of America's professional salespeople in domestic and world markets will become increasingly important to the health of our economy.

What Career Paths Begin with Personal Selling?

Many companies offer three career paths to newly hired salespeople: (1) professional selling, (2) sales management, and (3) marketing management. Figure 1-3 shows how the sales track branches out into multiple career path alternatives.

After completing an initial training program, the novice is promoted to sales representative and, depending on the industry and company, given a title similar to one of these: marketing representative, account representative, account executive, account manager, sales representative, sales engineer, sales associate, sales coordinator, sales consultant, market specialist, territory manager, or salesperson. Typically, newly designated salespeople spend a year or two in the field gaining essential experience before a decision is made regarding their long-term career with the company. The length of this field selling experience varies according to the industry, company, product, and market complexities. After the salesperson has achieved success in field selling assignments, he or she meets with the sales manager, and perhaps a human resources manager, to examine the salesperson's skills and performance record. On the basis of this in-depth evaluation, the best career path for the individual and the company is decided.

---

[16]F. B. Evans, "Selling as a Dyadic Relationship—A New Approach," *American Behavioral Scientist*, May 1963, pp. 76–79. Other studies supporting Evans's results include: M. S. Gadel, "Concentration by Salesmen on Congenial Prospects," *Journal of Marketing*, April 1964, pp. 64–66; Arch G. Woodside and J. W. Davenport, Jr., "The Effect of Salesman Similarity and Expertise on Consumer Purchasing Behavior," *Journal of Marketing Research*, May 1974, pp. 198–202; and Edward A. Riordan et al., "The Unsold Prospect: Dyadic and Attitudinal Determinants," *Journal of Marketing Research*, November 1977, pp. 530–537.

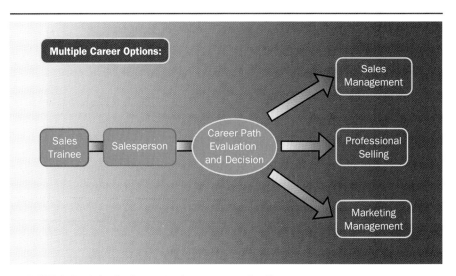

FIGURE 1-3 Multiple Career Paths in Personal Selling

Professional Selling

If the career path selected is professional selling, the salesperson may spend three to five years as a *sales representative* before being promoted to senior sales representative. After five to seven years in this capacity, the senior salesperson will be promoted to *master sales representative.* Top-performing master sales reps may be named *national or key account sales representatives* with responsibility for selling to a few major customers (e.g., national retail chains like Sears or K Mart).

Sales Management

When the career path selected is sales management, the senior sales rep will probably be promoted to sales supervisor or field sales manager, with responsibility for day-to-day guidance of a few other salespeople in a given sales branch. Next comes promotion to *branch sales manager,* then *district manager,* with successively larger territorial responsibilities. From district sales manager, the successive promotion steps would be *zone, division,* and *regional sales manager.* Finally comes promotion to *national sales manager* and, in some companies, *vice president of sales.*

A close alternative to the sales management career path is the *sales management staff* route. Here the salesperson might serve as a *sales analyst, sales training manager,* or *assistant to the sales manager.* Staff people are at every organizational level, and may hold positions in sales planning, sales promotion, sales recruiting, sales analysis, or sales training. Although people in sales management staff positions have no line authority over the sales force, they frequently hold impressive titles such as *assistant national sales manager* and often switch over to top positions in line management.

Marketing Management

Following success in field sales, the salesperson might be selected for the marketing management career path. This path often starts with promotion to *product*

Corporate CEOs Who Started in Sales

Lee Iacocca (Chrysler), Edwin Artzt (Procter & Gamble), Adolphus Busch (Anheuser-Busch), Phil Lippincott (Scott Paper), Marcel Bich (Bic Pens), Dr. William Scholl (Dr. Scholl's Foot Care Products), George McGovern (Campbell Soup), John Akers (IBM), Victor Kiam (Remington), John Hanley (Monsanto), Henry Heinz (Heinz Ketchup), H. Ross Perot (formerly Electronic Data Systems, now Perot Systems), W. W. Clements (Dr. Pepper), Frank Perdue (Perdue), Bruce Klatsky (Van Heusen), John J. McDonald (Casio), William Coleman (Coleman Camping Equipment), Roy Halston Frowick (Halston Fashions), John E. Pearson (Northwestern National Life Insurance Company), Adolph Coors (Coors Beer), Ronald G. Shaw (Pilot Pen Corporation of America), Estée Lauder (Estée Lauder Cosmetics), and John C. Emery, Jr. (Emery Air Freight)

---

or brand manager for a product category such as Quaker Oats' Ken'L Ration canned dog food or Pillsbury's Hungry Jack biscuits. Success in product management leads to promotion to *director of product management,* then *vice president of marketing* and maybe even *president and CEO.*

SUMMARY

Selling is a universal activity. At one time or another, everyone uses persuasive communication to "sell" products, services, ideas, opinions, or points of view. Commercial selling in the United States has evolved through the pioneer, production, sales, and marketing eras. Different selling strategies have been emphasized in each era. In today's Marketing Era, *consultative selling* and the *marketing concept* have changed the basis of professional personal selling from a short-run focus on the needs of sellers to a long-run focus on the needs of customers.

Consumers and *organizations* are the two basic categories of customers or markets. Organizational markets, which can be either profit-oriented or nonprofit, include *producers, resellers,* and *governments.* A *product* is anything offered to a market to satisfy its needs and wants. Every product is an amalgam of a *core product,* a *tangible product,* and an *augmented product.*

Professional salespeople carry out seven basic tasks in the selling process, from prospecting and qualifying to following up and servicing the account. Selling roles include order taking, order supporting, and order getting.

Sales careers offer opportunities for nearly anyone who is interested. Benefits include financial rewards, perquisites, a route to the top of an organization, job freedom and independence, personal satisfaction, and objective performance evaluation.

CHAPTER REVIEW QUESTIONS

1. Describe the myth of the "born" salesperson.
2. Briefly discuss selling in colonial America. What roles did "Yankee peddlers" play? Credit investigators? Greeters and drummers?
3. What are the names and approximate dates of the four eras of selling in the United States? Describe their characteristics.

4. Explain "consultative selling" and the "marketing concept."

5. List and briefly describe the three kinds of profit and nonprofit organizational markets.

6. What is a product? What are the differences between the core, tangible, and augmented product?

7. List the seven stages in the professional personal selling process. Why do we depict it as a wheel?

8. Name the three basic selling roles and describe the continuum of sales jobs ranging from simple response selling to complex creative selling.

9. What are the seven types of creative salesperson discussed in this chapter?

10. Discuss the benefits and drawbacks of a career in personal selling.

TOPICS FOR THOUGHT AND CLASS DISCUSSION

1. Have you ever known or met a person who appeared to be a "natural-born" salesperson? What made you think he or she was a good salesperson? Based on what you now know about professional personal selling, do you think you could call this person a truly professional salesperson? Why or why not?

2. What kind of selling do you think you would like to do? What products and customers would you prefer to work with? What do you think some of the advantages and disadvantages of each kind of selling would be for you personally?

3. Think about why you would want a career in professional personal selling. What would motivate you best? Money? The opportunity to contribute to society? Job independence? Discuss your thoughts and feelings with classmates.

PROJECTS FOR PERSONAL GROWTH

1. You have just inherited a pencil manufacturing business. Pencils are hardly a glamorous product, but there is a large and competitive market for them. See if you can develop a description of your product that would help your sales staff sell the core, tangible, and augmented product.

2. Use what you have learned about what professional salespeople do to "sell" one of your classmates something right there in the classroom—a pen, chair, book, pair of shoes, whatever. Once you've successfully sold to the classmate, try selling to your instructor!

KEY TERMS

Selling The use of persuasive communication to negotiate mutually beneficial agreements.

Yankee peddler Colonial American salesman who picked up goods from English merchants and colonial manufacturers and transported them throughout the colonies for sale to settlers.

Credit investigator Early-nineteenth-century investigator hired by manufacturers and wholesalers to collect overdue bills from customers and verify creditworthiness; often also sold goods.

Greeters and drummers Early-nineteenth-century salespeople hired by suppliers to meet and entertain retail merchants; worked on commission.

Social selling The use of personality and social skills to sell products.

Consultative selling Selling through understanding and helping to solve customer problems.

Marketing concept Business philosophy that holds that achieving organizational goals depends on determining the needs and wants of target markets and satisfying them more effectively than competitors.

Product Anything that is offered to a market to satisfy customer needs and wants, including tangible products and intangible services.

Core product What the customer actually seeks in terms of a problem-solving benefit.

Tangible product Combination of a core product and product characteristics.

Augumented product The complete product package: the core product plus product characteristics plus supplemental benefits and services.

Case 1-1

WHAT? YOU WANT TO BE A SALESPERSON?

Paula Majors is graduating from Ohio State University with a degree in marketing this June. Throughout her college studies, Paula maintained a B average, was active in several campus organizations, and worked 20 hours a week in a local retail artists' supply store. She comes from an achievement-oriented family. Her father is a certified public accountant who specializes in taxes, and her mother is a divorce lawyer in private practice. Everybody says that Paula has inherited her father's analytical approach to problem solving and her mother's drive and determination to do well in whatever she undertakes.

On her résumé, Paula felt it would be best to keep her job objective fairly general, so she wrote:

> **Job Objective:** Entry-level sales or marketing job that allows me to use my abilities creatively and offers an opportunity for career development.

After interviews with representatives of several companies who visited the campus during the fall and winter, Paula received three job offers, all in sales. Two of the jobs are sales trainee positions with large Fortune 500 companies, where she would complete an intensive training program before being assigned to a sales territory. The third job is a sales position with a small manufacturer of art supplies, where she would complete a three-week training course before assuming responsibility for a territory covering two-thirds of the Ohio market.

With either of the large companies, Paula would receive a straight salary the first year while completing her training program, then go on to 80 percent salary and 20 percent commission. At the small company, Paula would be paid 70 percent salary and 30 percent commission immediately. Because the small company has offered a slightly larger salary than the large companies, the compensation for all three jobs works out to be about the same. All three jobs also provide a company car.

Paula had asked three of her college professors for advice about which of the jobs she should take. Each of them gave her some perspectives on the three jobs, but said that the final decision was up to her.

Finally, Paula telephones her parents to get their views. She has been reluctant to call them because she knows that her mother and father view a sales career negatively. She discovers that her father is working late at his office and that her mother has to leave in a few minutes to meet an important client for dinner. After Paula quickly tells her about the three job offers, Paula's mother replies:

> Paula, you know that your father and I want you to make up your own mind about a career, but I think you should consider some alternatives besides sales. We'd like to see you use your education. It doesn't take any special abilities to be a salesperson, except the willingness to push unwanted products on people. And

where does a sales job lead? You can't be a salesperson all your life. With the constant travel and living out of a suitcase, we'd be concerned about your safety. A woman really doesn't belong in sales, especially if she plans to have children. When you raise a family, you've got to settle down and be home at night for your kids. Why don't you try to get into a large company's management training program so that you can have a chance for promotions and a good salary? Maybe I'm idealistic, but I'd also like to see you choose a career where you can make a positive contribution to society— you know, make a real difference. Honey, I've got to run now or I'll be late for my dinner meeting, but why don't you call us around 4:00 P.M. on Sunday after your father and I get back from the CPA luncheon. Love you, Paula! Bye for now.

Feeling a little depressed after hearing her mother's comments, Paula lies down on her sofa and begins to think about what she will say to her parents when she calls them on Sunday.

Questions

1. Why do you think Paula's parents are against her choice of a sales career? What are their misgivings? Are they right or wrong? Why do you think so?

2. In order to convince her parents that sales is the right place to begin her business career, what points should Paula make when she calls them on Sunday?

3. If Paula cannot persuade her parents to see personal selling in a positive light, what would you advise her to do?

Case 1-2

WHICH CAREER PATH?

Nearing completion of his third year as a sales representative for Admiralty Food Company in Chicago, John Stanley has just been notified that his annual evaluation with his sales manager is scheduled for this coming Monday morning at 9 o'clock. John feels confident about meeting with his boss for the evaluation because he is having an outstanding year, and even has a chance at winning the company's "Salesperson of the Year" award. Only 2 other salespeople out of a total of 43 in the Midwest region are selling at John's pace this year.

Most of Admiralty Food's products are sold through wholesalers or direct to large supermarket buying centers. John has over 100 customers, most of whom he calls on about every two weeks. He believes that his track record with Admiralty is impressive by almost anybody's standards. He sold 105 percent of his assigned quota the first year, 115 percent the second year, nearly 135 percent the third year, and is on track this year to reach 140 percent of

quota. During each of the three previous years, John made the "CEO's Sales Club" and won a week's vacation in the Bahamas, along with nine other top-performing Admiralty salespeople from around the country. John is proud to be working for Admiralty because the company has an excellent reputation for quality products and superior service as well as an excellent record of community outreach programs.

John knows that a part of the fourth-year annual performance evaluation for all Admiralty salespeople is a discussion of their desired career path. Although salespeople are not required to declare a career path in their fourth year, the sales manager has to indicate what the salesperson's preference seems to be at that time. John feels that he isn't ready to declare his career path preference, but is giving serious thought to his options.

With a degree in marketing from Central Michigan University and halfway through an evening MBA program at DePaul University, John believes that all three sales and marketing career paths are open to him at Admiralty. He can continue on the *personal selling track,* progressing from sales rep to senior sales rep to master sales rep. Or he can switch into the *sales management track,* which leads from sales rep to key account manager to district manager to regional sales manager—and perhaps eventually to senior vice president for sales. Finally, he can move into *marketing management* by becoming a brand manager for one of the company's product lines, then seek promotion to director of product management, then possibly vice president of marketing, and eventually perhaps CEO.

John is engaged to be married this coming summer to Sylvia Maplewood, a public relations manager for Admiralty. He knows he has to take into account how this might affect his career strategy. Admiralty has no official policy concerning in-house personal relationships, but both John and Sylvia are somewhat concerned that if he goes to work in marketing they might have to interact professionally almost every day, and that could prove awkward.

Professional Personal Selling Track. John loves the freedom and independence of personal selling. He isn't sure that he could stand being cooped up in an office all day long. By remaining a sales rep, John is sure he can maximize his income within five to seven years. However, he is uncertain whether he can maintain his intense selling pace for more than another five years. He feels that after his salary peaks, Admiralty will probably move him into a large national account where sales maintenance is most important. At that point, he thinks it might be nice to become a sales manager guiding the career development of younger salespeople, or to take on new challenges in marketing management.

Sales Management Track. As much as John loves selling, he does fear that the pressure of traveling and meeting sales quotas might become nerve-racking after he is married. He and Sylvia plan to have a couple of children, and John wants to be able to watch them grow up and share as much as possible in the responsibilities of their upbringing. In this light, a sales management position looks very inviting. Sales managers at Admiralty are, after all, really like field marketing managers in that they spend most of their time in the office doing such things as forecasting sales, preparing sales plans, setting sales goals and quotas for salespeople, recruiting, training, and evaluating salespeople, and analyzing sales volume, costs, and profits by territory, product, customer, and salesperson.

Marketing Management Track. John believes the brand management path is the most risky of the three. The success or failure of a brand manager's career seems to depend on the success of new products. He remembers one of the company's current brand managers commenting during a dinner session at the annual sales meeting last year:

> Brand managers have a lot of responsibility but little authority. Our job is to develop marketing strategies, improve present products, develop new products, and manage the marketing mixes for all of these products within a fiercely competitive and changing market environment. If a new product is successful, you can just hang onto its coat tails and let it pull you to success. But if you get identified with a product failure, you'd better get your resumé up to date. As a salesperson, you might get away with blaming poor headquarters marketing for unsuccessful products, but as a brand manager, it's hard to find anybody to blame but yourself.

Finally, Sylvia has told John that office politics are very "subtle" at headquarters and that he will probably have to tone down his natural tendency for candor "to avoid sticking your foot in your mouth the way you always do with me." Moreover, it seems to John that most of the top marketing people received their MBAs from Ivy League schools. Nevertheless, John believes that moving into marketing management is the best way to go if you want to become one of the top officers at Admiralty.

Questions

1. Do you think John should declare a career path now? Why or why not? If you were John's manager and John did not declare a career path goal, what would you indicate as his career path preference anyway?

2. What advice would you give John about each of the three career paths open to him? Outline the advantages and disadvantages of each for John.

3. Which career path do *you* think would be best for John? Explain why.

Chapter 2

Professional Salespeople in Today's Dynamic Selling Environment

If today's salespeople don't innovate and automate, they'll evaporate.

Profile

David Paul

"THROUGHOUT my sales career, I have attended sales training classes to help me improve and develop as a sales professional. Continual improvement through training and practice is imperative for staying successful in sales," says David Paul, now in his sixth year as a sales representative for Hewlett-Packard in Fort Wayne, Indiana. After four years of engineering curriculum at the University of Dayton, David set aside his original plan for a career in design engineering and turned his attention to field engineering or sales. "Sales easily won when Hewlett-Packard came to campus," continues David. "They had so much to offer. Hewlett-Packard is the number-one company in the electronics test equipment industry, and technical training is of the utmost importance."

David speaks glowingly of his first year in professional personal selling, and especially about his first big sale: "During the early part of the year, I met a customer who had never done business with Hewlett-Packard before. They needed to measure and control many parameters on a PC board so that it could be functionally tested for production. As soon as I realized that I had the perfect product to help them do this automatically, my face became noticeably flushed with excitement. I explained how our product system would solve their problem. By concentrating on the specific benefits of the system that were relevant to their problem, I was able to solidify and assume the sale. They became my fourth-largest customer that year. It was so exciting to see the customer become successful on a project with my help and my recommendations!" Since that sale, David's vigorous efforts to maintain customer satisfaction have earned him awards at two of his accounts, ITT (Vendor Excellence Award) and GTE (Partners in Quality Award), and he sincerely considers every new sale as exciting as that very first big sale.

With 20 percent compound annual growth in his territory over the last four years, David will probably have little difficulty realizing his short-term ambition of becoming a district sales manager with Hewlett-Packard. He feels that the transition from sales representative to sales manager will not be all that difficult because, he says, "a district managerial position is actually very similar to my current function as a sales representative. I am a manager of resources that are used to achieve $4.7 million in sales quota. I work with my customers to manage where their money will be best spent. I manage relationships between myself, sales support, product development, and other headquarters teams to ensure sales successes and customer satisfaction. In short, as a district manager, I will be managing many of the same resources I manage now, but—and this is the really exciting part—I will also be responsible for providing leadership and motivation for other sales professionals so they can do their best." ■

After reading this chapter, you should understand:

- How today's professional salespeople are much like micromarketing managers in their expanding job roles

- What megatrends are impacting personal selling now and will in the foreseeable future

- How developments in telecommunications and computer technology are dramatically changing personal selling

- Why rising personal sales costs are encouraging salespeople and their companies to make increasing use of alternative direct-marketing techniques

WANTED: A NEW BREED OF PROFESSIONAL SALESPEOPLE

In the words of an Amoco Chemicals vice president: "There is a need for a new professionalism in sales, a new pride in being a sales professional. It bothers me to still hear people say, 'But he's only a salesman.' They don't realize what it takes to be a good sales professional. In fact, most salespeople don't realize they need to become professionals."[1]

A new breed of uniquely talented professional salespeople is needed to meet the complex challenges and opportunities of the new professional selling era. Donald Beveridge, Jr., president of Beveridge Business Systems, has noted ten characteristics that he thinks identify today's professional salespeople:

1. They make initial contact with the purchasing agent, then get permission to work with other members of the customer team who are more interested in solving problems than in price.

2. They write sophisticated sales proposals that go beyond product specifications to identify the customer's needs and the systems and solutions that will satisfy those needs.

3. They are keenly aware of the need to continually upgrade their own professional selling skills and understand that their professional growth depends on seeking new sales challenges.

4. Professional salespeople don't sell or talk "product" during the initial sales call. They recognize that the objective of the first meeting is to uncover customer needs and to establish a problem-solver identity and a credible image. Immediately launching into a product "pitch" creates a one-way dialogue that the prospect perceives as amateurish.

5. They don't measure their performance by short-term earnings. Instead, they gauge the long-run potential of their markets or territories and the penetration of those markets.

[1]Michael P. Wynne, "The Time Has Come for Professionalism," *Sales & Marketing Management*, September 10, 1984, p. 18.

6. They demonstrate empathy, expertise, and problem-solving skills by working closely with customers to determine their current needs and to anticipate their future needs.

7. They work closely with other departments or support personnel in their company and never talk disparagingly about them. Professional salespeople think of themselves as "orchestrators" of a selling team trying to match the needs of customers with the product and service capabilities of their companies.

8. They understand that they will rarely have a long-term competitive advantage in product or price and feel that their company's real competitive advantage is *them*.

9. They see goals as something that they "must make happen." Although there may be logical, justifiable reasons for not attaining a goal, professional salespeople rise above such excuses.

10. Finally, professional salespeople feel that they are being constantly challenged.[2]

Typical Salesperson

Today's sales representatives are more productive, better compensated, and better educated than ever, according to a survey by the Dartnell Institute of Financial Research of 122,000 salespeople in more than 300 companies across 36 industries. As Figure 2-1 shows, the typical salesperson sells about $1.6 million yearly, makes 5.5 sales calls per day, spends 45 hours a week selling, and devotes another 15 hours to nonselling tasks.

[2]Donald W. Beveridge, Jr., "Fast-Talking Peddler of Professional? Rating Reps' Selling Skills," *Marketing News,* September 16, 1983, p. 13.

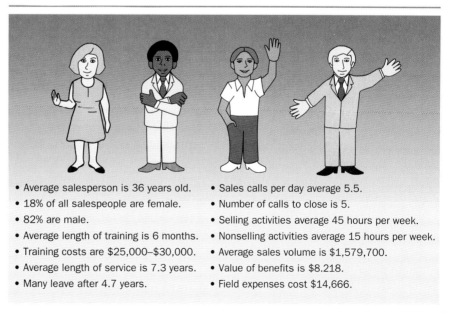

- Average salesperson is 36 years old.
- 18% of all salespeople are female.
- 82% are male.
- Average length of training is 6 months.
- Training costs are $25,000–$30,000.
- Average length of service is 7.3 years.
- Many leave after 4.7 years.
- Sales calls per day average 5.5.
- Number of calls to close is 5.
- Selling activities average 45 hours per week.
- Nonselling activities average 15 hours per week.
- Average sales volume is $1,579,700.
- Value of benefits is $8.218.
- Field expenses cost $14,666.

FIGURE 2-1 Profile of the American Sales Professional

PROFESSIONAL SALESPEOPLE
AS MICROMARKETING MANAGERS

The role of the professional salesperson has expanded and changed dramatically in recent years. Instead of merely selling products, today's sales representatives are expected to serve customers as *consultants* who offer expert advice on improving customers' lifestyles or making their business operations more profitable. They operate much like **micromarketing managers** in the field, with profit objectives for their designated territories or markets. Their expanding marketing responsibilities require them to perform in such diverse roles as:

MICROMARKETING MANAGER Another name for a sales representative who skillfully applies the latest professional personal selling principles and marketing techniques in his or her designated territory or market.

■ *Customer partner:* It is not enough for today's salespeople to know their own company's business; they must also thoroughly understand the business of their customers—as well as businesses of their customers' customers. They must develop partnerships with customers in order to help them achieve competitive advantages and increased profitability.

■ *Market analyst and planner:* Salespeople must monitor changes in the marketing environment, especially competitive actions, and devise strategies and tactics to adjust to these changes and satisfy customers.

■ *Buyer-seller team coordinator:* Modern salespeople must know how to use backup organizational specialists in marketing research, traffic management, engineering, finance, operations, and customer services from both seller and buyer teams to solve customer problems.

■ *Customer service provider:* Today's prospects and customers expect service, and if they don't get it, they'll buy from someone else. They want advice on their problems, technical assistance, arrangement of financing, and expedited deliveries. After making a sale, salespeople must continually check with customers to see how the product is performing. Keeping customers satisfied is largely a matter of providing good service, and top salespeople are as skillful at that as they are at persuading prospects to buy.

■ *Buyer behavior expert:* Salespeople must study customer purchase decision processes and buyer motivations in order to better communicate with and serve customers.

■ *Opportunity spotter:* Salespeople who remain alert to unsatisfied or unrecognized customer needs and potential problems are able to recommend new products, new markets, or innovative marketing mixes.

■ *Intelligence gatherer:* Providing informational feedback from the field to headquarters marketing for strategic and tactical planning purposes is an important part of the salesperson's job.

■ *Sales forecaster:* Sales managers need the sales representative's help in estimating future sales and setting sales quotas in the sales rep's assigned territory or market.

■ *Marketing cost analyst:* Professional salespeople concentrate on profitable sales, rather than on sales volume or quotas. Some companies have exempted their sales reps from routine duties, such as putting up displays in retail outlets, so they can devote more time to creative selling. Hunt-Wesson Foods, Allied Chemical, and Gillette are among the many firms that have freed their salespeople from some routine duties. Gillette, for example, employs part-timers to set up retail displays and replenish store stock. Salespeople now spend only about 15 percent of their time on such routine tasks as store displays, restocking shelves, and taking reorders, leaving 85 percent of their time to talk with customers.

■ *Allocator of scarce products:* When the company's products are in short supply and being demanded by customers, you might think that the salesperson's job is a "piece

Company Highlight

Allocating Instead of Selling at Armco Steel

In the mid-1970s, salespeople at Armco Steel came under tremendous pressure as a steel shortage put an end to sales calls on new customers and damaged relations with old ones. Only customers who had a "buying history" with Armco could be partially supplied, and a rationing plan based on previous buying experience had to be justified to oftentimes irate customers. Relations between Armco salespeople and their own company also became strained. Some Armco salespeople got angry with executives who promised steel to customers without informing the sales reps assigned to the accounts. They also found themselves in the position of promoting products that weren't available, and grumbled about plant managers who didn't notify them of production or delivery problems. "Not once in the last year has the mill said they'd do something to help a customer," complained one sales rep. "We always have to fight them." Eventually, the steel shortage ended and Armco salespeople gratefully returned to the challenge of selling rather than allocating products.

Source: Michael B. Rothfeld, "A New Kind of Challenge for Salesmen," *Fortune*, April 1974, pp. 156–166.

of cake," but consider some of the problems encountered by salespeople during a product shortage in the Company Highlight featuring Armco Steel.

■ *Field public relations person:* Because they deal with customers on a daily basis, salespeople must handle many customer problems and concerns that require sensitivity and public relations skills.

■ *Adopter of advanced sales technology:* Because of the rising cost of the sales force, sales reps must quickly adopt the latest technology to improve their efficiency and effectiveness. In the fierce competition of today and tomorrow, salespeople who don't innovate and automate may evaporate.[3]

MEGATRENDS AFFECTING PERSONAL SELLING

Change is inevitable in every field, of course, but eight megatrends make personal selling one of today's most volatile careers:

1. Buyers are more expert and demanding.
2. Customer expectations are rising.
3. Revolutionary advances in telecommunications and computer technology are happening all the time.

[3]Rolph E. Anderson and Bert Rosenbloom, "Eclectic Sales Management: Strategic Response to Trends in the 1980s," *Journal of Personal Selling & Sales Management,* November 1982, pp. 41–46.

Bill Gates, CEO of Microsoft Corporation (left), and Steve Jobs, CEO of NEXT (right), are two young entrepreneurs whose success is largely due to their ability to develop and sell their products on the basis of at least three current megatrends: (1) more expert and demanding customers, (2) rising customer expectations, and (3) advances in telecommunications and computer technology.

4. Consumer products sales forces are shrinking.
5. Women and minorities are flooding into sales.
6. Domestic markets are undergoing microsegmentation.
7. Foreign competition is intensifying.
8. Markets are being internationalized.[4]

No matter what kind of selling you decide to go into, your job will be at least indirectly affected by several, if not all, of these megatrends. Let's briefly discuss each of them.

More Expert and Demanding Buyers

Buyers of all kinds (producers, resellers, governments, and consumers) are becoming increasingly skillful at obtaining value for their expenditures. Organizations are developing more efficient purchasing processes and using buying committees composed of purchasing, engineering, finance, and operations managers. A talented new type of professional salesperson is needed to make sales presentations to buying committees and to consumers who treat purchases like long-term investments.

Rising Customer Expectations

Salespeople must reconcile themselves to the fact that human expectations are probably infinitely elastic. Consumers and organizational buyers are less and less tolerant of inferior products. Japanese automoblile manufacturers, for example,

---

[4]Bert Rosenbloom and Rolph E. Anderson, "The Sales Manager: Tomorrow's Super Marketer," *Business Horizons*, March–April 1984, pp. 50–56.

are pushing quality and service to such high levels that one American manufacturer found that it could not compete successfully in the international market.

> Armstrong World Industries has successfully manufactured and marketed automobile gaskets for years in the United States, so the company assumed it could become a major player in the world market. Unfortunately, Armstrong found limited success because, even though its gaskets exceeded all U.S. auto manufacturers' requirements, they weren't good enough for the Japanese producers. U.S. car owners are used to seeing an occasional drop of oil on the garage floor, especially from a car with over 50,000 miles on it. But in Japan, a single drop of oil is grounds for a complaint to the manufacturer.[5]

Sales representatives cannot afford to become defensive about their company's products. Instead, they must look at their offerings from the perspective of their most critical customers. Tomorrow's customers will expect even higher-quality products.

Advances in Telecommunications and Computer Technology

Successful salespeople in the coming years will be those who can make skillful and efficient use of communications and computer technology to increase their customer service, efficiency, and productivity. The most important technological innovations for personal selling are portable computers, electronic data exchange, videotape presentations, videoconferencing, mobile communications equipment (car phones and satellite pagers), voice mail, facsimile machines, electronic mail, and high-tech offices.

Portable Computers

Progressive companies realize that instant information on inventory availability, pricing, delivery dates, and competitive products must be available at the point of customer contact, where many decisions are made. Salespeople with companies such as L'eggs Products use hand-held computers in their territories for order entry, price verification, inventory control, field service, route accounting, and market research.

Laptop computers can place an enormous wealth of information literally at the salesperson's fingertips.

In a study comparing two groups of sales representatives, Hewlett-Packard found that salespeople using laptop computers spent 27 percent more time with customers, earned 10 percent more sales, and achieved three times the productivity of sales reps who did not use laptops. HP also found that laptop computers cut time spent in meetings by 46 percent and travel time by 13 percent. Based on these results, HP decided to invest over $6 million outfitting its entire sales force with laptop computers. With the laptop, HP salespeople can quickly call up account histories, track order status, reorder products, develop sales call schedules, and target direct mail at specific prospects. Each HP sales rep uses the Lotus 1-2-3 spreadsheet program to analyze product sales, identify developing trends, and maintain customer purchase and payment records.[6]

[5]William W. Locke, "The Fatal Flaw: Hidden Cultural Differences," *Business Marketing*, April 1986, p. 65.

[6]Thayer Taylor, "Hewlett-Packard Gives Sales Reps a Competitive Edge," *Sales & Marketing Management*, February 1987, pp. 36–37; and Jonathan B. Levine, "If Only Willy Loman Had Used a Laptop," *Business Week*, October 2, 1987, p. 137.

Electronic Data Interchange

Supermarket *scanners* have made consumer products salespeople more efficient by taking over the job of monitoring store inventories. Direct computer linkups with suppliers are allowing chain stores and many independent retailers to bypass sales representatives and order automatically when their computers determine that on-hand stocks have reached the reorder point. Many resellers rely on electronic data interchange (EDI) to transmit purchase orders, invoices, price quotes, shipping, and promotional information via interlinked computers. For example, independent retailers who sell Hallmark greeting cards at locations throughout the United States use EDI to transmit orders and receive aknowledgment within seconds from Hallmark's Kansas City, Missouri, headquarters. Orders are not only filled faster, thereby reducing store out-of-stocks, but are no longer lost in the mail.

As more customer buying is handled by EDI systems, fewer but more talented consumer products sales reps are needed to call on large national accounts such as Toys 'R Us, Sears, K Mart, and J. C. Penney. Because these top salespeople, usually called key account executives (KAE) or national account managers (NAM), possess outstanding marketing expertise and in-depth understanding of their customers' businesses, they can serve customers as sales/marketing consultants in developing profitable buying and selling strategies.

Videotape Presentations

Videotapes are being used instead of catalogs by over 480 salespeople at 27 branch offices of Fisher Scientific Company to demonstrate the company's diverse products, equipment, and furniture for educational, medical, and industrial laboratories. At American Saw & Manufacturing's industrial division, 50 salespeople share 20 portable videotape recorders. One profitable use of the equipment was the preparation of instructional tapes in Spanish to win the account of a Chicago manufacturer with a large number of Hispanic employees. American Saw also uses monthly tapes instead of a company newsletter to boost the morale of its employees both in the field and in the home office.

Videoconferencing

VIDEOCONFERENCING
The use of video technology in such a way that people in various locations can simultaneously participate in a meeting or conference.

Many companies have cut the cost of travel and employee "downtime" by substituting **videoconferencing** for national and regional conferences. Using a satellite network provided by VideoStar, Texas Instruments made a sales call simultaneously on 20 Hewlett-Packard facilities across the country to show a custom-designed line of semiconductor products. "This was the most cost- and time-effective way to get our message across to the people who use these specialized products, and to get input from them on how we might make the products better," says TI's media center manager. "A traditional sales call these days can cost from a few hundred to a few thousand dollars, including travel. Doing it by satellite costs about $40 per person reached, and the net effect is the same—increased sales and better service."[7]

Car Phones and Satellite Pagers

Mobile communications innovations, especially cellular car phones and satellite pagers (beepers), are helping salespeople keep in touch with customers and the home office even when they are traveling in their automobiles or walking across

---

[7]"Sales Via Satellite Net Lower Costs, Greater Mobility," *Marketing News*, March 1, 1985, p. 16.

The cellular car phone is fast becoming one of the most commonly used sales tools today.

parking lots hundreds or thousands of miles away. Car phones enable salespeople to obtain the latest information about a customer from the home office while en route to the customer's place of business, and to alert customers about unavoidable delays such as a car breakdown or a traffic jam.

By dialing a toll-free 800 telephone number and punching in a personal identification code, sales managers or customers can send information via satellite to one or more transmitters in over 50 cities coast to coast, where it is then transmitted to the salesperson's electronic pager. Kent H. Landsberg Company, a distributor of corrugated paper products in Montebello, California, has equipped its entire sales force with mobile telephones, pagers, and two-way radios. Landsberg's sales reps consider the equipment vital for maintaining constant contact with sales managers, key support people in the main office, and drivers in company delivery trucks who check on customer orders. Now that they have instant access to one another every day, the sales force meets only every two weeks or so for general sales conferences.

Voice Mail

Staying in touch with office support people, answering customer inquiries, keeping distributors informed about product availabilities and delivery dates, and carrying out numerous other telephone communications consume a lot of sales force time. AT&T has determined that 75 percent of all business communications are not completed on the first try.[8] The reasons for this failure are shown in Figure 2-2.

VOICE MAIL Various electronic methods of sending and receiving voice messages, ranging from a simple telephone answering machine to a complex, computer-driven "mailbox" message storage and retrieval system.

Voice mail—various electronic methods of sending and receiving voice messages—is dramatically improving the efficiency of sales force communications. The simplest type of voice mail is the telephone answering machine in your home that lets callers leave a message. But answering machines are limited in

[8]Sam Lobue, "Tired of Telephone Tag? Voice (Message) Your Opinion," *Marketing News*, November 7, 1988, p. 20.

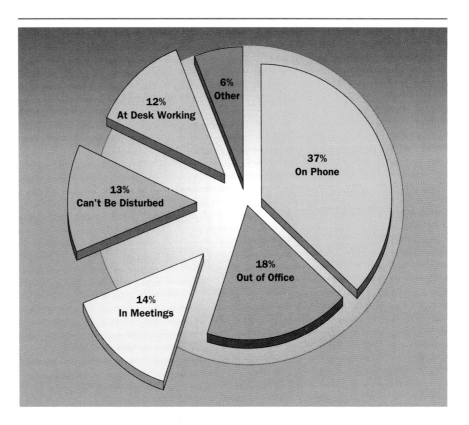

FIGURE 2-2 Where Are People When You Call Them?

what they can do, so the business version is a complete voice mail system. Users are assigned personal security-coded "mailboxes" or storage areas in a central computer. Using any push-button telephone (including the cellular phone in their car), salespeople can access their mailboxes to retrieve messages, send replies, and save or redirect messages. Voice mail keeps the time-wasting chitchat that occurs in most telephone conversations to a minimum. It offers you at least four major benefits:

1. All your phone calls become productive because you always reach the party called.
2. You can send messages to many people simultaneously.
3. You stop playing telephone tag with prospects who aren't there when you call or who return your call when you aren't in.
4. You and your sales manager can exchange complete messages for later pickup if you are both out on sales calls.

Over 850 salespeople who sell for Thomas J. Lipton of Englewood Cliffs, New Jersey, use voice mail to keep in touch with their sales managers while on the road calling on food chains, wholesalers, and independent retailers. Before they got voice mail, Lipton salespeople were on the phone every night bringing their managers up to date on their activities and discussing problems. Now their evenings are free because they can dial into the system whenever they like to leave messages and receive information left for them by their sales managers. It's like working for a different company now.[9]

Facsimile Machines

"Faxing," as it is commonly called, is transmitting text or graphic communications over telephone lines between two or more facsimile machines that look like small photocopiers with a telephone attached. In less than a minute, salespeople can "fax" anything that can be photocopied—letters, sales proposals, pictures, charts, diagrams, invoices—to several prospects and customers located almost anywhere in the world. To send a document, the salesperson just slips it into the fax machine and dials the telephone number of the receiving fax machine. The image of the document is transformed into electric signals that travel over the telephone line to the receiving fax machine, which prints out a copy of the document. A personal computer can also send and receive documents if it is equipped with a special circuit "fax board." Some salespeople use portable fax machines while traveling in their territories to instantly send in call reports, customer orders, expense sheets, and other documents.

Electronic Mail

"E-mail" is the transmission via modem of electronic messages between two or more computers. Electronic messages can be sent to a single receiver's E-mail identification number or written on an electronic "bulletin board" for thousands of computer users to see at the same time. Instead of enduring the frustration of playing "telephone tag" with a customer, salespeople using electronic mail always get through to the computer of the addressee, who can read it when convenient. Electronic mail is as fast as a phone call, but less subject to misunderstandings because the message is written out for the receiver to read several times if necessary. A company can cut its cost of handling information by 60 percent or more by replacing regular mail and filing cabinets with electronic mail and storage.

High-tech Sales Offices

Today's high-tech sales office provides salespeople and their customers with such services as remote dictation systems to reduce the paperwork burden, instant data and status reports, automatic ordering and scheduling, computer graphics, electronic and voice mail, and instant facsimile of documents.

Smaller Consumer Products Sales Forces

DIRECT-MARKETING TECHNIQUES Techniques for selling products directly to consumers in their homes, such as catalog marketing, automatic vending, television home-shopping channels, and electronic shopping services.

To reduce their costs in selling consumer products, many manufacturers are aggressively seeking alternatives to large national sales forces. Some are turning to independent brokers and manufacturers' agents, part-time salespeople, or inside telephone salespeople to help call on buying organizations such as wholesalers and retailers. Others are using **direct-marketing techniques** such as catalog marketing, automatic vending, television home-shopping channels, and electronic shopping services like videotex to reach consumers in their homes. An example of a successful catalog retailer is Lands' End.

[9]Thayer C. Taylor, "Voice Mail Delivers," *Sales & Marketing Management,* July 1988, p. 62.

Company Highlight

Lands' End: Catalog Retailer

Founded by Gary Comer, Lands' End originally sold only sailboat equipment through the mail. Adding a small clothing section proved so successful that the hardware products were soon dropped in order to focus on adult and children's apparel. Today Lands' End mails out 150-page catalogs to millions of consumers several times a year to encourage them to order by mail or via a toll-free 800 telephone number. Polite, friendly, and knowledgeable operators take the telephone calls in Dodgeville, Wisconsin, where the Lands' End warehouse is the size of ten football fields and employs 3,000 workers to fill orders. Offering quality products and outstanding service, Lands' End accepts credit cards, delivers goods to the consumer's house within a few days, and provides this unconditional money-back guarantee: "If you are not completely satisfied with any item you buy from us, at any time

during your use of it, return it and we will refund your full purchase price." A thick computer printout of customer comments is circulated each month to Lands' End managers to help them find ways to improve product and service offerings. Ordering by telephone or mail enables catalog shoppers to avoid parking problems, inclement weather, long check-out lines, and unfriendly retail store clerks. For Lands' End and other catalog resellers, the major advantage is smaller operating costs, including lower rents, fewer salespeople, and no shoplifting.

Source: Based on information from several sources, including: Susan Caminiti, "A Mail-Order Romance: Lands' End Counts Unseen Customers," *Fortune*, March 13, 1989, pp. 44–45; Susan Benway et al., "Presto! The Convenience Industry: Making Life a Little Simpler," *Business Week*, April 27, 1987, pp. 86–94; and M. John Storey, *Inside America's Fastest Growing Companies* (New York: John Wiley, 1989).

Influx of Women and Minorities into Sales

Over 50 million women work outside the home. Between now and the end of the century, women will make up more than half of all new entrants into the labor force and account for almost two-thirds of labor force growth. There will be a net increase of 13 million female versus only 7.7 million male workers.[10] Many of these women will enter the sales field.

The influx of minorities into the labor force will also be dramatic. The number of Hispanics, male and female, joining the work force will be more than five times the number leaving. Hispanic-Americans will account for nearly 28 percent and African-Americans for about 17 percent of total labor force growth between now and the end of the century. A recent issue of *Ebony* magazine listed marketing and sales as among the top ten career opportunities for African-Americans in the 1990s.[11]

[10]*The Wall Street Journal*, March 7, 1989, p. B1.
[11]"The 10 Top Careers for Blacks in the '90s", *Ebony*, February 1989, pp. 39–44.

Affirmative Action

The 1964 Civil Rights Act gave legal impetus to the hiring of minority sales reps, but for years many companies had little success in attracting minorities to industrial sales jobs. This began changing in the early 1980s as the number of minorities interested in business increased substantially and sales managers became more creative in recruiting them. Minority employees with sales potential serving in secretarial, clerical, or factory positions are now frequently considered for sales force openings. Local chapters of the National Association for the Advancement of Colored People (NAACP) and the Urban League have employment referral services that work closely with many employers. Colleges with large minority enrollments have become attractive recruiting grounds for companies seeking sales candidates, and college instructors of sales and marketing courses are often asked to recommend talented minority students who may be interested in sales careers. The Research Institute of America reports that roughly one-fourth of companies now employ African-American salespeople.

Even though the 1964 Civil Rights Act has stimulated the hiring of women and minorities, many companies claim that they would like to hire more than they have been able to attract to industrial sales jobs. The collective attempt by public- and private-sector institutions and organizations to correct the effects of discrimination against women and minorities in education and employment is called **affirmative action.**

AFFIRMATIVE ACTION The collective attempt by public- and private-sector institutions and organizations to correct the effects of discrimination in the education or employment of women and minorities.

All major companies doing business in the United States have policy statements reflecting legal requirements with regard to equal employment opportunities. Nearly all these policies state that the company does not discriminate against any employee or applicant for employment because of race, color, religion, sex, age, or national origin. The Equal Employment Opportunity Commission (EEOC) and state agencies may take legal action for noncompliance against employers and levy heavy financial penalties. Some time ago, AT&T agreed to make back payments of almost $15 million to 15,000 women and minority employees who alleged discrimination in pay and promotion. Today any company with 50 or more employees seeking federal government contracts must submit a written affirmative action program to the Office of Federal Contract Compliance (OFCC) of the Department of Labor.

Workforce 2000

Right now, there are expanding opportunities in sales careers for women and minorities who have a strong interest in the field. According to the U.S. Labor Department, there will be 4 to 5 million fewer people entering the work force in the 1990s than there were in the 1980s. Moreover, 75 percent of these new workers will be minorities and women.[12] White males now constitute only 45 percent of the country's 117.8 million workers, and their share will decline to 39 percent over the next few years.[13] At the same time, the demand for salespeople, especially business-to-business salespeople, is projected to increase faster than the average demand for new workers.[14] Organizations that want the most productive employees will have to think beyond traditional corporate stereotypes

---

[12]Lennie Copeland, "Learning to Manage a Multicultural Work Force," *Training,* May 1988, pp. 49–51, 55–56.

[13]Marcus Mabry et al., "Past Tokenism," *Newsweek,* May 14, 1990, pp. 37–38, 43.

[14]Thayer C. Taylor, "Meet the Sales Force of the Future," *Sales & Marketing Management,* March 10, 1986, pp. 59–60.

TABLE 2-1 Women in Sales by Industry

INDUSTRY GROUP	% OF WOMEN IN SALES FORCE
Communications	50.9
Printing/publishing	39.4
Electronics	35.0
Instruments	35.0
Office equipment	33.9
Business services	33.2
Retail	32.2
Wholesale (industrial)	30.9
Insurance	28.5
Rubber/plastics	26.9
Food products	24.9
Miscellaneous manufacturing	22.7
Utilities	20.2
Wholesale (consumer)	19.7
Fabricated metals	7.3
Chemicals	5.9
AVERAGE	**27.9**

Source: Dartnell Corporation, 25th Survey of Sales Force Compensation, 1989, as reported in *Sales & Marketing Management,* February 26, 1990, p. 81.

concerning age, sex, appearance, physical ability, and lifestyle and embrace the concept of on-the-job diversity. Some companies, like Ortho Pharmaceutical, Avon, and Pillsbury, have hired consultants to conduct "diversity seminars" for their employees.[15] There can be no doubt that *Workforce 2000* (the U.S. workforce in the year 2000) will include a greater number of women and ethnic minorities than U.S. business has ever seen.

Female Sales Reps

Women have already made significant progress in entering industries traditionally dominated by men. Nearly 70 percent of companies employ female sales reps today, and the percentage is climbing. During the 1980s, the proportion of women in sales rose more than two and half times, from 7 percent to 18 percent.[16] Women now hold key sales jobs in such diverse industries as steel, aluminum, life insurance, lumber, brewing, office equipment, computer equipment, and consumer packaged goods. Table 2-1 shows women as a percentage of the sales force in various industries.

Saleswomen are outperforming salesmen. Women in sales frequently perform better than men because they tend to have a greater ability to empathize with customers and to nurture long-term relationships. Studies also indicate that women tend to listen and speak better than men, and are more service-oriented.[17] Saleswomen at Exxon, for example, are outperforming salesmen in selling electronic and information-processing products, and their commissions are running 10 to 15 percent higher than salesmen's. Women are also outperforming men at Semispecialists of America, where a sales manager says that they tend to

---

[15]Mabry et al., "Past Tokenism," pp. 37–38, 43.
[16]"The Birth of a Saleswoman," *U.S. News & World Report,* February 6, 1989, p. 40.
[17]Ibid., pp. 40–42.

Selling in Action

Eight Cents or $100,000?

At Century 21, Vikki Morrison is one of the company's top salespeople, generating up to $9 million a year in sales. At age 29, she found herself in a dead-end job as a secretary. One day, after receiving an 8-cents-an-hour raise, she recalled her mother's advice: "Presidents are people who want to be presidents." Determined to prove that she was better than her 8-cents-an-hour increase suggested, Vikki began thinking bigger. She completed a real estate course and began selling properties in Huntington Beach, California. For three years, she ate, slept, and breathed real estate, 24 hours a day. To prevent burnout, she exercised regularly and maintained a positive attitude by reading upbeat books and magazine stories, avoiding negative people, and never watching television news. Today Vikki happily says that personal selling is the only field you can go into after a 90-day real estate course and earn $100,000 a year if you apply yourself.

Source: Stephanie Bernardo, Elizabeth Meryman, Hanna Rubin, and Judith D. Schwartz, "Superstars of Selling," *Success,* November 1984, p. 37.

be better team players than men and just as aggressive. In fact, some studies show that a woman can be far more aggressive than a man when dealing with a male customer.[18] The Selling in Action box that follows shows that opportunities in sales are waiting for women who are willing to take the initiative to move beyond dead-end jobs.

Assimilating women into sales. Hercules, Inc., a manufacturer of chemical resins, set up a special conference for its saleswomen to discuss problems unique to women in industrial selling. After listening to the saleswomen complain for an hour about late deliveries on customer orders, too much paperwork, and inadequate backup from the laboratory, the male moderator interrupted: "Hold on a minute, this is just what I hear from the guys."[19]

Although they may have many of the same problems as salesmen, saleswomen do have some special concerns, as discovered in a recent poll.[20] On a *personal level,* these are:

- Scheduling their travel to avoid problems at home, especially in taking care of children.
- Having to explain to customers and friends why they travel, how their husbands feel about their jobs, and who takes care of the children.
- Unwelcome advances from men, including strangers, hotel employees, customers, and colleagues.

[18]John T. Molloy, *Molloy's Live for Success* (New York: Bantam Books, 1983), p. 91.
[19]"The Industrial Salesman Becomes a Salesperson," *Business Week,* February 19, 1979, pp. 104–110.
[20]Bobbi Linkemer, "Women in Sales: What Do They Really Want?" *Sales & Marketing Management,* January 1989, pp. 61–65.

- Becoming dependent on male sales managers who assume a paternal or mentor role.
- Clients' perceptions of their relationships with sales managers or male colleagues when they travel together.
- The difficulty of maintaining a social life if they are single and must travel.
- Competition or lack of cooperation from husbands when they are more successful or have more "glamorous" jobs.

On a *professional level,* women worry about:

- Sustaining interest and maintaining credibility with the prospect from the beginning of the call to the close of the sale.
- Handling heavy luggage and sample cases.
- Getting lost or having the car break down on a strange road in unfamiliar territory— especially at night.
- Taking married male customers to dinner. Some customers bring their wives, some feel awkward, and others misinterpret the invitation.
- How they come across on the job—too feminine? too aggressive? too self-confident? too diffident?
- Dealing with customers or sales managers who believe "a woman's place is in the home" or in a typing pool.

Because of the flexibility in working hours, sales has become the field of choice for many women who want to have it all—marriage, children, and career.

■ The reactions of their sales managers or customers if they have to cancel an appointment, trip, or major sales presentation because of a sick child.

Women have come a long way in sales during the last decade or so. Many problems that today's saleswomen face are common to all salespeople, such as long and irregular working hours, frequent travel, entertaining customers, and dealing with difficult customers. But saleswomen are still more likely than salesmen to encounter unwelcome sexual overtures, exclusion from "good ol' boy" get-togethers, and condescension from an occasional Neanderthal customer who doesn't want to do business with a woman, especially in technical sales.

Saleswomen, marriage, and children. In a study on single and married saleswomen between the ages of 25 and 36 (over a third of whom had children at home), Kanuk concluded that "a career in industrial sales is not incompatible with marriage or having children."[21] In fact, because of the flexibility in working hours, sales has become the field of choice for many women who want to have it all—marriage, children, and career.

Female sales managers. Many women are also advancing into sales management positions. According to U.S. Labor Department statistics, manufacturing firms now employ almost 5,000 female sales managers. The experiences of such companies as Del Monte, General Tire & Rubber, Wang Laboratories, Viking Press, Continental Air Transport, Jewel Companies, and Xerox prove that women can perform successfully as sales managers. Over 3 million sales reps in the United States are women, and they will make up nearly 40 percent of all sales forces by the early 1990s. Thus, tomorrow's sales manager will more and more likely be female.

Support organizations for saleswomen. The National Association for Professional Saleswomen and the National Association of Business and Industrial Saleswomen are two sources of advice and support for new saleswomen or sales managers. After networking with successful saleswomen at meetings of these professional organizations, many women have found the self-confidence to leave dead-end jobs for higher-paying sales careers.

Minorities in Sales

As the number of women entering the sales profession is climbing, so too is the number of African-Americans, Asian-Americans, Native Americans, Hispanic-Americans, and handicapped and older workers. These and other minority groups are protected under civil rights law, and during the last two decades, employers have been subjected to legal and moral pressure to hire people from these groups. In the future, however, sales managers who seek qualified employees will stop thinking of these groups as literal minorities because the pool of people from diverse ethnic backgrounds and abilities is growing rapidly, while the number of white males aged 16 to 24 (who have traditionally been the majority of sales trainees) is shrinking.

The aging of the baby boomers and the baby-bust generation that followed them means that in the mid-1990s and beyond there will be intense pressure to raise compensation for new sales recruits, retain experienced, older salespeople, and attract salespeople from other companies. Texas Refinery Corporation is

American sales forces include such diverse people that the only valid stereotype of the salesperson today is "well-educated, well-trained professional."

[21]Leslie Kanuk, "Women in Industrial Selling," *Journal of Marketing,* January 1978, pp. 87–91.

leading the way in recruiting older salespeople. One-fifth of its sales force of 3,000 is over 65; the oldest salesperson is 84. A recent "rookie of the year" was a 74-year-old man who earned $45,000 in commissions. Studies of thousands of salespeople have found that a person of 50 may be more open-minded and vigorous than someone half that age.[22] In many situations, their age and experience actually give older salespeople a decided advantage over younger competitors.

In short, American sales forces in the near future will include such diverse people that the only valid stereotype of the salesperson will be "well-educated, well-trained professional."

Microsegmentation of Domestic Markets

Millions of immigrants (legal and illegal) will enter the United States in the decade ahead. America is becoming multicultural and multilingual. Selling in major parts of Miami, New York City, Los Angeles, Chicago, Philadelphia, Detroit, and San Antonio—in fact, in most large cities—will increasingly require an understanding of different cultures, languages, tastes, and preferences for everything from food and clothing to cosmetics. Any sales force that does not understand this rich mix of wants and needs will miss out on several large, fast-growing markets.

Recognizing that selling in America is becoming somewhat like selling internationally, Campbell Soup Company has divided the United States into 22 distinct markets based on unique cultural and ethnic tastes and preferences. In 1987, Campbell allocated about 15 percent of its $181 million advertising budget to regional promotion, and intends to increase its regional ad budget to around 50 percent. Products exemplifying Campbell's regional sales approach are spicy Ranchero beans and Nacho cheese soup in the Southwest, Creole soup in some southern markets, red bean soup in Hispanic-American areas, pepper pot soup only in the Philadelphia area, and Zesty pickles for Northwesterners who like their pickles very sour. Goya Foods, which employs a Spanish-speaking sales force that serves both large retailers and *bodegas* (Hispanic-American mom-and-pop stores), has already won a major share of the diverse Hispanic-American market by catering to the special tastes and preferences of consumers from Mexico, Puerto Rico, Venezuela, and Cuba.

Intense Foreign Competition

With its large population, high discretionary income levels, and political stability, the United States is the world's most attractive market. Companies based in Asia—notably in Japan, South Korea, Hong Kong, and Taiwan—have captured huge market shares of the most basic U.S. industries: automobiles, steel, electronic components, televisions, home appliances, industrial chemicals, textiles, and machine tools. Many foreign manufacturers and service companies are establishing operations in the United States. Foreign-owned assets now exceed $1 trillion and are growing by over $100 billion yearly. Unless the United States

---

[22]Herbert M. Greenberg and Jeanne Greenberg, "Job Matching for Better Sales Performance," *Harvard Business Review,* September–October 1980, pp. 128–133.

can learn to manufacture, market, and service innovative, top-quality, cost-competitive products, it will continue to lose domestic market shares to imports and world market shares to global competitors. The future economic health of the United States will depend partly on how well salespeople and sales managers do their jobs as competition from foreign products and services intensifies.

Internationalization of Markets

Over 20 percent of the U.S. gross national product comes from the export of goods and services, and that percentage will have to be increased if this country is to regain a healthy balance of trade. The United States is in global competition now, so American salespeople will have to learn how to sell in foreign countries. Language, customs, culture, politics, ethics, law, economies, market information, and distribution channels are just a few of the areas where differences can make international selling much more challenging and potentially more rewarding for salespeople willing to make the extra effort.

RISING PERSONAL SELLING COSTS

The increasing costs of personal selling are forcing salespeople and their companies to consider alternative direct-marketing methods for selling to consumers and organizations.

According to *Sales & Marketing Management*'s annual Survey of Selling Costs, the average cost of a sales call increased more than 11 percent a year during the last decade, at a time when the average annual sales volume per salesperson rose by only 5.5 percent. Over the same period, the average number of nonselling hours grew from 12.6 to 15 per week, resulting in an additional 120 nonselling hours per year, and the average cost of training a salesperson jumped 31 percent, from $11,000 to $14,435.[23]

The median cost of a business-to-business sales call is now more than $250. The cost varies by industry, from a high of over $300 for industrial machinery and equipment to a low of $155 for stone, clay, and glass products.[24] For some individual companies like IBM and Apple Computer, a sales call costs over $400 because of the unusual complexity of both the selling process and the product itself.[25] A survey by McGraw-Hill found that it takes, on average, 4.6 face-to-face calls to close the typical industrial product sale of $125,400.[26]

Several changes in the selling environment have contributed to rising sales costs: (1) the emphasis on market segmentation; (2) expensive national account selling; (3) the growth in customer service demands; (4) increased transportation costs; (5) a greater number of professional buyers; (6) the consolidation of distributors, giving them the power to demand more service and price concessions; and (7) reductions in the number of vendors approved by customers. According

[23]William A. O'Connell, "A 10-Year Report on Sales Force Productivity," *Sales & Marketing Management*, December 1988, pp. 33–36, 38.
[24]*Marketing News,* September 12, 1988, p. 5.
[25]*Sales & Marketing Management,* February 1989, p. 25.
[26]*Sales & Marketing Management,* November 1988, p. 27.

to the Conference Board, a growing number of large manufacturers are cutting costs by reaching customers through distributors, other middlemen, and direct marketing rather than with their own sales forces.[27]

DIRECT-MARKETING ALTERNATIVES

As the costs of personal sales calls continue to rise, companies are trying out new methods to reduce these costs. Rather than fear or fight these new selling methods, professional salespeople should jump on the bandwagon and make skillful use of the new techniques to improve their selling efficiency and effectiveness.

DIRECT MARKETING Any nonstore selling to consumers, including door-to-door selling, direct mail, telemarketing, electronic mail, and selling via television, videodisc, and automatic vending.

There are several available methods for selling to consumers besides retail store sales. Today in-store sales account for 85 percent of consumer purchases. Within ten years, nonstore selling—commonly called **direct marketing**—is expected to account for one-third of all consumer sales.[28] Direct-marketing methods reach out to consumers in their homes, saving them the inconvenience of having to go to a retail store. For generations, the traditional method of reaching consumers directly has been door-to-door sales.

Door-to-Door Selling

More than 600 companies, including pioneers like Fuller Brush Company, Electrolux (vacuum cleaners), World Book (encyclopedias), and Southwestern (books), sell to consumers in their homes or offices. Stanley Home Products in the 1930s, and later Tupperware and Mary Kay Cosmetics, put a different twist on door-to-door selling by popularizing "home-party sales" at which products and services are demonstrated and sold to friends and neighbors in a festive atmosphere at one of the customer's homes. Door-to-door selling offers consumers convenience and individualized attention, which are somewhat offset by higher prices resulting from labor costs—mostly commissions for the salespeople, who often receive 40 to 50 cents of every sales dollar.

Is Anybody Home?
The growth in the number of working-couple households has reduced the chances of salespeople finding anyone home when they call. Now that over 60 percent of American women work outside the home, companies in door-to-door selling are finding it difficult to recruit new sales reps and to retain those they do recruit. Recruitment of part-time salespeople on college campuses has not been very successful either, because of the negative image of door-to-door salespeople. A recent word-association study of personal selling done with 300 college students found that 68 percent of comments regarding door-to-door selling were negative.[29] Other impediments to door-to-door selling are local Green River

[27]*The Wall Street Journal,* November 25, 1986, p. 1.
[28]Richard Green, "A Boutique in Your Living Room," *Forbes,* May 7, 1984, pp. 86–94.
[29]William A. Weeks and Darrel D. Muehling, "Students' Perceptions of Personal Selling," *Industrial Marketing Management,* May 1987, pp. 145–151.

Ordinances that require the licensing of such salespeople and limit the hours or neighborhoods in which they may make calls.

Since many Americans don't like to meet door-to-door salespeople or participate in home-party sales, a rapidly growing trend is the replacement of door-to-door salespeople by less costly and less restrictive direct-marketing methods. There are several alternative channels to sell to consumers and organizational buyers: *direct mail, telemarketing, facsimile, electronic mail (E-mail), selling via television (direct-response and home-shopping channels), electronic shopping,* and *automatic vending.* Because of the speed with which they reach the customer, some direct-marketing methods, such as facsimile and E-mail, are called "salespeople on wings."

Direct Mail

Since the 1960s, several important developments have helped facilitate the growth of direct mail. First, the postal service introduced ZIP codes, which enabled direct marketers to segment their markets and efficiently reach target groups of people by mail. Now even more mailing precision is possible because business ZIP codes have nine instead of the former five digits. Second, widespread distribution of *credit cards* to people whose incomes and creditworthiness have been checked allow direct marketers to obtain mailing lists of affluent prospects. Third, high-speed electronic *computers* allow direct marketers to analyze huge customer-response databases and to generate specific lists of customers by desired market segments. Fourth, the creation and growth of *express mail* by such companies as UPS, Federal Express, and Emory have spurred the U.S. postal service to add express mail service, too. All of these overnight delivery services have helped to increase direct-mail sales dramatically.

Over 35 percent of Americans have bought a product or service after reading letters, brochures, advertisements, or catalogs received through the mail. The cost per thousand people reached is higher than with mass media such as television or magazines, but targeted mailing lists provide much better prospects. Profits for mail-order companies average nearly 60 percent more than those for retail stores selling similar items.[30] Applying **databased marketing techniques,** mailing-list companies use computers to generate lists of names and addresses for numerous demographic and psychographic dimensions stored in their data banks, including income level, education, home ownership, magazine readership, political party, and clothing preferences.

DATABASED MARKETING TECHNIQUES Using computers to compile and generate mailing lists and other information about prospective customers.

Direct mail accounts for nearly half of all direct-response purchases, while sales by telephone, circulars, magazines, and newspapers each account for 7 percent or less. The fastest-growing major segment of direct mail is catalog sales. With nearly 12 billion copies of more than 8,500 different catalogs being mailed out annually, the average household receives at least 50 catalogs a year, which generate sales of over $65 billion.[31] According to the Direct Marketing Association, consumer purchases by mail have been increasing by 10 percent a year for the past decade—double the growth rate of the rest of retailing. At the beginning

[30]"Caution: Retailing Without Marketing May Be Dangerous to Your Health," *ZIP/Target Marketing,* May 1983, p. 23.

[31]Eileen Norris, "Alternative Media Try to Get Their Feet in the Door," *Advertising Age,* October 17, 1985, p. 15.

of 1990, about 28 percent of all purchases were made by mail, and some experts predict that this figure will be at least 50 percent within ten years.[32]

Direct mail is not just for commercial companies. Nearly one-fourth of all direct-mail income is generated by nonprofit charities, which have raised over $35 billion in one year by direct-mail solicitation.[33] In the increasingly competitive medical field, hospitals, clinics, and some physicians regularly mail newsletters to patients and potential patients. Although some doctors write their own newsletters, others purchase a generic newsletter with their name and office address printed on it. Both kinds of newsletters are subtly effective marketing devices. Some doctors say they would give up their listing in the Yellow Pages before they'd stop sending out their newsletter.[34]

Telemarketing

A marketing strategy conducted entirely by telephone to support and sometimes substitute for face-to-face selling is called _telemarketing._ Employed by over 250,000 U.S. businessses, it can be either outbound or inbound. _Outbound telemarketing_ uses the telephone to call customers at their homes or businesses in place of making costly sales calls in person. While a sales representative can average 5 calls a day, a telemarketer can make up to 15 phone contacts per hour.[35] Although the final sale may not be closed over the telephone, telemarketers can qualify prospects for the sales force to call upon. _Inbound telemarketing_ responds to customers who call a toll-free number to obtain information or place orders.

Among the many reasons for the growth of telemarketing are:

- The rising cost of field selling.
- The lower cost of training inside salespeople.
- Lower expenses for inside salespeople compared to field salespeople's travel, housing, and entertainment expenditures.
- The greater efficiency of telemarketing compared to field selling (no travel or waiting) and the close control that can be exercised over the activities of inside salespeople.

At one of its sales offices, General Electric achieved a 94 percent cost reduction without losing sales volume by reassigning smaller accounts to telemarketing.[36] By the year 2000, there are expected to be 8 million new telemarketing jobs in the United States, the largest increase in any job category.[37]

Telemarketing got a big boost in the late 1960s with the introduction of inward and outward Wide Area Telephone Service (WATS). With IN WATS, marketers can use toll-free 800 numbers to handle customer service and complaints, or to receive orders generated by television and radio ads, direct mail, or catalogs. With OUT WATS, they can use the telephone to sell directly to consumers and businesses, generate or qualify sales leads, reach distant buyers, or service

---

[32]_Business Week,_ January 8, 1990, p. 33.

[33]Arnold Fishman, "The 1986 Mail Order Guide," _Direct Marketing,_ July 1987, p. 40.

[34]Ellen Paris, "Paper Medicine," _Forbes,_ January 23, 1989, p. 92.

[35]Joel Dreyfuss, "Reach Out and Sell Something," _Fortune,_ November 26, 1984, pp. 127–132.

[36]Louis A. Wallis, _Computers and the Sales Effort_ (New York: The Conference Board, 1986), p. 10.

[37]Earl Hitchcock, "Suddenly, Marketers Are Calling Up America," _Sales & Marketing Management,_ June 4, 1984, p. 36.

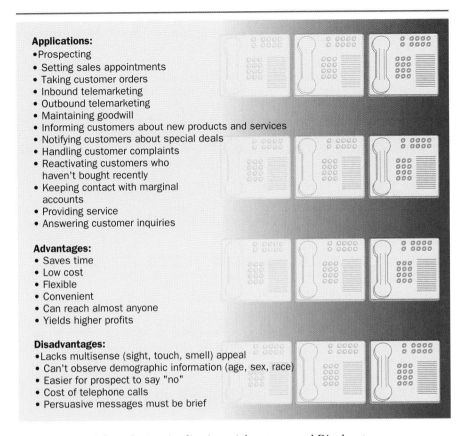

Applications:
- Prospecting
- Setting sales appointments
- Taking customer orders
- Inbound telemarketing
- Outbound telemarketing
- Maintaining goodwill
- Informing customers about new products and services
- Notifying customers about special deals
- Handling customer complaints
- Reactivating customers who haven't bought recently
- Keeping contact with marginal accounts
- Providing service
- Answering customer inquiries

Advantages:
- Saves time
- Low cost
- Flexible
- Convenient
- Can reach almost anyone
- Yields higher profits

Disadvantages:
- Lacks multisense (sight, touch, smell) appeal
- Can't observe demographic information (age, sex, race)
- Easier for prospect to say "no"
- Cost of telephone calls
- Persuasive messages must be brief

FIGURE 2-3 Telemarketing Applications, Advantages, and Disadvantages

current customers. As shown in Figure 2-3, telemarketing has many applications.

An estimated 250,000 U.S. companies are now using telemarketing to generate over $100 billion a year in sales, and the growth rate is 25 to 30 percent a year. More than $50 billion is being spent annually by telemarketers to sell products and services over the phone. Over 700 people dial an 800 number every minute in response to television commercials. Each year, the average household makes 16 calls to order products or services and receives 19 telephone sales calls. If a customer calls you, you have an 80 percent chance of making a sale, but if you call the customer, your chances for a sale drop to 20 percent.[38] Some telemarketing systems are fully automated. For example, automatic dialing and recorded message players dial telephone numbers, play a voice-activated advertising message, and take orders from interested customers on an answering machine or by forwarding the call to an operator.

Telemarketing is being used increasingly in business marketing as well as in consumer marketing. By the early 1990s, a new transmission technology called Integrated Services Digital Network (ISDN) will be installed in most major U.S. cities. ISDN will make telemarketing more like face-to-face selling in that it will

A TALKING COMPUTER COVERS CONSUMER FLOORS

Sands Woody, president of Woody Distributors in Roanoke, Virginia, uses a talking computer—an order-processing system that responds to callers in a natural-sounding human voice—to process orders for his $10 million floor-covering distributorship. The VCT Series 2000 microcomputer, bought from Voice Computer Technologies Corporation in Arlington, Virginia, can handle up to eight orders at a time, 24 hours a day, over an ordinary Touch-tone telephone. "We're not open Saturdays, but our customers are," says Woody. Callers simply press the appropriate buttons on the Touch-tone phone to enter their orders. The computer also checks and automatically updates inventories. Various contingencies can be handled, too. For example, if an item is not in stock, the computer can suggest an alternative. If that substitute is unacceptable, the computer will ask if the caller would like to talk with a salesperson. As the system expands and becomes more sophisticated, Woody hopes to free up current order takers to make more outgoing sales calls.

Source: Sara Delano, "Turning Sales Inside Out," *INC.,* August 1983, pp. 99–102.

enable salespeople to transmit their voices, video images, and computer data simultaneously to customers over the phone. One company has been very successful in using a "talking computer salesperson," as described in the above vignette.

How Telemarketers Help Field Salespeople
Telemarketing salespeople serve four basic functions in helping field salespeople: sales support, order taking, customer service, and account management.

Sales support. Telemarketing representatives are especially valuable to the outside salespeople in finding and qualifying prospects, scheduling sales call appointments, and leading prospects up the *hierarchy of effects* toward a pur-

In addition to their effectiveness as direct marketers, telemarketing representatives can help field salespeople in the areas of sales support, order taking, customer service, and account management.

chase decision so that the outside salesperson has an easier time closing the sale. Many insurance companies have cut their costs of doing business by using tele-marketing teams to prospect and qualify leads generated by direct mail or adver-tising, then giving the prospect list to independent sales agents. Some companies using this approach have achieved closing rates of over 70 percent.

Order taking. Telemarketing reps can save field reps time by handling rou-tine orders and reorders from present customers. Digital Equipment Corpora-tion's telemarketing staff for its Accessories and Supplies Group handles over 14,000 calls per month for a product line of 30,000 items, ranging in price from $20 to $15,000.[39] In consumer marketing, *Changing Times, Sports Illustrated, Time,* and other magazines advertise toll-free numbers for consumers to call to order a subscription. Many organizations, such as 3M, Xerox, and Blue Cross, routinely seek basic information about their 800 callers to build prospect and customer data banks.

Customer service. Telemarketers can ease the burden on the outside sales force by providing a number of customer services. They can respond to customer inquiries about order status, delivery date, price, returns and claims, and tech-nical information; handle complaints, sales literature requests, and liaison with other departments; conduct consumer surveys; and generally promote customer goodwill. Knowing that some knowledgeable, helpful person is always just a phone call away makes customers feel more secure and leads to higher customer retention rates. By talking daily to a cross section of customers, telemarketing reps learn a lot about customer needs and become an excellent source for new-product ideas.

Account management. Telemarketing staffs may be assigned account man-agement duties for specific customer groups. For example, one group of tele-marketing reps may handle all retail accounts, while another group handles all distributors and a third is responsible for government accounts. Account man-agement responsibilities include handling ordering, credit, billing, complaints, and product information. By serving just a specific group of accounts, the tele-marketing representative can build special expertise and rapport with particular customers instead of trying to be a "jack-of-all-trades" to a cross section of cus-tomers.

Facsimile

Direct marketers are making increasing use of "faxing" as an inexpensive meth-od to reach prospects and customers. Facsimile machines can send a letter, chart, photograph, or other document to customers almost instantly. Faxing promo-tions to target customers avoids the massive waste of unopened junk mail. And when a customer claims he didn't receive a sales proposal or invoice, the sales-person can fax him one in less than a minute.

While Federal Express and similar carriers charge at least $10 to deliver a single document the next day, a page of text or a chart can be faxed in about 20

[39]John I. Coppett and Roy Dale Voorhees, "Telemarketing Supplement to Field Sales," *Indus-trial Marketing Management,* May 1984, pp. 213–216.

Direct marketers are making increasing use of "faxing" as an inexpensive method to reach prospects and customers.

seconds at the cost of a very short long-distance phone call. Faxes overcome the problems of delayed transportation, unreliable couriers, and telephone tag. A fax can be sent virtually anywhere in the world at any time, whether the receiving office is open or not, and the information will be there upon the addressee's arrival.

Electronic Mail

Since most American businesses and over 40 million American homes now possess personal computers, electronic transmissions or E-mail from one computer to another is an inexpensive way to reach out to customers either at their home or in their office.[40] Computer "hackers" used electronic bulletin boards to communicate with one another for years before their direct-marketing potential was realized. Computerized reservation services for air travel and hotels were among the first large applications of electronic data transmission. The cost of sending a three-page letter by Federal Express overnight, with pickup, is $14, compared to about $1 for fax (day rates) and $1 for electronic mail.[41] By 1995, the cost of an electronic transmission is expected to fall to 8 cents. Some electronic mail systems permit the sender to attach a "receipt" to a message to ensure that it's read before a follow-up sales call is made.

Aggressive direct marketers are coming up with innovative schemes to contact prospects and customers electronically. Prodigy, a joint venture between Sears and IBM, is a low-cost, public, on-line service that will be available to about 90 percent of the U.S. population in the early 1990s. It provides news, banking, shopping, discount brokerage services, electronic mail, and dozens of other services, while keeping monthly fees low by selling advertising space to appear along the bottom of the user's computer screen.[42]

[40]David Churbuck, "Let Your Keyboard Do the Walking." *Forbes*, January 9, 1989, pp. 316–317.
[41]*Business Week*, February 20, 1989, p. 36.
[42]Kathleen A Hughes, "IBM-Sears Computer-Services Venture Shows Promise, But a Lot of Kinks Remain," *The Wall Street Journal*, February 8, 1989, p. B1.

Selling via Television

Television offers two ways to market products directly to consumers: direct-response selling and home-shopping channels.

Direct-Response Selling

This kind of selling usually includes a persuasive advertisement describing and demonstrating a product in 60- or 120-second spots, with a toll-free number for viewers to call with their order. Direct-response selling is often used for records, tapes, magazines, books, and small home appliances. Some successful direct-response ads have run for years and become classics. For instance, the ads for Ginsu knives ran for seven years and sold almost 3 million sets (over $40 million worth), and the long-running Armourcote cookware ads generated nearly $80 million in sales.[43]

Home-Shopping Channels

These are programs or entire channels devoted to selling products and services. More than half of all U.S. homes have access to one of a dozen home-shopping channels such as Home Shopping Network, Cable Value Network, Value Club of America, Home Shopping Mall, or Telshop. Home Shopping Network (HSN), which broadcasts its Home Shopping Club 24 hours a day, is the largest, reaching 15 million cable TV homes and 26 million UHF broadcast channel homes. The program's upbeat hosts promote general merchandise ranging from jewelry, lamps, collectible dolls, and clothing to power tools and consumer electronics. Hosts honk horns, blow whistles, make small talk, and praise viewers for their good taste, while making short sales presentations on each item shown. Viewers call an 800 number to order merchandise from over 400 operators handling more than 1,200 incoming lines. The operators enter orders directly into their computer terminals, and orders are shipped within 48 hours. Sales were $2 billion in 1987, and are expected to exceed $7 billion by 1992.

Electronic Shopping

Videotex and Videodisc are the major types of electronic shopping.

Videotex

VIDEOTEX A two-way electronic home-shopping system that links consumers with the seller's computer data banks via cable or telephone lines.

A two-way system that links consumers with the seller's computer data banks via cable or telephone lines, **videotex** provides a computerized catalog of products offered by manufacturers, retailers, banks, and travel and entertainment organizations. Consumers can connect into the system by telephone via modems on their home computers or through their televisions via special keyboard and cable hookups. Choosing from a list of several stores, they can select a department within the store and the specific products, brands, models, or price categories they want shown on their television screen. Viewers using the interactive system call up comprehensive directories or menus to select products like baby shoes, men's ties, vacuum cleaners, or more general categories such as "what's

---

[43]Jim Auchmute, "But Wait There's More!" *Advertising Age*, October 17, 1985, p. 18.

What Would You Do?

As a sales representative assigned a territory that includes New York City, you have become frustrated by traffic problems. Last week, while driving to two separate appointments with major accounts, you got stuck in traffic jams and arrived over a half-hour late each time. Both customers told you it would be necessary to reschedule the appointment about three weeks from now be-cause their calendars were so booked. You're afraid that missing appointment times will cost you a lot of business. You've even thought about using the New York subway system and taxis to get to appointments, but it would be difficult to carry all your sales presentation material and equipment by hand.

on sale." To order, the consumer enters the desired item number and a charge card number.

Videodisc

VIDEODISC An electronic shopping system that collects product information on a disk similar to an audio compact disc and allows merchants and consumers to "play back" this information in their stores and homes.

An electronic shopping system that collects digitalized product information on a disk similar to an audio compact disc, **videodisc** allows the storage of text, photographs, videotapes, and sound, all on the same disc. Currently, videodiscs are used primarily in stores and public places—like shopping malls, hotel lobbies, and airports—to assist people in obtaining information. Recently, however, J.C. Penney has experimented with a unique new service that allows consumers access to Penney catalogs in their homes. Pictures and printed information are stored on laser videodisc and transmitted via cable to the shopper's home television screen. Telaction, a Penney subsidiary, began testing the concept with 125,000 cable-connected homes in the northwest suburbs of Chicago in the summer of 1987.

Automatic Vending

It is estimated that there is one vending machine for every 40 people in the United States. Vending machines are virtually everywhere—in retail stores, gasoline stations, shopping malls, transportation and entertainment centers, factories, offices, hospitals, schools, and libraries—and sales are over $16.5 billion yearly, about 1.3 percent of total retail sales. Convenience products and services available from vending machines include cigarettes, gum, candy, beverages, yogurt, snack foods, newspapers, airline tickets, traveler's insurance, bloodpressure readings, shoeshines, cosmetics, paperback books, records and tapes, T-shirts, hosiery, photocopying, rides for children, and even fishing worms. Automatic teller machines (ATMs) provide bank customers with checking, savings, withdrawals, and funds-transfer services. Vending machines offer consumers 24-hour self-service, but customers and vendors must deal with such disadvantages as higher costs and prices, vandalism and machine breakdowns, change-making errors, out-of-stocks, low-quality image, and no returns on unsatisfactory goods.

SALESPEOPLE IN THE NEW ERA OF TECHNOLOGY

Flexible and resourceful salespeople should not fear the growing number of alternatives to sales reps in selling. All these methods still require human selling skills to design and effect major parts of the sales and customer service process. Some telecommunications and computer innovations will partially substitute for consumer products salespeople in carrying out certain parts of the selling process, such as prospecting and routine order taking. But the more dominant role of these innovations will be to help professional salespeople do their jobs more effectively and efficiently, especially in selling to organizations.

SUMMARY Today's professional salespeople work in dramatically changing selling environments and must increasingly operate like micromarketing managers in their territories. First, several megatrends are changing customers, markets, and the composition of America's sales forces. Second, revolutionary developments in telecommunications and computer technology are helping salespeople do their jobs better but, in some cases, partially replacing consumer products salespeople. Finally, rising personal selling costs have encouraged salespeople and their companies to make greater use of alternative direct-marketing techniques to reach consumer and organizational prospects and customers.

CHAPTER REVIEW QUESTIONS

1. Why must today's professional salesperson learn to function like a micromarketing manager in the field?
2. What are the duties and responsibilities of a professional salesperson today?
3. Describe eight current megatrends that impact personal selling.
4. Name some of the major advances in telecommunications and computer technology that are affecting personal selling and briefly describe how each one works.
5. Refer to Table 2-1, Women in Sales by Industry. Why do you think the communications, printing/publishing, electronics, instruments, and office equipment industries have higher percentages of saleswomen than do the chemicals, fabricated metals, wholesaling, and utilities industries?
6. Why do saleswomen often outperform salesmen in their jobs?
7. In your own words, define the term *direct marketing*. What tools and techniques are used in direct marketing?
8. Why do some companies see selling in the United States as increasingly like selling internationally?
9. Describe the type of assistance that salespeople may receive from the company's telemarketing staff. What can field salespeople do to increase the benefits they derive from telemarketers?

TOPICS FOR THOUGHT AND CLASS DISCUSSION

1. What would you recommend that companies do to attract more women and minorities into personal selling?

2. Which of the advances in telecommunications and computer technology do you think will provide the most help to salespeople over the next decade? What present or potential new technologies do you think will be most important to personal selling ten years from now?

3. How do you think the rising cost of personal selling and the growth of direct-marketing techniques will affect salespeople who sell door-to-door to consumers?

PROJECTS FOR PERSONAL GROWTH

1. Make a sketch of a very modern sales office showing the various computer and telecommunications technologies that are available to assist and keep in touch with the field sales force.

2. Campbell Soup Company has divided the United States into 22 regional markets based on different tastes and preferences for its food products. Assume that you have been asked by Campbell's CEO to prepare a map of the United States showing these regional markets. Don't worry about coming up with exactly 22; just try to identify as many as you can. Clearly label each region according to the way you identify it. For example, perhaps part of the southwestern United States may be identified as a regional market for Mexican-American tastes and preferences, whereas part of Florida may be identified with Cuban-American tastes and preferences. You may need to do some library research to complete your map.

KEY TERMS

Micromarketing manager   Another name for a sales representative who skillfully applies the latest professional personal selling principles and marketing techniques in his or her designated territory or market.

Videoconferencing   The use of video technology in such a way that people in various locations can simultaneously participate in a meeting or conference.

Voice mail   Various electronic methods of sending and receiving voice messages, ranging from a simple telephone answering machine to a complex, computer-driven "mailbox" message storage and retrieval system.

Direct-marketing techniques   Techniques for selling products directly to consumers in their homes, such as catalog marketing, automatic vending, television home-shopping channels, and electronic shopping services.

Affirmative action   The collective attempt by public- and private-sector institutions and organizations to correct the effects of discrimination in the education or employment of women and minorities.

Direct marketing   Any nonstore selling to consumers, including door-to-door selling, direct mail, telemarketing, electronic mail, and selling via television, videodisc, and automatic vending.

Databased marketing techniques   Using computers to compile and generate mailing lists and other information about prospective customers.

Videotex   A two-way electronic home-shopping system that links consumers with the seller's computer data banks via cable or telephone lines.

Videodisc   An electronic shopping system that collects product information on a disk similar to an audio compact disc and allows merchants and consumers to "play back" this information in their stores and homes.

Case 2-1

COMPUTER FEARS

Jerry Mollberg has been a salesperson for Spartan & Brown, a small New York City–based manufacturer of men's clothing accessories (belts, tie clasps, cuff links, and suspenders), for nearly 23 years. Jerry calls on independent retail clothing stores in the New England area and earns a comfortable income, based on 70 percent salary and 30 percent commissions. Respected and well-liked by his customers, he makes at least one sales call a month on each of his customers and does his best to provide them with quality service. At the end of each sales call, he invariably tells the customer: "Don't hesitate to call me at the office or my home if you should have problems with any of our products or need any special service."

Except for his annual vacation during the first two weeks of August, Jerry always returns customer calls within a day or two. When traveling his territory, it is his habit to call his Spartan & Brown office each weekday around 4:00 P.M. to obtain his phone messages from Phyllis Lauver, the national sales manager's secretary. Next, Jerry always calls his home in Newark, New Jersey, to ask his wife for his messages. This routine enables him to provide what he believes to be excellent service to his customers. Rarely does one of Jerry's customers complain about not being able to obtain a needed service, such as a rush order or a correction of an erroneous billing, on a timely basis.

Last month, Spartan & Brown's national sales manager—a close friend of Jerry's—retired after 38 years with the company. Gordon Marrs, a 35-year-old former district sales manager for a West Coast manufacturer of men's wallets, was hired as the new national sales manager. Gordon is an extroverted, fast-talking, fast-moving, decisive individual who during his first week on the job sent a memorandum to all 20 of Spartan & Brown's salespeople. In it he said that he intended to modernize field sales operations by "bringing the S&B sales force into the computer age." First, he stated that all salespeople would be required to carry an electronic pager ("beeper") on their person from 7:00 A.M. to 6:00 P.M. each weekday so that he could reach them with emergency messages. Second, all S&B salespeople would have to install a cellular phone in their cars. Third, within three months, salespeople would be expected to car-

ry laptop computers on their sales calls so that "vital customer information will always be at your fingertips." Each S&B salesperson would contribute $500 of commission earnings to the purchase of these items so that, in Gordon's words, they would "have a stake in the use and maintenance of the new equipment."

Jerry was unhappy with these dictates from the new national sales manager. He saw little need for the new equipment—in fact, he felt it would be a waste of money because his customers had no complaints about their access to information and customer service. Daily telephone calls were working just fine, he thought, so "why fix the system if it ain't broke"? Jerry felt he had no choice but to obtain the equipment, especially since he would be charged $500 for it, but he didn't intend to give up his normal practice of making daily phone calls to headquarters and home to receive his messages.

As Gordon promised, within three months, all S&B salespeople had a personal beeper, cellular phone, and laptop computer. It wasn't hard to learn how to use the beeper and the car phone, but Jerry was intimidated by the laptop computer. He had never felt comfortable with anything "high-tech," and the manual that came with the computer was so poorly written that it didn't help much. After spending several nights and a weekend trying to use the computer, Jerry gave up and put it in his car trunk. For several weeks, he forgot all about it.

Then, late one Wednesday afternoon, Gordon Marrs called Jerry on his car phone to tell him that he would be traveling with him all next week to see how the new equipment was working out in his territory. A wave of apprehension flooded over Jerry as he realized that he hadn't taken the computer out of his car trunk in several weeks and he still didn't know how to use it. He began thinking about his options. Maybe he could:

- Just tell Gordon that he hasn't learned how to use the laptop and that he doesn't really need it to serve customers in his territory.
- Call one of the younger S&B salespeople who is successfully using the laptop to see if the two of them might get together this weekend for some instruction.

- Go to a local computer dealer to learn how to use the laptop.
- Ask the high-school daughter of a neighbor if she will help him learn how to use it this weekend.
- Get the computer manual out and try one more time to understand it.

Jerry also wondered what to tell Gordon if he asked how the computer was helping him serve customers better. And how should he respond in front of Gordon if a customer asked about the laptop upon seeing him carry one in for the first time? Gordon knew that he called on each customer at least once a month, so it might be hard to explain why a customer hadn't seen the laptop before. Jerry worried about what other situations or questions might come up during the five days Gordon would be traveling with him. That Wednesday night, Jerry didn't get a wink of sleep, and he still didn't feel that he knew what to do when he rolled out of bed red-eyed early Thursday

morning. He was too nervous to read the morning newspaper, so he continued to stew about his problems while he drank his morning coffee.

Questions

1. With respect to learning how to use the laptop computer, which of the options would you advise Jerry to take? Are there other options that he ought to consider?

2. What should Jerry say if Gordon asks him how he is using the laptop computer to better serve customers?

3. What should Jerry say if a customer asks about the laptop computer?

4. What other situations and possible questions should Jerry prepare for during his five days of working with Gordon?

5. What overall strategy or tactical advice would you give Jerry?

Case 2-2

SAVORING SUCCESS AND CONTEMPLATING THE FUTURE

Gloria Pattengale is eating dinner with two of her United Business Technologies (UBT) colleagues, Vickie Brodo and Deborah Coyle, at one of the best restaurants in Chicago. The three of them have just completed a three-week training course for new sales representatives and this dinner is part of their reward from UBT for finishing at the top of their training class. Out of 20 new sales trainees (8 women and 12 men) participating in the program, Vickie finished third, Deborah second, and Gloria first in overall scores on the five training categories: (1) role plays, (2) product demonstrations, (3) case analyses, (4) written exams, and (5) peer ratings. Now, for the first time in weeks, they are able to relax and reflect on what they have been through and what might be ahead for them at UBT. They all know that it is standard UBT practice to quickly assign newly trained sales representatives to individual sales territories.

While sipping their drinks and nibbling on appetizers, the three friends talk about the intensive pressure of the training they just completed. They have had almost no time for relaxation over the last three weeks, even on weekends, because time-consuming projects, such as preparing sales proposals or presentations for hypothetical customers, were assigned each Friday night for completion by Monday morning. None of the three can remember undergoing such sustained, intense pressure before. Let's listen in on their conversation.

Gloria Pattengale: I'm sure glad I took that selling and sales management course in college. I'd done a lot of this stuff—like role playing and case analyses—before. Of course, I worked a lot harder here than I did in college. I'll bet some of the guys are mad because none of them ranked in the top three. They're

Vickie Brodo: probably having pizza tonight while we dine in the style I'd like to become accustomed to.

Vickie Brodo: Earning 98 percent on that last exam made the difference for me. I just barely beat out Tom Bajier, who messed up on the final exam.

Deborah Coyle: Well, we all made it. Let's drink a toast to UBT's next three superstar salespeople.

Vickie Brodo: It feels great to be a winner!

Gloria Pattengale: It sure does. But to be honest, I get a little nervous just thinking about going out into my own territory within a few days. Training didn't cover what it's like for a *woman* traveling a sales territory. I wish we'd had some female trainers. I'm not sure men really understand some of the problems we might run into.

Deborah Coyle: I agree. What are we going to do when we stay overnight at a hotel? I don't want to go down to the hotel lounge alone, and I know I'm going to get bored sitting around in the room. Guess I'll just watch a movie on television or read some good books.

Vickie Brodo: You know what really worries me? Some customer, whose order I can't afford to lose, coming on to me. It's going to take some real skill to maneuver out of those situations.

Gloria Pattengale: I don't think you have to worry about too many of those situations, Vickie. Most men today are pretty skittish about being accused of sexual harassment. Besides, I plan to come across as so businesslike and professional that no one will bother me.

Vickie Brodo: Maybe you're right. But I don't want to be viewed as another one of the "boys" either. I think that the fact we are female can actually help us in gaining respectful treatment and winning sales. I've heard stories about customers getting so mad at salesmen that they throw them out of their offices. I don't think that will happen to us—unless, perhaps, the buyer's a woman, too! Another thing that worries me, though, is what to do when some customer starts asking a lot of technical questions about one of our more complex products and I don't have the info right away.

Gloria Pattengale: Don't you think all the guys are wor-

ried about that, too? Just do the same thing they do: Tell them you don't know but you'll find out and get back to them shortly. Look, we just spent three weeks proving that we're the best new sales reps in the company. I'm not worried about my ability. In fact, my biggest concern is what happens when I start making more money than my husband. I could be outearning him in less than three years.

Deborah Coyle: I don't think you need to worry, Gloria. Your husband seems very secure, so he'll probably be delighted when you earn more than he does.

Gloria Pattengale: Well, I don't know. We've never talked about it. I hope you're right. Come to think of it, maybe there aren't that many unique problems for women in selling. In fact, we probably have some advantages over salesmen. Oh well, we'll soon know. Look, here comes the waiter with our entrées—and we haven't even finished our appetizers yet!

Questions

1. Do you think that Gloria, Deborah, and Vickie need to worry about any speical problems they may encounter as saleswomen? If so, what kinds of problems? How would you advise them to handle these situations?

2. How would you advise a woman to deal with a spouse or boyfriend who feels insecure about her traveling alone, making more money than he does, or spending so much time on the job?

3. Do you think it will be possible for Gloria, Deborah, and Vickie to stay in the field if they decide to have children a few years from now? If not, why not? If so, how will they manage to keep high-pressure field sales jobs and still raise children? (*Hint:* You might develop one or more answers by *not* assuming that raising children is solely the woman's responsibility!)

4. What general advice would you give Gloria, Deborah, and Vickie in managing their interactions with customers, sales colleagues, and sale managers?

Chapter 3

Ethical and Legal Considerations in Personal Selling

A Society with no other scale but the legal one is not quite worthy of man.

ALEKSANDR SOLZHENITSYN

Profile

Jeff Odell

"I feel that the best preparation for a sales career is to develop a thorough understanding of (1) how businesses operate and (2) how people [buyers] think," says Jeff Odell, a sales representative with NCR Corporation in Richmond, Virginia. Jeff knew early in his college experience that he wanted to go into selling, and he took a straightforward approach to achieving this goal. In addition to carefully including a broad range of business and psychology courses in his curriculum, Jeff sought out extracurricular activities that would simultaneously provide him with enjoyment and ample opportunities to develop speaking and negotiating skills. One of the most important of these activities was his involvement with the Intra-Fraternity Council at his school, the University of Virginia. According to Jeff: "The primary purpose of the IFC is to enhance relationships between the fraternities and local residents. My work with the IFC gave me the opportunity to learn how to sell the positive aspects of fraternities to the community—quite a challenge, I might add!"

Jeff began his sales career by signing up for an interview at his university's Office of Career Planning and Placement. After three further interviews, Jeff accepted a job offer from NCR and embarked on a comprehensive six-month training course that included several weeks of field selling with experienced salespeople. Now in his sixth year with NCR, Jeff emphasizes that his work has a very significant managerial component: "My title, Senior Account Manager, sums it up. I coordinate the selling activities of several different product specialists who serve some of our largest customers. My role is not only to manage the selling and installing of systems, but also to manage and nurture the relationships developed between NCR and our customers."

When asked about ethical dilemmas he has encountered on the job, it becomes obvious that Jeff has a truly professional attitude toward his work: "Oftentimes a customer has set in his mind that he needs 'X' and wants to buy 'X,' although I know that he won't be happy with it in the long run. It's sometimes tempting just to sell it to him rather than convince him that he needs 'Y.' However, I've found that it's much better to forgo short-term gains and maintain the long-term relationship." Applying this same high ethical standard to his dealings with the competition, Jeff never knocks his competitors, but uses a strategy of patient persistence: "My plan is to make continuous calls on all levels of management, from the highest decision makers to the end users, and watch for holes in the competitor's armor."

Jeff loves selling and regards it as the best business training ground he could have hoped for. He told us: "I have definitely decided to make marketing my career—product marketing would probably be my first choice for my next career move. It's an area of business that I find fun, challenging, and financially rewarding." ■

After reading this chapter, you should understand:

□ Organizational, individual, and professional ethics and their potential conflicts

□ The roles and applications of business codes

□ The ethical concerns of salespeople in dealing with customers, competitors, employers, and co-workers

□ What behavior salespeople have a right to expect from employers

□ Key applications of federal, state, local, and international laws affecting personal selling

On June 1, 1989, Sam Donaldson hosted a television special titled "Lying, Cheating, and Stealing in America." The program pointed out that many of us, in all walks of life, have stopped asking ourselves whether what we plan to do is morally and ethically right. Instead, we now simply ask: "Can I get away with it?" Many of us seem to have developed an immunity or at least an insensitivity to high ethical standards. We cheat in school, on our income taxes, on our résumés, on our insurance claims, and in numerous other situations where the chances of getting caught are low. Only 7 percent of the people polled for this show felt that American business leaders have high moral and ethical standards. While the television documentary bemoaned the declining moral and ethical standards in America, there is some good news. Americans seem to be getting fed up with this ethical decay, and are now demanding adherence to higher standards of conduct by politicians, businesspeople, and perhaps even themselves.

WHAT ARE ETHICS?

ETHICS The moral code that governs individuals and societies in determining what is right and wrong.

Ethics may be defined as the study of what is good and bad or right and wrong. Ethics constitute a moral code of conduct governing individuals and societies. They deal with things as they should be, not necessarily as they are. According to the great humanitarian Dr. Albert Schweitzer, ethics is "an obligation to consider not only our own personal well-being, but also that of other human beings." People may differ sharply about what is ethical and unethical behavior, especially in complex, competitive areas like business. Thus there is a need for thorough analysis and evaluation before developing ethical standards for business decision making.

Business Ethics

In business, "right" and "wrong" decision making usually are based on economic criteria. Some salespeople have the idea that if it's legal, it's ethical. But "ethical" behavior is not simply that which stays within the law. A salesperson can be dishonest, unprincipled, untrustworthy, unfair, and uncaring without breaking the law.[1]

Most of us would probably agree that it's unethical to do what we personally believe is wrong. Thus a salesperson who believes that it's wrong to pressure older people to buy life insurance they don't really need, yet does so anyway, is acting unethically. Salespeople must continually work at being ethical, for as University of Pennsylvania business ethics professor Thomas Dunfee says: "Following the path of least resistance has the same effect on people as it does on rivers: It makes them crooked."[2]

BUSINESS CODES OF ETHICS

Business activities, like all human relationships, cannot function well for long unless we have some "rules of the game" that all parties abide by. If we could not trust one another, most day-to-day transactions would eventually come to a standstill while we waited for our lawyers to draw up mutually acceptable contracts. What an inefficient, frustrating world that would create! Fortunately, most businesspeople and customers value their reputations enough to abide by the general rules of ethical behavior.

To provide guidelines for principled business conduct, many organizations have developed codes of ethics. Ninety percent of Fortune 500 firms and almost half of all other companies have codes in place.[3] Some of these codes are very simple and unspecific. Cigna, the giant insurance company, tells its employees that they "will abide by the highest legal and ethical standards without exceptions." Instead of going into specifics, Cigna places heavy reliance on the individual good judgment and character of its employees. Quaker Oats Company prohibits "behavior that would be embarrassing for you, your family and our company if it were revealed publicly." Smith Kline Beckman issues a four-page statement on ethics that all managers must reread and agree to every year.

There are three basic types of ethical codes in American business:

- ■ *Professional codes* for occupational groups such as doctors, lawyers, accountants, marketing researchers, advertisers, and sales representatives.
- ■ *Business association codes* for companies engaged in the same line of activity. Examples are the codes established by the Direct Selling Association of America and by the American Association of Advertising Agencies.
- ■ *Advisory group codes* suggested by government agencies or other special interest groups.

The move toward sales and marketing professional codes is being led by various professional groups such as Sales and Marketing Executives International, the American Marketing Association, and the American Association of Adver-

---

[1]Michael Josephson, "Ethics Begin with People, Not Law Books," *The Philadelphia Inquirer*, February 12, 1989, p. 7-E.

[2]Rose DeWolf, "Doing Business Right—Ethically Speaking," *The Philadelphia Daily News*, January 3, 1989, p. 27.

[3]Patrick E. Murphy, "Implementing Business Ethics," *Journal of Business Ethics*, December 1988, pp. 907–915.

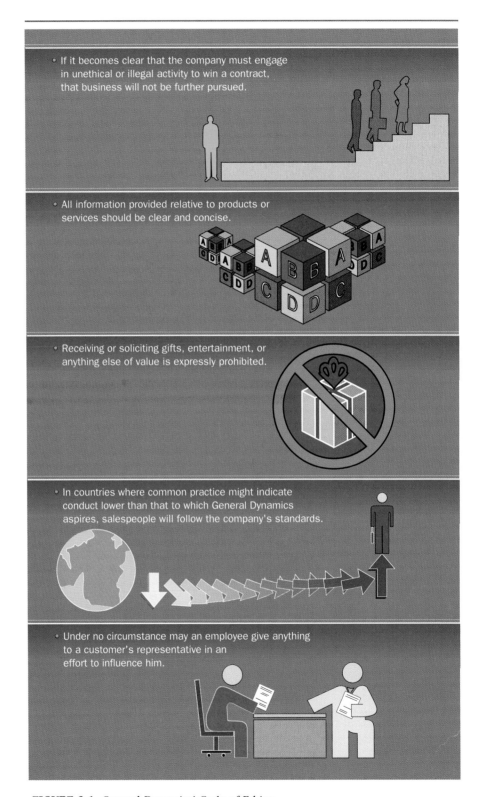

FIGURE 3-1 General Dynamics' Code of Ethics

Source: Arthur Bragg, "Ethics in Selling, Honest!" *Sales & Marketing Management,* May 1987, p. 44.

tising Agencies, each of which has adopted a code of ethics. According to the American Marketing Association's code of ethics, the basic rule of professional ethics is "not knowingly to do harm."

Formal codes of ethics must satisfy two requirements if they are to encourage ethical conduct. First, the codes must refer to specific practices such as kickbacks, payoffs, record falsification, and misleading sales claims. General platitudes about "good business practice" or "professional conduct" are not very effective. Second, organizational codes of ethics must be supported by top management and consistently enforced through a system of rewards and punishments. No code of ethical business practices is likely to be strictly adhered to by salespeople or anyone else unless violators are promptly given a punishment that matches the degree of infraction.

In 1977, the Foreign Corrupt Practices Act (FCPA) established a $1 million fine for the firm and a $10,000 fine and five years' imprisonment for any individual involved in bribing foreign officials to solicit new or repeat sales abroad. This stimulated most large companies to develop written codes of conduct focused on international business activities. These codes range from Gulf Oil's one-page "Statement of Business Principles" to lengthy codes for worldwide business conduct such as General Dynamics' 20-page "Code of Ethics" (Figure 3–1 is a condensed version of the latter). General Dynamics, which was charged by the U.S. government with engaging in unethical and illegal sales practices, now has a corporate ethics director and operates hot lines through which any company employee can obtain instant advice on ethical issues involving his or her work.

As illustrated in Figure 3-2, most of us rely on various sources to guide our beliefs about what is right or wrong and to develop an overall value system that forms the basis for our decisions and actions. No doubt, the major sources of ethical guidance are the examples and advice we receive from our parents, friends, and role models like schoolteachers, music and movie celebrities, and sports figures. Many people turn to their religion and their minister, rabbi, or priest for ethical leadership.

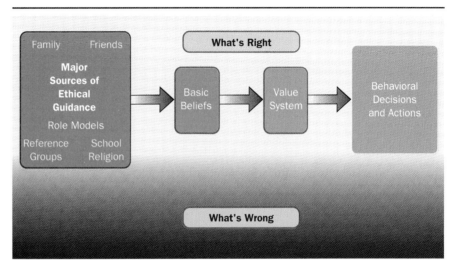

FIGURE 3-2 Developing the Individual's Value System

THE THREE FACES OF ETHICS

In analyzing business ethics, we need to specify whether we are talking about *personal, professional,* or *organizational* ethical standards. Ethical issues in business often involve conflicts and pressures between these three standards, as indicated in Figure 3-3.

When they join a business organization, individuals add a new dimension to the ethical standards they have developed in their personal lives. Now they must think of what is right and good for their companies with respect to customers and other companies, as well as what is right and good for themselves with respect to other people. In the rush to please every customer while engaged in vigorous competition with other companies, employees find that the organizational goals of survival, growth, and profit frequently override their personal ethical standards. Many people are guilty of unethical actions on behalf of their companies that they would never think of taking in their personal lives. In defending themselves against criticism and even legal action when they are discovered, these people usually give the tired old excuse of "I was only following orders." It is an unfortunate fact, however, that those courageous individuals who openly oppose unethical aspects of an organization's value system or "blow the whistle" on activities they consider unethical often jeopardize their careers.

In addition to their companies' formal organizational codes of ethics, salespeople need to develop and abide by their own personal and professional ethical standards.

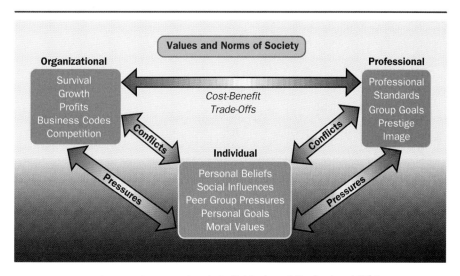

FIGURE 3-3 Balancing Organizational, Individual, and Professional Ethics

Professional ethics differ from *personal ethics* by emphasizing the collective viewpoint and acceptable practices of the members of a specific profession like accounting, law, or sales. They differ from *organizational ethics* by stressing the norms or values of the profession as a basis of authority rather than the norms or values of the organization. Sometimes one's allegiance to a profession and its own ethical codes of self-interest can lead to a very narrow perspective and a defensiveness toward outside criticism. "Ethical" bans on advertising professional medical, dental, and legal services, for example, have been criticized for being indirect means of preventing price competition.

Personal, organizational, and professional ethics provide valuable checks and balances on one another. Professional ethics can enforce high standards of business practice when the organization as a whole attempts to justify some proposed unethical action as "just doing what other companies are doing" or "fighting fire with fire." For example, a company's sales force may object to a company-approved advertising campaign that unfairly criticizes another company's product.

Organizational ethics, which stress profits and growth, serve to check overly zealous, self-serving professional ethics, such as when a lawyer applies "unreasonable" standards before approving new-product labels. Employees' own ethics help them to resist any excessive organizational or professional control that might violate their personal standards—for example, when a sales manager pressures a salesperson to offer bribes or expensive gifts to important customers in order to win their business.

In an ideal world, there would never be a serious conflict between any of these three types of ethics. Until this ideal world has been established, however, salespeople ought to ensure that the checks and balances system is working in their own decision making and that they are not allowing their personal value systems to be dominated by their organizational or professional ones.

Selling in Action

Ethics Pay

It was my first call as a district manager in Washington, in 1970. One of the major department stores there was not doing a lot of business with Maidenform, and we were looking to get some more penetration in the market. Surprisingly, the sale took only two sales calls. The first person I approached was a buyer. He was completely uncooperative. On the way out of the store, I popped my head into his boss's office and we set up a meeting with some higher-level executives later in the week. So there I was, a young kid facing a committee of nine tough executives, and I had to make my presentation. I was in the middle of my pitch when the executive vice president stopped me. He told me this was going to be a big program, about $500,000, and asked me, point-blank, how much of a rebate I was willing to give him to do business with the store, over

and above the normal things like co-op ad money. He was actually asking me for money under the table! I had to make a decision fast. I stood up and said, "If this is what it takes to do business here, I don't want anything to do with it." I then turned to walk out the door, and the guy started cracking up. I guess he was just testing me to see what lengths I'd go to in order to get my sales program into the store. This one incident taught me some very important things: You can't compromise your integrity, and you can't let people intimidate you. But most important, don't lose your sense of humor. Needless to say, we got the program into the store, and today, we do more than $2 million worth of business a year with it.

Source: Alan Lesk, "Strange Tales of Sales," *Sales & Marketing Management,* June 3, 1985, p. 46.

ETHICAL IMAGE OF SALESPEOPLE

Largely because of its persuasive nature, high visibility, direct contact with customers, and the presence of a few "con artists" in the profession, personal selling continually attracts criticism about its low ethical standards. Door-to-door salespeople and car salespeople are the classic objects of criticism, but apparently they aren't the only salespeople who have a tainted image. When *Chemical Engineering* magazine conducted a survey of over 4,000 readers, it found that 31 percent considered chemical equipment salespeople to be "moderately to extremely unethical." Just 24 percent rated them as "ethical." Lawyers and politicians were the only groups that ranked lower in the survey.[4] To counter this negative image, professional salespeople must hold themselves and their companies to a high standard of ethics: Like Caesar's wife, they must avoid even the appearance of questionable ethics. In this chapter's Selling in Action, Alan Lesk, now senior vice president for sales and merchandising for Maidenform, recalls one of his early sales calls where he had to make an on-the-spot ethical decision.

[4]*Sales and Marketing Management,* November 17, 1980, p. 28.

ETHICAL CONCERNS OF SALESPEOPLE

Professional salespeople must be ethically sensitive in their interactions with a variety of people and organizations, including customers, competitors, co-workers, and their own companies. And companies have ethical obligations toward their employees.

Customer Relationships

It is never smart to engage in unethical practices with customers, even when the customer is the instigator. Even dishonest and unethical customers don't trust, and will eventually not want to deal with, unethical salespeople. Losing the business of such customers in the short run may simply be the price an ethical salesperson has to pay for long-run success in selling. Professional salespeople try to build long-run relationships of mutual trust, respect, and confidence with customers. Any loss of personal or company integrity in the eyes of a customer will jeopardize that relationship.

Special Gifts

Bribes, payoffs, and kickbacks are clearly illegal and can bring serious legal problems to the violators. Nevertheless, some salespeople insist on "showing their appreciation" to customers by giving them expensive gifts. Sometimes, especially around the holiday seasons, some customers will drop subtle hints that they expect a nice gift for all the business they've been giving you. Many companies

Professional salespeople never show appreciation to their customers by engaging in activities like bribes, payoffs, or kickbacks.

What Would You Do?

You are a salesperson for Hercules Sports, Inc., a manufacturer of sports equipment and apparel. While you are trying to negotiate a $100,000 sale with a buyer for one of the largest retailers in New York City, the buyer says to you: "I saw an ad for those 'space-age balanced' golf clubs your company recently developed. With the holidays coming up, I sure would be grateful if somebody would surprise me with a set of those." If you negotiate this sale, your commission will be $5,000; the golf clubs would cost you $800.

refuse to allow their employees to accept *any* gifts from suppliers. Some companies have stopped the practice of giving Christmas gifts to customers, offering instead to contribute to the customer's favorite charity.

Entertainment
Taking a customer or prospect to dinner, out to play golf, or to a ballgame or special event is an acceptable and often expected part of doing business. But entertaining a prospect or customer must not become a disguised bribe to influence a purchase.

Entertaining a customer at lunch is a pleasant and legitimate part of doing business.

Overpromising

In order to win the sale, some salespeople will promise much more than they can deliver with the idea that the customer will later accept some reasonable excuse. Promising an unrealistic delivery date in order to make a sale is not only an ethical violation but poor business practice as well. Customers prefer to buy from salespeople whose word and promises can be relied upon.

Misrepresenting or Covering Up the Facts

A few salespeople will cover up the facts or distort the truth to make a quick sale. For example, one salesperson told a married couple that if they bought a car off the showroom floor, they could have air conditioning installed later. Rather than wait several weeks for a car with factory-installed air conditioning, the couple bought the car on the showroom floor. Later, when a custom air-conditioning unit was installed, it not only didn't work, but it literally fell out of the car. When they went back to the dealer, the couple learned that the car manufacturer had not installed air conditioning in that particular model for several years and, in fact, had recommended against custom installation. After filing a lawsuit for misrepresentation by the salesperson, the couple won their case, with the judge deciding that they "obviously relied upon the salesman's statements, and it is clear they had a right to."[5]

Manipulating Order Forms

During sales contests or as sales quota deadlines approach, some salespeople are tempted to finagle their actual sales records by shifting orders from one period to another or by overselling some products. Customers are not always aware of how much inventory they need, so the unethical salesperson may try to persuade them to overbuy. Overselling and order manipulation not only cheat customers but are also unfair to other sales colleagues competing in the contest or striving to make their quotas.

Disclosing Confidential Information

In an effort to ingratiate themselves with important customers, some salespeople reveal confidential and potentially harmful information about their customer's competitors. Customers who receive such information have to wonder whether these salespeople are also telling competitors confidential information about them. Thus a seed of mistrust is planted that will likely inhibit future communication with customers. Ethical salespeople play it straight with all their customers and earn a reputation for being honest and trustworthy.

Showing Favoritism

Salespeople will almost always like some customers more than others, but the ethical salesperson cannot afford to show favoritism by doing such things as (1) moving a favored customer's deliveries ahead of orders from other customers, or (2) making sure preferred customers receive scarce products while others do not. Customers who are discriminated against will deeply resent such unequal treatment and may refuse to buy from salespeople they even suspect of such behavior.

---

[5]"Salesman George Wingfield's Day in Court," *Sales Management*, January 22, 1973, p. 3.

Conflicts of Interest

Stockbrokers and real estate agents are good examples of salespeople who deal daily with potential conflicts of interest in working with both buyers and sellers. For instance, should a real estate agent convince the potential buyer to pay the highest price for a seller's house and thereby earn a higher commission, or try to secure a fair price that the seller will accept?

Treatment of Competitors

Perhaps it can be argued that "all is fair in love and war," but this is certainly not the case for ethical salespeople in dealing with competitors. Initiating unethical practices against competitors can stimulate unethical retaliatory action from them and lead to accelerating aggressive activity that soon crosses the line into legal violations.

Disparaging Competitors

Negative, exaggerated statements about competing products and companies are unethical practices that may invite retaliation from competitors. Moreover, disparaging comments about competing salespeople will often harm relations with customers, who will wonder what the salesperson is saying about *them* behind their backs. Even the best companies are sometimes guilty of disparaging their competitors. Minnesota Mining and Manufacturing's (3M) Static Control Systems Department was accused of using sales demonstrations that "unfairly" denigrated the competition by purposely misusing materials and static-measuring devices.[6]

Tampering with Competitors' Products

It is both unethical and illegal for salespeople to damage competitors' products, tamper with their displays and point-of-sale materials, or reduce their product shelf space in retail stores or elsewhere. Salespeople who stoop to such activities may also anger retailers and wholesalers, who naturally resent any unauthorized tampering with their displays.

Competitive Snooping

Salespeople use many different guises to obtain valuable information about competitors. To get competitive pricing information, they may request customers to solicit bids from competitors. Some salespeople will pretend to be customers at professional conferences, trade shows, and exhibits, or on plant tours of the competition. Such practices are neither uncommon nor illegal, and some would argue that they are okay because "nearly everybody does these things." But salespeople who are trying to maintain the highest ethical standards will see such practices as questionable at best. Recently, two Caterpillar equipment dealers, H. O. Penn Machinery Company in Armonk, New York, and Yancy Brothers in Atlanta, Georgia, used some graduate students to surreptitiously obtain information about their competitors. The dealers provided the students with the names and addresses of the competitors and suggested what questions to ask. Identifying themselves only as M.B.A. students working on a class project, the students persuaded the competitive companies to provide information about their inven-

---

[6]*Sales & Marketing Management*, May 18, 1981, p. 32.

What Would You Do?

You are a 23-year-old saleswoman for office equipment who has just finished making a sales presentation to the purchasing agent of a large manufacturer. It seemed to go well. Then the purchasing agent (a middle-aged male) says: "I liked your sales presentation and maybe we'll be able to do business. But there are many suppliers, so I prefer to buy from someone with whom I have a special relationship. How about dinner tonight so we can start developing that relationship?"

tory levels, sales volume, advertising expenditures, and potential new-product introductions. In corresponding with the dealers, the students even used their university's marketing department stationery. After learning of the deception, an angry competitor said: "I wouldn't give out that type of stuff if I knew it were going to someone other than students."[7]

Treatment of Co-workers

A few excessively aggressive salespeople will behave unethically even in competing with their own company sales colleagues. Unethical behavior among co-workers can destroy employee morale, work against company goals and objectives, and ruin the reputation of the company. Let's look at some examples of what would generally be considered unethical behavior in dealing with one's colleagues.

Sexual Harassment
Salespeople may become perpetrators or victims of subtle sexual harassment that violates both ethical and legal codes of conduct.

In 1980, the Equal Employment Opportunity Commission wrote guidelines defining sexual harassment as a form of sex discrimination and therefore illegal under Title VII of the Civil Rights Act of 1964. The EEOC definition is:

> **Unwelcome sexual advances, requests for sexual favors, and other verbal or physical conduct of a sexual nature constitutes sexual harassment when (1) submission to such conduct is either explicitly or implicitly a term or condition of an individual's employment, (2) submission to or a rejection of such conduct by an individual is used as a basis for employment decisions affecting that individual, or (3) such conduct has the purpose or effect of unreasonably interfering with an individual's**

[7]Clare Ansberry, "For These M.B.A.s, Class Became Exercise in Corporate Espionage," *The Wall Street Journal*, March 22, 1988, p. 37.

work performance or creating an intimidating, hostile, or offensive working environment.[8]

Clearly, an open demand for sexual favors is illegal. But with respect to *hostile environment harassment*—hazing, joking, and sexually suggestive talk—the law is fuzzy. Where does good-humored or just plain stupid kidding cease and harassment begin? Table 3-1 reveals what personnel managers believe is sexual harassment, and how they prefer to deal with each situation. Three-quarters of the personnel managers reported having a formal written sexual harassment policy. Over 90 percent of these were adopted after the publication of the EEOC guidelines. Note that co-workers, not just higher-level managers, can get into a lot of trouble for sexual harassment.

Some women fear filing a sexual harassment case because it may lead to humiliation for the woman, possible job loss, and threats to her family happiness. Many therefore prefer to leave the job or suffer in silence.[9] Nevertheless, many women have filed legal suits, and some have received substantial awards from juries. In a case against Murray Savings, a Texas savings and loan organization, five plaintiffs won $3.8 million. In California, the median jury verdict for sexual harassment cases litigated since 1984 is $183,000.[10]

Stealing Customers from Colleagues

Encroaching on another salesperson's territory and trying to convince a customer doing business in two different territories to make all purchases from your territory are unethical practices. Salespeople found guilty of poaching on other salespeople's territories may face reprimands from management and possible loss of their jobs.

Undermining Co-workers

Occasionally, salespeople become so obsessed with their own lust for success that they deliberately undercut their co-workers. Failing to relay a customer's telephone message to a sales colleague and telling the boss's secretary some disparaging remark made by another salesperson about the boss are examples of unethical activities. Such viciously self-serving salespeople usually underestimate other people, who will quickly size them up and begin to shun them. Few salespeople get ahead for long by cutting down their colleagues. Remember the moral of the old saying: "To hold someone else down, a part of you has to stay down, too."

Often less clear-cut are situations where two or more salespeople from the same company are selling different products to the same buyer. There may be some overlapping of products, or one sales rep may simply be preferred over another. In these cases, some companies have *cross claim* systems in place so that salespeople can easily "claim" and receive proper credit for their sales.

---

[8]"Discrimination Because of Sex Under Title VII of the Civil Rights Act of 1964 as Amended: Adoption of Final Interpretive Guidelines," U.S. Equal Employment Opportunity Commission, Part 1604, *Federal Register*, November 10, 1980.

[9]Gretchen Morgenson, "Watch That Leer, Stifle That Joke," *Forbes*, May 15, 1989, pp. 69–72.

[10]Ibid., p. 71.

TABLE 3-1 What Personnel Managers Believe Is Sexual Harassment and Their Preferred Response

TYPE OF ACTIVITY	SEXUAL HARASSMENT? % Agree	FORMAL DISCIPLINE/ LEGAL ACTION? % Agree
1. Higher-level manager threatening firing, demotion, etc., if the employee is not willing to comply with sexual proposition.	100.0	99.1
2. Higher-level manager promising rewards for sexual favors.	98.8	95.8
3. An employee grabbing, fondling, touching, or brushing up against intimate parts of the body.	98.8	94.5
4. Senior manager making persistent sexual advances after requested to stop.	98.4	86.1
5. Co-worker making persistent sexual advances after requested to stop.	97.1	70.0
6. Lewd sexual comments, innuendos, and gestures made in employee's presence.	93.4	39.9
7. An employee continues sexual joking after being asked to stop.	84.9	39.3
8. Higher-level manager repeatedly asking for dates after refusal.	80.0	41.3
9. Lewd photographs or obscene cartoons displayed in work area.	74.8	34.6
10. Co-worker keeps staring in a sexual way.	67.5	10.0
11. One employee alleging another employee got rewards after first employee refused sexual advances of boss.	65.1	41.4
12. An employee exposing self at organization social function.	63.7	86.7
13. Co-worker repeatedly asking for dates after being refused.	57.3	16.0
14. An employee commenting on a co-worker's moral reputation.	47.7	18.3
15. An employee touching nonintimate parts of another employee's body.	47.1	16.9
16. One employee alleging another employee got a raise, promotion, or better job assignment because the other employee and the boss were intimate.	41.7	24.9
17. Co-worker repeatedly asking for dates after some acceptances.	16.5	2.2
18. Male co-worker refusing to listen to female co-worker's work-related ideas or suggestions seriously.	15.1	3.6

Source: Robert C. Ford and Frank S. McLaughlin, "Sexual Harassment at Work," *Business Horizons,* November–December 1988, pp. 14–19.

Salespeople's Ethics vis-à-vis Their Company

Salespeople and other employees sometimes feel that standards of ethics don't fully apply when they are dealing with an organization, whether it's the Internal Revenue Service, an insurance firm, or their own company. After all, some employees seem to think, an organization is not something human, just a big bureaucracy with lots of money. But when large numbers of people start taking home a few ballpoint pens or paper tablets, padding expense accounts, or doing personal business on company time, the costs of doing business can go up dramatically. Eventually, these abuses translate into higher prices to customers, lower profits, fewer company employees, and lower wages and salaries as the company loses sales to lower-cost competitors.

Expense Account Padding
Salespeople can easily pad their expense accounts by taking friends out to dinner and claiming they were entertaining customers, or by submitting excess claims for meal expenses, mileage, taxi fares, tips, and the like. Padding one's expense account may be viewed as stealing by sales managers and can lead to dismissal if discovered. Occasionally, padding schemes involve massive collusion. For instance, 50 Tennessee Valley Authority nuclear power employees arranged with hotel and motel representatives to overcharge ratepayers for $189,000 of travel expenses over several years.[11]

Unauthorized Use of Company Resources
Making personal telephone calls on company phones, using company copying machines for personal purposes, keeping company promotional premiums intended for customers, taking home supplies from the office for personal use, and driving a company car on unauthorized personal trips are unethical activities that can significantly add to company costs. Beyond these morally shabby practices, American businesses lose an estimated $200 billion yearly to outright employee theft. Seven out of every ten dollars lost in retail stores is due to employee theft, not shoplifting. In a recent survey of more than 100,000 job applicants, an alarming 32 percent admitted stealing merchandise, ranging in value from $25 to $1,500, from a previous employer.[12] Some employees rationalize stealing from their own companies by claiming that the company owes it to them because it is underpaying them, or by telling themselves that they're just borrowing something they will pay back later, or by believing that because "everybody else does it," it must be all right.

Personal Use of Company Time
In a study of 500 corporations, Robert Half Associates asked employees to estimate how much *time* the average worker "steals" each week. From these responses, he estimated that U.S. workers may steal over $120 billion in time each year from their companies.[13] Some employees go beyond long lunch hours, personal telephone calls, and excessive socializing to actually "moonlighting" on

---

[11]J. Patrick Willar, *The Nashville Tennesseean,* November 24, 1987, p. 1A.
[12]Banning K. Lary, "Why Corporations Can't Lock the Rascals Out," *Management Review,* October 1989, pp. 51–54.
[13]Herbert Swartz, "The $120 Billion-a-Year Theft of Time," *Dun's Business Monthly*, October 1982, p. 75.

part-time jobs during the same hours they are supposed to be working for their primary employer. Because of their independence and freedom, salespeople have many opportunities to convert company time to personal use, but ethical sales reps will give their companies a full day's work even if they have made all of their scheduled sales calls for the day. There is always some customer servicing or paperwork that needs to be done.

Fabricating Sales Records

Because many companies base their performance evaluations of salespeople at least partially on their sales *activities* as well as on their sales *results*, some salespeople are tempted to falsify their number of sales calls, service calls, or promotional mailings to customers. Smart salespeople realize that activities quotas are guides designed to help them learn what it takes to achieve top performance. Falsifying sales activity records may become a habit that causes salespeople to become lazy, with consequent adverse effect on their sales performance.

Manipulating Customer Orders

To win sales contests or meet their annual quotas, salespeople may persuade customers to overorder products with the promise that they can return them after the contest or at the end of the year. Not only does this unethical practice harm sales colleagues who are competing fairly in the contest, but it also creates unnecessary costs for the company and hurts the image of the company and its salespeople with customers.

Ethical Eyes and Ears of the Company in the Field

Misguided managers sometimes employ unethical means to achieve short-run sales and profit levels. Professional salespeople should accept the role of customer representative or spokesperson whenever they spot questionable company activities.

Product quality and service Poor product quality, unsafe products, unreasonable return policies, and poor servicing of products after the sale are examples of unethical practices that salespeople should not have to tolerate from their companies. If the company persists in shady activities, a salesperson would probably be better off seeking a job with a more ethical company. Over the long run, unethical companies are not likely to prosper competing against ethical companies.

Pricing Some companies or salespeople routinely inflate list prices so they can appear to offer customers a discount. Salespeople are often accused of taking advantage of customers who are not well informed or are less aggressive in negotiating. Ethical salespeople, however, will not resort to price gouging or exploiting a naive customer. Though you may make the sale now, customers will eventually find out that they paid too much and refuse to buy from you again. Salespeople can legitimately offer price and quantity discounts that they make available on an equal basis to all their customers.

Distribution Lower-quality products and inferior services have sometimes been sold to young people, the elderly, non-English-speaking Americans, and poorly informed people at prices that are oftentimes as high or higher than those for better-quality products and services.[14] Unscrupulous salespeople tend to prey on people who are undereducated, dependent on credit, unaware of their legal rights, and unable to read or speak English.

Promotion Deceptive advertising, misleading product warranties, phony promotional contests, and dishonest fund-raising activities are unethical and perhaps illegal. Unfair or stereotypical representation of women, minorities, gays, the disabled, or senior citizens may be viewed as merely insensitive instead of unethical, but such promotions can turn off major customer groups. Whenever salespeople hear customers commenting negatively about the company's promotional efforts, they should relay this information to sales and marketing management. No salesperson should be expected to work under the cloud of unethical advertising.

EMPLOYER ETHICS WITH THEIR SALESPEOPLE

Ethical salespeople have a right to expect ethical treatment from their companies, especially with regard to compensation, sales territories, sales quotas, hiring, promoting, and firing policies.

Compensation

Prompt, accurate payment of salary, commissions, and bonuses as well as timely reimbursement of selling expenses are basic requirements for any ethical company in dealing with its salespeople. Any company that tries to delay payments or cheat salespeople out of their fair commissions or reimbursements for selling expenses will see its sales force turnover skyrocket.

Sales Territories

Sales managers must ensure that salespeople are involved in the fair assignment of sales territories. Whenever territories must be reassigned, split up, or moved to national accounts, the salespeople should receive early warning of the impending change and be given an opportunity to negotiate a new territorial assignment.

Sales Quotas

Setting unrealistically high sales quotas for salespeople, then applying constant pressure to produce the sales, is unfair and unethical. Salespeople should always

---

[14]Howard Kunreuther, "Why the Poor Pay More for Food: Theoretical and Empirical Evidence," *Journal of Business,* July 1973, pp. 368–383.

Company Highlight

Music for Little People

One company, Music for Little People, has found a way to increase sales, get favorable publicity, and attract dedicated telemarketers, while helping struggling environmental causes. In its mail-order catalog of cassettes, videotapes, and musical instruments for children, the company freely promotes nonprofit organizations that help clean up the planet. For 25 percent of the nonprofit groups spotlighted over the past three years, the Music for Little People catalog has been the best source of new members.

Source: INC., August 1989, p. 112.

be involved in setting their own quotas, so that they will view them as fair. An important aspect of sales force motivation and loyalty to the company is salespeople's perception that they are each being treated fairly and ethically.

Hiring, Promoting, and Firing

Although all forms of discrimination have been legally prohibited since the 1964 Civil Rights Act, which was made even more powerful by the Equal Employment Opportunity Act of 1972, there is continuing evidence that *sexism, racism,* and *ageism* still influence managerial decisions in hiring, promoting, and firing salespeople. Over the long run, the most successful companies are those that provide equal opportunities for all employees and base promotion decisions on job performance.

GOING BEYOND ETHICS: SOCIAL RESPONSIBILITY IN SELLING

Some progressive companies are committed to helping the ethnic communities where people buy their products. This includes placing advertisements in ethnic newspapers or on ethnic radio stations, emphasizing point-of-sale materials favorably depicting the ethnic group, sponsoring local festivals and holidays, and making sure products are available in ethnic community stores.

Over 40 U.S. companies have signed "fair share agreements" with the National Association for the Advancement of Colored People (NAACP) committing the companies to expand opportunities for African-Americans in employment in their industries. Coors and other national brewers run special ethnic-marketing programs, sponsor neighborhood events, and actively solicit ethnic suppliers.

Several soft-drink, grocery, and fast-food companies have signed convenants with Jesse Jackson's organization, People United to Save Humanity (PUSH), to fund sports teams, school programs, scholarships, and black cultural events. PepsiCo sponsored the Lionel Ritchie "Stay in School" tour, and Coca-Cola developed a traveling exhibit about Jackie Robinson. The specific form of benevolence will need to be specifically tailored for each ethnic group.

LAWS AFFECTING PERSONAL SELLING

Personal selling is affected by numerous federal, state, and local laws. Local and state laws tend to deal directly with personal selling. Federal laws are more indirect, but still powerful in their impact.

State and Local Regulations

Among the most important state and local laws and ordinances designed to regulate selling activities are the Uniform Commercial Code, state Unfair Trade Practices Acts, the Green River ordinances, and the "cooling-off rule."

The *Uniform Commercial Code of 1962* is a basic set of guidelines adopted by most states that sets forth the rules of contracts and the law pertaining to sales. The code includes specific provisions governing product performance, sellers' warranties, and the maximum allowable rates of interest and carrying charges. Court actions under this code usually concern buyers' claims that salespeople misrepresented the goods or made promises that were not kept. Companies and salespeople that are most successful in defending themselves against lawsuits are those that are able to provide the court with substantiating sales documentation, such as contracts or letters of agreement.

State Unfair Trade Practices Acts, passed in the 1930s, prohibit "loss-leader" pricing (selling below cost). These laws are still in effect in about half the states.

GREEN RIVER ORDINANCES Widespread local ordinances first established in 1933 in Green River, Wyoming, that require nonresidents to obtain a license to sell goods and services directly to consumers in that vicinity.

The **Green River ordinances,** first enforced in Green River, Wyoming, in 1933, are local ordinances requiring nonresidents to obtain a license to sell goods and services directly to consumers in that vicinity. Adopted in most metropolitan areas, the laws have discouraged some companies from trying to sell their products and services door-to-door on a national basis.

COOLING-OFF RULE A rule imposed by the Federal Trade Commission that requires door-to-door salespeople to give their customers a written notice stating that a customer who makes a purchase of $25 or more may cancel the purchase within three days without loss.

Closely connected to the Green River ordinances is the **cooling-off rule** imposed by the Federal Trade Commission. It requires door-to-door salespeople to give their customers a written notice stating that a customer who makes a purchase of $25 or more may cancel the purchase within three days without loss. This rule was imposed on companies selling door-to-door after years of consumer complaints about high-pressure sales tactics, false claims about product features and quality, high prices, and the failure of salespeople to identify themselves and their intentions properly.

The cooling-off rule requires salespeople to do three things at the closing of the sale:

give buyer contract ↖ 1. Give the buyer a copy of the written contract or a receipt of the transaction.

make sure statement is on first page ← 2. Make sure that the following statement is on the first page of the contract or receipt:

> **You, the buyer, may cancel this transaction at any time prior to midnight of the third business day after the date of this transaction. See the attached notice of cancellation form for an explanation of this right.**

make sure notice of cancellation ← 3. Make sure that the "notice of cancellation form," shown in Figure 3-4 is attached and read.

Notice of Cancellation

_____

(date of transaction)

You may cancel this transaction, without any penalty or obligation, within three business days from the above date.

If you cancel, any property traded in, any payments made by you under the contract or sale, and any negotiable instrument executed by you will be returned within ten business days following receipt by the seller of your cancellation notice, and any security interest arising out of the transactions will be cancelled.

If you cancel, you must make available to the seller at your residence, in substantially as good condition, as when received, any goods delivered to you under this contract or sale; or you may if you wish comply with the instructions of the seller regarding the return shipment of the goods at the seller's expense and risk. If you do make the goods available to the seller and the seller does not pick them up within twenty days of the date of your notice of cancellation, you may retain or dispose of the goods without any further obligation. If you fail to make the goods available to the seller, or if you agree to return the goods to the seller and fail to do so, then you remain liable for performance of all obligations under the contract.

To cancel this transaction, mail or deliver a signed and dated copy of this cancellation notice or any other written notice, or send a telegram, to (name of seller) at (address of seller's place of business) no later than midnight of

_____.

(date)

I hereby cancel this transaction.

_____   _____

                                           (buyer's signature)

FIGURE 3-4 Notice of Cancellation Form for Door-to-Door Sales

Federal Regulations

U. S. legislation of business operations can be divided into two major categories: (1) laws intended to protect companies from each other; and (2) laws intended to protect consumers from unfair business practices. Table 3-2 shows the major federal legislation that has had a direct or indirect impact on personal selling and marketing activities.

TABLE 3-2   Federal Laws Affecting Personal Selling

Sherman Antitrust Act (1890). Prohibits "monopolies or attempts to monopolize" and "contracts, combinations, or conspiracies in restraint of trade" in interstate and foreign commerce.

Pure Food and Drug Act (1906). Regulates labeling of food and drugs and prohibits the manufacture or marketing of adulterated food or drugs. Amended in 1938 by Food, Drug, and Cosmetics Act.

Meat Inspection Act (1906). Provides for the enforcement of sanitary regulations in meat packing and for federal inspection of all companies selling meats in interstate commerce.

Federal Trade Commission Act (1914). Established the Federal Trade Commission (FTC) as a body of specialists with broad powers to investigate and to issue cease and desist orders to enforce Section V, which declares that "unfair methods of competition in commerce are unlawful."

Clayton Act (1914). Supplements the Sherman Act by prohibiting specific practices (certain types of price discrimination, tying clauses, exclusive dealing, intercorporate stockholdings, and interlocking directorates) "where the effect . . . may be to substantially lessen competition or tend to create a monopoly in any line of commerce." Provides that violating corporate officials can be held personally responsible.

Robinson-Patman Act (1936). Amends the Clayton Act by strengthening the prohibition of price discrimination (subject to certain defenses). Provides the FTC with the right to establish limits on quantity discounts; to forbid brokerage allowances except to independent brokers; and to prohibit promotional allowances, services, or facilities except where made available to all "on proportionately equal terms."

Wheeler-Lea Act (1938). Amends the FTC Act; prohibits unfair and deceptive acts and practices whether competition is injured or not.

Lanham Trademark Act (1946). Regulates brands and trademarks.

Fair Packaging and Labeling Act (1966). Provides for the regulation of the packaging and labeling of consumer goods. Requires manufacturers to state what the package contains, who made it, and how much it contains. Permits industries to voluntarily adopt uniform packaging standards.

Child Protection Act (1966). Bans sales of hazardous toys and other unsafe articles. Amended in 1969 to include articles that pose electrical, mechanical, or thermal hazards.

Fair Credit Reporting Act (1970). Ensures that a consumer's credit report will contain only accurate, relevant, and recent information, and will be confidential unless requested for an appropriate reason by a proper party.

Consumer Product Safety Act (1972). Established the Consumer Product Safety Commission and authorized it to set safety standards for consumer products as well as to exact penalties for failure to uphold the standards.

Magnuson-Moss Warranty/FTC Improvement Act (1975). Authorizes the FTC to determine rules concerning consumer warranties and provides for consumer access to means of redress, e.g., class action suits. Expands FTC regulatory powers over unfair or deceptive acts or practices.

Equal Credit Opportunity Act (1975). Prohibits discrimination in a credit transaction because of sex, marital status, race, national origin, religion, age, or receipt of public assistance.

Consumer Goods Pricing Act (1975). Repeals federal "fair trade laws" and state laws allowing manufacturers to set retail prices.

Fair Debt Collection Practice Act (1978). Makes it illegal to harass or abuse any person and to make false statements or use unfair methods when attempting to collect a debt.

Trademark Counterfeiting Act (1980). Provides civil and criminal penalties against those who deal in counterfeit consumer goods or any counterfeit goods that can threaten health or safety.

FTC Improvement Act (1980). Provides the House of Representatives and Senate jointly with veto power over FTC trade regulation rules. Enacted to limit the FTC's powers to regulate "unfairness" issues. Reverses the trend toward more FTC protection of consumers.

Key Federal Laws

The most important federal laws regulating business competition are the *Robinson-Patman Act, Sherman Act,* and *Clayton Act.* These acts cover price discrimination, collusion, price-fixing, restraint of trade, exclusive dealing, reciprocity, tie-in sales, business and product descriptions, orders and terms of sale, unordered goods, secret rebates, customer coercion, and business defamation.

Price Discrimination

The Clayton Act prohibits a seller from discriminating on price or terms of sale among different customers when the discrimination would injure competition. It also makes it illegal for a buyer to knowingly induce or accept a discriminatory price.

Under the Robinson-Patman Act, a seller cannot sell at different prices in different markets, or charge different prices to different purchasers for the same quality and quantity of goods. Differences in price or terms of sale can be successfully defended only if (1) the price differential was given in good faith to match, not beat, a price offered by a competitor; and (2) the price differential is a cost saving resulting from different manufacturing techniques or quantities in which the products are sold or delivered. Price reductions are permissible when based on quantity ordered, closeout sales, lower shipping and selling costs, good faith meeting of competition, and lower commissions paid to salespeople. For their own legal protection, sellers should establish accounting procedures that can certify cost differences in selling to certain customers.

Price-Fixing

Two or more competing sellers who conspire to set or maintain uniform prices and profit margins are involved in price-fixing. Even the informal exchange of price information between competitors or the discussion of pricing policies at trade shows has been found to be illegal by the courts.

Collusion

Competing sellers who agree to set prices, divide up markets or territories, or act to the detriment of a third competitor are involved in an illegal arrangement called **collusion.**

COLLUSION An illegal arrangement in which competing sellers agree to set prices, divide up markets or territories, or act to the detriment of a third competitor.

Exclusive Dealing

Agreements in which a manufacturer or wholesaler grants one dealer exclusive rights to sell a product in a certain trading area or insists that the dealer not carry competing lines are illegal under the Clayton Act.

Restraint of Trade

Under both the Sherman Act and the Clayton Act, agreements made between competitors to divide a market into noncompetitive territories or to restrict competition in a market are restraints of trade. Dealers cannot be prohibited from selling competitors' products as a condition of receiving the right to sell the manufacturer's product.

Reciprocity

Purchasing from suppliers who buy from your company, a practice called **reci-**

RECIPROCITY An ethically and sometimes legally questionable business practice in which two parties have an informal agreement for the regular purchase of products from each other to the exclusion of competitors.

procity, is a controversial practice but is not uncommon. For example, General Motors buys transmissions from Borg-Warner, which buys its automobiles and trucks from GM. Industries such as chemicals, paints, and transportation, where products are homogeneous and similarly priced, are most likely to practice reciprocal purchasing. In times of raw material shortages, *reverse reciprocity* is used by some firms to allocate their scarce products to companies that will sell them needed materials in short supply.

Reciprocity agreements that eliminate competition are illegal, and the Department of Justice and the Federal Trade Commission will intervene to stop systematic reciprocal buying practices deemed to be anticompetitive. Because reciprocity forces purchasing agents to buy from designated suppliers, it discourages salespeople from other companies from competing for the business. It can also adversely affect the morale of purchasing agents, who may be forced to buy inferior products and services or to pay higher prices. Most purchasing agents and salespeople dislike reciprocity, and many believe it should be illegal.[15]

Chemical Bank, the New York–based financial institution with over 300 branches in the United States and abroad, has established policies and procedures to ensure fair and equitable treatment of all the bank's suppliers. Even its own printing subsidiary must compete against other suppliers for most of the bank's printing orders.

Tie-in Sales

A **tie-in** occurs when the seller requires a customer to buy an unwanted product along with the desired product.

TIE-IN Refers to an often illegal situation in which a seller requires a customer to purchase an unwanted product along with the desired product.

Unordered Goods

Section V of the FTC Act prohibits companies from shipping unordered goods or shipping larger quantities than customers ordered.

Orders and Terms of Sale

It is illegal for sellers to substitute different goods than those ordered, to misrepresent delivery dates, or to not fill an order within a reasonable time. Key terms of sale, such as warranties or guarantees, the ability of the buyer to cancel a contract or obtain a refund, and important facts in a credit or financing transaction cannot be concealed or misrepresented.

Business Descriptions

Salespeople must never misrepresent their company's financial strength, length of time in business, reputation, or particulars about its plant, equipment, and facilities.

Product Descriptions

It is illegal to lie about how a product is made. A salesperson may not state that a product is "custom-made" or "tailor-made" when it is actually ready-made. Furthermore, no statements can be made about "proven" claims unless scientific or empirical evidence is available to substantiate the truth of the claims. Beech-Nut Nutrition Corporation pleaded guilty and paid a record $2.2 million fine for selling phony apple juice for babies. The fine was small compared to the millions

[15]F. Robert Finney, "Reciprocity: Gone but Not Forgotten," *Journal of Marketing,* January 1978, pp. 54–59.

of dollars Beech-Nut lost in market share from negative publicity. In addition, two Beech-Nut executives received stiff fines and were sentenced to prison for their role in the consumer fraud.[16]

Secret Rebates

You cannot secretly reward a dealer's salespeople for sales of your company's products without the consent of their employer. And even if the dealer management approves such an incentive plan, this practice may violate the Sherman Act if it results in unfair discrimination among competing dealers.

Customer Coercion

It is unlawful to make fictitious inquiries that harass a competitor or pressure anyone into buying a product through scare tactics, coercion, or intimidation.

Business Defamation

BUSINESS DEFAMATION Any action or utterance that slanders, libels, or disparages the product of a competitor, causing the competitor financial damage, lost customers, unemployment, or lost sales.

Hundreds of companies and salespeople have been sued by competitors for making slanderous statements about them that caused financial damage, lost customers, unemployment, or lost sales. The Federal Trade Commission can impose cease and desist orders or obtain an injunction on companies that engage in unfair or deceptive practices through their salespeople. Private lawsuits may also be brought against the offenders. **Business defamation** can include the following offenses:

- *Business slander:* Unfair and untrue *oral* statements made about competitors that damage the reputation of the competitor or the personal reputation of an individual in that business.
- *Business libel:* Unfair and untrue statements made about a competitor *in writing* (usually a letter, sales literature, advertisement, or company brochure) that damage the competitor's reputation or the personal reputation of an individual in that business.
- *Product disparagement:* False or deceptive comparisons or distorted claims made during or after a sales presentation about a competitor's product, services, or property.

Unfair Competition

False advertising, misrepresenting the quality or characteristics of a product, and engaging in deceptive trade practices are all forms of unfair competition and are all illegal. Negative statements made by a salesperson during or after the sales presentation are especially dangerous. These statements are considered defamatory per se; that is, a defamed company or individual does not have to prove actual damages to win a favorable verdict, only that the statement is untrue. Below are the kinds of statements that may be judged defamatory:

- Untrue comments that a competitor is engaging in illegal or unfair business practices.
- Untrue remarks that a competitor fails to live up to its contractual obligations and responsibilities.
- Untrue statements regarding a competitor's financial condition.
- Untrue statements that a principal in the competitor's business is incompetent, of poor moral character, unreliable, or dishonest.

[16]Joseph A. Raelin, "Professional and Business Ethics: Bridging the Gap," *Managment Review*, November 1980, p. 40.

A reputation for integrity and high ethical standards in dealing with all people at all times is one of the most valuable possessions of the professional sales representative. Ethics will pay off in the long run because nearly all customers prefer to do business with a salesperson who is ethical.

INTERNATIONAL REGULATION OF SALES

Salespeople in international selling encounter different ethical standards and modes of behavior as they go from one country to another. Selling practices illegal in one country may be accepted ways of doing business in another. Yet salespeople who engage in certain practices that are acceptable abroad may be criticized or even prosecuted for violation of U.S. law. International salespeople are restrained by three different kinds of laws:

1. *U.S. law* prohibits American companies from trading with some foreign countries, including North Korea, Cambodia, and Vietnam.
2. Salespeople must obey the *laws of the host country* where they operate, even if they sharply differ from American laws. Some foreign countries actually have more restrictive business laws than the United States. For example, Greece sued Colgate for giving away razor blades with its shaving cream; France and Sweden regulate the transborder flow of mailing lists and data about citizens; and Japan restricts compilation of computerized mailing lists. More usually, American companies face difficult moral and ethical issues in foreign countries that have less restrictive business laws.

Salespeople in international selling should be prepared to deal with varying ethical standards and modes of behavior as they go from one country to another.

For instance, in some countries, paying high-level military officials to sell weapons to their government is not illegal, but merely the expected way of doing business.

3. The multinational firm is subject to *international laws* that are enforced across national boundaries. Gifts, bribes, and payoffs have consistently been identified in studies as the major abuses in international personal selling. One of the more recent cases involved payments of nearly $38 million made by Lockheed Aircraft Corporation to government officials in Japan, Italy, and the Netherlands to win sales for its L1011 Tri Star and F-104 Starfighter jet airplanes. Both the United Nations and the European Economic Community are standardizing commercial codes that deal with such issues as product safety and environmental standards, and making them binding on all companies whose nations endorse the codes.

In international negotiations, salespeople must not confuse ethical standards and the law. Ethical practices vary greatly from one country to another. "Lubrication bribery," or small amounts of money to grease the wheels of bureaucracy, is a deeply entrenched practice in some parts of the world. A lubrication bribe or *baksheesh* is often the accepted and expected way of doing business in the Middle and Far East. In Italy, a *bustarella* (an envelope stuffed with lire notes) gets a particular license clerk to do his job. By contrast, *mordida* ("the bite") ensures that a Mexican government inspector will *not* do his job. *Whitemail bribery* buys influence at high levels. One study of marketing ethics in ten countries—France, Germany, United Kingdom, Greece, India, Israel, Italy, Japan, Mexico, and the United States—ranked Germany, the United Kingdom, the United States, and France highest. Mexico ranked lowest, with India and Italy not far ahead.[17] Even though payoffs and bribes sometimes seem essential to doing business in certain countries, a study of 65 major American corporations (40 of which admitted to making questionable payments aboard) found that these payments usually just shift orders from one American company to another. If both companies were to follow the same ethical standards, no payment would be needed.[18]

Sales representatives planning to sell products or services to a foreign country should check with the U.S. Department of Commerce for information about that country's legal restrictions on imports and U.S. restrictions on exports to that country. For example, sales of some categories of technological equipment and processes are restricted by U.S. law or by edict of the State Department or Defense Department, and such items will not be allowed to leave the country. Then, before beginning any transaction within the foreign country, the sales representative should contact the commercial attaché at the U.S. embassy for information on the specific legal requirements in conducting business there.

MAKING ETHICAL DECISIONS

Whether selling domestically or internationally, ethical standards must be maintained in the salesperson's individual decision-making process or they will not be maintained at all. A five-step process for ethical decision making is suggested in Table 3-3.

[17]David J. Fritzsche and Helmut Becker, "Linking Management Behavior to Ethical Philosophy—An Empirical Investigation," *Academy of Management Journal*, March 1984, pp. 166–175.
[18]Barry Richman, "Stopping Payments Under the Table," *Business Week*, May 2, 1978, p. 18.

TABLE 3-3 Ethical Decision-Making Checklist Analysis

General Questions
- ■ Who is responsible to act?
- ■ What are the consequences of action? (Benefits-Harm Analysis)
- ■ What and whose rights are affected? (Rights-Principles Analysis)
- ■ What is fair treatment in this case? (Social Justice Analysis)

Solution Development
- ■ What solutions are available to me?
- ■ Have I considered all of the creative solutions that might permit me to reduce harm, maximize benefits, respect more rights, or be fair to more parties?

Select the Optimum Solution
- ■ What are the potential consequences of my solutions?
- ■ Which of the options I have considered does the most to maximize benefits, reduce harm, respect rights, and increase fairness?
- ■ Are all parties treated fairly in my proposed decision?

Implementation
- ■ Who should be consulted and informed?
- ■ What actions will ensure that my decision achieves the intended outcome?
- ■ Implement the decision

Follow-up
- ■ Was the decision implemented correctly?
- ■ Did the decision maximize benefits, reduce harm, respect rights, and treat all parties fairly?

Source: Adapted from Patrick E. Murphy, "Implementing Business Ethics," *Journal of Business Ethics,* December 1988, p. 913.

SUMMARY

Ethics is the study of what's right and wrong and serves as the basis for a code of conduct for interactions among people. Business ethics have usually been guided largely by economic criteria. Although codes of ethics have been adopted by most organizations, the degree of adherence varies widely. Organizational, professional, and individual ethical values often conflict. Salespeople need and want training in ethical conduct for dealing with customers, competitors, co-workers, and their own employers. Some companies and their sales forces are becoming actively involved in socially responsible community service.

There are a large number of local, state, and federal laws that affect personal selling either directly or indirectly. These laws focus on issues of product quality and safety, promotion, pricing, and distribution, as well as on fair competition. International selling is affected by U.S. laws, host country laws, and international laws enforced across national boundaries. Salespeople and their companies should bear in mind that what's legal or ethical in the host country may not be so in the United States, and that the seller may be held responsible in both countries. Cultural differences make it critical for salespeople to understand the legal, ethical, and social mores of any countries in which they are attempting to sell their company's products.

CHAPTER REVIEW QUESTIONS

1. What are ethics?
2. What are the three basic types of ethical codes in American business?
3. How do professional ethics differ from personal ethics? From organizational ethics?
4. Can you explain the difference between *sexual harassment* and *hostile environment harassment?*

5. Discuss some of the ways that professional salespeople can be the ethical "eyes and ears" of their companies.

6. Name and briefly describe several of the most important *state* and *local* laws affecting selling and the three most important *federal* laws regulating business competition.

7. What are the three most common kinds of business defamation?

8. What is "unfair competition"?

9. What three different sets of laws must international salespeople abide by?

TOPICS FOR THOUGHT AND CLASS DISCUSSION

1. How do you think your ethical values were formed? Who had the most influence on you? Why?

2. Why do salespeople need to concern themselves with ethical issues? Isn't it enough to understand and operate within the law?

3. Do you believe that ethical standards in the United States are relatively stable or changing? Do you think U.S. ethical standards are becoming higher or lower? Why?

4. Why do countries differ so sharply about what is ethical or unethical behavior? Do you think there might ever be an international code of ethical behavior in business that all countries would adopt?

5. Who do you think are the best role models for ethical or social behavior in business?

6. What is your definition of sexual harassment?

7. What do you think were the major ethical issues of the 1980s? What do you think might be the major ethical issues of the 1990s?

8. Do you have any personal guidelines for what is ethical or unethical behavior? Would you like to see everyone use your guidelines?

PROJECTS FOR PERSONAL GROWTH

1. Locate and interview two salespeople. Ask them how they decide whether a particular behavior is ethical or unethical. Did they receive any instruction in ethics during their sales training program? Do their companies have codes of ethics? What punishments or penalties are there for ethical violations?

2. Write down two ethical dilemmas that you have personally faced. How did you decide what to do in each case? In retrospect, do you think you made the right decision? Who was affected by your decision? How? Would you be willing to tell your friends the total truth about each dilemma and how you resolved it? How do you think they would react?

3. Go to your college or public library and look through issues from the 1940s or 1950s of popular magazines such as *Life* or *Time*. Then compare them with more recent issues. Do you think the advertisements seem more or less ethical than those of today? Why do you feel that way? What do you think might account for the differences?

KEY TERMS

Ethics The moral code that governs individuals and societies in determining what is right and wrong.

Green River ordinances Widespread local ordinances first established in 1933 in Green River, Wyoming, that require nonresidents to obtain a license to sell goods and services directly to consumers in that vicinity.

Cooling-off rule A rule imposed by

the Federal Trade Commission that requires door-to-door salespeople to give their customers a written notice stating that a customer who makes a purchase of $25 or more may cancel the purchase within three days without loss.

Collusion An illegal arrangement in which competing sellers agree to set prices, divide up markets or territories, or act to the detriment of a third competitor.

Reciprocity An ethically and sometimes legally questionable business practice in which two parties have an informal agreement for the regular purchase of products from each other to the exclusion of competitors.

Tie-in Refers to an often illegal situation in which a seller requires a customer to purchase an unwanted product along with the desired product.

Business defamation Any action or utterance that slanders, libels, or disparages the product of a competitor, causing the competitor financial damage, lost customers, unemployment, or lost sales.

Case 3-1

TO CHURN OR NOT TO CHURN
James T. Strong, University of Akron

After graduating from Rutgers University, Dan Murray started as a stockbroker with Spearhead and Peabody, a small financial firm in Baltimore, Maryland. Dan quickly learned the brokerage business, and after two years became number 2 in sales among the firm's ten salespeople. In his third year, Dan left the firm to join a more prestigious brokerage house in midtown Manhattan, where he expected to double his earnings his first year. Because the stockmarket suffered a down year, however, Dan only managed to earn $90,000, about the same as he had been earning at Spearhead and Peabody. Unfortunately, the higher living expenses in New York City made his income seem much lower than before.

Dan's wife, Sarah, gave up her position as a high-school history teacher when they moved to New York City and took a part-time job clerking in a retail store. In the past, Sarah's income helped give Dan a sense of security that the family (which included two children) could ride out the ups and downs of his commission checks. Now Sarah's part-time job brings in only about one-third her previous income in teaching.

With the stockmarket stagnation, the pressures to sell are starting to affect Dan emotionally. When his commissions were high, he felt great. Now in a dry period he feels increasingly frustrated. Several of his customers have dropped out of the stockmarket completely and put their money into money market funds because they no longer feel that they are benefiting from Dan's financial advice. The loss of customers has hurt Dan emotionally as well as financially, but he doesn't blame them. Recently, Dan has even thought about quitting and taking a job as a sales rep for a Baltimore wholesaler he worked for in the summers during college. Dan figures that he can earn about $60,000 a year at the wholesaling company, with the possibility for advancement after a few years.

Making "cold calls" to prospects, a necessity in the competitive brokerage business, has become harder and harder for Dan to do. He dreads the frequent rejection and the long hours on the phone at night. Perhaps most irritating, however, is the constant pressure from his sales manager to keep sales volume up. Dan resents his manager's not-so-subtle suggestions to "churn" his accounts in order to hit his annual sales quota. The manager has issued constant warnings that anybody who doesn't make the quota this year is in danger of being let go. Dan figures that he will reach only 75 percent of his quota at the current rate. The manager's daily greeting echoes in Dan's ears: "Remember, you're a salesman first, a financial adviser second." Dan knows that "churning" accounts can succeed only in the short run, because once customers realize that a stockbroker is pushing them to buy and sell stock just so the broker can receive commissions on the transactions, they usually drop the broker. But the sales manager counters Dan's arguments that "churning" is a bad long-run strategy with: "In the long run, we're all dead. Let's deal with today."

This morning Sarah calls Dan to tell him that she is pregnant again and will be quitting her part-time job in a few months. Sarah tries to keep Dan's spirits up by telling him to "just hang in there, honey, the good times will come again when the stockmarket heats up."

Questions

1. What do you think Dan should do about meeting his sales quota? Are there any innovative approaches he might take to obtain new customers and meet his quota?

2. Do you think Dan should "churn" his accounts a little if he can do it without hurting anyone much? If not, what should Dan say to his sales manager about his unwillingness to "churn" his accounts?

3. Do you think Dan should leave the brokerage business? Why or why not? If yes, what other types of selling would you recommend that Dan consider?

Case 3-2

FEAR OF FAILURE
James T. Strong, University of Akron

For nearly a year, Troy Rivera has been a salesman for SunFlooring, Inc., a major floor-covering distributor in the Southeast. Troy was performing fairly well, although inconsistently, when SunFlooring kicked off the most ambitious carpet display placement campaign in its history. All salespeople are now expected to sell twice as many carpet displays as they did before. Each display costs $75. Dealers can earn back the cost of the display if they sell a certain amount of carpet. But selling displays in the very competitive carpet business is tough.

Salespeople will be paid bonuses of $300 if they hit their quota, $500 if they are the highest over quota in their branch, and $1,000 if they are the highest in the sales force of 75. Bonuses will be given onstage in front of the entire sales force at the summer carpet show in Atlanta in two months.

Although the bonuses are attractive, what is worrying Troy is what will happen to a salesperson who doesn't make the assigned quota. Any salesperson who fails to make quota will be required to stand onstage before all the other salespeople and explain why he or she has not reached the quota. Troy and his sales colleagues shudder at the possibility of such humiliation. Troy has sold 15 displays out of his quota of 20, which is 5 more than he ever sold before,

but he doesn't know how he can place the remaining five displays. He has contacted all of his customers, and 15 is his best effort. Troy is worried enough to ask Pete Hamil, one of the veteran salespeople, what he should do. Pete tells Troy to "fudge" the remaining five displays. He says: "Listen, Troy, if they're going to give you a ridiculous quota, go ahead and give the last five displays away free. Just tell a dealer that you will write some phony complaints to cover the cost of the displays."

"But, Pete, what happens if I get caught?" Troy replies. "Don't get caught," smirks Pete. "I can show you how not to."

Questions

1. Do you think Troy should go ahead and "fudge" the remaining five displays? Why?

2. What other alternatives does Troy have to avoid public humiliation at the summer carpet show?

3. Should Troy say anything to the sales manager about his distaste for subjecting salespeople to ridicule in front of their colleagues? What effect do you think this "punish in public" practice will have on most salespeoples's motivation?

Chapter 4

Integrating Personal Selling and Marketing

Without teamwork, there soon will be no team and eventually no work.

Profile

"IN the business of supermarket retailing, where shelf space is paramount, outstanding customer service to the retailer is the key element of success for the consumer-products salesperson," says Mary Ellen Duffy, a Unit Manager for the Chicago Sales District of the Colgate-Palmolive Company.

Mary Ellen graduated from St. Norbert College in 1980 with a degree in marketing. Before joining Colgate-Palmolive in 1987, she worked for two other large consumer-products companies with similar product lines. This experience, along with her college background, made her an ideal candidate for a Unit Manager position with Colgate-Palmolive. After working with experienced Unit Managers in an extensive training program, Mary Ellen was assigned a unit (a geographically defined territory) in the Chicago District. Within this unit, she provides sales and service support to customers who carry Colgate brands. These customers are a diverse group of businesses that include large discounters, drugstores, and supermarkets. At sales calls, Mary Ellen introduces new products, sells store managers on participating in product promotions, writes orders, and keeps tabs on competitors' activities. She currently handles 70 retail grocery and drugstore accounts.

When it comes to teamwork, Mary Ellen's job sometimes sounds more like choreography than selling. She enjoys telling this story: "When a new Cub Foods store recently opened in my territory, I worked closely with my managers and headquarters marketing personnel to structure a promotion that would attract customers to my client's store while selling Colgate-Palmolive product. I got approval to purchase a new car to be raffled off at the store's grand opening. In return for my efforts, the client purchased a large quantity of Colgate-Palmolive detergent and toothpaste and agreed to fill the car with Colgate merchandise. I made sure to give the local press the date of the raffle drawing, and after the grand opening, I gave them the story about the promotion along with a photograph of the happy winner and the store manager. In addition to selling a great deal of Colgate product, I was able to establish credibility and an outstanding business relationship with a very large customer."

Mary Ellen regards dependability, communication, and convenience as the most important aspects of customer service. When one of her retailer customers places an order, Mary Ellen works very closely with Colgate's customer service department to make absolutely certain that the order arrives (1) on time, (2) undamaged, (3) in the correct quantity, and (4) correctly priced.

"I frequently meet with my customers to ensure that no problems arise in the course of a transaction and to be alert for new opportunities to sell Colgate products," explains Mary Ellen. Also routine is Mary Ellen's attendance at customer "resets," which involve positioning items on the store shelves in order to highlight Colgate products. ■

Mary Ellen Duffy

After reading this chapter, you should understand:

☐ How important it is for field sales and headquarters marketing activities to be coordinated

☐ How sales support people affect the earnings of field sales representatives

☐ Ways for salespeople and headquarters support people to work more effectively together

☐ Personal selling as the key tool in the promotional mix

☐ Strategies for substitutability of promotional tools to improve sales force effectiveness and efficiency

PERSONAL SELLING IN TODAY'S MARKETING ENVIRONMENT

In their book *A Passion for Excellence*, Tom Peters and Nancy Austin state that "the heart of marketing is selling."[1] It is the salesperson who represents and defines the company in the eyes of the customer. Few customers interact with or even know anybody else in the seller organization. Because selling is the critical frontline contact with customers, all other marketing activities should be designed to support the sales force.

In her book *Mary Kay on People Management*, the founder of Mary Kay Cosmetics writes: "Ideally every employee in the company should be sales oriented. It doesn't matter if that person is in research, accounting, or shipping—everyone's job supports the sales organization. Not a single major decision is made at Mary Kay Cosmetics without first weighing the consequences to our sales force."[2] It is essential to understand that modern marketing departments are composed of two groups of people—the field sales force and the headquarters marketing staff—who must work closely together if the organization is to achieve its goals.

COORDINATING SALES AND MARKETING ACTIVITIES

Although personal selling is one of the key functions of marketing management, some businesspeople, and even a few academicians, still treat sales as if it were completely separated from headquarters marketing activities. Under this misguided view, inadequate communication and lack of cooperation can develop

[1]Tom Peters and Nancy Austin, *A Passion for Excellence* (New York: Random House, 1985), pp. 91–92.
[2]Mary Kay Ash, *Mary Kay on People Management* (New York: Warner Books, 1984), p. 140.

between the headquarters marketing group and the sales force. Rosenbloom and Anderson sum up the problem this way:

> Too many think of . . . sales as an activity isolated from marketing planning and strategy development. So it is not surprising that poor communication and even rivalry separate the headquarters marketing staff and the sales force in some companies. Instead, they need to understand that they are on the same team and must cooperate to achieve organizational objectives. . . . The sales force must be seen as an integral part of the marketing organization—that critical part which brings the marketing plan to fruition by generating sales revenues.[3]

Professional sales and marketing people must understand the interrelationship of selling and marketing and the benefits to be derived for each group through close cooperation. One of the findings in a national study by the Forum Corporation of North America was that building relationships with internal staff is a key factor in the success of salespeople. The report stated:

> Salespeople generally have no subordinates; they get their work done through others over whom they have little or no direct control. Influencing others to change their priorities, accept new responsibilities, interrupt their schedules, or fulfill any other request for attention or special action is a major part of the job. High performers generally do a much better job than moderate performers in this area.[4]

Sales Aren't Made by Salespeople Alone

Working closely with customers and sales reps, sales support personnel exert a direct influence on sales results. Successful sales operations have always depended on many people, not just on the field salesperson, but this fact is only now becoming manifest to all. At John Deere & Company in Moline, Illinois, where sales of farm and construction equipment topped $4 billion in 1987, it is recognized that farmers and contractors alike are interested in a product's overall cost rather than merely its initial price. The company believes in a multilevel service approach. When unusual service problems crop up, product support and parts specialists from headquarters come in to back up the field sales team. As key Deere managers see it: "The field salesperson may sell the first machine, but the product support group will continue to sell those customers for years to come. We feel the two are inseparable."[5]

Dividing Up Sales Activities
Because of the growing complexity of products and services, various parts of the sales function are being delegated to people who work inside the company. Inside salespeople and other sales support staff are being assigned to routine sales tasks such as qualifying prospects, soliciting reorders, expediting delivery, redressing complaints, handling sales paperwork, doing missionary work, providing customer service, and maintaining good customer relations. Among the

---

[3]Bert Rosenbloom and Rolph E. Anderson, in "The Sales Manager: Tomorrow's Super Marketer," *Business Horizons*, March–April 1984, pp. 51–52.

[4]William M. deMarco and Michael D. Maginn, *Sales Competency Research Report* (Boston: Forum Corporation of North America, 1982), p. 29.

[5]Kate Bertrand, "Sales and Service: One Big Happy Family?" *Business Marketing*, December 1988, pp. 36–42.

many employees who contribute directly or indirectly to sales results are technical support people and customer service employees (both of whom often go on sales calls with the sales rep), material handlers, expediters, accounts receivable and credit clerks, switchboard operators, receptionists, and truck drivers. At SecondWind Company, which sells athletic shoe-care products, sales order pads hang from the desk of every employee in the company's Paso Robles, California, headquarters. Since everyone from the CEO on down has been trained to fill out the sales forms, anyone who answers a phone call from a prospect or customer is a potential salesperson.

Incentives for Sales Support People

Traditionally, sales representatives have been the only group of employees below management levels to participate in incentive programs. But the time may have come to make support staff people eligible for incentives, too, not only to motivate them to work harder but also to discourage resentment toward the salespeople.

Tom Shane, owner and CEO of Western Stone and Metal, an importer and retailer of precious stones, has developed a profit-based plan that considers the individual's level of performance and contribution to the sales effort. He explains: "Since we believe that every employee supports the sale in some way, it seemed only natural to provide all of our employees with the opportunity to share in the rewards of increased sales."[6] Western Stone and Metal's incentive plan provides for a bonus pool to be distributed quarterly, with 50 percent going to salespeople, 35 percent to the support staff and supervisors, and 15 percent to the store manager. Salespeople earn their bonuses by exceeding their sales quotas, while sales support employees earn their bonuses based on a point system that weighs each person's responsibility and authority against the store's performance.

HEADQUARTERS MARKETING SUPPORT FOR SALES

While the sales force is usually out in the field talking with customers face-to-face, the headquarters marketing people provide advertising, sales promotion, publicity, and a number of other sales support functions. Although most of these support activities are handled by marketing department personnel, some may be subcontracted to outside specialists in advertising, marketing research, consulting, or public relations. Briefly, headquarters support for salespeople includes the following:

Sales Promotion

Brochures, catalogs, and direct-mail flyers provide customers with advance information about special offers and new products.

---

[6]William Keenan, Jr., "Should Sales Support Employees Get Incentive Pay?" *Sales & Marketing Management*, January 1989, pp. 30–33.

This computer trade show in Chicago is just one of the thousands of large trade shows held every year in cities throughout the world.

Selling Aids

Audiovisuals, flip charts, and videotapes are prepared for salespeople to use in their sales presentations.

Advertising

Advertisements in consumer and trade publications, television, billboards, and newspapers help smooth the way for salespeople by identifying the company, its products, and its *unique selling propositions (USPs)* in advance of the sales call.

Trade Shows and Exhibits

Large exhibitions and demonstrations of a line of company products are provided for special shows to which the trade and sometimes the general public are invited. The Detroit Auto Show and the Atlanta Home Show are just two of over 9,000 trade shows that are now held annually. This is double the number held a decade ago, and the number is expected to grow 8 percent each year through the 1990s, partly because of the expansion of trade shows and exhibits into consumer markets.

EXHIBIT MARKETING Demonstration of a line of company products at a special show to which the trade and sometimes the general public are invited.

At companies like Texas Instruments, **exhibit marketing** is one of the fastest-growing areas of marketing. Since exhibiting at a large show can cost $200,000 or more and can divert sales force efforts from territorial work, it is essential that attendees be potential customers. On average, 67 percent of the visitors to an exhibit are truly interested in seeing the exhibited product and 31 percent are planning to buy it.[7] One of the largest private trade shows in the United States is Digital Equipment Corporation's DecWorld, a nine-day invitation-only show that costs over $20 million to stage. DecWorld allows DEC to show off their products to a large captive audience of over 30,000 customers and prospects.

[7]Jonathan M. Cox, "Trade Shows Provide Easiest Media Evaluation," *Marketing News*, May 10, 1985, p. 13.

What Would You Do?

Your district sales manager has just asked you if you would attend a three-day trade show outside your territory because he is unable to go himself. You are complimented by his asking you to substitute for him because it means you will be interacting with the national sales manager and several marketing managers from headquarters, as well as with people from the sales promotion and advertising departments. However, you are reluctant to leave your territory for three days right now because you're about to close two major sales worth several thousand dollars in commissions to you. In both cases, the prospects were impressed with your tailored service to them, especially your readiness to make an appearance in person when they had any questions or concerns. If you're absent for three days, you're afraid your competition may use this period to offer these two prospects some special inducements to buy. Unless you're there to counter these offers, you may lose the sales. You know that one of the telemarketers at your company's headquarters is acquainted with both of these prospects since she set up the original sales call appointments for you.

Product Publicity
News releases are prepared and distributed to various mass media about new products and services. Innovations such as filmless cameras and high-resolution televisions receive considerable free press that paves the way for product introductions and sales.

Market Research
Valuable data concerning markets, products, customers, sales trends, and sales problems are collected, analyzed, interpreted, and distributed. Without up-to-date market research, salespeople may try to sell to a market that doesn't exist. Markets are like a parade; they continually change. If you look away for a while, new performers have replaced earlier ones.

Marketing and Sales Planning
Overall marketing and sales goals, sales forecasts, and strategic plans are developed to guide sales force efforts.

New-Product Development
New-product ideas are generated and converted into commercially feasible new products.

STAKEHOLDERS An organization's publics, including employees, the media, special interest groups, suppliers, government agencies, legislators, the financial community, stockholders, and the general public.

Public Relations
Informational and persuasive communications are distributed to the company's **stakeholders** or publics (employees, the media, special interest groups, suppliers, government agencies, legislators, the financial community, stockholders, and the general public) to win support for management initiatives and to enhance the company's reputation.

SALESPEOPLE AND SUPPORT PEOPLE WORKING TOGETHER

Studies have shown that most salespeople and headquarters marketing service personnel could do a much better job of working together.[8] Many of the people who supply critical marketing services for the sales force do not have much understanding of the sales job. Instead of disparaging the efforts of the support people, however, salespeople should help them understand how they can provide better support. Resourceful salespeople and sales managers foster friendly, cooperative relationships with their headquarters marketing specialists to obtain extra support and services that can measurably improve selling performance. Some sales training experts advocate that salespeople actively participate in the training and supervision of sales support personnel to obtain better coordination between the sales force and marketing staff.[9]

Cross-Selling

In our increasingly specialized marketplace, it isn't unusual for more than one salesperson from the same company to call on the same customer. For example, an office supplies wholesaler may have one salesperson selling paper and pencils and another selling office furniture and electronic typewriters to the same company. These two salespeople, however, may never run into each other because they are assigned to separate sales force groups or they are calling on two different purchasing agents or buyers. Salespeople who aren't aware of their counterparts' activities often miss big **cross-selling** opportunities.

CROSS-SELLING Situation in which a salesperson gets a referral to a customer from a colleague within the company.

Smart salespeople know that they can obtain referrals on new prospects from headquarters marketing people, who are in a position to know which sales forces or salespeople are calling on which customers. Continuing our example, the customer who normally buys paper and pencils may at some point need a new desk and typewriter. If there is good communication between the paper and pencil salesperson and the headquarters marketing staff, the marketing staff will be able to tell the office furniture salesperson about the potential sale. Good salespeople, however, do not simply wait for such referrals to happen. Instead, they try to develop strong relationships with headquarters marketing people as well as with their counterparts in the field. At the very least, salespeople from two different sales forces in the same company should share knowledge about customers and selling strategies. (See the Company Highlight featuring Cigna for one cross-selling success story.)

Other Headquarters Support for Sales

Besides the marketing department, salespeople ought to cultivate good working relationships with people in credit, production, traffic or shipping, billing, quality control, and customer service. Knowing the right people in each of these areas

---

[8]Vaughan C. Judd, "Help Marketing Services Get with It," *Sales & Marketing Management*, October 6, 1980, p. 46.

[9]"Selling and Training for the 21st Century," *Sales & Marketing Management*, July 1988, p. 22.

Company Highlight

Cross-Selling at Cigna

Cigna, the giant insurance company, is seeing dramatic payoffs from cross-selling. In 1983, Cigna's income from cross-selling totaled only $30 million, primarily from property-casualty referrals into the employee-benefit organization. However, in 1987, cross-selling was responsible for $352 million in revenue, or 34 percent of Cigna's total revenue growth and 15 percent of new-customer sales. The number of referrals between offices increased from 1,151 by 152 offices in 1986 to 2,868 by 216 offices in 1987. To promote cross-selling, Cigna publishes local personnel directories for field salespeople to contact their counterparts elsewhere, uses an integrated customer database, maintains a Cross-Selling Hotline, organizes local trade fairs, and makes awards each year to the most successful cross-sellers.

Source: Harry J. Lew, "Cross-Selling Bears Fruit," *National Underwriter* (Life/Health/Financial Services), September 5, 1988, pp. 12–13.

Salespeople should try to cultivate good working relationships with people in credit, production, shipping, billing, quality control, and customer service.

can enable salespeople to solve problems for customers more quickly and easily. For example, when customers need credit, want to return defective products, have questions about their invoices, or need more products in a hurry, salespeople who have taken the time to establish rapport with key people in each of these areas can cut through some of the bureaucratic red tape to help their customers (and themselves in the eyes of their customers).

Of course, support is a two-way street, so salespeople must be willing to do favors now and then for headquarters people. For example, a salesperson might collect payment from an overdue account, pick up erroneous small shipments from customers and return them to shipping, or bring back unsatisfactory products to quality control and take the time to explain the customer's complaints. In dealing with diverse personalities at headquarters, salespeople might keep in mind some advice from J. C. Penney: "No rewards are handed out for cooperating merely with people we like. It's cooperating with the stinkers that counts."[10]

Understanding Headquarters Marketing Departments

Before they can work more closely with headquarters marketing people, salespeople must understand the different jobs in headquarters marketing departments. Salespeople employed by smaller companies sometimes work most closely with a single headquarters marketing manager and a single headquarters national sales manager (in addition to a regional or district field sales manager). At larger companies, however, it is not unusual for salespeople to work with a general marketing manager, several specialist product managers, an advertising manager, a distribution manager . . . and just about any other kind of specialist manager you can think of. Table 4-1 presents the major headquarters marketing

[10]Quoted in *Sales & Marketing Management*, December 1988, p. 24.

positions, their alternative titles, and their responsibilities. As you study this table, keep in mind that these positions are all possible career goals for people with strong professional personal selling experience.

TABLE 4-1   Marketing Positions and Responsibilities

POSITION	ALTERNATIVE TITLES	DUTIES
Marketing Manager	Vice President of Marketing, Director of Marketing	Directs all the company's marketing activities, including planning, organizing, staffing, directing, controlling, and evaluating performance
Product Manager	Brand Manager	Develops goals, objectives, plans, strategies, and marketing mixes for a product line or brand
Advertising Manager	Advertising Director, Director of Communications	Devises advertising policy and strategy, selects advertising agencies, develops promotional campaigns, selects media, and allocates advertising expenditures
Distribution Manager	Logistics Manager, Traffic Manager, Transportation Manager	Manages the distribution system, including storage and transportation, for all products and services
Purchasing Manager	Director of Purchasing, Director of Procurement	Manages all purchasing activities, including buying of product ingredients or components, supplies, equipment, and needed materials
Marketing Research Manager	Director of Commercial Research, Director of Market Research	Develops research designs to solve specific problems, then collects, analyzes, interprets data, and presents results to top management
Public Relations Manager	Director of Public Relations, Director of Communications, Public Affairs Officer	Manages all communications with the media and various company stakeholders to gain support for company positions and to present favorable public image
Customer Service Manager	Director of Customer Relations	Provides customer service, manages and handles customer complaints
Sales Manager	Vice President of Sales, Director of Sales, National Sales Manager, Regional, District, or Branch Sales Manager	Organizes, develops, directs, controls, and evaluates the sales force

Selling in Action

Integrating Outside and Inside Sales Forces at General Foods

A few years ago, managers at General Foods' Food Service Division recognized the need to set long-term goals in order to stay ahead of competitors who also sold a full range of food products to institutions such as restaurants, hotels, universities, corporations, and hospitals. Meetings between top executives, sales and marketing managers, and sales and marketing support personnel yielded several goals:

- Provide increased coverage to consumers while maintaining alignments with distributors.
- Reduce the high cost of cold-calling and prospecting for accounts.
- Target and identify the largest new-customer opportunities.
- Free the field sales force from nonselling maintenance activities to current customers.
- Support products currently undersupported by a field sales force with many priorities.
- Listen better to the needs of the marketplace.

- Provide a medium that would provide a direct two-way link to a broader segment of current and potential customers.
- Improve support and tracking of merchandising and promotional programs.

To achieve these objectives, an in-house telemarketing sales team was set up to help both field sales and headquarters marketing. The diversity of GF's product line required professionally trained inside sales reps whose knowledge of all GF products enabled them to answer diverse inquiries and to identify cross-selling opportunities. Called "GF Central," these inside salespeople identified and qualified new high-volume accounts for the field sales force. An in-house sales force gave upper management an opportunity to stay in closer touch with customers and enabled them to obtain more timely market information. Being situated at headquarters also allowed the telephone sales reps to tap internal expertise and resources to answer customer questions and resolve customer problems.

Telemarketing reduced the cost of sales prospecting and freed field sales reps from non-

THE TOTAL SALES TEAM

No ship captain, no matter how well-charted the course, can reach the intended destination without the crew's help. Nor can any salesperson, no matter how individually talented and prepared, reach territorial goals without the help of a strong backup team. Today's professional sales team, especially when calling on large national accounts, may include top management, customer service representatives, technical specialists, inside salespeople, manufacturer's representatives, and many others, such as warehouse and delivery people. Each of these sales team members has a valuable role to play in developing ongoing positive

selling activities, such as routine order taking and customer service for current customers. It also allowed General Foods to dramatically increase customer contacts because telemarketers were able to contact five times as many food service operators in a day as could field reps making in-person sales calls. Most important, the telemarketing unit served as a central clearing house that improved communication and coordination of GF's various selling and marketing programs.

Initially, each telephone sales rep participated in a three-week training course, including one week working with GF field sales reps. This field work helped the inside salespeople to gain the support of the outside salespeople and to learn more about the art of selling. After completing the training, the telemarketers identified many high-volume opportunities for one of GF's most successful products: Crystal Light. Ninety-five percent of the leads turned over to the field sales reps resulted in sales. Normally, only 44 percent of the leads turn into sales. An automated telemarketing system used by the inside salespeople when placing calls created a proprietary database of current and potential customers.

GF understood the importance of integrating the unit with the field sales force and went to great lengths to deal with any field sales force fears. Outside sales reps were won over when they saw how the telemarketing reps at headquarters helped them earn their bonus checks. To ensure that the inside reps cooperated with the field reps, bonuses were awarded to telemarketers and field reps only when the outside sales force reached its sales goals. An electronic messaging service helped maintain constant communication between the inside and outside sales force, and enabled the field reps to get back to customers within hours of any telephone call. One revealing anecdote involved a lead given a field salesperson for a restaurateur whom he had known for years as a fellow Kiwanis Club member. The outside rep hadn't even considered his friend as a potential customer for Crystal Light and was delighted when the lead given him by a telemarketer resulted in a high-volume account for Crystal Light.

Source: Adapted from David C. Barnard, "Integrating an In-House Center," *Direct Marketing,* December 1988, pp. 72–75, 87.

relationships with customers. The sales representative, who may be called a *national account manager (NAM)* or *key account executive (KAE),* serves as coordinator of the buyer and seller team interactions.

Top Management

At some companies, top managers are key members of the national account selling team. For example, Singer Business Machines' initial sales approach is for a top manager to request a meeting with the prospect company's chief operating officer. Singer is rarely turned down at this level. At this first meeting, the regional sales manager, the local salesperson, and a systems engineer accompany the top manager to discuss how they can benefit the client. If all goes well, this meeting is followed by a series of conferences and demonstrations that may involve people from throughout the seller's and the buyer's organization. At Emery Air Freight Corporation, chairman and CEO John C. Emery, Jr., has a standing offer for any of his salespeople: Just ask, and he'll call the prospect to say that Emery wants the business. "People almost fall off their chairs when they realize it's the president calling," laughs Emery.[11] All top company officers at Emery have sales jobs in addition to their normal duties; John Emery himself handles IBM and General Electric.

Technical Specialists

Many companies assign technical specialists to work with their sales representatives as part of a consultative team that anticipates and solves customer problems. Companies like IBM and Xerox have specialists who work with sales representatives to provide technical advice and information needed by the customer before, during, and after the purchase.

Customer Service Representatives

Installation, maintenance, and regular servicing of the products and systems that customers purchase are handled by customer service representatives. It is often the salesperson's responsibility to initiate contact between a new customer and the customer service department.

Specialized Salespeople

Many sales organizations have two specialized categories of salespeople to round out their selling efforts or sometimes to substitute for a direct sales force: (1) inside salespeople and (2) manufacturers' representatives.

INSIDE SALESPEOPLE or TELEMARKETERS Salespeople who sell from the office by answering unsolicited inquiries and generating leads and prospects for the field sales force.

Inside salespeople or **telemarketers** sell from the office using telephones. Their main job is to answer unsolicited inquiries from prospects and generate leads for the field sales force. They also confirm appointments, make travel arrangements, and look up customer data. A single inside support person can handle several salespeople and increase sales significantly when linked to field salespeople by "beepers" or cellular phones. Since 70 percent of business calls do not reach the person intended, it is best to have inside salespeople make them for the field salesperson, whose productive selling time is often eroded by games of "telephone tag" with customers. WATS lines and incoming 800 numbers make cellular phone communications with a remote base support person practical.

MANUFACTURERS' AGENTS Independent salespeople who specialize in certain markets and sell for several noncompeting manufacturers on a straight commission basis.

Manufacturers' agents, as mentioned in Chapter 1, are independent salespeople who specialize in certain markets and sell for several noncompeting manufacturers on a straight commission basis. Hiring manufacturers' reps is a relatively low-risk way to expand the sales force because the cost-to-sales ratio is fixed by the commission percentage. Working closely together, the direct sales force, inside salespeople, and manufacturers' representatives can create a synergistic selling team.

---

[11]Sherry Siegel, "Selling Your Way to the Top," *Success*, January–February 1987, p. 43.

SELLING: THE FOCAL POINT OF MARKETING

In their 1988 book *Bottom-Up Marketing*, Al Ries and Jack Trout contend that one of the major mistakes marketing managers make is to persist in devising top-down strategies that don't work. Ries and Trout believe that tactics should dictate marketing strategy, and that any strategic plan is useless unless it can be implemented tactically.[12] Given this assumption, one can argue that selling is *the* critical organizational function and that the primary role of marketing planning and strategy is to provide support to the sales force. A Los Gatos, California, company that puts this view into practice is XA Systems Corporation, which develops and markets applications software that sells for prices starting at $40,000. XA Systems' marketing department does not make any strategic or positioning decisions, but concentrates on increasing the productivity of XA salespeople.[13]

Probably few marketing managers are ready to accept this radical view, but there is no doubt that personal selling plays a major role in the success of most companies. Within overall corporate goals and strategy, headquarters marketing formulates the marketing goals and strategy that guide the sales force in carrying out field tactics and other detailed activities. The bottom line is that unless products can be profitably sold, the most ingenious strategic marketing plans will be barren. To better understand the job of the marketing manager who sets the marketing goals and strategy for the sales force, let's look at what the marketing manager does.

DESIGNING THE MARKETING MIX

PROMOTION *Informs* prospective buyers about the benefits of a product or service, *persuades* them to try it, and *reminds* them later of the benefits they enjoyed the last time they used it.

Marketing managers are responsible for skillfully designing marketing strategies by manipulating the four components of the marketing mix: product, price, distribution, and promotion. Of these four variables, salespeople most actively participate in **promotion,** which enables the company to communicate directly with customers. Promotion *informs* prospective buyers about the benefits of a product or service, *persuades* them to try it, and *reminds* them later about the benefits they enjoyed the last time they used it. Promotion, too, may be seen as a "mix" of several variables.

The Promotional Mix

An organization's promotional mix includes four components—advertising, personal selling, publicity, and sales promotion—which can be combined in innumerable ways with the other elements of the organization's marketing mix. Figure 4-1 illustrates that personal selling is a substrategy of promotional strategy, which, in turn, is a substrategy of the marketing mix.

ADVERTISING The promotion of products by an identified sponsor who purchases mass media time or space.

Advertising is the promotion of products by an identified sponsor who

[12]Al Ries and Jack Trout, *Bottom-up Marketing* (New York: McGraw-Hill, 1988).
[13]"Sell Mates," *INC.*, December 1980, p. 126.

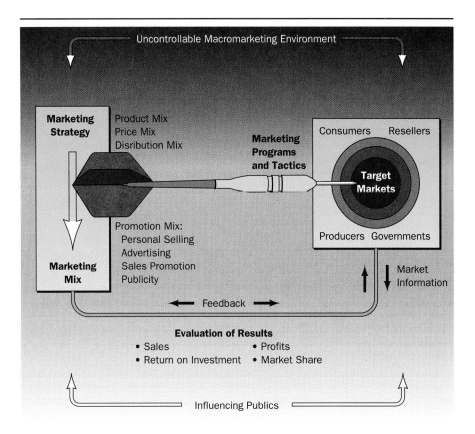

Figure 4-1 How All the Elements of a Marketing Strategy Work Together to Hit Target Markets

purchases mass media time or space in television, radio, magazines, newspapers, or billboards. By paying for the advertising, the company controls precisely *what* is said and, to a lesser extent, *whom* the message reaches because the ad will be run in media aimed at the target market.

PERSONAL SELLING
Interpersonal presentation of products to one or more prospective customers to develop or maintain mutually beneficial exchange relationships.

Personal selling is the interpersonal presentation of products to one or more prospective customers to develop or maintain mutually beneficial exchange relationships. Personal selling is the only part of the seller's promotional mix that is typically carried out on an interactive person-to-person, or at least voice-to-voice, basis with potential buyers. Effective personal selling requires communication *with*, not just *to*, buyers. All other elements of the promotional mix—advertising, sales promotion, and publicity—are one-way flows from seller to buyer.

One of the most important advantages of personal selling is its flexibility. Salespeople can usually see or hear the prospect's reaction to the presentation and make adjustments on the spot. On the downside, personal selling is the most expensive of the four promotional elements on a per-customer contact basis. With advances in telecommunications technology, more marketing organizations are using video conferencing and interactive computer linkups with potential customers, so face-to-face and even voice-to-voice interaction may gradually be replaced by more cost-effective technology in selling.

PUBLICITY Providing
newsworthy releases of
information to the mass
media in order to achieve
favorable communications
and goodwill for an
organization, a product, a
service, or an idea.

Publicity seeks to achieve favorable communications and goodwill for an organization, a product, a service, or an idea by providing newsworthy releases of information to mass media representatives. Publicity is nonpersonal and unpaid promotion: The company attempts to have favorable news stories covered for free by the mass media. (Of course, there are some costs to the company—it must pay its public relations people.) A special benefit of publicity is the credibility a company release gains by its appearance as an objective news story. A disadvantage of publicity is the inability of the company to control how, when, where, or whether the release is finally presented in the media. Media people generally have their own styles and priorities, and abbreviate or add their own touches to any story, if they decide to run it at all. And even if the publicity release is run in a form, time, and place that pleases company management, it is usually a one-shot effort because it's news only once.

SALES PROMOTION A
short-run incentive or
inducement offered to
prospective customers to
stimulate sales or to
enhance the distribution of
a product.

Sales promotion is a short-run incentive or inducement offered to prospective customers to stimulate sales or to enhance the distribution of a product. Sales promotion activities cover a wide variety of trade and consumer programs; examples are trade shows, exhibitions, point-of-purchase displays, product and service demonstrations, coupons, rebates, dealer incentives, free samples, contests, games, sweepstakes, trading stamps, special price offers, catalogs, premiums, toll-free numbers, and sponsorship of special events and various other one-time promotional efforts. A few years ago, when British Airways feared a loss of American tourists because of the threat of terrorism, the airline ran a sweepstakes that gave winners free plane tickets plus the use of a London townhouse and a Rolls-Royce.

More than $100 billion is spent annually on trade and consumer sales promotion, an amount roughly equal to all advertising expenditures. Moreover, sales promotion expenditures are growing at an annual rate of 12 percent, versus only 7.5 percent for advertising.[14] The most frequently used forms of consumer-oriented sales promotion are coupons (66 percent), price discounts (11 percent), refunds (10 percent), premiums (8 percent), prize promotions (4 percent), and samples (1 percent). About 6.5 billion coupons (4 percent of which are issued by packaged-goods manufacturers) are redeemed every year by U.S. consumers.[15]

Many companies use an internal form of sales promotion, *sales force promotion,* to stimulate extra selling efforts from their salespeople. A company that wants a big sales increase for a specific product over a short period of time may offer its salespeople and sales support staff special bonuses and prizes.

Substitutability of the Promotional Tools

A significant feature of the four promotional tools is their partial substitutability for one another. It may be possible to achieve a sales forecast by increasing advertising expenditures or personal selling efforts or sales promotions, or even through special publicity for an innovative new product. Recognition of this substitutability of promotion tools explains why nearly one-fourth of industrial firms

[14]Steven W. Hartley and James Cross, "How Sales Promotion Can Work for and Against You," *Journal of Consumer Marketing*, Summer 1988, p. 35.
[15]Monograph titled *Consumer Promotion Report* (New York: Dancer, Fitzgerald, Sampel, 1982).

have integrated all promotion under one person whose title may be *manager of marketing communication, director of marketing services,* or *communications manager.* Product improvements, lower prices, better customer service, and increased distribution can all be effective in stimulating sales. Promotional efforts, however, are essential for initiating customer awareness of a product and for moving customers toward purchase decisions.

Sales Transaction Stages

Findings of a study on the contribution of the different promotion tools in successive sales transaction stages suggest that advertising (backed by publicity) is more important than "cold" sales calls in obtaining customer *awareness* of new products and services. Customer *comprehension* is affected about equally by advertising and personal selling, whereas *closing* sales is largely influenced by the salesperson. Thus it appears that organizations can improve their promotional efficiency by increasing advertising and minimizing personal selling in the early stages of the customer adoption process, and then relying mainly on salespeople in the later stages.

All types of promotion, especially advertising and follow-ups by salespeople, can improve customer evaluation and satisfaction with products even after purchase and use. When Fortune 500 company vice presidents of marketing and planning were asked how promotional strategy components will change in importance by 1995, they reported that the greatest increase will be in personal selling activities.[16]

Consumer versus Business Markets

The optimal mix of promotional elements will depend on the type of market. In consumer marketing, advertising is the most effective promotion tool, while personal selling is most productive in industrial marketing (selling to business organizations). Sales promotion and publicity have proved to be much less important in both types of markets, although about equally effective. Factors that are most favorable for emphasizing either personal selling or advertising in the promotional mix are shown in Table 4-2.

Some salespeople, sales managers, and marketing managers have the impression that advertising is unimportant in selling to business organizations and that personal selling is unimportant in selling to consumers. Neither impression is accurate. Richard Manville, president of Manville International Corporation, cites studies to support his belief that advertising is even *more* important in selling to businesses than to consumers.[17] Consumer goods have built-in point-of-sale advertising by their presence on retail shelves when customers are in the store, but industrial products have no such exposure to potential buyers. Advertising is therefore necessary to prepare industrial buyers for the sales representative's presentation. McGraw-Hill has dramatically made this point in its well-known advertisement, shown in Figure 4-2.

[16]Gene R. Laczniak and Robert F. Lusch, "Environment and Strategy in 1995: A Survey of High-Level Executives," *The Journal of Business and Industrial Marketing,* Winter 1987, pp. 16–17.

[17]Richard Manville, "Why Industrial Companies Must Advertise Their Products . . . and Consumer Companies Should Advertise Theirs," *Industrial Marketing,* October 1978, p. 46.

TABLE 4-2 When to Use Personal Selling or Advertising

FACTORS	PERSONAL SELLING	ADVERTISING
Customers		
Customer type	Industrial	Consumers
Number of customers	Few	Large
Location of customers	Concentrated	Dispersed
Contact with customers	Direct	Indirect
Customer feedback desired	Direct	Indirect
Stage of purchase decision	Purchase	Prepurchase
Number of people involved in the decision	Large	Small
Products		
Product cost	Expensive	Inexpensive
Product complexity	Complex	Simple
Product uniqueness	Unique	Standardized
Size of purchase	Large	Small
Service		
Postpurchase services	Many	Few
Delivery	Required	Not required
Installation	Required	Not required
Repair	Much	Little
Trade-ins	Frequently	Seldom
Cost/Price		
Cost	High	Low
Price elasticity	Inelastic	Elastic
Risk in purchase	High	Low
Channels of Distribution		
Channels	Short	Long
Channel strategy	Push	Pull

PERSONAL SELLING IS NUMBER 1

In many organizations, personal selling costs (salaries, commissions, travel and other expenses, and operation of sales branches) are the largest single operating expense—often as much as 15 percent of total sales revenues. By contrast, advertising expenditures average less than 2 percent of all industry sales revenues. As shown in Table 4-4, personal selling is considered the most important of the promotion tools by over two-thirds of industrial goods manufacturers, nearly half of consumer durable goods manufacturers, and more than one-third of consumer nondurable goods manufacturers.

For many organizations, the time, money, and effort put into other elements of business strategy would be profitless without successful personal selling. As the national sales manager for Veeco Instruments sees it:

> The order that I must get tomorrow will be responsible for our purchasing agent ordering more material; our engineering department producing new designs; our manufacturing department producing more merchandise; our personnel department hiring more people; and for me and my family, and all the other Veeco employees and their families, enjoying the better life that all begins with professional salesmanship.[18]

[18]T. G. Povey, "Spotting the Salesman Who Has What It Takes," *Nation's Business*, July 1972, pp. 70–71.

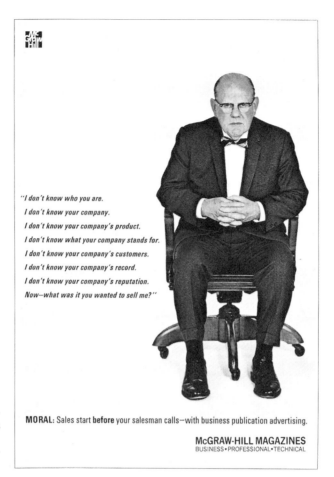

Figure 4-2 Business advertising is just as important as consumer advertising. *Source:* Reprinted with permission of McGraw-Hill, Inc.

SALESPEOPLE AS FIELD MARKETING MANAGERS

With their expanding responsibilities for marketing support coordination and profits, today's salespeople must operate like field marketing managers for their territories. One of the most critical tasks of the professional salesperson/field marketing manager is to optimize the mix of direct-selling activities and marketing support in his or her territory.

Optimizing Sales Calls and Promotional Support

Many salespeople incur high average costs for each successful sale because they overutilize direct-selling activities and underutilize marketing team support. By cooperating with the marketing specialists in advertising, marketing research, and sales promotion, the sales rep can often work much more efficiently.

Different combinations of selling and supporting marketing efforts are needed to achieve different sales objectives. The relationship between marketing efforts (inputs) and sales results (outputs) is a measure of selling efficiency. As

TABLE 4-3   Relative Importance of the Elements of Promotion

PROMOTION ACTIVITY	INDUSTRIAL GOODS	CONSUMER DURABLES	CONSUMER NONDURABLES
Personal selling	69.2	47.6	38.1
Broadcast media advertising	0.9	10.7	20.9
Print media advertising	12.5	16.1	14.8
Special promotional activities	9.6	15.5	15.5
Branding and promotional packaging	4.5	9.5	9.8
Other	3.3	0.6	0.9
Total	100.0	100.0	100.0

Note: Firms were asked to rate the relative importance of each of the above promotional mix elements using a scale of 100. Responses came from 336 industrial, 52 consumer durable, and 88 consumer nondurable goods manufacturers.
Source: Jon G. Udell, *Successful Marketing Strategies in American Marketing* (Madison, Wis.: MIMIR Publications, 1972), p. 47.

illustrated in Figure 4-3, if a regional sales organization has the objective of selling 1,500 facsimile machines for $1,000 each with a gross margin of $500 each, the input would be the mix and level of direct-selling and supporting marketing efforts required to achieve the sales target. As inputs, it is expected that the sales force will have to make 2,200 sales calls. In addition, the inside sales force will accept about 900 collect telephone calls (many long distance) inquiring about the new machines. An efficiency ratio of 2.26 is derived by dividing the dollar outputs by the dollar inputs ($750,000 ÷ $331,350).

Instead of using 2,200 sales calls, it may be more efficient to mail out 5,000 sales promotion brochures about the new product and make only 1,100 sales calls on the best prospects as identified by marketing research. By reallocating the mixture of direct-selling and marketing support activities, the same sales might be achieved with greater efficiency ($750,000 ÷ $171,350 = 4.38), as shown In Figure 4-4.

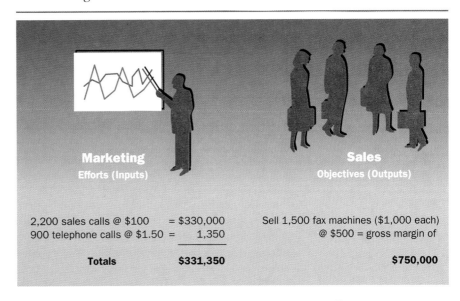

Marketing
Efforts (Inputs)

Sales
Objectives (Outputs)

2,200 sales calls @ $100   = $330,000
900 telephone calls @ $1.50 =   1,350

Totals   **$331,350**

Sell 1,500 fax machines ($1,000 each)
@ $500 = gross margin of

$750,000

FIGURE 4-3 Optimizing Sales Force and Marketing Support Efforts: Efficiency Ratio = 2.26

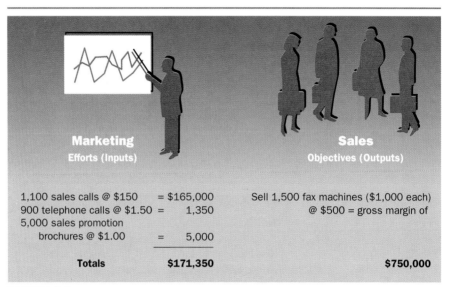

FIGURE 4-4 Optimizing Sales Force and Marketing Support Efforts:
Efficiency Ratio = 4.38

TEAMWORK HELPS EVERYBODY

As salespeople increase in professionalism and assume the role of field marketing managers for their territories, they become even more aware of the value of headquarters support. They understand that no one can become a supersalesperson without the help of his or her teammates in marketing and sales. Each time they make a major sale, the best sales reps remember to send a personal note or a small gift to the key sales and marketing support people who helped accomplish the sale. Even the toughest, most experienced salespeople are often surprised by how delighted support people feel when their contribution to sales is recognized and appreciated. Like professional football quarterbacks and backfield runners who send gifts to their linemen after a successful performance, salespeople can gain renewed commitment from the support staff by simply showing a little gratitude. Don't forget it. *You need your teammates!*

SUMMARY

Since selling is the heart of marketing, marketing activities should be designed to support the sales force. Professional salespeople work at building close relationships with headquarters marketing and sales support people. Headquarters support personnel provide sales support through sales promotion, selling aids, advertising, trade shows and exhibits, product publicity, market research, marketing and sales planning, new-product development, and public relations. Many companies offer incentives for sales support people to cooperate with salespeople. Significant *cross-selling* opportunities can come from marketing and sales support people or from company salespeople who handle other products. Successful selling is increasingly accomplished by a professional sales team composed of top management, technical specialists, customer service representatives, and specialized salespeople such as telemarketers and manufacturers' agents.

Personal selling is an integral component of an organization's *promotional mix,* which is an integral component of the organization's *marketing mix.* Personal selling and the other promotional tools—advertising, publicity, and sales promotion—are partially substitutable for each other. The optimal mix of promotional tools depends on the type of market. As salespeople are increasingly required to assume the role of field marketing managers, they will need to become adept at optimizing sales calls and promotional support activities.

CHAPTER REVIEW QUESTIONS

1. Name and describe at least six ways that headquarters marketing personnel support the sales force.

2. What is cross-selling and how does it work?

3. How can salespeople get support for their efforts from headquarters personnel who are not specifically involved in marketing activities? Provide an example of a situation where such support might be necessary.

4. Fill in the information missing from the following table:

Position	Alternative Titles	Duties
Advertising Manager	*Advertising Director / Director of Communications*	*Devises Adv Policy & Strategy, selects Adv agencies, develops promotional campaigns, selects media & allocates advertising expenditures*
Marketing Manager	Vice President of Marketing, Director of Marketing	*Directs all company's marketing activities — planning, organizing, staffing, directing, controlling & evaluating.*
Customer Service Manager	*Director of Customer Relations*	Provides customer services. Manages and handles customer complaints.
Product Manager	Brand Manager	*Develops goals, objectives, plans & strategies & marketing mixes for product line or brand.*
Sales Manager	*VP of Sales / Director of Sales / National Sales Manager / Regional District or Branch Manager / Sales Manager*	*Organizes, develops, direct, controls & evaluates the Sales force.*

5. What is a NAM? a KAE? *→ NAM → National Account Manager   KAE → Key Account Executive / serves as coordinator of buyer & seller team interactions*

6. Name and describe the two specialized categories of salespeople that many sales organizations have.

7. List the four components of the promotional mix. What is meant by the "substitutability" of the promotional tools? *Advertising, Personal Selling, Publicity & Sales Promotion*

8. What are the responsibilities of a field marketing manager?

TOPICS FOR THOUGHT AND CLASS DISCUSSION

1. Who supports whom: Should marketing activities be aimed primarily at supporting the efforts of field salespeople, or should salespeople's efforts be primarily focused on carrying out the plans and strategies of marketing?

2. What types of sales and marketing support do salespeople receive in doing their jobs? Which type of support do you think is most helpful to them?

3. Name and describe the duties of two categories of specialized salespeople who support and supplement the company's field salespeople. Why are these specialized salespeople sometimes necessary even for a major corporation with a large field sales force?

4. With respect to customers, products, cost/prices, service, and distribution, give two or three examples of when personal selling is more likely to be used than advertising.

5. "Today's salespeople must increasingly be able to function like field marketing managers." Write a brief essay on this statement.

6. In the decade ahead, do you think that field salespeople will have more or fewer duties and responsibilities? Why?

PROJECTS FOR PERSONAL GROWTH

1. Assume that you are CEO of a medium-sized consumer products company located in Los Angeles. Outline a total plan (including organization, training, compensation, motivation, and evaluation) for getting your company's marketing department and sales force to work more closely together. Use your library's *Business Periodicals Index* to locate articles that can help you in deciding what to do.

2. Conduct a small survey of nine people (three salespeople, three sales managers, and three marketing managers) using the two following questions:
   a. In your company, does marketing work for the sales force, or does the sales force work for marketing?
   b. Is this the way you think it should be? Why?
   Tabulate your answers by respondent categories and type of company. Any surprises?

KEY TERMS

Exhibit marketing Demonstration of a line of company products at a special show to which the trade and sometimes the general public are invited.

Stakeholders An organization's publics, including employees, the media, special interest groups, suppliers, government agencies, legislators, the financial community, stockholders, and the general public.

Cross-selling Situation in which a salesperson gets a referral to a customer from a colleague within the company.

Inside salespeople or **telemarketers** Salespeople who sell from the office by answering unsolicited inquiries and generating leads and prospects for the field sales force.

Manufacturers' agents Independent salespeople who specialize in certain markets and sell for several noncompeting manufacturers on a straight commission basis.

Promotion *Informs* prospective buyers about the benefits of a product or service, *persuades* them to try it, and *reminds* them later of the benefits they enjoyed the last time they used it.

Advertising The promotion of products by an identified sponsor who purchases mass media time or space.

Personal selling Interpersonal presentation of products to one or more prospective customers to develop or maintain mutually beneficial exchange relationships.

Publicity Providing newsworthy releases of information to the mass media in order to achieve favorable communications and goodwill for an organization, a product, a service, or an idea.

Sales promotion A short-run incentive or inducement offered to prospective customers to stimulate sales or to enhance the distribution of a product.

Case 4-1

ANY PROBLEMS IN YOUR SALES TERRITORY?

At the monthly sales meeting held at the Chicago regional sales office of Stafford Products, Inc., a manufacturer of office supplies, Michael Stranahan, the regional sales manager, has just completed his formal agenda. After putting his notes aside and taking a quick sip of coffee, he goes around the room asking each of the six salespeople present if they have any problems.

Glen Baker: No problems, Mike. This month looks like a big one in my territory. We just landed the Krumm Company account. After working on it for three years, we finally wrestled it away from our major competitor. I think the thing that really clinched it was that beautiful full-color product catalog we got from sales promotion. My hat's off to those people, especially to Peggy Wrigley, who included a couple of my suggestions about product descriptions in the catalog when I asked her for a copy of the preliminary version. She's sharp and a delight to work with. That catalog has sure helped me show off our product line to best advantage. All of my competitor's product catalogs are still black and white.

Mike Stranahan: Good going, Glen! Okay, Steve, have you got anything?

Steve Feinman: It's tough following Glen, with his good news. I'm afraid that one of my major accounts, Murphy Brothers, is going to switch to a competitor. Bill Murphy told me that he's fed up with all the problems he has to deal with in buying from us. First, it seems our billing department sent him an invoice that failed to include the 15 percent discount for five of the products on his last order. He says it took him three days on the phone to straighten that one out. Then the delivery was two weeks late—seems the shipping department delivered his order to Murphy Brothers' old address, which is now occupied by a YMCA. You'd think the driver could figure out that a YMCA wouldn't be one of our customers. Finally, when I asked him if he wanted to order any of the new tape dispensers that have been selling like hotcakes, he said that he'd never gotten any information on our tape dispenser. Seems that somebody in the marketing department deleted his company from the mailing list for sales promotions when they moved to their new location. Bill says when he phoned, he was shuffled to three different people before he finally got someone who could put him back on the mailing list. Then when I called the warehouse to set aside two cartons of the new tape dispenser for Murphy Brothers, I was told that there was no inventory and that production was running three weeks behind orders. Boy, it's frustrating trying to work with customers when the headquarters backup team keeps dropping the ball. Can't you do anything, Mike, to make those headquarters clowns get their act together?

Mike Stranahan: I'll check into it, Steve. We can't let longtime customers like Murphy Brothers slip away. Why don't you send Bill Murphy one of our promotional samples, like the transistor radio, to smooth his ruffled feathers? Candy?

Candice Hawsey: No major problems, Mike. The only complaint I have is about our sexist advertisements that keep appearing in trade magazines. Don't the advertising people understand that a lot of the buyers and office managers today are women who are offended by seeing bikini-clad models promoting our products? I've apologized to three prospects during the last month about these ads. When are those advertising guys going to get in touch with the times?

Mike Stranahan: You've got a good point, Candy. I've got a college-age daughter myself, and I don't like the image those advertisements are projecting for our company. I'll pass on your complaint to our national sales manager. Walt, you look perplexed—what's up?

Walter Zoltners: Everything's going fine in my territory, Mike, except for those darn survey forms that marketing research is asking us to deliver to customers. With my daily sales call schedule, I don't have time to be doing work for marketing research, too. If they want to find out how satisfied our customers are with our products and services, why don't they hire an independent firm to conduct the survey instead of using up our selling time?

Mike Stranahan: They claim that their return rate sharply increases when the surveys are hand-delivered. But I agree with you, Walt. They shouldn't be asking us to do their work. I'll try to keep them from foisting any more surveys on us. Joan, how are you doing?

Joan Runyon: No problems, Mike, but you might be interested to know something about the big annual office products trade show I attended last weekend at the McCormack Center. It ran from Wednesday until Sunday evening. Wish I could've been there when it opened—I heard that some of my biggest customers were there only on Wednesday. But it was really quite a spectacle—first time I've ever attended a trade show, and I really got a lot out of it. Passed out my business card to about 80 prospects. I thought our Stafford Products booth exhibit was very professionally done. It was a small office setting, about one-third normal size, with nearly all our products prominently displayed on desks, tables, and cabinets in the room. I understand that Leon Mescon, one of our marketing managers, designed it. I sent him a little note telling him what a good job he did. I think it would be a good idea if the whole regional sales force attended at least this trade show—maybe we could take turns hanging out at our booth. I really found it a wonderful place to learn about competitors' new products and to do some prospecting for new customers.

Mike Stranahan: Thanks, Joan. Maybe each of you should take a day off to go to the annual office products trade show. I think I can fit it into our budget. Larry?

Larry Pascarella: Well, I'd like to have some fun at a trade show, too, Mike, but I can't afford to leave my customers alone with the competitors' salespeople during a business day—I'll take a weekend day, if we're going to take turns! Mike, I've got only one problem. It's with our credit department. They're giving one of my potential customers a hard time about approving his credit. Osgood & Paley Company have been in business over five years now, and they're just starting to turn the corner toward profits. Credit claims that their D&B report says that Osgood & Paley has a poor credit rating, and they won't approve anything but cash sales. Mike, Osgood & Paley want to buy $20,000 worth of supplies a year. Can't we do something to get their credit approved? It really irritates me when I work my tail off to win a customer, only to see the Credit Department stop me dead in my tracks.

Mike Stranahan: I hear what you're saying, Larry. Ever since that new guy, Norback, became credit manager, it's been like pulling teeth to get credit approvals for new customers. I'll call the VP of finance to see what I can do for you. Meanwhile, try to reassure Osgood & Paley that we're working on getting their credit approved.

Okay, it's 10:00 A.M., does anybody have anything else? If not, let's go sell 'em.

Questions

1. Based on this dialog at the monthly sales meeting, which of the salespeople do you think are probably the most successful?

2. Which of the salespeople do you think are the least successful? Why?

3. What do you think of Mike Stranahan as a sales manager? Why?

4. If you were to replace Mike Stranahan as sales manager, what would you tell these six salespeople at the next monthly sales meeting?

Case 4-2

DESIGNING THE PROMOTIONAL MIX FOR A SALES TERRITORY

Recently hired to replace a previous sales representative for Neuberger Plumbing Supplies, Inc., George Gellerman will be calling on large apartment complexes, public and private institutions such as hospitals and colleges, and a few large retail stores in the Middle Atlantic sales region. In all, he will have about 4,000 current and potential customers. George has divided these customers and prospects into three categories: large, medium, and small volume.

Large Volume. About 800 of these 4,000 customers and prospects are large-volume buyers who purchase over $10,000 of plumbing supplies a year. Approximately 200 of George's present customers are in this large-volume category, and their average purchase is nearly $12,000. Of the remaining 600 large-volume prospects, George thinks that he can sell to 25 percent of them after three sales calls, and he expects their average purchase to be about the same as for his present large-volume customers.

Medium Volume. Nearly 1,000 of the customers and prospects in George's territory are medium-volume purchasers of between $4,000 and $10,000 worth of plumbing supplies yearly. Roughly 300 of these medium-volume buyers are present Neuberger customers, and their average order is around $6,000. Among the remaining 700 prospects, George thinks he can successfully sell to about 100 of them after two sales calls.

Small Volume. Finally, there are the rest of the 2,200 customers and prospects, who buy less than $4,000 worth of plumbing supplies a year. Nearly 500 of George's present customers fall into this category; their average annual purchase is only $500. George thinks he can sell to another 300 in this small-volume category after one sales call on them.

Even if he made an average of eight sales calls per day, George figures that he could call just one time on about half of his 4,000 customers and prospects during an entire year. Recognizing this reality, George is trying to design the best promotional mix to cover his territory. Recently, his company implemented a telemarketing program that requires all sales reps to spend one full day a week in the office telephoning prospective customers in their territories. Using tailored prospect lists purchased from a commercial list company, each salesperson is expected to average about 30 completed phone calls daily. Neuberger's national sales manager estimates that about 20 percent of customers or prospects reached by telephone will buy.

In addition to telemarketing activities, all salespeople are now required to mail out product catalogs and brochures to 25 percent of their customers and prospects every quarter, along with a form letter. Whenever appropriate, the salespeople are supposed to write a short personal note on the form letter to give the mailing a personal touch. Based on past performance, about 10 percent of these catalog and brochure mailings will result in a sale.

George thinks to himself: "So much potential, so little time." Pouring himself a hot cup of coffee, he sits down with his pad and pencil to figure out a plan that will provide maximum results for his efforts.

Questions

1. How would you advise George Gellerman to allocate his territory promotional mix among personal sales calls, telemarketing, and catalog/ brochure mailings for his three categories of customers and prospects?

2. If Neuberger's national sales manager asks each salesperson to estimate his or her next year's annual sales, what approximate dollar amount should George forecast? How did you arrive at this figure?

Chapter 5

Consumer Markets

Understanding people is 90 percent of sales success.

Profile

Ed Van Campenout

DURING spring break in his senior year, Ed Van Campenhout travelled to Seattle and loved it. That's one reason why, when he graduated from college with a degree in communications, Ed moved from Green Bay, Wisconsin, to Seattle, Washington, and went to work in a restaurant. Sound like an unlikely beginning for one of Maytag Company's top regional representatives? That's not how Ed sees it. "I also knew that Seattle was a booming market—a good place to get my feet wet in the business world," says Ed, who carefully planned the route to his true goal: a sales career.

After Ed's 18 months of solid performance as manager of the restaurant, its owner—a well-known and well-liked Seattle personality—was happy to give Ed an enthusiastic recommendation for his first sales job. "It was with a company that provides wholesale inventory financing services," explains Ed. "Although I soon decided that I didn't want to be in the financial services industry, the job gave me the opportunity to learn a lot about wholesale and retail businesses. During that time, I began a 2½-year research process in which I asked the wholesale and retail sales reps I met with about three areas: (1) qualifications their companies looked for in hiring them; (2) company sales training programs; and (3) how the products and companies were perceived by the public." Ed's research led him straight to Maytag Company, who hired him in January 1988 for a territory in the Erie, Pennsylvania, area.

Ed's approach to his new selling job and territory career were as well thought out as his previous research process. Immediately focusing on long-range goals rather than short-range objectives, Ed set out to help his customers—who included retail centers the size of small, family-owned stores to large, chain-store accounts—build their markets over the long term with Maytag products. There was some resistance at first. Says Ed: "I was a little more aggressive than my predecessor, and that alienated two of my largest clients. These accounts had the most potential in my territory, but Maytag wasn't getting its share. I had to show them that I was sincerely interested in helping them sell *their* customers on my product and that I was serious about a strong, lasting business relationship. After all, unless I help them develop a good retail environment, how can I hope to sell wholesale?" Ed went on to design a merchandising plan that included profitable retail and wholesale programs. His plan resulted in 50 percent sales increases for both clients.

Since then, Ed has cultivated a keen understanding of each of his customers' businesses and what kinds of consumer selling techniques work best for each of them. Ed believes that even though he is an "organizational" salesperson, he needs to understand his end-users—consumers—just as well as his retailer customers: "Appliance sales is an unusual form of organizational selling because it's retail and merchandising driven. My job involves a lot of activities to help my customers sell my product—planning advertising, product sales training, and special events such as grand openings and private sales. Whenever possible, I try to get my customers to allow me to help their salespeople work the retail floor. That allows me to get closer to consumers and promote my products directly to them and to my customers' retail sales staff." ∎

"A lot of marketers are shocked to realize that the traditional American family (father, nonworking mother, and two children) is less than 10 percent of the American public," says Ogilvy & Mather research development director Jane Fitzgibbon. "They are much more comfortable marketing to Norman Rockwell's vision."[1]

WHO IS THE CONSUMER MARKET?

The consumer market consists of all those individuals like you and me who buy products for personal consumption. We buy a huge variety of goods, from toothpaste and corn flakes to automobiles and homes. Why we buy a particular product at a particular time is seldom easy to understand. An ad for the magazine *American Demographics* puts it this way:

> Exasperating, aren't they? I'm talking about human beings. Americans. Consumers. The public. The markets. The crazy decision-making jury out there you're paid to understand—and whose whims and flights of fancy you're rewarded for predicting. Just what do they want? And what will they want tomorrow?

Consumers: The Big Picture

About 250 million consumers live in the United States today. Our population growth is slowing down, however, and we are getting older as a nation. The median age of Americans will increase 10 years, from 33 years in 1990 to 43 in 2040, with significant impacts on consumer tastes and preferences. A birth rate of 2.1 per couple is needed merely to maintain population size, and the United States has been hovering around this rate for several years since the birth rate peaked in 1957. Using current assumptions about fertility, mortality, and immigration, the number of U.S. consumers will grow to about 268 million people in the year 2000, peak at around 300 million by 2025, and then begin to decline.[2] Thus food manufacturers and other companies whose sales are closely related to population growth will have to devise strategies to defend and capture market shares from competitors.

[1]Thomas Moore, "Different Folks, Different Strokes," *Fortune*, September 16, 1985, pp. 65–68.
[2]Ibid.

Consumer Market Segments

Marketing professionals have tried over the years to better understand consumers by classifying them into *market segments* based on such factors as age, income, and ethnic group. A market segment is a group of prospective consumers who can be expected to respond in similar ways to the same marketing and sales strategy. Most large market segments can be subdivided into several smaller, relatively homogeneous groups for better targeting of marketing and sales strategies. Let's briefly discuss some of today's largest consumer market segments and their characteristics.

Baby Boomers

BABY BOOMERS The huge generation born between 1946 and 1964.

Over 76 million babies, almost one-third of the current U.S. population, were born between 1946 and 1964. The number of **baby boomers** entering middle age (considered to be 35 to 54) will increase by more than 40 percent over the next decade, and their buying power will grow by 70 percent. Many new markets are being created by this baby boomer generation, who often have two incomes per household and sizable discretionary income to spend.

Baby Busters

BABY BUSTERS The much smaller generation born between 1964 and 1976.

People born between 1964 (when the birth control pill was introduced and many women started to work outside the home) and 1976 (when baby boomers began to have babies) are called **baby busters.**. As any McDonald's manager or college recruiter can tell you, not enough people were born in those years to fill fast-food restaurant jobs or to satisfy the enrollment goals of America's colleges and universities through the 1990s. And the situation will get worse before it gets better. By 2000, the number of 18-to-24-year-olds is expected to fall 8 percent, and the number of young adults aged 25 to 34 to drop from 44 million to 37 million.

Older People

The average American alive today can expect to survive to age 76, which is nearly 27 more years than the life expectancy in 1900. Sixty-two million people—25

Salespeople must be careful to avoid stereotypes about older consumers as "elderly" people who buy mainly denture cream, medicines, and other geriatric products.

Selling in Action

Still Selling at 90

"I just love sales work," says 90-year-old Charlie Tucker. "I'm no high-pressure salesman, but maybe I'll try to create a desire sufficient to overcome your resistance." For 59 years, Charlie Tucker has been selling household products for the Fuller Brush Company. When he started work in 1931, Fuller Brush offered only about a dozen products. Today the company has 400 products sold by 13,000 sales representatives, all of whom work strictly on commission.

Charlie still knocks on a few doors in his hometown of Chattanooga, Tennessee, but most of his sales are now made over the telephone to repeat customers who pick up their goods at Mr. Tucker's home. A 61-year-old customer, who has known Mr. Tucker since she was a teenager, estimates that she has bought about every product Fuller has ever made. She says: "I love them, and I think Mr. Tucker has been a part of that because he is so knowledgeable and tells you how . . . to use them." At one time, Charlie Tucker was a district sales manager supervising 35 salespeople. When Fuller Brush was sold in the 1960s to Consolidated Foods of Chicago, however, the district sales offices were eliminated. As Mr. Tucker puts it: "I was too old to go out and hunt for a new job, but I figured I could sell Fuller brushes."

Source: Dan George, "Fuller Brush Man Going Strong at 90," *The Courier Times,* Bucks County, Pennsylvania, April 16, 1990, p. D1.

percent of the U.S. population—are over the age of 50. The number of people aged 55 to 74 is expected to grow just 5 percent to the year 2000, but they will control over 40 percent of the nation's discretionary income. In fact, the older the age group, the more discretionary money the people belonging to that group appear to have. Many older people remain active in the work force long after normal retirement age (65), as illustrated in this chapter's Selling in Action box.

As the baby boom generation ages, it will swell the ranks of the older population from 30 million people in 1991 to 68 million people by 2040. Although the number of people aged 65 to 74 will actually decline by 3 percent between 1995 and 2005, the 75-and-older population will more than compensate for this decline by growing 20 percent. Within this older population, the number of people aged 74 to 84 will increase by 25 percent, and those over 85 by 62 percent by the year 2000.[3] The projected age composition of the U.S. population for the year 2000 is shown in Figure 5-1.

Salespeople must be careful to avoid stereotypes about older consumers as "elderly" people who buy mainly denture cream, medicines, and other geriatric products. Consumer research has shown that older buyers see themselves as 12 to 15 years younger than their chronological years and that their lifestyles are as varied as those of younger age groups.

[3]*Sales & Marketing Management,* July 1988, p. 19.

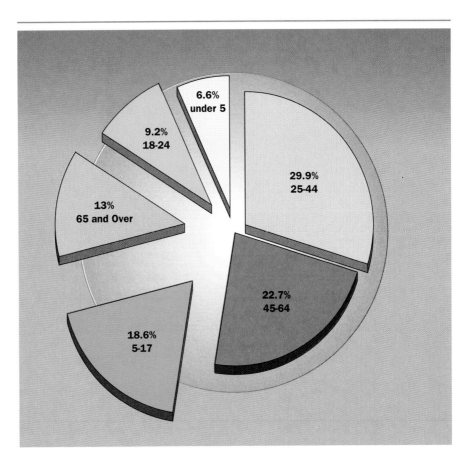

FIGURE 5-1 Age Distribution of U.S. Population in the Year 2000

Smaller Families

Today about 25 percent of America's roughly 95 million households consist of one person living alone, another 32 percent are two-person families, 17 percent include three people, and about 26 percent have four or more members.[4] Just looking at one of these segments, the one-fourth of our population living alone, reveals tremendous market opportunities for single-serving sizes of all kinds of food, entertainment and recreational activities, single-housing units, specially tailored financial plans, and special services for busy career-oriented singles or for elderly singles confined to their homes.

The New Immigrants

Most of the projected U.S. growth in population will come from immigration. During the 1960s only 16 percent of U.S. population growth was due to immigration, but today immigration accounts for about 27 percent of population growth. The Census Bureau projects that the share of population growth due to immigration will soar from 33 percent in 2000 to 54 percent in 2020. By 2028, deaths are expected to outnumber births, and immigration will be the only

[4]Blayne Cutler, "Meet Jane Doe," *American Demographics,* June 1989, pp. 25–63.

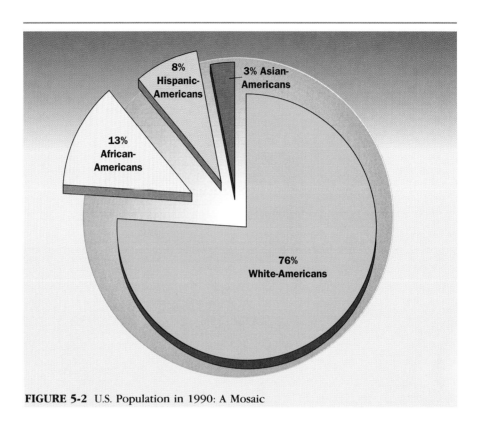

FIGURE 5-2 U.S. Population in 1990: A Mosaic

source of new population, but even immigration won't be enough to continue replenishing our population by 2038. While the number of immigrants from Europe and Canada has declined sharply over the last two decades, the proportion of immigrants coming from Latin America and the Caribbean has risen dramatically. And the percentge of immigrants from Asia has soared from only 6 percent in the 1950s to 50 percent in the 1980s. Understanding the composition and special product tastes and preferences of the *new immigrants* will be very important for developing effective sales strategies and tactics. An emerging subculture with long-run market potential for salespeople is the Asian-American market, as described in the following vignette.

Mosaic of Minorities

A senior vice president for marketing services at Kraft USA says: "The mythological homogeneous America is gone. We are a mosaic of minorities. All companies will have to do more stratified or tailored or niche marketing."[5] As seen in Figure 5-2, Asian-Americans make up about 3 percent of the U.S. population, Hispanic-Americans about 8 percent, African-Americans about 13 percent, and non-Hispanic-American whites nearly 76 percent. By 2080, the U.S. population is forecast to be 11 percent Asian-American, 19 percent Hispanic-American, 16 percent African-American, and 55 percent non-Hispanic white.

[5]"Stalking the New Consumer," *Business Week*, August 28, 1989, p. 55.

ASIAN-AMERICANS: AN EMERGING MARKET

A market segment that has been called the "Sleeping Dragon" and the "Super Minority" was virtually nonexistent a decade ago. Today Asian-Americans are the fastest-growing ethnic group in the United States, and they have some of the most attractive demographics of any market. For example, Asian-Americans have an average household income of $23,671, higher than whites ($21,173), Hispanics ($16,271), and blacks ($14,051). Nearly one-third of Asian-Americans over age 25 have completed four or more years of college, which is almost twice the ratio for whites (17.1 percent) and four times that for blacks (8.4 percent) and Hispanics (7.6 percent). Over half (53.3 percent) of all Asians employed in the United States hold managerial or professional positions.

More than 42 percent of all Asians living in the United States in 1980 arrived here after 1970. Two-thirds live in just three states—California, Hawaii, and New York. Although they represent only about 3 percent of the U.S. population now, projections from the Population Reference Bureau show the number of Asian-Americans in the United States increasing by 165 percent between 1980 and the end of the century. By the year 2000, it is expected there will be 10 million Asians living in the United States, mostly in California, New York, Texas, and Hawaii. Unlike the larger, more homogeneous black and Hispanic markets, the Asian-American market includes highly fragmented groups of Chinese, Koreans, Vietnamese, Filipinos, Japanese, and Asian Indians, who tend to maintain their independence within the larger Asian framework. Each of these nationalities has its own distinct language, culture, and tastes and preferences for products and services. Thus, a sales approach effective for Chinese consumers probably won't work with Koreans or Filipinos. Sales campaigns that violate cultural taboos, as in mentioning death or other misfortune in discussing life insurance or health care, will fail. Two success stories in selling to the Asian-American market are Remy Martin Cognac and Metropolitan Life, companies that have stressed security, family, longevity, and company track records.

While incredibly diverse, Asian-Americans do share some consumer qualities. They tend to live in larger households with higher percentages of dual-income sources than the rest of Americans, they share strong family orientations, they value educational and business achievements and security, and they usually rate quality over price. Because Asian-Americans tend to be well educated, work in professional or technical fields, and exhibit a high rate of savings, they present a new upscale market segment for insurance and other financial products aimed at providing college educations for children and ensuring against financial risks. Alert smaller companies like New York's G. Fried Carpet and San Francisco's East/West Securities are already profitably cultivating the growing Asian-American market. Younger Asians seem to be more attracted by appeals to lifestyle than to ethnicity. For example, Kirshenbaum & Bond of New York has been successful in selling its Kenneth Cole shoes to Asians by using a "hip" appeal rather than an ethnic one.

Sources: Richard Kern, "The Asian Market: Too Good to Be True," *Sales & Marketing; The Wall Street Journal,* July 20, 1989, p. B1; *Management,* May 1988, pp. 39–42; and Tracey L. Longo, "New Immigrants, New Markets?" *Managers Magazine,* January 1987, pp. 12–13, 30.

WHY AND HOW CONSUMERS BUY

Because no two consumers are exactly alike in their purchase decisions, tailoring each product to meet the needs of each individual consumer in each new buying situation is a major part of the salesperson's job. By studying *whole groups* of people, however, sales and marketing professionals can develop models of consumer behavior that provide a good general idea of what *individual* consumers want. Market researchers regularly analyze demographics and psychographics to try to understand the factors that influence the behavior of groups of consumers, and then compare their findings with the demonstrated behavior of individual consumers.

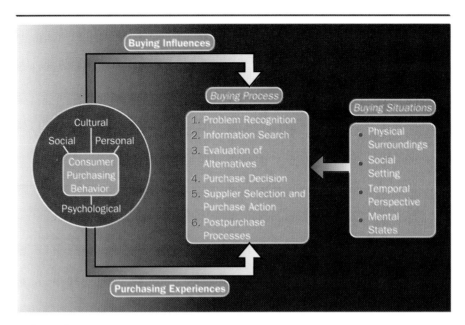

FIGURE 5-3 Consumer Behavior Model

Demographics are the readily identifiable characteristics of consumers, such as age, sex, education level, occupation, marriage status, family size, race, religion, social class, and income. **Psychographics** describe the activities, interests, opinions, and lifestyles of consumers. Social and psychological factors work together to determine how each consumer spends time and money. *Social factors* include culture, social class, reference groups, opinion leaders, stage in the family life cycle, and activities. *Psychological factors* include personality, attitudes, opinions, motivation, innovativeness, and perceptions. Social and psychological factors overlap and complement each other in determining why a particular consumer purchases a specific category and brand of product. Some consumers spend a great deal of time evaluating alternatives; others spend little time considering alternatives before making their decisions. Consumer decision making varies not only between individuals but also for the same person in different situations at different times. A man may easily buy a new car every four years, yet agonize over the purchase of a new suit each year.

Figure 5-3 depicts a consumer behavior model that tries to account for the complex mixture of factors that influence the consumer *before, during,* and *after* the purchase. Individual consumers begin the buying process armed with a unique set of behavioral characteristics. The top line, *buying influences,* represents the consumer's purchase criteria based on his or her social, cultural, personal, and psychological makeup. The lower line, *purchasing experiences,* represents the consumer's purchase criteria derived from his or her past buying experiences. Note that Figure 5-3 also includes the *buying situation,* which is most closely associated with the fifth stage of the buying process: supplier selection and purchase action. Sales and marketing professionals know that any consumer purchase decision is likely to be a complex mixture of many interacting personal and situational variables. Let's discuss some aspects of the consumer behavior model in Figure 5-3 in more detail.

BUYING INFLUENCES

Learning why people buy a certain product at a given time from a particular seller is the key to successful selling. If salespeople do not appeal to the right motive at the right time with the right product, they will probably lose the sale. For example, it is probably futile to try to sell a risky growth-oriented mutual fund to a man who is retired and primarily concerned about preserving his lifetime savings and avoiding risk. Understanding the role of different buying influences on various market segments helps salespeople to select the most effective approach, sales presentation strategy, and closing tactics in each particular situation. Influences on consumer buying behavior can be categorized as either *internal* or *external* to the individual.

Internal Buying Influences

In their attempts to comprehend human thought and action, behaviorial scientists have discovered much information that is useful to salespeople engaged in their own struggle to understand the individual consumer's internal buying influences. To facilitate our study of these consumer influences, we will group them into seven different conceptual frameworks: consumer (1) needs, (2) motivations, (3) perceptions, (4) personality, (5) self-concept, (6) learning, and (7) attitudes and beliefs.

Consumer Needs

HIERARCHY OF NEEDS
Maslow's conceptual framework of motivation in which lower-level human needs (physiological, safety and security) must be satisfied before higher-level needs (belongingness and love, self-esteem, and self-actualization) become activated.

Abraham Maslow's **hierarchy of needs** provides us with an excellent conceptual framework for better understanding human needs.[6] Maslow, who was a psychologist, reasoned that needs are arranged in a hierarchy from most urgent to least urgent. Lowest-level needs are largely biological or physiological, like hunger and thirst. Higher-level needs tend to be emotional or psychological, like personal esteem and self-fulfillment. Here are brief descriptions of Maslow's five levels of needs and some examples of how certain companies appeal directly to them:

1. *Physiological:* Biological needs such as the demand for food, drink, sex, shelter, and relief from pain. (Examples: "Give your mouth sex appeal"—Close-Up toothpaste; "Rub out the pain"—Ben-Gay [products: toothpaste, analgesics].)

2. *Safety and Security:* The need for freedom from threat; the security from threatening events and/or surroundings. (Examples: "Michelin. Because so much is riding on your tires"; "Rock solid. Market wise"—Prudential-Bache [products: automobile tires, securities investments].)

3. *Belongingness and love:* The need for friendship, social interaction, and affiliation. (Examples: "When you care enough to send the very best"—Hallmark cards; "Stay with someone you know"—Holiday Inns [products: greeting cards, hotel accommodations].)

4. *Esteem:* The need for status and respect from others. (Example: "The only way to travel is Cadillac Style"—Cadillac [products: Luxury cars].)

5. *Self-actualization:* The need to fulfill oneself by maximizing the use of one's abilities, skills, and potential. (Examples: "Explore a world of your own creation"—Canon

[6]A. H. Maslow, *Motivation and Personality* (New York: Harper & Row, 1954), pp. 80–116.

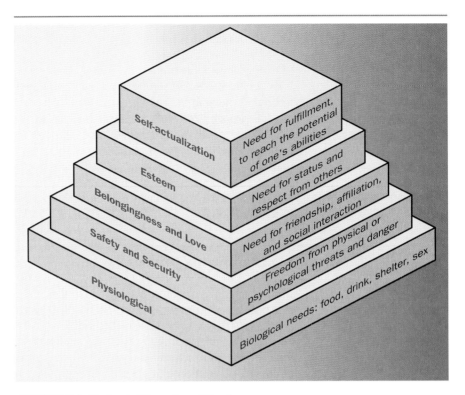

FIGURE 5-4   Maslow's Hierarchy of Needs

cameras; "Be all that you can be"—U.S. Army [products: photographic equipment, military service].)

People are driven to satisfy their most pressing needs (physiological, safety) before they turn toward satisfying less pressing needs (esteem, self-actualization). But as soon as lower-order needs are reasonably well satisfied, higher-level needs spring forth as motivating influences, as depicted in Figure 5-4. For example, Bill Smith is not going to be very attentive to a sales presentation on life insurance at a breakfast meeting until his hunger pangs have been at least partially satisfied. Cathy Hughes has a secure, high-paying job as a computer programmer, but still feels a lack of self-actualization, so she enrolls in an evening accounting course at a nearby college and wears business suits instead of the more casual attire of her programming colleagues.

Can salespeople influence consumer needs? As a salesperson, you can have a powerful influence on consumer needs.

First, you can *make consumers aware of their specific needs*, including latent needs, and offer them a means of fulfilling those needs. A good salesperson can make Mr. and Mrs. O'Malley aware that they must establish a sound savings and investment plan now if they expect to be able to send their three small children to college in the future. And to ensure their children's education in case of their own untimely deaths, the O'Malleys can be encouraged to increase the amount of their life insurance.

Second, you can *increase the intensity of needs*. You can stimulate consumers to want something badly. For example, even though most people don't want to think about their own funeral, a sensitive salesperson can show the O'Malleys the advantages of buying their burial plots now by stressing how important it is to make these arrangements while there are still some good plots left and how considerate it is to spare loved ones the trauma of having to decide on a burial place during a time of bereavement.

Third, you can help consumers *solve several needs in a single purchase* by a technique called **motive bundling.** Motive bundling can increase a consumer's desire to purchase a product or service by showing how one purchase will solve several problems simultaneously. If Mrs. O'Malley needs a reliable writing instrument, but thinks prestige, conspicuous status symbols, and personalization are also important, she might be persuaded to buy a Mont Blanc or Waterman fountainpen with her name engraved on it.

MOTIVE BUNDLING
Increasing a consumer's desire to purchase a product or service by showing how one purchase will solve several problems simultaneously.

Empathy To influence consumer needs, salespeople must learn to *empathize* with prospects and customers. If you can put yourself in your prospect's frame of mind and think as he or she does (at least during the purchase consideration), you'll gain an enormous advantage over salespeople who see things only from their own perspective. The best way to achieve empathy is to *really care* about people and their problems. In fact, if you do not sincerely care about other people, you will never be able to truly empathize. Most people will see through your act and refuse to buy from you.

Consumer Motivation

All purchase behavior starts with motivation. A motive or drive develops from an *aroused need* that an individual seeks to satisfy. Very little is known about what goes on in a buyer's mind before, during, and after a purchase. We do know that when a buyer makes a purchase decision, he or she is trying to accomplish something. Table 5-1 represents an attempt to depict buyer motives in terms of

TABLE 5-1   Why Consumers Buy

To Increase:	To Improve:
Status	Efficiency
Income	Earnings on investments
Safety	Social life
Wealth	Personal satisfaction
Convenience	Education
Opportunities	Appearance
Quality	Health
To Protect:	**To Reduce:**
Family and pets	Risks
Employees	Costs
Customers	Competition
Property	Complaints
Money	Problems
Personal privacy	Worry

To Save:
Time
Money
Energy
Space

what the buyer wants to accomplish. Mrs. Burrus, for example, might want *to increase her health* by joining a health spa. Paul Toland may intend *to protect his property* by purchasing an alarm system for his automobile.

We also know that a purchase is rarely the result of a single motive and that various motives may conflict. In addition to improving her health, Mrs. Burrus may also want *to reduce the worry* her stressful office job causes her through a daily workout. Unfortunately, she also wants *to save money* and finds that all the local health spas have expensive membership fees.

Moreover, purchasing behavior can vary over time as an individual's internal and external buying influences change. If Mrs. Burrus leaves her office job to start a career in selling, she will quickly become interested in nice clothing and computer hardware and software that will help her in prospecting, planning sales presentations, and servicing her customers.

Finally, one can have *latent or unfelt needs and motives* that do not affect behavior until they become aroused or stimulated. For example, a teenage boy may become less interested in playing baseball when he becomes interested in a teenage girl. He may suddenly feel the daily need to use a mouthwash and an underarm deodorant. Even in today's high-powered business world, many executives are reluctant to interact with others without the psychological security provided by an array of personal deodorants and sprays, though their grandparents managed to survive nicely without them.

Are consumers aware of their real motives? The great psychologist Sigmund Freud believed that the real motives or drives that channel a person's behavior are largely *subconscious or unknown* to that person. When Sam Steiner buys an expensive brand-name briefcase, he may tell others that he needs a high-quality, durable briefcase for work. Subconsciously, however, Sam may have been influenced by the briefcases his superiors at work carry. He may feel that carrying the same brand and type of briefcase will help him to fit in and be accepted by this reference group. Of course, other motives may come into play as well. Perhaps Sam wants a heavy, rugged-looking black briefcase with a rich leather smell so that the people in his office will see him as more professional. The style, size, color, smell, material, and design may convey strength and independence to him and, he hopes, to others.

Salespeople should be careful about readily accepting consumers' initial explanations for purchasing a particular product because sometimes people are embarrassed by their real motives for buying. For example, few young people will admit that they like prunes. Motivational researchers have learned that people associate prunes with old age and constipation problems.

Table 5-2 illustrates four basic types of consumer buying motives: *rational, emotional, patronage,* and *product.* Good salespeople use different appeals to sell the same products, depending on the particular buying motives of an individual consumer.

Consumer Perceptions

Two people with the same motivation in the same purchasing situation may behave quite differently because their perceptions of the salesperson and the sales situation are very different. Tony Verzilli may not purchase an expensive diamond necklace for his wife because the salesperson reminds him of a person he once knew who was pushy and insincere. However, Ruth Verzilli may see the

TABLE 5-2   Consumer Buying Motives

Rational	Based on the desire to save time and money, increase financial gain, obtain quality service, guarantee durability, or ensure safety. *Product examples:* home appliances, stock and bond investments, home office equipment, insurance policies, health-care plans, self-improvement programs, encyclopedias, business travel, real estate, education or child-care services.
Emotional	Based on the desire for pleasure, comfort, social approval, status, or romance. *Product examples:* fashionable clothing, perfume, deodorants, self-improvement programs, paintings or sculptures, health clubs, vacation travel, holiday hotel accommodations, cosmetics, sports cars, antique furniture, recreational vehicles.
Patronage	Based on the desire to buy from a particular seller because of perceived superior total benefits. Motives may be rational or emotional. For example, a consumer may be willing to pay a higher price in order to buy from a local seller or friend. *Examples of patronage motives:* product quality, exchange or return policies, product assortment, credit services, seller reputation, helpfulness of salespeople, convenience, check cashing policies, affection or empathy for the seller.
Product	Based on the consumer's preference for one product over another. Motives may be rational or emotional. *Examples of product preference motives:* brand name, price, quality, image, durability, style or design, size, engineering, ease of maintenance, installation, delivery, method of payment, repair services.

same salesperson as enthusiastic, intelligent, and knowledgeable, and thus purchase the necklace for herself.

Perception is the way a person "makes sense" of his or her world. In a nutshell, perception can be defined as the *process by which an individual selects, organizes, and interprets information to create a meaningful picture of the world.* Although we receive information through our five senses (sight, hearing, smell, touch, and taste), each of us receives, organizes, and interprets this information uniquely.

Three perceptual processes determine how each of us forms perceptions: selective exposure, selective comprehension, and selective retention. Figure 5-5 shows how these three processes combine to form the individual consumer's "perceptual filter."

Selective exposure is the process by which a person filters information, disregarding data that are not important at the time. Sam Steiner may disregard the salesperson's comment that the handle on this particular briefcase model is fragile because he is predisposed to buy the same brand and style executives at

SELECTIVE EXPOSURE The process by which a person filters information, disregarding data that are not important or of interest at the time.

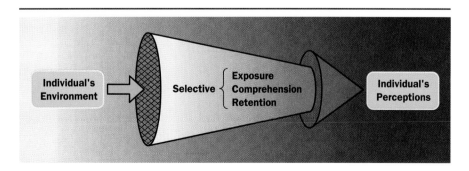

FIGURE 5-5 The Individual Consumer's Perceptual Filter

SELECTIVE COMPREHENSION The tendency to understand and interpret information so that it is consistent with what an individual already feels and believes.

SELECTIVE RETENTION The tendency to retain in memory only that information that supports preconceived attitudes and beliefs.

his company carry. **Selective comprehension** describes the tendency to understand and interpret information so that it is consistent with what an individual already feels and believes. Even when a sales message grabs the prospect's attention, it may not be comprehended in the way the seller intended. Instead of rejecting the salesperson's comment that the briefcase's handle is fragile, Sam might perceive this information as substantiation of the briefcase's slim, attractive design. From Sam's perspective, the handle doesn't need to be "rugged" because he does not intend to stuff the briefcase with heavy materials. **Selective retention** occurs when a person retains in his or her memory only the information that supports preconceived attitudes and beliefs. Sam is not likely to remember the good points about competing briefcases. Rather, he will remember the good points about the brand and style he bought and recall them every time he needs reassurance about the wisdom of his purchase decision.

Consumer Personality

Another individual determinant of consumer buying behavior is personality. *Personality* is the pattern of traits, activities, interests, and opinions that determine a person's unique behavior. Many psychologists have tried to classify human personality. One interesting approach, developed by Karen Horney,[7] identifies three types of personalities:

- *Compliant:* People who "move *toward* others," seeking acceptance and approval. They want to fit in with others in purchasing products and services, so they are largely influenced by reference groups and opinion leaders.
- *Aggressive:* People who "move *against* others" in what they see as a very competitive world. Because they want to excel and gain prestige through their buying choices, they may be susceptible to appeals that a product or service will enable them to outshine others. People who buy a Corvette or Porsche automobile exemplify this type of personality. One study showed that aggressiveness is also the primary personality trait of consumers who buy designer clothes.[8]
- *Detached:* People who "move *away* from others" into a more solitary, self-contained lifestyle. They "march to their own drummer" and tend to ignore others in their buying decisions. These people will not be influenced by opinion leaders or by sales appeals not based on logic and objective evidence.

Another way of looking at consumer personalities comes from the work of Carl Gustav Jung, who divided people into four basic types: (1) thinker, (2) feeler, (3) intuitor, and (4) senser. Although most people are a mixture of these types, you can usually classify prospects on the basis of which quality dominates their personality. Table 5-3 offers help to salespeople trying to identify these personality types.

Would you characterize these consumers as compliant, aggressive, or detached personality types?

Thinkers In making sales presentations to *thinker* types, you should carefully preplan the presentation to include many facts and strong supporting evidence. Material should be presented in a precise, orderly, and logical way. If you are unable to close the sale during the sales call, say something like: "Why don't you

[7]Karen Horney, *Our Inner Conflicts* (New York: Norton, 1945); see also Joel B. Cohen, "An Interpersonal Orientation to the Study of Consumer Behavior," *Journal of Marketing Research,* August 1967, pp. 270–278.

[8]Marvin A. Jolson, Rolph E. Anderson, and Nancy J. Leber, "Profiles of Signature Goods Consumers and Avoiders," *Journal of Retailing,* Winter 1981, pp. 19–38.

TABLE 5-3   Prospect Personality Types

CUES	THINKER	FEELER	INTUITOR	SENSER
General Orientation	Detail-oriented, very precise	People-oriented, emotional	Future-oriented, innovative	Action-oriented, energetic
Typical Strengths	Objective, rational, analytical, effective communicator	Spontaneous, empathetic, introspective, acts on what has worked in past	Imaginative, idealistic, conceptual, original, charismatic	Pragmatic, results-oriented, down-to-earth, bases opinions on what he/she sees
Potential Weaknesses	Indecisive, overly cautious, unemotional, rigid, nitpicking, overly analytical	Impulsive, manipulative, guilt-ridden, stirs up conflict, sentimental, subjective	Unrealistic, devious, out-of-touch, dogmatic, impractical, poor listener, fantasy-oriented	Impatient, short-run focus, status seeker, won't delegate, doesn't trust people, impulsive
Time Focus	Past, present, and future	Past	Future	Present
Home or Work Environment	Usually neat, analytical look, reference books, computer printouts	Warmly decorated, antiques, family pictures, personal mementos	Abstract art, trend charts, unusual books, far-out look	Generally chaotic, piles of paper, action pictures of products
Clothes	Conservative, neat	Informal, current styles	Unconventional, rumpled	Functional work clothes, no jacket or tie

think it over, and I'll call you tomorrow about 10:00 A.M. to get your decision, okay?"

Feelers   *Feelers* are very people-oriented and like to engage in small talk first. You should wait until they suggest you begin the sales presentation. Usually, they'll say something like: "Well, what can I do for you today?" or "What's on your mind today?" In the sales presentation, use emotion-packed words and phrases, such as: "We feel this is a revolutionary new product that will excite your customers and motivate your workers." Keep the sales presentation personal. Try to entice the prospect away from the office for lunch or a coffee break so you can talk in a less formal environment. Since feelers are very sensitive to other people's needs, you can use a strong personal close, such as: "Okay, Mr. Peters, should I go ahead and place the order now for the new Poland Spring water cooler so that your family can soon begin enjoying pure, refreshing water?"

Intuitors   Because *intuitor* personalities value ideas, concepts, innovation, and long-run planning, you should try to fit your sales presentation into the consumer's "big picture" or overall planning objectives. Intuitors are good prospects for new products, services, and creative approaches to doing things. A small gift along the lines of a daily planner with a built-in calculator and digital clock can help gain their attention and interest in your sales presentation. In closing, stress the value of fast results and creative benefits by saying something like: "Let's place the order for the *Learning French the Easy Way* software so you and your whole family can learn to speak French before your vacation in Paris next summer. I'll bet your friends will be impressed when they hear you ordering dinner in French."

Sensers Be brief and to the point with *sensers* because they value fast action. Employ visual aids, demonstrations, models, and samples to help sensers use their five senses in understanding and appreciating your sales presentation. Start with conclusions and results, but be armed with supporting data to back up your summary. Outline an action plan, then wrap it up with a comment like this: "I know you're busy, so if you'll just sign on the dotted line, I'll get moving on this immediately." If you cannot make the sale that day, leave a sample of the product with the senser prospect so he or she can explore further when alone.

Consumer Self-Concept

Another personal characteristic closely related to personality is the consumer's self-concept. Our *self-concept* determines the way we see ourselves and how we think others see us. Self-concept theory has four interacting components: (1) the *real self*—people as they actually are; (2) the *self-image*—the way people see themselves; the *ideal self*—what people aspire to be; and (4) the *looking-glass self*—how people think others see them. Understanding self-concept theory can be a big plus in personal selling. If you can pinpoint the potential buyer's self-image or ideal self, you can present the product in such a way that the potential customer realizes it fits his or her self-concept. For example, Lucy Brown might be reached by this *looking-glass self* appeal: "With your reputation as one of the most innovative photographers in our community, people will be expecting you to be one of the first to own this revolutionary new Nishika 35mm 3-D camera." Sidney Wilson may respond best to this *ideal-self* appeal: "After you pass your CPA exam this fall, won't you want to own the Zenith laptop computer that six out of ten CPAs carry?"

Consumer Learning

Professional salespeople can also benefit from an understanding of human learning theories. The fundamental idea underlying many of these theories is that most human behavior, except for instinctual responses, is learned through experience. At its rudimentary level, human learning occurs in an interplay of forces called *stimuli, drives, motives, cues, responses,* and *reinforcement.*

A *stimulus* is anything that excites or increases action. For example, Susan Erving is a successful salesperson who has been thinking about buying a new car for months now. Her company car—a new Oldsmobile Cutlass Ciera—is very nice, but she feels that it doesn't "fit" her personality and activities outside of work. Lately, several things have become appropriate stimuli coaxing her toward taking buying action, such as steadily falling interest rates and automobile rebates. These stimuli combine with Ms. Erving's substantial year-end sales bonus to form a *drive,* which is a strong *internal* stimulus that impels action. One week after she receives her bonus check, Ms. Erving rides by an automobile dealership and sees a fire-engine-red Ford Mustang GT parked on the showroom floor. Now her drive becomes a *motive,* which is a drive that is directed toward a *specific, drive-reducing* stimulus object (the car).

Cues are minor stimuli that help to determine how, when, and where the person will respond. Ms. Erving may be elated by the thought of owning this particular Mustang because she loves the flamboyant color, the dealership is close to her home and the salesperson is friendly, and she has read magazine articles praising the Mustang as one of the most popular sports cars in America. It is thoughts and feelings like these that establish her *response* to all the stimuli and cues relating to the car by buying it.

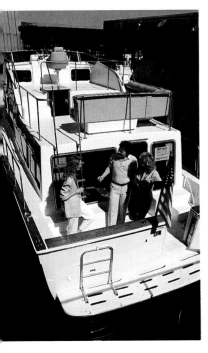

If you can pinpoint the potential buyer's self-image or ideal self, you can present the product in such a way that the potential customer realizes it fits his or her self-concept.

POSITIVE REINFORCEMENT Reinforcement that rewards a certain behavior and thus makes it likely that that behavior will be repeated.

NEGATIVE REINFORCEMENT Reinforcement that punishes a certain behavior and thus makes it unlikely that that behavior will be repeated.

Finally, there are two basic kinds of *reinforcement:* **positive reinforcement,** which *rewards* a certain behavior; and **negative reinforcement**, which *punishes* a certain behavior. Behavior that is positively reinforced will most likely be repeated. Thus when prospects obtain satisfaction (positive reinforcement) from the purchase and use of products, they are on their way to becoming loyal buyers of those products from those sellers.

Returning to Susan Erving's purchasing situation, the car salesperson may be in a position to *reward* Ms. Erving with a special cash rebate and interest rate on her loan if she decides to purchase the car within a given period of time. If she delays her decision, she may be *punished* by a lower cash rebate and a higher interest rate on her loan.

Generalization and discrimination Learning theory applies directly to personal selling in that salespeople can stimulate demand for their brands by (1) associating them with strong drives, (2) providing appealing stimuli and cue configurations, and (3) ensuring plenty of positive reinforcement. Learning theory also tells us that there are two strong tendencies in human behavior that can potentially help or hurt an entire line of products: *generalization* and *discrimination.*

Sales professionals realize that consumers are prone to *generalization,* that is, to respond in the same way to similar stimuli and cues, to *generalize* their responses across a line of products. Salespeople who become expert at providing their customers with consistently positive stimuli and cues have little trouble selling the same customers entire families of products. For example, a salesperson who has sold one brand and style of dress shoe to a customer might sell another style of the same brand to that customer by providing the same cues and stimuli that successfully appealed to the customer's desire for the first shoe style.

Buyers are also more likely to transfer their loyalty to familiar products. "Me-too" products that are somewhat lower priced, such as the various clones of IBM portable computers, are often successful.

The opposite reaction to generalization is *discrimination.* If Mr. Morales has an opportunity to compare two CD players on a trial basis and finds one more rewarding than the other, his ability to discriminate between similar product configurations in the future improves. *Discrimination* means that one has learned to recognize differences between sets of stimuli and to adjust one's responses accordingly. For this reason, salespeople who are trying to switch customers to a new brand will often carry comparison charts or even competitive products with them so that prospects can make side-by-side product comparisons.

Consumer Attitudes and Beliefs

Attitudes are one's enduring feelings toward an object or idea. People have attitudes about almost everything, from "big" things, like religion, to "small" things, like toothpaste. Attitudes put people into a frame of mind to either like or dislike something. Thus, if a young man goes to buy a new suit holding such attitudes as "American-made suits are poorly tailored" and "Italian-made suits are more stylish and prestigious," he may purchase an Italian-made suit simply because it fits his preexisting attitudes.

Because attitudes are relatively long-lasting, people display fairly consistent behavior toward similar classes of objects and ideas. Attitudes economize our

Company Highlight

Honda Changes Consumer Attitudes

Honda entered the U.S. motorcycle market facing two major marketing alternatives. It could either sell its small motorcycles to a small market of people already interested in motorcycles, or it could try to increase the number of people interested in motorcycles. The second alternative was more expensive because many people had nega-tive attitudes toward motorcycles and motorcycle riders; they associated them with such elements as gangs, black leather jackets, drugs, and crime. Honda chose the second alternative anyway, and launched an attitude-change campaign based on the theme: "You meet the nicest people on a Honda."

energy and thought so that we do not have to interpret and react to everything in a fresh way. Changing consumers' attitudes toward something often requires a painful readjustment on their part and a costly promotional (educational) effort by the seller. Therefore salespeople are well advised to try to fit their products to existing consumer attitudes. Still, some companies have become successful because they took the risk and managed to change people's attitudes.

A *belief* is any thought, idea, or fact a person accepts as true on the basis of authority or evidence. Salespeople need to be very interested in the beliefs people have about products because buying behavior is partly a function of these beliefs. For instance, a woman wishing to buy a camera may believe that a Kodak Instamatic takes great pictures, holds up well through rugged use, and is relatively inexpensive. This belief may be based on fact or opinion, and may or may not be susceptible to changes in attitude. Perhaps the woman's mother owns a Kodak Instamatic and achieves excellent results with it. A salesperson trying to sell this woman a compact automatic 35mm camera might want to indicate that Instamatic cameras were previously the choice of people intimidated by expensive, complex 35mm cameras, but that today's 35mm cameras are easy to use and produce professional-looking photographs. Or the salesperson might try a "new generation" approach similar to the advertisement Oldsmobile used in the 1980s: "This is NOT your father's Oldsmobile."

External Buying Influences

Now let's examine six buying influences external to the individual consumer: (1) culture, (2) subculture, (3) social class, (4) reference groups, (5) family decision roles, and (6) family life cycle.

Culture

Culture is the most fundamental determinant of a person's wants and behaviors. Whereas the behavior of animals is based largely on instinct, human behavior is mostly learned. Human beings learn a basic set of values, perceptions, preferences, and behaviors through a process of socialization involving such key institutions as the family, educational systems, and religious affiliations. *Culture* may be defined as the complex of symbols, customs, values, attitudes, and artifacts passed on from one generation to the next that influence human behavior in a given society. Cultural symbols may be intangible (attitudes, values, language, religion) or tangible (tools, housing, works of art).

Subculture

A *subculture* is a group within the larger, more complex culture that retains its own values, customs, and behavioral patterns. Important subcultural influences on consumer behavior are religion, race, nationality, age, sex, occupation, and social class. One's subculture can influence one's choice of neighborhood to live in, food, music, TV programs, toys, clothing, and recreation. For the Hispanic-American submarkets, Mattel makes a Hispanic Barbie doll and Eastern Airlines encourages Puerto-Ricans to fly to the island for a visit. When formulating sales presentations, it is important for salespeople not only to understand subcultures but also to recognize that there are many different market segments within each subculture. Breaking down each subculture by income, education, or lifestyle is usually more effective than appealing to a broad-based ethnic category.

Minority Markets. Most of the consumer behavior literature and models have focused on the white majority in the United States. But special opportunities are opening up for sellers who are attuned to the cultural diversity of America, especially the fast-growing minority markets. Today Asian-Americans buy about $35 billion worth of goods and services a year, Hispanic-Americans $134 billion, and African-Americans $218 billion (see Figure 5-6). These three important minority groups now account for about 20 percent of the U.S. population and will be 30 percent by the year 2000.[9] While some sellers still erroneously think of minority markets as homogeneous, the perceptive ones know that selling approaches must be tailored to various target segments within each minority group. Rock star Michael Jackson, for example, has been successful in reaching 12-to-20-year-olds, the elderly, and Japanese Pepsi drinkers, but not very effective with 25-to-40-year-old African-Americans, who think he is rejecting his cultural heritage through plastic surgery and eccentricities.[10]

Minority consumers do show some common traits, however. David Chen, vice president for Asian marketing for the Los Angeles company Muse, Cordero & Chen, claims that African-Americans, Hispanic-Americans, and Asian-Americans all have strong family loyalties, a desire to preserve their native language and culture, an emphasis on education, achievement, and bringing honor to their families, and a strong preference for well-known American products even when those products are the most expensive.[11] Nearly 70 percent of Asian-Americans and 50 percent of Hispanic-Americans are immigrants, and the majority are under 25 years of age. These immigrants usually have an unquenchable desire for information about their new country—most of which they get from television—and they are strongly influenced by their peers.

[9]Marty Westerman, "Dean of the Frito Bandito," *American Demographics*, March 1989, pp. 28–32.

[10]Ibid., p. 32.

[11]Ibid., p. 31.

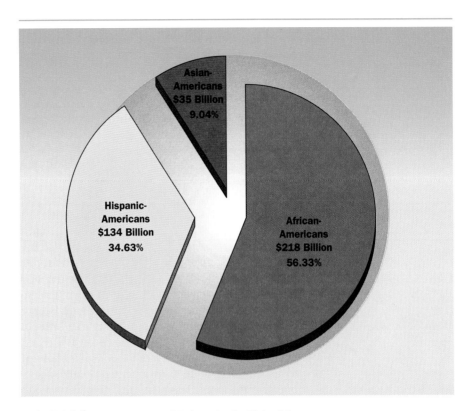

FIGURE 5-6 Major Minority Markets in the United States

Social Class

Social class may be defined as a relatively permanent and homogeneous category of individuals or families sharing similar values, lifestyles, interests, and behavior. Traditionally, social class has been measured in terms of socioeconomic factors such as source of income, occupational status, level of education, and location and quality of housing. Such socioeconomic information appeals to salespeople because it is easily collected through questionnaires or U.S. census reports. Social class is an important influence on consumers' values, attitudes, lifestyles, and behavior. Different social classes have distinct product form and brand preferences for homes, home furnishings, clothing, automobiles, and leisure activities.

Reference Groups

Choices among products, services, and sellers are influenced for many consumers by their evaluation of how others feel toward a particular choice. The individuals or groups to which a person looks for values, attitudes, and/or behavior are called **reference groups.** Three categories of reference groups are important:

REFERENCE GROUP The group to which a person looks for values, attitudes, and/or behavior.

- ■ *Primary groups* (face-to-face groups): Family, friends, neighbors, and co-workers.
- ■ *Secondary groups:* Fraternal and professional associations to which one belongs.
- ■ *Aspirational groups:* Groups to which one might relate or aspire to belong, if only in one's fantasies, like sports heroes, movie stars, or prominent leaders.

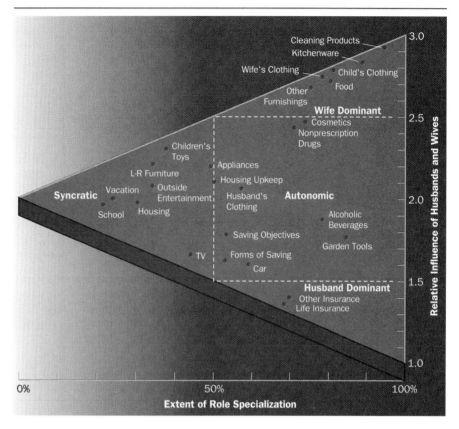

FIGURE 5-7 Decision-Making Influence in Families
Source: Harry I. Davis and Benny P. Rigaux, "Perception of Marital Roles in Decision Processes,"
Journal of Consumer Research, June 1974, p. 57.

Family Decision Roles

An individual's family undoubtedly plays the most influential role in shaping attitudes, opinions, and values. Family decision making is a complex process. It is often very difficult to determine which family members initiate a purchase decision, which members decide different parts of the decision, which members are most influential in making the final decision, and which members make the actual purchase and ultimately use the product. It is crucial for salespeople to learn which members of a household are most influential in particular purchase decisions. Remember, it isn't always the user of the product or service. For example, in most households, women select and purchase underwear and most outer clothing for their husbands and unmarried sons.

The majority of family decision-making responsibilities can be categorized into four major types: (1) *autonomic*—where the husband and wife make an equal number of decisions independently; (2) *husband-dominant;* (3) *wife-dominant;* and (4) *syncratic*—where most decisions are made jointly by husband and wife. As the above Figure 5-7 shows, salespeople will be faced with different family decision makers according to the type of product they are selling.

Family Life Cycle

The concept of *family life cycle* can help salespeople identify prospective customers because wants, attitudes, and values tend to match the family situation over time. A family consisting of four preteen children and parents in their 40s is a better prospect for bicycles, videotapes, stereo equipment, life insurance, encyclopedias, and clothing than a childless couple in their 40s. Similarly, the products and services bought by a 30-year-old bachelor differ sharply from those bought by a 30-year-old father of two children under 6. Salespeople can find a lot of information about the life-cycle stage of families living in a particular neighborhood by reviewing U.S. census tract data (available in most libraries).

WHERE INTERNAL AND EXTERNAL BUYING INFLUENCES MEET: LIFESTYLE

LIFESTYLE The manifestation of myriad influences acting on people to form their self-concepts, perceptions, and attitudes toward life, as well as their goals as consumers.

Perhaps the best way to view a customer as a complete human being rather than as a multitude of internal and external dimensions is to look at his or her lifestyle. **Lifestyle** is how one lives. It is the manifestation of myriad influences acting on people to form their self-concepts, perceptions, attitudes toward life—and their goals and desires as consumers. Because people buy products and services that they feel will maintain or enhance their desired lifestyle, salespeople will find each consumer's lifestyle reflected in his or her particular blend of past purchasing experiences and future purchasing plans. Lifestyle is not just a motivator of buying behavior, however; it also directs the type of search and information sought for purchase decisions, and it determines the consumer's level of satisfaction with products as well. Interaction of the internal and external factors discussed above—culture, subculture, social class, reference groups, family decision roles, stage in the life cycle, and personal characteristics—determines the lifestyle of an individual consumer.

People may have dramatically different lifestyles even though they have the same income, education, and occupation and come from the same subculture and social class. One excellent way for salespeople to understand consumer

Perhaps the best way to view a customer as a complete human being is to look at his or her lifestyle.

PSYCHOGRAPHIC
PROFILE Depiction of a
consumer's activities,
interests, and opinions
(AIOs) as measured in a
survey questionnaire or
personal interview.

lifestyles is to study **psychographic profiles** (you may wish to review the earlier discussion of demographics and psychographics). A psychographic profile
depicts a consumer's activities, interests, and opinions (AIOs) as measured in a
survey, questionnaire, or interview. Marketers of Miller Lite beer, Kentucky Fried
Chicken, and Dewar's White Label Scotch have been able to conduct highly successful promotional efforts thanks to psychographic research. In the case of Kentucky Fried Chicken, it was found that the target consumer was highly conven-
ience-oriented and enjoyed parties and group activities like bowling. This information led Kentucky Fried Chicken to keep its outlets largely carry-out, use a
party theme in advertising, and offer premium coupons good for free bowling
and cases of Coca-Cola.

Sales and marketing professionals have also tried to develop broad classifications of consumer lifestyles. One system of lifestyle classification that has
proved highly successful is *VALS (Values and Life Styles)*, which divides consumers into nine lifestyle groups as depicted in Table 5-4. VALS can help salespeople

TABLE 5-4   The VALS American Lifestyles

LIFESTYLE GROUP	% OF POPULATION	CHARACTERISTICS
Survivors	4 %	People marked by poverty and little education who have given up on life. They find little satisfaction in life and concentrate on just making it from day to day. Survivors tend to be conservative and are "despairing, depressed, and withdrawn."
Sustainers	7 %	People also marked by poverty but who are striving toward a better life. They are "angry, distrustful, rebellious, and combative" and have a deep distrust of "the system." Despite their strong need for status and group acceptance, sustainers see themselves as having low social status.
Belongers	33 %	Traditional, conforming, family-oriented people with a strong need for acceptance who would rather be followers than leaders. They prefer the status quo and tend to lead happy and contented lives.
Emulators	10 %	"Ambitious, competitive, and ostentatious" people who are striving to move ahead by emulating those richer and more successful than themselves. They tend to be hard-working, less conservative, and more successful than belongers, but less satisfied with life.
Achievers	23 %	The "driving and driven" people who made the system and are now at the top. They are hard-working, successful, and self-confident, and tend to feel good about the system, themselves, and their accomplishments.
I-Am-Me's	5 %	Typically young people in transition between the old and the new. They find life confusing, contradictory, and uncertain; experience emotional ups and downs; and live life "intensely, vividly, and experientially." They are seeking and finding new interests and new life goals.
Experientials	7 %	Seek intense personal experiences and emotions. Actions and interaction are the important things in their lives. They are politically and socially liberal, independent and self-reliant, and fairly happy with life. They appreciate nature and seek spiritual meanings in things.
Societally Conscious	9 %	People driven by social ideals—by concern with societal issues and events such as consumerism, conservation, pollution, and wildlife protection. They tend to be well educated, successful, influential, mature, sophisticated, and politically effective.
Integrateds	12 %	Mature and balanced people who have a broad perspective and can find solutions to opposing views. They combine inner directedness and outer directedness. They lead when action is called for, and they have high social status even though they do not seek it.

Source: Arnold Mitchell, *The Nine American Life Styles* (New York: Macmillan, 1983). Used with permission of the author and
publisher.

define the buying potential of individual prospects and whole market populations quickly and accurately. For example, VALS studies have shown that *belongers* tend to buy family-sized domestic cars, while *emulators* and *I-Am-Me's* buy domestic and foreign "muscle cars" (like the Chevy Camaro and Porsche). *Achievers* usually buy luxury foreign cars because these cars represent achievement and status. *Societally conscious* consumers might also buy luxury foreign cars, but would be motivated more by safety records than by what their purchases represent to other people.

CONSUMER BUYING PROCESS

Now that we have discussed the potential influences on consumer buying behavior, let us turn to the buying process itself. Salespeople who understand the different stages of the consumer buying process have multiple opportunities to influence the final purchasing decision by influencing the outcome of each particular stage of the process. Although each consumer has unique reasons for making a purchase, we can identify six basic buying process stages that all consumers go through in reaching their final purchase decision:

- Problem recognition
- Information search
- Evaluation of alternatives
- Purchase decision
- Supplier selection and purchase action
- Postpurchase evaluation

Sometimes consumers complete these stages almost instantaneously or subconsciously, as in impulse purchasing. At other times, they pass through these stages over a long period of time, perhaps months, as in buying a new car or home. Let's discuss each of the six consumer buying stages.

1. Problem Recognition

Either internal or external stimuli can trigger the problem recognition stage. Hunger pangs can stimulate the desire for food; a television advertisement for a steaming hot breakfast at Denny's can do the same thing. Once the problem is recognized, the consumer begins to "solve" it. Sales and marketing professionals have postulated three basic levels of consumer problem solving, which can be placed on a continuum ranging from *programmed decision* to *complex decision,* as depicted in Figure 5-8.

Routine Problem Solving
The simplest kind of buying behavior, routine problem solving usually involves the purchase of inexpensive, frequently repurchased items with low personal involvement, such as groceries and household supplies. Sellers must ensure product quality and availability for present customers, while making special

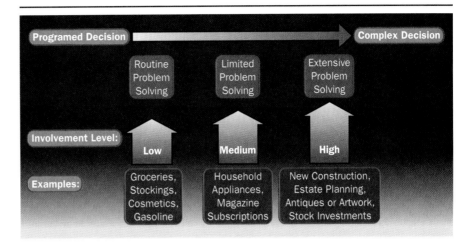

FIGURE 5-8 Continuum of Consumer Problem Solving

efforts to attract new customers by sales presentations stressing special benefits and discount coupons. As the old saying goes: "There ain't no brand loyalty that 20 percent off can't overcome."

Limited Problem Solving

This is a situation in which buyers are aware of the product category and their own evaluative criteria, but are unfamiliar with the various features of alternative brands. A salesperson selling products like over-the-counter medicines, vacuum cleaners, or refrigerators should favorably educate the prospect about the brand while striving to increase the prospect's confidence in that brand.

Extensive Problem Solving

This is the most complex of buying situations because buyers are not familiar with the product or what evaluative criteria to use. The seller must understand the information search and evaluation process of potential buyers (described below) in order to effectively promote the benefits and features of the product category. Personal computers were in the problem-solving situation when they were introduced in the late 1970s.

2. Information Search

If the problem is a routine one frequently solved by the consumer with the purchase of a known product or service, there is little or no search for information. Consumer search efforts vary directly with the perceived severity of the problem, the amount of information already available, the value of additional information, and the perceived cost (time, money, effort, or psychological discomfort) necessary to obtain additional information. Consumers may turn to several sources of information, including:

■ *Personal sources:* personal experience, family, friends, and associates.

■ *Commercial sources:* advertising, salespeople, retailers, and point-of-purchase materials.
■ *Public sources:* government information, consumer organizations, magazines and newspapers, and product rating services.

3. Evaluation of Alternatives

The consumer evaluation process varies by consumer and buying situation. Each consumer sees a given product as a bundle of attributes. For example, a portable photocopier might be evaluated on the following attributes: special features, quality of copies, style, color, size, weight, guarantee, price, delivery date, brand prestige, and service contract. Individual buyers will differ on which attributes are most important in the buying situation.

Evaluative Criteria

To learn what evaluative criteria are used by consumers for specific product-buying decisions, salespeople should ask their in-house market research people what information is available or can be obtained, perhaps by purchasing a study from a commercial market research firm. Salespeople may be surprised by the amount and variety of in-house information supplied to marketing managers but not passed on to the sales force. Cultivating a close relationship with the marketing research staff can give them access to studies that often provide significant insights for selling to consumers.

Armed with knowledge of the consumer evaluation process, salespeople can develop appropriate selling strategies and tactics to reach prospects. For instance, if you learn that buyers of a certain product make their evaluations by comparing their perceptions of the product brand with their ideal brand, then you can try one or more of the several tactics described in Table 5-5 to close the sale.

TABLE 5-5   Closing the Perceptional Gap

■ **Modify the product:** Make some physical adjustment in the product to better satisfy the consumer's specific needs. You might arrange to add a special sound or flashing light to an office copier to indicate when it's about to run out of paper.
■ **Alter the customer's perceptions:** Persuade the potential customer that the product is better than he or she initially believes. You could allay customer concerns about durability by putting the copier through some rigorous tests or by obtaining testimonials from similar customers who have used the product for a long time.
■ **Shift the relative weights of the attributes:** Persuade the customer that one or two product features are critical to his or her needs. For example, the copier customer may have little mechanical ability, so you might emphasize how easy it is to maintain the copier in good working order.
■ **Point out neglected attributes:** Stress overlooked attributes, such as the special two-sided copying feature that will significantly cut the cost of paper supplies.
■ **Shift the customer's ideal product:** Persuade the customer that the customer's perceived ideal product is not the best one for his or her particular needs. Initially, the customer may prefer a small, portable copier that won't take up much space and can be carried from room to room. But you can point out that the portable copier makes only 20 copies at a time, and that its master unit must be replaced twice as often as the larger model's.

What Would You Do?

You are a rug and carpet salesperson for a large department store located in South Bend, Indiana. Two weeks ago, you sold Jim and Marci Hawes a beautiful beige-colored carpeting for their living room. You went along with the carpet installers to make sure they did a good job, and you were impressed by how well the carpet complemented the furniture and decor of the room. This morning at work you receive a phone call from Mrs. Hawes saying that she's not satisfied with the way the carpeting looks in her living room. She says that the dim lights in your store showroom fooled her into thinking that the carpet sample was a darker color. She asks if she can exchange the carpeting.

4. Purchase Decision

Having evaluated alternative products for solving the problem, the consumer has developed a ranking for the alternatives and will normally attempt to purchase the preferred product. Salespeople can help themselves and the consumer in this stage by promoting the ready availability of the product, credit or financing policies, warranties and guarantees, repair and service facilities, and liberal return or exchange policies. Any one of these may prove critical to consumers in making the purchase decision for a particular brand.

5. Supplier Selection and Purchase Action

The consumer's selection of the supplier from whom to buy the product or service depends on the unique combination of consumer and supplier characteristics interacting in a given purchase decision.

Consumer Characteristics

Consumer self-confidence has been found to have a strong impact on the consumer's choice of supplier. Highly self-confident women shopping for clothing prefer discount stores, whereas less self-confident women tend to patronize neighborhood retailers.[12] Shoppers' personalities even influence the type of salesperson they prefer to deal with. Dependent consumers favor more assertive salespeople who make purchasing suggestions, while independent consumers prefer less assertive salespeople.[13]

[12]H. Lawrence Isaacson, "Store Choice," Ph.D dissertation, Graduate School of Business Administration, Harvard University, 1964, pp. 85–89.

[13]James E. Stafford and Thomas V. Greer, "Consumer Preference for Types of Salesmen: A Study of Independence-Dependence Characteristics," *Journal of Retailing*, Summer 1965, pp. 27–33.

Supplier Characteristics

A consumer considers several factors in choosing a supplier, including the seller's reputation, product assortment, prices (perceived value for the dollar), advertising credibility, purchasing convenience, attitudes of friends toward the supplier, and characteristics of the salesperson.[14] With respect to the individual salesperson, research has shown that the most valued factors are: (1) reliability, credibility; (2) professionalism, integrity; and (3) product knowledge.[15]

6. Postpurchase Evaluation

After purchasing and using a product, consumers make a postpurchase evaluation that will determine their level of satisfaction or dissatisfaction and future purchasing behavior. The more important the purchase to them, the more likely they will experience postpurchase anxiety or dissonance about whether they bought the best product. Consumer satisfaction or dissatisfaction with a product depends largely upon prior expectations for the product's performance and the consumer's perception of actual performance (after use) compared to these expectations. Two theories are of particular interest in anticipating the possible reactions of consumers in the postpurchase evaluation of products or services.

Assimilation Theory

ASSIMILATION THEORY Asserts that psychological tension arises when consumers perceive a disparity between their expectations of a product and its performance. They will resolve the tension by altering their perception of performance to better match their expectations.

Based on Festinger's theory of cognitive dissonance,[16] **assimilation theory** assumes that psychological anxiety or tension will arise when consumers perceive a disparity between their expectations and actual product performance. Consumers usually resolve this conflict by altering their personal perceptions of product performance to better match their expectations. Recommendations for salespeople using this theory are to exaggerate product claims to encourage higher consumer evaluations of the product. Owner manuals, brochures, warranties, repair service, and follow-up letters and phone calls by salespeople can help alleviate *postpurchase dissonance* by reassuring consumers that they have purchased a superior product.

Assimilation-Contrast Theory

ASSIMILATION-CONTRAST THEORY Asserts that consumers have latitudes of acceptance and rejection for product performance. They will assimilate minor discrepancies but exaggerate major ones.

Assimilation-contrast theory asserts that consumers have ranges or latitudes of acceptance and rejection for product claims. Minor discrepancies between expectations and product performance will be assimilated toward the consumer's expectations, whereas larger discrepancies will be exaggerated. Using this theory, salespeople should create expectations slightly above actual product performance, but still within the consumer's range of acceptance. Anderson's work supports this theory of consumer satisfaction and dissatisfaction.[17] Repeat pur-

---

[14]Ronald Stephenson, "Identifying Determinants of Retail Patronage," *Journal of Marketing,* July 1969, pp. 57–61.

[15]"PAs Examine the People Who Sell to Them," *Sales & Marketing Management,* November 12, 1985, p. 39.

[16]L. Festinger, *A Theory of Cognitive Dissonance* (Stanford, Calif.: Stanford University Press, 1987.

[17]Rolph E. Anderson, "Consumer Dissatisfaction: The Effect of Disconfirmed Expectancy on Perceived Product Performance," *Journal of Marketing Research,* February 1973, p. 39.

chases, consumer attitudes, and word-of-mouth promotion are all affected by the consumer's postpurchase evaluation, so it is essential for salespeople to learn all they can about this process and what influences it.

In studying consumers, it's a good idea to keep in mind the humble words of India's great peaceful revolutionary Mahatma Gandhi: "There go my people; I must hurry and catch up with them for I am their leader." The consumer market is like a fast-moving parade. You can't look away for long without missing major themes, developments, and participants.

SUMMARY In this chapter we discussed who the U.S. consumer market is and how and why they buy. We began by identifying several current consumer *market segments,* including the "baby boomers," "baby busters," older people, smaller families, the "new immigrants," and minorities. We then examined how sales and marketing professionals use *demographics* and *psychographics* to understand the factors that influence consumer behavior and developed a consumer behavior model based on internal and external buying influences.

We grouped *internal buying influences* into seven conceptual frameworks: consumer (1) needs, (2) motivation, (3) perception, (4) personality, (5) self-concept, (6) learning, and (7) attitudes and beliefs. Turning to *external buying influences,* we saw that each consumer is affected by six important factors: (1) culture, (2) subculture, (3) social class, (4) reference groups, (5) family decision roles, and (6) family life cycle. Although it is useful to be able to examine specific consumer buying influences, we concluded that it is best to examine *lifestyle* as a way of gaining a broader understanding of individual consumers and consumer groups.

Finally, we discussed the six stages of the consumer buying process.

CHAPTER REVIEW QUESTIONS

1. Discuss the present U.S. consumer market. Who are the "baby boomers"? The "baby busters"? Why is it important for salespeople not to treat older consumers as "elderly"? Who are the "new immigrants" and what are some of their consumer characteristics?
2. What are demographics and psychographics? Why are they important in trying to understand consumers?
3. Construct a figure or list representing Maslow's hierarchy of needs.
4. How can salespeople influence consumer needs? What is "motive bundling"?
5. Identify and describe the three perceptual processes that determine how people form their perceptions.
6. Jung divided people into four basic personality types. What are these types and how would you approach them as a salesperson?
7. Use the example of a consumer buying a house to outline and briefly describe the interplay of forces that accomplish consumer learning.
8. How can a salesperson use generalization and discrimination to increase sales?
9. Describe the six basic stages in the consumer buying process.

TOPICS FOR THOUGHT AND CLASS DISCUSSION

1. How do you think the changing characteristics of American consumers will change their lifestyles? Do you believe that the current VALS American Lifestyles presented in Table 5-6 will still be valid by the year 2000?

2. As the cultural mix of the United States changes because of immigration, will understanding consumer buying behavior be more or less important to salespeople? Why?

3. Think of four different brands of toothpaste. In terms of Maslow's hierarchy of needs, what is the specific consumer need to which each brand's advertising and promotional effort appeals?

PROJECTS FOR PERSONAL GROWTH

1. Think about an important purchase decision you made recently. On a piece of paper, be as honest as you can in identifying the rational, emotional, patronage, and product motives for the purchase. Were some of these motives more important to you than others? If a salesperson influenced your choice, how?

2. In making your purchase, how did you proceed through each of the six consumer buying stages? (a) problem recognition, (b) information search, (c) evaluation of alternatives, (d) purchase decision, (e) supplier search and purchase action, and (f) postpurchase evaluation. Was any stage more difficult or easier than the others? Why?

3. Write down the names of five of your friends. How would you classify them in terms of the two personality classifications discussed in the chapter: (a) compliant, aggressive, or detached; and (b) thinker, feeler, intuitor, or senser? How would you classify yourself?

4. In your family, how are the decision-making responsibilities divided for the following purchases: automobile, breakfast cereal, furniture, restaurant food, annual vacation, soft drinks? Classify each of these purchase decisions as to whether it is autonomic, syncratic, or one-person dominant.

KEY TERMS

Baby boomers The huge generation born between 1946 and 1964.

Baby busters The much smaller generation born between 1964 and 1976.

Demographics The readily identifiable characteristics of consumers, such as age, sex, occupation, and income.

Psychographics The activities, interests, opinions, and lifestyles of consumers.

Hierarchy of needs Maslow's conceptual framework of motivation in which lower-level human needs (physiological, safety and security) must be satisfied before higher-level needs (belongingness and love, self-esteem, and self-actualization) become activated.

Motive bundling Increasing a consumer's desire to purchase a product or service by showing how one purchase will solve several problems simultaneously.

Selective exposure The process by which a person filters information, disregarding data that are not important or of interest at the time.

Selective comprehension The tendency to understand and interpret information so that it is consistent with what an individual already feels and believes.

Selective retention The tendency to retain in memory only that information that supports preconceived attitudes and beliefs.

Positive reinforcement Reinforcement that rewards a certain behavior and thus makes it likely that that behavior will be repeated.

Negative reinforcement Reinforcement that punishes a certain behavior and thus makes it unlikely that that behavior will be repeated.

Reference group The group to which a person looks for values, attitudes, and/or behavior.

Lifestyle The manifestation of myriad influences acting on people to form their self-concepts, perceptions, and attitudes toward life, as well as their goals as consumers.

Psychographic profile Depiction of a consumer's activities, interests, and opinions (AIOs) as measured in a survey questionnaire or personal interview.

Assimilation theory Asserts that psychological tension arises when consumers perceive a disparity between their expectations of a product and its performance. They will resolve the tension by altering their perception of performance to better match their expectations.

Assimilation-contrast theory Asserts that consumers have latitudes of acceptance and rejection for product performance. They will assimilate minor discrepancies but exaggerate major ones.

Case 5-1

SELLING FIDELITY MUTUAL FUNDS

Darlene Schmidt has been a sales representative for Fidelity Mutual Funds for nearly three years now, ever since she graduated from St. John's University with a major in psychology. Unable to find desirable work in her chosen field, Darlene had interviewed with several companies before taking the Fidelity job, expecting it to be only temporary until she found an opening in her field. Instead, Darlene found that she really enjoyed the freedom and independence of sales work and the attractive earnings tied directly to her achievements. Selling mutual funds also gave her a chance to meet a lot of interesting people and to use her training in psychology to try to figure them out. It is a challenge to try to find a consumer's "hot button" and make the sale. It usually takes her two or three calls on a prospect to close the sale, and Darlene has become quite adept at using the first call to gather information and size up the potential customer prior to making a comprehensive sales presentation in subsequent calls.

On Friday evening while unwinding at home in front of a mindless situation comedy on TV, Darlene begins to think about the best approach to sell two prospects she has met this week. She tries to visualize each in her mind. "Let's see, there are Luther Raymond and Harold Stauffer . . ."

Luther Raymond. Darlene selected Luther Raymond's card from among those who had written for more information in response to the company's newspaper advertisements. She recalls he claimed to be too busy for a luncheon appointment until he discovered that she was a 26-year-old single woman. Luther—or Luke, as he prefers to be called—is a tall, ruggedly attractive man in his mid-30s who has recently been divorced. He was fastidiously dressed and somewhat arrogant in manner at their first meeting, but very enthusiastic about his career and future with his company—a medium-sized cosmetics producer that has recently promoted him to marketing manager for the Starlight line of perfumes. Luke confided that he hopes to become a vice president of marketing within three years and that he has begun taking M.B.A. courses at night. During the luncheon conversation, he did a lot of name dropping and boasting about his marketing skills, but Darlene detected some insecurity in his braggadocio, especially when he asked her how she felt he came across to people. He seemed especially concerned about his image with his management superiors.

As a single man with a promising future and no dependents, Luke no doubt has considerable disposable income, and Darlene wonders what evaluative criteria he would use in selecting a mutual fund. Fidelity offers a range of investment funds—from very conservative income funds to speculative growth funds. Luke drives a late-model sports car identical to the one his immediate boss drives, and he talked enthusiastically about being a member of the same health club as his company's top managers. One word that cropped up frequently in his conversation was "contacts." "Without contacts," he said, "you don't have a chance to make it big." He seems to see himself as a "smooth operator" (both at work and in social settings), but somewhat unappreciated at times. Darlene smiles to herself as she remembers how Luke had subtly tried to make a date for that weekend, but she politely put him off with an excuse about a prior commitment. As she is thinking about her meeting with Luke, Darlene's mind suddenly jumps to Harold Stauffer, who seems to be a sharp contrast to Luther Raymond.

Harold Stauffer. A senior vice president for Jefferson Savings and Loan in his late 40s or early 50s, Harold Stauffer has a wife (his second) and five children, two in college, two in high school, and one in elementary school. Although cordial, Mr. Stauffer was very businesslike in manner when Darlene called, but did agree to see her at his home on Wednesday evening.

Mr. Stauffer's wife was a surprise. About ten years younger than her husband, she is a vivaciously attractive woman who enjoys teasing him about his conservative ways and kiddingly calls him "party-poop." Obviously proud of his lovely young wife, Mr. Stauffer frequently calls her by the pet name "Princess." Talking quietly with Mr. Stauffer, Darlene could almost see the pressures in his face from supporting five children and a wife who had put her

career on hold for their youngest child, who had just started elementary school. It was evident that Mr. Stauffer did not make decisions quickly, and he wanted to know nearly everything about the various Fidelity funds—from their comparative performance records to the procedure for redemption of shares. He purchased shares in a mutual fund about eight years ago and lost about 40 percent of his original investment when the stock market declined sharply and he had to sell during his divorce settlement. His current wife has been urging him to make some investments that could help put their children through college.

Glancing at the clock, Darlene sees that it is past midnight, so she decides to sleep on the information she's acquired before attempting to devise sales tactics for each prospect.

Questions

1. How would you evaluate Luther Raymond and Harold Stauffer as potential customers for mutual funds? What kind of funds would they most likely want to invest in?

2. Think about the internal and external buying influences for both Luther Raymond and Harold Stauffer. Using the limited information presented, what kind of consumer lifestyle profile would you draw for each man? What kinds of needs or motives would each have for buying?

3. Many of Darlene's friends are salespeople and she would like to provide some of them with referrals for Luther Raymond and Harold Stauffer. What kinds of products would her friends have to sell in order for Darlene's referrals to be worthwhile for each of her two prospects? What advice should Darlene give these friends about selling their specific products to each prospect? (Give three or four examples for each. For example, if one friend is a real estate agent, what would Darlene say to him about Luther Raymond and Harold Stauffer?)

Case 5-2

IDENTIFYING MARKET SEGMENTS

As one of nearly 20 million Hispanic-Americans in the United States, Juan Sanchez feels that he can capitalize on his knowledge of Hispanic cultures in his job as a life insurance sales representative for Pioneer Mutual Life Insurance Company. Although he has been moderately successful during his three years with Pioneer, Juan believes that he could do better by focusing all his efforts on the large Hispanic-American market in New York City instead of remaining in his Albany territory. He knows, however, that Pioneer does not currently segment its markets or assign its salespeople on the basis of their ethnic background and probably does not even consider the Hispanic-American market as having much immediate potential.

While living in New York City during his college and graduate student years, Juan was involved in several Hispanic-American organizations and acquired a first-hand familiarity with the diversity of the Hispanic community there. He knows that Hispanic-Americans are an up-and-coming minority, and that the Cubans, Puerto Ricans, and Mexicans who immigrated to the United States earlier than other South Americans have established themselves as much as any other minority. These people, Juan feels, are certainly an important market for his product. And the newer, mostly South American immigrants are working hard, so Juan believes that it won't be long before they, too, will be interested in protecting their earnings and property with insurance.

While researching some specific market characteristics in the city library, Juan learned that the median income of Hispanic-Americans is about 75 percent of the national average and gaining steadily. Hispanics already have a purchasing power of over $60 billion a year, and are expected to be the largest minority in the United States within the next decade. It has become clear to Juan that these people do not represent one huge, homogeneous market, but rather a mixture of many submarkets with varying origins, goals, lifestyles, and product preferences. They do, however, share some important characteristics. In addition to the Spanish language and their concentration in a few large cities across the United States, Hispanic-Americans also share love of music, brand loyalty for particular kinds of products, large and close families, and disproportionately large expenditures (compared to other Americans) on high-quality food and clothing.

Carol Minelli, who is both the northeastern U.S. regional sales manager and Juan's district sales manager, is always telling her sales reps to "go after the big fish first and the minnows last." Juan is afraid that Carol might regard the Hispanic-American market as a "minnow" unless he can present their case to her in a thoroughly convincing manner. Even if he succeeds in doing that, Juan knows that he will further have to convince Carol that he should be assigned to New York City. Since that might require the creation of another sales territory just for him, his presentation to Carol is going to have to be one of the best presentations of his career!

Questions

1. What would you advise Juan to say to his sales manager to convince her that his moving into a New York City territory would be the best thing for the Pioneer Mutual Life Insurance Company?

2. What kinds of product benefits do you think Juan should tell his manager he will stress in selling life insurance to the Hispanic-American market?

3. One important aspect of a Pioneer rep's job is to work closely with headquarters marketing and marketing research people to develop the most effective promotional and advertising materials for specific markets. What are some ways that Juan could show his manager his resourcefulness in gathering and interpreting information about the Hispanic-American market?

Chapter 6

Organizational Markets: Industrial, Reseller, Government, and Nonprofit

If selling were just a matter of the low bid meeting specs, the world wouldn't need salespeople.

HARVEY MACKAY

JANET Hober, a sales and marketing representative for Du Pont in New York City, opted for the self development rather than the career development path in college, but that certainly hasn't hindered her success at Du Pont; in fact, it may have enhanced it. Janet told us: "I graduated from Lehigh University with a liberal arts degree. My majors were English and Political Science. I believe liberal arts courses teach people to listen and communicate well, two skills that every superior salesperson possesses. Getting in the door of large companies is no doubt more difficult without a technical or business degree, but people who are trained to communicate effectively learn the business quickly and can often develop relationships easily." Janet got "in the door" with Du Pont through an internship during the summer between her junior and senior years, an opportunity that allowed her to show the company that she had energy and could do fine work. "I did plenty of grunt work and took on projects that full-time employees avoided. When I interviewed with Du Pont during my senior year, they had already built a sizable file on me; I was a very low risk. I worked with a few recruiters and decided that sales would be a good fit for me," says Janet.

During her 18 months of training as a customer sales coordinator, Janet learned the internal workings of Du Pont's Fibers Department. She now does end-use marketing in a newly established sales position—for which she wrote the job description, objectives, and strategies. Working in the field with retailer customers, Janet supports a whole team of direct salespeople who sell Dacron®, nylon, and Lycra®. Her position represents Du Pont's closest link between its in-house activities and consumers.

Profile

Janet Hober

It was difficult for us to figure out where Janet's *selling* activities end and her *marketing* and *managing* activities begin, so we asked her to discuss her job: "I act as a team coordinator between fabric development people, technical sales representatives, product managers, and marketing strategists. When working with retailers, I strive to find new market needs and gather market intelligence. As Du Pont's eyes and ears at the retail level, I communicate what I learn back to my internal organization. Much of my job involves market knowledge and leadership. As producers of the raw materials that go into what retailers sell, we have to give retailers a good reason to specify Du Pont fibers when they purchase garments for their stores. I share a lot of market research that Du Pont commissions, and often, via direct mail or telemarketing, I let retailers know where we think the business is headed."

When asked whether she thinks she faces any special problems because she is female, Janet gave us a refreshingly candid answer: "Yes, I do believe women face some unique problems selling in industrial markets. Our golf tees are placed closer to the holes, so you miss all the good bashing taking place on the men's tee! . . . Seriously, there are still many old boy networks out there left to dissolve. Young women often get treated as daughters, while older women are seen as having abandoned the family model. The only way to deal with these problems is to work out solutions with which you feel comfortable." ■

After reading this chapter, you should understand:

□ Four types of organizational markets

□ Differences between consumer and organizational markets

□ Why, what, and how organizational markets buy goods and services

□ Major steps in the buying process and the types of buying situations

As a college graduate pursuing a profession in selling or sales management, you will probably spend most of your career selling to organizations rather than to consumers. The highest-earning professional salespeople sell to industrial, reseller, government, or nonprofit market types. All the organizations represented by these market types purchase a vast assortment of goods and services in order to carry out their administrative and production activities. In this chapter, we discuss the kinds of buying processes that salespeople must understand in order to sell successfully in organizational markets.

ORGANIZATIONAL MARKETS

From the salesperson's perspective, there are four types of organizational markets:

■ *Industrial markets:* Also called *producer* or *manufacturer markets,* these are organizations that buy goods and services for the production of other products and services that are sold, rented, or supplied to other organizations and final consumers.

■ *Reseller markets:* Individuals and organizations (retailers, wholesalers, and industrial distributors) that buy goods to resell or rent to other organizations and final consumers.

■ *Government markets:* Federal, state, and local governmental units that buy goods and services for conducting the functions of government.

■ *Nonprofit markets:* Organizations such as public and private universities, colleges, hospitals, nursing homes, prisons, museums, libraries, and charitable institutions that buy goods and services for carrying out their functions.

SEGMENTING ORGANIZATIONAL MARKETS

BUYING CENTER In a buying organization, a group of organization members responsible for making purchases.

Like consumer markets, organizational markets can be divided into smaller, more homogenous submarkets for better tailoring of marketing mixes. Almost every organization can be segmented into three levels with respect to its buying activity: (1) the *buying organization* as a whole; (2) the **buying center,** made up of the organization members responsible for purchases; and (3) the *individ-*

TABLE 6-1 Segmentation Variables for Organizational Markets

I. Characteristics of the Buying Organization

■ *Type of organization*—manufacturing firm, educational institution, hospital, retailer or wholesaler, government agency, public utility.

■ *Organizational "demographics"*—industry affiliation, geographic location, annual sales volume, number of employees, domestic/international markets, standard industrial classification (SIC), standard metropolitan statistical area (SMSA), ZIP code.

■ *Product application*—how the product is used by the organization.

■ *Type of buying situation*—straight rebuy, modified rebuy, new task.

■ *Degree of source loyalty,* and whether the supplier is "in" or "out."

■ *Types of purchasing contracts*—"open" or "blanket" purchase agreements, sealed bid, stockless purchasing.

■ *Organizational purchasing characteristics*—purchasing policies and procedures, buying process, average order size, frequency of purchase, inventory requirements.

■ *Reciprocity*—whether or not buyer expects reciprocal purchasing by the supplier.

■ *Supplier/customer relationship*—current or past customer, or new prospect; light, medium, or heavy user; single- or multiple-source buyer.

II. Characteristics of the Buying Center (within the Buying Organization)

■ *Composition*—membership and roles of individual members.

■ *Specific buying functions* of the center.

■ *Types of pressures on center members*—e.g., time, political, and budget limitations.

■ *Purchasing strategies and decision rules*—specific product benefits sought.

■ *Method of conflict resolution used in the center*—persuasion, compromise, bargaining, or negotiation.

■ *Types of uncertainty perceived in the center*—needs, markets, or transaction uncertainty.

■ *Confidence*—how secure the center is in its own purchasing ability.

III. Characteristics of Individual Decision Participants (within the Buying Center)

■ *Individual buying criteria used*—price, quality, delivery reliability, service.

■ *Organizational role*—position in organization structure and within the buying center.

■ *Perceptions of rewards or punishments* for risk taking.

■ *Demographics*—age, education, occupation, industry experience.

■ *Psychographics*—attitudes toward various suppliers, degree of self-confidence, buying personality or style, lifestyle, self-image, risk tolerance, professional affiliations outside the organization.

Source: Adapted from Yoram Wind and Richard Cardozo, "Industrial Market Segmentation," *Industrial Marketing Management,* April 1974, pp. 153–166.

ual decision participants. Salespeople can examine these three levels together or separately, depending on their priorities and goals, keeping in mind that each of the three levels has several special characteristics, or *segmentation variables.* Table 6-1 provides a handy overview of some of the segmentation variables for all three organization levels.

Segmentation Variables

Among the segmentation variables based on the *characteristics of the buying organization* are the type of organization, organizational demographics (such as size and geographic location), product application, the type of buying situation, degree of loyalty to suppliers, types of purchasing agreement, organizational purchasing policies and procedures, reciprocity arrangements, and the buyer-seller relationship. Narrowing our perspective from the organization as a whole to the specific group of people responsible for purchasing decisions, we can identify several *buying center characteristics:* the membership composition of the buying center and the roles of the individual members, buying functions, pressures on buyers, purchasing decision rules and strategies, approach to conflict resolution, and types of uncertainty prevailing in the center. "Uncertainty" suggests an often overlooked variable that can be used to segment organizational markets: the confidence the buying organization has in its own purchasing ability. Some companies do not trust their own judgment, so they rely on the reputation of a manufacturer. At one time, for example, the computer market was segmented into two groups: customer organizations that believed they had the expertise to evaluate computer options; and the remaining, less confident organizations (the majority) that were captives of IBM.

Finally, organizational markets can be segmented on the basis of the *characteristics of the individual decision participants:* their buying criteria, organization role, perceptions of rewards and punishments, demographics, and psychographics. Although people tend to think that organizational markets buy for purely rational reasons, it must be remembered that organizational buyers are human beings with needs and motivations that cannot help but influence their purchase decisions. For instance, a multimillion-dollar jet airplane can seldom be sold to a corporation unless the CEO becomes personally excited about the plane's beauty and the prestige of owning it.[1] The following are some examples of rational and emotional motives in organizational buying:

Rational	*Emotional*
Price	Reward/punishment system
Quality	Effect on buyer status
Delivery reliability	Image of supplier
Service	Perceived purchase risk
Reciprocity	Friendship with salesperson
Continuity of supply	Buyer self-confidence
Return/replacement policy	Attitude toward seller company

WHAT ORGANIZATIONAL BUYERS WANT FROM SALESPEOPLE

Organizational buyers want to buy from salespeople they can trust to deliver on their promises, provide continual service, and supply them with precise, accurate, and complete information. They expect sales reps to forewarn them about upcoming price changes, product shortages, employee strikes, delivery delays, or anything else that might affect them and their organizations. Buyers want to do business with a salesperson who is truly looking out for their organization's best interests and who helps them to look good personally—in other words, they want a trusted friend and partner.

---

[1]Thomas V. Bonoma, "Major Sales: Who Really Does the Buying?" *Harvard Business Review,* May–June 1982, p. 112.

As an industrial salesperson, your negotiations with buyers must always be *win-win,* never *win-lose.* You do not succeed over the long run in professional selling by beating customers in negotiations. Even if you have the power to take advantage of a customer, never yield to the temptation. It is folly for a sales rep who wishes to develop a trusting long-lasting buyer-seller relationship to mislead or withhold information or manipulate the buyer in any way. Instead, strive to make sure that all parties are satisfied in all transactions. In dealing with organizational customers, it might help to keep in mind the slogan Vidal Sassoon used to sell hair-treatment products: "If you don't look good, we don't look good."

INDUSTRIAL MARKETS

Largest and most diverse of all the organizational markets, industrial markets offer outstanding opportunities for anyone considering a professional selling career. There are more careers in industrial selling than in other kinds of selling because almost all industries buy from and sell to one another in creating products for the final consumer. The dollar volume of industrial marketing transactions far exceeds that for consumer markets. Included in the industrial market are about 350,000 manufacturing firms that together employ over 20 million people and account for about $3 trillion in sales annually. Table 6-2 shows the large number of industrial selling transactions that must take place before a pair of shoes reaches the final, single-consumer buying transaction.

The large number of industrial selling transactions that go into the creation of one consumer product also point to the enormous diversity of industrial markets. Industrial markets include several types of industries:

Agriculture	Mining	Banking	Transportation
Forestry	Manufacturing	Insurance	Public utilities
Fishing	Construction	Finance	Real estate

Usually, industrial organizations have one or more of these motives for buying: (1) to make profits, (2) to cut operating costs, or (3) to carry out social or legal obligations (for example, the installation of wheelchair ramps for handicapped people).

TABLE 6-2 Transactions Required to Produce and Sell Shoes

HIDE DEALER	TANNER	SHOE MANUFACTURER	WHOLESALER	RETAILER	CONSUMER
Buys: Animal skins Chemicals Equipment Labor Energy	*Buys:* Hides Chemicals Equipment Labor Energy	*Buys:* Leather Heels Equipment Labor Energy	*Buys:* Shoes Space Equipment Labor Energy	*Buys:* Shoes Space Fixtures Labor Energy	*Buys:* Shoes
Sells: Hides	*Sells:* Leather	*Sells:* Shoes	*Sells:* Shoes	*Sells:* Shoes	

Source: Philip Kotler and Gary Armstrong, *Principles of Marketing* (Englewood Cliffs, N.J.: Prentice Hall, 1989), p. 165.

Industrial Market Characteristics

Industrial markets differ significantly from consumer markets in the areas of demand, buyers, purchasing process, and marketing mix, as outlined in Table 6-3.

Demand

DERIVED DEMAND Demand that is created as a result of consumer demand; typical of industrial markets.

PRICE INELASTICITY OF DEMAND Demand that hardly changes with a small change in price; characteristic of industrial markets.

Industrial demand is **derived demand.** For example, Chrysler Motor's demand for sheet steel from USX as an input in manufacturing automobiles is *derived* from consumer demand for Chrysler automobiles. If the demand for automobiles weakens, so will the demand for sheet steel to produce them. **Price inelasticity of demand** is another characteristic of industrial demand, especially in the short run, when industrial producers find it difficult to make changes in production methods. In consumer markets, sometimes even a small upward change in price will have a large negative impact on consumer demand, meaning that demand is *elastic* with respect to price. In industrial markets, however, a comparatively small change in price usually will have little or no impact on overall demand, meaning that demand is *inelastic* with respect to price. Finally, industrial demand is characterized by *volatility*. Because industrial goods are so impacted by final consumer demand, a *small* (less volatile) change in *consumer* demand creates a much *larger* (more volatile) change in the demand for *industrial* goods and services.

Buyers

Industrial buyers tend to be geographically concentrated. Half of the nation's producers are in seven states: New York, California, Pennsylvania, Illinois, Ohio,

TABLE 6-3   Industrial versus Consumer Market Characteristics

CHARACTERISTIC	INDUSTRIAL	CONSUMER
Demand	Derived	Direct
	Price inelasticity	Price elasticity
	More volatile	Less volatile
Buyer	Few buying centers	Many individuals or households
	Professional	Amateur
Purchasing process	Long negotiations	Short negotiations
	Infrequent purchases	Frequent purchases
	Large order size	Small order size
	Servicing expected	Servicing not expected
	Reciprocity demanded	No reciprocity demanded
	Often lease	Seldom lease
	Buyer centers	Individual or household buyers
Marketing Mix: Products/ services	Customized	Standardized
	More technical	Less technical
Price	Formal bids	List prices
Promotion	Emphasis on personal selling	Emphasis on advertising
Distribution	Shorter channels	Longer channels
	Buy direct from producers	Buy through middlemen

New Jersey, and Michigan. Industrial buyers are also usually grouped into buying centers or committees, which typically include technical experts and top management. Sales representatives need to be well trained and well prepared to make presentations before such groups of professional buyers.

Purchasing Process
Industrial buyers do not shop for goods or seek out salespeople the way consumers do. Instead, sales representatives usually go to them. Industrial purchases are less frequent and normally require a longer negotiation period than do consumer purchases, both because the industrial product is generally made to order, so exact specifications must be agreed upon, and because industrial buyers often require formal bids, so the seller needs time to prepare precise cost estimates. If the product is complex and expensive, many industrial organizations will buy directly from the producers instead of through middlemen. Major airlines, for example, buy their aircraft directly from manufacturers like Boeing and McDonnell Douglas.

RECIPROCITY A mutual exchange of benefits; in industrial buyer-seller relationships, an informal agreement between two or more organizations to exchange goods and services on a systematic and more or less exclusive basis.

Reciprocity. Taking our cue from the old saying "If you scratch my back, I'll scratch yours," we can define **reciprocity,** in the context of industrial organizations, as a mutual exchange of benefits. A company that produces hardwood veneers and laminates, for example, might buy its office desks and bookcases from its biggest customer, an office furniture maker. Most reciprocal arrangements like this are not backed by a formal contract, though some companies have a "trade relations" department to keep track of their reciprocal buying arrangements with various customers and suppliers.

Although reciprocity might sound like a reasonable practice, the Federal Trade Commission and the Justice Department's antitrust division prohibit it if it results in unfair competition. Buyers must be able to show that they are getting competitive prices, quality, and service from suppliers with whom they are practicing reciprocity. Most contracts requiring an exclusive supplier arrangement, exclusive dealing, and tying agreements are found illegal in court. The systematic practice of reciprocity can also hurt the morale of a company's sales force and purchasing departments. Surveys show that most purchasing agents and salespeople dislike reciprocity, and many feel that it should be made altogether illegal.[2]

Leasing. Leasing in lieu of purchasing is a rapidly growing option in industrial organizations. Each year American companies lease over $100 billion of equipment, ranging from power plants and offshore drilling rigs to office copiers and forklift trucks. Company cars, computers, and machine tools that have high obsolescence are frequently leased to save capital investment funds and ensure the latest technology.

Marketing Mix
The many differences between industrial and consumer markets in terms of demand, buyers, and purchasing process (see Table 6-3) require that companies selling to industrial organizations develop marketing mixes that are tailored to

[2]F. Robert Finney, "Reciprocity: Gone but Not Forgotten," *Journal of Marketing,* January 1978, pp. 54–59.

Company Highlight

Training Industrial Salespeople at Xerox

Xerox is known throughout the world for its copying machines. Its brand name is so dominant that many people use it as a verb, as in "I'm going to xerox this article." Xerox maintains its world-class image by providing its salespeople with excellent training, and each year its sales force is ranked among the best in its industry. Every applicant for Xerox's sales force receives the following information about training.

Before you make your first sales call, Xerox will have invested thousands of dollars in your training. Our sales training programs are recognized as the most thorough and effective in the reprographics industry. And, in reality, training never really stops. As you become ready for more responsibilities, you're prepared for them with the appropriate advanced training.

Initial training, which takes place at your branch, consists of our "Foundations for Success" program. For seven weeks, you'll learn basic selling skills and product knowledge. For the next four months, much of your time will be spent calling on prospects and customers. At the same time, you'll receive ongoing coaching and training from your Sales Manager.

Then you'll go to Leesburg, Virginia, to attend an intensive one-week course at our one-thousand-student International Center for Management Training and Development. This course covers all aspects of a sales call, as well as product demonstration and self-motivation tech-

niques. At Leesburg, you'll be exposed to the newest instructional methods and materials, including videotaped role plays and hands-on experience with our equipment.

Back at your branch, training continues under the guidance and direction of your Sales Manager. You'll gain broader experience in writing proposals, conducting surveys, and demonstrating equipment.

Your next step will be assignment to a specific account or accounts. You'll prepare for this by studying a series of self-paced training materials concentrating on knowledge of the competition and skills needed in major account marketing. Then, you'll return to Leesburg for a two-week Account Management course. Here you'll focus on presentation skills, survey techniques and decision making.

As your career progresses, you'll have the opportunity to take part in seminars and courses that will prepare you to meet the needs of specialized markets or assignments. Your Sales Manager will be the critical link between your formal training and your ongoing, informal training. At Xerox, you're not only trained for success to begin with, you're also trained for continued success as Xerox grows and changes to successfully compete in an ever-changing and more competitive marketplace.

Source: Courtesy of Xerox Corporation.

specific customer groups and their unique needs. Products are frequently custom-designed for industrial customers, whereas consumer products are more often standardized for large numbers of consumers. Industrial products are usually very technical in nature, while most consumer products are nontechnical. Industrial marketers stress personal selling, whereas consumer marketers emphasize advertising. Because sellers must anticipate and satisfy the changing needs of industrial customers who, in turn, are trying to satisfy the needs of their own customers, it is easy to understand why personal selling is the most important factor in their marketing mixes. Every successful company knows that the only way to sell to industrial organizations is to have salespeople who make it their job to understand their customers' organizations inside and out. For this reason, companies like Xerox feel compelled to make a major investment in training their industrial salespeople, as described in the Company Highlight featuring Xerox Corporation.

Standard Industrial Classification System

One of the best ways to learn about industrial markets is to study the Standard Industrial Classification (SIC) system set forth in the SIC manual published every five years by the U.S. Office of Management and Budget. The SIC system categorizes nearly all industries into 11 major divisions according to their economic activities. Look at Table 6-4 and trace the SIC classification route from the general industry of mining to the specific industry of placer gold. All companies assigned the number 10 as the first two digits of their SIC code are involved in metal mining. Within metal mining, the mining of gold and silver ores has been assigned a third digit, making that number 104. Finally, different types of gold and silver ores are subdivided into categories with four-digit SIC numbers. Thus, if buyers or sellers are interested in learning about mining companies that retrieve placer gold (gold that comes from bodies of water or glaciers rather than from lodes deep in the earth), they can refer to all the companies listed under SIC code 1043. Where necessary, the SIC further classifies industrial subgroups with increasing specificity up to seven digits. Many industrial salespeople make regular use of this handy reference system in locating new customers, estimating market potentials, and improving sales forecasting accuracy. Once you have a solid knowledge of the SIC system, you can gather more information by consult-

TABLE 6-4 Standard Industrial Classification System: Finding Placer Gold

MAJOR SIC DIVISIONS	INDUSTRY GROUP (2 DIGITS)	INDUSTRY SUBGROUP (3 DIGITS)	SPECIFIC INDUSTRY (4 DIGITS)
01–09 Agriculture, forestry, fishing	10 Metal mining	101 Iron ores	1042 Lode gold
10–14 Mining	11 Anthracite mining	102 Copper ores	1043 Placer gold
15–19 Contract construction	12 Bituminous coal	103 Lead and zinc ores	1044 Silver ores
20–39 Manufacturing	13 Crude petroleum and natural gas	104 Gold and silver ores	
40–49 Transportation, communications, electric, gas	14 Nonmetallic minerals	105 Bauxite	
50–59 Wholesale and retail trade		106 Ferroalloy ores	
60–67 Finance, insurance, and real estate		108 Metal mining services	
70–89 Services		109 Miscellaneous metal ores	
90–93 Government			
99 Others			

ing national input-output analysis tables published by the Commerce Department's Office of Business Economics in its monthly *Survey of Current Business*. These input-output tables present basic industries in a matrix format showing how an industry's sales (outputs) are distributed among its customer industries. Since each sale is also a purchase, the tables show an industry's purchases (inputs) as a percentage of the seller's output. In another table, the percentages are converted to dollars to provide the value of the flow of goods and services between industries.

The Role of the Industrial Buyer

INDUSTRIAL BUYER Also called the purchasing agent; the buying expert for an organization.

The **industrial buyer,** frequently called the *purchasing agent,* is the buying expert for his or her organization. Large companies have purchasing departments with many purchasing agents, each specializing in buying a particular product or service from sales reps who visit them. Over the past few decades, the industrial buyer's role and responsibilities have expanded from those of little more than a clerk to those of an executive. With increasing competition worldwide, the industrial buyer has had to become a highly sophisticated career professional. Skillful purchasing, especially during times of resource shortages, is a major determinant of the profitability of an organization. The success of industrial buyers depends largely on their ability to:

- Negotiate favorable prices and purchase terms.
- Develop alternative solutions to buying problems while keeping organizational departments informed about negotiations.
- Protect the organization's cost structure (its cost of doing business).
- Assure reliable, long-run sources of supply.
- Maintain good relationships with suppliers.
- Manage the procurement process (reorder procedures, order expediting, order receipt, and record control).

Professional buyers have strong views about what they like, dislike, and just plain hate in salespeople, as revealed in Table 6-5.

TABLE 6-5 How Buyers See Salespeople: The Good, the Bad, and the Ugly

THE GOOD	THE BAD	THE UGLY
Is honest	Does not follow up	Has a "wise" attitude
Loses a sale graciously	Walks in without an appointment	Calls me "dear" or "sweetheart"
Admits mistakes	Begins by talking sports	Gets personal
Has problem-solving capabilities	Puts down competitors' products	Thinks purchasing people are fools
Acts friendly but professionally	Has poor listening skills	Whines
Is dependable	Makes too many phone calls	Shoots the bull
Is adaptable	Gives a lousy presentation	Wines and dines me
Knows my business	Fails to ask about my needs	Plays one company against another
Comes well-prepared	Lacks product knowledge	Is pushy
Is patient	Wastes my time	Smokes in my office

Source: Adapted from "PAS Examine the People Who Sell to Them," *Sales & Marketing Management,* November 11, 1985, p. 39.

New Strategies in Industrial Buying

In searching for higher-quality products and services, progressive companies have turned to new purchasing strategies, including (1) supplier reduction, (2) single sourcing, (3) cost-based procurement, (4) supplier analysis, (5) supplier partnering, and (6) early supplier involvement.[3]

Supplier Reduction

Leading companies are cutting the number of suppliers they deal with by 50 percent or more to lower administrative expenses, develop closer relationships, and gain more control over suppliers.

Single Sourcing

Some customers take supplier reduction to an extreme by buying everything from one supplier. This can be risky, however, because of the possibility of strikes, fires, or unsatisfactory supplier performance. To obtain the advantages of single sourcing while guarding against risks, most organizational buyers give about 75 percent of their business to one supplier and the rest to backup suppliers. This, they feel, will protect them in an emergency and prevent overconfidence and mediocre performance in the major source.

Cost-Based Procurement

Fewer and fewer companies evaluate their suppliers solely on the basis of price. Today the primary consideration for many top companies is cost. What's the difference between price and cost? *Price* is what you pay up front for what you purchase. *Cost* is what your purchase ends up costing you over the long run. For instance, purchasing low-quality parts that are delivered late usually ends up costing more in terms of late shipments and product failures than paying a little more up front for high-quality parts delivered on time. Additional costs for poor-quality products include higher inspection costs, more scrap and returns, higher inventory costs, increased customer complaints, and more service calls. Industrial customers are learning that it's better to purchase a part for $100 that will cost them $100 in the long run than to pay $70 for a part that will ultimately cost them $120. This is known as **cost-based procurement.**

COST-BASED PROCUREMENT A buyer strategy that considers *cost* over the long run rather than only *price* in the short run.

Supplier Analysis

To determine whether suppliers can satisfy demands for quality, cost containment, delivery, and technological advancement, organizational customers send teams of experts from their purchasing, quality assurance, marketing, engineering, manufacturing, logistics, and finance departments to visit suppliers. These teams check on quality control, inventory management, financial strength, management depth, technical competence, business plans, and employee training. Suppliers who survive these grueling investigations and show promise of further improvements are welcomed as "partners" and given a larger share of the customer's business.

Supplier Partnering

Many buyers and sellers form a partnership that resembles a marriage. The two parties promise to care for each other "in sickness or in health, for richer and for

[3]Ibid., pp. 18–22.

When customers accept suppliers as partners, they give them the opportunity to become involved early in solving their problems and developing specifications for new products.

poorer"—in short, no matter what the economic times. If you make buyers look good, you will strengthen the "marriage." If you make buyers look bad, you will be "divorced" and replaced by another supplier. A survey of industrial buyers by Learning International of Stanford, Connecticut, found that when a buyer drops a supplier, the reason is usually a "breach of partnership." In a partnership, the relationship goes far beyond price. The buyer shares more internal company data with the supplier than is typical in buyer-seller relationships, and expects reciprocal commitments and loyalty. Some companies confirm the supplier's commitment to them by tracking the supplier's performance. When Union Pacific Railroad monitored suppliers' on-time performance in 1987, it found that 40 percent of orders arrived late. Since then, late arrivals are down to 14 percent.[4]

Early Supplier Involvement

When customers accept suppliers as partners, they give them the opportunity to become involved early in solving the customers' problems and developing specifications for new products. Called "quality function deployment" (QFD) or "voice of the customer" by the Japanese, this partnering strategy uses buyer-seller teams to design, produce, and ship products that will fully satisfy customers' needs and help them sell to their customers.

[4]*The Wall Street Journal,* July 27, 1989, p. 1.

Selling in Action

The Typical Industrial Salesperson

■ Works nearly 9 hours per day, 240 days a year.

■ Spends 25 percent of working time in actual face-to-face selling, 25 percent traveling and waiting, 22 percent on reports, paperwork, and attending sales meetings, 17 percent selling to customers and prospects by telephone, 8 percent on service calls, and 3 percent on other activities. Exact use of time varies widely, depending on the industry. In the chemical industry, 34 percent of the salesperson's time is spent in face-to-face selling and only 13 percent on the telephone. In the instruments industry, 16 percent of the salesperson's time is taken up by face-to-face selling and 27 percent is spent on the telephone.

■ Uses both face-to-face and telephone selling methods to call on 179 active and 216 prospective accounts annually for a total of 395 companies.

■ Makes 5 personal sales calls per day, spending 25 minutes with each individual.

■ Makes about 9 telephone calls daily to customers and prospects.

■ Contacts about 1,272 prospects and customers in person and 2,088 by telephone in the course of a year.

■ Sees assigned buying influencers about 3 times per year for a total of only about 70 minutes a year with each of these people.

■ Makes 4 sales calls to close an average industrial sale, but may make as many as 11.

Nearly 20 percent of industrial salespeople will leave their present job within a year. Of these, 38 percent will resign, 27 percent will be fired, 6 percent will retire, and the remaining 29 percent will leave for various other reasons.

Source: Based on information from McGraw-Hill Research Department, Dartnell Corporation, and *Sales & Marketing Management* magazine, as summarized in Robert W. Haas, *Industrial Marketing Management,* 4th ed. (Boston: PWS-Kent, 1989), pp. 302–303.

General Motors and Ford Motor Company have publicly acknowledged the important role suppliers of all their products and services play in their companies' success. GM ran a full-page message of appreciation in *The Philadelphia Inquirer,* which read in part: "To our GM family: Thanks for making us number one again. . . . Our success has been a direct result of the caring and dedication of all the people in our worldwide GM family—our 775,000 employees, 15,000 dealers, and more than 35,000 suppliers."[5] In a full-page ad in *The Wall Street Journal,* Ford Motor Company listed the names of its suppliers who were awarded its Q1 Preferred Quality Award for "helping us in our goal to build the highest-quality cars and trucks in the world."[6]

The Role of the Industrial Salesperson

Modern industrial sales reps must not only solve their own customers' problems, they must also help their customers satisfy *their* customers' needs. Today's industrial customers recognize that they cannot produce better-quality products and

[5]*The Philadelphia Inquirer,* February 12, 1990, p. 8-B.
[6]*The Wall Street Journal,* September 27, 1980, p. B3.

services without obtaining better-quality products and services from their suppliers. Since raw supplies and services make up about 60 percent of a company's expenses, sales reps must help their business customers become more profitable, not just sell them products. To win larger market shares and become more profitable, customers are demanding ever-improving quality levels, JIT (just-in-time) shipments, and information on the latest technologies. The challenging work of the typical industrial salesperson is described below.

WHAT DO INDUSTRIAL MARKETS BUY?

The industrial buying process, with its diverse buying influences and products, can be put into perspective by classifying industrial goods on the basis of their relationship to the organization's production process and cost structure. Industrial buyers are interested in three basic categories of goods and services: (1) foundation goods, (2) entering goods, and (3) facilitating goods. Let's briefly consider each of them.

Foundation Goods

FOUNDATION GOODS
Goods that are used in the production process but do not become part of the finished product, such as fixed major equipment and office equipment.

Foundation goods are those used in the production process that do not become a part of the finished product. They usually consist of installations and accessory equipment. Installations are the fixed major equipment (turbines, electric generators, huge machine tools); accessory equipment includes portable or light factory tools (forklift trucks, hand tools) and office equipment (file cabinets, typewriters).

Are these industrial robots foundation, facilitating, or entering goods?

ENTERING GOODS
Ingredients or components that become part of the finished product, such as raw materials and semimanufactured goods.

Entering Goods

Entering goods are components that become part of the finished product. They include raw materials (wheat, iron ore, livestock), semimanufactured goods (flour, sheet steel, textiles), parts (automobile batteries and tires, electric motors), and contract manufacturing services (dyeing, casting, shaping).

Facilitating Goods

FACILITATING GOODS
Goods consumed while assisting in the ongoing production process, such as maintenance and repair items.

Usually budgeted as expenses because they are consumed while assisting the ongoing production process, **facilitating goods** include maintenance and repair items (repair parts, paint, nails), operating supplies (lubricants, paper, pencils), and business services (janitorial, consulting, or advertising services).

HOW DO INDUSTRIAL MARKETS BUY?

Buying Centers

In larger organizations, it is realistic to refer to industrial purchasing operations as "buying centers" because there are several people involved in the purchasing decisions. A buying center includes everyone in the organization who plays any of the following six roles in the buying process:

- *Initiators:* People who first recognize or anticipate a problem that may be solved by buying a good or service.
- *Gatekeepers:* People who control information or access to decision makers. Purchasing agents, technical advisers, secretaries, and even telephone switchboard operators can assume this role by preventing salespeople from seeing users or deciders. By the way, never snub secretaries. Almost 40 percent of the secretaries at smaller companies can buy items costing up to $100 without consulting their boss. One in eleven secretaries can make purchases of $2,100 or more. In situations where sales reps cannot win over gatekeepers, they will have to find ways to subtly go around them to make sales.
- *Influencers:* People who influence the purchase decision by helping to set specifications or by providing information about evaluating alternatives. Technical specialists are usually important influencers.
- *Deciders:* Normally higher-level managers who have the power to select or approve suppliers and final purchase decisions. For routine purchases, the purchasing agents are the deciders.
- *Buyers:* People with formal authority to order supplies and negotiate purchase terms within organizational constraints.
- *Users:* People who will actually use the product or service purchased. Users are generally people in production, including machine operators, shop foremen, and supervisors. They often initiate the buying proposal and help decide product specifications.[7]

[7]Thomas V. Bonoma, "Major Sales: Who Really Does the Buying?" *Harvard Business Review,* May–June 1982, p. 113.

Company _____

Address _____

Telephone _____ Fax _____

Products/Services Purchased _____

Role	Name	Position	Available
Initiator	George Gipp	Foreman	MTWTH 1-3 p.m.
Gatekeeper	Cathy Sullivan	Secretary	MWF 9-11 a.m.
Influencer	David Swartz	Engineer	TTH 10-12 a.m.
Decider	Wanda Perez	Plant Manager	MWF 2-4 p.m.
Buyer	Ivan Piccolo	Purchasing Agent	MWTH 9-12 a.m.
User	Gene Anders	Machinist	TWTH 3-5 p.m.

FIGURE 6-1 Buying Center Organization Chart

In most buying centers, many people are involved in the purchase decision, and the most successful sales reps get to know them all and the roles they play. In fact, it is common for sales reps to virtually move in with large customers (that is, to work with them on a daily basis) so they can stay attuned to the shifting multiple buying influences in order to do multilevel, in-depth, consultative selling. Ask the salespeople in any company if, with most of their customers, they are dealing with the same purchasing agents today as they were five years ago, and usually the answer is no. Farsighted salespeople try to get to know all the members of the purchasing department so that their relationship with the company doesn't depend on just one person. In other words, they don't put all their eggs in one basket. Many industrial salespeople maintain an up-to-date Buying Center Organization Chart like the one shown in Figure 6-1 for each of their customers. What other information would you include on this chart?

Types of Buying Situations

In making a purchase, industrial buyers face a series of decisions that depend on the buying situation. As illustrated in Figure 6-2, there are three basic types of buying situations: (1) straight rebuy, (2) modified rebuy, and (3) new task. Purchasing agents are most influential in straight and modified rebuys, which involve, respectively, routine and limited problem-solving skills, while engineers are most influential in new-task buying, which involves extensive problem-solving skills.[8]

Straight Rebuy

When a buyer routinely reorders a product from a supplier, the purchase is called a *straight rebuy*. The buying decision is usually made by a single purchas-

[8]Earl Naumann, Douglas J. Lincoln, and Robert D. McWilliams, "The Purchase of Components: Functional Areas of Influence," *Industrial Marketing Management,* May 1984, p. 118.

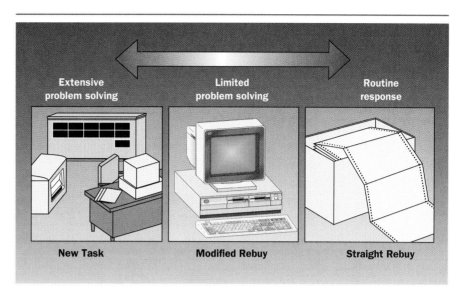

FIGURE 6-2 Three Types of Industrial Buying

ing agent. Examples of straight rebuys are the purchase of office supplies, utilities, and bulk chemicals. Once suppliers have been placed on the customer's approved list of suppliers, they strive to maintain product and service quality and encourage automatic reordering systems that have the double benefit of saving the purchasing agent time and keeping out other suppliers. Suppliers not on a company's approved list must offer the prospective customer something new or provide incentives like price discounts or broader service guarantees to get their foot in the door.

With the increasing computerization of purchasing departments, competition among sellers of industrial goods has become more intense because more suppliers are solicited for proposals and higher standards are being applied for supplier performance. For companies that handle routine ordering by computers following programmed decision rules, it is essential for the supplier to be in the computer's "memory banks" as one of the company's regular suppliers. Sales reps must keep abreast of changing computer buying routines and the enlarged responsibilities of industrial buyers.

Modified Rebuy

A more complex decision-making process is required for the *modified rebuy,* in which the buyer seeks a change in product specifications, prices, or supplier performance. Several people may be involved in the final buying decision. In this situation, "in" suppliers run scared and "out" suppliers try to induce the buyer to try them. Examples of modified rebuys are the purchase of consulting services, company vehicles, and heavy equipment.

New Task

The most complex buying situation is the *new task,* in which the buyer considers the purchase of a relatively complex product for the first time. Many people may be involved in the final buying decision. The new-task situation represents the greatest opportunity for new suppliers, who can use specialized teams of mis-

TABLE 6-6 Strategies for "In" and "Out" Suppliers

BUYING SITUATION	"IN" SUPPLIER	"OUT" SUPPLIER
Straight Rebuy	Reinforce buyer-seller relationship by meeting organization's expectations. Be alert and responsive to changing needs of customers.	Convince organization that the potential benefits of reexamining requirements and suppliers exceed the cost. Attempt to gain a position on the organization's approved list of suppliers even as a second or third choice.
Modified Rebuy	Act immediately to remedy problems with customer. Reexamine and respond to customer needs.	Define and respond to the organization's problems with existing supplier. Encourage organization to sample alternative offerings.
New-Task Buying	Monitor changing purchasing needs in customer organization. Isolate specific needs. If possible, participate actively in early phases of the buying process by supplying information and technical advice.	Actively search for leads. Isolate specific needs. If possible, participate actively in early phases of buying process by supplying information and technical advice.

Source: Adapted from P. J. Robinson, C. W. Faris, and Y. Wind, *Industrial Buying and Creative Marketing* (Boston, Mass.: Allyn & Bacon, 1967), p. 28.

sionary salespeople and technical experts to make comprehensive presentations that "sell" the supplier company to the prospective buyer. Examples of new-task situations are the purchase of a huge installation such as a heating plant or the construction of a new building.

To some extent, there will be "in" and "out" suppliers in all three buying situations, though this phenomenon is perhaps easiest to understand in the context of the straight and modified rebuys. You might think that everybody is "out" in the event of a new-task situation, but this is not necessarily so. Past or discontinued business transactions between a prospective supplier and a prospective buyer or any number of changes in circumstances can suddenly provide enormous "in" leverage in a new-task situation. It is the alert, well-informed sales rep who is most often aware of and able to seize such opportunities. Table 6-6 suggests how "in" and "out" suppliers should approach the three different buying situations.

Stages in the Buying Process

Today's industrial buyers usually know much more about industrial selling behavior than the industrial salesperson knows about industrial buying behavior. So unless salespeople learn how their potential customers make their buying decisions, they will be severely disadvantaged. Thoroughly researching and understanding the customers' buying process is one of the selling secrets of supersalespeople. There are eight major stages in the industrial buying process: (1) recognizing the problem, (2) describing the basic need, (3) developing product specifications, (4) searching for suppliers, (5) soliciting proposals, (6) evaluating proposals and selecting suppliers, (7) setting up the ordering procedure, and (8) reviewing performance.

Recognizing the Problem

The window of opportunity opens for the alert salesperson whenever a prospect complains about another supplier's equipment or products, a new problem arises, or the prospect is considering the purchase of additional equipment or products. Of course, if it is *your* products that are not performing well, you're challenged to address the complaints or problems fast enough to keep the customer's business. You must remain continually sensitive to means of improving the profitability of your customers' operations by anticipating problems and alerting customers to opportunities.

Describing the Basic Need

After recognizing the problem, the industrial buyer tries to better define the general characteristics of the needed item through discussions with company engineers, research and development scientists, or line managers. At this stage, the buyer organization usually runs a feasibility study to determine whether it would be better off making the item or buying it.

Developing Product Specifications

Detailed technical specifications are developed by the buying organization to ensure that no error is made and that suppliers will provide the exact item needed. Any confusion about specifications (dimensions, quality, or quantity) can result in costly manufacturing delays for the customer and lost business (rejected items) for the supplier. Many times, especially with government customers, suppliers help to write tight specs to enable their own companies to get the business. Most buyers, however, oppose product specifications that are so rigid that they limit consideration of alternative suppliers. No buyer wants to be at the mercy of a sole supplier.

Searching for Suppliers

Using product specifications as the guide, the buyer tries to identify qualified potential suppliers. Trade directories and recommendations from other industrial buyers are useful in this search phase. Aggressive sales organizations will probably have already solicited business with most potential customers, but unsolicited "call-ins" are still a valuable source of sales. (The inside salespeople who handle these call-ins need to be as well trained as outside salespeople.) Beyond this, salespeople need to do all they can to ensure that their company and its offerings are listed in all appropriate trade directories and that the company's reputation as a supplier remains favorable. Repeat business and referrals from satisfied customers are the fastest, most secure ways to a profitable sales operation.

Soliciting Proposals

Industrial buyers will usually invite qualified suppliers to submit sales proposals and bids for producing and selling the specified items. After reviewing these proposals, the buyer will often invite the more promising potential suppliers to make a formal presentation. Thus professional salespeople must be trained to research, prepare, and present proposals so that they "sell" the company as well as the technical product. In preparing and presenting sales proposals, salespeople should keep in mind the five basic decision criteria used by nearly all organizational buyers:

1. *Performance criteria:* How well will the product or service do the required job?
2. *Economic criteria:* What are the total costs associated with buying and using the product or service?
3. *Integrative criteria:* Will the supplier be flexible and responsive in working closely with us to meet our changing requirements and expectations?
4. *Adaptive criteria:* How certain is it that the seller will produce and deliver according to specifications and terms?
5. *Legalistic criteria:* What legal or policy parameters must be considered in buying the product or service?[9]

Evaluating Proposals and Selecting Suppliers

In reviewing the proposals prior to awarding a contract, industrial buying organizations will evaluate the potential supplier on various criteria. These criteria vary according to the size and nature of the buying organization as well as the type of product. Delivery capability, product quality, service, technical ability, and price are usually most important in buying technically complex products.[10] Within the buying center, the engineering department is the most influential in new-task buying, while the purchasing department has the most influence in straight rebuys and modified rebuys.[11] Indicating the importance of supplier performance to successful marketing, the most serious concerns that Japanese companies have about ventures in America focus on suppliers, not competitors. Says one executive: "In Japan our suppliers deliver on schedule. But in America they are sometimes behind. That delays all our production schedules; our investment is dead, our capital tied up."[12] Table 6-7 lists the rules of thumb industrial buyers use in selecting suppliers.

Setting Up the Ordering Procedure

Instead of preparing a new contract for each periodic purchase order, most industrial buyers prefer *blanket contracts* that establish an open purchase arrangement over a stated period at a certain price. Computerized ordering procedures are common for staple supplies. An order is automatically printed out and teletyped or faxed to the designated supplier whenever inventory reaches a specified level. Sales reps usually encourage blanket purchase agreements when they win an order because such agreements promote single-source buying.

Reviewing Performance

Many industrial buyers regularly contact the end-user departments in their company to obtain feedback on the performance of suppliers. Sometimes taking the form of detailed, formal ratings, these performance reviews shape relationships with suppliers by continuing, modifying, or terminating purchase orders. Sales representatives should constantly review their own performances so that potential problems are "nipped in the bud."

[9]Robert W. Haas, *Industrial Marketing Management: Text and Cases,* 4th ed. (Boston: PWS-Kent, 1989), p. 105.
[10]William A. Dempsey, "Vendor Selection and the Buying Process," *Industrial Marketing Management,* August 1978, p. 259.
[11]Earl Naumann, Douglas J. Lincoln, and Robert D. McWilliams, "The Purchase of Components: Functional Areas of Influence," *Industrial Marketing Management,* May 1984, p. 118.
[12]*Business Week,* July 16, 1980, p. 98.

TABLE 6-7   How Industrial Buyers Select Winning Bidders

Based on interviews in 18 industrial buying centers, these are the decision rules used by members of industrial buying centers to simplify the process of selecting a winning bidder:

■ Find potential vendors for the bidders' list. For straight and modified rebuy products, use existing lists of potential suppliers kept by buyers. For new buys, talk to design engineers and other buyers, draw on past experience, and search trade journals.

■ Qualify satisfactory vendors. Use local distributors when immediate availability of large numbers of parts in small quantities is essential. Use manufacturers and avoid distributors' margin of profit when a predictable usage pattern exists for a large quantity needed; establish that manufacturers have the capacity, quality, and reasonable transportation costs to fill the order.

■ Invite bids from vendors. Try to get bids from at least three suppliers. Relax criteria when necessary to achieve this number. Increase the number of bids when the size and importance of the purchase warrant it. Tighten criteria when necessary to restrict the number of bidders to six.

■ Evaluate the bids. Have the purchasing department conduct a commercial evaluation, including price, transportation, and tooling costs, delivery schedule, and past performance. Have engineering and production people conduct a technical evaluation to assess the bidder's ability to meet specifications. Drop bidders who are not within 3–6 percent of the lowest bid price or who do not satisfy technical requirements.

■ Select the winning bidder. Select two suppliers if the volume and importance of the product warrant it, dividing the contract equally if their prices are within 1 percent of each other or giving a larger contract to the lower bidder. Otherwise select a single supplier. Select the lowest bidder unless past performance justifies choosing the second lowest.

Source: Niren Vyas and Arch Woodside, "An Inductive Model of Industrial Supplier Choice Processes," *Journal of Marketing,* Winter 1984, pp. 30–45.

SYSTEMS BUYING AND SELLING

Buyers often prefer to purchase a whole system rather than make a series of smaller decisions. Instead of buying separate components and trying to put them together, the buyer solicits bids from suppliers to assemble the entire package or system. An example of systems buying is the federal government's purchase of a

Organizational buyers often prefer to purchase a whole system rather than make a series of smaller decisions.

major weapons system. In this instance, systems selling involves two steps. First, the supplier company's proposal must show that the supplier can produce and provide all the interconnected products and services—delivery devices, repair parts, maintenance equipment and supplies, and training of operating personnel as well as the basic weapon. Second, the supplier must prove that it has a management system capable of smoothly handling production, inventory control, distribution, and other necessary services.

An international example of systems selling is a Japanese company that won a huge contract (even though its price was much higher than competitors') to build a cement factory for the Indonesian government by providing a more complete system than the lower-bidding American firms. In their proposal, the Japanese agreed to choose the site, design the cement factory, hire the construction crews, assemble the materials and equipment, hire and train workers to run the factory, export the cement through their trading companies, and use the cement to build needed roads and office buildings.[13]

RESELLER MARKETS

Resellers include all those intermediary organizations that buy goods for reselling or renting to others at a profit or for conducting their own operations. Since resellers serve as purchasing agents for their customers, they buy products and brands they think will appeal to their customers. There are three categories of resellers:

- *Industrial distributors,* which sell to manufacturers and producers.
- *Wholesalers,* which sell to retailers.
- *Retailers,* which sell to consumers.

Industrial Distributors

There are approximately 12,000 industrial distributors; their average yearly sales volume is about $4 million each. Industrial distributors handle a variety of products: maintenance, repair, and operating (MRO) supplies; original equipment that becomes part of the manufacturer's finished products; and tools, equipment, and machinery used in the operation of the manufacturer's business. There are three kinds of industrial distributors. *General-line distributors* (mill supply houses) are the "supermarkets" of industry because of the broad range of products they carry. *Specialist firms* stock a narrow line of related products, such as bearings, abrasives, and cutting tools. Because general-line houses have developed specialist departments, the difference between them and specialist companies is not always clear. Finally, a third type, the *combination house,* often operates like both a wholesaler and an industrial distributor by selling to retailers and institutions in addition to manufacturers and construction firms.

---

[13]Philip Kotler and Gary Armstrong, *Principles of Marketing* (Englewood Cliffs, N.J.: Prentice Hall, 1989), p. 172.

TABLE 6-8 Types of Middlemen Serving Retailers

TYPE OF MIDDLEMAN	CHARACTERISTICS
Service (regular) wholesaler	Serves as the retailer's buying agent by assembling, collecting, and storing goods, providing fast delivery, extending credit, and furnishing market information. These services appeal especially to small and medium-sized retailers.
Limited-function wholesaler	Charges less but provides less service; e.g., does not grant credit or offer delivery service. Offers only fast-moving items; may do business only by mail.
Rack jobber	Supplies mainly nonfood items to supermarkets. Sets up displays, maintains merchandise assortment, and receives payment only on goods actually sold, thereby guaranteeing a prespecified percent markup to the outlet.
Broker	Receives a commission to bring retail buyers and suppliers together; does not handle merchandise or take title to goods. Handles only a few lines—mainly grocery specialties, dry goods, fruits, vegetables, drugs, and hardware.
Commission agent	Similar to broker but physically handles merchandise; does not take title to goods; supplies mainly large retailers with dry goods, grocery specialties, fruits, and vegetables.
Manufacturer's agent	Provides services similar to those of a salesperson; restricted to a limited territory and has limited authority to negotiate price and terms of sale; sells only part of client's output.
Selling agent	Similar to manufacturer's agent, except that selling agent is responsible for selling the entire output of client.
Auctioneer	Places product on display and sells it to highest bidder. Used mainly to sell livestock, fruits, and vegetables to small restaurants, large chains, or other wholesalers.

Wholesalers

Over 370,000 wholesaling organizations operate in the United States. Their total annual sales volume is well over $1 trillion, and they employ more than 4.2 million people. Contrary to predictions of a few decades ago that wholesalers would decline in numbers and importance, they have more than doubled over the past 40 years and their sales volume has tripled. Almost half of all manufactured consumer goods go through wholesalers. They handle 90 percent of all hardware goods and nearly 70 percent of all drugstore merchandise. Salespeople who sell to retailers work for various types of wholesalers and other middlemen, whose characteristics are listed in Table 6-8.

Retailers

Employing 15 percent of the civilian labor force, about 2 million retailers in the United States annually sell over $1.5 trillion worth of goods and services to consumers. Chain stores—centrally owned and managed groups of retail stores—account for over one-third of all retail sales, even though they make up less than 1 percent of all retail establishments. Despite the growing importance of chains, single-unit independently owned stores still dominate retailing. This ownership category accounts for over 90 percent of all retail stores and nearly 60 percent of sales. Most retail store salespeople (often called *salesclerks*) are little more than order takers and have traditionally been paid poor hourly wages. Only recently have a few large chains begun offering commissions on sales to all their retail salespeople.

A large part of the reseller's job is to decide what merchandise mix to offer customers.

WHAT AND HOW DO RESELLERS BUY?

Both wholesaler and retailer resellers purchase everything produced except for goods that manufacturers sell directly to ultimate consumers such as custom-made industrial equipment and products sold only door-to-door or via direct mail. Because there is such a vast array of products and services that might be sold or rented, a large part of the reseller's job is to decide what product mix (*merchandise mix* is the term more commonly used by retailers) to offer customers. Retailers generally look at product or merchandise assortments from three planning perspectives: *width, support,* and *dollars.*

Width

Merchandise assortments must match market demands and meet competition in terms of product brands, sizes, colors, fabrics, and prices. Consider the decisions determining the width of a store's assortment of shirts that creates 1,920 line items:

Brands (5)	5
Sizes (small, medium large, extra large)	× 4
Colors (8)	× 8
Fabrics (knit, cotton)	× 2
Prices (6)	× 6
	= 1,920

Support

Using his or her knowledge of the consumer market segment served, the retail buyer must decide how many shirts to buy in each of the 1,920 categories. Sales representatives can assist buyers in this risky task by sharing the experiences of other retailers. It is important that sales reps not take advantage of the buyer's uncertainty in such situations if a trusting, long-run relationship is the objective.

Dollars

Retail managers restrict the flexibility of buyers in planning the width and support of merchandise ordered by limiting the number of dollars that can be invested in inventory. In each planning period, buyers must work with a certain purchasing budget, known as an "open-to-buy" (OTB). The retail manager's job is to try to obtain the highest merchandise turnover rate without creating frequent "out-of-stock" situations that may cause customers to shop elsewhere.

Most industrial distributors, wholesalers, and retailers are independently owned reseller businesses. But those that have evolved into chains or that participate in a cooperative operation usually have centralized resident buying offices with purchasing specialists for each type of product. A common practice is to use a "buying committee" as a buffer between the sales rep and the buyer. Although some buyers have great latitude to buy or reject items, most often they merely screen items for presentation at the regular buying committee meeting. Of course, as the expert in the product category, the individual buyer serves as a "gatekeeper" who decides what to tell the committee members. Normally, the buyer's recommendations to buy or reject an item are followed. Buyers for resellers tend to fall into one of seven categories in terms of what influences them most:

1. *Loyal buyer:* Remains loyal to a supplier year after year as long as performance is satisfactory.
2. *Opportunistic buyer:* Selects vendors according to which will best serve his or her short-term interests.
3. *Best-deal buyer:* Selects the best deal available at a given time.
4. *Creative buyer:* Tells the seller what he or she expects in terms of product quality, services, and prices.
5. *Advertising buyer:* Tries to obtain advertising money as part of every purchase.
6. *Chiseler:* Attempts to negotiate extra price concessions on every purchase. Usually chooses vendor offering the highest discount or special deal.
7. *Nuts-and-bolts buyer:* Selects the products that are made the best.[14]

Reseller Buying Situations

Sales representatives dealing with reseller buyers should know that resellers regularly find themselves involved in three particular types of buying situations. Let's discuss each briefly.

[14]Roger A. Dickinson, *Buyer Decision Making* (Berkeley, Calif.: Institute of Business and Economic Research, 1967), pp. 14–17.

The *new-product situation* arises when suppliers are seeking distribution for a newly developed product. Since storage and display space are always at a premium, the buyer must often determine what item to drop when ordering a new product for stock. Many buyers estimate potential *profit per cubic foot* before making a decision. A panel of supermarket buyers identified six criteria most often used to make decisions on purchasing new products: (1) pricing and profit margins, (2) the product's uniqueness and the strength of the product category, (3) the seller's intended positioning and marketing plan for the product, (4) the test market evidence of consumer acceptance of the product, (5) advertising and sales promotion support for the product, and (6) the selling company's reputation.[15] Many supermarket chains also demand "slotting allowances" or payments up front before they will make room for a new product on their shelves. Some supermarkets even demand "pay to stay" payments to keep the manufacturer's products on the shelves.

The second reseller buying situation is *selection of the best supplier* from several when space limitations permit only one or two brands in a product category, or when a private-label supplier is needed for the reseller's own house brand. For example, K Mart chose Sherwin-Williams to make its private-label paints.

The third buying situation comes about when the reseller wants to obtain *a better set of terms from current suppliers.* McDonald's, the world's most successful food franchiser, decided a few years ago to buy all its food and nonfood products from one supplier. Golden State Foods Corporation, which was supplying McDonald's burgers, buns, and potatoes, was forced to take on a line of paper products to keep McDonald's business, which accounted for 80 percent of Golden State's sales at the time. Even though the Robinson-Patman Act prohibits *suppliers and their sales reps* from practicing price discrimination among similar buyers (unless true cost differentials can be shown), sales reps know that *buyers* will often pressure *them* for more services, higher discounts, or easier credit terms.

Reseller Information Systems

PROFESSIONAL RESELLER MANAGER A modern-day scientific- and information-oriented buyer for a reseller.

The 1980s saw the rise of the **professional reseller manager,** who is more scientific and information-oriented than his predecessor. Although electronic point-of-sale (POS) systems and in-store computers began appearing in retail outlets in the early 1970s, computer software packages that efficiently provide inventory, purchase, cash flow, and accounts payable information were slow in arriving. Installation of checkout scanners has generated an abundance of timely and specific data about consumer response. Instead of receiving monthly or bimonthly reports about how a brand is doing, retailers now get weekly data for every item and size. They are learning precisely how a price cut, promotional coupon, store display, or discount to the retailer actually affects their sales and profits. Nestlé Foods Corporation discovered that a combination of store displays and newspaper ads resulted in large-volume increases for its chocolate drink Quik. Warner-Lambert Company found that store displays were far more effective than newspaper ads or price promotions, and its sales force now focuses on providing incentives to supermarket managers to set up in-store displays.

---

[15]"Retailers Rate New Products," *Sales & Marketing Management,* November 1986, pp. 75–77.

What Would You Do?

Your company, Celestial Creations, has developed an exciting new line of colognes for men called Manly Aromas that will be aimed at successful, confident men who "are unafraid to be adventurous." Gross margins on these colognes will be nearly 60 percent for the exclusive department stores who handle them. Although the market for men's cologne is small, its growth potential seems great. One medium-sized department store chain has already bought the entire line of Manly Aromas products. As a sales rep for a small, relatively unknown company, however, you are having a hard time getting to see buyers to make your sales presentation. Most buyers' receptionists and secretaries keep giving excuses for not scheduling an appointment for you. You're wondering how best to get around these *gatekeepers* to talk to the buyers.

Computer-Assisted Buying and Merchandising

More and more reseller buyers are using computer programs to solicit vendors for proposals, prepare purchase orders (especially under blanket purchase agreements), calculate economic order quantities (EOQ), control inventories, and keep track of unit and dollar volumes of sales with each supplier. Gaining admittance to the buyer's computer memory as a qualified supplier and becoming familiar with the buyer's computer purchasing routines are critical tasks for sales reps. Many buyers use computers to send orders directly to the supplier's receiving computer terminals, and the supplier's computer automatically prepares shipping invoices so that buyer stocks are replenished quickly.

Programmed computers may even carry out assortment and merchandising strategies. For instance, Sears, Roebuck and Company is testing a central merchandising system in which headquarters merchandise managers use a CRT (cathode-ray tube) screen to analyze inventory and stock movements on an outlet-by-outlet basis and make decisions to shift merchandise among stores or drop lines. Casual Corner, the 235-unit specialty store chain, has over 800 electronic point-of-sales terminals that feed sales and inventory information via telephone lines into the chain's central computer in Connecticut. Giant Foods has its entire chain, from computerized store cash registers to distribution centers for automatic stock replenishment, connected to a single information network. Information can readily be collected at the point of sale because of the availability of standard stock marking technology such as the universal product code (UPC) for the food industry and OCR-A (optical character recognition, font A) for general merchandise retailing.

Computer-Assisted Selling to Resellers

Peg Fisher, a sales consultant in Racine, Wisconsin, says: "Today's customers place increasing value upon having information. The person who has access to

TABLE 6-9   Special Inducements in Selling to Resellers

Automatic reordering systems: Seller sets up system and provides forms for automatic reordering of products by reseller.

Preticketing: Seller places a tag on each product listing its price, color, size, manufacturer, and identification number so that the reseller can keep track of products sold.

Stockless purchasing: Seller carries the inventory and delivers goods to the reseller on short notice.

Cooperative advertising: Seller pays part of the reseller's costs when advertising the seller's products.

Advertising aids: Seller provides in-store displays, glossy photos, broadcast scripts.

Special prices: Seller reduces prices for store promotions that attract customer traffic.

Sponsoring in-store demonstrations: Seller sets up a demonstration in the store to show shoppers how a product works and to persuade them to buy it.

Generous allowances: Seller gives good allowance for reseller returns, exchanges, and markdowns of seller products.

Source: Based in part on Philip Kotler, *Marketing Management: Analysis, Planning, Implementation, and Control* (Englewood Cliffs, N.J.: Prentice Hall, 1988), p. 227.

the best information is the person on the inside."[16] After outfitting its salespeople with laptop computers, Evan-Picone Hosiery sharply reduced the turnaround time between receiving, manufacturing, and delivering sales orders. In addition, Evan-Picone can spot fashion trends earlier now that they know the status of every order for every product.

As reseller information systems based on computerized purchasing operations increase in sophistication, the professional salesperson's job will rapidly shift toward providing buyers with detailed and comprehensive data. There will always be room for salespeople with special flair and talent, but most will find themselves relying less on personality and persuasive skills and more on extensive preparation to supply potential buyers with timely information in the desired format for purchase decisions. Some large manufacturers' salespeople have already gotten an edge on the competition by providing retailer customers with individualized merchandising service. For example, sales reps for R. J. Reynolds show retailers various ways to increase profits by better use of display space, new merchandising techniques, and improved inventory control. (See Table 6-9 for several other sales and marketing tools that can help salespeople make their offerings more attractive to resellers.)

GOVERNMENT MARKETS

The United States government, the 50 state governments, over 3,000 county governments, and nearly 86,000 local government units purchase more than $1 trillion worth of goods and services every year. The federal government, accounting for over 40 percent of the total spent by all government levels, is the largest customer in the nation.

Government markets offer opportunities for both producers and middlemen to sell all sorts of products from spacecraft to toothpaste—everything needed to provide citizens with necessary services like national defense, fire and police protection, education, health care, water, postal service, waste disposal,

[16]Sara Delano, "Turning Sales Inside Out," *INC.,* August 1983, p. 200.

and public transportation. Government purchasing patterns sometimes change abruptly in response to budget constraints or the service demands of citizens, which can present a problem—or an opportunity—to sellers.

How Do Governments Buy?

Because governments spend public funds derived largely from taxes, the law requires that they make purchases on the basis of bids or written proposals from vendors. Although purchasing procedures are rigorous in order to ensure honest, efficient expenditures, selling to governments can be very profitable for sellers willing to wrestle with the inevitable bureaucratic red tape. The basic goal of government purchasing agents is to obtain goods and services from qualified suppliers at the lowest cost. Sometimes, however, this goal takes second place to such objectives as favoring small businesses, minority-owned companies, or suppliers from economically depressed areas. For example, a 5 percent differential in price is allowed to firms with fewer than 600 employees.[17]

Federal buying is done for two sectors, the civilian and the military. For the civilian sector of the federal government, the General Services Administration (GSA), through its Office of Federal Supply and Services, buys all general goods and services (such as office furniture, equipment, supplies, vehicles, and fuels) for use by other government agencies. Defense Department purchases are made by the Defense Supply Agency (DSA) and the three military services, the army, navy, and air force. The DSA operates specialized supply centers that function as "single managers" for purchasing and distributing construction materials, electronics, fuel, personnel support, and industrial and general supplies used in common by the army, navy, and air force. In addition, each branch of the military buys for its specialized needs through its own supply system.

Both the DSA and the GSA function like wholesalers and resellers for other government units. Together they account for most federal contracts for goods and services, although nearly 500 other offices in Washington have their own buying functions and procurement policies. In most states, there are procurement offices to help carry out these massive federal government purchasing activities. Booklets explaining the procedures to follow in selling to the federal government can be obtained from the Government Printing Office or from most state governments.[18]

Fear of dealing with the federal bureaucracy prevents many companies from submitting bids for federal government contracts. One survey found that industrial suppliers have the following complaints about the government purchasing process: excessive paperwork, unnecessary regulations, too much emphasis on low prices, delays in decision making, frequent shifts in procurement personnel, and continual policy changes.[19] Suppliers ought to keep in mind, however, that nearly 20 percent of all government contracts are awarded on the basis of only one bid. In other words, there is often little or no competition for government contracts.

---

[17]Stewart W. Husted, Dale L. Varble, and James R. Lowry, *Principles of Modern Marketing* (Boston: Allyn & Bacon, 1989), p. 134.

[18]See Warren H. Suss, "How to Sell to Uncle Sam," *Harvard Business Review*, November–December 1984, pp. 136–144.

[19]Ibid., pp. 44–46, 48, 50, 52.

Government Contracts

Government policy is to encourage supplier competition. Thus most purchases are made by either negotiated contracts or open bids. *Negotiated contracts* are used for buying nonstandard or complex products such as defense-related purchases involving major research and development efforts and high risk. In *open bid buying,* the government invites bids from qualified suppliers on specified items and usually awards the contract to the lowest-cost bidder. Almost all contracts awarded through competitive bidding are firm, fixed-price contracts. This means that the contractor agrees to deliver the purchased item at the price that was bid regardless of actual production costs. It is assumed that the bidding competition will eliminate excessive profits. Suppliers can request to be placed on the bidders' list to receive regular "invitations to bid."

Use a Systematic Approach

In pursuing government contracts, the sales rep must use a systematic approach to keep from being overwhelmed by the size and complexity of government agencies. The federal government has different procedures for purchases over and under $25,000. For those under $25,000, the Small Purchase program provides for preferences for small business, and informal procedures are used. Purchases over $25,000 are determined by formal bidding procedures. In most cases, the low bidder wins if its bid conforms precisely to the bid specifications and the company can demonstrate it has the financial and operational capability to perform as promised. If you expect the government contracts for which you are bidding to be over $25,000, study the *Commerce Business Daily.* Experienced government salespeople say that this daily list of government procurement invitations, contract awards, subcontracting leads, sales of surplus property, and foreign business opportunities is actually more valuable as an indicator of procurement trends than as a source of leads. To learn the names of the senior officers in over 70,000 federal offices, consult Carroll Publishing Company's *Federal Executive Directory* (issued semimonthly). The *United States Government Manual* (put out annually by the Government Printing Office) provides general sketches of each government agency. Finally, the latest *President's Budget Message* will indicate government budgeting and purchasing priorities.

If you expect your bids for government contracts to be under $25,000, you will find the Small Business Administration (SBA) a help. First, purchase a copy of the *U.S. Government Purchasing and Sales Directory* from the Government Printing Office to learn which agencies are most likely to buy your products. Then get a list of the purchasing contract requirements for those agencies from the SBA district or regional office. Obtain Standard Form 129, Bidders Mailing List Application, from any federal contracting office and send a copy to each buying activity in which you have an interest. Include a letter asking that you be notified when your company has been placed on any bidders' list. Register with the SBA's Procurement Automated Source System (PASS) by filing a form at any SBA regional office. This computerized general bidder's list is often used by agencies to search for businesses by product, location, or other characteristics. Finally, make a personal sales call on the agency you want to sell to and meet and develop a personal relationship with the procurement center representatives and the procurement people. If your product is bought through a federal buying office, check the office's bulletin board display of current solicitations. It is important to get to know each agency's representative in charge of Small and Disadvantaged

Business Utilization (SDBU) because these people can be very helpful in describing the workings of their respective agencies and advising marketers how to approach them.

Government Sales Representatives

Many companies have specialized sales forces operating out of Washington, D.C. Goodyear Tire & Rubber Company has a dozen salespeople calling on procurement officials and engineers, and Eastman Kodak assigns a sales manager to Washington for each of its product divisions. Sony has a "government marketing manager" in Washington to ensure that Sony products are on the *multiple awards schedules* that list vendor products, technical descriptions, and prices that the GSA and other agencies use as shopping catalogs. Some large companies (Eastman Kodak, Zenith, and Goodyear) have established special marketing and sales operations to coordinate bids, gather competitive information, and propose projects and products to meet government needs rather than merely respond to government requests. Largely as a result of such efforts, over half of all Zenith's computer sales come from the government market.

According to many salespeople, government selling isn't any more difficult than selling to a commercial customer, though they dread the paperwork and extra time they must devote to finding the right procurement agent and satisfying the frequently changing requirements. But once a salesperson establishes a relationship, repeat sales can be relatively easy and profitable. In dealing with the federal government, a sales representative for J.I. Case Company, a Racine, Wisconsin, manufacturer of cranes and industrial equipment, says: "My job is to keep day-to-day contact with all the federal agencies, looking for sales leads."[20]

Small Businesses

About one-third of all federal purchases are made from small businesses.[21] Even when a large company wins a contract, about 50 percent of the award is subcontracted to smaller companies. Small-business representatives who want to sell to government markets should take the following steps:

- Contact the local field offices of the Small Business Administration (SBA) to obtain detailed directories identifying what products and services are bought by what government agencies and where those agencies are located.
- Contact the Business Service Centers of the General Services Administration, which act as purchasing agents for many items bought by federal agencies.
- Subscribe to *Commerce Business Daily,* which provides detailed listings of government invitations for bids, subcontracting leads, contract awards, and foreign business opportunities.

Many government purchasing agents are becoming more visible and aggressive in soliciting new suppliers by attending trade shows, industry meetings, and professional seminars. Salespeople can often obtain an inside track on government sales by talking with the government representatives at these events.

[20]"Selling to the Government: Out of the Maze," in *1980 Portfolio Sales & Marketing Plans* (New York: Sales and Marketing Management, 1979), pp. 121–126.

[21]Don Hill, "Who Says Uncle Sam's a Tough Sell?" *Sales & Marketing Management,* July 1988, pp. 56–60.

PUBLICATIONS TO HELP YOU SELL
TO THE U.S. GOVERNMENT

Commerce Business Daily. Available from the Department of Commerce. Lists proposals for doing business with the federal government and provides leads and information on foreign government procurements in the United States.

The United States Government Manual. Available from the Government Printing Office. Lists all government agencies, names, and numbers of key officials, field offices, sources of information, and functions of agencies.

Doing Business with the Federal Government. Available free from Business Service Centers of the General Services Administration. Describes policies and procedures, tells whom to contact for information, and advises what agencies buy what products.

Small Business Subcontracting Directory. Available free from Small and Disadvantaged Business Utilization (SDBU) offices at various government agencies or from the Office of Procurement Assistance, SBA. Lists major contractors to the federal government that subcontract to small businesses.

U.S. Government Purchasing and Sales Directory. Available from the Government Printing Office. Designed to tell small businesses what products are purchased by specific agencies.

How to Sell to the U.S. Department of Commerce. Available free from the Department of Commerce, Small and Disadvantaged Business Utilization. Tells what the department buys and how. (Similar books are published by other government agencies.)

NONPROFIT MARKETS

Nonprofit organizations, also called *noncommercial* or *not-for-profit* organizations, include colleges, hospitals, libraries, charities, churches, museums, and such organizations as the National Organization for Women (NOW), the American Association of Retired People (AARP), and the Red Cross. Many nonprofit organizations use buying processes similar to those of commercial businesses, and buy everything from janitorial services to automobiles. Nevertheless, nonprofit organizations do have several distinct characteristics.

Services and Social Change

Rather than marketing and selling a tangible product, nonprofit organizations are involved in distributing ideas and services with the intention of changing people's attitudes and behavior. One of the Sierra Club's goals, for example, is to increase public awareness and concern for environmental issues and problems.

Public Scrutiny

Because of their dependence on public support, tax-exempt status, and operation in the public interest, nonprofit organizations are often under close public scrutiny. For instance, if the director of a prominent charitable organization were to make racist remarks during an evening television interview, that organization might soon find itself with greatly reduced public support.

Multiple Publics

In addition to scrutiny from the general public, nonprofit organizations—like commercial organizations—must answer to multiple stakeholding publics when planning their marketing and distribution campaigns. For example, a college must design its marketing program to reach not only prospective students but also current students, parents of students, alumni, faculty, staff, and business and government organizations.

Today, the Franklin Mountain State Park is one of the unique state parks in America. With 25,000 acres in the heart of El Paso, it is the largest state park in Texas and a wilderness area inhabited by mountain lions, mule deer, bobcat, eagles and hawks...all within a metropolitan area.

But it could just as easily have fallen prey to developers. The Chihuahua Desert mountain range splits the city of El Paso and any developer would regard it as prime real estate. And so Sierra Club member LeBron Hardie and other concerned environmentalists went to work.

Because of their efforts, the 500,000 citizens of El Paso enjoy a wilderness recreation area in their own back yard.

When you join the Sierra Club, you join LeBron Hardie and over 600,000 other dedicated members. People who care about the protection of our parks, forests and wildlife habitat. Your membership will help assure our continued effectiveness. Join Today!

Sierra Club People Make A Difference.

MEMBERSHIP FORM

☐ **Yes,** I want to join! I want to help safeguard our nation's precious natural heritage.

New Member Name _____

Address _____

City/State _____ Zip _____

MEMBERSHIP CATEGORIES

	Individual	Joint
Regular	☐ $33	☐ $41
Supporting	☐ $50	☐ $58
Contributing	☐ $100	☐ $108
Life	☐ $750 (per person)	
Senior	☐ $15	☐ $23
Student	☐ $15	☐ $23
Limited Income	☐ $15	☐ $23

All dues include subscription to *Sierra* ($6) and chapter publications ($1). Dues are not tax deductible.

Enclose check or money order and mail to:

Sierra Club

Dept. H-109, P.O. Box 7959
San Francisco, CA
94120-7959   W-

It is easy to see from this ad piece that this nonprofit organization has a nonfinancial bottom line.

Multiple Objectives

Instead of profits, the "bottom line" for nonprofit organizations consists of multiple financial and nonfinancial goals. For example, a museum might measure its progress by the number of visitors it attracts, the amount of donations it inspires from patrons, the impact of its special monthly exhibits, and the kinds of artwork it acquires for its collection.

DUAL MANAGEMENT Especially of nonprofit organizations, a management system in which both professional managers and specialists without managerial training run an organization, sometimes resulting in conflict.

Dual Management

Finally, nonprofit organizations usually have both professional managers and specialists with managerial responsibilities, and this dual leadership sometimes leads to conflict. A manager with an MBA might find it difficult to agree with a museum curator on specific financial goals; the business manager of a theater may oppose the artistic director's preference for doing little-known modern plays that attract only small audiences.

Sales representatives whose companies have not yet examined their potential sales in nonprofit markets would be wise to study where nonprofit organizations are located and how they operate. Many large charitable, special interest, and political action groups have one national or international headquarters office and several smaller offices in other geographical regions. Thus it is possible for a salesperson who wins an account with the headquarters office to simultaneously win accounts with some or all of the regional offices. For example, boards of education often adopt textbooks for an entire township's or city's public school system. Like selling to government agencies, selling to nonprofit organizations sometimes involves working through bureaucratic red tape. Still, the rewards for sales reps who are persistent can be great.

SUMMARY   In this chapter, we identified the four kinds of *organizational markets* and discussed the various buying processes they employ. After briefly describing ways to segment them, we examined *industrial, reseller, government,* and *nonprofit* organizational markets in detail.

Industrial markets are the largest and most diverse of all the organizational markets and differ significantly from consumer markets in the areas of demand, buyers, purchasing process, and marketing mix. The *Standard Industrial Classification (SIC)* system, set forth in the SIC manual published by the U.S. Office of Management and Budget, provides an excellent source of information for studying industrial markets.

We briefly looked at the roles of individual industrial buyers and industrial salespeople. *Industrial buyers,* the buying experts for their organizations, have turned to such new purchasing strategies as *supplier reduction, single sourcing,* and *cost-based procurement.* Industrial salespeople know that to be successful in the long run they must not only solve their own customers' problems but also help their customers to solve *their* customers' problems.

The rest of the chapter was devoted to the three other types of organizational markets. *Resellers* include *industrial distributors, wholesalers,* and *retailers* who buy goods for reselling or renting to others at a profit or for conducting their own operations. The 1980s saw the rise of the *professional reseller manager* and *computer-assisted buying* in reseller markets. *Government markets* include the federal government and all state and local governments, which purchase goods and services in order to provide citizens with necessary services like fire and police protection, education, and health care. *Nonprofit markets,* which include institutions and organizations like colleges, hospitals, libraries, and charities, purchase goods and services in order to provide people with services, attract donations, or change public attitudes about social concerns and problems.

CHAPTER REVIEW QUESTIONS

1. What are the three levels into which most organizations can be segmented with respect to their buying activities? List some of the individual segmentation variables for each of the three levels.
2. Explain why industrial demand is *derived* demand. Why are industrial markets more price inelastic and volatile than consumer markets?
3. Describe four of the abilities a purchasing agent must have in order to be successful.
4. Name and briefly describe the three categories of goods and services that industrial markets buy.
5. What are the six roles that different members of a buying center can play in the industrial buying process?
6. List and discuss the three types of industrial buying situations.
7. Name and describe the eight stages in the industrial buying process.
8. What are the three kinds of reseller industrial distributors? How do they, as a group, differ from wholesaler and retailer resellers?
9. Briefly discuss government markets. What are the two sectors the federal government buys for? How are most government purchases made?
10. What are the five characteristics that distinguish nonprofit markets from the three other organizational markets?

TOPICS FOR THOUGHT AND CLASS DISCUSSION

1. Why do you think partnerships are becoming increasingly important in buyer-seller relationships? What are the responsibilities of the seller and the buyer to ensure a lasting partnership?
2. Reread the description of "The Typical Industrial Salesperson" on page 169. How does this portrait strike you? Bearing in mind that industrial sales representatives are some of the best trained and most highly paid salespeople of all, do you think you would like the job? Why or why not?
3. Compare the stages in the industrial buying process with the stages in the consumer buying process presented in Chapter 5 by setting up a side-by-side list of the stages. How are they similar and different? How would you account for the similarities and differences between the two processes?
4. In selling to resellers, what are some of the major reasons why sales are lost? What special inducements would you offer as a sales rep to a reseller buyer?

5. If you were a small-business owner who wanted to obtain some federal government contracts, how would you find out how to sell to the government? List, in order, the steps that you would take.

PROJECTS FOR PERSONAL GROWTH

1. Your company's R&D department has developed a chemical compound made from corn by-products that provides airtight sealing properties when coated over various substances. R&D scientists believe that this product, tentatively named Sealatron, will have many uses in the heavy construction industry. They say it may be appropriate for a final coating on top of the outer insulation wrappings for large oil and gas pipes, power lines, and perhaps sewer and water mains. It might also be used for waterproofing the exteriors of commercial buildings. Go to your school library and use the Standard Industrial Classification (SIC) to research the potential markets for this new chemical sealant. How specifically can you define the potential markets by SIC digits?

2. Find a college, university, or public library that subscribes to *Commerce Business Daily* (you can simply telephone the reference desk and ask). Next, call or visit the local field office of the Small Business Administration (SBA) to obtain directories and whatever other information you can to help you identify goods and services bought by various government agencies. Make a list of ten of these products. Then go to the library and, in the latest issue of *Commerce Business Daily*, find the listings of government purchases and proposed purchases. Are any of your ten products listed? If so—and at least one of them should be!—are they civilian or military purchases? Are they listed under invitations for bids, subcontracting leads, contract awards, or foreign business opportunities? (For further study, apply what you have learned in this exercise to the fifth *Topic for Thought and Class Discussion* above.)

KEY TERMS

Buying center In a buying organization, a group of organization members responsible for making purchases.

Derived demand Demand that is created as a result of consumer demand; typical of industrial markets.

Price inelasticity of demand Demand that hardly changes with a small change in price; characteristic of industrial markets.

Reciprocity A mutual exchange of benefits; in industrial buyer-seller relationships, an informal agreement between two or more organizations to exchange goods and services on a systematic and more or less exclusive basis.

Industrial buyer Also called the purchasing agent; the buying expert for an organization.

Cost-based procurement A buyer strategy that considers *cost* over the long run rather than only *price* in the short run.

Foundation goods Goods that are used in the production process but do not become part of the finished product, such as fixed major equipment and office equipment.

Entering goods Ingredients or components that become part of the finished product, such as raw materials and semi-manufactured goods.

Facilitating goods Goods consumed while assisting in the ongoing production process, such as maintenance and repair items.

Professional reseller manager A modern-day scientific- and information-oriented buyer for a reseller.

Dual management Especially of non-profit organizations, a management system in which both professional managers and specialists without managerial training run an organization, sometimes resulting in conflict.

Case 6-1

LEVERAGED BUYOUT CREATES BUYER TURNOVER

Eaton Electronic Company, a manufacturer of electronic motors and controls with annual sales of about $150 million, was a steady customer of Mectronic Supplies Company for nearly four years. Eaton regularly bought all of its rheostats and resistors from Mectronic, and the relationship between the two companies had become almost like a partnership based on mutual trust and respect. Keith Shepherd, a senior sales rep for Mectronic who has serviced the Eaton account for the past four years, developed a particularly close relationship with two Eaton buyers, Debbie Roseman and Roger Dommermuth.

Then, three months ago, a leveraged buyout of Eaton Electronic Company by National Electric Corporation brought about several changes in Eaton's management, from the senior level down through middle management. Eaton's 55-year-old director of purchasing took early retirement and was quickly replaced by Herb Cuthbert, a purchasing manager from National Electric. Three senior Eaton buyers, including Debbie Roseman and Roger Dommermuth, resigned within the last two weeks to take jobs with other companies. Keith Shepherd was surprised by the sudden turnover of so many people. He only learned about Debbie and Roger leaving late last week, and neither has gone to a company that would be interested in buying anything Mectronic sold.

Early this morning, when calling on the new director of purchasing, Keith was told that all current purchasing arrangements would be reviewed for total performance and that, based on that review, there might be some "changed relationships" with current suppliers. From his preliminary review, Mr. Cuthbert said: "It looks like we're going to be dropping some suppliers. In fact, I'm not very impressed by the performance of your company, Keith. You were up to a week late on three out of twelve shipments last year. Late shipments can cost us several thousand dollars in production downtime, and such poor performance will no longer be tolerated. I haven't looked at the number of defective parts or the quality of service that we've gotten from each supplier, but those will be other factors in our decisions to drop or retain current suppliers. Finally, I should alert you that we will be requesting new sales proposals from present and potential new suppliers before signing any purchasing agreements for the coming year. In the future, we will expect our suppliers to be price competitive in addition to supplying quality products and total service."

Ever since his interview with Mr. Cuthbert, Keith has been trying to think what he might do to keep the Eaton business. He doesn't really know how well his company has performed over the past year; in fact, he was surprised to learn of the late deliveries because nobody at Eaton ever complained to him about the shipments. Perhaps, he thinks to himself, he has taken the Eaton account for granted because of the good relationships he enjoyed with Debbie Roseman and Roger Dommermuth. The three of them even used to get together for an informal lunch every other Thursday. Herb Cuthbert, on the other hand, seems to be all business. Keith doubts that Cuthbert ever does anything in an informal way! The people who are replacing Debbie and Roger won't be starting until next Monday, so Keith doesn't know what to expect.

Keith can't afford to lose the Eaton account. It represents almost 15 percent of his annual commissions, and losing that amount would be a severe blow to his family's standard of living. Also, the loss of such a large account might jeopardize his promotion to sales supervisor—a promotion Keith's sales manager has hinted might be forthcoming.

Keith decides to drive to a local café for a cup of coffee to calm his nerves and take a little time to think. While slowly drinking his coffee, Keith considers the changed situation at Eaton and tries to devise a strategy to keep this important account.

Questions

1. Do you think Keith has been doing a good job in serving the Eaton account? Why or why not?
2. In what stage of the buying process is the new purchasing organization at Eaton? What is the buying situation from their perspective?
3. What specific actions would you advise Keith to take now?
4. If Keith manages to retain the Eaton account, what advice would you give him for long-run maintenance of the account?

Case 6-2

UNDERSTANDING THE BUYING CENTER

Linda Stephens is a sales engineer for McDonnell-Cummins Company, which sells specialty chemicals, plastics, and polymer products to large consumer goods companies. After graduating from Michigan State University with a degree in chemical engineering, Linda interviewed with several companies and received three job offers. She decided to take the job as sales engineer with McDonnell-Cummins because it offered the best overall compensation package (including perks like a new car and an expense account) as well as a career path that could lead to top management. After three months of intensive training that included classroom lectures and discussions, laboratory demonstrations of products, videotapes, lots of reading material, and several examinations, Linda feels confident of her knowledge of the company's products and believes that she is prepared to make effective sales presentations to customers.

Still, on her first sales call at the headquarters of Gamble & Simpson, a large consumer products manufacturer, Linda is a little apprehensive as she walks into the huge lobby and sees many other people—apparently salespeople—waiting. After she introduces herself to the receptionist and says that she is here for a 9:00 A.M. meeting with Bill Constantin in the purchasing department, she takes her Gamble & Simpson visitor's pass and sits down in a comfortable chair to wait for Mr. Constantin. (She learned his name from the call reports that the previous sales engineer handling this account had submitted.) Within a few minutes, Mr. Constantin's secretary, Marie Doyle, comes down to the lobby to greet Linda and escort her back to Mr. Constantin's office. Marie says that Mr. Constantin can spend only about 15 minutes with Linda because he has to prepare for an emergency meeting scheduled for 9:30 A.M. with the vice president of purchasing.

Arriving at Mr. Constantin's office, Linda introduces herself and gives Mr. Constantin her business card. Bill Constantin seems somewhat harried and preoccupied, so Linda thinks she had better forget the small talk and get down to business. Handing a packet of product brochures to Mr. Constantin, she tells him that her company will be introducing several new products over the next few months and that she wants to give him some preliminary information about them. Linda makes a short presentation on each of five new products while Mr. Constantin listens and leafs through the brochures. Upon finishing her presentations, Linda asks if he has any questions. Mr. Constantin replies: "Not at the moment, but I'll probably have some later when I get a chance to read the brochures and talk to some of the R&D people. Right now, I've got to get ready for my 9:30 meeting."

At that moment, Mr. Constantin's manager, Esther Hughes, pokes her head in the door and says that she'd like to talk with Bill after his meeting with the VP. Bill quickly introduces Linda to Esther and leaves for his meeting. Esther was hired as purchasing manager only a month earlier, so she is still progressing up the learning curve at Gamble & Simpson. She asks Linda a few questions and requests copies of the product brochures to bring her up to date on what McDonnell-Cummins is offering. She remarks that at her previous company she bought from a competitor of Linda's company. Ms. Hughes soon excuses herself and asks Marie if she would mind taking Linda out to the laboratory to introduce her to some of the research and development people who use the products that Bill buys for them.

In the laboratory, Linda meets Dr. Stuart Forbes and Dr. Li Chu, two scientists who provide detailed specifications to Bill for products they need in their work. Li Chu says that he is working on a new idea for a laundry detergent for which he needs a polymer with particular properties. He asks Linda if her company can provide such a product. Linda admits that she isn't sure, but says that she will talk to her company's R&D people and get back to him as soon as possible. While in the laboratory, Linda also meets Fred Burnett, a laboratory technician who carries out most of the experiments designed by Drs. Forbes and Chu. Mr. Burnett is an uninhibited young man about Linda's age who cracks a couple of lighthearted jokes along the line of "What's a nice person like you doing in a place like this?" Finally, on the way out of the laboratory, Marie introduces Linda to the director of R&D, Dr. Leland Birsner, whose approval has to be obtained for any product requests submitted to purchasing. Dr. Birsner seems rather dour, but he is polite enough and says that he hopes Linda will keep him informed about any new products her company is developing. Taking this as her cue, Linda hands him another packet of brochures from her briefcase.

Later, while walking back to the lobby with Marie, Linda asks who will make the purchasing decision on her products. Marie responds: "Oh, lots of people have input. It's usually more of a group decision than any one person's, although the director of R&D and the purchasing manager have final say on any purchase decision."

Leaving Gamble & Simpson, Linda is a bit overwhelmed by the possibility that each of the people she's met might have an input in deciding whether or not to purchase her company's products. Her first job, she feels, is to prepare an organization chart of the Gamble & Simpson buying center to help her understand the multiple roles played by the different people. Then she will need to develop some strategy and tactics for developing and keeping good relationships with all of these people.

Questions

1. In terms of buying center roles (initiators, gatekeepers, influencers, deciders, buyers, and users), how should Linda classify each of the seven people (Marie Doyle, Bill Constantin, Esther Hughes, Dr. Stuart Forbes, Dr. Li Chu, Fred Burnett, and Dr. Leland Birsner) she met at Gamble & Simpson?

2. Which of these people do you think has the greatest input on purchase decisions? Why?

3. What advice would you give Linda in her efforts to think up a strategy and tactics to develop and maintain good relationships with all of these buying center members?

4. Now that her first sales call is over, what do you think Linda should do to follow up with some or all of the Gamble & Simpson people?

Chapter 7

Communicating with Customers

Good, the more communicated, more abundant grows.

JOHN MILTON, *Paradise Lost,* Book V, 1.71

Profile

"AS an undergraduate at the University of Pennsylvania, I majored in marketing. I guess it's pretty ironic that, when I started job hunting, I didn't give much thought to a sales position, but I just didn't consider myself to be aggressive enough for selling," says Maxine Dennis of Somerset, New Jersey, a sales representative for Prentice Hall. "Luckily, I was soon able to realize that you don't have to be really aggressive to be a good salesperson. Prentice Hall realizes that, too. That's one of the reasons why my first job after graduation was, and still is, with PH."

In fact, aggressiveness is probably not the best trait to display when dealing with the kind of customers Maxine commonly sees: college instructors. "My job involves meeting with professors and discussing their textbook needs with them. Prentice Hall publishes a huge variety of texts, so chances are we've got a book that will fit the professor's needs in either a lower- or higher-level course. My basic objective is to get a commitment from the professor that she or he will use a Prentice Hall textbook in a particular course for the coming semester. Professors are smart people; they appreciate open, honest communication without any pushiness. And because most major textbooks are revised every three years or so, I am interested in cultivating long-term relationships with my professor-customers so that they will consider future editions of the books I sell. I listen carefully to their evaluations of the current editions of Prentice Hall and competing texts and communicate their comments and critiques to our home office marketing and acquisitions staff people. To us, the professors' input is just as important as their choice of books, and I try to make sure that they realize this."

Maxine Dennis

Maxine has also found, however, that professors are usually very busy people and that one-on-one, face-to-face interviews are not always possible. Says Maxine: "In these cases, I have a variety of quick, simple communication techniques: A handwritten note on personal stationery or a brief message on my business card, a thank-you note, a postcard confirming an action I've taken, brief outlines of product information, a copy of an appropriate textbook that I've 'tabbed' for the professor's quick reference, phone calls—there are endless possibilities for getting a dialogue going and keeping it going, even with those professors who are so busy that they miss their own office hours. I also enjoy talking with groups of professors. Sometimes department heads or heads of textbook committees are able to corral all of the professors I need to speak with for one or two big meetings. These group meetings are not only wonderful for sales presentations but also for figuring out the dynamics of a department or committee. Even if I don't make a sale, I'm able to gather an incredible amount of information for next time!"

Maxine believes that the ability to listen is probably the single most important characteristic a salesperson can possess. "Over the years I've made many good friends among my customers. Our rapport always begins, I think, with my listening to them carefully and patiently. It's probably no coincidence that my best friends are also my best customers." ∎

After reading this chapter, you should understand:

- The five modes of communication
- Four communication styles and sources of conflicts between them
- How to respond to the diverse communication styles of prospects and customers
- Techniques for improving your verbal and nonverbal communication skills
- Barriers to effective communication

Successful salespeople, like most successful professionals, are excellent communicators. So central is communication to successful selling and marketing that

> More and more it is becoming apparent that marketing is almost entirely communications. The product communicates; the price communicates; the package communicates; salespeople communicate to the prospect, to the trade, to management and to each other; also, prospects, dealers, management and competitors communicate.[1]

WHAT IS COMMUNICATION?

COMMUNICATION
A process in which information and understanding are conveyed in a two-way exchange between two or more people.

PROMOTION Typically, a one-way flow of persuasive information from a seller to a buyer.

Communication is a process in which information and understanding are conveyed between two or more people. Communication should not be confused with promotion. **Promotion** is typically a one-way flow of persuasive information from seller to buyer, whereas *communication is a two-way exchange*.

There are five distinct modes of communication: (1) listening, (2) writing, (3) talking, (4) reading, and (5) nonverbal communication. Of the first four modes, researchers have found that people normally spend the most time listening, as depicted in Figure 7-1. But we have drawn a thin line around the circle in Figure 7-1 to indicate the constant presence of nonverbal communication during every one of the other four modes. Nonverbal communication, sometimes called "body language," is expressed through the actions of our bodies (faces, arms, hands, legs, and posture) and our voices (rate of speech, volume, pitch, tone, accent, rhythm, emphasis, and pauses).

Active listening is by far the most important mode of communication for sales representatives. You can't learn anything about prospects or customers and their needs while *you* are doing the talking. In fact, you must become more than a good listener. You must learn to be an *expert* listener, one who shows sincerity and respect for prospects and continually enhances rapport with customers.

[1]Marion Harper, Jr., "Communications Is the Core of Marketing," *Printers' Ink,* June 1, 1962, p. 53.

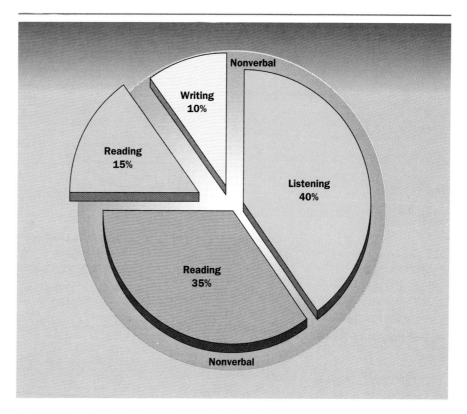

FIGURE 7-1 Time Spent in Communication Modes
Sources: Harold P. Zelko, *The Art of Communicating Your Ideas* (New York: Reading Services, 1968), p. 3; and H. Herzfield, "The Unspoken Message," *Small Systems World,* February 1977, pp. 12–14.

Here's a good rule of thumb for salespeople: *Always use your mouth and ears in proportion to how many you have of each.*

Keep in mind that you, the salesperson, are not the only one with a message to communicate. Customers want you to understand them and comprehend *their* message *first.* Among 43 sales communication practices industrial customers indicated were important in their purchasing activities, the 16 identified in Table 7-1 received the highest ratings. Note that nearly all of them depend directly on communication skills.

MESSAGES AND COMMUNICATION STYLES

COMMUNICATION STYLE
The way a person gets his or her message across to other people.

People have lots of messages, and every person has a particular **communication style,** which is the way that person gets his or her message across to others. Figure 7-2 is a schematic depiction of any communicative exchange between two people. The *source* in the left oval space, representing one frame of reference, sends a message to the *receiver* in the right oval space, representing another frame of reference. The message "works" only in the area where these two

TABLE 7-1   How Customers Recognize the Pros

SALES COMMUNICATION PRACTICE	SIGNIFICANCE LEVEL[a]
1. Makes effort to understand concerns	.01
2. Presents logical arguments	.01
3. Gives evidence of product effectiveness	.05
4. Prepares effective responses to objections	.05
5. Asks questions about customer's needs	.05
6. Asks about needs of customer's company	.05
7. Explains product drawbacks	.05
8. Answers questions about products	.05
9. Is concise and to the point	.05
10. Maintains eye contact	.05
11. Shows enthusiasm	.05
12. Is aware of customer's needs	.10
13. Understands economic conditions	.10
14. Is trustworthy with confidential information	.10
15. Is sensitive to customer's personal situation	.10
16. Is able to restate terms accurately	.10

[a]Significance level of .01 means that there is only 1 chance in 100 that a cited practice was selected randomly; .05 means 5 chances in 100; etc.

Source: Reported in Thayer C. Taylor, "Anatomy of a Star Salesperson," *Sales & Marketing Management,* May 1986, p. 233.

people's frames of reference overlap. The size of the overlapping area depends on how well the source succeeds in *encoding* the message to fit the receiver's frame of reference and/or how well the receiver succeeds in *decoding* the message in the way the source intended it to be understood. Obviously, the more different the source's and the receiver's frames of reference, the more work both will have to do to understand each other.

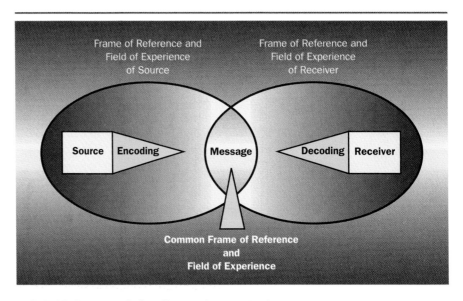

FIGURE 7-2   Essentials for Effective Communication
Source: Adapted from Wilbur Schramm, *The Process and Effects of Mass Communication* (Urbana: University of Illinois Press, 1960), p. 6. Copyright © 1960 by the Trustees of the University of Illinois.

As a salesperson, you will constantly meet people with many different frames of reference. You should realize right now that the majority of these people will expect *you* to do most of the work necessary for mutual understanding. Therefore, your basic messages—"I am a professional," "I am here to help and serve you," "You have my personal guarantee of highest product quality and service"—should be couched in a highly flexible communication style. The bad news is that a highly flexible communication style may take a very long time to develop. You will make mistakes, and customers will become upset, and so will you. The good news is that there are general theories and principles that will set you on the road to learning a flexible style of communication that will prove effective with almost any kind of customer imaginable. And remember, even the best salespeople make mistakes. They are the "best" precisely because they are eager to learn from their mistakes and are *always* trying to increase their communication style flexibility. Let's begin your communication style studies with a look at ego states.

EGO STATES IN COMMUNICATION

In his book *Games People Play,* Eric Berne discusses transactional analysis (TA) and three *ego states* in communication: (1) *adult,* (2) *parent,* and (3) *child.*[2] This concept has provided many people, professional and nonprofessional, with a valuable general principle for effectively communicating with others. It's a commonsense approach to a very complex problem. Most of us, after all, have some idea of how adults, parents, and children *should* behave. Berne asserts that each of us displays all three ego states at various times in our communication with others, and that the ideal exchange occurs when both communicating persons or parties are in the adult ego state.

Communicating as adults—logically and rationally, with respect for one another—is without doubt the best kind of communicative exchange between salespeople and their prospects or customers. Although some effective communication can take place *whenever ego states* of the salesperson and prospect *match,* the most effective communication is in the adult-to-adult ego state— depicted as a heavy two-way arrow in Figure 7-3. Communication usually breaks down when the ego states are mismatched, as indicated by the diagonal broken lines in the figure. Thus, if you employ the parent ego state to converse with prospects who are in the adult or child ego state, you will be perceived as condescending or domineering. Conversely, if you communicate in the child ego state to prospects in the adult or parent ego state, you may appear immature, insecure, and peevish.

As a salesperson, you have essentially two solutions to the problem of mismatched ego states: (1) You can shift to your customer's ego state, or (2) you can delay the sales presentation and return another day. The problem with the first solution is that it will be effective only if the customer is already in the adult ego state and it is you who are required to switch to that state. (For instance, you may have just finished chastising your teenage son about poor grades in school and

---

[2]Eric Berne, *Games People Play* (New York: Grove Press, 1964).

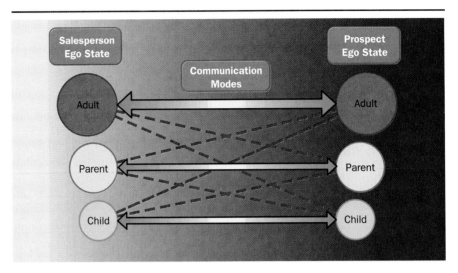

FIGURE 7-3 Salesperson-Prospect Ego States in Communicating

unconsciously continued in the parent ego state with your customer.) The problem with the second solution is that if the communication problem you are having with the customer is chronic (a customer who works for a very demanding and intimidating superior may operate in the child ego state most of the time), making another appointment won't change the situation.

In your professional selling career, you are bound to encounter customers who persist in trying to communicate with you in a parent or child ego state. *It should be your goal to stay within the boundaries of the adult ego state as much as possible,* for even parents and children respond best to the civility and respect shown by people in the adult ego state.

What Would You Do?

As a salesperson for Jiffy Tools Company, you sell a wide variety of small tools like hammers and screw drivers to industrial distributors and home building supply stores. Although you are 24 years old, you look several years younger. One of your regular customers always calls you "kid" instead of using your first or last name. Whenever you call on him, he makes a little joke about your youthful appearance, like: "Well, how's the teen-age salesboy?" or "Did school get out early this afternoon?" He never seems to take you seriously. Nevertheless, he is a steady and profitable customer. One time when he needed tools in an emergency, he even called your sales office and asked for "the kid" because he couldn't remember your name. This embarrassed you when your sales manager found out about it and some of the office staff began to call you "the kid."

COMMUNICATION STYLES

Our prospects and customers are continually sending us verbal and nonverbal signals about their personalities and how to communicate with them more effectively. Because everyone is a mixture of diverse personality characteristics, it may be simplistic to set up categories for classifying people. Yet in order to begin to understand the complex personalities of our prospects and customers, we need ways to classify them.

Classifying Communication Styles

ASSERTIVENESS The degree to which a person attempts to control or dominate situations and direct the thoughts and actions of other people.

RESPONSIVENESS The level of emotions, feelings, or sociability that a person openly displays.

Expanding on Jung's pioneering work in human behavior (outlined in Chapter 5, Consumer Markets), David Merrill, Roger Reid, Paul Mok, Larry Wilson, and Anthony Alessandra, among other researchers, have developed new models for classifying people's behavior and communication styles.[3] Most of these behavior models divide people into four distinct categories based on two dimensions: assertiveness and responsiveness. **Assertiveness** is the degree to which a person attempts to control or dominate situations and direct the thoughts and actions of other people. **Responsiveness** is the level of emotions, feelings, or sociability that a person openly displays.

Using the graph in Figure 7-4, we can plot an individual's levels of assertiveness and responsiveness and classify him or her into one of four communication styles: (1) amiable, (2) expressive, (3) analytical, or (4) driver.[4] Let's discuss the people who use these four communication styles and how you can sell to them.

Amiables

Open, relatively unassertive, warm, supportive, and sociable people who "wear well" with others, amiables are the most people-oriented of all the four categories. As shown in the upper-left-hand corner of Figure 7-4, they are high in responsive and low in assertive behavior. When communicating, they are congenial and their body language is warmly animated. Co-workers and salespeople perceive them as compliant and easygoing because they emphasize building trustful relationships and work at a relatively slow pace. They readily share their personal feelings and are often charming storytellers. Generally, they are very deliberate in making decisions because they want to know how others feel before they take an action. Amiables prefer friendly, personal, first-name relationships with others. They dislike interpersonal conflicts so much that they will often say what others want to hear rather than what they really think. Amiables are understanding listeners and easily make and keep friends. They don't like

[3]See David W. Merrill and Roger H. Reid, *Personal Styles and Effective Performance* (Radnor, Pa.: Chilton Book Co., 1981); Paul Mok, *Communicating Styles Technology* (Dallas, Tex.: Training Associates Press, 1982); Larry Wilson, *Social Styles Sales Strategies* (Eden Prairie, Minn.: Wilson Learning Corp., 1987); Anthony Alessandra, Phil Wexler, and Rick Barrera, *Non-Manipulative Selling* (Englewood Cliffs, N.J.: Prentice Hall, 1987).

[4]For an in-depth explanation of communication styles, see Anthony Alessandra, Phil Wexler, and Rick Barrera, *Non-Manipulative Selling* (Englewood Cliffs, N.J.: Prentice Hall, 1987); J. Ingrasci, "How to Reach Buyers in Their Psychological Comfort Zones," *Industrial Marketing*, July 1981, pp. 60–64; Anthony J. Alessandra and Phillip S. Wexler with Jerry D. DeenHugh, *Non-Manipulative Selling* (San Diego, Cal.: Courseware, 1979).

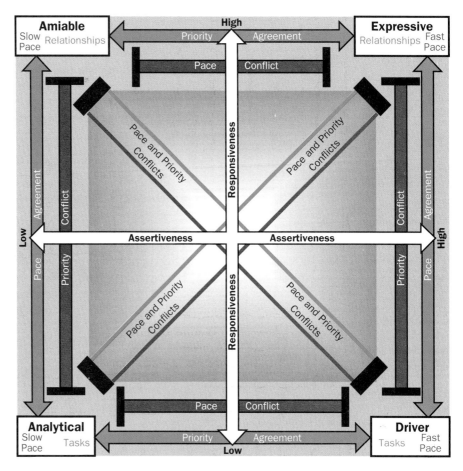

FIGURE 7-4 Communication Styles
Source: Adapted from Anthony Alessandra, James Cathcart, and Phillip Wexler, *Selling by Objectives* (Englewood Cliffs, N.J.: Prentice Hall, 1988), p. 43.

President George Bush is a good example of an "amiable" personality type.

SELLING TO AMIABLES

- Approach amiables in a warm, friendly manner, beginning with a sincere smile and a cordial handshake. Use the prospect's first name frequently. Adapt an informal, easygoing pace to build trust, friendship, and credibility.
- Sell yourself and develop a positive relationship before starting the sales presentation for the product.
- Try to get to know the prospect personally. Ask nonthreatening questions about the prospect's interests and activities. Be agreeable and supportive, professional but friendly. Show the prospect that you genuinely like him or her.

- Involve the prospect in the sales presentation and demonstration as much as possible, so that the interaction between you is open, comfortable, and relaxed.
- Negotiate resistance and objections by using testimonials from other people, personal assurances, and guarantees.
- Close in a warm, reassuring way. Avoid any hint of pushiness or aggressiveness.
- Follow up with friendly personal letters, notes, and phone calls to make sure that the prospect is satisfied with the product and to further the friendly relationship.

pushy, aggressive behavior. Cooperative team players, their theme song might be "People" or "Getting to Know You."

Amiables' offices will probably be decorated in a comfortable, open, friendly style with informal seating arrangements conducive to close contact. On their desks you'll probably find family pictures and various personal items. Family or group pictures and personal mementos are likely to be hanging on their office walls. Among famous people, television show host Pat Sajak and President George Bush are considered amiables.

Expressives

Expressives, placed in the upper-right-hand corner of Figure 7-4, are high in both responsiveness and assertiveness. Enthusiastic, spontaneous, talkative, and extroverted, they work at a fast pace. They operate largely on intuition and express their views dramatically. They dislike being alone. If no one's around, they'll spend a lot of time on the telephone. Full of ideas, expressives may daydream and "chase a lot of rainbows." Their persuasive skills are usually excellent, enabling them to get others excited about their ideas. They seek approval and recognition for their accomplishments and achievements. They are usually very creative and have the ability to think on their feet. Uninhibited in giving verbal or nonverbal feedback, they readily share their personal feelings. They believe that success depends more on "who you know than what you know." Expressives tend to become involved in too many things and may not be strong on follow-through because of their impatience and relatively short attention span.

Their desks often look cluttered and disorganized. You will see awards, provocative posters, pictures taken with celebrities, and motivational slogans hanging on their office walls. Their offices are usually decorated in an open, friendly style, with a seating arrangement that invites interaction and contact. Comedienne Carol Burnett and minister and presidential candidate Jesse Jackson are examples of expressives. The song Carol Burnett used to close each segment of her long-running television show is an appropriate theme song for expressive personalities. The song began: "I'm so glad we had this time together, just to have a laugh or sing a song. . . ."

The Reverend Jesse Jackson is a good example of an "expressive" personality type.

Analyticals

Analyticals, shown in the lower-left-hand corner of Figure 7-4, tend to be low in both assertiveness and responsiveness. Logical, controlled, and self-contained, they are not very demonstrative in their verbal or nonverbal communication. They like organization, structure, and self-discipline, and they work at a deliberate pace. Systematic problem solvers who ask many detailed questions, analytical buyers like sales presentations to be based on facts. They will probably be most persuaded by objective product tests conducted by independent research orga-

---

SELLING TO EXPRESSIVES

■ In an exuberant and open manner that says you're delighted to meet the prospect, extend your hand and enthusiastically introduce yourself.

■ Converse in a cheerful, sociable, and confident manner for a few minutes before beginning your sales presentation.

■ Ask questions that will allow the prospect to brag a little. You can obtain clues from the pictures, trophies, awards, and interesting art objects you are likely to see in his or her office.

■ Ask questions that show you are genuinely interested in learning about the prospect's interests, needs, goals, hopes, and dreams. Readily share your personal feelings.

■ Show appreciation for the prospect's abilities and achievements. Compliment the prospect on his or her accomplishments if you can do so sincerely.

■ Be spirited and fast-paced throughout your presentation and demonstration. Spice up your sales presentation with interesting stories and illustrations.

■ Negotiate resistance and objectives candidly and confidently.

■ Close with lively appeals that provide positive support for achieving the prospect's personal goals as well as the company's.

■ Follow up by confirming the purchase in an enthusiastic and friendly telephone call or letter.

SELLING TO ANALYTICALS

■ Approach an analytical prospect in a gracious, congenial, understated manner, then state the purpose of your visit.

■ Be prepared to answer in-depth questions about the product, its construction, features, applications, and benefits.

■ Make your sales presentation in a logical, objective, and unemotional way and at a deliberate pace. Use facts and statistics to support your statements.

■ Negotiate resistance and objections by providing detailed analysis and research findings.

■ Close by summarizing the advantages and disadvantages in purchasing and using the product.

■ Follow up with reassuring scientific information from surveys or research that supports the analytical customer's purchase decisions.

nizations, expert testimonials, and comprehensive warranties. Very security conscious, they prefer predictability. They want to know how a product or service works and what proof there is of its quality. Analyticals dislike becoming too involved with other people. They work slowly and precisely by themselves and prefer an intellectual work environment that allows them to self-actualize. They rarely share their personal feelings and are slow in giving nonverbal feedback. Precise, detail-oriented, and time-conscious, they are likely to be critical of their own and other people's performances. They exhibit a skeptical "show me" attitude and prefer to have agreements in writing. They like salespeople to be organized and very professional, with all the facts at their fingertips. In their desire for information, analyticals may compulsively go on collecting data past the time when a decision is needed. Most analyticals would probably be pleased to have a baroque concerto (usually characterized by strict rhythms and standardized forms and ornamentation) as their "theme song."

You will find an analytical person's office highly organized and functional, with all furniture and equipment in their proper places. The office walls may be covered with charts, graphs, and pictures relating to their job; pictures of people are unlikely. Decor and seating arrangements are formal and impersonal. Astronomer Carl Sagan and *National Review* editor William F. Buckley are good examples of the analytical type.

Drivers
Drivers, found in the lower-right-hand corner of Figure 7-4, tend to be assertive and unresponsive. Controlled and decisive, they operate at a fast pace and are very goal-oriented in their relationships with others. Strong-willed, impatient, tough, "take-charge" personalities, drivers have a low tolerance for the feelings, attitudes, and advice of others. Since they believe that their success depends on themselves, they feel a need to control situations and people, and actively seek leadership roles. They thrive on decision making and getting things done. Inflexible, impatient, and poor listeners, they tend to ignore facts and figures and to rely on their "gut feeling" for things. A theme song for drivers might be "My Way."

Clues identifying the driver personality are desks that are piled high with work projects. These people's offices are decorated to indicate power and control; the walls may contain honors and achievement awards or an elaborate plan-

SELLING TO DRIVERS

- Approach the driver prospect directly with a firm handshake in a confident, businesslike manner.
- Be well prepared, organized, fast-paced, and to the point.
- Present your selling points clearly and directly by showing how the product will help the prospect achieve his or her goals. Involve the prospect in a hands-on demonstration of the product.
- Negotiate resistance and objections directly. Do not try to avoid or gloss over the prospect's questions and concerns because drivers are very persistent in getting the answers they want.
- Close in a straightforward, professional way by emphasizing bottom line results or benefits.
- Follow up by asking how well the product is doing in helping the driver achieve his or her goals. Suggest ancillary products that may improve results.

ning schedule. Seating arrangements are likely to be closed, formal, and positioned for power. Some drivers even raise their own chair's height and choose an extra-large desk to project their dominance over others. Hotel owner-manager Leona Helmsley and Chrysler Corporation CEO Lee Iaccoca are examples of drivers.

Although most people show characteristics of all four communication styles at least occasionally, every prospect and customer will have a preponderant communication style. It is the salesperson's job to identify that style early on and adapt the presentation accordingly. Table 7-2 provides a quick reference tool for the four communication styles, with their respective characteristics listed by key variables.

DEVELOPING COMMUNICATION STYLE FLEXIBILITY

Pairing a salesperson and a prospect with different styles can be tricky. Besides differences in levels of responsiveness and assertiveness, their styles may clash in terms of pace and priority. *Pace* is the speed at which a person moves. People who are high in assertiveness (expressives and drivers) prefer a fast pace in talking, thinking, and making decisions; those who are low in assertiveness (amiables and analyticals) prefer a slow pace. *Priorities* identify what a person considers to be important. Goals, objectives, and task achievement are highest in priority for those who are low in responsiveness (analyticals and drivers), while relationships with other people are the top priority for those who are high in responsiveness (amiables and expressives). Table 7-3 shows the types of conflicts that can occur when people with different styles try to communicate. As you can see, amiables paired with drivers and expressives paired with analyticals will encounter both pace and priority problems when they try to communicate with each other. All the other communication style pairings (except, of course, for those with identical styles) will produce either a pace or a priority problem.

TABLE 7-2   Summary of Communication Styles

VARIABLES	AMIABLES (George Bush, Pat Sajak)	EXPRESSIVES (Jesse Jackson, Carol Burnett)	ANALYTICALS (Carl Sagan, William F. Buckley)	DRIVERS (Lee Iacocca, Leona Helmsley)
Communication style	Responsive, nonassertive	Responsive, assertive	Nonresponsive, nonassertive	Nonresponsive, assertive
Presentation pace	Slow and easy-going	Quick and spontaneous	Deliberate and disciplined	Fast and decisive
Orientation toward risk	Avoids risks	Takes risks	Calculates risks	Controls risks
Personal focus	Human relationships	Social interaction	The analytical process	Results
Wants to be	Liked	Admired	Accurate	In charge
Prefers salespeople who are	Friendly	Stimulating	Precise	To the point
Decision process	Participatory	Spontaneous	Methodical	Decisive
Office design	Informal	Stimulating	Functional	Efficient
Clothing	Casual	Stylish	Conservative	Businesslike
Wants to ensure . . .	Relationships	Status	Credibility	Success
Salesperson should appreciate prospect's	Feelings	Creativity	Knowledge	Goals and achievements
Fears	Confrontation	Loss of prestige	Embarrassment	Loss of control
Likely reaction to pressure	Compromise	Argument	Reconsideration	Confrontation
Dislikes salespeople who are	Insensitive	Boring	Unpredictable or inexact	Inefficient or indecisive
Places high value on	Compatibility, close relationships	Recognition, prestige	Precision, accuracy	Results, progress toward goals
Wants to know	How product will affect personal relationships	How product will affect status	How to justify the purchase on rational grounds	How product will help to achieve goals

TABLE 7-3   Agreement and Conflict in Paired Communication Styles

STYLE MATCHUP	SHARED QUALITIES	AREA OF AGREEMENT	AREA OF CONFLICT
Amiable with Expressive	High responsiveness	Priorities	Pace
Analytical with Driver	Low responsiveness	Priorities	Pace
Amiable with Analytical	Low assertiveness	Pace	Priorities
Expressive with Driver	High assertiveness	Pace	Priorities
Amiable with Driver	None	None	Both
Expressive with Analytical	None	None	Both

Style Flexing

The many possible conflicts between salesperson and prospect communication styles illustrate the need for every salesperson to cultivate the ability to *flex* with prospect communication styles. *Style flexing* will enable you to sell to your prospects *in the way they want to be sold to.* If prospects talk and move quickly, then you should adjust your rate of speech and movements to match theirs. If they like to take their time and engage in light conversation, relax and allow more time for the appointment. If prospects are task-oriented, shift your focus to tasks. If they are relationship-oriented, stress relationships. When you meet another person's communication style needs, a climate of mutual trust is created. As the bond of trust develops, the other person will begin to tell you what he or she really wants.

DEVELOPING COMMUNICATION SKILLS

Today's top professional salespeople continually increase the effectiveness and efficiency of their communication by improving their skills in (1) listening, (2) asking questions, (3) persuasion, (4) using space, (5) nonverbal communication, (6) reading, and (7) writing. Let's discuss these skills and ways that you can develop and use them in your sales career.

Listening

On any given day, you will hear or have the opportunity to hear an incredible number of different things. While there may be plenty to hear, however, there are only a few things that you will really want to listen to and only two basic ways to listen to those things: selective listening and concentrated listening.

Selective Listening

People talk at a rate of between 130 and 160 words per minute, but they can listen to over 800 words per minute. Because of the relative ease of listening compared to talking, many people become lazy listeners, retaining only about half of what they hear. Most of us use a different listening style for social occasions than we do for work. On social occasions, many of us engage in *selective listening* in that we listen only to parts of a person's conversation while we peer around the room or reach for a handful of peanuts.

CRITICAL LISTENING
A type of concentrated listening in which you attempt to analyze the ideas presented by the speaker and make critical judgments about the validity and quality of the information presented.

Concentrated Listening

The opposite of selective listening is *concentrated listening,* in which you give your rapt attention to the entire message. There are two types of concentrated listening: (1) critical and (2) discriminative. In **critical listening,** you attempt to analyze the ideas presented by the speaker and make critical judgments about the validity and quality of the information presented. This is the kind of listening that citizens may do in deciding which political candidate to vote for. But many customers also listen critically to sales presentations, especially when they don't

DISCRIMINATIVE LISTENING A type of concentrated listening in which you listen to understand and remember. This is the type of listening most often used by salespeople.

quite trust the salesperson. In **discriminative listening,** you listen to understand and remember. *Discriminative listening is the kind most often used by salespeople,* and it can be done at four different levels of increasing intensity:

- Attentive Listening: Simply paying attention to the message.
- *Retentive Listening:* Attempting to comprehend and remember the message.
- **Reflective Listening:** Paying attention and remembering the message, then attempting to evaluate it to identify relationships and draw conclusions.
- **REACTIVE LISTENING:** Paying attention, remembering, and reflecting on the meaning of the message, then providing verbal or nonverbal feedback to the speaker. Top-performing salespeople become effective *reactive* listeners!

Listening Effectively

Effective listening is obviously not a passive activity. Even when salespeople hear a prospect's words, they must listen carefully for voice inflection and tone and observe body language (discussed later) to fully understand what the words mean. There are at least six different messages in communicating:

1. *What you mean to say:* "This BMW is a very classy car that would be ideal for someone like you."
2. *What you really say:* "Based on our sales, we've found that people who drive BMWs tend to be mature, college-educated, upwardly mobile professionals with incomes in the top 10 percent of the population."
3. *What the other person hears:* "People who drive BMWs tend to be mature, mobile professionals with incomes in the top 10 percent."
4. *What the other person thinks he or she heard:* "BMWs are driven by middle-aged people who move around a lot because they're wealthy and have free time."
5. *What the other person says about what he or she thinks you said:* "Oh, I don't think I'm too young to buy a BMW because I see a lot of young people driving BMWs in my hometown."
6. *What you think the other person said about what you thought you said:* "A lot of young people drive BMWs, so it's not really that classy a car."

Salespeople can convey to prospects and customers that they are actively listening by nodding their heads, by maintaining good eye contact, and by asking an occasional question or making a comment like "I see," "Okay," or "Mmm-huh." Xerox Learning Systems suggests these actions for active listeners:

Paraphrase what you hear. In paraphrasing, you restate the prospect's key words for emphasis and understanding. You have to be careful when using this technique to avoid annoying customers by echoing everything they say. A *confirmatory* or *summary paraphrase* is simply a restatement of a prospect's comment or series of comments to confirm an attitude or a fact. This technique can help build rapport and a climate of empathy and mutual understanding. For example, you can say: "Then it's my understanding that you feel that our Just-in-Time Inventory Response program is something that your plant manager would like us to implement quickly."

A *leading paraphrase* is a bit trickier. Here you subtly try to get prospects to reexamine and modify their views by interpreting their words to make your point. For instance, when the prospect comments: "Your product may be the best, but it is just too expensive," a leading paraphrase would be: "If I understand you correctly, you feel that price is more of a concern than product quality." You have to be careful in using leading paraphrases because your interpretation of their words can irritate prospects. A miffed prospect might retort: "I didn't say that quality is less important than reasonable price. I said we need both." Hearing this response, you would be wise to back off a little and reply: "I'm sorry I misunderstood. I know that you just want the best value for your company. And I assure you, Ms. Snyder, that our product will be your best buy over the long run because our quality is much higher and our price is only a little higher."

Clarify the information.   Conversation with prospects sometimes becomes a little hazy. To make sure that you understand exactly why, where, when, and how the product is desired, you should ask follow-up questions to clarify your understanding. For example, you can say: "Now, let me make sure I understand exactly *when* you need the stronger steel and *where* it should be delivered, Ms. Snyder. If one of our big trailer rigs dumped a load of steel in the wrong place, you'd probably come looking for me with a baseball bat. You said to deliver one trailer load to 12th and Market Streets on the morning of August 31st at 7:30 A.M.—right?"

Use pauses and silences.   Don't fear long pauses or silences in communicating with prospects. A common mistake of rookie salespeople is to try to fill any gap in communication with words. Short pauses or longer silences give both you and the prospect some time to think and to make sure that you haven't overlooked anything. Silences by the salesperson also encourage the prospect to continue talking and providing more information about the purchase decision and reasons for buying.

Summarize the conversation.   At the conclusion of the sales call, it's a good idea to summarize the sales interview so that the prospect has a final chance to correct any errors or misunderstandings. This summary can also reassure the prospect that you are a very thorough and conscientious professional.

Can You Really Sell More by Listening?

An executive with Forum Corporation, a Boston-based sales training firm, claims that ineffective salespeople have an inability to listen to or care about prospects. They can't get off their own agenda long enough to focus on the customer's agenda. They tend to have preconceived notions about each customer, do most of the talking during sales calls, belittle the prospect's objections, and ignore the customer after making a sale.

As a salesperson, your most important tool is not a clever sales pitch but a probing question. Probing allows you to uncover a sales opportunity. Further questions can stimulate a need for your product and ultimately transform the prospect into a customer. This approach is taught to over 200,000 salespeople yearly by such major sales training companies as Xerox Learning Systems, Wilson Learning Corporation, and Forum Corporation. After Commerce Clearing House put some of their salespeople through "selling by listening" sales training, one of its trained divisions increased sales by nearly 34 percent, while an untrained division increased sales by less than 3 percent.[5]

[5]Monci Jo Williams, "America's Best Salesmen," *Fortune,* October 26, 1987, pp. 122–134; "Sales Training," *Training,* special issue, February 1988; and Jeremy Main, "How to Sell by Listening," *Fortune,* February 4, 1985, pp. 52–54.

Asking Questions

Research has substantiated that the more questions salespeople ask, the more successful they are in closing sales.[6] Top salespeople have long known that superior selling is *less talking* and *more asking*. The most successful salespeople are nearly always excellent questioners, knowing exactly what information they need, so that each of their questions has a specific purpose. They develop questioning skills and approaches that enable them to quickly find out:

1. Who the best prospects are
2. What the prospect's needs are
3. What, when, how, and why they buy
4. Who influences the purchase decision
5. What product benefits they want
6. How quickly the prospect wants the product
7. Who the competition is and what they offer
8. Why prospects prefer one brand over another
9. How the prospect will pay for the order
10. What kinds of postpurchase service the prospect will require

Question Formats

Before calling on a prospect, you should outline a questioning plan and make a prioritized list of the information you need just in case the sales call gets cut off early. There are three basic question formats: (1) open-ended, (2) closed, and (3) semi-open questions.

Open-ended. Open-ended questions usually begin with words like *who, what, why, where, when,* and *how*. They allow prospects to answer in their own words, and are best for eliciting general background information and prospect feelings, verifying understanding of a comment, and probing for subconscious feelings. Here are some examples of open-ended questions:

■ What kind of benefits are you seeking from this product?
■ How do you think you will use it?
■ Why do you believe that brand C is better than brand D?

Closed. Closed questions can usually be answered directly with a simple "yes" or "no." They are best for ensuring that you are on the right track, confirming information, and narrowing the focus of the discussion. Closed questions often begin with some form of the verbs *be, do,* or *have*. Some examples of closed questions are:

■ Are your office computers networked?
■ Do you think Mr. Burris would be interested in buying laptop computers for the sales force?
■ Will he be back from vacation next Monday?

Semi-open. Semi-open questions resemble open-ended questions, except that they seek precise information. They are used to obtain specific facts. By the time

[6]Camille P. Schuster and Jeffrey E. Davis, "Asking Questions: Some Characteristics of Successful Sales Encounters," *Journal of Personal Selling and Sales Management*, May 1986, p. 17.

you are using semi-open questions in a sales interview, you probably have obtained all the general information that you need (through open-ended questions) and have only one or two more closed questions to ask ("Are you ready to buy?"). With semi-open questions, you can help the customer define exactly what he or she really needs and wants. Examples of semi-open questions are:

- When can we set up an appointment?
- What day do you want us to deliver the equipment?
- What's your preference—the red one or the blue one?
- Do you want to pay by cash or credit card?

Types of Questions

In addition to general question formats, there are six specific types of questions. Probing, evaluative, strategic, tactical, dichotomous, and multiple-choice questions each have a different purpose and appropriate time for use.

PROBING QUESTION
A type of question used to "dig" or "probe" for information when prospects and customers have difficulty articulating their precise needs.

Probing questions. The **probing question** is an essential tool for digging deeper for information when prospects find it difficult to articulate their precise needs. Surface-penetrating questions are appropriate at almost any time after initial rapport has been established. An example of a probing question is: "Bob, what 'preparation time' do you think the plant manager meant when he said that our equipment requires too much preparation time before each shift?"

There are several approaches to probing for more information, including: silence, clarification, encouragement, elaboration, consequence, change of topic, directive, verifying, leading, and loaded approaches.

- *Silence* can be an effective probing tool because it encourages the prospect to talk. One way to make the silence seem natural is to take notes while the prospect talks, and to look up with pen poised whenever the prospect stops talking.
- *Clarification* is a request that the prospect provide additional information on a specific subject. "Would you explain what you mean by that?" is an example of a clarification approach to a probing question.
- *Encouragement* is a technique to get a prospect to continue talking and expanding on a topic by providing support such as nodding one's head in agreement, looking interested, giving positive responses ("Mmmm-huh," "I see," "Go on," "Right"), and leaning toward the prospect.
- *Elaboration* is merely asking the prospect to elaborate on what he or she has said. For example: "Will you tell me a little more about the problems you're experiencing with your current product?"
- *Consequence* questions point out the disadvantages of the prospect's continuing to use the present product. These questions usually need to be asked with tact and diplomacy. An example: "Ms. Byrd, don't you think that continuing to use a dot matrix printer now that you've been promoted to senior buyer will make your reports seem, well, kind of unprofessional?"
- *Change of topic* is used when the salesperson feels that he or she has obtained all the information needed on a given topic and wants to move on to another subject. To switch topics, the salesperson might say: "May I ask you a question on a somewhat different topic?"
- *Directive approaches* are used to obtain direct responses to specific questions. For instance, the question "Who will be making the decision on the textbook for spring term?" calls for the prospect to respond with specific names.

- *Verifying questions* seek to obtain the prospect's confirmation of information. Examples are: "Is Charlie Sampson still the purchasing agent for truck axles?" and "Do you expect to buy about 5,000 axles this year?"
- *Leading questions* are used to obtain feedback, determine product preferences, and secure confirmation of the purchase decision. Example: "You appear to me to be somewhat more sophisticated than my average customer. You'll prefer the deluxe model, won't you?"
- *Loaded questions* bring out strong prospect feelings with emotionally charged words. This approach is most effective in the later stages of the sales presentation or during the close, *after* you've gotten to know your prospect or customer better. Example: "I'm pleased that you like our synthetic fur coats. Doesn't it make you mad to see people wearing animal fur coats?"

EVALUATIVE QUESTION
A type of question used within the open-ended question format to stimulate prospects and customers to talk about their general or specific goals, problems, and needs.

Evaluative questions.   The open-ended question format stimulates prospects to talk about their goals, problems, and needs. **Evaluative questions** can be very effective in discovering what the prospect thinks, feels, wants, or hopes. "How do you feel about our proposed design for your new office?" and "What do you think are the problems with your current inventory system?" are examples of questions that call for an evaluative response from prospects. There are two basic types of evaluative questions: direct and indirect.

- *Direct questions* are straightforward questions meant to obtain the views and opinions of prospects on uncomplicated issues, especially when "yes" or "no" is an acceptable answer. "Are you ready to buy the product today?" and "What color would you like?" are examples of direct questions.
- *Indirect questions* are designed to learn what the prospect thinks or feels without forcing the prospect to reveal his or her own opinion. These questions allow prospects to project their own feelings by responding for other people. For instance, some buyers feel uncomfortable saying anything negative to you about your product or company, but may be willing to tell you what their boss or colleagues are saying. An example of an indirect question is: "What are most people in your company saying about our new advertising campaign for your company?"

Strategic questions.   The strategic approach allows you to productively question a prospect even when that prospect is very negative. Strategic questions are appropriate at any time during the sales call to uncover the real needs and attitudes of a generally negatively responding prospect. "Why do you think our mainframe computer isn't even in the same league with the IBM computer, Mr. Wiekowski?" is an example of a strategic question.

Tactical questions.   Whenever the prospect asks a sensitive, irritating, or tough question in an effort to put you on the defensive, you can "hit the ball" back into the prospect's court by asking a tactical question. For example, assume that a prospect says: "We don't normally do business with firms as small as yours." To hit the ball back to the prospect, you might say: "Yes, we are a relatively small firm, Ms. Kimmons, but what if I can show you that our small business is as capable as any large firm of providing the service you expect?"

DICHOTOMOUS QUESTION A type of question used to set up a clear-cut "either-or" answer for prospects and customers.

Dichotomous questions.   Set up clear-cut "either-or" alternatives for prospects by asking **dichotomous questions.** They are most effective when used in the close to nudge a prospect toward a final purchase decision or to compel an indecisive prospect to make a choice between specific product types. For example: "Would you prefer the table model or the floor model projector?" or "Do you want the regular strength or the industrial strength solvent?" Be careful not to mistake the prospect's positive answer to a dichotomous question for a solid close. For instance, a prospect who is willing to indicate a preference for the floor model projector is not necessarily telling you that he or she is definitely ready to buy *your* floor model projector. Always follow this type of question with a direct question: "Will delivery by the end of next week be all right, or do you need it sooner than that?"

Company Highlight

Salespeople or Art Consultants at Hanson Galleries?

Each of Hanson Galleries' eight storefront galleries annually sells about $3 million worth of limited-edition art by popular artists like Marc Chagall, Peter Max, Thomas McKnight, and Erté to middle-class, usually novice, art buyers. Because of their locations in such vacation meccas as Sausalito, Beverly Hills, New Orleans, and San Francisco, the Hanson Galleries don't normally attract traditional art collectors. But its salespeople, called *art consultants,* are taught to view all browsers as potential art collectors and to ask questions to learn about them, whether or not they buy anything. During their conversations with prospects, Hanson Galleries consultants gently educate them about art and try to adjust their attitude toward purchasing it. People have to be persuaded that buying art is not frivolous, that they are capable of buying art intelligently, and that there is little risk in buying from Hanson Galleries. When prospects show interest in a particular sculpture or painting at a Hanson gallery, they are given about 30 minutes of information about the artist, his work, his techniques, and where he ranks compared to his contemporaries. Videotapes, catalogs, and private viewing rooms are often used to help educate customers and change their attitudes toward buying art. Throughout the interactions, salespeople ask customers for information about themselves and record this information on customer cards for later follow-ups. HG art consultants use newsletters, postcards, thank-you notes, and telephone calls after a store visit to close a sale. For instance, about a week after the initial visit to a store gallery, a vacationer's home or office may be called by the HG art consultant, who will likely continue their previous conversation by saying: "Hi, Mr. Morelli, how did you enjoy the Napa Valley wine tour?" Then the consultant will tell Mr. Morelli about some special showing or new work by the artist they discussed in the store, or perhaps the possibility of purchasing the artist's work at a prerelease price. Hanson Galleries requires its art consultants to spend roughly half their time on the phone, the other half on the gallery floor. By working the floor, they continually develop their customer lists and lay the groundwork for future sales. And in working the phones, they close the sale set up during the customer's visit to the Hanson Galleries.

By asking customers the right questions, Hanson Galleries' average art consultant sells about $500,000 worth of art a year. Top HG art consultants sell twice that amount.

Source: Adapted from Tom Richman, "Come Again," *INC.,* April 1989, pp. 177–178.

Multiple-choice questions. Offer the prospect a range of choices when you are pushing for a purchase decision. Like dichotomous questions, multiple-choice questions are most effective during the sales close to force a prospect to reach a decision. Where possible, the salesperson should offer just three choices to avoid confusing the prospect and delaying a decision. "Which of the three do you prefer—the regular, queen size, or king size?" is an example of a multiple-choice question. The same warning we applied to dichotomous questions applies here: Be careful not to mistake the prospect's positive response to a multiple-choice question for a definite close.

One exceptional retailer that understands the importance of asking customers the right questions is Scott Hanson's art galleries, featured in the Company Highlight on the opposite page.

PERSUASION IN THE COMMUNICATION CONTEXT

At the beginning of this chapter, we stated that *communication,* a two-way exchange, should not be confused with *promotion,* a one-way flow of persuasive information. Advertising, sales promotion, and publicity—the three areas of a company's promotion mix besides personal selling—are often more concerned with promotion than with communication. There are two major reasons for this: (1) Advertising, sales promotion, and publicity personnel normally do not have intensive daily contact with final customers; and (2) they must plan the most effective promotional campaigns for the largest number of customers possible. They therefore tend to understand *persuasion* in the context of *promotion.*

Salespeople, however, because they intensively work with individual customers every day and tailor promotional materials to fit each individual selling situation, must try to understand *persuasion* in the context of *communication.* In other words, when you think about persuasion, don't just think about how you're going to sell that product. Instead, think about *selling yourself and your company* to every prospect and customer in every new selling situation through effective communication. People buy from people they trust. Your customers must be persuaded that you and your company are honest, competent, conscientious, and thoroughly professional before they will be persuaded to buy your product. The best salespeople, of course, know how to work these two angles of persuasion simultaneously.

As salespeople should understand it, **persuasion** is a carefully developed communication process built upon a firm foundation of mutual trust and mutual benefit shared between buyer and seller. Occasionally, you will have difficulty getting this process started with some prospects and customers. Perhaps a prospect has not yet realized that he or she has a real need for your product. In cases like these, there are persuasive techniques that, if properly employed, can "jumpstart" the persuasion process. We will briefly discuss three of these techniques: testimonials, bandwagon, and association.

Testimonials from famous athletes and movie stars have been used by advertisers to sell everything from Hertz rental car service to Polygrip denture cream. Although many professional buyers would not be impressed by testimonials from sports or movie celebrities, they are often impressed by testimonial letters and statements from satisfied customers. A sales rep trying to sell radio adver-

PERSUASION As salespeople should understand it, persuasion is a carefully developed communication process built upon a firm foundation of mutual trust and benefit shared between buyer and seller.

tising services to a small business, for example, could gain an edge over competitive media salespeople by carrying testimonial letters from other small business owners in the area relating how the radio ads helped increase their sales and profits.

BANDWAGON A persuasive technique that encourages a prospect or customer to buy a product by implying that the product is extremely popular among other customers with similar needs and requirements.

Bandwagon, as the name implies, is a technique that suggests that everybody's buying a product, so the prospect had better jump on board the moving wagon to keep from being left behind. It is most effective with fashionable or trendy products such as clothing, hairstyles, and "in" activities, and with people who look to opinion leaders and reference groups for guidance. The bandwagon technique is used in all kinds of selling, ranging from garnering support for a political candidate to peddling shares in a "hot" new stock. For example, a stockbroker might encourage small investors to buy shares of a stock by letting them know that a big-name client has recently purchased a large number of shares of the same stock.

Association of a product with a pleasant outcome or benefit is another effective persuasive technique. For many years, Old Spice after-shave cologne experienced excellent sales using a television ad that depicted a rugged young sailor who used the cologne before going ashore and was subsequently mobbed by attractive local women. On a slightly more professional level, a communications equipment salesperson might show sales managers how supplying their salespeople with cellular car phones and electronic pagers would allow them to obtain instant contact with salespeople no matter where they were in the field.

When using any persuasive technique, keep in mind that your most important assets as a sales rep are your reputation and your customer's trust and respect. Any compromise in your standards of honesty, integrity, and professionalism may mean a sacrifice of sales opportunities.

Using Space or Proxemics

PROXEMICS Refers to the spatial relationships (positions) of people and objects.

The spatial relationships of people and objects are referred to as **proxemics.** Salespeople need to be aware of the proxemics of every sales situation, especially with new prospective customers, because their spatial relationship to prospects has a proven impact on the outcome of the sales presentation. You must be careful about getting too close to the prospect who wants a little more space, or too far away from the prospect who needs a little more intimacy. The first prospect may think you're trying to be dominating, intimidating, or even sexy. The second prospect may perceive you as callous and formal. Believe it or not, where you stand or sit in the prospect's office may well be the determining factor in your winning or losing the sale.

Americans appear to recognize four *proxemic zones* in interactions between two or more people: (1) intimate, (2) personal, (3) social, and (4) public, as pictured in Figure 7-5. Let's briefly discuss how the salesperson can determine and use these four zones in dealing with prospects.

Intimate Zone

The intimate zone is about arm's length, or roughly 2 feet, and is reserved for loved ones or close friends. Once a prospect has become a loyal customer, an occasional pat on the back or hand on the shoulder might be in order, but only if the customer initiates such practices. Until then, stay out of the customer's intimate zone.

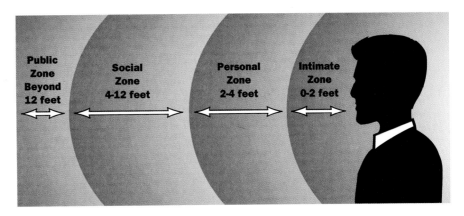

FIGURE 7-5 The Four Zones for Communication

Personal Zone

The personal zone, which begins at 2 feet and ends at about 4 feet, is a zone that business acquaintances and strangers are normally allowed to enter. Some prospects, however are uncomfortable with new salespeople in this zone.

Social Zone

When beginning a sales presentation, it is best to stay in the social zone, which is 4 to 12 feet away from the prospect. Actually, in many cases, you will have to stay 6 to 8 feet away because that is where most business office furniture arrangements will place you. Later, as rapport grows, the prospect may invite you into his or her personal zone by coming out from behind the desk or pulling a chair up to you. If the prospect seems "glued" to the chair, you might attempt to get a little closer by handing the prospect a sample product and some sales literature and then leaning toward the prospect in order to point out special features. It has been shown that highly successful salespeople gradually move closer to prospects as they prepare to close the sale.[7]

Public Zone

Finally, you will most likely make use of the *public zone* when giving a sales presentation to a group of people. The distance of 12 feet or more is about the same as between a teacher and students in a classroom. It is nonthreatening and allows people to feel comfortable and secure in their own territorial zones.

You should also keep in mind that the appropriate distance for communication varies from one culture to another. Smart salespeople and their companies study the proxemics of the foreign country they are going to be working in *before* they arrive. For example, many people in Spanish-speaking countries prefer to speak at close range and may be offended if you move back. In contrast, people in German-speaking countries feel more comfortable with formality and spatial distance.

[7]John T. Molloy, *Live for Success* (New York: Perigord Press, 1981), p. 99.

Nonverbal Communication: Kinesics or Body Language

KINESICS Describes bodily gestures and movements with regard to what these gestures and movements communicate to other people.

Studies show that over 70 percent of human communications is nonverbal, even though most of us are not aware that we are communicating this way.[8] **Kinesics** is a term describing any movement in our bodies that communicates something to others, including shifts in posture (body angle), facial expressions, eye movements, and arm, hand, and leg movements. Every movement or gesture we make, from shrugging our shoulders to crossing our legs to subtly winking an eye, is a part of this body language. Unconscious movements or changes, such as the throb of a neck muscle, heavy breathing, or blushing, can reveal many emotions, including tenseness, frustration, anger, and embarrassment.

Reading Body Language

Everybody "reads" and uses body language to some degree. Many professional athletes are expert readers and users of body language, and this ability gives them a competitive edge. For example, clever opponents observed that Miami football quarterback Dan Marino always slapped the center with the back of his right hand a split second before the snap.[9] In baseball, catchers call pitches with their fingers and coaches use various body language signs to tell batters to bunt or base runners to steal. Some players reveal when they are going to try to steal a base by the way they crouch just before running, and some pitchers make an unconscious facial expression when they are about to throw a curve or a fast ball.

Some salespeople become expert at reading body language and use this ability to determine prospects' mental states during a sales call. Prospects are always sending signals with body language, and some of the messages are obvious. For instance, when the prospect looks at his watch, starts stacking up his desk papers, or reading his mail, he is signaling that he wants to end the interview. When this happens, you should acknowledge the value of the prospect's time and try to close the sale quickly. If it appears that your close won't be successful this time, ask for another appointment, thank the prospect, then exit. Most body language is more subtle. One successful salesperson claims that there are two unmistakable clues of intent to buy: (1) When prospects put their fingers on their chins, they are ready to buy; and (2) when they put their hands over their mouths on or near their noses, they are not yet ready to buy.

Sending Body Language Messages

Learning to use nonverbal language is very important to sales success. In a pioneering study of nonverbal communication, Edward T. Hall was able to predict 74 percent of the time whether or not a sale would take place by observing nonverbal language only.[10] You will make better sales presentations if your nonverbal language is harmonious with your verbal expression. We have all seen speakers whose body language was out of synch with their words and voice inflections. It's almost like watching a movie where the sound and the action are not synchronized.

[8]C. Barnum and N. Wolniansky, "Taking Cues from Body Language," *Management Review,* June 1989, p. 59.
[9]"Body Language," *Special Report on Sports,* February–April 1989, p. 38.
[10]Wilbur Schramm, *The Process and Effects of Mass Communications* (Urbana: University of Illinois Press, 1960), p. 3.

Nonverbal messages have several channels or vehicles: (1) general appearance and personal hygiene, (2) body postures and movements, (3) eyes and facial expressions, (4) arm, hand, and leg movements, and (5) voice characteristics. We have already seen how an understanding of proxemics can help you in the selling situation. Let's see how the other aspects of body language can help you, too.

General appearance and hygiene. Good grooming and personal hygiene are essential to salespeople if they want to send positive messages to prospects and customers. Shined shoes, neatly pressed shirt or blouse and suit, clean and trimmed fingernails, and neatly combed hair will enhance your communication effectiveness. Bad breath or body odor will cause everybody to give you plenty of space and little time. After that third cup of coffee each morning, salespeople should refresh their mouths by brushing their teeth, gargling with a mouthwash, or using a breath mint or spray before calling on the next customer.

Body postures and movements. Almost like people who are shaking their heads "no" or nodding their heads "yes," prospects who make side-to-side movements with their bodies are usually expressing negative feelings—perhaps anxiety and uncertainty—while prospects who are moving their bodies back and forth are expressing positive feelings. When prospects lean toward you, they are interested in what you're saying and showing a positive reaction. When they lean away from you, they are communicating negative emotions—perhaps disinterest, boredom, hesitation, wariness, or distrust.

A rigid, erect posture conveys defensiveness, while a sloppy posture suggests disinterest or boredom. People who share the same opinion in a group uncon-

Company Highlight

Timex Dresses for Success

After a year of fighting the corporate bureaucracy at Timex, Mike Jacoby, worldwide vice president for marketing and sales, got permission to reimburse Watch Division salespeople for 67 percent of their clothing purchases each year—as long as the new clothes conform to corporate standards of attire. The company set an annual payout limit of $1,500 for each salesperson. Eligible salespeople just send their clothing receipts to Timex for reimbursement; the subsidies are treated as taxable income for each employee. Jacoby gives the salesmen a list of recommended stores and brands, including Brooks Brothers, Paul Stuart, and Hickey-Freeman. They are free to shop elsewhere as long as their purchases are guided by a dress-for-success booklet Jacoby gives them. As for the saleswomen, Jacoby says he wouldn't dare give them clothing advice. He just gives them the money and tells them to make their own selections. Entry-level salespeople receive an extra $500–$1,000 allowance to help them build a basic wardrobe. What the program comes down to, argues Jacoby, is an investment in the company's image.

Source: "Perks: Timex Subsidizes Suits and Ties," *Sales & Marketing Management,* November 1986, pp. 26–30.

Does this buyer look pleased to see you today? Why or why not? How would you address him?

sciously tend to assume the same body postures. When prospects agree with you, they often mirror your body posture. This is a signal for you to try to close the sale.

Deliberate medium-speed strides send a message of confidence. Slumped posture and shuffling feet send a message that you lack self-confidence. But an overly erect posture, like that of a military cadet, suggests rigidity and lack of warmth.

Eyes and facial expressions. Some people have "rubber faces" that openly show approval, disapproval, concern, relaxation, frustration, impatience—the whole range of human emotions. Other people have "stone faces" that seem to reveal little about what's going on inside their heads. Eyes are the most important feature on our faces. When we are interested or excited, our pupils tend to enlarge. Magicians have long known this and use their eye-reading skills to identify which card we picked out of a deck. Jewelry salespeople are often so expert at reading people's eyes that professional jewelry buyers sometimes wear dark glasses so that salespeople cannot see their level of interest in different pieces.

Eye contact in our culture conveys sincerity and interest, while eye avoidance suggests insincerity and dishonesty. Long contact usually indicates rapt attention, but overlong eye contact may invade the prospect's privacy and be considered threatening. People can smile with their lips or with their eyes. In fact, unless the eyes are smiling, the person's lip smile may be insincere.

John Molloy, author of several books on dressing for success, gives a different perspective on eye contact and smiling for women, as described in the following vignette.

Arm, hand, and leg movements. Like an orchestra conductor's, our arm movements express our intensity of feeling. If we wave our arms frantically, we are in distress or trying to get someone's attention. Similarly, when we make stiff, jerky movements with our arms, we are expressing determination or aggression.

DO EYE CONTACT AND SMILES
KILL SALES FOR SALESWOMEN?

Molloy claims that present methods of sales training often do not work for women because they are based on the assumption that women use body language the same way men do. Every saleswoman he interviewed said that their male sales trainers gave them the same selling advice they gave the men. For instance, the trainers told them to maintain eye contact or they would turn their buyers off. But the women knew that keeping steady eye contact with a male buyer often turned him on. Some saleswomen were instructed to smile all the time, even though they intuitively knew that if they smiled too much, they wouldn't be taken seriously. One woman summed up the results of Molloy's research on saleswomen by saying: "Smiles kill sales." Being taken seriously is one of the main problems women have in business, so they must start by looking serious. Molloy advises women not to smile for at least the first ten minutes of the initial sales call. Only after "you have established the fact that you're a serious businessperson" can you afford to smile if you're a woman.

SOURCE: John T. Molloy, *Molloy's Live for Success* (New York: Bantam Books, 1983), p. 91.

If we move our arms gracefully and slowly, we are expressing warmth and gentleness. People from some cultures have even been ridiculed for being incapable of communicating without using their hands. The language of hands is not easy to read because hand movements must be interpreted in the context of a given situation. People often show impatience by tapping their fingers on a desk. Clenched fists are a strongly defensive or offensive gesture. Touching the fingertips of one hand to the fingertips of the other hand to form a kind of steeple indicates dominance or weighing of alternatives. When prospects handle a product roughly, they are suggesting that they find it of little worth. When they handle it gingerly, they are suggesting that they feel the product is valuable. To suggest

How can you tell that this buyer is willing to talk openly with you?

This buyer feels that she can beat these two sales reps at their own game! Can you *see* why?

high quality, clever salespeople often carefully and dramatically use their hands to remove their products, whether knives or perfume, from fancy packages in front of prospects. Prospects who cross their legs in an open position toward the salesperson are sending a message of confidence, interest, and cooperation. But prospects who cross their legs away from a salesperson are sending a negative message. In an Arab country, you must be careful about body shifts because showing the soles of your shoes may be seen as an insult.

Voice characteristics.   Voice qualities such as volume, pitch, sound articulation, resonance, inflection, and tempo, and nonlanguage sounds or vocalizations such as laughing, yawning, grunting, and expressions like *uh-uh* for "no," *uh-huh* for "yes," and *ah* or *er* for hesitation, are called *paralanguage.* If you go into international sales, you will find that people in some cultures will start making a hissing sound as they breathe, which means: "I hear you, but I'm not sure that I agree—I'm thinking about it."

It's a good idea for you to tape your sales presentation practice sessions so that you can critique your voice characteristics and nonverbal communication (see Table 7-4). Varying your speech pattern by increasing its volume or pace can help emphasize key points. Speaking in a very quiet voice can sometimes draw

TABLE 7-4   Salesperson Vocal Qualities

VOICE QUALITY	POTENTIAL PROBLEMS
Volume	Do you speak too loudly or too softly?
Pitch	Is your voice too high or too low?
Clarity	Do you slur your words, or do you enunciate clearly?
Resonance	Is the timbre or tone of your voice unpleasant?
Inflection	Do you speak in a monotone, or do you use changes in inflection to emphasize points?
Speed	Do you speak too fast or too slowly?

Watch out! How can you recognize that you are pushing these buyers too much? Now, how do you get out of this situation?

attention to your points as well. The pace or speed of delivery should be determined by the preference of the prospect and the complexity of the presentation. Material that is easy to grasp can be covered at a faster rate of speech, but slowing down will give emphasis to whatever point you are making. Voice quality can be improved. Any salesperson with a significant vocal problem ought to enroll in a speech class or work with family members, friends, or colleagues to correct it.

Reading

Salespeople must become outstanding readers because there is so much material to absorb from headquarters, customers, and general business sources. Some salespeople take speed-reading courses to overcome bad habits (such as lip synching or subvocalizing every word) that slow down their reading pace. Learning to scan or skim material to quickly ferret out the essence is an important skill that all salespeople need to develop.

Writing

One of the little secrets of top salespeople is writing to prospects and customers. Notes to thank customers, alert them to upcoming price changes, and confirm appointments; letters that cover sales proposals, summarize sales calls, and provide interesting information—all these can give you a significant edge over competitive salespeople.

Reports

Nearly all sales managers require their salespeople to prepare daily or weekly sales and activity reports covering essential information about sales, customer needs, competitive actions, and market conditions. It is to your career advantage to do a good job in completing these reports and to submit them on time, because they indicate how you might perform as a sales manager. Keep a copy of your reports as an aid in analyzing your personal sales activities and use of time.

Taking Notes

Like reporters, good salespeople know that taking notes during or after a sales call aids their recall and improves their communications with prospects and customers. Writing down key words or an outline that you can review later will help ensure that you don't forget critical details of a conversation. On your daily sales calls you'll often pick up bits of information on customers and their needs that are worthy of jotting down for later reference. Over the months and years this daily note-taking habit will enable you to build a file on customers, prospects, and general information that will give you an edge on competing salespeople.

Here are some suggestions for improving your writing skills:

- Outline the key points you want to make in your letter or memorandum.
- State your most important points first.
- Express your thoughts clearly and succinctly in simple words.
- Use conversational words that paint a vivid verbal picture of what might be experienced through the senses: seeing, tasting, touching, smelling, and hearing.
- Use the vocabulary or special jargon most familiar to the individual to whom you're writing.
- Use strong, action-oriented verbs. Avoid passive verbs such as forms of "to be."
- Focus on the prospect by using "you" frequently. For example: "We invite you to visit our booth at the trade show" is stronger than "Our booth will be conveniently located for a visit."[11]

BARRIERS TO COMMUNICATION

There are many barriers that can distort or completely inhibit communication between salespeople and prospects. Even though they learn to recognize and avoid these barriers, the best salespeople know that they may not be able to overcome all of them all the time. Some of the biggest barriers are (1) an uncomfortable physical environment, (2) poor personal chemistry, (3) inappropriate words and phrases, (4) irritating personal habits, (5) interference, (6) fatigue, (7) absent partner, (8) bad mood, (9) withdrawal, and (10) a lack of empathy for customer problems. We will devote the rest of this chapter to a discussion of these barriers and how you, the salesperson, might deal with them.

Uncomfortable Physical Environment

Unless people are physically comfortable, they're not likely to communicate well. If a room is too cold, hot, smokey, noisy, or otherwise annoying, you should try to move to another room. If that is impossible, attempt to change the conditions by politely suggesting that the heat or air conditioning be turned on or by offering to open or close a window or door.

[11]Based partially on Bruce B. MacMillan, "Seven Ways to Improve Your Writing Skills," *Sales & Marketing Management,* March 11, 1985, pp. 75–76.

Poor Personal Chemistry

Sometimes two people just don't hit it off. A sales rep may remind the buyer of his former high-school math teacher who flunked him. Or the prospect may be a quiet, pipe-smoking man and the salesperson a hyperactive nonsmoker. Occasionally, an entire organization may project an unpleasant aura, like arrogance or disdain toward outsiders. For instance, some publisher's representatives have complained that they don't like to call on certain colleges and universities because the professors are rude or treat them like inferiors. Salespeople dealing with customers with whom they have poor chemistry must work harder to understand those customers and find ways to improve the relationship. This chapter's Selling in Action box features the story of how one salesperson overcame potential chemistry problems—without realizing it until after the sale was made.

Inappropriate Words and Phrases

You must not allow yourself to slip into jargon that has little or no meaning to customers. Using highly technical words when talking to a nontechnical prospect about a piece of equipment will probably be an intimidating turnoff. Another barrier to effective communication is the use of offensive words such as profanity or negative words and phrases. In talking to most prospects and customers, you should avoid curse words, street slang, bad grammar, racial, sexual, and ethnic slurs, and insulting words like *stupid, worthless, ignorant, dumb, idiot,* and *terrible.* Finally, excessively repeated irritating words and phrases such as "You know," "I couldn't care less," "Ah" or "Um," "like," "Are you with me?", "Know what I mean?", "Right," and "You got that right" can inhibit communication with prospects and customers. Even the popular "How may I help you?" is heard by some prospects as condescending.

Irritating Personal Habits

Prospects and customers can also be offended by the salesperson's personal habits. Smoking is never a good idea, even if your present prospect is smoking. The smell may cling to you, and your next prospect could very well be an ardent nonsmoker. Some other personal habits to avoid are: audible clearing of your throat, frequently pushing your glasses back on your nose, continually straightening your tie, clicking your ballpoint pen on and off, chewing gum, biting your fingernails, cracking your knuckles, putting your fingers on your nose, and twitching your face or shoulders. Videotaping your sales presentations will reveal many of these habits so that you can become more conscious of them on sales calls and eventually eliminate them.

INTERFERENCE In communication, anything that hinders or stops a communicative exchange. Interference may be external (like loud office equipment) or internal (like negative opinions about new products).

Interference

Communication can also be hindered or stopped by external or internal **interference.** A salesperson who must speak with a prospect while noisy machines clang in the background and telephones ring continually is a victim of *external interference.* A salesperson who must first try to overcome a prospect's stubborn

Selling in Action

Even Tough Guys Have a Soft Spot

After earning his college degree in marketing, Marvin Gibson took a job with Universal Building Supplies, headquartered in Delaware. After a six-week training course, Marv was assigned a territory in southeast Pennsylvania that was notorious for one very tough purchasing agent, Mike Bitters of Henderson Modular Homes (HMH). A warning from the previous salesperson in the territory unnerved Marv about calling on Mr. Bitters, even though the account had a high-volume potential. The previous salesperson had been insulted and thrown out of Mr. Bitters's office on the first sales call for "wasting his valuable time," so he never called on HMH again. He told Marv that "Mike Bitters is a domineering jerk. Nobody can sell him anything. He hasn't changed suppliers in 20 years, so there's no use even calling on him." Marv avoided the HMH account during his first three months on the job. But one day when he was in a particularly upbeat mood, Marv decided to give the notorious Mike Bitters a try. After arriving at Henderson Modular Homes headquarters, Marv felt a lump in his throat as he asked the receptionist if he could see Mr. Bitters. The receptionist smirked and called Mr. Bitters's secretary. To Marv's and the receptionist's surprise, Mr. Bitters decided to grant him exactly five minutes. So off Marv trotted to Mr. Bitters's office where, through a half-opened door, he saw a large, rough-featured man in his early 60s staring down at some papers. Knocking on the door, Marv said: "Mr. Bitters, I'm Marv Gibson from Universal Building Supplies. May I come in?" "Yeah, but get straight to the point. I'm busy and

don't have time to waste bullshooting with a salesman." Nervously glancing around the office, Marv noticed a plaque on the wall to the right of Mr. Bitters's desk and blurted out without thinking: "That's an impressive plaque, what's it for?" Well, those turned out to be the magic words. Mr. Bitters launched into a story about how he had been chosen Pennsylvania's top purchasing agent five years ago and exactly what led to his selection. Marv didn't say a word for 30 minutes. He just listened intensely while making a few appropriate nods of his head and "mmm-huh" sounds. At the end of the half hour, Mr. Bitters said curtly: "I've got to go to a meeting. Leave your product brochures with my secretary." Then he got up and left without so much as a good-bye or a handshake.

Thinking he had failed like his predecessor, Marv felt a little depressed as he drove home after his last sales call that night. But the next morning, to his delight, he learned that Mr. Bitters had called and placed a large order and given Marv credit for being a persuasive salesperson. After that, Marv called on Mr. Bitters regularly, and within two years, HMH had become Marv's biggest customer. According to Marv, what really won over Mr. Bitters was that "I unwittingly encouraged him to tell his own story. No other sales rep had ever shown any interest in Mr. Bitters personally. They were all too intimidated by his gruff reputation."

Source: This story was related to the author by a former student who became a professional salesperson. The names of the people and companies have been changed.

preconceptions about new products before making a sales presentation is a victim of *internal interference.*

Although you can often remedy external interference by doing something as easy as closing a door or suggesting a move to another room, remedying internal interference can be a difficult and time-consuming task. Attitudes and beliefs about old and current products can interfere with the acceptance of new and different products. You may hear prospects say things like: "We tried something like that a couple of years ago and it didn't work" or "We've always used this brand and see no reason to change now." Your golden rule for handling prospects with this kind of attitude should be: *Never directly attack the prospect's beliefs about a current product or preconceptions about a new product.* Be patient. Find out what the prospect likes and dislikes about the current product and how he or she thinks it could be improved. Use this information to custom-tailor your sales presentation to that prospect's particular needs and demands.

Fatigue

No salesperson should work so hard as to fall into a state of physical or mental exhaustion. Fatigue keeps people from performing at their best and prevents them from effectively communicating. If either the salesperson or the prospect is in a state of exhaustion or mental fatigue, it is best to reschedule the appointment for another day.

Absent Partner

In the middle of a sales negotiation, you may suddenly be confronted with your prospect's real or imaginary *absent partner*. Usually, the prospect will indicate the absent partner's presence by saying something like: "Oh, my boss wouldn't like these terms at all" or "I'm not sure if my wife likes these colors." Most prospects use the absent partner in one of two ways: (1) as a defense mechanism or (2) as a genuine indication of the need to confer with the partner before making a buying decision.

If you believe the prospect is using the absent partner in the second way, you might have to find out everything you can about what the absent partner could want, give the prospect the appropriate information and materials to show the absent partner, and schedule another appointment for after the prospect has consulted with the partner.

More often, however, the prospect is using the absent partner as a defense mechanism. Perhaps the prospect simply wants to be relieved of the pressure to make the buying decision. In this case, you could ask the prospect a question that reflects your interest in the absent partner's opinion, like "What features especially interest your boss?" This kind of question might help you discover the real cause of the prospect's defensive attitude so that you can redirect your questioning. It could be, however, that the prospect is trying to signal an end to your sales presentation. Maybe the prospect has an important meeting coming up, is tired, or has simply seen too many salespeople already that day. You might carefully continue questioning, but if the prospect resists, don't push your luck. Schedule an appointment for another day.

Bad Mood

Occasionally, you will encounter a customer who is upset, angry, or depressed, and therefore grouchy, insulting, or sullen—and just about impossible to communicate with. Recognize that you are not the target, but have just wandered across a shooting range where someone is firing randomly. So what do you do? Quickly but graciously get off the firing range and come back some other day.

Withdrawal

Prospects will withdraw and stop paying attention to a salesperson when they feel duress or stress. You need to become sensitive to the prospect's withdrawal symptoms and any actions you may have taken to trigger them so that you can avoid those actions on future sales calls.

Lack of Empathy for Customer's Problems

Actor and comedian George Burns used to say: "If you want to be successful in Hollywood, you've got to be sincere. And if you can fake that, you've got it made." Few salespeople can fake sincerity and fool prospects into thinking they really care when they don't. Instead of working hard to fake sincerity, the best salespeople work hard to develop genuine empathy with their customers. *Empathy* is the ability to identify with another person's feelings in a given situation. Salespeople who are successful over the long run really do care about their customers, and they display sincere empathy and understanding for their situations. They are able to make their customers' problems more important than their own, at least during the work day.

SUMMARY   In this chapter, we examined principles and theories of communication and communication skills for the professional salesperson. After stating that *active listening* is the most important communication skill for the salesperson to learn and practice, we discussed various methods for classifying and understanding the ways people communicate with each other.

The concept of three ego states—adult, parent, and child—provides a good general principle for understanding human communications. Salespeople should stay in the *adult ego state* as much as possible with their prospects and customers.

Turning to specific *communication styles,* we saw how an individual's levels of *assertiveness* and *responsiveness* could be plotted in four directions, yielding four basic communication styles: (1) *amiable,* (2) *expressive,* (3) *analytical,* and (4) *driver.* Quickly comprehending each new prospect's communication style and *flexing* to that style will enable the salesperson to sell to prospects in the way they want to be sold to.

The chapter concluded with a discussion of communication skills for the salesperson. The best salespeople are constantly sharpening their ability to (1) listen, (2) ask questions, (3) persuade, (4) use space, (5) communicate nonverbally, (6) read, and (7) write.

CHAPTER REVIEW QUESTIONS

1. What is the difference between communication and promotion?

2. Name and list some of the characteristics of the three ego states. Are they of any possible significance to selling? Why or why not?

3. Briefly describe how you would sell to each of the four communication styles: amiable, expressive, driver, and analytical.

4. What is "style flexing" and why is it important to salespeople? Give an example of style flexing in a selling situation.

5. What are the differences between "selective" and "concentrated" listening? Under concentrated listening, what are the four kinds of discriminative listening, and which of them is most important for salespeople to learn?

6. Name the three basic question formats. What kind of response would you expect from a customer for each format?

7. Make a simple two-column chart on a separate piece of paper (or on your computer)—a "T" design will do. In the left-hand column, list the six specific types of questions salespeople use, leaving plenty of space between each entry. In the right-hand column, put down as much information as you can about each question type—how and when to use it, the expected or desired response, and examples.

8. How should salespeople understand "persuasion"? Discuss three persuasive techniques.

9. How would you describe the difference between "proxemics" and "kinesics"?

10. Name and briefly describe six barriers to effective communication.

TOPICS FOR THOUGHT AND CLASS DISCUSSION

1. Can you think of any people—in your own life or in public life—who appear to be very effective communicators? What do you think makes them so effective? Is there any way that you could incorporate some of their communication techniques into your own repertoire of techniques? How?

2. If your class is small enough, designate a student—or the instructor—to ask everyone in the class where he or she fits into the four communication styles: amiables, expressives, analyticals, drivers. Which style appears to be most prevalent in your class? Now discuss how a salesperson with that communication style would interact with prospects and customers—what would be some of the advantages and disadvantages of "coming from" this communication style?

PROJECTS FOR PERSONAL GROWTH

1. Prepare a 20-minute sales presentation on a product with which you are very familiar. Rehearse it several times, then ask a friend to watch you while you give your presentation and note positive and negative verbal and nonverbal communication. Compare the effect *you* thought you were having to the effect *your friend* thought you had during the presentation. Any surprises? (If you have the resources, try doing this exercise with a video camera and/or a cassette tape recorder/player. For the video camera: After taping your presentation, play it back while observing and listening to all modes of communication, then play it back with the sound off so you can analyze body language only. For the cassette tape recorder: Record yourself doing your

presentation and analyze your voice. Whether you make your presentation to a friend, videotape it, or merely record it, ask yourself the following questions: Do I look and sound sincere? Would I buy from myself? With respect to verbal and nonverbal communication, what do I like about my presentation? What don't I like?)

2. Over the next two days, find two people who are giving a speech or an address, whether in person or on television, and take the time to hear and watch the whole presentation. Evaluate their verbal and nonverbal communication. What advice would you give these people to improve their communication effectiveness? Do you think they got their points across? What did you find convincing and/or inspiring about what they said and did? Did they look or sound at all insincere? What was basically good about their "performances," and what was basically bad about them?

KEY TERMS

Communication A process in which information and understanding are conveyed in a two-way exchange between two or more people.

Promotion Typically, a one-way flow of persuasive information from a seller to a buyer.

Communication style The way a person gets his or her message across to other people.

Assertiveness The degree to which a person attempts to control or dominate situations and direct the thoughts and actions of other people.

Responsiveness The level of emotions, feelings, or sociability that a person openly displays.

Critical listening A type of concentrated listening in which you attempt to analyze the ideas presented by the speaker and make critical judgments about the validity and quality of the information presented.

Discriminative listening A type of concentrated listening in which you listen to understand and remember. This is the type of listening most often used by salespeople.

Probing question A type of question used to "dig" or "probe" for information when prospects and customers have difficulty articulating their precise needs.

Evaluative question A type of question used within the open-ended ques-

tion format to stimulate prospects and customers to talk about their general or specific goals, problems, and needs.

Dichotomous question A type of question used to set up a clear-cut "either-or" answer for prospects and customers.

Persuasion As salespeople should understand it, persuasion is a carefully developed communication process built upon a firm foundation of mutual trust and benefit shared between buyer and seller.

Bandwagon A persuasive technique that encourages a prospect or customer to buy a product by implying that the product is extremely popular among other customers with similar needs and requirements.

Proxemics Refers to the spatial relationships (positions) of people and objects.

Kinesics Describes bodily gestures and movements with regard to what these gestures and movements communicate to other people.

Interference In communication, anything that hinders or stops a communicative exchange. Interference may be external (like loud office equipment) or internal (like negative opinions about new products).

Case 7-1

DEVISING COMMUNICATION STRATEGIES

Sally Blakemore is beginning her first field day on her job as missionary salesperson or "detail person" for Bevan-Warner Pharmaceutical Company. Having completed a three-month training program, she is now ready to call on hospitals and medical offices in the Philadelphia area to introduce and explain her company's pharmaceutical products to health-care professionals. Called a "detail person" because her job is to give doctors all the details needed to convince them to prescribe the Bevan-Warner pharmaceuticals for their patients, Ms. Blakemore will not directly sell or take orders for her company's products. Instead, her job is to influence the doctor "decider" in the purchasing process for Bevan-Warner pharmaceuticals.

As she learned in her training program, few doctors are able to keep up with the latest pharmaceutical products because of their hectic daily schedules. Most tend to rely heavily on detail people to keep them up-to-date. Sally Blakemore's job is to provide in-depth information on the chemical make-up of each product, how it interacts with other medicines a patient might be taking, and the potential side effects from using it. To gain the trust of the medical professionals, detail people must know their products thoroughly and be able to answer questions in a straightforward, professional way. In addition, the detail person must be able to communicate effectively with diverse physician personalities.

On this first day of field work, Sally is calling on three doctors: (1) Dr. Peter Hartman, an orthopedic surgeon; (2) Dr. Elizabeth Butterfield, a general practitioner; and (3) Dr. Janice Winer, a gynecologist. Her predecessor, who was promoted to district sales manager after three years in the field, tried to help Sally understand the personalities of the three physicians. Here's the way he described each one:

Dr. Peter Hartman is a tall, thin man about 55 years old who tends to be somewhat irritable and generally preoccupied. He's definitely not Mr. Warmth. I always get the feeling in talking to him that he doesn't quite believe me. I can never keep him listening to me for more than ten minutes, and he always sits on the edge of his chair like he's ready to jump up at any time. He's got a reputation as a loner in that he doesn't socialize with any of the other doctors or

nurses. His wife divorced him three years ago after they raised three children—two of whom are doctors. I think the other one is a struggling artist. With Hartman, you'll need to get right to the point because his favorite line is: "Give me the short version and nothing but the facts, please." He won't ask many questions, but he'll expect you to provide very precise answers. And he'll want to see the research that backs up product claims, so leave him all the technical product literature you can and send him more in between visits. I've found that he actually reads those reports, so it will help you on your next call to have him high up on the learning curve.

Dr. Elizabeth Butterfield is one of the nicest, least pretentious people you'll ever meet. She's everybody's mother. Although she sees a heavy load of patients every day, her spirits never seem to be dampened. She's always laughing and telling playful little one-liners, often about her size—she's over six feet tall and "full-figured," as they say. Her husband's a high-school principal and they have five children, ranging in age from 4 to 20. Her patients love her, and so does nearly everyone else. Dr. Liz will always find at least 15 or 20 minutes to see you no matter how backed up her schedule is. I hear that she often stays in her office until 10 o'clock at night seeing patients. And her nurses say she's just as upbeat at the end of a long day as at the beginning. The thing that always amazes me is that she remembers your name after meeting you once, and she'll remember the names of any family members you've talked about, too. She always asked how my mother was doing. It's a joy to call on her because she makes you feel that she likes, trusts, and respects you.

Dr. Janice Winer is a superintelligent woman about 35 years old who I heard was number one in her class at medical school. She's perpetual motion and all business. She moves fast, talks fast, thinks fast, and makes decisions fast. I don't think I've ever met anyone who's more organized and efficient. Her whole office staff is the same way. You know how most doctors always seem to have a lot of patients in the waiting room. Well, I've never seen more than two or three patients in her waiting room at any one time. At first, I thought it was because she didn't have many patients. Then her receptionist showed me her appointment book—she's booked up solid for months ahead of time, but she's simply one of those rare doctors who's nearly always ready to see you at approximately the time of your scheduled appointment. You don't want to waste her time with chit-chat. She'll greet you politely, then say: "Okay, what have you got?" You can be halfway through a product presentation and she'll stop you and say: "Okay, I'm sold on it. What else do you have?" I never really got to know her personally, but I understand she got married last year to a corporate executive who is 20 years her senior.

Ever since listening to her colleague describe the people she will meet on her first three calls, Sally has felt anxious about whether her own personality will mesh or clash with the personalities of the three physicians. In college, her classmates used to kiddingly call her "grind" because of her unwillingness to break her habit of studying at the university library every weeknight from 7 to 11 P.M. True, she graduated with a 3.8 average on a 4.0 scale, but she certainly doesn't think of herself as a grind because she was an officer in the student marketing club and a sorority member. She saved her partying for the weekends. Thinking about how others might describe her, Sally imagines them saying things like: quiet, reserved, intelligent, hard-working, coopera-

tive, organized, goal-oriented, determined, and likable. "Hmmm," she thinks to herself, "I'm not sure what personality type I am. I seem to be a mixture of several types, like most people. Oh well, no use worrying any more—best to just get going."

Questions

1. How would you categorize the personalities of each of the three physicians Sally will be calling on?
2. What personality type is Sally?
3. Which of the physicians do you think Sally will be able to communicate with best? Why? Which one will she have the most difficulty communicating with? Why?
4. What advice would you give Sally before she calls on each physician?

Case 7-2

SELLING ADVERTISING SERVICES

Clare Suzuki is an account representative for Burton, Dirksen, & Lipton, a New York advertising agency. She and Earl Webb, a vice president of the agency, are in the midst of making a sales presentation designed to win the advertising account for the Lovable Tramp line of dry dog food manufactured by National Foods Corporation. The account could be worth over $5 million to B, D & L. Sitting at a big round table in a comfortable conference room are seven National Foods representatives: the vice president of marketing, the director of brand management, the brand manager, two assistant brand managers, a product development manager, and a marketing research manager.

Mr. Webb and Clare carefully rehearsed their presentation for two days before flying to National Foods headquarters in Milwaukee. Mr. Webb's part of the presentation was timed to last about an hour, and Clare's was to be about 25 minutes. As Mr. Webb is about to finish his part of the presentation—which has taken 75 minutes because of some questions from the National Foods people—Clare glances around the room to see how it is going over. Even

though the room is darkened so people can view Mr. Webb's color transparencies better, she can see what everybody is doing. Two people in the audience are doodling on the handouts that she and Mr. Webb passed out. George Mason, National's vice president of marketing, is resting his head on his cupped hand and quietly tapping his fingers on the table. Another person is leaning back in his chair with his hands clasped behind his head. The director of product management has just gotten up to get a cup of coffee from the table in the corner of the room. And the two assistant brand managers are whispering to each other and smiling.

During Mr. Webb's presentation, Clare knew that he was nervous because he repeatedly cleared his throat and uttered "uh" several times. Although Mr. Webb has a deep, resonant voice, he spoke very slowly and rarely changed his inflection to emphasize key points. In the darkened room, these little speech and voice problems seemed magnified.

Clare has 15 transparencies to show in her presentation, so she feels she will have to keep the lights dimmed. The original plan was not to take a break

between Mr. Webb's presentation and her own because the two presentations are so interconnected.
But now Clare fears that Mr. Webb was so engrossed
in his detailed presentation that he didn't notice how
bored and weary the audience was getting. Still, calling for a break after Mr. Webb's part will upset the
game plan, and Clare doesn't think she can suggest
this on her own initiative. Mr. Webb might really
blow his top if he feels the presentation didn't go
right. One of his favorite sayings is: "Sales presentations are our bread and butter. They're what we're
really selling. They're our real product. The advertisements we prepare later for the client are just confirmation of what we've already sold."

Soon Mr. Webb finishes, briefly introduces
Clare, then sits down. Standing up and glancing over
at Mr. Webb for an indication of whether there
should be any change in the presentation strategy,
Clare sees him pick up the presentation booklet and
turn to her part without looking up.

Questions

1. How do you think Mr. Webb's presentation was
received by the audience? Why? What visual aids
should he have used? Should he have tried to
involve the audience in the presentation?
How?

2. What do you think Clare should do? Should she
suggest a ten-minute break? Continue with her
part of the presentation as planned? Forget
about using the 15 transparencies and turn up
the lights in the room? Or turn up the lights and
show the 15 transparencies anyway?

3. Can you suggest anything else that Clare might
do to make sure that her part of the presentation
goes over well?

4. Depending on what you suggest, what should
Clare say to Mr. Webb when the two of them
discuss the presentation later? Should Clare offer Mr. Webb any suggestions on improving his
sales presentations? If so, how should she
broach this delicate matter? What would it be
appropriate for her to say to her boss?

Chapter 8

Personal Preparation for Sales Success

To be happy, set yourself a goal that commands your thoughts, liberates your energy and inspires your hopes.

DALE CARNEGIE

Profile

Peter Nordstrom

P ETE Nordstrom is one of the most experienced salespeople profiled in this book, with over 25 years of professional personal selling and marketing management behind him. Pete spent the first 23 years of his career selling for the Office Products Division of IBM. When IBM sold its Copier Division to Eastman Kodak, he accepted a job offer from Kodak and joined its Copy Products Division in Bellevue, Washington. He is definitely a "career rep" who loves the freedom, independence, and rewards of the selling job.

Pete considers sales motivation his specialty. He stresses the importance of self-motivation in the context of developing long-term business relationships with customers: "Like everything else on earth, selling operates on the Law of Exchange. You plant seeds, you reap a harvest. Certainly there are 'flash in the pan' salespeople who seem to get fantastic results right away, but generally that happens just for a season. Long-term, consistent results occur only by continuously planting seeds of value into the territory."

The core of every salesperson's motivation is a good attitude, which Pete believes to be one of the most important aspects of the salesperson's job. Pete explains: "Your attitude is your greatest asset or hindrance. It is your stock in trade. It empowers your creativity and controls your desire to excel. Your customers' opinion of you comes from *your* attitude, positive or negative. You are in control of your attitude. You decide how you will feel each day. If you expect good things to happen, they will. If you fear that mediocre or bad things will happen, they will. If your job has lost its excitement, it's because you have stopped putting excitement into it. Don't look for a new product, a new territory, or a promotion to spice up your job, because after a few months it will be old hat once again. You must be the one to keep yourself up all the time. You must make a decision to be excited about your job. Use your driving time to pump yourself up by listening to motivational cassette tapes. Don't space out on the radio. Stay away from negative people, no matter how much you like them. Certainly you should talk with them and be friendly, but don't allow them into your inner circle of friends. Spend your time with people who put good things into you, not with those who take goods things out of you."

At the same time, Pete cautions new salespeople about getting too caught up in the daily activities of making a living to provide themselves with security. "Don't deny yourself the time to make money. Regularly make appointments with yourself to go aside to a quiet place and get your creative juices flowing. Think of things you can do to push yourself outside of your 'comfort zone.' 'Possibilitize' on how you could approach a large, untapped opportunity. Remember: If you wanna' get big fleas, you gotta' hang out with big dogs!"

Pete attributes the power of his own personal and professional success and happiness to his strong religious beliefs, which, says Pete, "changed my entire life dramatically, including my sales results. I became more concerned about my customers' needs and desires than my own—and it showed. Customer loyalty that had never been there before started to develop. You can't sell on your own steam over the long haul—you need 'something higher.' " ∎

After reading this chapter, you should understand:

□ What it takes to become a successful salesperson

□ Some key characteristics and behaviors of super-achieving salespeople

□ What sales managers look for in new salespeople

□ various approaches for reprogramming your self-image and inspiring and motivating yourself toward sales success

SUCCESSFUL PEOPLE ARE GOOD SALESPEOPLE

In his book *Molloy's Live for Success,* John T. Molloy says:

> When we asked the wives, husbands, friends, and associates of some of the most successful men and women in America to describe them, the word they used most often was *supersalesperson.* In spite of the fact that more than 85 percent of the people being described never held a job in direct sales, they sold all the time. . . . When I told these executives that most of their associates saw them primarily as salespeople, they were in most cases flattered. In fact, two of them suggested an experiment. They sent select middle-management people through my sales training program to see if it would improve their performance. The results were so positive that several of our corporate clients now send all their middle managers to our sales training course.[1]

WHAT DOES IT TAKE TO BE A SUCCESSFUL SALESPERSON?

Today's professional salesperson has a more challenging, rewarding, and interesting job than the salesperson of any earlier time. Fantastic innovations in telecommunications and computer technology, increasingly complex products and services, continual change in customer tastes and preferences, expanded support from headquarters marketing, greater buyer professionalism, higher expectations for product and service performance, growing diversity of markets, and intense global competition even for domestic markets—all these conditions demand that salespeople be better prepared than ever to achieve success. The salesperson of yesteryear would have a tough time making it in sales today.

In this complex selling environment, no one is a "born salesperson." Some people may exhibit more extroverted personalities and higher energy levels than others, but it takes a lot more than personality or energy to survive and prosper in sales. Let's find out what it does take to be a successful salesperson now and in the years ahead.

[1]John T. Molloy, *Molloy's Live for Success* (New York: Bantam Books, 1983), p.87.

Attributes of Successful Salespeople

McMurry and Arnold identified six attributes of successful salespeople: (1) a high energy level, (2) solid self-confidence, (3) a strong desire to be paid well, (4) an ability to work hard without close supervision, (5) perseverance, and (6) a natural tendency to be competitive.[2]

At Eastman Kodak, four "nontrainable qualities" are sought in recruiting potential high-performing salespeople: *self-confidence* (not modesty); *job commitment* (unafraid to get hands dirty in doing the job); *persistence* (always finds another reason for going back when a customer says no); and *initiative* (in solving problems, gathering information, and asking direct questions).[3]

Hewlett-Packard believes that two qualities characterize top salespeople: They know how to get special things done smoothly for the customer inside or outside of normal policies and systems, and they always know where they stand with customers, in terms of their performance, stage in the selling process, positioning, and knowledge of the customer's situation.[4]

When 25 San Francisco Bay Area retail computer store sales managers were asked: "What kind of traits/qualities do you look for when hiring a salesperson?" 20 named *competitiveness* as most important. One sales manager replied that he hires only athletes who have competed in team sports because they've learned fear of failure and know how to deal with pressure. Other sales managers stated that participation in team sports demonstrates a high energy level and the ability to work with other people toward common goals.[5] Of course, these same qualities are demonstrated by people who participate in other extracurricular activities, such as writing for the school newspaper or serving as an officer in a student organization. A young saleswoman who displays the confidence, self-motivation, enthusiasm, competitiveness, and persistence needed for success in sales is presented in the following Selling in Action box.

Who Are the Supersalespeople?

After studying 1,500 superachievers over a period of 20 years, Charles Garfield, professor of clinical psychology at the University of California, is convinced that it takes mastery of several fields to become a supersalesperson. He sees certain common characteristics in peak sales performers:

■ *They are willing to take risks and to innovate.* Unlike most people, supersalespeople shun the "comfort zone" and strive constantly to surpass their previous levels of performance.

■ *They have a powerful sense of mission* and are able to set the short-, intermediate-, and long-term goals necessary to achieve that mission. Supersalespeople establish personal goals that are higher than the sales quotas given them by their sales managers.

[2]Robert McMurry and James Arnold, *How to Build a Dynamic Sales Organization* (New York:

[3]Thayer C. Taylor, "Anatomy of a Star Salesperson," *Sales & Marketing Management,* May 1986, p. 51.

[4]Ibid.

[5]Sharon M. Chase, "Competitiveness in the Sales Force," *Sales Management Update,* a publication of the Marketing and Sales Management Division of the American Marketing Association, Spring 1989, p. 3.

Selling in Action

Freedom, Challenge, and Opportunity

Twenty-four-year-old Krestin Haser, who sells office forms for the Arnold Corporation in Pittsburgh, says "freedom" was the major reason she was attracted to a career in selling. "You have your own schedule," says Ms. Haser. "It's fun to be able to meet your boyfriend for lunch or go to the mall" while other people are cooped up in an office. A college graduate with a degree in marketing, Ms. Haser took the job as a way to make money before pursuing a graduate degree in business. She had enjoyed a previous job promoting Gatorade and thought that selling might be similar. Ms. Haser was right; in fact, she likes selling even better. Her friendly personality, self-motivation, and determination seem to be the main ingredients of her success in selling business forms. On the job for 18 months, Ms. Haser can still remember the thrill of her first big sale—an order from North Side Deposit Bank for 100,000 drive-through teller envelopes, which earned her a $200 commission. "I was so happy I ran back to the office and blurted it out to everybody," she said.

Ms. Haser has already faced most of the unpleasant aspects of selling: disappointment, rejection, and anxiety. For example, a few months ago, she learned that a hospital in Pittsburgh was soliciting bids for its paper contract. It was an opportunity for a long-term contract worth around $15,000 a year in commissions. "I thought I had it all sewed up. Then the other company flew in six guys from out of town. They got it. I was depressed for a month."

"I think about going back to school or doing something with less pressure, but it's hard to quit," says Ms. Haser. "The longer you stay, the better you do. A couple of people in our office make over $100,000 a year."

Source: Sharon M. Chase, "Competitiveness in the Sales Force," *Sales Management Update,* a publication of the Marketing and Sales Management Division of the American Marketing Association, Spring 1989, p. 3.

- *They are more interested in solving problems than in placing blame* or bluffing their way out of situations. Because they view themselves as professionals, supersalespeople readily accept responsibility for what they do, and they are always trying to upgrade their skills.
- *They see their customers as partners and themselves as team players* rather than superstars or adversaries. Super-achieving salespeople believe that their job is to communicate with people. By contrast, mediocre salespeople tend to psychologically convert their customers into objects and talk about the number of calls and closes made as if these statistics are unrelated to human beings.
- *Supersalespeople accept each rejection as information they can learn from,* whereas mediocre salespeople personalize rejection.
- *They use mental rehearsal.* Before every sales call, supersalespeople rehearse each stage in the selling process in their mind's eye, from shaking the customer's hand to asking for the order.[6]

[6]"What Makes a Supersalesperson?" *Sales & Marketing Management,* August 13, 1984, p. 86.

Super-achieving salespeople see their customers as partners and themselves as team players.

Needs That Motivate Supersalespeople

One study of several thousand top sales producers found seven needs that motivate most of them:

1. *Need for status.* They are aware of and concerned about their image and reputation. Superior performance brings them recognition and proof of their status.

2. *Need for control.* They enjoy interacting with people and delight in using persuasive skills to influence them.

3. *Need for Respect.* They want to be seen as experts, and they view themselves as well-intentioned people helping others.

4. *Need for routine.* Contrary to the popular belief that supersalespeople are impulsive and undisciplined, most follow definite routines and dislike having them upset.

5. *Need for accomplishment.* Top performers constantly seek new challenges and go after the "impossible sales" to sustain their enthusiasm. Money is used more as a measure of success than as a prime motivator. Most top salespeople earn so much money that they take material things like a beautiful home, expensive clothing, and a luxury car for granted.

6. *Need for stimulation.* Supersalespeople are generally rather calm, relaxed people on the outside who internally thrive on continual stimulation and effectively channel their high physical energy.

7. *Need for honesty.* Supersalespeople have a strong need to believe in the product they are selling. They will often quit a company if they develop serious doubts about a new product line or if the company's reputation slips. In general, however, they are not rigidly moralistic and are willing to accept normal imperfections in people and products.[7]

[7]Donald J. Moine, "The Fire Within," *Psychology Today,* March 1984, pp. 37–44.

What Characteristics Are Most Important?

Forum, a Boston-based sales training company, surveyed three groups—customers, internal support staffs, and salespeople—to find out their perspectives on eight basic characteristics of top-performing salespeople. As revealed in Table 8-1, each group named different characteristics as most important. *Customers* rated knowledge, creativity, aggressiveness, and interpersonal skills about equally. *Internal support staff* judged knowledge and professionalism as most important to high performance. *Salespeople,* however, rated professionalism almost twice as high as any other characteristic and placed aggressiveness last. Probing deeper, Forum researchers found that it was not product knowledge so much as knowledge of the customer's situation coupled with the ability to orchestrate support resources for the customer that differentiated top performers from average salespeople.

What Do Sales Managers Look for in Salespeople?

When sales executives of some leading U.S. corporations were recently asked what they look for in new salespeople, the major conclusion was that they aren't looking for the popular stereotype of a fast-talking, joke-telling bundle of personality. Instead, they prefer ambitious, enthusiastic, well-organized, and highly persuasive individuals, preferably with some solid sales experience. In the opinion of sales managers, high-performing salespeople are those who:

- Maintain two-way advocacy, representing the interests of their companies and their customers with equal skill.
- Bring added value to the sales task through their enthusiasm, sensitive interpersonal skills, and sense of professionalism.
- Analyze the sales process, actively planning and developing strategies that will maximize their impact on the customer's time and provide for efficient internal support relationships.
- Are committed to the selling process as an "art form" or a way of life.[8]

Sales managers across 44 major manufacturing firms ranked ten desired attributes for salespeople in the following order (including two ties): (1) enthusiasm, (2) good organization, (3) obvious ambition, (4) high persuasiveness, (5) general sales experience, (6) high verbal skill, (6) specific sales experience, (7) good recommendations, (7) ability to follow instructions, and (8) sociability.[9]

[8]Thayer C. Taylor, "Anatomy of a Star Salesman," *Sales & Marketing Management,* May 1986, pp. 49–51. Other studies identifying key variables for successful salespeople include Stan Moss, "What Sales Executives Look for in New Salespeople," *Sales & Marketing Management,* March 1986, pp. 46–48; Melany E. Baehr and Glenn B. Williams, "Predictions of Sales Success from Factorially Determined Dimensions of Personal Background Data," *Journal of Applied Psychology,* April 1968, pp. 98–103; Robert Tanofsky, Ronald R. Shepp, and Paul J. O'Neill, "Pattern Analysis of Biographical Predictions of Success as an Insurance Salesman," *Journal of Applied Psychology,* April 1969. pp. 136–139.
[9]Stan Moss, "What Sales Executives Look for in New Salespeople," *Sales & Marketing Management,* March 1986, p. 47.

TABLE 8-1   Perspectives on Characteristics Accounting for Success of Top-Performing Salespeople

CHARACTERISTICS OF TOP SALESPEOPLE	CUSTOMERS	INTERNAL SUPPORT STAFF	SALESPEOPLE
Aggressive	14.8%	8.0%	3.4%
Creative	16.6	4.5	10.0
Disciplined	9.4	15.2	16.9
Interpersonal	14.8	16.1	16.9
Knowledgeable	17.3	25.9	15.7
Professional	12.9	23.2	29.2
Verbal	7.4	7.1	4.5
Well-groomed	6.8	0.0	3.4

Source: Sales and Marketing Management, May 1986, p. 49.

LOOKING FOR THE SUPERSALESPERSON IN YOU

Now that you have seen what customers, support staff, established salespeople, and sales managers look for in salespeople, how do you go about finding the supersalesperson in *you?* Before you start looking, remember that most successful salespeople didn't start out with any special advantages over other people. They just worked harder than others to overcome their weaknesses and develop their abilities to the fullest potential. Their achievements are largely the result of persevering self-development, not extraordinary gifts or talents. You can become a supersalesperson if you are willing to thoroughly plan and tenaciously execute a self-development program. Begin your program with an honest, thorough appraisal of yourself.

Your Self-Appraisal

Before you can make progress in any area, you must first know where you are now and where you're headed if *you make no changes.* The first step in self-appraisal is therefore to identify and categorize your present (1) strengths and weaknesses, (2) self-image and goals, and (3) likes and dislikes in reference to a present or future sales career. Perhaps the easiest way to take this first step is to get your information down on paper or in your computer's memory. Although there are many ways to format and compile your information, I suggest that you use the kind of "self-appraisal chart" depicted in Figure 8-1, which combines comparative lists and broad questions corresponding to the three categories presented above. Let's briefly discuss the kind of information you'll need to consider for your chart.

Strengths and Weaknesses
Consider your *strengths* first. What accomplishments have you had in school, in jobs, at home, in extracurricular activities? Have you taken the initiative to lead or help organize some activity—in sports, a school newspaper or play, a charity, or a

Your Self-Appraisal Chart

I.

Strengths	Weaknesses
_____	_____
_____	_____
_____	_____
_____	_____

- Describe the most rewarding experience you have had in school or in a job.
- Describe the worst experience you have had in school or in a job.
- In what activities do you feel most confident?
- In what activities do you feel most insecure?
- What are your special abilities?

II. Self-Image and Goals

- In comparison to other students, how do you rate yourself on the following attributes?

Self-Image

	Above Average	Average	Below Average
Intelligence	_____	_____	_____
Speaking Ability	_____	_____	_____
Writing Ability	_____	_____	_____
Maturity	_____	_____	_____
Sense of Humor	_____	_____	_____
Resourcefulness	_____	_____	_____
Dependability	_____	_____	_____
Ambition	_____	_____	_____
Integrity	_____	_____	_____
Interpersonal Skills	_____	_____	_____

Examples of Self-Image Questions:

- What is most important to you — security, money, prestige, or power? Why?
- If you could change one thing about yourself, what would it be?
- What do you like most about yourself?
- What do you like least about yourself?

Goals

1. _____
2. _____
3. _____
4. _____
5. _____

Examples of Goals Questions:

- What are your career goals? What do you want to have accomplished in one year, five years, ten years?
- Name the things you have done to prepare yourself for a sales career.
- List the things you are looking for in a sales job.

III.

Likes	Dislikes
_____	_____
_____	_____
_____	_____
_____	_____

Examples of Likes and Dislikes Questions:

- What things would you really dislike in a sales job?
- What do you think you would like about a sales job?
- What kinds of activities do you enjoy? Not enjoy? Relate these to aspects of professional personal selling.

FIGURE 8-1 Your Self-Appraisal Chart

campaign for some cause? Have you voluntarily done more than your share on some project, perhaps a group assignment? Have you been elected to a leadership position in school or a social organization? Have you won some competition such as an essay contest, a bowling or tennis tournament, or for selling the largest amount of candy for the annual band boosters club? Have you held a part-time job while going to school? Do you usually do what you say you are going to do? Do you generally finish projects that you start? On time? Do you feel confident of your own ability? Do you get along well with others? Do you set your own goals? Do other people tend to look to you for leadership? Do you like taking responsibility? Do you enjoy challenges? Do you like doing things well? How would someone who really likes you describe you?

What about _weaknesses?_ Do you seldom volunteer for any job, especially a leadership role? Do you rarely finish projects that you start? Is your word something that others cannot depend on? Do you make excuses or blame others for your failures to do things? Do you seldom do more than your share in a group assignment? Do you find it difficult to make and keep friends? Do you feel that life is generally unfair to you? How would someone who really dislikes you describe you?

Self-image and Goals

The act of gathering data about your strenghts and weaknesses will soon give you an idea of how you really think and feel about yourself. If you then combine this information with how you believe other people think and feel about you, you will arrive at your **self-image.**

SELF-IMAGE The combination of your own thoughts and feelings about yourself and how you believe other people think and feel about you.

Although some people are driven to high achievement to overcome feelings of inferiority,[10] a positive self-image can be a tremendous advantage in professional personal selling. Very few people seem to be blessed with a positive self-image from childhood on. In fact, studies with grammer school children have found that most find it more difficult to name positive things about themselves than to name negative things. If your self-image requires work, don't worry, most of us are in the same boat. Many of us are consciously or unconsciously working on our self-image all the time. When was the last time you subtly let someone know about one of your recent achievements or did something extra to make an impression? Perhaps you recently bought an expensive new outfit to wear to a party or enrolled in a public speaking course. Maybe you stayed up late last night preparing for a seminar so that you might impress the professor with your knowledge. Possibly you volunteered to take some handicapped children to the zoo this weekend or sent a donation to a favorite charity. All of these actions, even the apparently unselfish and noble ones, probably are motivated at least partly by the desire to maintain or improve your self-image. And that's okay, because when you can help others while improving your self-image, it's a "win-win" situation.

Being positive about yourself and knowing that other people think well of you won't just make you feel good, it will also help you to set _goals._ For many years Prudential Insurance Company has used the Rock of Gibraltar as its corporate symbol to emphasize strength and security. You may have seen some of Prudential's print and television ads that advise: "Get a piece of the Rock." Well,

---

[10]Gerald W. Ditz, "Status Problems of the Salesman," _MSU Business Topics,_ Winter 1967, p. 77; and Lawrence M. Lamont and W. J. Lunstrom, "Identifying Successful Industrial Salesmen by Personality and Personal Characteristics," _Journal of Marketing Research,_ November 1977, pp. 517–529.

your positive self-image can be your "Rock of Gibraltar," the firm foundation on which to confidently establish your future goals and plan your strategy to achieve them. The best salespeople are the most goal-oriented, and it isn't coincidental that they usually also display the most positive self-images.

After you have written down your thoughts about your strengths and weaknesses, your self-image, and your goals, you may want to ask teachers, friends, or parents (if they can be reasonably objective) to evaluate your strengths and weaknesses, how you "look" to other people, and how reasonable your goals seem. Whatever the answers now, be confident that you can steadily improve in all these personal areas, though it will take conscientious work, as we will discuss in more depth later in this chapter.

Likes and Dislikes

A large part of every goal-setting decision consists of what you like or do not like. If you don't like mathematics, for example, you will certainly not want to become a mathematics professor. Now think about what you like and dislike in terms of selling. What kinds of products and activities do you especially enjoy—airplanes, computers, motorcycles, music videotapes, books, stocks and bonds, food, stylish clothes, dancing, swimming, reading, travel, sports? Sales careers offer opportunities to work with any of these or almost any other product or service you can think of. What kinds of people would you like to work with—high-school coaches, farmers, doctors, lawyers, college professors, accountants, business managers? You name the occupation—there are selling jobs there, too.

For each product or type of activity, there is great diversity in the sales jobs available. If you like travel, you might get a sales job with a tourist center, convention service, airline, ship line, or travel agency. If you like cosmetics, you might sell for a cosmetics manufacturer to wholesalers or to retailers. If you like swimming, you could sell swimwear and related clothing and equipment to wholesalers, retailers, high schools, and colleges.

You also need to be honest with yourself about the amount of travel you're willing to do, geographical locations where you're willing to work, and how much time and effort you're willing to put into your work. If you dislike what you're doing, you'll probably be unhappy and will not excel.

Self-Awareness and Acceptance

Good salespeople continually study themselves and seek feedback from others.

No matter what the results of your self-appraisal, you have gained more of the self-awareness that is essential to self-development. Most of us have relatively low self-awareness because we have never really wanted to scrutinize ourselves. To avoid the risk of facing up to our own irritating habits and personality flaws, we have become desensitized and unable to perceive subtle cues and feedback about ourselves from others. So, we go through life largely oblivious to how others see us. All of us know people who talk too much and listen too little, who wear bizarre clothes, who unintentionally say hurtful things, who have poor table manners, who are careless about personal hygiene, or who just generally embarrass themselves. Good salespeople continually study themselves and seek feedback from others. They cultivate sensitive antennas because their stock in trade is knowing how they "come across" to other people.

Accepting Yourself

After gaining self-awareness, you must not dwell on the negative. You are neither inferior nor superior to other people, but a unique individual. Successful sales-people forgive themselves any past failings or misdeeds and accept themselves as they are now while keeping clearly in mind what they want to become. Some things you can't do much about. If you're short, or don't have a "quick" mind, or are only average-looking, don't fret. Accept these largely unchangeable things and work on those you can change.

In his book *I'm OK—You're OK,* Thomas A. Harris classifies people, on the basis of their attitudes about themselves and others, into four categories:

- *I'm OK—You're OK.* People in this group accept and respect themselves and others. This attitude is fundamental to healthy interpersonal relationships. This is the most beneficial way to think for long-run success in sales.
- *I'm OK—You're Not OK.* People in this group have a high regard for themselves but hold unfavorable views of others. Intolerant of other people's individuality, they tend to be independent and avoid close relationships with anyone. Since such negative feelings are quickly detected by other people, this type of person seldom achieves long-run success in sales.
- *I'm Not OK—You're OK.* People in this group tend to think of themselves as failures and see others as successful and happy. Unable to accept their imperfections, they become their own worst enemy. Without continual support and approval from others, they cannot maintain the drive and energy levels to succeed in sales.
- *I'm Not OK—You're Not OK.* People in this group have negative attitudes toward everyone—themselves as well as others. Effective interpersonal communication becomes nearly impossible because of the lack of mutual confidence, trust, and respect. No salesperson can succeed with this attitude.[11]

Dr. Maxwell Maltz, author of *Psycho-Cybernetics,* sums up the case for self-acceptance best:

Accept yourself as you are—and start from there. Learn to emotionally tolerate imperfection in yourself. It is necessary to intellectually recognize our shortcomings, but disastrous to hate ourselves because of them. Differentiate between your "self" and your behavior. . . . Don't hate yourself because you're not perfect. You have lots of company.[12]

LOOKING AT YOURSELF FROM ALL SIDES

Human beings are complex, multidimensional creatures with at least three sides: *mental, physical,* and *spiritual.* Unless all three sides are healthy, you will remain less than what you could become.

[11]Thomas H. Harris, *I'm OK—You're OK* (New York: Harper & Row Publishers, 1967).
[12]Maxwell Maltz, *Psycho-Cybernetics* (Englewood Cliffs, N.J.: Prentice Hall, 1960), p. 116.

Your Mental Side

Sages down through the ages have recognized that "as a person thinks, so a person is" and "action follows thought." Our mental side can limit us and hold us captive as surely as strong ropes. I can remember when running a mile in under four minutes was thought to be something no human being could ever do, so nobody ever did it. But in the same week that one runner did it, a second one did it, too. Today you can't win a world-class race without a time considerably under four minutes for the mile. What was the barrier all those years? Unlike in some other track and field events, there isn't much that equipment can do here. So the major barrier had to be a mental one. As soon as someone proved it could be done, other athletes broke through their mental barriers, too.

Your Physical Side

Most of us pay more attention to our physical sides (eating, working out, playing) than to our mental or spiritual sides. Nevertheless, physical health and overall appearance play a vital role in sales success. The phrase "A healthy mind in a healthy body" may seem trite, but it is as true today as it was when the ancients coined it. No one is truly successful, even with wealth and a powerful position, unless he or she has the time and good health to enjoy the rewards of success.

Sales reps need tremendous energy and vitality to get up early and be upbeat and generally "on" all day long in interacting with customers. Old Ben Franklin wasn't far off when he said so many years ago: "Early to bed and early to rise make a man healthy, wealthy, and wise." The ancient philosopher Aristotle advocated moderation in all things as the way to health. Sleep, exercise, and a good diet all contribute to making you a healthy person in mind and body. Good health gives you that extra sparkle and positive attitude that come across to customers.

One especially important ingredient for good health is the ability to laugh at yourself and your human frailties. Most children are able to really let go and let out a big belly laugh when they do something funny, but few adults can because they fear being seen as foolish. Hearty laughter is a purifying process that clears the cobwebs from our minds and saves us from taking ourselves too seriously. Laughter will help you keep your life in perspective. As the Bible says: "A merry heart doeth good like a medicine" (Proverbs 17:22).

Here are some guidelines for maintaining or building a healthy mind and body.

Respect and Appreciate Yourself

As one recent poster says: "God Don't Make No Junk." You are a worthy human being who has something valuable to contribute to others. Your contribution may not be on a world stage that brings celebrity status, but it is extremely important to your friends, your co-workers, your customers, your family, and maybe even as a role model to someone you may never really know. Establish personal standards for yourself in all endeavors and be faithful to your own value system.

Accept Yourself Like a Good Friend

We all love people who accept us as we are so that we can just be ourselves with them. No human being is perfect. We all have many physical, mental, and character flaws. Yet many of us are very harsh and unforgiving toward ourselves, much more so than we would be toward a friend. Successful people learn to be their own best friends by accepting themselves despite their imperfections and failings, just as good friends do. Wipe the slate clean by forgiving yourself for any past mistakes and get on with making the future better.

Visualize Yourself as Successful and Act Like It

Paraphrasing from the famous Broadway show *The King and I:* Whenever I feel afraid, I draw myself up tall and whistle a happy tune, and soon I don't feel afraid at all. Visualizing success—actually seeing something come true in your mind's eye—will help you draw a mental picture of yourself as confident and successful. Feeling successful will reinforce your mental image and affect your behavior until you seem successful to others as well as to yourself. Learn to visualize a success over and over again until you actually achieve it.

Reinforce Your Positive Self-Image by Regular Self-Praise

When you accomplish something or behave in a highly positive way, reinforce this activity and your self-image by praising yourself in private. Muhammad Ali, the former boxing champion, even practiced this technique in public by referring to himself as "The Greatest." Unless you're a flamboyant and charming personality like Muhammad Ali, to keep others from thinking of you as egotistical or vain, it's probably preferable to do your self-praising in quiet meditation. Nevertheless: do it.

Be Honest and Dependable in All Your Dealings with Others

Nearly everyone wants to do business with honest individuals. Even crooks generally prefer to deal with honest people when they're trying to buy something. And honesty is a much easier policy than dishonesty because you don't have to remember any lies, you just tell the truth. If prospects and customers feel that you are being dishonest with them or trying to manipulate them, your sales career will come to an abrupt halt. People buy from people they trust, and your personal integrity is as important to your succuss as your company's brands, trademarks, and goodwill are to its success.

Project a Positive Personal Appearance

Your dress and general appearance affect the way customers react to you and how you feel about yourself. You will feel more confident and project more confidence if you make sure that your dress and personal grooming are appropriate for the image you want to project. If they are sloppy or bizarre, some prospects and customers will find you less professional and less credible—and may become reluctant to do business with you. It's probably better to dress on the conservative side rather than the flamboyant or weird side. One man who worked with me at a Fortune 500 company was a bright, attractive, energetic person who had only one little hang-up. He loved horses so much that every day he wore a tie with a large horse's head on it. Well, he drew so much attention to himself with his horses' heads that he became the subject of jokes by customers and co-workers. Slowly, his credibility was damaged and his performance fell off until he finally quit.

Pay Attention to Personal Hygiene

Personal grooming is especially important to a salesperson's professional image. Such manageable things as bad breath, body odors, unkempt hair, dirty finger-nails, and general sloppiness will undercut your professionalism. Many people will think that if you don't have enough pride and energy to take care of your personal appearance, you can't be relied upon to deliver the goods on time or to provide quality service.

Eat Right

As a salesperson, you will frequently find yourself in situations that don't allow you to enjoy a wholesome breakfast, lunch, or dinner. Many successful salespeo-ple get so wrapped up in their daily activities that they sometimes *forget* to eat right! Pulling into a fast-food joint is all right once in a while, but you should make every effort to maintain a regular schedule of good, nutritious meals.

Continue Self-Development All Your Life

You can never stop improving your knowledge and yourself if you expect to keep your outlook positive and to remain successful. Reading professional magazines, journals, and books, listening to and watching sales and marketing-related audio- and videotapes, enrolling in educational courses, and staying involved in profes-sional organizations and community affairs will keep you learning and develop-ing your skills and self-image. Many successful salespeople listen to tapes in their cars while driving from one prospect to another, and some carry around infor-mational or inspirational books to read while waiting to see prospects.

Stay in Control, Don't Let Things or Habits Control You

If you smoke, drink, eat excessively, stay up all hours of the night, or use con-trolled substances, try to stop this behavior. Don't be too proud or embarrassed to seek help from physicians, psychologists, clergy, or other qualified people in regaining control of your life. Most people have to fight habits and temptations of various kinds, and overcoming these problems is not easy, but your health and well-being are worth the struggle.

Your Spiritual Side

Although many people are uncomfortable talking about religion or God, writers and businesspeople like Norman Vincent Peale, W. Clement Stone, Maxwell Maltz, Bishop Fulton Sheen, and Robert Schuller have stressed faith or belief in a higher power as an important source of personal strength and success. Thus, it is important that we not ignore this third dimension of our selves.

Affirmations or Self-Empowerment

Norman Vincent Peale stresses the benefit of starting out each day by "charging" your personal "battery" with an affirmation such as: "I feel good this morning. I am going to have a great day." Affirmations are one of the most potent forms of self-direction. Saying "Boy, I wish I felt better today" is not an affirmation. But when you say "I feel great today and I'm going to have a fantastic day," your subconscious mind listens to this powerful statement and reacts in a strong, positive way. An affirmation confirms your personal strength and activates the power inherent in you.[13] Another word for the action of affirming yourself is **self-empowerment.** This is an important daily activity for any salesperson. For the religiously oriented, Dr. Peale suggests saying something like: "Dear God, I know that you're going to be with me all day long and that you're going to help me do my very best."

SELF-EMPOWERMENT
A term that describes the action of affirming yourself—an important daily activity for salespeople.

This doesn't mean that you needn't work hard. The following story illustrates the old saying that "God helps most those who help themselves":

> A man bought an old run-down farm with weeds over his head. He worked it into a beautiful cultivated farm. The local minister came by one day and said to him: "My, what you and God have done with this place!" The man said: "Yes, sir! But you should have seen it when just God had it."[14]

Believing that everything depends on God and working as if everything depends on you is a valuable formula for success in any field.

Inspiring and Motivating Yourself

When you are traveling out of town, it can often be lonely and boring in the evening, and these feelings can drain off your energy and motivation. Carrying good motivational books and tapes on business trips for solitary reading or listening can saturate your mind with inspirational and motivational thoughts. You go to sleep with positive thoughts that your subconscious will absorb, so that you're in a positive frame of mind in the morning. Here are some self-help books and tapes that have inspired salespeople and many others throughout the years:

- *How to Win Friends and Influence People*—Dale Carnegie
- *Psycho-Cybernetics*—Dr. Maxwell Maltz
- *I'm OK—You're OK*—Amy Harris and Thomas Harris
- *How to Be Your Own Best Friend*—Mildred Newman and Bernard Berkowitz
- *Think and Grow Rich*—Napoleon Hill
- *The Power of Positive Thinking*—Norman Vincent Peale
- *A Treasury of Success Unlimited*—Og Mandino

The first author in this list—Dale Carnegie—not only wrote a great, inspiring book, but also founded a company that offers courses to people who want to inspire themselves to new and greater successes, as outlined in the full-page box featuring Dale Carnegie & Associates. Originally, Dale Carnegie & Associates offered one comprehensive course in effective communication, human relations, and public speaking. Today they offer many specialized courses, including the Dale Carnegie Sales Course.

Finally, remember that you cannot be at the emotional or spiritual mountaintop all the time, nor would you want to be. You'd probably begin to take such

[13]Gerhard Gschwandtner and L. B. Gschwandtner, "Dr. Norman Vincent Peale," *Personal Selling Power,* July/August 1986, p. 7.
[14]Maxwell Maltz, *Psycho-Cybernetic Principles for Creative Living* (New York: Pocket Books, 1974), p. 255.

Training for Success at Dale Carnegie & Associates

The Dale Carnegie Sales Course

Have you ever wondered why you close some sales and not others? Does it sometimes seem that you are selling by accident rather than on purpose?
If your answer to these questions is yes, then you should consider taking the Dale Carnegie Sales Course.

Course Materials

Dale Carnegie, Founder

Dale Carnegie & Associates, Inc.   Background

Dale Carnegie & Associates, Inc., specialists in developing business and personal relations skills, was founded in 1912 by Dale Carnegie. Headquartered in Garden City, New York, it includes 90 licensed sponsors in the United States and Canada, 41 sponsors in 67 other countries, and 14 company-operated institutes.

What It Offers.   Training in effective communication, human relations and public speaking (the original Dale Carnegie Course), management, sales, customer relations, employee development, executive image awareness, executive presentations. Also available: specialized company programs, motivational seminars and workshops.

Why It Trains.   To develop the individual's potential... the skills needed for greater success and satisfaction in business, family, and social life.

How It Trains.   Participants are coached by instructors, thoroughly trained in The Dale Carnegie Method and kept up-to-date in periodic workshops. Members participate actively in all class meetings. These are spaced to permit immediate application and practice of newly learned skills so they become "second nature."

Who Is Trained.   Individuals—many of them with the help and support of their companies—enroll in "public classes." "In-house" courses are sponsored by companies and other organizations to augment their own training programs.

Where It Trains.   In sponsor and institute headquarters, selected local sites and location chosen by clients.

When It Trains.   Schedules of public classes are set locally. In-house classes are arranged for client convenience.

The Dale Carnegie organization is accredited in the United States and Canada by the Accrediting Council for Continuing Education and Training, Inc. It is recognized, too, by the American Council on Education, which recommends college transfer credits for noncollegiate courses.

The Dale Carnegie Course®, The Dale Carnegie Sales Course®, The Dale Carnegie Method®, and Dale Carnegie Training® are registered trademarks of Dale Carnegie & Associates, Inc.

For more information about Dale Carnegie Training, contact:

Dale Carnegie & Associates, Inc.
1475 Franklin Avenue
Garden City, NY 11530
or call
1-800-231-5800

Benefits of the Dale Carnegie Sales Course

In the Sales Course you can learn how to:
- Close sales;
- Set, implement and meet sales goals;
- Manage and organize your day to maximize selling time;
- Evaluate your prospects ability to purchase;
- Prepare effective sales presentations;
- Maintain enthusiasm throughout the selling day;
- Make yourself, your company and your product more interesting to prospective buyers;
- Use the telephone as an effective sales tool;
- Overcome customer objections;
- Improve the image you project through effective sales presentations;
- Nurture and manage accounts to increase business;
- Understand the essential steps of the buying/selling process: attention, interest, conviction, desire, and the close.

Some Dale Carnegie Graduates

Walter Anderson, editor, *Parade*
Mary Kay Ash, Mary Kay Cosmetics
William E. Brock, former Secretary of Labor
Macdonald Carey, actor
Warren Buffett, chairman, Berkshire Hathaway
Linda Gray, actress
Lee Iacocca, chairman, Chrysler Corporation
Stew Leonard, owner, Stew Leonard's
Harvey Mackay, author, *Swim with the Sharks*
Thomas Monaghan, CEO & board chairman, Domino's Pizza
Charley Nishioka, "Small Businessman of the Year" (1987)
Frank Perdue, Perdue Farms, Inc.
Senator Paul Simon

Courtesy of Dale Carnegie & Associates, Inc.

If you were at the emotional or spiritual mountaintop all the time, you might begin to take such heights for granted and lose the exhilarating joy of gaining them.

heights for granted and lose the exhilarating joy of gaining them. Learn to appreciate the struggle as well as the success.

Your Attitudes and Attitude Change

Coaches, businesspeople, and teachers sometimes explain somebody's under-performance by saying: "He's got an attitude problem." What they usually mean is that the person lets negative thinking keep him from doing his best. Attitudes can be negative, neutral, or positive. Attitudes are simply the way you think and feel about things and how you tend to respond to different ideas or situations. Attitudes put you into a frame of mind of liking or disliking things and cause you to behave consistently toward those things.

Cognitive, affective, and behavioral components combine to make up your overall attitude toward people, objects, ideas, concepts, or anything else. The *cognitive* component refers to your knowledge or beliefs about an object or concept; the *affective* component covers your feelings or emotional reactions; and the *behavioral* component determines your behavioral tendencies. For example, if a salesman *believes* that governments are inefficient bureaucracies and *feels* that the "red tape" involved in government purchases is overwhelming, then his basic *behavior* will be to shun potential customers that are government agencies. Another salesperson who believes that government agencies are generally fair and reasonably efficient organizations, and who feels that their detailed procedures are designed to allow more objective purchasing, will probably successfully sell to governments. In this example, the difference between making profitable sales or no sales at all can be attributed to the difference between the two salespeople's attitudes toward government agencies. Negative attitudes are like self-fulfilling prophecies: People who think negatively and feel like failures generally find some way to fail. According to Aetna Life & Casualty, winners can be distinguished from losers in the following ways:

- A winner credits good luck for winning, even though it isn't luck. A loser blames bad luck for losing, even though it isn't luck.
- When a winner makes a mistake, he or she says: "I was wrong." When a loser makes a mistake, he or she says: "It wasn't my fault."
- A winner isn't nearly as afraid of losing as a loser is secretly afraid of winning.
- A winner works harder than a loser, but a winner has more time. A loser is always "too busy" to do those things that are necessary.
- A winner goes through a problem. A loser attempts to go around a problem and never seems to get past it.
- A winner makes commitments. A loser gives alibis.
- A winner knows what to fight for and what to compromise on. A loser compromises on the wrong things and fights for those things that aren't really worthwhile.
- A winner says: "I'm good, but not nearly as good as I ought to be." A loser says: "I'm not nearly as bad as a lot of other people."
- A winner listens. A loser simply waits until it's his or her turn to talk.
- A winner would rather be respected than liked, although he or she would prefer both. A loser would rather be liked than respected, and is even willing to pay the price of mild contempt for it.

■ A winner respects superiors and attempts to learn from them. A loser resents superiors and attempts to find chinks in their armor.

■ A winner paces him or herself. A loser has two speeds, hysterical and lethargic.

Salespeople may have many attitudes: an attitude of teamwork or independence; an attitude of confidence or insecurity; an attitude of service or indifference; an attitude of determination or helplessness; an attitude of self-improvement or resignation; an attitude of friendliness or hostility; an attitude of optimism or pessimism; or any number of other attitudes. Attitudes are not innate, but learned over time through experience, so they can be changed. However, they are enduring and difficult to change because they are so much a part of your overall personality pattern. Thus, to change your attitude in one area may require you to make substantial attitude adjustments in related areas. Attitudes are most likely to change when you recognize inconsistencies among your cognitive, affective, and behavioral components. Because the affective and behavioral parts flow largely from the cognitive, one of the best ways to change an attitude is to open yourself to new information that, if accepted as fact, will be inconsistent with your present feelings and behavior. In order to return to equilibrium or harmony, you will have to adjust your affective and behavioral attitude components to become compatible with your revised cognitive component. Effective sales training programs are usually designed to bring about positive changes in all three attitude components by first changing sales trainees' beliefs and perceptions.

You can often change your attitudes about people, products, or companies by learning more about them and overcoming stereotyped thinking. Research has shown that the mere processing of information about someone or something usually leads to a more positive attitude toward that person or object. Oftentimes it is necessary to change our attitudes about ourselves before we can effectively change our attitudes toward others. One of the best places to start the attitude change process is with our own self-image.

CHANGING YOUR SELF-IMAGE

Dr. Maxwell Maltz, the plastic surgeon who wrote *Psycho-Cybernetics,* found that although he could improve people's physical appearances dramatically, many of his patients retained their old, negative self-images.[15] He realized that unless a patient's *mental* self-image was changed, plastic surgery was of little avail in improving the patient's overall attitude.

Even though the analogy doesn't do justice to the complexity of the human mind, it is convenient to compare the mind to a powerful and highly efficient computer. Viewed as a magnificent computer, the human mind is "programmed" daily by whatever thoughts the individual allows to enter. As you go through life, you accumulate many "floppy disks" full of files containing life experiences. Your interpretation of those files of experiences continually writes the new programs for your mental computer. Over time, you develop a subconscious pattern of loading the appropriate file automatically whenever you encounter a new situation that somehow resembles a previous one. For example, if in the past you

[15]Maxwell Maltz, *Psycho-Cybernetics* (Englewood Cliffs, N.J.: Prentice Hall, 1960), pp. 1ff.

responded to a failure by becoming sad and depressed, it's likely that you stored that reponse away in a particular file and that you'll load it again and respond the same way to a present or future failure. This analogy allows you to think about changing your self-image in terms of rewriting the files that go into your mind-computer.

You will probably never meet a successful salesperson who has *not* had to rewrite a mental file or two. Most top performers diligently work at programming themselves to view every failure as a kind of success. Every failure is, after all, at least a learning experience, even if it is not a very *nice* experience! You must train to "catch" yourself before you respond to a *new* tough situation in the same way you responded to a similar *old* tough situation.

Though much of our self-image was formed in childhood, it is never too late to repair or change a damaged self-image. The vignette below reproduces a series of guidelines for parents to help their children develop positive self-images. A review of this series might help you locate the sources of your own negative feelings and enable you to work toward a change for the better. A positive self-image is a tremendous advantage in a sales career, and the good news is that you *can* reprogram your self-image for the better.

Reprogramming Yourself

Your "reprogramming" need not be a terribly complex process. In its most basic form, reprogramming yourself for a positive self-image comprises two essential steps: (1) thinking positively about yourself and (2) counting your blessings.

Think Positively About Yourself

It will take time to rewrite all those negative files that you have in your mental computer, but it can be done. You can start by realizing and accepting one basic concept: *The road to a positive self-image is paved with positive thoughts and feelings about yourself.* Mildred Newman and Bernard Berkowitz, authors of *How to Be Your Own Best Friend,* tell us that whenever we achieve a goal or do something good, we should take time to praise ourselves, to relish the experi-

---

CHILDREN LEARN WHAT THEY LIVE

- If a child lives with criticism, he learns to condemn.
- If a child lives with hostility, he learns to fight.
- If a child lives with ridicule, he learns to be shy.
- If a child lives with shame, he learns to feel guilty.
- If a child lives with tolerance, he learns to be patient.
- If a child lives with encouragement, he learns confidence.

- If a child lives with praise, he learns to appreciate.
- If a child lives with fairness, he learns justice.
- If a child lives with security, he learns to have faith.
- If a child lives with approval, he learns to like himself.
- If a child lives with acceptance and friendship, he learns to find love in the world.

—Dorothy Law Nolte

ence, to bring it to our mind's attention. Unfortunately, few of us feel comfortable congratulating ourselves because we've been taught not to be vain or proud. When something goes wrong, of course, we tend to mull it over and over, berating ourselves. Think about it: Do you attack and criticize a friend for his or her failure? Probably not. On the other hand, do you congratulate a friend on some achievement? Your friend would probably feel hurt if you didn't. Well, you should be equally willing to congratulate yourself, at least privately. If you're not your own best friend, who is?

Count Your Blessings

Dr. Maltz suggests counting all the positive experiences in your life each night before you fall asleep. Start at the earliest age you can remember, and think of every positive thing you can: the time you won the school playground race, the praise your teacher gave you for the picture you drew, the compliment you received from your coach about the game you played, the top grade you earned in history, the praise you got on that school project, the promotion you earned on your part-time job, or the time a classmate called you "smart," "cute," or "nice." All these things, no matter how small they may seem to you now, are worth storing in your mind as you rewrite your old negative files with fresh, positive information.

Start now to write your new master program of files titled "Positive Self-Images." Make a list of all the positive things you've ever experienced, heard, or thought about yourself. Keep adding to the list each day, and reread it daily from beginning to end so that it's constantly brought to your mind's attention. You won't accomplish a self-transformation overnight, or even in a few weeks, but each day you can make some progress . . . and before you know it, you will have a positive self-image. Success will surely follow. Why not start counting your blessings today?

Techniques for Fast Positive Energy

Besides thinking positively about yourself and counting your blessings—which you should learn to do on a regular basis—there are various techniques you can use whenever you need a powerful boost of positive energy fast. What do you do,

What Would You Do?

Wilbert Washington was beginning to lose confidence in himself. He hadn't sold any life insurance during the entire month, and his sales manager was coming down hard on him. Wilbert's self-image was suffering. He began to worry that people weren't reacting well to him. Perhaps his personality had soured, or maybe he had some personal hygiene problem. He lacked his former confidence on sales calls, and almost took it for granted that he wouldn't make the sale. Lately, Wilbert had started looking for excuses not to make a sales call.

for example, when you're minutes away from walking into a sales presentation for a prospect who is especially demanding? You feel positive and optimistic, but you need a little extra something. Try using these two techniques: (1) synthetic experience and (2) self-talk.

Synthetic Experience

SYNTHETIC EXPERIENCE The technique of using imagined or simulated experiences, thoughts, and feelings in order to force yourself to act, think, or feel in a positive way.

As its name implies, **synthetic experience** consists of imagined or simulated experiences, thoughts, and feelings that you deliberately create and temporarily use to force yourself to act, think, or feel in a different—hopefully, positive!—way. We have already discussed *visualizing* success and *acting* successfully, both of which you need to do continually as a salesperson. The technique of synthetic experience requires you to reach deep into your mind (understanding), heart (feeling), and imagination (imagining) and retrieve what you need for success in a particular situation. No, I'm not talking about fooling other people with false displays of happiness, sadness, or excitement. I'm talking about making yourself effectively understand, feel, and imagine the good, winning side of a situation and actively grasping the very real possibility of your success in that situation.

We have all seen actors who are able to transform their personalities to play a new role. Onstage or onscreen, they actually become someone else. Great athletes regularly "psyche" themselves up in order to achieve top performance. You have probably already used synthetic experience of one form or another in your life. Think about the last time you gave yourself a "pep talk" before an important test or athletic competition, or carefully rehearsed how you would ask someone out on a date.

Self-Talk

SELF-TALK The technique of literally talking to yourself in order to help shape or reshape your attitudes and behavior.

People who talk to themselves have almost always been regarded with amusement or fear. After all, what reason could someone possibly have for talking to him or herself but befuddlement or even outright insanity? Psychologists Shad Helmstetter, author of *What to Say When You Talk to Yourself,* and Pamela Butler, author of *Talking to Yourself,* have convincingly described **self-talk** as a valid and powerful technique for helping to shape or reshape attitudes and behavior. Although you might want to reserve talking out loud and in a full voice to yourself for the privacy of your home or car, in most situations you can whisper to yourself or respond positively to that inner voice that keeps telling you to "go for it!"[16]

WHAT IS SUCCESS TO YOU?

Each person defines success in his or her own way. Success is not necessarily measured by income, education, or celebrity status. If success is defined narrowly as "being no. 1," then only one person in any activity can be called successful!

Success can be a much quieter, but more satisfying, longer-term feeling that may come from helping people solve their problems, doing a first-rate job day in

[16]For a fine summary of this technique, see Robert McGarvey, "Talk Yourself Up," *USAir Magazine,* March 1990, pp. 88–90.

and day out, providing extra service for your customers, feeling good about the quality and integrity of your work, or appreciating the value of the work you do even if it seems to affect only a few people. Success may not even be defined as "happiness," as the following excerpt from *Reader's Digest* indicates:

> Nothing on earth renders happiness less approachable than trying to find it. Historian Will Durant described how he looked for happiness in knowledge, and found only disillusionment. He then sought happiness in travel and found weariness; in wealth and found discord and worry. He looked for happiness in his writing and was only fatigued. One day he saw a woman waiting in a tiny car with a sleeping child in her arms. A man descended from a train and came over and gently kissed the woman and then the baby, very softly so as not to waken him. The family drove off and left Durant with a stunning realization of the real nature of happiness. He relaxed and discovered that "every normal function of life holds some delight."[17]

Abraham Lincoln put it this way: "Most people are just about as happy as they make up their minds to be." Happiness and success must be defined by each individual. No doubt, Mother Theresa of Calcutta suffers heartache and pain along with the poor people with whom she works, and certainly she has none of the material trappings of wealth or success, but who would doubt that she is fulfilled and successful?

Success Must Be Earned

I remember, when I was a navy officer aboard an aircraft carrier, assigning a seaman the job of scrubbing the deck in one of the crew's living quarters. About a half hour later, I returned to find that the deck had still not been scrubbed. When I asked the seaman what the problem was, he said: "I'm too smart to be doing low-level work like this. Give me something to do that challenges me." Instinctively, I responded: "You had a challenge and you didn't meet it. This is a job that must be done. Unless you prove that you can do the low-level jobs well, you'll never get the chance to do the higher-level ones." A couple of years later, after I had been assigned to shore duty and was about to leave the navy, I chanced to meet that young man again at Great Lakes Naval Base, and his rating was still "seaman." Apparently, he never learned that success must be earned.

Success is not an overnight thing. It comes slowly but surely over time to those who always do their best no matter what the job. Most people, whether movie stars, athletes, astronauts, politicians, or supersalespeople, have worked hard for many years to become successful. They've seen many others get discouraged and give up. People with "the right stuff" fight through hardships, obstacles, discouragements, and even pain to keep getting the job done.

More effective salespeople show less variance in their behavior than do less effective salespeople.[18] They consistently put out the extra effort that makes them winners. If you watch professional athletes, you'll notice that the best usually

---

[17]June Callwood, "The One Sure Way to Happiness," *Reader's Digest,* October 1974, as reported in Wayne W. Dyer, *Your Erroneous Zones* (New York: Avon, 1976), p. 243.

[18]Harish Sujan, Mita Sujan, and James R. Bettman, "Knowledge Structure Differences Between More Effective and Less Effective Salespeople," *Journal of Marketing Research XXV* (February 1988): 81–86.

Everyone has a different image of success. What's yours?

keep on trying as hard as they can whether their team is way ahead or way behind. True professionals give 100 percent all the time.

In the words of former President Calvin Coolidge: "Nothing in the world can take the place of persistence. Talent will not; nothing is more common than unsuccessful men with talent. Genius will not; unrewarded genius is almost a proverb. Education will not; the world is full of educated derelicts. Persistence and determination alone are omnipotent."[19]

[19] "The Invincible Vince," *Sales Manual* (Memphis, Tenn.: Southwestern Publishing Co., 1980), p. 62.

Your Goals

Napoleon Hill spent 25 years studying why superachievers are so successful. His conclusion, as outlined in his book *Think and Grow Rich,* was that people have to have a purpose in life.[20] Each superachiever he studied had goals and worked hard at achieving them.

Hill stresses the need to write down one's goals in as much detail as possible, then visualize their achievement and success. Make sure your goals are realistic, unequivocal, worthwhile, and meaningful to you. Don't merely accept someone else's goals as your own. Only you can judge what's important to you. Ambiguous or conflicting goals can lead to lack of commitment and failure. Clear-cut career and personal goals will give you self-confidence and make decision making easier for you. Hill recommends reinforcing your personal goals every day by repeating them aloud each morning and night. And don't be afraid of setting your goals high. As Thomas J. Watson, Sr., the man who made IBM a worldwide leader in computers, often said: "It is better to aim at perfection and miss than it is to aim at imperfection and hit it."

Set Goals for Yourself

To be successful, you need goals so you will know in which direction to head as well as how to judge your progress along the way. Establish realistic goals for yourself, visualize your goals, and envision their achievement. Write them down, say them out loud, and review them daily. You will dervive many benefits from this process because goals:

- Force you to evaluate your strengths and weaknesses.
- Help you to think in realistic and measurable terms.
- Improve your confidence and self-image because you are working toward something worthwhile.
- Give you a sense of urgency in taking action toward achieving them.
- Provide you with direction and focus that make decision making easier.
- Compel you to set priorities in all your activities.
- Reinforce your positive self-image when they are achieved and prepare you for more success.

Make the Goal-Achieving Process Fun

Few people achieve all their goals, but that doesn't make goals any less important to set or less fun to work toward. In sales, as in many other fields, you're judged mainly by your successes, not your failures. If you make ten sales calls in a day and only one person buys, your sales manager may still be delighted and probably won't even ask about the other nine calls!

Never be afraid of making a mistake because a failure is only a failure if you label it as such. Highly successful people see what other people call "failure" as merely information gained to use toward achieving success the next time. When the great inventor Thomas Edison was asked about his countless unsuccessful attempts to produce a long-burning incandescent lightbulb, he snapped: "I haven't failed a thousand times, I've discovered a thousand ways that don't work."

[20]Napoleon Hill, *Think and Grow Rich* (New York: Hawthorn Publishing, 1967) pp. 31, 77–78.

Successful people know that they are going to succeed, it's just a matter of time. Each turndown moves you closer to the next success. The only shame is to quit trying. Babe Ruth is remembered for the 714 home runs he hit over his baseball career, not the 1,330 times he struck out.

Often there is more fun in striving to obtain a goal than in its actual achievement. Try to make the selling process fun, so that closing a sale puts "icing on the cake." Meeting new people and telling them about your company, your products, and yourself can be a highly enjoyable social process in itself. Don't think about each contact as a success or failure. It's all part of the selling process. Nobody bats 1.000. For some products, batting .100 or less may make you a supersalesperson. Very few sales are made on the first call, and today's sales call may have moved you closer to a sale the next time you call. Noted economist Kenneth Boulding even makes a strong case for the value of failure:

> Nothing fails like success because you do not learn anything from it. The only thing we ever learn from is failure. Success only confirms our superstitions. Think of it. Without failure we can learn nothing, and yet we have learned to treasure success as the only acceptable standard. We tend to shun all experiences which might bring about failure. Apprehension of failure is a big part of fear of the unknown. Anything which doesn't smack of guaranteed success is to be avoided. And fearing failure means fearing both the unknown and the disapproval that accompanies not doing your best.[21]

Lee Iacocca is a great example of an enormously successful person who has known failures but doesn't know how to quit, as the following vignette shows.

[21]As quoted in Wayne W. Dyer, *Your Erroneous Zones* (New York: Avon, 1976), p. 136.

"YOU NEVER GIVE UP. YOU NEVER QUIT."

One of America's greatest salespeople, Lee Iacocca— CEO and Chairman of Chrysler Motor Corporation— was rejected when he applied for his first sales job. After graduating from Lehigh University, earning a master's degree at Princeton, and completing a training program at Ford Motor Company, Iacocca decided that the best opportunities for advancement at Ford were in sales and marketing. Applying at the truck sales department in Ford's New York district office, he was interviewed by two assistant managers. As Iacocca recalls: "One of them never put down his *Wall Street Journal,* so he never really saw me, and the second assistant manager snapped: 'If you're a college graduate, number one, and from the home office, number two, get the hell out and go back to Detroit.'" Even after this brusque treatment, Iacocca waited for the district manager, whose advice was: "You'll never make it in sales. I think you ought to try to get into engineering."

Dejected by their rejection, Iacocca thought about leaving Ford. But he remembered his father's often-repeated words, "You never give up. You never quit," and approached another sales manager, who saw something special in Iacocca and hired him. Many years later, after facing another shocking setback when Henry Ford II fired him, Iacocca bounced back to invigorate a nearly bankrupt Chrysler Motor Company by personally persuading people in television commercials to buy Chrysler cars. Later he used his promotional skills to raise $230 million from the American people to restore the Statue of Liberty. Nothing can defeat someone with that kind of drive and determination.

Source: Based on Lee Iacocca with William Novak, *Iacocca: An Autobiography* (New York: Bantam Books, 1984), pp. 31–32; Martin Gottlieb, "Statue of Liberty's Repair: A Marketing Saga," *The New York Times,* November 3, 1985, p. 1; "Can Iacocca Keep Chrysler Moving?" *The New York Times,* August 25, 1985, Sect. 3, p. 1.

After you have determined your goals and prepared yourself mentally, physically, and spiritually as well as you can, all you need to succeed in professional personal selling is the drive and persistence to keep on doing your best whether things are going well or not. The following verse should spur you on when the going gets a little rough:

If you want a thing bad enough to go out and fight for it,
Work day and night for it,
Give up your time and peace and sleep for it,
If only desire of it
Makes you quite mad enough
Never to tire of it,
If you'll gladly sweat for it,
Fret for it, plan for it,
If you'll simply go after the thing you want,
With all your capacity,
Strength and sagacity,
Faith, hope and confidence, stern pertinacity,
If neither cold poverty, famished and gaunt,
Nor sickness nor pain
Of body or brain
Can turn you away from the thing you want,
If dogged and grim, you besiege and beset it,
YOU'LL GET IT![22]

SUMMARY

Many studies and individual companies have identified a broad range of basic characteristics of successful salespeople, and sales managers always look for some of these characteristics when interviewing prospective salespeople. To prepare yourself for success in personal selling, you should start a self-development program. The first step in this program is to conduct a self-appraisal. Accepting yourself, complete with all your strengths and weaknesses, is essential if you are to make progress. Human beings are complex creatures with mental, physical, and spiritual dimensions, and you can only become a top performer if all three dimensions are healthy. Several self-help books and tapes can inspire and motivate the salesperson in you. Your attitudes toward people, objects, and concepts are made up of cognitive, affective, and behavioral components.

Your self-image is developed over time by how you "program" your mind. Synthetic experience and mental reprogramming can improve your self-image. Success is defined uniquely by each individual, but always requires meaningful purpose in work and life. Successful people refuse to label setbacks as failures; instead, they see them as learning experiences. Finally, nothing succeeds like persistence: Never give up on your goals or striving to be all that you can be!

[22]Robert S. Tralins, *How to Be a Power Closer in Selling* (Englewood Cliffs, N.J.: Prentice Hall, 1971), p. 188.

CHAPTER REVIEW QUESTIONS

1. What six attributes of successful salespeople have been identified by McMurry and Arnold?
2. From the perspectives of customers, internal support staff, and salespeople, what eight characteristics account for the success of top salespeople?
3. What characteristics do sales managers look for in new salespeople?
4. What are the elements of a self-appraisal? How can performing a self-appraisal benefit you?
5. What are some basic guidelines for maintaining a healthy mind and body?
6. What is meant by "affirmation" or "self-empowerment"?
7. Distinguish between cognitive, affective, and behavioral components of a person's overall attitude toward people, objects, and concepts.
8. What benefits can be derived from setting goals?

TOPICS FOR THOUGHT AND CLASS DISCUSSION

1. As revealed in his book *Molloy's Live for Success,* John T. Molloy's research found that successful people are most often described as "supersalespeople." Why do you think successful people in various types of careers are often viewed as supersalespeople?
2. This chapter presents the results of several research studies designed to determine the personal characteristics most important for success in sales. Which basic characteristics are mentioned most often? Do you think these are always the most important characteristics for sales success? Why or why not?
3. What is your attitude toward a potential career in sales? How was this attitude formed?
4. What is meant by "synthetic experience"? Have you ever benefited from synthetic experience? Explain how.
5. How is one's self-image formed over time? Why do you think so many people have a negative self-image? What can be done to make one's self-image more positive?
6. How would you define "success" for yourself? Who or what do you think has most influenced your definition of personal success?
7. Have you ever failed at something? Describe the experience. How do you define "failure"? Do highly successful people define "failure" in the same way as less successful people?

PROJECTS FOR PERSONAL GROWTH

1. Contact five sales managers and five salespeople and ask them to name the three characteristics/attributes that they feel are most important for success in sales. Do the opinions of the two groups differ? Try to explain any differences between the perspectives of the two groups.
2. Visit a convenient library and check out a motivational tape (try to get one with a "sales and marketing" theme). After listening to the tape, write a report about it. Be sure to include the following information in your report: (a) the tape's overall theme or message, (b) the major points it made, (c) your overall attitude toward the tape, and (d) your thoughts about how this motivational tape might be applied to sales.
3. Prepare your own self-appraisal, then ask a friend to read and react to it. Does your friend think your self-appraisal is accurate? What are the areas of agreement and

disagreement between your friend's assessment of you and your own self-appraisal? After comparing the two, do you think you have been too hard or too easy on yourself?

4. Make a list of all the positive things you can think of about yourself. Include all your accomplishments, good personal qualities, and positive feedback you have received from others over the years, as far back as you can remember. Read this list over at least once a day for a week. Do you feel more positive about yourself at the end of the week? (If not: Try once more *with feeling!*)

KEY TERMS

Self-image The combination of your own thoughts and feelings about yourself and how you believe other people think and feel about you.

Self-empowerment A term that describes the action of affirming yourself—an important daily activity for salespeople.

Synthetic experience The technique of using imagined or simulated experiences, thoughts, and feelings in order to force yourself to act, think, or feel in a positive way.

Self-talk The technique of literally talking to yourself in order to help shape or reshape your attitudes and behavior.

Case 8-1

MAKING AN IMPRESSION

By Paul F. Christ, Delaware Valley College

Jennifer Loren is a 32-year-old district sales manager for Unity Pharmaceutical Company who has just completed her second day at a large state university interviewing candidates for a sales representative position. After four years as district sales manager, she has discovered that it usually requires interviewing from six to ten candidates to find the right person for the job. When she first became a sales manager, she found it difficult to remember conversations with candidates because there were always so many of them and usually so few ways to differentiate them. However, she quickly learned that taking notes during these meetings is a great help in recalling the details of each interview. Jennifer's notes are brief phrases summarizing her impressions from observations and candidate responses to questions.

In the screening process, Jennifer evaluates three areas that she feels are strong indicators of success in pharmaceutical sales, largely to wholesalers and drugstore chains. First, she tries to ascertain an interviewee's *personality*. In particular, she looks for someone who is personable, enthusiastic, energetic, motivated, and willing to work hard. Second, she evaluates the individual's *communication skills*.

Third, she looks at the candidate's *background*. It is preferred that candidates have some understanding of biology or chemistry as well as prior sales experience.

Earlier today, Jennifer interviewed six candidates, and now she is sitting in her office and studying her notes while trying to decide which ones should be called back for a more in-depth second interview. Her notes read as follows:

Alice Livingston—9:00 A.M.
Arrived at 9:15 A.M. Looks nervous—flowery dress seems unprofessional—speaks softly—stammers a little in answering questions for the first few minutes—body language suggests insecurity. Recent college graduate—major in biology—good grades, B+ average—no previous sales experience, but says she is a quick learner. Didn't work while in college—parents paid college tuition. Took two business courses but no sales course in college. Says she likes to meet people, so thinks sales might be right for her—had trouble answering question about her major strengths and weaknesses because she'd "never really thought about it before." Treasurer of hon-

orary sorority. Doesn't have any particular goals at this point in her life, wants to experience more first—likes to travel—didn't ask any questions about Unity. Left at 9:30 A.M.

Louis Granger—10:00 A.M.

Arrived at 10:00 A.M. Tall with strong handshake. Dressed conservatively—very businesslike, no small talk—body language a little stiff—speaks in a loud, forceful voice. Spent two years in Marine Corps—has worked for past six months as a testing lab supervisor—plans to leave at the end of the month because the job offers "no challenge." No sales experience but has talked to several sales reps at work. Degree in chemistry—paid own way through school—ROTC. Average grades. Member of wrestling team. Likes sales because "that's where the money is"—says he is a hard worker and expects others to work hard too. Claims major strength is "drive to succeed"—major weakness is "tendency to be abrupt with people who are losers." Expects to be top salesperson by second year and sales manager within five years—wanted to know what career path options Unity offered. Said his philosophy of life is "winning is what it's all about." Left at 10:40 A.M.

Judith Campeau—11:00 A.M.

Arrived at 10:55 A.M. Very friendly person, smiles a lot—dressed conservatively. Work experience includes three years as a cashier in a Kroger grocery store and five years with a small advertising agency. Just finishing business degree in night school, took almost eight years, 2.9 GPA on a 4.0 scale. Showed enthusiasm in answering questions—positive body language. Says she likes sales because it will give her the chance to "make good money while helping people solve their problems." Only science background is biology course taken four years ago, earned a B. Likes drug industry because her neighbor, a physician, says it's a growing field. Claims she gets along with nearly everyone. Says major strength is her "gracious assertiveness"—only weakness is some fear of public speaking but is taking a Dale Carnegie course to overcome the problem. Expects to be one of the top sales representatives in the company in three to five years because she "will do whatever it takes to succeed." Says she wants the Unity job very badly and will call in a few days to see how she did. Asked several questions about how Unity salespeople were compensated. Left at 12:10 P.M.

Michael Jasper—1:00 P.M.

Arrived at 1:02 P.M. Muscular-looking, lifts weights on regular basis. Well-dressed, though tie is too loud. Initiated small talk about Unity, seemed to know a

lot. Worked last two years as one of six sales reps for small medical supply firm but company went bankrupt. Won "sales rep of the quarter" award twice. Called on doctors and hospitals. Wife works in public relations—has a 2-year-old daughter in nursey school—father is national sales manager for medium-size textile company. Earning degree in biology, minor in business, overall GPA is 2.8 on a 4.0 scale—took a sales course in school, earned an A. Likes sales lifestyle and rewards—says customers like him because he takes good care of them. Claims his major strengths are being "well-organized and energetic"—weakness is "impatience with people who have negative attitudes." Wants to be a sales manager or a marketing manager in a few years. Asked several questions about Unity's retirement plan. Left at 1:50 P.M.

Mary Ellen Porter—2:00 P.M.

Arrived at 2:05 P.M. Looks very young, well-dressed, kept thanking me for the interview. Recent college graduate with very good grades, 3.4 on 4.0 scale—majored in marketing but had three courses in sciences—earned A's—vice president of student marketing organization. Selected to Beta Gamma Sigma, National Business Administration honor society for top 10 percent of class, and elected president of Beta Gamma Sigma in senior year. Father is a pharmacist. Spent two summers selling advertising for hometown newspaper. Paid for 50 percent of her college tuition. Feels her major weakness is initial shyness with people—major strength is "I wear well with people." Says she wants to eventually move into marketing management. Seems to know a lot about Unity and cited several statistics in asking questions about Unity's business strategy for the future. Says she already has two job offers. Left at 2:45 P.M.

Scott Kissick—3:00 P.M.

Arrived at 2:57 P.M. Dressed neatly but shoes need polishing. Seems open and personable—dirty fingernails! Has worked as lab technician for six years—enjoys fixing automobiles in his spare time. Recently received M.B.A. majoring in marketing, GPA=3.3 on 4.0 scale. Vice president of student MBA Club. Likes health-care field but wants to start in sales "to learn about the business from customer perspective." Says people think that he is a natural for sales—claims "resourcefulness in getting projects done" as major strength—couldn't think of any weaknesses. Sees himself as sales manager in four years and marketing vice president in 10 to 15 years. Says he'd prefer to stay in local area because of family. Impressed with quality of Unity products, which he has used for years. Left at 3:35 P.M.

After reviewing her notes, Jennifer thinks that several of the candidates have some potential for sales, but feels that only two should be called back.

Questions

1. What do you think of Jennifer Loren's approach to interviewing sales candidates?

2. How would you evaluate the six candidates for the job in pharmaceutical sales? Which two candidates do you think Jennifer will call back for a second interview?

3. What do you think the two candidates invited back might do to enhance their chances of being hired by Unity?

Case 8-2

MAKING THE RIGHT MOVES

John Wilson is about to begin his first year at Delaware County Community College (DCCC). At Middlebury High School, he was a varsity baseball and basketball player and maintained a B average. Although he would like to have a B.A. degree "under his belt," John has never been especially fond of academic work, and the prospect of spending another four solid years in school earning a B.A. is a little daunting. However, he is undecided about a career and feels that two years at DCCC will help him make up his mind. John worked as a lifeguard for the past two summers in Ocean City, New Jersey, and saved enough money to pay for his first year of college. Upon earning his associate's degree, he plans to transfer to a private four-year college with a cooperative education program in order to obtain some actual experience in a career field.

John's father owns a small hardware store where Mrs. Wilson often works in the afternoons and on weekends. John also works in the store occasionally when his father needs extra help, but his mom has discouraged her husband from asking John to do this too often for fear his schoolwork might suffer. Neither parent graduated from college, and both are very anxious that their only child earn the college degree they feel will open the door to a good future for him. They hope that John will major in accounting and eventually acquire his C.P.A. credentials because that seems like a secure field that pays well. Their tax man is a C.P.A. who lives in a beautiful home and always seems to be busy. John wants to please his parents, but he isn't sure that he would like being an accountant, or a "bean counter," as

some of his high-school classmates jokingly call him whenever he mentions the possibility.

If he had to choose right now, John would prefer to become a sporting equipment salesperson like his uncle, Bob Wilson. Bob sells for Champion Athletes Company and has given John quite a lot of sports equipment over the years. Bob earned all-state honors as a basketball player for Middlebury High School about 25 years ago, and still goes to most of the home games. He was John's biggest fan in high school because John's dad doesn't care much for sports and usually works evenings in the store anyway.

John's uncle loves his job and every so often invites John to go with him on his daily sales calls. The job seems easy to John. All Bob does is call on high-school athletic departments and sporting goods stores and explain what new equipment his company has to offer. Bob seems to know everybody and always exchanges some funny sports stories with the coaches and store managers he calls on. John is especially impressed that his uncle knows two big league baseball players whom he first met while they were high school stars.

Still, John wonders if he has the skills to be a good sporting equipment salesperson. His teachers have usually described him as quiet and somewhat shy, but, of course, most of them saw him only in the classroom. None of John's teammates has ever called him quiet or shy. In fact, his nickname is "Mad Dog" because of his habit of diving to the gym floor for loose basketballs and throwing himself left or right from his shortstop position to trap hard-hit baseballs.

John's legs and elbows were almost always skinned after a basketball or baseball game.

One day, Bob gave John a self-appraisal booklet that his company has sales candidates fill out. It took John about two hours to complete the self-appraisal, but he tried to answer all the questions as honestly as he could. Bob has promised to take John's completed booklet back to the Champion Athletes personnel office for evaluation. Here are excerpts from the self-appraisal booklet and John's answers:

Champion Athletes Company
Self-Appraisal Booklet

1. Rate yourself on the below attributes:

	HIGH	AVERAGE	LOW
Intelligence		X	
Maturity		X	
Ambition	X		
Honesty	X		
Speaking Ability		X	
Writing Ability			X
Resourcefulness		X	
Dependability	X		
Self-Confidence		X	
Initiative		X	
Willingness to Work	X		
Interpersonal Skills		X	
Perseverance	X		
Ethical Behavior	X		
Sensitivity to Others	X		
Creativity		X	
Assertiveness		X	
Social Skills		X	

2. What are your three major weaknesses?
Tendency toward shyness
Poor writing skills
Somewhat disorganized

3. What are your three major strengths?
Hard-working
Cooperative team player
Strong need to succeed

4. What are the five major accomplishments in your life?
Making the varsity basketball team
Earning second-team, all-conference honors in baseball
Being named captain of the baseball team
Graduating from high school with honors
Saving enough money on my summer job to pay for my first year of junior college

5. What are your three major goals over the next five years?
Graduate from college
Get a good job
Buy a car

6. Which of the following is closest to how you would define success in your career?
a. _X_ Looking forward to going to work each day
b. ____ Earning a lot of money
c. ____ Being admired or envied by others
d. ____ Helping other people solve their problems
e. ____ Having enough free time to enjoy other interests

7. Which five of the following words would you say best describe you?
a. Impatient ____   **i.** Aggressive ____
b. Enthusiastic ____   **j.** Introverted ____
c. Hesitant ____   **k.** Good
d. Energetic _X_   communicator ____
e. Disciplined _X_   **l.** Goal-oriented _X_
f. Extroverted ____   **m.** Bookish ____
g. Successful ____   **n.** Analytical ____
h. Helpful _X_   **o.** Confident ____
                            p. Practical _X_

8. How would you describe your self-image?
a. Highly positive ____
b. Somewhat positive _X_
c. Neutral ____
d. Somewhat negative ____
e. Highly negative ____

After filling out the booklet and giving it to his Uncle Bob, John is now very excited about the possibility of becoming a sales rep right away. Instead of pursuing a college degree full time, he thinks he wants to become a salesperson and go to evening school.

Questions

1. We have included only an excerpt from the self-appraisal booklet that John filled out. What additional questions do you think the booklet contains or should contain to help John determine whether or not a sales position is right for him?

2. Based on what you have learned about John from the information in the narrative and his partial self-appraisal form, what do you think of his overall attitude? Would he be a good salesperson? Why or why not?

3. What do you think about John's impression of his uncle's job? Why do you think that John sees his uncle's job as "easy"? Do you think that John would be making the right move by starting a sales career immediately, without exploring some other career areas first? If you were John's friend, what would you advise him to do?

Chapter 9

Understanding the Company, Products, Competition, and Markets

Customers don't care how much you know *about your products until they know how much you* care *about them and their needs.*

A FTER graduating from Georgia Tech with a B.S. in Industrial Management, Pete Brandt ventured out into the tough job market of the 1958 recession and eventually found a job selling industrial wire cloth and screening machinery to the mining and pulp and paper industries. Today, Pete is a manufacturer's representative and simultaneously president of Chapman Associates, Inc., a firm in Charlotte, North Carolina, that specializes in sales representation for capital equipment manufacturers. Like Kodak's Pete Nordstrom in the previous chapter's profile, Pete Brandt is a veteran sales representative who has accumulated more than 30 years' selling experience.

In that first job, Pete continues, "there was no formal one-on-one sales training, but I learned the value of knowing your product and the customer's application of the product. I also learned two rules that were and are basic to all selling: (1) plan your schedule as far ahead as possible, and (2) allocate at least one half of your time to cultivating new customers and penetrating high-potential accounts. Most importantly, however, I learned that service is a key to selling."

Pete now realizes that the first five years of his selling career were all training years that gave him the opportunity to develop a sales style that complements his personality and recognizes his interest in the sale of capital equipment, which, he explains, "is high-dollar, low-volume business, rather than replacement item selling, which tends to be low-dollar, high-volume business. The fine sense of timing and high degree of technical knowledge usually required in capital equipment selling also appealed to me as a challenge. It was with this background that I jumped at the chance to become a manufacturer's representative with Chapman Associates, an established representative firm." Among the manufacturers Pete now represents is Chemineer, Inc., based in Dayton, Ohio, and featured in this chapter's Company Highlight.

Profile

Pete Brandt

Although Pete could speak volumes about all of the sales situations he has worked in over the years, he decided to tell us about a recent situation that was especially tough: "It involved a sales presentation for a job for which three competitors applied. I knew that the meeting was controlled by a consulting engineer who, based on past dealings, could be considered hostile. I made sure I brought to the meeting all of the descriptive literature and technical backup that applied to the job. Although the customer didn't indicate beforehand that it would be a large meeting, a $300,000 order was at stake and 18 customer representatives—engineers, operating personnel, and purchasing agents—attended. It was mind-boggling to walk into a room that, without previous warning, was filled with the customer's people! The meeting began with my sales presentation and lasted for a grueling 3½ hours. At the end, it looked like we had the order. After returning to my office that afternoon, I answered several minor questions for them by fax, and then waited. The next morning I received the verbal order. This success was possible because we could show the customer a full knowledge of our manufacturer's product line, a full understanding of the customer's problem and intended product application, and because we kept calm and stuck to the solid basics of selling before, during, and after the presentation." ■

After reading this chapter, you should understand:

☐ Why in-depth knowledge about the company, products, competition, and markets will enable you to become a more successful salesperson

☐ Products from the perspective of customers

☐ The growing professionalism in purchasing and its impact on personal selling

☐ What industrial buyers like most about salespeople

☐ How to keep current on product developments and markets

More effective salespeople have richer and more interrelated knowledge about their customers and selling strategies than do less effective salespeople.[1] How do salespeople acquire this knowledge? At one time, they were given a price book and told: "Go make some sales calls to see if you can get some orders." With no training and little product knowledge, most of these salespeople failed miserably and soon left the company. Because today's products are complex and customer needs are diverse, new salespeople must receive thorough training about their company, its products, competitors, and markets before calling on customers.

THE COMPANY TRAINING PROGRAM

Most companies provide much of this essential knowledge in formal training programs that make use of videotapes, lectures, demonstrations, role-playing sessions, and trainee interaction with one another and seasoned salespeople. Before or after an initial training program, a junior salesperson may even be assigned to work with one of the "old pros" to learn *on the job*. Though sometimes effective, this approach can be inefficient and may teach new salespeople bad selling habits.

Xerox Corporation uses a three-tiered sales training program that extends over three or four years. The first tier includes two weeks of classroom and demonstration lab work in the company's modern training center in Leesburg, Virginia. Most of the second training tier is done in the district sales offices where the manager's monthly staff meetings are followed by two hours of sales training. Each district office includes a library of training modules on VCR cassettes for use by the sales trainees. The third training tier takes place in the homes of the sales reps. Each rep is given a Xerox PC or workstation on which he or she completes computer-assisted homework exercises in preparation for classes at the district

---

[1]Harish Sujan, Mita Sujan, and James R. Bettman, "Knowledge Structure Differences Between More Effective and Less Effective Salespeople," *Journal of Marketing Research*, February 1988, pp. 81–86; Steven P. Schnaars, *Megamistakes: Forecasting and the Myth of Rapid Technological Change* (New York: Macmillan, 1989).

TABLE 9-1 Instructional Methods Used in Training

TRAINING METHOD	% OF COMPANIES USING
Videotapes	89.3
Lectures	87.9
One-on-one instruction	70.3
Role plays	58.1
Slides	55.1
Films	47.2
Computer-based training	44.0
Games/simulations	43.9
Case studies	41.6
Self-testing instruments	40.3
Noncomputerized self-study	32.4
Videoconferencing	10.6
Teleconferencing	8.9
Computer conferencing	4.1

Source: Adapted from the October 1989 issue of *Training: The Magazine of Human Resources Development.*

office. The in-home PCs are networked so that messages, such as the preclass exercises, can be broadcast simultaneously to the reps.[2]

Modern sales training at most companies is facilitated by a variety of audio-visual and telecommunications equipment used alongside traditional instructional methods. A survey of different industries and job types found that the most popular instructional methods used in training are videotapes, lectures, one-on-one instruction, and role plays, as shown in Table 9-1.

Initial sales training programs vary widely from one company to another, depending on organizational culture, policies, philosophies, products, markets, competitors, and the trainees' experience levels. But, in general, information is provided about four basic areas: (1) the company, (2) products, (3) markets, and (4) the selling process. We will deal with the selling process in depth in Chapters 10–15, so the focus here will be on the first three areas. As indicated in Table 9-2, 35 percent of total sales training time at large companies is spent on product information, 30 percent on sales techniques, 15 percent on market information, and 10 percent on understanding the company.

[2]Thayer C. Taylor, "Xerox's Sales Force Learns a New Game," *Sales & Marketing Management,* July 1, 1985, pp. 48–51.

TABLE 9-2 Median Time Devoted to Subject Areas in Sales Training Programs of Large American Companies

TYPE OF SALES TRAINING	% OF TOTAL TRAINING PROGRAM
Product information	35
Sales techniques	30
Market information	15
Company information	10
Other topics	10
Total	100

Source: Earl D. Honeycutt, Jr., Clyde E. Harris, Jr., and Stephen B. Castleberry, "Sales Training: A Status Report," *Training and Development Journal,* May 1987, p. 43.

UNDERSTANDING THE COMPANY

Company history, organization, mission statement, culture, philosophy, goals and objectives, strategies and tactics, policies, and procedures are among the first things taught to sales trainees. Companies take different approaches to teaching these basics. Some present the information in formal training programs, while others provide it in manuals and handouts. Whatever the approach, every salesperson needs to thoroughly understand the company in order to knowledgeably respond to customer questions.

Company History

Studying the company's history may not seem particularly interesting at first, but this knowledge provides perspectives and insights that will serve the salesperson well throughout a career. It may be intriguing to see how humbly the company began. What new sales trainee would not be inspired by the story of young Steve Jobs and Steve Wozniak? They raised $1,300 by selling Jobs's Volkswagen bus and Wozniak's Hewlett-Packard handheld calculator, then built the first personal computer "for the rest of us" in a tiny garage.[3] Today Apple computers are known all over the world. Most companies were started by one determined individual with a marvelous vision. Henry Ford dreamed of building inexpensive automobiles for the common man, and Thomas Monaghan wanted to deliver "piping-hot pizza in less than 30 minutes" to people's homes. Monaghan started with one tiny unit in Ypsilanti, Michigan, in 1960, and today Domino's Pizza is the second-largest pizza organization (after Pizza Hut) in the world. Because a company's present business philosophies and slogans can often be traced to its founder, a study of company history generally begins with the founder's life and philosophies. Usually the company's librarian or personnel manager can recommend a good book on the company and its founder. Many customers will enjoy hearing the story of a company's origins, and relating it may help win respect for the salesperson's professional knowledge.

Growth and Development

Another aspect of a company's history is its record of growth in sales, market share, profits, and new products. Reading annual and quarterly reports or independent financial analysts' (e.g., Value Line, Standard & Poor's) evaluations of the company can enable a salesperson to keep current about its growth and development and give the salesperson an advantage in closing sales. A potential customer may ask: "How's this new product been selling so far?" A knowledgeable salesperson might truthfully answer: "It's the fastest-growing new product in the industry . . . we're barely able to keep up with orders. Your two major competitors have already placed large orders." Sharing this information not only reassures but also helps persuade the customer to make the purchase *now* in order to keep up with competition. Without such timely knowledge, the salesperson might have to answer: "Gee, I don't know. Let me check with the home office." Most likely, the customer will delay buying until the salesperson reports back— or buy from someone else in the interim.

[3]Robert F. Harley, *Marketing Successes* (New York: John Wiley, 1985), p. 203.

Studying the company's history provides perspectives and insights that will serve the salesperson well throughout a career.

Company Organization

Many companies carefully maintain one or more organization charts. An organization chart provides an overview of a company's chain of command, communication flows, and overall structure. The organization chart might be anything from a single sheet of paper giving the names of company officers and executives to an elaborate wall chart kept in the company's main boardroom. New salespeople can learn a lot about the positions and unique roles of key individuals by studying the organization chart. Most companies maintain a separate, detailed organization chart for the sales department showing the hierarchy of sales managers, sales support people, and the most important people in the sales organization: the salespeople. Figure 9-1 illustrates some of the ways a sales force can be structured. The choice among these options suggests what's really important to top management. If a sales force is structured by geographic location, for example, this could suggest that management considers specific geographic markets large enough to justify special attention. A sales force structured by customer type, however, may reflect management's emphasis on identifying and solving problems and its concern to serve specific customers or customer types.

Mission Statement

The mission statement provides an understanding and feel for the organization's orientation, goals, basic values, and sense of purpose. In describing the essence of the company's business and what it seeks to accomplish, the mission statement lays out the vision and direction for the company over the next 10 to 20 years. It is also a document that can help motivate salespeople to extraordinary performances. For example, it is much more satisfying and challenging for salespeople

A. Geographic

Appropriate when:

Customers are widely disbursed; customers in similar industries tend to be located near one another; regional differences in customer behavior are great; personal relationships are important in the marketing effort; geographic markets are large enough to justify special attention.

B. Product

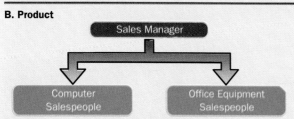

Appropriate when:

Product complexities and differences are great; there is a need to coordinate all aspects of the marketing program at the customers' level; product introductions are frequent; there are large differences in locations of products or life cycles; products or product groups are sufficiently important to justify special attention.

C. Function

Appropriate when:

Activities, such as sales development, require special expertise; number of products is small and similar; functions (activities or jobs) are sufficiently important to justify special attention.

D. Customer

Appropriate when:

Customer needs and products purchased vary greatly from one industry to another; it's important to avoid duplication of effort in serving customers; customer groups are large enough to justify special attention; the need to identify and solve customer problems is substantial.

E. Combination (organized by geography, products, and customers)

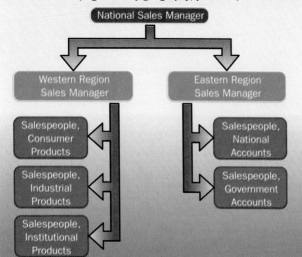

Appropriate when:

Products are unique and complex; customer needs and products purchased vary widely from one industry to another; customers are dispersed but tend to be located near one another by industry or type of product needs; customer groups are large enough to justify special attention—e.g., large national accounts.

FIGURE 9-1 Sales Force Organization Options

to think of their jobs as helping to create cleaner, healthier, more attractive home environments for families than as merely selling vacuum cleaners.

Culture

CULTURE In an organization, a set of formal and informal values that establishes rules for dress, communicating, and behavior.

Every organization has its own unique culture or operating climate. This **culture** may be defined as a set of formal and informal values that establish rules for dress, communicating, and behavior on everything from problem solving to ethics. A highly centralized organization run by authoritarian management will create a sales climate sharply different from that of an organization where authority is decentralized and management employs a more consultative or democratic style. There may not be one pervasive climate in the organization, but a number of different climates depending on the department or unit. Consider the organizational climate where a marketing executive gave the following talk to the sales force:

> I've been out there in the field just like every one of you in this room. And, believe me, I know every trick there is. If any of you think for one moment that you're going to pull the wool over my eyes, you're making a big mistake. There's nothing you can do that I haven't already done. So if you're thinking I don't trust salespeople, you're right, I don't. It takes one to know one, if you know what I mean![4]

Contrast that with another organizational climate where the CEO delivered this talk:

> It's you salespeople gathered here tonight who are responsible for this company's record performance during the past year. It's true that our company's plant has the latest state-of-the-art facilities, and we've got an outstanding backup system to serve you. But we all know very well that nothing happens until somebody sells something. Production minus sales equals scrap. I'm proud to be associated with such fine men and women. I think you're the finest sales organization in the world.[5]

Every organization has formal and informal cultural values. Formal values are *idealized* values set forth in the company's mission statements, philosophies, goals, policies, and procedures. Informal values are more *realistic* indicators of the company's values. They are evident in top management's attitude and behavior toward customers, employees, suppliers, and other stakeholders; the extent and quality of management's involvement in various activities such as sales and customer service; the stories and folklore that circulate in the company; and the degree of consistency in operations.

Customer satisfaction is a key cultural value at IBM. Salespeople know that they can change or postpone a meeting with the chairman of the board in order to meet with a customer. They also know that they are expected to do whatever is necessary to keep a customer's operations running smoothly. These beliefs are strengthened by the "living memory" of the organization—the stories told by IBM employees and customers of performance miracles.

Jaguar Company provides an example of how culture can both help and hinder a company's ability to maximize customer satisfaction. In the 1970s, as a subsidiary of British Leyland, Jaguar treated customers with indifference. By 1980,

[4]Mary Kay Ash, *Mary Kay on People Management* (New York: Warner Books, 1984), p. 143.
[5]Ibid.

its U.S. sales had dwindled to 3,000 cars and the company was losing $1.5 million a week. Its cars had such a poor reputation for durability that a common joke was that if you wanted a Jaguar, you had to buy two of them—one to drive while the other was in the shop.[6] Then a new management team, headed by new CEO John Egan, turned the company around by initiating an ongoing customer service/ market research program to learn about customers' experiences and complaints. Discovering over 150 problems, Egan set up multidisciplinary task forces to analyze and fix product flaws and ensure on-time deliveries of new models. Soon employees, dealers, and prospective owners began to see that Jaguar was again standing behind its cars, improving its reliability record, and doing everything possible to satisfy its customers.

A new salesperson should try to size up the organizational culture quickly and learn what is acceptable and expected behavior. A few coffee breaks or lunches with more experienced salespeople and staff can prove invaluable in understanding the corporate culture and managerial climate.

Philosophy

PHILOSOPHY In an organization, a program or system of beliefs and attitudes passed down from the founder to successive managers.

An organizational **philosophy** is a program or system of beliefs and attitudes passed down from the founder through successive managers. Basic philosophies are often incorporated into the company logo, like J. C. Penney's "The customer is always right" or Zenith's "The quality goes in before the name goes on." However, a strong CEO can install a new corporate philosophy, especially in times of stress or crisis such as a sharp decline in market share or profits. Salespeople must stay alert to shifting management philosophies because flexibility in adjusting to a new regime's philosophies is essential for continued success and happiness on the job. For example, if new management insists that customers who order less than $10,000 worth of items yearly should be dropped, then the salesperson may have to sever ties gently with many loyal but small customers.

Goals and Objectives

Goals are long-run, qualitatively defined targets. An example of a goal might be a company's desire for recognition as the most service-oriented company in the industry. *Objectives* are short-run, quantitatively defined targets. An example of an objective might be a company's desire to achieve a 10 percent market share by the end of the year. Good salespeople are aware of the goals and objectives of the company, the marketing department, and each successive organizational unit (sales region, division, branch) in which they work. This knowledge enables them to formulate more compatible and realistic personal goals and objectives. It would probably be unrealistic for a salesperson to forecast an increase of 30 percent in territorial sales if the company's and the region's overall forecast is for a 5 percent sales decline. Awareness of the company and sales department forecasts would keep a salesperson from making this serious forecasting error.

---

[6]Samuel C. Certo, *Principles of Modern Management,* 4th ed. (Boston: Allyn & Bacon, 1989), p. 371.

Strategies and Tactics

A *strategy* is a total program of action for using resources to achieve a goal or an objective. A tactic is a short-run, specific action that is part of the larger strategic plan. An example of a sales strategy is Honeywell's concentration of its field sales force in small cities in competing against IBM, whose resources are concentrated in large cities. Sales tactics might include use of a videotape and brochures in Spanish for sales presentations to Hispanic customers. Salespeople who understand their companies' strategies and tactics will have useful guidelines for making decisions in the field. In order for any organization to succeed, every member of the team needs to know the overall plan (strategy) as well as the individual tasks (tactics).

Policies

POLICIES Predetermined decisions for handling recurring situations efficiently and effectively.

To ensure consistency, continuity, and expeditious organizational decisions on routine matters, general rules of action called *policies* are necessary. **Policies** are predetermined decisions for handling recurring situations efficiently and effectively. A knowledge of company policies helps salespeople in making field decisions and serving customers more efficiently. For example, a salesperson who is familiar with the company's policy of not shipping goods until payment has been received for the previous shipment can prevent customer embarrassment. In order to negotiate price and terms with the buyer, the salesperson must thoroughly know the company's credit policies and credit terms. Sometimes discounts are available for quantity purchases. Cash discounts may be offered to buyers who pay the invoice within a specified number of days. Typical cash discount terms are 2/10, net 30, meaning that the buyer will receive a 2 percent discount if he pays within 10 days of the invoice date, but after 10 days the total invoice must be paid within 30 days. Even for the salesperson's own family financial planning, it is critical to know whether the company's policy is to pay com-

What Would You Do?

One of your better customers has just called you to complain about the latest batch of business forms that your company delivered. It seems that the customer's telephone number is incorrect on all 12 cases of the forms. You check the order to see how such a mistake could have been made, and you notice that the customer himself made the mistake in filling out the order. Your company's policy is to take back any misprinted forms that are its fault, but to hold customers responsible for any errors they make on the order form. This customer has been increasing its purchases with you by about 10 percent a year, and last year bought $900 worth of goods from you. The invoice price of the 12 cases of misprinted forms is $208.32.

missions when the order is accepted, when the goods are shipped, or when the customer pays the invoice. Most companies pay commissions to their salespeople when the goods are shipped.

Procedures

PROCEDURES Descriptions of the specific steps for accomplishing a task.

Procedures describe the specific steps for accomplishing a task, such as accepting an order or taking back an unsatisfactory product. Good procedures are designed to get the job done quickly and correctly. Sometimes salespeople become impatient with standard procedures and spend a lot of time and energy trying to get around them, thereby alienating the sales support staff. It's usually better to follow the procedure while trying to get it changed. Poor procedures usually have short lives.

UNDERSTANDING PRODUCTS

Studies consistently show that more effective salespeople have greater knowledge about their company's products.[7] Few customers will respect or buy from a salesperson who isn't fully informed about the technical details of the product and its application to their problems. A vice president of purchasing and supply for Ford Motor Company says: "Today's salespeople have to be more technically qualified and more knowledgeable about their products than their predecessors. At the very least, they have to understand what their products can and can't do for us and how they can best be used. If they are not technically qualified beyond that point, we expect them to find experts in their own organizations who can interface with our technical teams."[8] Salespeople who really understand their products develop a pride and confidence that comes through to customers and helps gain their confidence and trust—and most likely, the sale.

As product cycles shorten and technology advances at an ever-increasing pace, salespeople have to work harder to keep informed about company products. What do salespeople need to know about their products? The answer is simple: EVERYTHING! A purchasing manager for the Honda auto plant in Marysville, Ohio, gives an idea of what is expected from sales reps: "Salespeople should know how the parts they sell are made, packaged, shipped, received by the customer, unpackaged, sent to the line, picked up, installed on the final product, adjoined to other parts, and function."[9]

Listed below are a few of the many questions that a salesperson should be able to answer about the product line:

■ Where does the product come from? Where is it mined, grown, assembled, or manufactured? How does it get shipped to the present location? Does shipping significantly affect its quality or price?

[7]Harish Sujan, Mita Sujan, and James R. Bettman, "Knowledge Structure Differences Between More Effective and Less Effective Salespeople," *Journal of Marketing Research,* February 1988, pp. 81–86.
[8]William Atkinson, "Know Thy Customer: Purchasers Redefine Supplier Relationships," *Management Review,* June 1989, p. 22.
[9]Ibid., p. 21.

- Who designed the product? How is the product made? What kind of machines produced it?
- How should the product be used? What are the manufacturer recommendations regarding care and maintenance? What can be learned from other customers who have used the product? Are there any special features or advantages that distinguish this product from competitive products on the market?
- What kind of guarantee or warranty does the company offer on the product? What kind of repair and maintenance service does the company provide? Does the company have a service department or service centers? Where are they located?
- What happens if a product is broken in delivery? Is the customer protected? How can the customer return the product if it proves unsatisfactory?

Products from the Customer's Perspective

Most products and services offer a range of functional, psychological, and sensory (sight, hearing, smell, touch, and taste) attributes. A bar of soap may become much more appealing and satisfy a wider array of the customer's functional and psychological needs when it is conveniently and attractively shaped, contains a special moisturizing agent, gives off a pleasant scent, feels good to the touch, and has a pleasing, eye-catching wrapper. Earth-moving equipment becomes much more appealing to industrial buyers when the seller guarantees that it will be replaced or repaired within 24 hours of any breakdown.

It is not enough simply to explain to a customer the basic functions or general uses of a product. A customer is really looking for personal benefits or solutions to his or her problems before anything else. Salespeople must use their product knowledge to present products in ways that match the needs and desires of customers. The identical product may be viewed quite differently by customers, depending on their individual needs. Consider the following conversation between a computer salesperson and a prospective customer.

Customer: What different types of personal computers do you sell?

Salesperson: Well, I sold you a personal computer to help you manage your stock and bond investments. Your friend Wayne Kimmel, the novelist, bought one to help him write books. Mary Pritchard, the owner of a public relations firm, bought a computer to keep records on her customers and to develop creative presentations for clients. Ruby Sloan bought hers to keep better track of food recipes, address changes for relatives and friends, and to balance her checkbook. Professor Doug Gallagher, the physicist, bought one to analyze the statistical results of his experiments.

Customer: Wow, sounds like you sell a wide range of computers.

Salesperson: No, I sell just one basic personal computer, but people buy it for a lot of different reasons.

The FAB Approach

FAB SELLING APPROACH A method of selling that first uncovers the customer's needs and wants, then presents the product's features, advantages, and benefits.

Salespeople must first uncover each customer's needs and wants, then present their product's FAB—features, advantages, and benefits—that will appeal most to that customer. Let's briefly discuss the three parts of the **FAB selling approach.**

1. *Features* are the relatively obvious characteristics of a product or service. These are what the customer can see, touch, hear, taste, or smell. In the case of a wristwatch, features may be a rich-looking gold finish, a sweep second hand, a date window, an expandable band, and a special alarm.

2. *Advantages* are the performance characteristics of the product that show how it can be used to help the customer. A salesperson may inform the customer that this wristwatch is the most reliable on the market and that it is completely shock resistant and waterproof. Claims like this, however, must be provable. The salesperson could drop the wristwatch into a glass of water after banging it on a table, then show its second hand still going around. This might adequately demonstrate the watch's advantages to the prospect.

3. *Benefits* are what the customer wants from the product. The salesperson should consider what problems a product solves or what satisfaction it provides for the prospect. A very busy salesperson may want a watch only to indicate the precise time so that she is never a minute late for her appointments with clients, whereas a scuba diver or tennis player may want a wristwatch that will keep reasonably accurate time but, more important, "take a licking and keep on ticking."

Professional salespeople using the FAB selling approach know that they must *describe* the product's features, *prove* its advantages, and *sell* its benefits. These three aspects of the FAB approach need not be covered in any particular order, though it's usually best to present the customer benefit first because that's the customer's "hot button," or reason for buying. Consider the following illustrations of the FAB selling formula:

■ You'll be able to produce dazzling full-color reports and memos *(benefit)* more quickly and inexpensively *(advantage)* with this new Hewlett-Packard Paintjet printer with its interface kit for Macintosh computers *(feature)*.

■ Your batting average should dramatically increase *(benefit)* with this new lightweight but incredibly strong titanium baseball bat *(feature)* because it enables you to hit the ball up to 50 percent harder *(advantage)*, thus changing many former soft line outs into smashing line drives *(advantage)*.

These two illustrations point to the broad range of use for the FAB selling approach. All products have features, advantages, and benefits, whether they are "low-tech" or "high-tech" products.

Low-Tech Products

Low-tech products are things like baseball bats, matches, safety pins, and mousetraps. Although they sound simple, there may be a lot for salespeople to learn about these products. In today's economy, the world will probably not beat a path to your door if you build a better mousetrap, but there is still a considerable market that responds well to changes in mousetrap design, such as a built-in scent that makes it unnecessary to bait the trap. Woodstream Corporation, near Lancaster, Pennsylvania, sells over 10 million mousetraps a year, and its sales are climbing. Woodstream recently introduced an innovative trap called Havahart, which merely traps a mouse without harming it so that people can release it outdoors.

One product that hasn't changed much over the years is the paper clip. Over 10 million are sold each year. Selling paper clips may sound easy, but supplier competition is fierce. Imports from Taiwan have cut market prices by about 20 percent. Moreover, although customer benefits from paper clips may seem self-evident, consider how every 100,000 paperclips are actually used.

Out of every 100,000 paperclips:	
3,196 are used as pipe cleaners,	
5,308 are used as nail cleaners	
5,434 are used as toothpicks,	
14,163 are twisted or broken during phone calls,	
15,556 are dropped on the floor and swept away,	
17,200 are used as suspender hooks,	
19,143 are used as chips in card games, and	
20,000 are actually used to clip papers together.	

Source: James Braham, "Ho-Hum, How Do You Peddle a Low-Tech Product?" *Industry Week,* June 9, 1986, pp. 53–56.

High-Tech Products

High-tech products change in response to developing technology. Illustrations are the Hewlett-Packard printer, a videocamera, and a computer-controlled manufacturing system. Because many of these products are so complex, some high-tech companies consider their salespeople to be little more than "bird dogs": They are supposed to sniff out the sales opportunity, and then the product managers and engineers will carry the technical load with the customer. Often, however, the inside technical staff is stretched so thin with other duties that it can't get involved soon enough, and the company loses the opportunity.

Some companies employ specially trained sales engineers to sell highly technical products like industrial tools or medicines. These salespeople must work harder than most to keep abreast of the latest technical aspects of their products. Sometimes a scientific or engineering education or orientation is important in selling technical products. Presenting genetically engineered pharmaceuticals to physicians requires a salesperson with a broad scientific background who is continually studying the newest developments in the field. Selling artificial vision machines used in measuring systems calls for an engineer's grasp of industrial processes and industrial computers.

Because today an engineer's knowledge is current for only five years,[10] and a scientist's for an even shorter period of time, a well-informed sales engineer or sales rep may find an important sales tactic in the customer's technical confusion. Chemineer, Inc., of Dayton, Ohio, has been able to do just that, as related in the next Company Highlight.

Product Knowledge Training

Better-managed companies know that the more knowledge a new salesperson gains in training, the more confident he or she will be and the more likely this

Company Highlight

Taking Advantage of Technical Confusion at Chemineer

There is so much complex machinery in the typical manufacturing plant that it's hard to tell where one supplier's equipment ends and another's begins. Chemineer, Inc., a manufacturer of corrosion-resistant fluid agitation and mixing equipment, knows that customer confusion can often lead to a sales opportunity. When customers phone and complain mistakenly to Chemineer about a piece of malfunctioning equipment that actually came from a competitor, the in-house customer service people are taught to befriend the customers, rather than chastise them for getting suppliers confused. Chemineer people try to find out what the trouble is, then have a local Chemineer representative contact the customer to see if Chemineer equipment can help solve the problem.

After the sale of each new piece of machinery, Chemineer has a technique for helping its sales force of independent manufacturers' representatives get past the purchasing agent's desk.

Chemineer's tactic is to have a technically trained sales representative offer to check the newly installed Chemineer equipment to make sure it's working properly. "Very few customers turn down the opportunity for a free inspection." says Rick Powell, manager of parts and field service for Chemineer. Besides generating customer goodwill, the visit provides a chance for the representatives to talk with the operators and maintenance people who work with the machinery to find out what kind of problems they encounter. The sales rep then suggests a solution to the problems that includes the replacement of the competitor's machinery with Chemineer's. As a final incentive to switch to Chemineer equipment, the sales representative will usually offer to take the competitor's defective equipment in trade.

Source: Edward Doherty, "How to Steal a Satisfied Customer," *Sales & Marketing Management,* March 1990, pp. 40–45.

will translate into sales success with customers. Salespeople must totally know the products they're selling, and the customer has to perceive that they know them. With technical products, it isn't unusual for new salespeople to spend six months in training before being allowed out into the field to sell. After the initial sales training program, salespeople ought to continue updating their product knowledge through such methods as absorption training, computer simulations, videoconferences, and job rotation.

Absorption Training

ABSORPTION TRAINING A system for training salespeople in which product manuals, videotapes, and other learning materials are sent directly to the salesperson for self-study.

To update and reinforce earlier product knowledge training and to quickly introduce new materials and products to the salespeople, many companies use an approach called **absorption training.** In absorption training, product manuals, videotapes, memoranda, and sales bulletins are sent directly to the salesperson for self-study. Although absorption training does not allow for immediate feedback and questioning, it is still an effective way to disseminate materials and information quickly. Many companies provide sales manuals that cover nearly everything the company wants the sales trainee to know. When these manuals are comprehensive, clearly written, well indexed, and regularly updated, they become the salesperson's "bible" in the field.

Computer Simulation

Computer simulations or games are helping companies present product knowledge to salespeople in highly effective, yet enjoyable ways. Both new sales trainees and experienced salespeople can work on a computer simulation or exercise at their convenience and progress at their own rate. Because computer sales training usually requires people to actively use at least three of their senses (sight, sound, and touch), the learning process becomes more interesting and less tiring. Some companies are using computer game competition to train salespeople about products, as described in the following vignette.

Videoconferences

To minimize the loss of field selling time and the costs of travel, many companies are conducting sales training seminars on new products and programs via videoconference. Salespeople go to a central location such as a branch sales office or Holiday Inn that has videoconferencing facilities and interactively participate in nationwide or even worldwide meetings. Just as on Ted Koppel's *Nightline* and other television programs, videoconferencing allows people from all over the world to see and talk to one another. Besides the savings on travel costs and selling downtime, a major advantage of videoconferences is that they permit the same information to be presented in the same way simultaneously to all salespeople, which minimizes confusion and misunderstanding. Some companies

---

COMPUTERS CAN MAKE LEARNING FUN

Chase Manhattan Bank, Caterpillar, BMW's Motorcycle Division, and Ford's Heavy Truck Division use a computer game developed by Atlanta-based Management Campus to enable salespeople to enjoy the fun and personal rewards of competition while learning about company products. The competition can become quite intense because winners often receive valuable prizes—besides prestige and ego satisfaction. One Caterpillar salesperson who won his competition says the game "forced me not only to read about the technical aspects of the Caterpillar engines, but to study and learn that material thoroughly. All of us who entered the competition had absolutely no idea of how really good a product we had to sell."

SOURCE: Christopher Payne-Taylor and Henry G. Berszinn, "Sales Reps Win with Product Knowledge," *Marketing News*, May 8, 1987, pp. 9–10.

even conduct their annual national or international sales meetings by videoconference. As costs for videoconferencing facilities continue to decline, more companies will find that videoconferences provide nearly all the advantages of traditional sales meetings held in a central location.

Job Rotation

JOB ROTATION "Rotating" employees through various jobs in an organization in order to help them obtain a better understanding of the organization's products, personnel, and ways of doing business.

In order to expose employees to as many aspects of a company's departments and processes as possible, some companies insist on employee **job rotation.** Japanese companies normally rotate their new employees, especially salespeople and others destined for management positions, through the different jobs involved in producing, packaging, and distributing the company's products. Some American companies rotate salespeople through various sales support and headquarters marketing jobs so that they will better understand how market research, advertising, sales promotion, publicity, pricing, and distribution strategies are developed for products. By working for a short time in different manufacturing and marketing jobs, salespeople learn how the products are made and what specific materials go into them, as well as the process of developing overall marketing and customer service strategies.

Selling Multiple Products

Product knowledge problems are compounded when salespeople must handle several lines of products. If a salesperson carries five product lines, it is nearly five times as much work to know all the products and keep them straight. In seeking a systematic way to stay informed about these products, salespeople should consider developing, maintaining, and carrying for ready reference a simple multiple-product knowledge worksheet. They can update and add relevant questions to this worksheet as they receive new questions from prospects and customers.

Interaction with Other Products

Not only must salespeople know their products thoroughly, they must also know how these products work with other products. For example, a customer may ask: "What color printers are compatible with the Macintosh IIcx?" or "Will Microsoft Word 4.0 run on the Macintosh IIcx with 1 megabyte of RAM?" Without understanding how their products interact with various other equipment and ancillaries, the salesperson cannot reassure the customer and will risk losing the sale. It is especially important for salespeople to know everything about the product and its ancillaries when selling a product without an established brand name. Even though its technology lagged behind that of Apple Computer, IBM was eventually able to achieve a higher market share in personal computers because people had confidence in the IBM brand name.

Overlooked Sources of Product Knowledge

Top salespeople pay careful attention to the numerous little details of product knowledge that less successful salespeople often overlook or take for granted

The company's service team is an often overlooked source of knowledge about the company, its products, and its competition.

because such details are not glamorous or exciting. Overlooked sources of product information include the tags, brochures, and operating manuals that come with each product. Salespeople should be familiar with these and try to anticipate what questions they might raise in the customer's mind.

Another underrated source of company, product, and competitor knowledge is the company's warehouse and service team. Because they make deliveries, install, and repair products, the warehouse and service personnel obtain unique perspectives on their own company's as well as competitors' products. They usually hear the comments and complaints of customers before salespeople do—and often in much more candid language.

Knowledge about Product Service

Most products, whether tangibles like appliances or intangibles like stocks and bonds, require service. Appliances eventually need repairs, and people investing in stocks and bonds expect advice as market conditions change. Professional sales reps know what services their companies provide on each product, the costs of those services, and how they can be obtained.

Sales reps have quite an advantage when they can offer postsale service such as Black & Decker began providing on its Master Series line of industrial power tools in 1987. Black & Decker guaranteed that any tool would be serviced within four hours if brought into one of the company's over 100 authorized service centers. If customers could not wait the four hours, a loaner tool was provided until the defective tool could be repaired. Black & Decker's move was market-motivated. In the fiercely competitive power tool industry, U.S. manufacturers had lost market share to Japanese and East German manufacturers who were able to accomplish warranty and routine repairs within 72 hours. U.S. manufacturers usually required from two to four weeks.[11]

Sales can also be lost because of lack of knowledge about presale service to potential customers. Salespeople and their companies are judged by prospects on the basis of the accuracy and timeliness of the information they provide. Salespeople, telemarketers, or even secretaries who fail to respond, erroneous information given to prospects, delays in providing requested information, proposals not delivered to prospects on the date promised—all these send distinct messages to prospects that a supplier will probably do a poor job in providing postsale service. In any business or human relationship, it's doing many little things well that oftentimes differentiates you from the also-rans. Salespeople must work at winning the confidence of prospects by ensuring that they get all their questions answered fully and accurately, in a timely fashion. It is the salesperson's responsibility to promptly obtain whatever product or service information the prospect needs. The next Selling in Action box tells of a salesperson who goes that extra mile in keeping her customers informed.

[11]Y.D. Scholar, "Faster Delivery Seen as Edge for Foreign Power Tools," *Industrial Distribution,* February 1984, p. 45.

Selling in Action

Keeping Customers Informed

Wendy Snyder, a field sales representative of the Torrington Company, was chosen in *Purchasing* magazine's annual poll of over 100,000 professional buyers as one of the top industrial field sales reps in the country. Snyder, who holds a master's degree in engineering, was cited for possessing a great deal of technical expertise and the ability to understand customers' problems and work with them toward solutions.

Working closely with the customers' production and quality control people, she monitors the buyers' MRP (materials requirement planning) schedules for the best fit with Torrington's MRP. She enabled one company to cut its inventory by 50 percent on some very costly bearings. Professional buyers rate her willingness to follow through and keep customers informed as one of her strongest sales attributes. One buyer who was interviewed by *Purchasing* commented that Snyder never fails to confirm the details of every meeting with a memorandum outlining what was decided. Such thoroughness minimizes the misunderstandings and communication problems that can sour the relationship with a customer. Wendy Snyder is a thorough professional who pays careful attention to the little details as well as the big tasks in a customer-supplier relationship.

Source: Adapted from Somerby Dowst, "Super Sellers Get Green Light to Go Extra Mile," *Purchasing* Magazine, August 25, 1983, pp. 45–46.

UNDERSTANDING THE COMPETITION

Because salespeople are nearly always selling in a competitive environment, they must understand competitors' products and services almost as well as their own company's. Customers will have confidence in a salesperson who can knowledgeably compare his or her own product's features and advantages with those of a competitor. This confidence, however, can be undermined if the salesperson gives in to the temptation to disparage the competition in front of customers. Negative comments like "Our competitor's machine is pathetically slow and has one of the worst repair records on the market" often work against the salesperson who is trying to win the trust and respect of customers. It's always better to make product comparisons in positive terms, such as: "Our table-top copiers average about 5,000 copies before you need to change the toner cartridge—nearly twice as many as any other comparable machines—and our repair record is one of the best."

In order to be able to compare their products with those of competitors, salespeople must learn all they can about competitive products. A surprising ally in this effort is the United States government. Since the passage of the Freedom of Information Act, which requires the federal government to release documents in its files to anyone making a request, companies have gained access to valuable information about competitors, including some of their secrets. For instance, in 1982, the Environmental Protection Agency released Monsanto's confidential formula for the herbicide Round-Up to competitors. And a Swedish ball-bearing maker obtained copies of a Federal Trade Commission document that discussed Ingersoll-Rand's marketing tactics for bearings.

One of the most comprehensive and widely used sources of information about who makes what products and where they can be purchased is the *Thomas Register of National Manufacturers*. A study of purchasing agents in Fortune 500 companies found that 98 percent use the *Thomas Register* as their primary source for locating suppliers.[12] Published annually in 25 volumes, it provides informa-

---

[12]"Reaching All the Industrial Prospects," *ZIP Target Marketing,* April 1984, a promotional publication of the Thomas Publishing Company.

What Would You Do?

One of your major competitors has been telling customers that your company is having problems making deliveries on time. One recent delivery was a week late because of a mixup in your company's shipping department, but all other shipments, to your knowledge, have been on time. Some customers have asked you if your company is having a problem meeting delivery dates.

TABLE 9-3 Competitive Analysis Worksheet

For each dimension below, rank our company versus competitors on a scale of 1–5, with 1 being the highest.

DIMENSION	OUR COMPANY	COMPETITORS A	B	C	D
Sales	___	___	___	___	___
Market share	___	___	___	___	___
Growth rate	___	___	___	___	___
New products	___	___	___	___	___
Financial strength	___	___	___	___	___
Marketing strategy	___	___	___	___	___
Marketing mix	___	___	___	___	___
Image/reputation	___	___	___	___	___
Product quality	___	___	___	___	___
Pricing	___	___	___	___	___
Installation	___	___	___	___	___
Delivery	___	___	___	___	___
Billing/invoicing	___	___	___	___	___
Repair	___	___	___	___	___
Customer service	___	___	___	___	___

Source: Adapted from Anthony Alessandra, James Cathcart, and Philip Wexler, *Selling by Objectives* (Englewood Cliffs, N.J.: Prentice Hall, 1988), p. 88.

tion about manufacturers of product categories, specific products, names of the companies, branches, top executives and their job titles, affiliation data, and credit rating. Volumes 1–16 list in alphabetical order all the products of manufacturers in the United States. A companion publication is the *Thomas Register Catalog File* (called *Thomcat*), which consists of manufacturers' catalogs bound together in alphabetical order and cross-referenced by product.

Many professional salespeople maintain well-organized files on competitors and their offerings. They keep running files on each of their competitors—products they sell, competitive advantages and disadvantages, major customers, products that each customer buys and for what use, names of competitive salespeople, and their estimated sales volume. A competitive analysis worksheet like the one in Table 9-3 can help the salesperson systematize information about competitors' product and service offerings versus his or her own company's.

UNDERSTANDING MARKETS

Where are the company's present and future markets? Who are and will be its customers? Economic, technological, political-legal, cultural-social, ethical, and competitive environments are continually changing in a largely uncontrollable way. Companies that have prospered most over the years are those that have successfully anticipated and responded to the many dynamic changes in the macromarketing environment, depicted in Figure 9-2.

Timely customer feedback is critical to the company's response to a dynamic macromarketing environment. Salespeople are supposed to be the "eyes and ears" of the company in the marketplace, but sales and marketing managers often ignore this information-gathering function of salespeople. Thus, the company loses a valuable early-warning system about changing customer needs and the evolving marketing environment. Most salespeople and their companies' man-

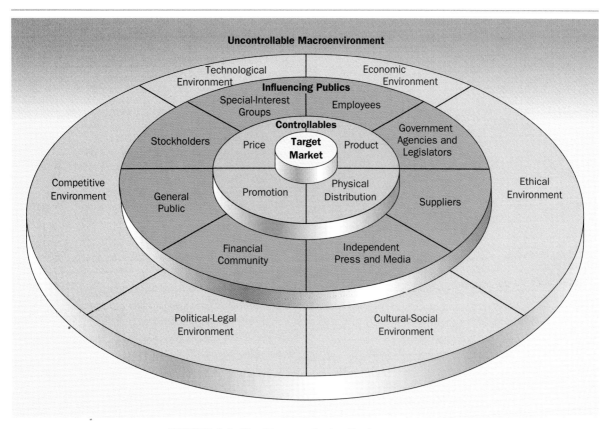

FIGURE 9-2 The Macromarketing Environment

agers feel that they know the market thoroughly. Yet the evidence is overwhelming that they do not. Important innovations rarely come from firms that are currently dominant in a given industry. Numerous industry leaders have been slow to recognize technological developments that changed their markets forever, as Table 9-4 shows.

TABLE 9-4 Slow Recognition of Opportunities in Markets They Dominated

COMPANY OR INDUSTRY	INNOVATIVE PRODUCT OR SERVICE
Parker Brothers, Mattel	Video games
Kendall (cloth diaper cleaners)	Disposable diapers
Levi Straus	Designer jeans
Goodyear, Firestone, Goodrich	Radial tires
Swiss watchmakers	Digital watches
Anheuser/Busch, Miller	Light beer
Coke, Pepsi	Diet soda
Wine producers	Wine coolers
Eversharp/Eberhard Faber	Ballpoint pens
IBM	Microcomputers
Converse, Keds	Running shoes
Keuffel & Esser (leading manufacturer of slide rules)	Calculators

TABLE 9-5   Understanding the Role of Company Stakeholders

PUBLIC	COMPANY OBJECTIVES
Customers	Increase sales, profits, customer satisfaction
Government	Encourage favorable legislation
Independent media	Create favorable corporate image
General public	Develop image as a good corporate citizen
Special interest groups	Show support for issues or present company side of issues
Stockholders	Encourage purchases of stock
Suppliers	Obtain credit, prompt delivery, and service
Financial community	Obtain short-run and long-run capital at favorable interest rates
Employees	Create job satisfaction, motivate workers for increased production and product quality

Beyond anticipating and adjusting to the changes in the macromarketing environment, an organization must apply marketing and sales planning to its relationships with all its influencing publics, not just its customers. All of these publics should be considered *stakeholders* in the company. Since, as shown in Table 9-5, each of these publics influences the operation of sales and marketing organizations for better or worse, each must be considered in developing strategies and tactics.

Keeping Informed

Successful salespeople work at staying well informed about the industry they serve and about business in general. They regularly do individual market research in local university or college libraries. They stay alert to trends in their customers' industries, and they read publications about their customers' industries. They join trade associations that publish current developments in the industry and can supply membership lists that may lead to new customers. Successful salespeople attend trade shows and seminars where they can interact with customers and learn more about their customers' businesses. They become familiar with basic bibliographical guides and directories like these:

- *Business Information Sources*
- *How to Find Information About Companies*
- *World Sources of Market Information*
- *Directory of Industry Data Sources*
- *Marketing Information: A Professional Reference Guide*
- *Encyclopedia of Trade Associations*
- *Directory of Directories*
- *Guide to American Directories*
- *County Business Patterns*

CREDIT MANAGER The person in the selling company who researches a customer's ability to pay and often makes the financing decision for customers who need to postpone or finance all or part of their payment.

The Credit Manager

Top-performing salespeople also cultivate an excellent relationship with their company's **credit manager,** the person who often makes the financing decisions for big and small orders alike. Most credit managers have immediate access

Dun & Bradstreet Business Credit Services is a well-known resource that many credit managers use for fast, accurate credit information about prospective customers.
Courtesy of the Dun & Bradstreet Corporation.

to a wealth of financial and other information about prospects and customers. You would be very wise to discuss with your credit manager the prospect's ability to meet financial obligations before closing a sale that requires the prospect to finance all or part of a large payment to your company.

Published Information
Sales professionals read the annual reports of their customers, their competitors, and their own companies, and study analyses of all these companies prepared by financial companies like Dun & Bradstreet, Standard & Poor's, and Value Line. They periodically review data from Dun & Bradstreet's *Million Dollar Directory*

TABLE 9-6   Sources of Information

TRADE ASSOCIATION DIRECTORIES

■ *Encyclopedia of Associations* (Gale Research Company, Detroit):
  —*Vol. 1. National Organizations of the U.S.:* Lists organizations alphabetically (by name, address, convention schedules).
  —*Vol II. Geographic and Executive Index:* Contains an alphabetical list of the association executives with a cross-reference to Vol. I by city and state.
  —*Vol. III. New Associations and Projects:* Continually updates information between editions of Vols. I and II.
■ *National Trade and Professional Associations of the United States and Labor Unions* (Columbia Books, Washington, D.C.): Contains data on over 4,700 organizations, trade and professional associations, and national labor unions.
■ *Directory of Corporate Affiliations* (National Register Publishing Company, Skokie, Ill.): Cross-references 3,000 parent companies with their 16,000 divisions, subsidiaries, and affiliates.

BUSINESS GUIDES

■ *Moody's Industrial Manual* (Moody's Investor Service, New York): Provides seven years of statistical records and financial statements on each company, principal officers and directors, major plants, products, and merger and acquisition records.
■ *Reference Book of Corporate Managements* (Dun & Bradstreet, New York): Identifies over 30,000 executives who are officers and directors of 2,400 large corporations.
■ *Thomas Register of National Manufacturers* (published annually in 25 volumes): Vols. 1–16 list alphabetically all the products of manufacturers in the United States. Vols. 17–18 lists alphabetically the manufacturers of those products; it also provides the names of the companies, their branches, top executives and their job titles, affiliation data, and credit rating.
■ *Standard & Poor's Corporation Services* (Standard & Poor's Corporations, New York): Provides various services, including: *Industry Surveys* (trends and projections); *Outlook* (weekly stock market letter); *Stock Guide* (monthly summary of data on 5,000 common and preferred stocks); *Trade and Securities* (monthly listing of statistics on business, finance, stocks and bonds, foreign trade, productivity, and employment).
■ *Standard & Poor's Register of Corporations, Directors and Executives* (Standard & Poor's Corporation, New York): Three volumes containing thousands of listings.

INDEXES

■ *Business Periodicals Index* (H. W. Wilson, New York): Cumulative subject index listing business articles from over 160 periodicals.
■ *The Wall Street Journal Index* (Dow Jones, Princeton, N. J.): Index of all *Wall Street Journal* articles arranged into corporate news and general news.
■ *F&S Index of Corporations and Industries* (Predicasts, Cleveland, Ohio): Covers company, industry, and product information on American companies from 750 business-oriented newspapers, financial publications, and trade magazines.
■ *F&S Index of International Industries, Countries, Companies* (Predicasts, Cleveland, Ohio): Provides information on foreign companies classified by SIC code and alphabetically by company name.
■ *Applied Science & Technology Index* (H. W. Wilson; New York): Cumulative subject index to periodicals in the fields of science (e.g., aeronautics, chemistry, construction, engineering, telecommunications, and transportation).

GOVERNMENT PUBLICATIONS

■ *Survey of Current Business* (U.S. Department of Commerce, Bureau of Economic Analysis, Washington, D.C.): Updates 2,600 different statistical series in each monthly issue. Includes data on gross national product, national income, international balance of payments, general business indicators, employment, construction, real estate, domestic and foreign trade.
■ *Monthly Catalog of United States Government Publications* (Superintendent of Documents, U.S. Government Printing Office, Washington, D.C.): Comprehensive list of federal publications issued each month, by agency.
■ *Monthly Checklist of State Publications* (Superintendent of Documents, U.S. Government Printing Office, Washington, D. C.): Lists state publications received by Library of Congress.
■ *Census Data:* Extensive source of information on the United States. Includes:
  —*Bureau of the Census Catalog of Publications*
  —*Census of Retail Trade*
  —*Census of Wholesale Trade*
  —*Census of Selected Services*
  —*Census of Housing*
  —*Census of Manufacturers*
  —*Census of Population*
  —*Census of Agriculture*

and *Ward's Directory of Major U.S. Private Companies.* They go to the *Business Periodicals Index* to find specific business articles on a company, product, or problem. They also regularly read general business publications such as *Business Week, The Wall Street Journal, Forbes,* and *Fortune* in order to project a more informed image. They don't rely on only one source for information, but rather compare and corroborate data among various sources, like those listed in Table 9-6.

Understanding Professional Buyers

Once able to rely on personal creative selling skills, salespeople now usually deal with professional buyers or purchasing agents who base their buying decisions on the representative's delivery of quality and service and on how a product will affect their company's profits. Major customers are demanding greater service and more concessions in price, while restricting the number of approved vendors for their local operating units. Rapid centralization of distributors has given middlemen more power as well. Increased transportation costs and changes in tax laws have reduced the number of distributors. The remaining distributors— now larger, more efficient, and more sophisticated—can demand better discounts and service.

Salespeople who can demonstrate that they have studied the customer's business and understand the customer's problems will help build a long-term relationship based on mutual trust, respect, and professionalism. Although friendliness and an outgoing personality help, professional knowledge is becoming increasingly important for success in sales. When buyers were recently surveyed about what they like from salespeople, several of the ten items named were directly related to knowledge, as shown in Table 9-7.

The rapidly growing sophistication of professional buyers and their increasing access to information will continue to challenge sales representatives to find new sources and faster methods of obtaining information. One particularly fast and valuable source is the company's management information system (MIS).

SMIS The abbreviation for a sales management information system, which is any system that collects, sorts, and analyzes information for the development of sales strategies.

Obtaining Information from the SMIS

In some progressive companies, a subset of the management information system is the sales management information system, or SMIS. An **SMIS** is a system that

TABLE 9-7 What Industrial Buyers Like from Salespeople

> 1. Thoroughness and follow-through.
> 2. Knowledge of product line.
> 3. Willingness to go to bat for buyer within the supplier's firm.
> 4. Market knowledge and willingness to keep the buyer informed.
> 5. Imagination in applying products to the buyer's needs.
> 6. Knowledge of the buyer's product line.
> 7. Diplomacy in dealing with operating departments.
> 8. Preparation for well-planned sales calls.
> 9. Regularity of sales calls.
> 10. Technical education.

Source: Alvin J. Williams and John Seminerio, "What Buyers Like from Salesmen," *Industrial Marketing Management 14* (May 1985): 76.

The Products & Services Section

The Thomas Register is a three-part, multi-volume reference work that is an invaluable resource for all companies that *buy* and *sell*. This is a description of the "Products and Services Section" (Vols. 1-16). The other two are "Company Profiles Section" (Vols. 17-18) and "Catalog File Section" (Vols. 19-25).

Courtesy of Thomas Publishing Company.

When you need a product or service—and want to find out what's available and who can supply it—use the Products & Services Section (Vol. 1-14).

■ Here you'll find detailed sourcing information under each of more than 50,000 separate product and service headings.

■ Product and service headings are listed alphabetically, using the "modified noun" system. For example, if you're looking for "Conveyor Belting," look under the heading "BELTING: CONVEYOR" . . . for "Electric Motors," look under "MOTORS: ELECTRIC."

■ As a fast alternative to the modified noun system, you can also use the alphabetical Product Index found at the end of Volume 14. Here "Conveyor Belting" is listed under "C". . .and "Electric Motors" is listed under "E". This index will give you the page number where the appropriate "modified noun" product heading begins.

■ Once you've found the product or service heading you want, you'll see a list of all known manufacturers or sources listed alphabetically by state and by city within each state.

■ Supplementing these listings are informative advertisements with more details about the product, service and supplier. These ads help you make side-by-side comparisons of vendors.

■ Look for the reference **"see our catalog in THOMCAT."** This tells you that a company's catalog is available to you instantly in the Catalog File Section (Vol. 17-23).

Volume 14 also includes a Product Index—
You'll find this convenient, when you're looking for a particular product.

collects, sorts, classifies, stores, analyzes, interprets, retrieves, and reports information in an ongoing process for the development of sales strategies and tactics. More companies are insisting that salespeople assume responsibility for gathering marketing intelligence on a continual basis for the company MIS. For instance, at American Cyanamid, a large industrial and consumer chemical manufacturer, salespeople are told: "Don't just sell—get information. What do our customers need? What's the competition doing? What sort of financial package do we need to win the order?"

With the information explosion, ever more complex products, the shift from local to national and international selling, the growing professionalism of buyers, and the continued development of management information systems by customers to determine the sizes of orders and potential suppliers, it becomes increas-

ingly important that salespeople have access to essential information readily available from the SMIS instead of operating on the basis of rumors and hunches. Pillsbury Grocery Division understands this and has dealt head-on with the problem. See the Company Highlight for details.

An SMIS will vary from company to company, depending on the structure, culture, and current needs of the sales organization. Specific purposes for which an SMIS can be used include:

■ Sales planning and profit analysis by customer, territory, product, or individual salesperson
■ Inventory control
■ Customer service monitoring
■ Accounts receivable management
■ Analysis of call reports
■ Time and territory management
■ Market trend projections

A study of large and small companies across different industries indicated that salespeople need all the help they can get for the following reasons:

■ Less than half the companies knew the profitability of their individual product lines.
■ Nearly one-third had no regular review process for spotting and dropping weak products.
■ Half the companies did not regularly compare their prices to the competition's, analyze their warehousing and distribution costs, determine the reasons for returned

Company Highlight

Pillsbury Grocery Goes On-Line

At Pillsbury Grocery Division, several hundred sales representatives are equipped with hand-held computers, and account executives and district managers with laptops. All are on on-line with two-way capability to a central mainframe computer maintained by FasTech, Inc., of Broomall, Pennsylvania, which tailored its Sales Information System (SIS) software for Pillsbury. Pillsbury's sales automation effort, says Dave Gillman, director of sales operations, evolved from the "realization that the account executives and sales supervisors who call on chain headquarters must have more timely information and it must be easily accessible." Pillsbury's information

loop begins with the sales reps, whose handheld computers contain a list of Pillsbury products that should be on the shelves. After each sales call, the reps input information on out-of-stocks, case sales of products ordered, and number of displays of both Pillsbury and competitive products. Each night the reps send this information to FasTech's mainframe for retrieval in the morning by the account executives they report to. Previously, it sometimes took Pillsbury up to two months to obtain reports from the field.

Source: Adapted from Thayer C. Taylor, "How Pillsbury's Reps Turn Buyer's 'No' Into 'Yes'," *Sales & Marketing Management,* February 1988, p. 67.

merchandise, evaluate advertising effectiveness, or review their sales force call reports.

■ Many companies took four to eight weeks to develop control reports, and they were often inaccurate.[13]

There will be continuing pressure on salespeople to become more and more knowledgeable in order to keep up with customers whose purchasing behavior is becoming increasingly sophisticated. Only the energetic salespeople who maintain up-to-date knowledge about their industries, companies, product lines, competitors, and customers will prosper.

SUMMARY

Sales training programs vary widely among industries and companies, but they all tend to cover four basic knowledge areas: the company, products, markets, and the selling process. Whether selling low-tech or high-tech products, salespeople must present those products' features, advantages, and benefits (FAB) that match their customers' needs and wants. After completing the company's training program, the most successful salespeople read professional and general business magazines, and make use of trade association directories, business guides, indexes, and government publications in searching for specific information about markets and products. The roles of professional buyers for organizations are expanding dramatically as their impact on profitability is understood by top management. To keep pace with professional buyers and computerized purchasing systems, many salespeople are using laptop computers to communicate on-line with the company's mainframe computer in order to tap its sales management information system (SMIS).

CHAPTER REVIEW QUESTIONS

1. What topics are usually covered in company training programs?
2. Discuss the various publics or stakeholders that influence a company and its selling organization.
3. What is a company mission statement?
4. Describe five alternatives for organizing the sales force.
5. Explain and give an example of the FAB concept.
6. Name as many as you can of the ten things that industrial buyers say they like in salespeople.
7. How are salespeople using their laptop computers?
8. For what specific purposes can an SMIS be used?

TOPICS FOR THOUGHT AND CLASS DISCUSSION

1. Why do you think so many product innovations come from smaller companies instead of the dominant companies in many industries?
2. In what ways might the company's stakeholders, other than customers, affect personal selling?

[13]Philip Kotler, *Marketing Management: Analysis, Planning, Implementation, and Control,* 6th ed. (Englewood Cliffs, N. J.: Prentice Hall, 1988), p. 729.

3. Do you think the Freedom of Information Act, which requires the U.S. government to release documents in any government file to anyone making a request, has an overall positive or negative impact on personal selling?

4. If you were a new sales trainee about to start a two-week training program, what instructional methods would you prefer? Why?

5. Why do you think that the role of company purchasing agents is expanding?

6. Do you think it's necessary for salespeople to know nearly as much about competitive products as they do about their own company's? Or is it sufficient to just know the major strengths and weaknesses of competitive products? Why?

PROJECTS FOR PERSONAL GROWTH

1. Contact two sales representatives and ask what their firms' policies and procedures are for:
  a. Processing "special rush" orders
  b. Approving customer credit
  c. Delivery and installation of products
  d. Opening new customer accounts
  e. Handling returned or damaged goods
  What do the sales reps think about the policies and procedures in their own companies for each of these five areas?

2. Choose a company of interest to you, then use (a) a trade association directory, (b) a business guide, (c) an index, and (d) a government publication to learn as much as you can about the company's history, mission, sales force organization, products sold, markets served, and major competitors. Write a three-page report summarizing what you found out about the company and which source(s) proved most helpful.

3. Prepare a lecture for new sales trainees describing how to present the features, advantages, and benefits of the following products or services:
  a. Central air conditioning
  b. Computerized payroll service
  c. Radio advertising
  d. Laser printers

KEY TERMS

Culture In an organization, a set of formal and informal values that establishes rules for dress, communicating, and behavior.

Philosophy In an organization, a program or system of beliefs and attitudes passed down from the founder to successive managers.

Policies Predetermined decisions for handling recurring situations efficiently and effectively.

Procedures Descriptions of the specific steps for accomplishing a task.

FAB selling approach A method of selling that first uncovers the customer's needs and wants, then presents the product's features, advantages, and benefits.

Absorption training A system for training salespeople in which product manuals, videotapes, and other learning materials are sent directly to the salesperson for self-study.

Job rotation "Rotating" employees through various jobs in an organization in order to help them obtain a better understanding of the organization's products, personnel, and ways of doing business.

Credit manager The person in the selling company who researches a customer's ability to pay and often makes the financing decision for customers who need to postpone or finance all or part of their payment.

SMIS The abbreviation for a sales management information system, which is any system that collects, sorts, and analyzes information for the development of sales strategies.

Case 9-1

TRYING TO REPLACE AN ENTRENCHED COMPETITOR

By Paul F. Christ, Delaware Valley College

"You can find him in the warehouse," says the store clerk in response to Marty's question. Marty Simpson begins to walk toward the back of the store, but stops and inspects some of his chief competitor's products displayed prominently at the end of the aisle. They sell some good products, he thinks, but ours are better. He smiles and feels confident that the next time he comes to this store, he will be looking at his own company's aisle display.

Marty is here to see Arnold Burke, owner of Burke's Kitchen and Bath Store. Marty has just returned from Dallas, where his company, Consolidated Cabinet, held their annual sales meeting. At the meeting Consolidated unveiled its new line of kitchen cabinets. The cabinets, which are high-quality, premium-priced, all-wood construction, are a step up for Consolidated, which in the past marketed low- to mid-priced cabinets made of particleboard and wood veneer. The low-end cabinets were mainly segmented toward the do-it-yourselfer and were primarily sold in retail home center stores. However, the company feels the best market for its new line of products is the kitchen contractor. Kitchen contractors shop at specialty stores for their cabinets, where quality products are sold at prices much higher than at home center retailers. For Consolidated, this represents a new channel of distribution, and for Marty, this is his first meeting with Arnold. Marty sees Arnold in the warehouse talking with two men and waits until Arnold finishes his conversation. Then Marty approaches him.

Simpson: Mr. Burke, my name is Marty Simpson, and I represent Consolidated Cabinet Company. I was wondering if you might have a few minutes to hear about our great new line of high-quality kitchen cabinets.

Burke: Well, actually, I'm a little busy at the moment. What was the name of that company again?

Simpson: Consolidated Cabinet Company. I promise this will only take a few minutes, and I also promise it will be worth your time.

Burke: Well, O.K.

Simpson: Great. [*Marty pulls out his selling aids and begins to explain the new cabinet line.*] We call this line the Classic America. You can see from the picture in the brochure that it is a beautiful piece. Let me tell you a few things about it. It features all-wood construction, no fillers or particleboard, and is available in the finest hardwoods. As you know, the main benefit of all-wood construction is that the product looks great and retains its quality look forever. Each piece is hand-crafted and fitted so that you can be assured of the highest quality with the fewest defects. The hardware is all metal, in stainless steel or solid brass, no plastic parts, and the hinges are made of the highest grade of steel available. And these cabinets are available in 32 different designs, all of them time- and market-tested classics. Well, what do you think?

Burke: Frankly, I'm happy with the line I'm carrying now. I've done business with them for a long time, and they provide excellent service. Both your price ranges are about the same—in fact, you're a little higher—and their product seems to have the same features as yours. I just can't see any compelling reason to change suppliers or add you on now.

Simpson: Well, Mr. Burke, think it over and in a few weeks I'll check to see if you've changed your mind.

Marty leaves wondering what he will say to Mr. Burke when he calls again.

Questions

1. Did Marty give a good presentation to Mr. Burke? If not, what was wrong with it? What was good about it? How would you change it?

2. What do you think about Marty's approach? Do you believe that he was ready to speak with Mr. Burke? What steps could he have taken to prepare himself better?

3. What should Marty do to prepare for another meeting with Mr. Burke? What should Marty say to Mr. Burke next time?

Case 9-2

DEALING WITH A STRONG COMPETITOR
By Paul F. Christ, Delaware Valley College

Beth Morelli is in her first year of selling business forms for Forms International. She is walking down the hall to the office of Chuck Stoner, purchasing agent for Forest Building Supply. Beth is not very familiar with Forest. About all she knows is that it is a division of a large multinational organization and that it opened this office only two months ago. Even before Beth walked through those sparkling new glass double doors, she was apprehensive because she always finds it difficult to approach new accounts, especially ones she doesn't know much about.

The sight of Bill Reilly has now made her even more concerned. Reilly, a sales representative for Troy Corporation, a major competitor of her company, has been her nemesis from day one. Seeing him leave Chuck Stoner's office makes Beth realize that she has a major selling job ahead of her. Beth's boss, who covered the territory before her, warned her about the tough competition from Troy Corporation's Bill Reilly. Not only has Reilly covered the same territory for six years, but he is well liked and respected by customers.

Within her first three months on the job, Beth found out how right her boss was about Reilly. Even though Beth is confident that her products are superior to those of any competitor's, including Troy Corporation, Reilly has managed to beat her out at four different accounts.

As they pass each other in the hallway, Bill Reilly greets Beth cordially and asks: "How are things going?" Beth is always a little surprised by Reilly's friendly greeting each time they meet because they are in head-to-head competition on many accounts. After a lighthearted chat, Beth excuses herself so she won't be late for her appointment with Stoner. Reilly calls to her: "Good Luck." As she walks toward Stoner's office, Beth thinks: "If he wasn't such a tough competitor, I might really like him."

After being ushered into the office by Stoner's friendly secretary, Beth is pleased to see him stand up, smile, and extend his hand. Shaking hands, Beth says: "Good morning, Mr. Stoner. You seem to be in a good mood."

Stoner: Yes, I am. Bill Reilly just gave me two tickets to tonight's baseball game. My son's going to be thrilled.

Morelli: Well, that's nice, but I heard there's a 50-50 chance of rain tonight.

Stoner: [*Looking a little annoyed*] I sure hope not. What do you have to show me today? [*Beth goes through her sales presentation, explaining her company's services and showing examples of her company's business forms.*]

Morelli: So, Mr. Stoner, what do you think?

Stoner: Well, your products do look good. But I'm not sure they're any better than Troy's.

Morelli: [*Thinks for a moment. She wants desperately to win this account.*] From what I've seen, I'm not sure why anyone would be interested in Troy's products. They have slow service, old-fashioned-looking products, and high prices. Our company's a lot more progressive. Troy's been messing up right and left lately. Did you know they sent 100 cases of business forms to Metropolitan Hospital last month and all had the wrong address on them? Every one of them had to be returned, and for two weeks the hospital had to ration forms to keep from running out. Customers can't afford many mistakes like that, can they? Well, Mr. Stoner, how many cases of forms can I order for you?

Stoner: Well, I've got to run to a 10 o'clock meeting now, but I'll get back to you when I decide. Thanks for coming in.

Before Beth can say another word, Stoner is standing up and heading out the door to his meeting. As Beth gathers up her presentation materials, she wonders what her chances are of getting a big order.

Questions

1. What do you think Beth should have done differently? Why?
2. How would you compete with a salesperson like Bill Reilly?
3. What advice would you give Beth if Mr. Stoner calls her later? What should Beth do if Mr. Stoner doesn't call her?

Chapter 10

Prospecting and Qualifying Prospects

Successful salespeople are resourceful in finding real prospects,
not just people to talk to.

Profile

Claire Kerr

CLAIRE Kerr, a Division Major Account Manager with NCR Corporation, maintains that she has been a sales representative her whole life: "Throughout my childhood, I was always selling something—Girl Scout cookies, things like popcorn and candy for school and church fund-raisers, and even babysitting services. My first 'real' job at 16 was selling luggage and leather goods in a retail store. It seemed like a natural progression for me to major in business administration and to concentrate on marketing when I got to college."

After receiving her B.S. in 1983 from the University of North Carolina at Chapel Hill, Claire became a sales representative with NCR in Richmond, Virginia, and began the company's comprehensive training program, which is a mixture of self-instruction, classroom study, and on-the-job experience. Claire told us that she felt like she really knew her job after about a year in the field. She also eventually found, however, that the job is much more involved than the job description indicates. Selling is only one aspect of the total organizational sales effort. "Selling computers for NCR encompasses a lot more than traditional face-to-face selling. I am directly involved with many areas and departments at NCR in addition to sales and marketing, including inventory, accounts receivable, production scheduling, delivery, sales training, and the coordination of personnel from several divisions. My work also involves a lot of reading to keep up with changes in the industry, market, technology, and competition, as well as with NCR's product lines," says Claire.

From prospecting to customer service, Claire provided us with a very straightforward summary about her selling philosophy: "My selling style includes flexibility to adapt to each unique selling situation. My approaches to new prospects are more formal and reserved than those to old customers. I find that presentations are most effective when they are clear, concise, and simple. The same rules apply to the close. Customers respect salespeople who are direct and come straight to the point. I don't use 'ulterior motive' closes, play games, or use tricks. Finally, customer service in this selling environment involves a lot of handholding. You can't just walk away after the sale. Since I depend on long-term business relationships for future sales and referrals, timely follow-up and follow-through on commitments are extremely important. Generally, in dealing with any customer, there is no substitute for good manners and common sense!"

True to her strong interest in sales and marketing, Claire would like her next career step to be in the direction of industry marketing. But she's in no hurry. Claire explains: "Although I am eligible for promotion at this time, I have the opportunity in my current position to expand my personal selling skills in a new area of selling—major accounts. Experience in selling to major accounts is vital to a long-term career with NCR because major account development is a key component to NCR's growth and success." ■

After reading this chapter, you should understand:

- □ The steps in the sales process

- □ Why the stages of the selling and buying processes must be compatible

- □ How to qualify leads as prospects

- □ Several prospecting approaches

THE WHEEL OF PROFESSIONAL PERSONAL SELLING AND THE SELLING PROCESS: AN INTRODUCTION

SELLING PROCESS The seven-stage process of professional personal selling, from prospecting and qualifying prospects to following up and servicing customers.

Chapter 10 is the first of six chapters that examine the heart and soul of selling: the **selling process.** Much of what you read in Chapters 10–15 will look somewhat familiar to you. That's because these six chapters draw on everything you already learned in Chapters 1–9. More importantly, these chapters try to place what you have learned into the context of actually selling to prospects and customers. That is why it wouldn't be going too far to say that the selling process presented in Chapters 10–15 is the focal point of this book.

The Wheel of Professional Personal Selling

For quick reference, we have included a figure that we think will help you keep track of where we are and where we are going in our discussion of the selling process: The Wheel of Professional Personal Selling (which we briefly introduced to you in Chapter 1). At the beginning of each selling process chapter, you will find the wheel with the appropriate selling process stage highlighted. For example, you will see that "Prospecting and Qualifying" is highlighted on the wheel for Chapter 10, which concerns this first stage of the selling process.

We strongly suggest that you read each of the selling process chapters at least two or three times and that you make a serious effort to put the information you learn here to use as soon as possible, perhaps through membership in a student marketing or sales organization, a part-time job, role playing with friends or fellow students, or in-class discussion. This will have three important benefits for you right now or in the near future: It will (1) acquaint you with the principles and methods of real-world selling, (2) show you what real-world selling is like and help you decide if professional selling is the right career choice for you, and (3) give you more confidence in interviewing for professional personal selling jobs.

The Stages in the Selling Process

Professional sales representatives need first to master basic selling strategies and tactics, and then to develop their own styles for dealing with specific customer

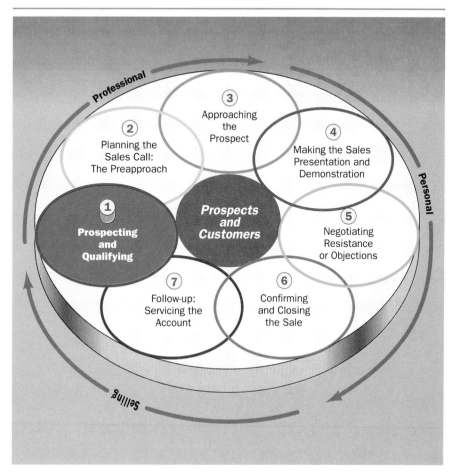

The Wheel of Professional Personal Selling

types and selling situations. The countless small tasks in the professional selling process may be divided into seven major stages:

1. Prospecting and qualifying prospects
2. Planning the sales call (the preapproach)
3. Approaching the prospect
4. Making the sales presentation and demonstration
5. Negotiating prospect resistance and objections
6. Confirming and closing the sale
7. Following up: Servicing customers to build the long-term relationship

Matching Stages in the Selling and Buying Processes

To describe it in the simplest theoretical terms, selling success depends on how well sales representatives match their selling processes with their prospects' buying processes. It is thus the salesperson's job to make sure that his or her activities in each stage of the selling process are compatible with the activities of the consumer or organizational buyer in the corresponding stages of the buying process. Unless sales reps understand how, when, why, and by whom each stage of the purchase decision is carried out and coordinate their selling activities with the buying activities of their prospects, their chances for making sales will be diminished—or nonexistent. For example, trying to *close a sale* when the consumer is still in the *information search* stage or an organizational buyer is in the *search for qualified suppliers* stage will nearly always be futile.

Organizational buyers, in particular, usually follow a very deliberate buying process that calls for specific input from sellers at designated times. When government or industrial purchasing agents ask for proposal solicitations from qualified suppliers, they are not going to be receptive to pressures from salespeople to confirm and close the sale until they have finished their evaluations of the proposals. Successful salespeople are usually adept at synchronizing their selling activities with their prospects' buying stages so that both the selling and the buying process flow together. As we stressed in Chapters 5 and 6, this is why it is so important for salespeople to thoroughly understand the buying processes of different customers. Table 10-1 shows how the stages of the selling process match up with typical stages in the consumer and organizational buying processes.

PROSPECTING AND QUALIFYING PROSPECTS

As long as there are market economies like those in the United States, Europe, Canada, and Japan, the selling process will never end. As depicted by the Wheel of Professional Personal Selling, this process is a continuous cycle, each stage of which connects with and indeed overlaps other stages. The entire wheel turns around its most important part: its "axis" of prospects and customers. Although every stage of the selling process is just as important as the next one, the extreme importance of prospects and customers tends to make the first and seventh stages

TABLE 10-1 Matching Selling and Buying Stages

SELLING PROCESS	CONSUMER BUYING PROCESS	ORGANIZATIONAL BUYING PROCESS
■ Prospecting and qualifying prospects ■ Planning the sales call (preapproach)	■ Problem recognition	■ Problem recognition ■ General need description ■ Product specifications
■ Approaching the prospect ■ Making the sales presentation and demonstration	■ Information search ■ Evaluation of alternatives	■ Search for qualified suppliers ■ Proposal solicitation and evaluation
■ Negotiating prospect resistance and objections ■ Confirming and closing the sale	■ Purchase decision ■ Supplier selection and purchase action	■ Supplier selection ■ Placing order and setting up ordering procedure
■ Following up: servicing customers to build the long-term relationship	■ Postpurchase evaluation	■ Performance review

Even if your sales territory and customer base appear to be stable now, you would be unwise not to do some prospecting activities every working day.

LEAD Anything that points to a potential buyer.

of the process seem especially significant. After all, it is the promise of potential customers and the security of satisfied current customers that gives the wheel its initial forward movement and its continued momentum. "Prospecting and Qualifying Customers" is the stage of the selling process that gives the wheel its initial push.

The Importance of Prospecting

To increase or just maintain sales volume, sales reps must continually seek out and prospect for new customers. Even if your sales territory and customer base appear to be stable now, you would be unwise not to do some prospecting activities every working day. Prospecting is necessary for several reasons: (1) customers switch to other suppliers; (2) customers move out of your territory; (3) customers go out of business because of bankruptcies, illness, or accidents; (4) customers die; (5) customers' businesses are taken over by other companies; (6) customers have only a one-time need for the product; (7) relationships with some customers deteriorate and they stop buying from you; (8) your buying contacts are promoted, demoted, transferred, fired, retired, or resign; or—the obvious—(9) you need to increase total sales.

Qualifying: How a Lead Becomes a Prospect

Most professional salespeople spend a large chunk of their time prospecting for new business. Prospecting involves discovering and working with leads on people who may have a need for your company's product. In professional selling, a **lead** is anything that points to a potential buyer. The most basic lead usually consists of a name, a phone number, and an address. Armed with this basic information, you must qualify the lead in terms of the following criteria:

- Need or want
- Authority to buy
- Ability to buy
- Eligibility to buy

PROSPECT A lead that has been qualified as a definite potential buyer.

NAME An abbreviation for the process of qualifying a lead in terms of Need for the product, Authority to buy, Money to be able to buy, and overall Eligibility to buy.

The lead becomes a **prospect** if the potential buyer meets all four of the qualifying criteria. A simple way to remember this qualifying process is to think of getting another **NAME:** First, qualify the lead's **N**eed, then **A**uthority, **M**oney, and **E**ligibility to buy before adding the potential buyer's name to your list of prospects. Let's take a closer look at each of the four qualifying criteria.

Need or Want

It's a waste of your time and efforts to try to sell your products to people who neither need nor want them. Not only would such efforts usually be unproductive, but many people would consider them unethical. You can usually quickly find out in your initial contact with leads whether there is a genuine need or want for your products and services. Sometimes, however, you may see that the customer has an unrecognized need or is unaware of a product that can satisfy a latent need. When a customer doesn't recognize his or her need for a product, you have an opportunity to explain and demonstrate your product's benefits. For example, an office manager may not appreciate the cost and timesaving advantages of having a facsimile machine to communicate with his customers and suppliers until you point out the benefits. Similarly, a consumer may not be familiar with a product such as a lightweight camcorder that will allow her to videotape her vacation without the bother of lugging around a lot of camera equipment.

Authority to Buy

One of the biggest mistakes that novice salespeople make is spending too much time with people who have insufficient decision-making authority to make the purchase. Neither the salesperson in the men's clothing store who talks to a man picking out a new suit, but overlooks the man's wife who is giving her husband nonverbal feedback on each suit, nor the industrial sales rep who tries to sell the drill press to the purchasing agent in the office, but doesn't bother to see the machine operator and his supervisor in the factory, understands the concept of authority to buy. Whether presenting to an individual, a couple, or a group of people, you first need to find out whose approval is necessary for the purchase. Sometimes merely asking "Whose approval is needed for this purchase?" will put you on the right track.

Money to Buy

Prospects, whether individual consumers or organizational buyers, must have the money or credit to buy before they can be qualified. Selling products to someone who has little or no chance of paying is a waste of your time and company resources because the products may have to be repossessed later or written off as bad debts. Selling to people who cannot pay is especially detrimental to a service organization because services performed cannot be repossessed. Salespeople selling services like commercial loans, advertising, financial investing and estate planning, executive recruiting, management consulting, security, and computer timesharing must be particularly careful to make sure that a lead is financially able to buy. Because services are intangible and perishable in that they are simultaneously produced and consumed, service organizations often demand prior payment. Hospitals are frequently criticized because they painstakingly qualify incoming patients before they allow them to see a doctor. But hospital administrators have learned from bitter experience that once a doctor has treated a patient or performed an operation, there is little recourse other than a collection agency if the patient refuses to pay the bill. You can't put the diseased gallbladder back into the patient's body or repossess a physical examination.

Credit cards have been a godsend to service organizations because they allow the individual's credit to be instantly checked. You can check up on a large organization's financial situation with national credit-rating services such as Dun & Bradstreet. Financial information about smaller companies can be obtained through Better Business Bureaus, commercial banks, and local credit-rating services.

Of course, if a buyer simply has a temporary cash flow problem, a resourceful sales rep may be able to arrange an installment or time-payment plan to enable the lead to be qualified as a prospect. Lee Iacocca became, in his words, "an overnight success" when he came up with an innovative idea to help people buy automobiles, as he explains in this excerpt from his book *Iacocca: An Auto-biography:*

> While sales of 1956 Fords were poor everywhere, our district was the weakest in the entire country. I decided that any customer who bought a new 1956 Ford should be able to do so for a modest down payment of 20 percent, followed by three years of monthly payments of $56. This was a payment schedule that almost anyone could afford, and I hoped that it would stimulate sales in our district. I called my idea "56 for '56." At that time, financing for new cars was just coming into its own. "56 for '56" took off like a rocket. Within a period of only three months, the Philadelphia district moved from last place in the country all the way to first. In Dearborn, Robert S. McNamara, vice president in charge of the Ford Division—he would become secretary of defense in the Kennedy administration—admired the plan so much that he made it part of the company's national marketing strategy. He later estimated it was responsible for selling 75,000 cars. And so, after ten years of preparation, I became an overnight success. Suddenly I was known and even talked about in national headquarters. I had toiled in the pits for a good decade, but now I had a big break. My future suddenly looked a lot brighter. As a reward, I was promoted to district manager of Washington, D.C.[1]

Eligibility to Buy

Many consumers would like to purchase products wholesale. But manufacturers and wholesalers would alienate their retail merchant customers if they sold directly to the general public. Similarly, in most cases, it would be a mistake for manufacturers to bypass their wholesalers to sell to some retailers. Feeling threatened by the manufacturer, the bypassed wholesalers may retaliate and refuse to carry the manufacturers' line for distribution to other retailers.

Many ineligible people seek to buy products and services such as life or health insurance and alcohol. People who are ill, unaffiliated with the seller's designated eligibility group such as the American Association of Retired Persons (AARP), or teenagers may not be eligible for health, membership, or legal reasons to buy a certain product or service. Unless you screen out these ineligible people in the qualifying process, your judgment, thoroughness, and perhaps your ethics will be questioned by your sales manager.

SOURCES OF PROSPECTS

There are two basic ways to search for leads to qualify as prospects: (1) random searching and (2) selective searching. But, as shown in Table 10-2, there are several random searching methods, and numerous selective searching methods, which can be further divided into direct and indirect sources. Direct sources allow leads to be identified by name or approached directly by salespeople, whereas indirect sources require leads to identify themselves by responding to a general call. Each of the random or selective searching methods can be useful to

[1]Lee Iacocca with William Novak, *Iacocca: An Autobiography* (New York: Bantam Books, 1984), pp. 39–40.

TABLE 10-2   Searching for Prospects

Random-Lead Searching Methods	
Door-to-door canvassing	Advertising
Territory blitz	Print media
Cold calls	Broadcast media
Selective-Lead Searching Methods	
Direct Sources	Indirect Sources
Friends, neighbors, acquaintances	Direct mail
Personal observation	Trade shows, fairs, exhibits
Spotters or "bird dogs"	Professional seminars and conferences
Endless chain	Group or party plans
Centers of influence	Newsletters
Former prospects and customers	Contests
Junior salespeople and sales associates	Free gifts
Noncompeting sales representatives	Surveys
Professional sales organizations	Unsolicited inquiries
Attending professional gatherings	Caller ID
Directories and lists	Telemarketing

professional salespeople, depending on the product and customer mix in a given situation.

Random-Lead Searching

RANDOM-LEAD SEARCHING The generation of leads by randomly calling on households or businesses. Sometimes called "blind" searching.

When names and addresses of leads are not available, they can be generated by randomly calling on households or businesses (door-to-door canvassing) or by mass appeals (advertising) to prospects to come forward. This process is called **random-lead searching** (it has sometimes also been called "blind" searching). There are several ways to carry out random-lead searching.

Door-to-Door Canvassing

DOOR-TO-DOOR CANVASSING Literally knocking on every door in a residential or commercial area to locate prospects.

Only when other lead-generating approaches are not available or don't seem to be working should you turn to door-to-door canvassing. **Door-to-door canvassing** is literally knocking on every door in a given residential or commercial area to see if you can find some prospects. It can be a time-consuming, ineffective, and therefore very costly method, so it should be used only to supplement other methods for obtaining leads.

Territory Blitz

TERRITORY BLITZ An intensified version of door-to-door canvassing in which several salespeople join efforts to call on every household or organization in a given territory or area.

A version of door-to-door canvassing is the **territory blitz,** a method in which several salespeople join efforts to swoop down on every household or organization in a given territory or area. Any leads developed during this blitz are turned over to the regular territory salesperson for follow-up.

Cold Calls

COLD CALLING Approaching or telephoning a home or business without an appointment for prospecting or selling.

Approaching or telephoning a home or business without an appointment and introducing yourself to whoever will talk to you is called **cold calling.** Many salespeople dread cold calls more than any other prospecting technique because they never know what kind of reception they will get. Sometimes they have no more information than a house or telephone number or a name on an apartment

Only when other lead-generating approaches are not available or don't seem to be working should you turn to door-to-door canvassing.

mailbox. Door-to-door canvassing and the territory blitz prospecting approaches necessarily involve cold calls. Within an apartment complex, sales pros look for the mailboxes with the clean, new nameplates because this indicates that the people have just moved in and probably have not yet been saturated with sales calls.

A great deal of face-to-face canvassing has been replaced by telephoning and faxing initial sales messages to potential customers, then following them up with face-to-face calls if the prospects show any interest in the product. In both consumer and organizational selling, the best salespeople develop excellent telephone skills and can fearlessly call prospective new accounts. A slow afternoon's paperwork can be livened up considerably with such cold calls, and they often yield at least a few definite appointments, if not an actual sale.

In general, however, all forms of cold calling are very time-consuming and wasteful unless you do a little careful qualifying and planning first. While you're driving to and from regular appointments, pay attention to the characteristics of the neighborhoods you pass through. If you are selling to consumers, make note of the kinds of houses and cars you see. If you are in organizational sales, size up the sales potential of individual businesses in an industrial park or a large office building by observing how many cars are parked in a particular company's lot, the number and types of deliveries coming and going, and what other salespeople are making calls.

Advertising

Various forms of print media (newspapers, magazines, Yellow Pages, billboards, and posters) can be used to stimulate people to inquire about a product or service and thus identify themselves as good leads. Broadcast media (television and radio) can be used to generate leads among audiences who are less likely to obtain information through the print media. After receiving inquiries, some companies prepare prospects for the salesperson's call by mailing videocassettes

---

SUGGESTED HOURS FOR COLD CALLS ON VARIOUS PROFESSIONALS

Accountants	April 16 to December 31: 9:00 A.M. to 5:00 P.M.
Attorneys	11:00 A.M. to 2:00 P.M.
Bankers	Before 10:00 A.M. and after 3:00 P.M.
Building contractors	Before 9:00 A.M. and after 5:00 P.M.
Business owners	10:30 A.M. to 3:00 P.M.
Businesspeople	10:00 A.M. to 12:00 P.M. and 2:00 to 5:00 P.M.
Clergy	8:00 A.M. to 8:00 P.M., Tuesday through Friday
Dentists	Before 9:30 A.M.
Druggists	1:00 P.M. to 3:00 P.M.
Engineers, chemists	1:00 to 5:00 P.M.
High-school teachers	Before 8:15 A.M. and after 2:30 P.M.
Homemakers	9:30 to 11:00 A.M. and 1:30 to 4:30 P.M.
Professors, teachers	Before 9:00 A.M. and after 4:30 P.M.
Retail merchants	1:00 to 3:00 P.M.
Stockbrokers	Before 10:00 A.M. and after 3:00 P.M.
Top executives	10:00 A.M. to 12:00 P.M. and 2:00 P.M. to 5:00 P.M.

SOURCE: Based on Jack Kinder, Jr., Garry D. Kinder, and Roger Staubach, *Winning Strategies in Selling* (Englewood Cliffs, N.J.: Prentice Hall, 1981), pp. 87–97; and conversations with several professional salespeople.

---

demonstrating the product or service so that the salesperson's selling time can be more efficiently used during the actual sales call.

Selective-Lead Searching

SELECTIVE-LEAD SEARCHING The application of systematic strategies to generate leads from predetermined target markets.

Instead of randomly searching for leads, most professional salespeople employ systematic strategies to generate leads from predetermined target markets. This approach to lead generation is called **selective-lead searching.** Let's discuss some methods and strategies for selective prospecting.

Direct Sources
Direct sources are those that are controlled largely by the field salespeople themselves, which allows them to identify leads by name or directly approach them. Direct sources are usually handled by the salesperson without his or her company's help. Let's briefly discuss some of the most widely used of these sources.

Friends, neighbors, and acquaintances. Probably the easiest sources of leads for a new salesperson are friends, neighbors, and acquaintances. It's hard to say no to a friend, so most friends will try to help you in your career if they can. Life insurance companies and other direct sellers usually tell new salespeople to write down the names and addresses of all their neighbors, friends, and acquaintances who might buy the product, then make telephone or personal sales calls on each.

Direct sellers are not the only salespeople who can benefit from the knowledge, experience, and acquaintances of their friends, neighbors and acquaintances. Technical reps and other business-to-business salespeople can also find many valuable leads this way. Perhaps you sell printing services to small businesses, and your best friend's husband just opened his own flower shop. Or maybe while chatting with people after church or temple services, you learn that one of them is planning to open up a new business location and another expects to replace the furnace in her home this fall.

When contacting friends, neighbors, and acquaintances, do it in a very low-key way. If you come on too much like a salesperson, your friends may start avoiding you.

Personal observation. All successful salespeople pick up leads from personal observations while carrying out their daily routines. While reading newspapers and magazines, or listening to their car radio, or watching television in their easy chairs, they spot leads. Notices of people graduating from schools or earning job promotions, announcements of two companies merging or opening new offices in another town—all provide direct leads for goods and services ranging from insurance, homes, and automobiles to office supplies, cleaning services, and communications and computer equipment.

Spotters. People who work in ordinary people-contact jobs are often excellent **spotters** (sometimes called "bird dogs") who can help you obtain good leads. Bartenders, doormen, taxi drivers, and service personnel such as beauty shop operators and barbers hear the intimate conversations of many people. They learn who's looking for financial advice, a larger home, an exciting vacation, office furniture, a personal computer. Other excellent spotters are carpenters, plumbers, and various service workers who learn about people's needs as they service or repair products, and retail sales clerks who hear about customers'

SPOTTERS People working in ordinary people-contact jobs who can help salespeople obtain leads. Sometimes also called "bird dogs."

People who work in ordinary people-contact jobs are often excellent spotters or "bird dogs."

plans to buy expensive jewelry, pleasure boats, or recreational vehicles. People buying "big ticket" items such as yachts and mobile homes are potential customers for many related products like accessories and special insurance. Within organizations, secretaries, workers on the receiving dock, maintenance people, and even mail room personnel can be valuable spotters for leads. Occasionally rewarding such spotters with a small gift is an inexpensive way to generate many excellent leads.

Endless chain. A classic way to obtain leads is ask your most recent satisfied customers to refer you to other people who might be interested in the benefits of your product or service. This method of prospecting is often referred to as the **endless chain.** Author and former self-proclaimed "world's best" car salesman Joe Girard got his customers to do the prospecting for him by offering them a $25 fee for any referrals who later bought a car from him. Unknowingly, these customers did much of the qualifying work for Girard before sending him a name.

I know a former podiatrist who was making about $80,000 a year treating people's foot ailments before he was persuaded by a salesperson friend to become a part-time life insurance agent. Now making over $200,000 a year selling life insurance full time, this ex-podiatrist is an avid proponent of building endless chains of leads. After successfully selling a new client, he says: "Now that I've helped you and your family obtain the security of a total insurance package, would you give me the names of the five most prominent people you know whom I can help obtain these benefits, too?" His clients are usually pleased—and their egos are tickled pink—to name the five most important people they know, and these leads often turn into customers who buy several million dollars' worth of insurance. Still in his early 40s, the doctor-salesman is thinking about retiring soon to a Florida beach. His commission earnings grow yearly even if he doesn't make any new sales because his old customers regularly increase the amount of their insurance coverage.

Centers of influence. Stockbrokers, life insurance and real estate agents, and other professionals such as dentists, accountants, and lawyers subtly cultivate potential customers by joining professional, social, and civic organizations whose members are potential customers and opinion leaders. From organizations like these, whether formal or informal, salespeople can develop **centers of influence,** which consist of individuals or groups of people whose opinions, professional activities, and lifestyles are respected among people in the salesperson's target markets. Health clubs, country clubs, university alumni associations, hobby groups, professional associations, and civic organizations offer salespeople the opportunity to develop contacts and centers of influence that can lead to many potential customers.

There are two unspoken rules that salespeople should be aware of and abide by when using a center-of-influence prospecting method. The first and most important is that you should only join clubs or associations that you would join even if they were not potential sources of leads. If you don't enjoy your membership, you probably won't make many worthwhile contributions, and other members will quickly recognize your poor attitude. The second thing to remember is that even salespeople with a solid record of involvement and a great attitude will be ostracized or avoided if they become too aggressive or obvious in their pursuit of leads among fellow association members. It's best to be very

ENDLESS CHAIN A classic method of prospecting in which the salesperson simply asks recently satisfied customers for prospect referrals.

CENTERS OF INFLUENCE Individuals or groups of people whose opinions, professional activities, and lifestyles are respected among people in the salesperson's target markets.

Health clubs and other associations offer the salesperson an opportunity to develop contacts that can lead to potential customers.

patient and low-key when networking with these influential people. They will not buy from you or refer you to their friends or business associates unless they are convinced that you are totally professional, ethical, trustworthy, and are not likely to embarrass them. Do let the people in the center of influence know what you do for a living, but never launch into obvious sales pitches. Only when you can really help people should you mention your company's products and services. When these opinion leaders provide you with a lead that turns into a customer, thank them in a professional way by sending them a tasteful gift or buying them a nice dinner. Such gestures of appreciation will enhance your rapport and may encourage them to suggest other leads.

Here are four handy strategies for dealing with centers of influence:

- Join appropriate professional, social, and civic organizations to develop contacts.
- Network with influential people who may become customers or provide you with referrals.
- Cultivate a solid record of involvement with professional and community groups.
- Only join clubs or associations that you would enjoy even if they were not potential sources of leads. Purely mercenary motives for joining will quickly become transparent to other members.

Former prospects and customers. Information available on prospects and customers from internal company records, such as warranty cards, repair service, unsolicited inquiries, and even complaint letters, can indicate who could use a related product, who hasn't bought anything for a long time, or who is having a problem with their present product that might be solved by a new product. Timely follow-ups on these leads can be very profitable. Unsolicited inquiries are usually "hot" prospects, and the first salesperson to call on them will probably make the sale.

Even when prospects decide not to buy or customers stop buying from you for some reason, they may still be willing to give you referrals to other potential

Selling in Action

Cold Calls, Gifts, and Former Customers

Nicholas Barsan is a top performer among the 75,000 U.S. real estate brokers affiliated with Century 21. Born in Romania, he emigrated to the United States in 1968 and owned a wholesale food company and then a restaurant before he began selling property several years ago. Recently, he sold $27 million of homes in Jackson Heights, Queens, netting $1.1 million in commissions. Homes in this middle-class New York City neighborhood average $225,000, so Barsan had to sell a lot of homes to make that kind of money. Though a millionaire, he still knocks urgently on strangers' doors, hungry for new business. He also still hands out key chains and car window scrapers imprinted with his name, lest anyone forget that he's around. But Barsan knows he can sell more homes with less effort by dealing again with customers he has already satisfied. So he also calls on the people who bought their homes from him. His selling style is a model of friendly persistence. "You ready to sell yet?" he asks playfully. A third of Barsan's sales are to repeat customers.

Source: Adapted from Monci Jo Williams, "America's Best Salesmen," *Fortune*, October 26, 1987, pp. 122–134.

customers if you ask. Former prospects often appreciate your honest efforts to sell to them and may feel a little guilty about not buying from you. If they are nice people, they may want to make it up to you by giving you the names of other potential customers. Former customers often feel the same way—provided your relationship with them ended on good terms. But *never* try to "guilt-trip" former prospects or customers into giving you referrals. Upon getting in touch with former prospects or customers for referrals, first politely remind them of who you are and then simply ask if they know of any other people or organizations who might be interested in your product.

Keep in mind that calling former prospects or customers for a referral is also a perfectly legitimate method of keeping in touch with *them* and their needs. You might start out by asking for a referral and end up with a former prospect or customer turning into a new customer! It is essential, however, to retain each customer's trust and respect if you expect to get referrals to other potential customers.

Junior salespeople and sales associates. By taking on much of the responsibility for developing leads and qualifying them, junior salespeople or sales associates can help make senior salespeople much more efficient. Freed from some of this time-consuming prospecting work, senior salespeople can spend their time more profitably in developing sales presentation strategies and actually selling to prospects.

Noncompeting sales representatives. Salespeople in your company who are selling different products can sometimes provide you with leads from the customers they call upon. Noncompetitive salespeople from other companies can also be a source of leads, especially if you can reciprocate in some way. Even competitive salespeople may unintentionally provide you with a lead during casual conversation at a restaurant or bar. Of course, you may unwittingly do the same for them.

Professional sales organizations. Today's professional salespeople often join local chapters of the *International Sales & Marketing Executives* or more informal local *tip clubs* that meet regularly over breakfast, lunch, or dinner to share information, ideas, and perspectives on selling. Both the IS&ME and tip clubs enable you to obtain information, exchange referrals, cross-sell, and learn new selling techniques.

Attending professional gatherings. Seminars, workshops, conferences, and conventions that many potential customers are likely to attend can be lead-generating "supermarkets." Attend as many of these professional gatherings as you can to network with the attendees and engage them in conversations about where they work, what they do, and their special interests. Exchange business cards with them and take some notes on the cards following your conversations. Obtain a list of attendees and collect all the literature, programs, brochures, and handouts that seem relevant. After the conference, telephone or write the most promising leads and prospects, remind them of where and how you met, recall a few pleasantries, and see if you can set up a luncheon or breakfast meeting.

Directories and lists. Another way to obtain leads is to acquire directories, registers, public records, and membership books of likely prospects. Directories of virtually every conceivable type and variety are available at public or university libraries or for a price from companies in the list preparation business.

Probably the best place for most salespeople to start is at a local library with a helpful reference librarian. You'll be directed to directories on almost anything you can imagine. If a reference librarian is not available, try using the *Directory of Directories* or the *Gale Directory of Publications* (formerly the *Ayer Directory*), both of which contain vast listings of directories currently published in the United States and Canada. Some directories are simply jazzed-up phone books, with the names, addresses, and job titles of influential people. Others provide in-depth biographical and demographic information about particular individuals and organizations. *Who's Who in America,* for example, is a good first stop if you're looking for a brief biographical description of an important American. Government agencies can also be excellent sources of lists. Voter registration lists, license records, and new construction applications can help you prepare your own directories or lists of potential customers. Most professional salespeople maintain their own lists of prospects, often based largely on business cards they've collected.

Indirect Sources

Many companies use general announcements or calls to potential markets, hoping that prospects will come forward and identify themselves. The names of these prospects are usually turned over to the appropriate territory salespeople for in-person sales calls. Let's now turn our discussion to some of the more popular indirect prospecting sources.

TABLE 10-3   How Industrial Companies Use Direct Mail

TYPE OF DIRECT MAIL	PERCENT OF COMPANIES USING
Sales letters	23
Catalogs	19
New-product mailings	17
Invitations	11
Samples	5
Research	5
Direct selling	5
Advertisement reprints	5
Company newsletters and bulletins	5
Editorial reprints	5

Direct mail. Direct mail is sometimes used by salespeople to prospect, but more often this approach is employed by a company to generate leads for the sales force. Using a lead directory, companies can do one-time mailings to obtain quick responses from prospects, or they can conduct strategic mail campaigns to steadily convince more people to become prospects. About 88.5 million Americans bought something through the mail in 1988, and the average mail-order purchase was $74.[2] Anybody who has ever ordered anything by mail or telephone, requested product or service information, obtained a credit card, or applied for a mortgage or loan is probably on one or more lists. Compilation of mailing lists is big business because "targeting"—reaching the highest-potential customers—is the name of the prospecting game.

Prospect mailing lists can be purchased from companies such as R. L. Polk & Company, National Business Lists, Hitchcock Business Lists, Burnett, Thomas Publishing Company's List Services, and the Marketing Services Division of Dun & Bradstreet. Polk's prospect list contains about 117,000 executives in the country's top 22,000 companies, with an average of five officers in each company. The files of National Business Lists contain more than 4 million businesses, institutions, and professional firms, all classified by four-digit SIC numbers. Thomas Publishing Company's "Industrial Buying Influence" list contains about 295,000 key decision makers by name and title.

Direct mail offers many subtle alternatives in prospecting for new customers. A survey by the Cahners Publishing Company, summarized in Table 10-3, found ten types of direct mail being used by industrial marketing companies.[3]

When preparing a direct-mail piece to develop prospects, salespeople ought to consider the following guidelines:

- ■ *Address your letter to an individual.* Nothing is more likely to be thrown in the trash than an obvious form letter addressed without the person's name and with a salutation like "Dear Consumer" or "Dear Business Manager." At the opposite extreme, overuse of the individual's name, as in the letter in Figure 10-1, can also be a turn-off that will get the letter tossed into the trash can!

- ■ *Use an attractive format.* An attractive, easy-to-read letter accompanied by a brochure filled with helpful illustrations and color will have eye appeal and increase yield.

[2]Mike Feinsilber, "The Direct-Marketing People Don't Deal in Small Numbers," *The Philadelphia Inquirer,* September 29, 1989, p. 12-C.

[3]*Ads for Chemicals Pay Off in Sales When They Run in Chemical & Engineering News* (Northfield, Ill.: Chemical & Engineering News, 1978).

Big Wheel Industries, Inc.
22 Shady Lane, Westmontville, IL 63423

AN URGENT MESSAGE FROM BIG WHEEL MAGAZINE CLEARING HOUSE

$ $ $ $ $ $ $

June 1, 1990

Ms. Susan Brophy
1407 S. Washington St.
Arlington Heights, IL 47401

Dear Susan Brophy:

YOU MAY WIN $10,000!!!

Big Wheel Magazine Clearing House, a leading Midwestern magazine publisher's clearing house for over 8 months, is making you, Susan Brophy , a one-time special offer!

If you act now, Susan Brophy , **you could win up to $10,000 in our special "Avoid Chapter 11 Sweepstakes."**

All you have to do, Susan Brophy , is send in your filled-out entry form by April 15 and we will enter your name for our Big Blast Bonus Sweepstakes offering $50 a week for one year, a 16-foot luxury yacht, an Imported miniature Italian motor scooter, or maybe even our

GRAND PRIZE OF $10,000!!!!!!

Yes, Susan Brophy , there is no purchase necessary to enter Big Wheel's"Avoid Chapter 11 Sweepstakes." But, Susan Brophy , **YOU MUST ACT TODAY!!!**

See the enclosed information for details, and thank you from the bottom of our hearts, Susan Brophy .

Very Sincerely,

B. Slick

Bob Slick, Chairman
Big Wheel Magazine Clearing House

YOU MAY BE AN INSTANT WINNER!!

FIGURE 10-1

■ *Keep it simple.* Trying to tell too much in a letter is a temptation that you must not yield to. An idea or two presented in straightforward, sincere language and covered in about a page is likely to be most effective in winning a positive response. Remember to apply the KISS formula: Keep it simple, salespeople. Figure 10-2 is a KISS letter.

■ *Stress benefits.* Emphasize *customer benefits* instead of *product functions and features.* People want solutions to *their* problems, not descriptions of how *your* product or service works.

■ *Provide proof.* Use testimonials from satisfied customers and scientific proof, if available, to reassure prospects.

■ *Ask for action.* No matter how small the action, you should ask people to do something after reading your letter, like calling a toll-free number or mailing in an enclosed card to obtain more information. At the close of the letter, offer an incentive to get prospects to buy now, such as "Send in your check before August 1st and take 20 percent off the regular price."

■ *Follow up your mailing.* A prompt telephone follow-up to all those who respond, and even to those special customers you wish had responded, may enable you to qualify them and schedule a personal sales call. Don't ask "Did you get the material I sent?" The prospect may honestly answer, "No, I didn't," and this response leads to a dead end. A better way is to ask a question such as "May I come by to show you how our product can save you hundreds of dollars a year?" or "May I send you a price estimate to show you how inexpensively you can start enjoying the full benefits of this exciting new product?"

■ *Keep records of mailing results.* Not all mailings are equal; some will produce better results than others. It's important to calculate your response rate for each mailing, and then what percent of those responding eventually bought. Dividing your income by your expenses can give you a figure we shall call "return on mailings," or ROM. For instance, if the mailing cost you $1,500 and you eventually earned $23,500, your ROM is 15.67 (23,500 ÷ 1,500). If your earnings were only $12,500, your ROM would be 8.33 (12,500 ÷ 1,500).

Trade shows, fairs, and exhibits. Special shows of consumer products, like home appliances, boats, and automobiles, and organizational products, like computer and telecommunications systems, office furniture, and specialized manufacturing equipment, attract many potential customers. Some are "just looking," but most are interested in eventually buying the products or they wouldn't be at the show (remember, consumer shows often charge admission fees). Names and addresses of attendees can be obtained in various ways—from simple requests to mail-product literature to registrations for prizes and business card raffle drawings. While at the show, attendees may be favorably moved by being shown videotape presentations and product demonstrations. Salespeople should not be afraid to be creative in their attempts to attract customers to their company exhibits. Creating a "party" atmosphere by using balloons, streamers, and noisemakers or by offering a large bowl of fruit or small candies is an inexpensive way to get people to stop, look, and sign up for information.

Setting up seminars and videoconferences. Brokerage houses, consulting firms, advertising agencies, accounting firms, and marketing research companies are among the many organizations that put on seminars, workshops, or conferences covering timely topics to attract prospects. Either in-house or outside experts run these programs. Invitations to attend the events are sent to people selected from a targeted directory or mailing list. Oftentimes the territory

Johnson & Williams Investment Planning, Inc.
916 W. Touhy Ave., Suite 34, Chicago, IL 34790

June 1, 1990

Ms. Susan Brophy
1407 S. Washington St.
Arlington Heights, IL 47401

Dear Ms. Brophy:

Congratulations on your recent graduation from the Wharton School! You are no doubt on the road to an exciting and rewarding career in Chicago's business world. As you begin to travel that road, we would like to offer you our services as investment portfolio managers.

In business since 1974, Johnson & Williams has earned a reputation for sound, shrewd investments and friendly, attentive client service among many leaders in the Chicagoland business community. We offer a wide variety of services and specialize in tailoring investment programs to meet the individual needs of each of our clients.

Perhaps you are thinking, "But I've just started out and am not really ready to begin thinking about an investment portfolio." We sincerely believe that it is never too soon to begin planning a financial future.

To this end, we would be very pleased if you would accept our invitation for an individual investment consultation. This consultation is absolutely free of any charge or obligation and is intended to help you assess (1) your financial readiness for investment and (2) the kinds of investments you would like to make. In order to schedule a consultation, or if you would simply like more information about Johnson & Williams, please use the enclosed reply card and postage-paid envelope to indicate where and when you prefer to be reached by telephone, or please call us at 1-800-368-PLAN. One of our investment managers will be happy to visit you.

With thanks for your attention, I am,

Very truly yours,

Cynthia Johnson

Cynthia Johnson, President

CJ/me
4 encl.

FIGURE 10-2

Seminars and workshops that combine traditional sales presentation techniques with videoconferencing facilities allow salespeople to develop leads and qualify prospects quickly in an attractive and impressive setting.

salesperson signs the invitation and includes his or her business card. At the seminar, product brochures and promotional materials are distributed to each participant. An informal social hour after the seminar enables company salespeople to learn the needs of individual participants and identify the best prospects for later sales calls.

Salespeople can also develop leads by serving as occasional guest lecturers at a local college or doing some public speaking before professional, social, and civic organizations such as the Kiwanis, Lions, Optimists, or Toastmasters Clubs. Some students in the college classes or attendees at your speaking engagements are likely to be prospects or be able to lead you to other prospects. During your talks, emphasize the imparting and sharing of information, not your persuasive selling skills.

Group or party plans. To multiply prospecting effectiveness, direct-to-consumer salespeople and occasionally industrial salespeople use group meetings or parties. Tupperware, Aloe Charm, Mary Kay, Amway, Shaklee, Home Interiors, and other direct sellers train their salespeople to set up meetings or parties at the home of a customer or prospect. The host or hostess invites several friends to enjoy light refreshments and participate in a product demonstration show presented by a skilled salesperson. Most of the attendees feel obligated to buy something, and the names and addresses of those who don't are leads to contact later.

Newsletters. In this age of personal computers and desktop publishing programs, a few enterprising salespeople and numerous companies prepare periodic newsletters to mail to their prospects. Some companies, such as real estate agencies, personalize their newsletters by printing the territory salesperson's picture and a personal note from him or her on the cover sheet of the newsletter.

What Would You Do?

As a salesperson for Megadisc Software Corporation, you have been assigned to work two days at one of the biggest trade shows of the year. Your company has invested a small fortune in display and demonstration equipment for the show. The Megadisc exhibit features a bank of five computers set up so that interested prospects can run a demo version of Megadisc's newest product offerings. In addition, two large video monitors, featuring laser disc technology, allow passersby to play their choice of 30 specialized film segments describing different aspects of the Megadisc programs, which are intended to help businesses streamline their computer and telecommunications hookups. Your company has sent along plenty of brochures, and there is a sign-up sheet at the exhibit for people who would like more information. During your first day at the exhibit, dozens of people stopped to look at your video segments and to try out the demo programs, but only two put their names on the sign-up sheet. You are very concerned that Megadisc management will think that you did not do a good job of generating prospects. It is now 9:00 A.M. on your second and last day of handling the exhibit.

If you don't feel that a newsletter is right for you, you can simply photocopy articles that you see in your reading and mail them to prospects with Post-it notes attached saying something like: "Thought you'd be interested in seeing the attached article. Best regards, Sally—Sales Representative, Menotti Coletrane Supply."

Contests. Who among us hasn't excitedly opened a letter from Publisher's Clearing House or Reader's Digest that says: "You may have already won ten million dollars!"? Many of us do the tearing, scraping, and pasting tasks necessary to enter these contests, even though our chances of winning anything are very slim. Few people can resist entering a contest, especially if little effort is required. Those who do enter are presumed to be interested in the prize offered winners, so they may be good prospects to buy if they don't win. At trade shows and exhibits, in newspapers and magazines, and in your favorite supermarket, contests are nearly always going on. You or your company may be in a position to sponsor small or large contests or sweepstakes. One word of advice: Check with your sales manager and public relations department about your plans.

Free gifts. Life insurance companies offer inexpensive free gifts such as keycases, pocket flashlights, and miniature screwdriver sets to people who send in their date of birth so life insurance proposals can be prepared for them. Although only about 4 percent of people receiving such letters send in their birth dates, nearly half of those who do eventually buy the product.

Another method of attracting potential customers is to offer them a special prize to visit your facility for a product demonstration. For example, some firms selling resort property send letters—usually in off-size brown envelopes to grab

Company Highlight

Getting a Grip on the Market at American Breeders Service

The American Breeders Service in DeForest, Wisconsin, mailed a single leather glove to each of 3,700 farmers and cattle breeders who might be interested in an artificial insemination service. The glove was imprinted with the ABS logo and came with a brochure entitled *Get a Better Grip on Beef A.I.* To get the matching glove, prospects only had to mail in the reply card. Respondents were called on by a sales rep, who brought the other glove with him to complete the pair. A follow-up mailing to those who didn't respond advised prospects: "You still have time to get a better grip on Beef A.I." The company reported a 47 percent total response to the two mailings and over $110,000 in additional sales.

the addressee's attention (important letters from government agencies such as the IRS often come in similar envelopes)—implying that homeowners have won some valuable prizes that they can claim within 14 days by scheduling an appointment to visit the resort. The odds against winning the top prizes are obviously astronomical, but many prospects show up anyway and submit to a high-pressure sales pitch. The ethics of such prospecting methods are questionable at best, and not recommended for sellers who value their long-run reputations.

American Breeders Service used an innovative adaptation of the free gift approach to obtain the names of prospects interested in its unique service, as described in this chapter's Company Highlight.

Surveys. Although legitimate pollsters and marketing researchers do not like it, many small companies generate leads by conducting so-called surveys by mail, telephone, or personal interview. Some unscrupulous surveys pretend to want to know a respondent's opinion on some issue when, in reality, the questions are trying to qualify the individual. Anyone who doesn't use the survey method honestly should be prepared for angry reactions from people who feel manipulated.

To screen out nonprospects quickly, surveys often use opening questions such as: "Do you use oil to heat your home?", "Are you interested in investing in tax-free bonds?", or "Does your home have central air conditioning?" Computers that randomly dial people's homes and play preprogrammed messages (sometimes from celebrities) are frequently used to conduct surveys. Virtually anyone who has a telephone is reachable this way, whether their phone number is listed in the telephone book or not. Those people who complete the survey have usually qualified themselves as prospects for the salesperson to call.

Unsolicited inquiries. Unsolicited telephone calls and letters from people asking for information are usually excellent leads because the inquirers have

Legitimate pollsters and marketing researchers generate leads by conducting surveys by mail, telephone, or personal interview.

often qualified themselves in terms of need, authority, money, and eligibility to buy the product or service. Inside telemarketing salespeople should respond to these calls and letters, then turn the names of prospects over to the territorial salesperson. Surprisingly, some salespeople and their companies do not even follow up on telephone and letter inquiries. A survey by the Center for Marketing Communications found that:

- 18 percent of all inquirers never got the information requested.
- 43 percent of them got it too late to be of value.
- 72 percent were never contacted by a sales representative.[4]

Caller ID. A controversial new technology that is opening up new concepts in prospecting is caller telephone number identification service, generically termed **caller ID.** It is offered throughout the United States by AT&T, US Sprint Communications, and MCI Communications. This service reveals any caller's telephone number—even unlisted numbers. American Express and J. C. Penney are already using this technology, and various oil companies, insurance companies, mail-order companies, stockbrokers, banks, bill collectors, and fund-raisers are quickly adopting it. When callers phone in for information about a product advertised in a catalog or brochure previously sent out by the company, caller ID allows the callers' numbers to be captured. With a computer that is tied into a customer list or database, the telephone number can be used to retrieve the name and address of the caller, as well as information like credit history, income, occupation, marital status, and number of children. At J. C. Penney catalog offices, callers are instantly identified with detailed account information on a service representative's computer screen.

CALLER ID A controversial new technology that identifies the caller's telephone number before the call is answered.

Credit card companies, fund-raisers, and major retailers are particularly eager to match phone numbers with names and addresses. From a sales stand-

[4]*Business Week,* July 21, 1980, pp. 196–205.

point, the service can link and fine-tune databases by determining who is interested in what products. The system shortens the average call by 12 seconds (that's 3.6 cents per call) and enables agents to answer about 7 percent more calls. Some companies have total estimated savings of nearly $500,000 per year.[5]

If left unregulated, caller identification services will no doubt change the way consumers and businesses use their telephones. However, many people are no longer as enthusiastic about caller ID as they were when the technology was being developed in the late 1980s. Their major concern is the individual's right to privacy. One will not be able to make an anonymous call to the police, the Internal Revenue Service, or a child-abuse hotline from home. Caller ID will make it virtually impossible for people to inquire about some service or respond to an advertisement without revealing their potential interest in a product. The big question is whether a public utility has the right to release phone numbers, particularly unlisted ones, to individuals and institutions who pay a fee for the information. Some civic leaders and consumer organization representatives have objected to businesses collecting information "behind the consumers' backs" or under false pretenses, such as when a company sets up a toll-free weather or sports information line in order to get a potential customer's telephone number. Whatever the moral or ethical ramifications of this new technology, the privacy debate could soon be over anyway because several small communications companies are working on a device that will allow individuals to block or garble caller ID signals, rendering the service useless!

Telemarketing. Most large companies, such as IBM and General Electric, use telemarketing to prospect. Numerous leads come to the company via toll-free telephone and mail-in responses to advertisements in magazines and newspapers, and ads on billboards, radio, or television. Leads are called and asked if and when they expect to be ready to make a purchase decision. Determining follow-up priorities is easy: The sooner the prospect is ready, the sooner the follow-up. Sometimes telemarketing strategies generate more leads than the sales staff can realistically follow up on. One IBM program received 13,000 computer sales leads for 70 salespeople to handle over a ten-month period.[6]

PROCESSING PROSPECT INFORMATION

MARKETING INFORMATION SYSTEM (MIS) Any systematized, continuous process of gathering, analyzing, and distributing market information.

Many industrial companies, like General Electric and IBM, generate so many thousands of leads each year that they need a continuous computerized marketing information system to handle them all. Similar to a sales marketing information system (SMIS), which we briefly discussed in Chapter 9, a **marketing information system,** or **MIS,** is any systematized, continuous process of gathering, analyzing, and distributing market information to marketing decision makers. Let's see how one successful company uses its MIS as a prospecting approach.

University Mechanical and Engineering Contractors of San Diego, California,

[5]*The Wall Street Journal,* November 28, 1989, p. 1.
[6]Chuck Wingis, "Telemarketing: A Great Idea Whose Time Has Come," *Industrial Marketing,* August 1981, pp. 71–79.

the nation's seventh-largest mechanical contractor, designs, manufactures, and installs plumbing, instrumentation, heating, ventilation, air-conditioning, and fire protection equipment. Its major sales opportunities come from construction projects such as high-rise office buildings, commercial complexes, manufacturing and processing plants, wastewater treatment plants, and nuclear generating plants. University Mechanical recognized that it could not profitably wait for bid lists to be published on a specific job and then submit a bid in competition with numerous other bidders. Under such conditions, bids were really price wars. And even when an award was won, it meant conforming to job specifications determined without University Mechanical's input. To overcome the disadvantages of straight-bid work, University Mechanical began marketing its engineering and construction management capabilities as well as its traditional construction abilities. In order to become involved with construction projects early in their development, University Mechanical developed a marketing information system to identify leads on a continuous basis, as depicted in Figure 10-3.

Typical lead sources for University Mechanical are: (1) *National Building News' Weekly Construction Preview,* which provides advance data on leading construction projects in the United States and Canada; (2) Herb Ireland's *Sales Prospector,* which contains advance reporting of regional and national industrial, commercial, and institutional construction on a monthly basis; (3) bid listings, such as those put out by the *Dodge Green Sheet, Engineering News Record,* and the *Journal of Daily Commerce;* (4) trade journals in their respective markets, which often report news items regarding plant construction plans and relocations; and (5) major city newspapers in the company's market areas. This intensive search of secondary sources is designed to uncover information on upcoming jobs as early as possible. These leads provide such information as the type of job (commercial, industrial, or federal), a job description, the dollar value of the project, its status (whether just at the proposal stage or at the stage where architects, engineers, or construction firms have already been selected), the target date of the project, and the name of the owner, architect, and structural engineer. The marketing manager then screens these sales leads for conformity to company objectives in terms of job size, job type, and so forth. Leads that pass this initial screening are discussed with the field sales engineers in whose territories the jobs will be done. With the sales engineer's comments added, the lead is entered into the company's computer. Figure 10-3 also shows that field sales engineers uncover leads on upcoming jobs while calling on general contractors, architects, and engineers. These leads are also screened, and those that are accepted are entered into the computer prospect file.

Leads that pass this first screening stage are forwarded to top management for another screening. This second review is based largely on whether or not the company can perform the job by the designated time in the specific locale. Its main purpose is to set priorities on available potential jobs so that the best jobs will be sought first. Leads that pass this second review are assigned to a field sales engineer via a *sales lead record form.* Shortly after receiving the lead, the sales engineer calls on the customer and completes a sales lead form. One copy of the form is returned to the vice president of marketing so the file in the company's computer can be updated for managerial review, and the other copy goes into the sales engineer's project notebook for later follow-up.

The MIS approach to generating prospects has enabled University Mechanical to steamline its marketing and sales strategies, concentrate the efforts of its

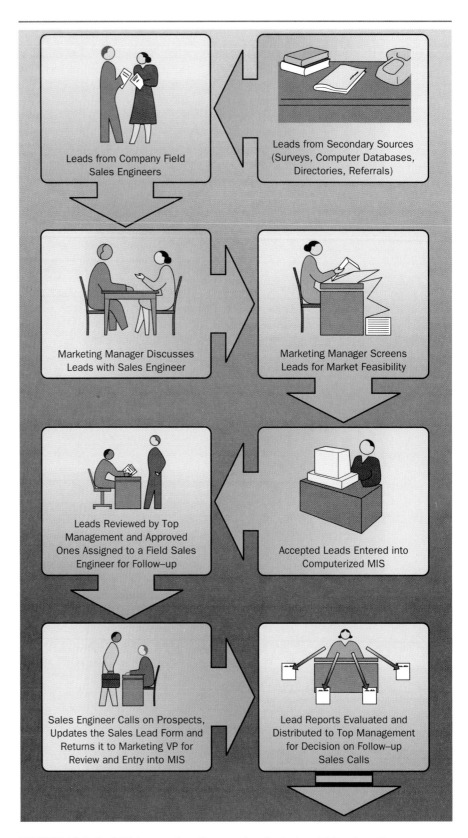

FIGURE 10-3 An MIS Approach to Prospecting for Industrial Product Customers

sales force, and secure more work on a profitable negotiated-bid basis instead of a low-margin straight-bid basis.[7]

PROSPECTS: THE SALESPERSON'S POT OF GOLD

Without prospects, the selling process never gets off first base. Whatever the method for generating prospects and whoever does it—telemarketers or field salespeople—prospects are essential to the continuous health of any sales organization. Consciously or subconsciously, whether making sales calls on present customers, listening to the car radio while driving to their next sales appointment, relaxing at home while reading the evening newspaper, or attending a party with friends and acquaintances, top professional salespeople are always prospecting.

Prospects not only provide every selling organization with the promise of future business, but also furnish special solace for individual salespeople who must deal with the rejection and frustration that accompany every selling job. When a salesperson hasn't made a sale in some time, a long list of prospects can keep him or her motivated to make the next sales call and continue looking for that "pot of gold" at the end of the faint rainbow peeking through an otherwise cloudy day.

Although we have discussed many different approaches to generating leads and prospecting, professional salespeople have their own favorite methods and adapt each to their own individual styles. They may discover that some methods work best with certain products in certain markets at certain times and choose the most useful method accordingly, like professional golfers who choose the best club for each situation on the green—or in the rough or the sand trap. So whenever you think you've done "enough" prospecting for the day or week or year, remember: Prospecting skills and professional selling success usually go hand in hand. Always try for that next prospect. After all, that next prospect could become your best customer ever.

SUMMARY There are seven basic stages in the professional selling process. These stages should not be viewed as separate, mutually exclusive steps toward a sale, but rather as a process in which the stages overlap and integrate in a continuous cycle. This cycle may be depicted as the Wheel of Professional Personal Selling. The best salespeople are highly skilled at matching the appropriate stage of the selling process with the corresponding stage of the consumer's or organization's buying process. Leads that are qualified on the basis of need, authority, ability, and eligibility to buy are called *prospects*. Prospecting methods can be categorized as either random searching or selective searching approaches. Because of the volume of leads they generate, large industrial firms often use computerized marketing information systems (MIS) to handle them. Prospecting is a never-

[7]Modified from Robert W. Haas, *Industrial Marketing Management,* 4th ed. (Boston: PWS-Kent, 1980), p. 179.

ending process for professional salespeople because new prospects are always needed to replace present customers who stop buying for various reasons.

<table>
<tr><td>

CHAPTER REVIEW QUESTIONS

</td><td>

1. Name and describe the seven basic stages in the selling process.
2. What are the four criteria that determine whether a lead becomes a prospect?
3. Give several reasons why a salesperson's present customers stop buying.
4. Distinguish between random searching and selective searching for leads. Give some examples of each.
5. What is the centers-of-influence approach to finding potential customers? Why is it the preferred method of many professionals like doctors, lawyers, and accountants?
6. Provide some basic guidelines for preparing a direct-mail piece to obtain leads on potential customers.
7. How can internal company records, such as warranty cards, be of value in developing lists of prospects?
8. Describe the survey approach to generating leads.
9. What is a marketing information system (MIS) and how can it help manage leads?

</td></tr>
</table>

<table>
<tr><td>

TOPICS FOR THOUGHT AND CLASS DISCUSSION

</td><td>

1. Why is prospecting and qualifying prospects such a crucial stage in the selling process? With innovations in telecommunication, do you think field salespeople will be required to do more or less prospecting and qualifying of prospects? Why?
2. If you were hired by Merrill Lynch to sell stocks and bonds, which prospecting methods do you think you would most likely use?
3. In making a cold call on a medium-size manufacturing company to sell a building maintenance service on a contractual basis, how would you go about qualifying the company?
4. It's October 1 and your first day on the job as a salesperson for central air conditioning in a town of about 35,000 people. Your boss, the owner of Stibb's Air Conditioning, has told you: "Go out and get some customers." Until now, Mr. Stibb has relied on a small advertisement in the Yellow Pages to generate sales, but because sales are particularly slow during the fall and winter months, he has hired you as his first salesperson. Your earnings will come solely from commissions. How will you prospect for potential customers?
5. Your spouse and two of her colleagues have recently graduated from dental school, pooled their limited resources, and opened up a small dental clinic in three rooms on the 16th floor of an office building in a West Coast city of nearly a million people. Because of the fluoridation of water and improved dental education in schools and at home, the market for dental services does not seem to be growing. Thus there is intense competition among dentists for fewer total patients. Because you are a professional salesperson with an automobile parts manufacturer, your spouse has asked you to help bring in patients for her dental clinic. Although you know very little about selling dental services, you promise to come up with a strategy. What prospecting methods do you think might be best for the dental clinic at this start-up stage?
6. What prospecting strategies would you recommend be used by a marketing research firm that specializes in carrying out research projects and developing marketing plans for colleges and universities?

</td></tr>
</table>

PROJECTS FOR PERSONAL GROWTH

1. Prepare a list of ten organizations in your area that you think would be good prospects for the products listed below. Describe your sources and criteria for selecting the companies and explain how you would go about qualifying them.
   a. Automobile leasing
   b. Overnight package or freight delivery
   c. Professional nursing uniform supplies
   d. Bottled water for offices

2. In business or trade magazines, find five examples each of (a) companies using telemarketing and (b) companies using mail-in response cards to generate leads on potential customers. Try to explain the reasoning behind the lead-generating strategy of each company.

3. After watching public concern about waste management grow rapidly in recent years, one of your father's friends has started a diaper-cleaning business for people who, for ecological reasons, are changing from disposable diapers to cloth diapers. Because you are a bright, hard-working young person and a sophomore in college, the owner of the business has asked you to work as a telemarketer prospecting for customers this summer. Upon beginning the job today, you are surprised when he hands you the phone book and simply says: "Call as many people as you can and ask them if they or anyone they know would like a diaper-cleaning service. If you can think of any better way, go ahead and try it." You're not sure that the telephone book is the best source for finding prospects. Moreover, you feel that you must first work out a simple telephone script and a method of qualifying people over the phone before you call anyone. Outline your overall strategy for prospecting for the cloth-diaper cleaning service.

4. Research and prepare a report on the trade show or exhibit marketing industry. In your report, cover the following points:
   a. What is a trade show or exhibit?
   b. Who attends trade shows?
   c. How can a company generate leads or prospects by participating in a trade show?
   d. What industries hold the largest shows? Why?
   e. What cities hold the most? Why?
   f. Is the number of trade shows increasing or decreasing each year? Why?

5. While reading your local newspaper over the next few days, find two industrial firms, two nonprofit organizations (such as a church, zoo, or library), and two professionals (such as a doctor or lawyer) who are prospecting through advertising. Critique the effectiveness of the six advertisements in accomplishing their objectives. How would you change each?

KEY TERMS

Selling process The seven-stage process of professional personal selling, from prospecting and qualifying prospects to following up and servicing customers.

Lead Anything that points to a potential buyer.

Prospect A lead that has been qualified as a definite potential buyer.

NAME An abbreviation for the process of qualifying a lead in terms of Need for the product, Authority to buy, Money to be able to buy, and overall Eligibility to buy.

Random-lead searching The generation of leads by randomly calling on households or businesses. Sometimes called "blind" searching.

Door - to - door canvassing Literally knocking on every door in a residential or commercial area to locate prospects.

Territory blitz An intensified version

of door-to-door canvassing in which several salespeople join efforts to call on every household or organization in a given territory or area.

Cold calling Approaching or telephoning a home or business without an appointment for prospecting or selling.

Selective-lead searching The application of systematic strategies to generate leads from predetermined target markets.

Spotters People working in ordinary people-contact jobs who can help salespeople obtain leads. Sometimes also called "bird dogs."

Endless chain A classic method of prospecting in which the salesperson simply asks recently satisfied customers for prospect referrals.

Centers of influence Individuals or groups of people whose opinions, professional activities, and lifestyles are respected among people in the salesperson's target markets.

Caller ID A controversial new technology that identifies the caller's telephone number before the call is answered.

Marketing information system (MIS) Any systematized, continuous process of gathering, analyzing, and distributing market information.

Case 10-1

WHEN COLD CALLING TURNS COLD

By Paul F. Christ, Delaware Valley College

The Betex Publishing Company has been in business for 15 years producing reference books that provide financial and market information on major corporations located in the United States. These publications are sold primarily to public and college libraries. Betex reference books, which compete with similar publications sold by *Standard and Poor's* and *Moody's,* are typically published once a year in a comprehensive hardcover format. Unlike many of their rivals, Betex does not provide monthly or quarterly updates to their reference books. Instead, Betex has chosen to update their product on a biannual basis, thereby saving subscribers as much as 50 percent on the price of reference products from competitors. Price is an important selling point for many small college, city, and county libraries, whose funds for reference materials are constrained by limited budgets.

In order to keep prices below those of competitive products, Betex also provides fewer company profiles in their publications. For example, Betex's main publication, *The Betex Industry Report,* a two-volume set, provides the user with extensive financial and market data on the top 3,000 publicly held companies in the United States. The competition provides information on over 10,000 companies. Betex management does not believe that including only 30 percent of all the company profiles of competitive products is a serious disadvantage because studies indicate that about 75 percent of all users of reference materials are primarily interested in information on the top 3,000 companies. Besides the *Industry Report,* Betex's product line includes financial summaries on the top 1,000 privately held U.S. firms and specific industries such as health care, financial services, and manufacturing. Most competitive products profile about 5,000 privately held U.S. firms.

Betex salespeople usually open new accounts by selling *The Betex Industry Report.* Within two weeks of the account's establishment, the sales rep makes a follow-up call to attempt to sell other Betex publications. Betex's 20 salespeople are a diverse group of 8 women and 12 men whose average age is 39. The youngest Betex sales rep is 26 and the oldest 51. After a two-week training program, new reps are dispatched to their territories to look for new accounts. Their compensation is 60 percent salary and 40 percent commission. Sales reps who achieve their annual quotas receive a $5,000 bonus and a one-week, all-expenses-paid vacation trip.

The principal duties of the field sales reps are to (1) locate and sell to new accounts and (2) maintain sales to existing accounts by superior customer service. Betex salespeople have been known to deliver, within hours, a new volume to a library that loses or damages a Betex publication.

As described in the sales training manual, written 13 years ago by the company's founder, Jeffrey

Breslin, the chief method of prospecting for new subscribers is cold calling. In bold type on the second page of the *Betex Sales Training Manual* are these words of Mr. Breslin:

> **In the introductory and growth periods of the product life cycle for Betex reference publications, cold calling is the most effective method of locating and selling new accounts. Cold calling provides the best opportunity for maximizing sales because we are competing with several well-known companies. Unless we arrive on the doorstep of prospects with our quality products in hand, it is too easy for prospects who don't recognize our name to refuse to give us that initial sales appointment. Once prospects see the quality of our reference volumes and hear our low prices, they will realize that their dollars go further with Betex. Your job, as a resourceful Betex salesperson, is to reach the buyer and make the sale on that initial in-person call. Remember that we are all family here at Betex and headquarters is always ready to help whenever you need us.**

Betex's sales force has been very successfully using the cold call approach. Last year alone, sales increased 10 percent over the previous year. However, within the last few years sales reps have begun to experience increasing difficulty in selling to *new* accounts. In fact, sales to new accounts actually declined last year for the first time in the firm's history. The management of Betex is quite concerned with this development. At the annual sales meeting last month, they asked the sales force to discuss the problems they were encountering. Among the problems cited by the salespeople are the following:

■ Many sales reps feel that the public and college libraries in their territories are close to the saturation point for reference books. One salesperson wondered whether other markets existed for Betex products besides public and college libraries.

■ Reference librarians who are not now purchasing the Betex publications have become increasingly difficult to get in to see. Recent cuts in library budgets have forced many library staffs to reduce personnel and increase workloads. Consequently, librarians in charge of purchasing reference materials are under more time pressure and will not talk to sales representatives without an appointment. Thus the Betex

sales rep often ends up talking to someone who is not the decision maker.

■ Several sales reps expressed the opinion that budget cuts, space limitations, and rising prices for library books and materials of all kinds are preventing libraries from purchasing new reference materials. The tendency among librarians who are in this predicament is to stick with established, well-known products that they know people are familiar with and will use.

Betex executives have expressed mixed responses to the sales representatives' comments since the sales meeting. Some managers feel that a problem does exist and that the company should listen to what the sales force is saying and adjust to the changing environment by developing new markets. However, other managers say that some of today's reps lack the old competitive spirit and drive that made Betex so successful in the past. These executives suggest substantial increases in the sales quota for each sales representative to force them to work harder on cold calls. This would bring about a "survival of the fittest" atmosphere in which those who couldn't "cut the mustard" would leave and more hardcharging reps could be hired to replace them, thus strengthening the sales force in the long run. Currently, Betex's sales force turnover is 25 percent a year, about average for the industry. After more than two hours of discussions, the Betex executives decide to implement the "survival of the fittest" program by increasing the quotas of each sales rep by 20 percent for the coming year. The following Monday, each Betex sales rep will be telephoned by the national sales manager and told about the new quota policy.

Questions

1. What do you think are the underlying reasons that Betex sales reps are having an increasingly difficult time selling to new accounts?

2. If you were a sales rep for Betex, what would be your reaction to the new "survival of the fittest" program? What would be your reaction if you were the 51-year-old sales rep? If you were the 26-year-old rep?

3. What advice would you give top management about selling Betex reference publications? How should you approach your company's top management to convey your suggestions? Should you ask other sales reps to join you in going to top management?

Case 10-2

PROSPECTING BY DRIVING AROUND

By Paul F. Christ, Delaware Valley College

When the phone rings, Charlie Preston knows exactly who is on the other end. It is eight o'clock Wednesday evening and his sales manager, Melinda White, is making her weekly checkup call to see how Charlie did last week. Charlie and Melinda work for RealVoice Corporation, a distributor of electronic communications equipment. One of the company's exciting new products is a portable voice-mail device that can be installed in company cars or even carried in a large briefcase. RealVoice is a small player in this growing but highly competitive market, and they are trying to carve out a niche by marketing their products mainly to small- and medium-sized companies. Customers and prospects for RealVoice products include firms that have a number of employees who do not report to a central headquarters office and companies that have widely scattered offices with only a few employees staffing each one.

Charlie, who has been with RealVoice for less than four months, is not looking forward to this conversation because he did not have a particularly impressive week. He completed only one sale, and that was to a very small account with limited potential for generating long-term profit for RealVoice. Although the three-day company training program for new salespeople covered a lot of different methods of prospecting, Charlie prefers to prospect by getting out into his territory in the Portland, Oregon, area and becoming familiar with the companies and people in it. During his first three months on the job, he had fairly good luck in selling products by driving around until he spotted an industrial park or a company whose parking lot contained a lot of look-alike middle-range cars—the kind usually assigned to salespeople. Even during his daily routine of putting gas in his car, eating meals, and doing little errands, he makes it a point to subtly prospect for business by starting conversations with people. He has found some of his best prospects and three customers by opening up a conversation with a stranger. But this past month his sales have really slowed, probably because a lot of companies in the area are cutting costs.

Charlie: Hello.

Melinda: Hi, Charlie, this is Melinda. How are you doing? Just calling to see how your week went.

Charlie: Well, it was not one of my best weeks, but I've got a lot of kettles on the old stove. *[Charlie has a few accounts that he is working on that hold promise, but he knows Melinda is really interested in how many sales he made for this week.]*

Melinda: First, tell me about your week. How many sales did you make?

Charlie: Unfortunately, I sold only one account last week. *[Charlie is sure he will hear Melinda's notorious wrath—another rep in the company has told him about Melinda's bad reaction when a salesperson's weekly numbers aren't good. Instead, he is surprised to hear her reply in a mild, comforting tone.]*

Melinda: Well, why don't you give me an idea of what happened on each call and maybe we can figure out a way to change your luck. *[Feeling relieved by Melinda's approach, Charlie proceeds to describe the past week on the road.]*

Charlie: Let me start on a positive note. I did develop three prospects that should turn into customers eventually. Last Thursday, while I was having coffee in a doughnut shop down in Salem, I met a guy named Carl Avery, who turned out to be the sales manager of Lixon Foods—a very nice guy who has ten sales reps located in four states. He said he has a hard time reaching his sales reps during the day and has been thinking about equipping each with a portable voice-mail device. So I followed him back to his office and showed him some of our product brochures. He seemed impressed. He even called to ask Joe Lixon, the company president, to sit in on a demonstration, but Mr. Lixon had gone for the day. Anyway, I tried to close Carl and get him to buy, but he said he wasn't quite sure he was ready and asked that I call back in about three weeks, after he's had a chance to educate himself more about the options.

On Monday I had an appointment to see the president of Waller Rubber Company. I found out about this company through a friend of mine who buys tires from them for his bicycle repair business. The president told me that they sell products throughout the United States and Canada and that they have a sales force of 25 manufacturers' reps. I told him that his company sounded just right for our RealVoice voice-mail product. But he wasn't sure. He said his company's present situation did not require voice mail, but he was pretty sure that they'd be interested about a year from now. Just as I was asking him to explain why he didn't think he needed our product now, his secretary buzzed to remind him of a meeting. So he quickly thanked me for my time and walked me to the door. As he was leaving, he yelled back to me: "Why don't you try our MR's, they might be interested." I didn't know what he meant by MR's, and he was gone before I could ask. Over the long run, I think this account shows promise.

Today, while I was having a flat tire fixed at a service station, I talked with the sales manager for a company that sells auto parts to service stations. He told me that they currently sell in 20 states and have 35 sales reps, but are planning to cut back in the near future. He wasn't sure how many reps they are going to keep, but he liked the idea of voice mail and thought they would eventually go to it. He even said that our product was the best-looking one that he had seen, although he thought the price was a little high. He seemed extremely interested and looked over the product and our brochure very closely. He asked whether the payments could be spread out over a longer period of time, and I told him I would get back to him on that. I got his business card, and I'll call him on Monday to set up an appointment. I think this account offers good potential.

I averaged about six in-person calls a day last week, but my other contacts were pretty much flat rejections. I didn't even get in to see about a third of my prospects because they were indisposed. Things are really tight in my territory now because of budget restrictions, but I'll keep charging until things turn up again.

Questions

1. After hearing Charlie describe his week, what do you think his sales manager ought to say to him?

2. What prospecting strategies do you think might be more effective and efficient for Charlie?

3. Do you think RealVoice should help Charlie generate leads? What prospecting methods could RealVoice use in order to help Charlie and other company salespeople?

Chapter 11

Planning the Sales Call, Then Approaching the Prospect

Planning and preparation are the keys that open the doors to opportunity and success.

Profile

Kathy Smith

I N her last summer before graduating from the University of Texas with a degree in textile science, Kathy Smith went home to Wilmington, Delaware, and talked herself into a job in the textile dyeing labs of Wilmington-based Du Pont Company. "I wasn't sure what I wanted to do with my degree," explains Kathy. "Most other textile science students were headed into merchandising, and that seemed like the surest career route. But the summer I worked at Du Pont really opened my eyes not only about the dyeing and finishing of fabrics, but also about the business end of the textile industry. After that, I knew for sure that I wanted to go into marketing."

Now a Marketing Specialist with Du Pont, Kathy emphasized to us the incredible diversity of her work, the heart and soul of which she sums up in two words: flexibility and communication. "Du Pont doesn't just churn out a new product and throw it at the market," says Kathy. "We really work with our customers to research and develop new products. This means that we have to be flexible and that we have to stay in constant communication with our customers to be effective." Du Pont's commitment to constant research and development provides the company's marketing representatives with ample opportunities to approach prospects as well as old customers with new ideas. In fact, Kathy explained to us that most of her prospecting and preapproach activities center around product research and development activities: "I've made it a practice to send a letter about appropriate new-product developments to prospects and customers to pique their interest. Initially, I'm not interested in getting them to think about our products. I'm mainly interested in getting them to think about their own business strategies and goals. Once a meeting has been arranged, I take the prospect some of the newest products and ideas we've developed and tell them the story of how they came about. Then I turn specifically to how Du Pont can help them, too. Our best ideas have come from our prospects and customers, and I think our success in this area is a direct result of our hard work in fostering an atmosphere of mutual teaching and learning with our customers."

According to Kathy, networking is one of the most important tools for success in industrial selling. "You've got to stay on top of your market, within each company you're dealing with and between companies and areas of industry. You quickly learn that nothing is set in stone. There is a constant flow of new ideas to work with and new people to meet, who are, after all, your prospects." Kathy uses a variety of technological improvements that help her in her work. "All of my customers now have voice mail, which is really the next best thing to an in-person discussion, and both my customers and I have found that faxing is the most convenient way to exchange letters and other documents." Recently, Kathy invested in a cellular car phone. "I have a 35-minute commute to my office, not to mention travel time between customers. With my car phone, I've 'found' at least a couple of productive hours every day." ■

After reading this chapter, you should understand:

☐ Why it's important to plan and prepare for the sales call

☐ How to plan the sales call

☐ How to prepare prospects for the initial sales call

☐ Strategies for approaching the prospect

WHY PLAN THE SALES CALL?

PREAPPROACH The approach planning stage of the selling process.

"Failing to plan is planning to fail" is an old saying in sales that remains true today. Unless each sales call has been carefully planned and prepared before the prospect is approached, the chances for sales success are slim. The approach planning stage of the selling process is often called the **preapproach.** Many sales managers view the preapproach as even more important than the next stage, which is the approach itself. This is because the comprehensive planning that goes into the preapproach provides salespeople with an overall framework for decision making, not only *before* the sales call but *during* and *after* the sales call as well. We will consider both the preapproach and the approach stages of the selling process in this chapter.

There are many reasons why professional sales representatives take so much care in thinking about and planning their approaches. We will list and briefly discuss five of these reasons.

The establishment of definite objectives for the sales call. Each sales call should have a realistic, meaningful, and measurable objective. Bell Telephone Company salespeople are taught to plan all their sales calls to achieve one or more of three objectives:

1. *Generate sales:* To sell particular products to target customers on designated sales calls.
2. *Develop the market:* To lay the groundwork for generating new business by educating customers and gaining visibility with prospective buyers.
3. *Protect the market:* To learn the strategies and tactics of competitors and to protect relationships with current customers.[1]

The choice of what selling strategies to use. Sometimes the objective of the sales call is simply to gather more information about the prospect's needs or to develop a closer relationship. At other times, the objective may be to win a large order. Each objective, depending on the stage in the selling process and on the prospect's needs and personality, requires a different sales presentation strategy.

---

[1]Philip Kotler, *Marketing Management: Analysis, Planning, and Control,* 4th ed. (Englewood Cliffs, N. J.: Prentice Hall, 1980), p. 569.

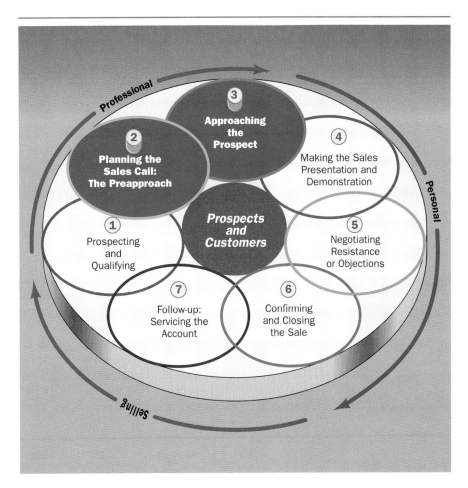

The Wheel of Professional Personal Selling

The improvement of effectiveness and efficiency. Salespeople must be concerned not only with *effectiveness* (how quickly and directly they accomplish their sales call objectives) but also with *efficiency* (how many resources they use in the process). Inefficient use of resources, like a salesperson's travel and selling time, expense account, and promotional materials, can make sales unprofitable.

Preparation for customer reaction. Top salespeople prepare for sales calls by anticipating the possible responses of prospects to each step and statement in the selling process. It's always a good idea to analyze every step of the planned sales presentation from the perspective of a very inquisitive and demanding potential customer.

The enhancement of self-confidence and professionalism. *Planning is preparing for the future,* and the most prepared salespeople are usually the most confident, professional, and successful. The very process of planning helps build the salesperson's confidence and professionalism.

PLANNING FOR THE SALES CALL: SIX STEPS TO PREAPPROACH SUCCESS

Depending on the type of sales situation, the type of customer, and the products to be presented, preapproach planning and preparation may vary widely. Some salespeople call on hundreds of small accounts, others call on only a few big ones. Some salespeople are coordinators of a selling team, others operate on their own. Some salespeople spend weeks or months gathering preapproach information about large potential customers, others (such as retail salespeople) must size up a customer quickly in the store or showroom, improvise a plan, and make an approach.

Sales call planning increases in importance when the customer's potential purchase is an expensive, complex, high-involvement one. In such cases, salespeople must keep in mind that they will have ongoing negotiations with the customer, that the customer has a range of alternatives, and that the customer's needs are unique.[2] Although the planning and preparation steps will differ for initial sales calls as compared to subsequent sales calls, and for organizational prospects as compared to consumer prospects, there are six basic steps to preapproach success, as depicted in Figure 11-1. As you read through the following discussion of these six steps, imagine a selling scenario in which you are the salesperson and think about ways you would prepare your preapproach for that scenario. Start by picking a product you like. Now, how would you prepare yourself to approach a prospect with a sales proposal for this product using the six steps to preapproach success?

Prepare the Prospect for the Initial Sales Call

If you don't properly "warm up" a prospect before making that first sales call, you may get an icy reception. Two approaches for favorably preparing a prospect for the sales call are seeding and sales promotion.

Seeding

SEEDING Prospect-focused activities, such as mailing pertinent news articles, carried out several weeks or months before a sales call.

Sales and marketing professionals frequently use the agricultural metaphor of **seeding** to describe prospect-focused activities that are carried out several weeks or months before a sales call. These activities are intended to "sow" the "seeds" of a potential sales "harvest." In this technique, the salesperson first identifies industries or customer categories that offer high sales potential, then creates a file for each. Second, the salesperson quickly learns as much as he or she can about the most important concerns of these industries, such as return on investment, employee turnover, and product quality. Third, the salesperson keeps these needs in mind while regularly reading newspapers, trade journals, and general business magazines, making copies of any pertinent articles. Fourth, the salesperson selects specific companies with high sales potential from each of

[2]Barton A. Weitz, "A Critical Review of Personal Selling Research: The Need for Contingency Approaches," in *Sales Management: State-of-the-Art and Future Research Needs,* edited by Gerald Albaum and Gilbert A. Churchill, Jr. (Eugene, Ore.: Division of Research, College of Business Administration, University of Oregon, 1979), p. 110.

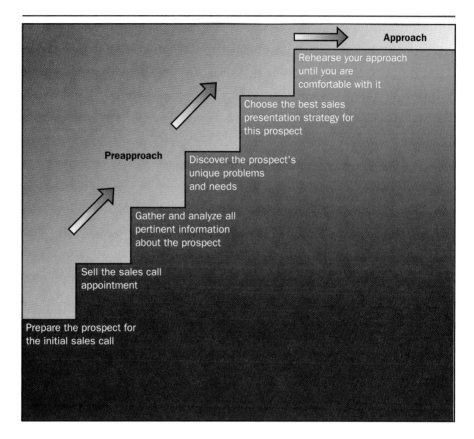

FIGURE 11-1 Six Steps to Preapproach Success

the industries and finds out the names of the key people in the buying center at each company. Fifth, the salesperson begins the campaign to develop a positive preapproach image for himself or herself by picking a relevant article from the appropriate file folder and mailing it to the prospect along with a business card and a handwritten note saying something like: "Hope you'll find the attached article interesting." No promotional materials should be enclosed with the article because seeding is essentially a *serving,* not a *selling,* activity. After mailing four to six articles to a prospect over a period of several weeks, the salesperson has created a relationship that will probably ensure a positive reception for the initial call.

Sales Promotion

We defined sales promotion in Chapter 4 as a short-run inducement offered to prospective customers to stimulate sales or enhance distribution of a product. Sales promotion materials, provided by the sales or marketing staff, can prepare the prospect for the sales call by identifying the salesperson's company, philosophy, products, price level, distribution methods, product advantages and benefits, and credit terms. Printing this information on a useful premium such as a desk or pocket calendar encourages the prospect to use the item and thus be consciously or subconsciously reminded of your company and its offerings.

Sell the Sales Call Appointment

No one wants to have his or her time wasted, so the salesperson must develop a persuasive strategy for "selling" the prospect the initial sales appointment.

Prenotification

About one step beyond seeding and sales promotion is the technique of **prenotification.** Whereas the former techniques simply make a prospect aware of you and your product, the purpose of prenotification is to send a strong signal to the prospect that you would like to make the initial sales call very soon. Using an in-person cold call, a mailing, or a telephone call, the salesperson "prenotifies" the prospect of his or her intention to make the first sales call and persuades the prospect to set a specific date, time, and place for the appointment.

Prenotification by cold call. One resourceful salesperson for a large office equipment supplier often sets up appointments by making an in-person cold call on the prospect. If the prospect is willing to see her on the cold call, great! However, if the prospect is unavailable, this salesperson writes a date and time on her business card, hands it to the prospect's secretary, and says: "I've written a day and time on my business card to meet with Mr. Barley. Would you ask him to call me if that time is inconvenient so we can schedule another time? Otherwise, I'll see him on May 3rd at 10 A.M. Thanks very much." This technique might not work for everyone, but this saleswoman has such a friendly personality that she readily wins over secretaries, who then help sell the appointments to their bosses.

Prenotification by mail. Salespeople for FrederickSeal Inc., a marketer of industrial sealing devices based in Bedford, New Hampshire, use written prenotifications to obtain their first sales appointments. A week before they call on a prospect, they send a postcard with a list of the product categories the company sells and a message saying that they look forward to visiting the prospect next

Many professional salespeople find that an in-person cold call is an excellent way to "prenotify" a prospect of their intention to make a sales presentation.

week at a certain time. This way, when they arrive at the prospect's office, they can honestly tell the secretary that their sales call is expected. Customers generally feel obligated to accept a sales call that has been announced in advance. The technique makes Frederickseal salespeople seem more professional than salespeople who show up unexpectedly at the prospect's office.

Prenotification by telephone.   One marketing researcher has found a three-stage approach to telephone prenotification to be very effective. First, introduce yourself, your company, and your product to the prospect and obtain the prospect's permission to send product literature. Second, mail the product literature and any samples. Third, after allowing the prospect a little time to "digest" your mailing, make a follow-up phone call and request a personal appointment.[3] An illustration of this process is provided in Figure 11-2.

Like most telephone prenotification strategies, this three-stage approach is effective because it requires a commitment from the prospect on three different occasions. At the first stage, the prospect expresses an interest in you, your company, and/or your product. At the second stage, the prospect receives and, you hope, reviews the materials you mail. At the third stage, the follow-up phone call, you attempt to (1) discover whether or not the prospect read the product literature, (2) determine what the prospect's reactions are to the literature, (3) encourage questions, which are the best indicators of interest in the product, and (4) arrange a day and time for a personal visit.

Executive to Executive

If all other methods for obtaining a sales appointment fail, an almost sure-fire method is to ask one of your company's top executives to call a top executive in the prospect company to set up a meeting for key members of the seller and buyer teams. Top executives almost never refuse such a request from a peer in another company. In advance of the scheduled meeting, each member of the prospect team should be sent a unique sales promotion gift as a reminder, along with a personal letter and brochure providing basic product information. It is important that the two key executives both be present at least during the early part of this initial meeting to provide credibility and encourage continuing cooperation among the participants.

AIDA

AIDA Attention, interest, desire, and action: a well-known "canned" or "formulaic" selling approach that is also an effective method for selling the sales appointment.

Another method for selling the appointment is actually a well-known four-stage selling approach called **AIDA,** which stands for *attention, interest, desire,* and *action* (we will discuss AIDA again briefly in the next chapter). An effective "canned" or "formulaic" approach for selling products, AIDA attempts to move the prospect swiftly through the stages of attention and interest into desire and buying action. For the purpose of selling the sales appointment, it is necessary to concentrate only on the first two stages, stimulating the prospect's attention and interest enough to "close" the appointment. Several specific approaches can be used in these two stages:

■ *Ask benefit-focused questions* to arouse the prospect's interest and curiosity. Examples: "Would you like to know how to legally cut your company's annual taxes by

[3]Marvin A. Jolson, "Prospecting by Telephone Prenotification: An Application of the Foot-in-the-Door Technique," *Journal of Personal Selling and Sales Management,* August 1986, p. 41.

After learning the name of the purchasing agent or key decision maker, the salesperson using the prenotification phone call approach to obtain an appointment might continue along the following lines.

When the prospect's receptionist answers the call, the salesperson can say:

Hello! My name is _____ and I'm trying to reach Mr. _____ to tell him some exciting news. Is he in?

When the prospect answers the phone, the salesperson can say:

Hello, Mr. _____, my name is _____ and I'm a marketing representative for _____ Company. We've developed some outstanding new materials-handling equipment and customer service concepts that can save your company many thousands of dollars yearly. Several of our current customers have already increased their profits from 10 to 20 percent by using our products. Since yours is a progressive company, you might be interested in seeing our latest literature on these products. I didn't want to clutter up your mailbox with something you might discard as junk mail, so I thought it best to call first and get your permission to mail the literature. May I send you this information?

Good! I'll mail it today. I'll put it in a large blue folder with our company name and red horse trademark on the outside, so you'll be able to readily identify it. Is there any special departmental code I should type on the folder to make sure that it gets routed to you as fast as possible? I'll give you a call in a few days, after you've had a chance to review the literature, to see what questions you have. Will that be okay? Good! I'll put the information in the mail today. I think you'll be pleased to see what we can offer you. Look forward to talking with you again soon, Mr. _____. Thank you for your time!

POSSIBLE PROSPECT OBJECTIONS

— Our company is not interested in any materials-handling equipment at this time.
— We're perfectly happy with the equipment we've got now.
— We don't do business over the phone.

Response:

Ms. _____, I'm calling purely in the spirit of "there's no harm in asking." You've got absolutely nothing to lose—and possibly a lot to gain—by looking over the literature I'll send you. I'm confident that you'll find our new equipment offers you substantial potential savings while providing better service to your customers. We're getting very positive testimonials from other customers. Two companies in your area, _____ and _____, are using the equipment and are very pleased. After you've reviewed the literature, I'd be delighted to visit your offices to answer any questions you may have about the specific benefits you can expect. And I'll also give you a videotaped demonstration in your office or a live demonstration at our local plant, whichever you prefer. So, you can't lose, Ms. _____. May I mail you the literature today?

Tactical Hints: Don't try hard-sell prospects. Talk to them like a friend or neighbor. Make reassuring statements like "Some of our satisfied customers were initially skeptical about the potential benefits from the material-handling equipment until they observed it in action and saw how it improved their company profits."

FIGURE 11-2 Prenotification Phone Call Approach to Obtain Sales Call Appointment

over 30 percent?" "Are you interested in something that will increase productivity by 20 percent or more for every member of your office staff?"

■ *Supply impressive testimonials* (from competitors or prominent businesspeople if possible) to show the prospect the success others are having using the product. Example: "Bob Dexter, the head of production management at Apex Industries, says that inventory costs have been sliced by 22 percent since installing our new computerized system. May I have an appointment to show you how we helped Apex?"

■ *Convey the idea that time is important to both you and the prospect,* and that you won't waste it. Suggest an appointment time and place that will not disrupt the prospect's normal routine—perhaps meeting for breakfast or on the train commuting to work or home, over a coffee break during the day, or while sharing a common interest like exercising at a health club.

■ *Ask for just five minutes to explain why an appointment will be of value to the prospect,* then spend that time outlining the major benefits you can provide.

■ *Send the prospect some unique and personally useful promotional item along with product literature that stirs interest and helps sell the appointment.* For example, mail the prospect a pocket telephone/address booklet (stamped with your company name, address, and telephone number) that includes a few pictures, descriptions, and applications of the products you sell.[4]

If the salesperson is successful in arousing and maintaining attention and interest, the prospect's desire to learn more will probably be piqued. To secure the appointment, the salesperson can be graciously assertive and presume that the prospect is agreeable to an appointment by giving him or her a specific choice such as: "Would next Tuesday at eight in the morning or Friday at noon be better for you?" "Do you prefer to meet in your office or the cafeteria?" After receiving a favorable reply, the salesperson should cordially conclude the conversation, holding back any further information until the actual sales call.

> The more information a salesperson has about a prospect, the better prepared he or she will be to handle any situation during a sales call.

Gather and Analyze Information about the Prospect

Today's and tomorrow's successful salespeople will be those who have the best information about their target consumers. Although some basic qualifying information about the prospect was gathered in the prospecting stage, it is usually necessary for the salesperson to acquire more in-depth information for the actual sales call.

Gathering Information About Consumer Prospects

The more information a salesperson has about a prospect, the better prepared he or she will be to handle any situation during a sales call. Almost any relevant information can be useful. Essentials include the prospect's name (or nickname, if preferred), job title, duties, education, work experience, level of technical expertise, purchasing authority, buying behavior, personality, after-work activities and interests, and family members. Let's briefly discuss two important sources of preapproach information about consumers: consumer credit bureaus and market research.

[4]L. Perry Wilbur, "Sell the Appointment First," *The American Salesman* 29 (January 1984): 40–42.

SUPERBUREAU SNOOPING

Using just the names and addresses of two of his colleagues, an editor of *Business Week* magazine decided to find out what he could learn about them from credit bureaus. For $20 each, one superbureau provided their credit reports and their social security numbers. A superbureau manager warned that one colleague's mortgage was ominously large and offered to fax the reports. Intrigued by these findings, the editor went for bigger game. For a $500 initial fee, the editor got access via his home computer to the superbureau's database. Exploring at will, the editor requested a credit report on Dan Quayle. Using an Indiana address he found for the vice president in an old *Who's Who in the Midwest,* the editor got an "a.k.a. J. Danforth Quayle" with a Washington-area address. The report listed the vice president's 16-digit credit card number at Merchants Bank in Washington, D.C., revealed the size of his mortgage, and showed that he charges more at Sears, Roebuck and Company than at Brooks Brothers.

SOURCE: Adapted from "Is Nothing Private?", *Business Week,* September 4, 1989, pp. 74–82.

Consumer credit bureaus.   One of the most accessible and rapidly growing sources of information about consumers is the consumer credit bureau. Credit bureaus sell consumer information broken out in over 300 categories, such as sex, age, income, occupation, education, and even likelihood of falling into bankruptcy. TRW in Orange, California, Equifax in Atlanta, Georgia, and Trans Union Credit Information in Chicago have 400 million records on 160 million individuals. TRW offers its Financial Lifestyle Database for as little as 10 cents per name. Any customer—phone solicitor, mail-order house, charity, or political group—can buy names, addresses, and phone numbers of people categorized by their income, number of credit cards, and amount of credit authorized. National Decision Systems, recently purchased for $21 million by Equifax, sells computerized breakouts of neighborhoods and towns with profiles of the residents' spending habits. National plans to incorporate Equifax's credit data into its own database to provide information on the purchasing behavior of individual households. National's financial services marketing director says that no longer will two neighbors be considered alike just because each has two kids and nearly identical houses. National will know, for example, that one heavily uses five different credit cards, whereas the other has none.[5]

In addition to their own records, the credit agencies supply "superbureaus," a second tier of about 200 credit agencies that serve small business customers. For a modest price, considerable financial and personal information is readily obtainable about almost any U.S. citizen, as the following vignette illustrates.

Market research.   To obtain information on potential prospects as a group or market segment, many sales organizations turn to market research. Information on consumer purchases can be bought from numerous market research suppliers, including A. C. Nielsen Company, Selling Area Marketing, Inc. (SAMI), Market Research Corporation of America (MRCA), Pulse, Inc., Market Facts, Inc., Donnelley Marketing, Opinion Research Corporation (ORC), and Information Resources, Inc. MRCA gathers its data from a consumer mail panel comprising 7,500 households that report weekly on their purchases of products. For a fee, com-

[5]L. Perry Wilbur, "Sell the Appointment First," *The American Salesman,* (January 1984), pp. 40–42.

panies can subscribe to one or more of over 3,000 on-line databases or information search services that estimate consumer markets and develop segmentation strategies. For example, the Donnelley Demographics Database provides household data based on U.S. census information in addition to Donnelley's own projections broken out by state, city, or zip code. Computerized Marketing Technologies (CMT) mails out millions of detailed consumer questionnaires and coded coupons to households yearly. CMT compiles data on product and brand usage, income, family size, hobbies, travel habits, and other activities of over 25 million households.[6]

As a professional salesperson, it is up to you to ask your company's sales and marketing managers for any market research studies that may be of value to you in preparing for sales calls. Other selected internal and external sources for gathering information that can help define prospects demographically, psychographically, and in terms of purchase behavior are presented in Table 11-1.

Consumer prospect profile. When gathering information on individual consumer prospects, it is important to build a consumer prospect profile. Where feasible, the prospect database should be transferred to a computer for ready reference and analysis. One straightforward format is presented in Figure 11-3.

Gathering Information About Organizational Prospects

There are many sources of information to help salespeople strategically plan sales calls on organizational prospects. These sources, several of which were discussed in Chapter 9, include (1) information available through the company's marketing, accounting, credit, purchasing, data processing, and other departments; (2) federal, state, and local government publications; (3) trade association

[6]"Stalking the New Consumer," *Business Week,* August 28, 1989, pp. 57–58.

What Would You Do?

On your first month in your new sales territory assignment for Inland Metals Corporation, you make a brilliant sales presentation to a buying committee at Wilcox & Elgin, a medium-size machine tools manufacturer. After you finish the presentation, you receive an order for $300,000 worth of sheet metals. Thrilled by this large order and thinking about the $15,000 commission you'll receive, you call your district sales manager to tell him the good news. He's delighted and congratulates you several times during your phone conversation. Just before hanging up, he says something about checking with the credit manager to make sure that the customer's credit is okay. In your excitement, you don't pay much attention to that comment and immediately call your wife to share the success. About a week later, after you've ordered a new $14,500 car for your wife, the credit manager at your company calls you to say: "We can't accept your $300,000 order from Wilcox & Elgin because their credit rating is bad."

TABLE 11-1   Selected Sources of Customer and Prospect Information

INTERNAL COMPANY SOURCES		
Sources	*Documents*	*Information*
Company libraries	Trade magazines; industry and company newsletters. Commercial clipping services like Burrells', Packaged Facts, and Bacon's.	Current market trends and developments. Current magazine and newspaper articles about the company, its products, and customers.
Accounting or sales departments	Sales invoices.	Customer names and addresses; products sold, unit and dollar sales, terms of sale, method of payment, special services provided.
Sales or marketing departments	Call reports.	Prospects and customers called on; products discussed; customer needs and usage, products now used, order size, competitors, orders obtained, annual purchases.
	Customer and prospect records.	Names and addresses of prospects and customers; sales calls made by company salespeople, unit and dollar amount of sales, products purchased, annual purchases.
EXTERNAL SOURCES		
Sources	*Documents*	*Information*
Public and university libraries	Various indexes, directories, and registers, such as *Who's Who in America* and *Who's Who in Commerce and Industry.*	Biographical sketches of prominent people—birth date, achievements, job title, education, names of spouse and children, positions held, memberships and affiliations.
City directories	Small-town city directories.	Family members' names and ages, addresses, telephone numbers, places of employment, job titles, and education.
Banks	Bank statements; savings and checking accounts.	Credit standing from checking accounts and savings records.
Local newspapers		Stories about civic or social activities, job promotions, hospital stays, and family activities such as athletics, plays, weddings, baby births, and school graduations.

Name _____   Address _____

Employer/Position/Responsibilities _____

_____

Telephone Numbers: Home (   ) _____ Work (   ) _____

Personality Type: Amiable_____ Analytical _____ Driver _____ Expressive _____

Demographic/Psychographic Profile: Age _____ Sex _____ Life-Cycle

    Stage _____ Marital Status_____Education_____

    Company _____

    Years with Company _____ Approximate Income _____

    Subculture _____ Spouse Occupation _____

    Children (names/ages) _____

    Favorite Activities _____ Interests_____

    Strong Opinions_____

Decision Making: Autonomic_____ Spouse Dominant_____

                   Syncratic_____ Not Sure _____

Dominant Buying Motives: (1)_____ (2) _____

General Comments:_____

_____

_____

_____

FIGURE 11-3 Consumer Prospect Profile

newsletters, brochures, and literature from trade shows and exhibits; (4) trade journals; (5) directories, indexes, and bibliographies; and (6) mailing lists bought from commercial companies. Let's discuss two sources that can be especially helpful: in-house purchasing agents and electronic directories and databases.

In-house purchasing agents. Buyers in your company's purchasing department are a good source of information on business prospects because they are buying goods and services from several companies that were investigated before they were accepted as suppliers. Because reciprocity is a widespread practice, it's always a good idea to see if your company is already a buyer as well as a seller to the company you're calling on, especially if your company is very large and has many different departments or groups that individually buy and sell.

Electronic directories and databases. Business data can also be purchased for computer analysis. The *Electronic Yellow Pages,* containing listings from nearly all the nation's 4,800 phone books, is the largest directory of American companies available. Standard & Poor's *Compustat* provides detailed balance sheet and income statement information for more than 5,000 companies. *Industry Data Sources* compiles information from trade association reports, governmental publications, and industry studies by brokerage firms on 65 major industries. *TRINET Data Base of U.S. Business Information* gives sales and market share information for 500,000 businesses, including addresses, number of employees, SIC code, decision makers, sales, and market information. *Dun's Market Identifiers* reports information on over 2 million U.S. businesses with ten or more employees, including address, product, and financial and marketing information.

Hundreds of on-line database vendors, including CompuServe, Inc., Bibliographic Retrieval Service (BRS), Dow Jones News Retrieval, and Dialog Information Services, Inc., provide access to over 200 databases in a variety of business and scientific fields. Some can give you electronic access to hundreds of business databases, newsletters, company annual reports, and investment firm reports. As computer data banks proliferate and laptop computers become more versatile, salespeople will be able to obtain instant access to prospect data. Only a few minutes before meeting the prospect, perhaps while waiting in the car or reception area, the salesperson will be able to electronically call up and review relevant information about the prospect, including the objectives and strategy for this particular sales call. Some companies, such as Monsanto Polymer Products, have made rapid progress toward this scenario, as described in the next Company Highlight.

Company Highlight

On-Line Information System for Monsanto Salespeople

At Monsanto Polymer Products in St. Louis, sales representatives obtain needed information from OACIS (On-Line Automated Commercial Information System). OACIS updates the salespeople daily on their accounts, products, and performance. Once a field salesperson signs on at a terminal, menus appear on the screen that present different options, depending on the type of information sought. Before making a sales call, the salesperson can obtain an order status report summarizing shipments, along with an explanation of the reasons for unfilled orders. Data can also be secured on specific products the customer bought this month, the previous month, and for the year to date. After obtaining data on buying activity, the salesperson can switch to another menu that shows sales forecasts for each product and the progress toward those objectives. The system was designed to make the terminals as user-friendly as possible. After less than four hours of training, the salesperson can get the information wanted 95 percent of the time with just two keystrokes. Salespeople are assured of the latest data because OACIS is hooked into Monsanto's automated order billing system. As new orders come in and shipments go out, the database is updated constantly. Thus salespeople can get data on everything that occurred up to 6:00 P.M. the previous day.

Source: Sales & Marketing Management, January 1988, p. 70.

Organizational prospect profile. Using a basic format like the one shown in Figure 11-4, salespeople can develop an organizational prospect profile on each of their business-to-business prospects and customers. As relevant information is uncovered, they can add it to the Insights and Comments section of this form. Ideally, they will maintain all this information on their laptop computer so that they can call it up for review just before they see a prospect.

International organizational prospects. Much less information is available on international markets than on domestic markets, but there are nevertheless an impressive number of sources to draw upon. As a starting point, you could contact the International Trade Division (ITD) of the U.S. Department of Commerce located in Washington, D.C., and other major cities. The ITD maintains reference libraries where salespeople can talk to trade experts and find statistical data on foreign companies. One U.S. company planning to try to sell toilets with microwave automatic flush mechanisms to Nigeria avoided a costly mistake when it learned that most parts of Nigeria still lacked basic sewage systems. Table 11-2 provides a selection of other sources for information about international organizational markets.

Identify the Prospect's Problems and Needs

Prior to the initial sales call, it is difficult to know the prospect's specific needs. However, by carefully analyzing the preapproach information gathered about the prospect, you can often identify basic problems that the prospect is facing and establish the general area of that prospect's needs.

Consumer Problems and Needs

As you learned in Chapter 5, the homogeneous American consumer, even within ethnic groups, is a myth. Today's consumers come from many backgrounds and cultures. They have diverse needs and product preferences for fulfilling those needs.

Organizational Problems and Needs

It usually takes an initial sales call to uncover the specific problems and needs of an organizational prospect. During this initial sales call, some salespeople use a technique referred to as SPIN to quickly zero in on prospect needs and achieve a commitment. Here's what SPIN stands for:

- ■ **S**ituation: First, the salesperson tries to learn about the prospect's situation. For example, a Xerox salesperson might ask such questions as: "How many copies do you make a month in your office?" "What kinds of documents do you most often copy?" "Who usually makes the decision to buy copier equipment?"
- ■ **P**roblem: Second, the salesperson identifies a problem that the prospect regularly encounters with present products. For example: "Do you have problems copying blue ink?" "Do you find that your present copier is so complex that only a few people use it?" "Do you find that your present copier seems to break down frequently?"
- ■ **I**mplication: Third, the salesperson learns the implication or result of the problem. For example: "Do you have to go to the trouble of changing the copier setting or have to do the messy job of changing the copier's ink supply in order to copy blue ink?" "Do you have to do the photocopying for a number of people because they don't

Company Name _____

Address _____

Telephone Number (   ) _____ Fax Number _____

Organization Profile

Type of Business: ____ Manufacturer ____ Wholesaler ____ Retailer ____ Service
                       ____ Government   ____ Petroleum   ____ Not-for-Profit ____ Utility
                       ____ Mine/Quarry   ____ Other_____

Buying Pattern: ____ Weekly   ____ Monthly   ____ Semiannually   ____ Yearly
                      ____ Seasonal ____ As Needed ____ Other_____

Purchasing Pattern

	Products Purchased	Annual $ Amount	Company Share	Brand Preferred	Competitive Suppliers
1.					
2.					
3.					
4.					
5.					
6.					
7.					
8.					
	Totals				

Customer Contacts

Initiators:
1. Names/Responsibilities   Department   Calling Hours
2. _____   _____   _____
    _____   _____   _____

     Contacts _____   Dates _____   Results _____

Gatekeepers:
1. Names/Responsibilities   Department   Calling Hours
2. _____   _____   _____
    _____   _____   _____

     Contacts _____   Dates _____   Results _____

Influencers:
1. Names/Responsibilities   Department   Calling Hours
2. _____   _____   _____
    _____   _____   _____

     Contacts _____   Dates _____   Results _____

Deciders:
1. Names/Responsibilities   Department   Calling Hours
2. _____   _____   _____
    _____   _____   _____

     Contacts _____   Dates _____   Results _____

Buyers:
1. Names/Responsibilities   Department   Calling Hours
2. _____   _____   _____
    _____   _____   _____

     Contacts _____   Dates _____   Results _____

Users:
1. Names/Responsibilities   Department   Calling Hours
2. _____   _____   _____
    _____   _____   _____

     Contacts _____   Dates _____   Results _____

Insights and Comments:

FIGURE 11-4 Organizational Prospect Profile

TABLE 11-2 Sources of Data on International Industrial Markets

DATA SOURCE	REGIONS COVERED	DATA PROVIDED
Business International	Eastern and Western Europe, Middle East, Latin America, Asia, Africa, and Australia	Growth, relative size of market, degree of concentrated power.
Foreign Trader's Index (FTI)	143 foreign companies	Listings by country and product according to SIC codes.
Datastream International (recently acquired by D&B)	Europe	Information and credit reports on over 7 million European companies.
Export Advisory Service (offered by Information Handling Services)	World	Information on trade regulations, legislation, statistics, and various pertinent periodicals.
Encyclopedia of Business Information Sources	World	1600 subjects covering 500 geographic areas.
Trade Opportunities Program (TOP)	World	Information about export opportunities is transmitted by U.S. Foreign Service posts to a TOP computer in Washington, D.C.
Automated Information Transfer System (AITS)	World	Market information and export sales leads available at offices of the International Trade Division.
Dun & Bradstreet's Principal International Businesses	135 countries of the world	Names, addresses, number of employees, products, CEO, up to 6 SIC classifications for each organization; over 144,000 business units classified by 4-digit SIC and by alphabetical order.
Ulrich's International Periodicals Directory (R. R. Bowker Co., New York)	Covers 61,000 periodicals throughout the world	Biannual publication with information arranged by subject; includes titles of publications of various international companies.
Japan Company Handbook (Tokyo Keizai Shinposha, LTD, Tokyo)	Over 1,000 Japanese corporations	Biannual publication that provides sales breakdowns, financial statistics, and forecasts for over 1,000 Japanese corporations.
World of Information	Middle East, Africa, Asia and the Pacific, Latin America and the Caribbean	Annual surveys of the general business environment in regions covered.

know how to use your present complex copier?" "Do you have to go to another department to try to get your copying done when your copier breaks down?"

■ **N**eeds payoff: Finally, the salesperson proposes a solution to the problem and asks for some kind of commitment from the prospect. For example: "If I could get you a machine that would copy blue ink, would you be interested?" "If I could get you a copier that's so simple to operate that even the CEO can use it, would you be interested?" "If I could get you a copier that seldom breaks down, would you be interested?"

Note that the first commitment asked for in all of these sample questions is simply one of "interest." In most organizational selling situations, the main purpose of the initial sales call is to allow salesperson and prospect to meet and learn about each other. Pushing too hard for a close at this time might alienate the prospect. Once the prospect has indicated that he or she is "interested," however, it's usually easy to get the prospect to commit to another sales call—and a full sales presentation.

Choose the Best Sales Presentation Strategy

After discovering the prospect's unique problems and needs, the next step to preapproach success is to choose an appropriate sales presentation strategy. Although we will discuss various sales presentation strategies in detail in the next chapter, this is a good time to recall two concepts from earlier chapters. Together, they provide an excellent guide for choosing the most appropriate sales presentation strategy for each prospect.

First, we saw in Chapter 1 that *consultative selling* is the selling approach preferred by most of today's sales professionals. The truly consultative salesperson strives at all times to identify and solve customer problems. Second, we saw in Chapter 7 how important it is for the salesperson to understand *style flexing*. The most successful salespeople easily "flex" their communication styles with their prospects' communication styles.

In choosing a sales presentation strategy, it might be helpful to think of consultative selling as an effective general *approach* and style flexing as an effective specific *method* for sales negotiations. Obviously, the goal of both consultative selling and style flexing is maximum flexibility in the selling process as a whole.

Rehearse Your Approach

As top athletes, public speakers, and professional salespeople know, the more they practice their skills, the more successful they become. So, rehearse, rehearse, rehearse until you have mastered your total sales performance and feel comfortable and confident about it. Do not memorize a canned spiel. Just keep in mind the key points you want to make in each part of the sales presentation and other stages of the selling process. Thorough planning, preparation, and rehearsal of each sales call will lead you to sales success.

INITIAL SALES CALL RELUCTANCE— SALES STAGE FRIGHT

INITIAL SALES CALL RELUCTANCE A kind of sales stage fright that renders many salespeople reluctant to make the initial sales call.

Once you have marched up all six steps to preapproach success, you may still have one barrier to overcome, especially if you are a new sales rep. One of the biggest problems new salespeople face is fear of making the initial contact with prospects. But **initial sales call reluctance** is a "disease" that hampers the careers of a wide range of salespeople, both experienced and novice. It is a kind of sales "stage fright" that can persist regardless of what you are selling, how well you have been trained, or how much you believe in your product and company. This reluctance can take many forms:

- *Social or self-image threat:* Belief that things are sure to go wrong, resulting in personal humiliation.
- *Intrusion sensitivity:* Fear of upsetting prospects by interrupting and intruding on them.
- *Analysis paralysis:* Overanalyzing and overpreparing for the sales call, then becoming too petrified to take action.
- *Group fright:* Fear of making presentations before groups of people. This fear is akin to the widespread dread of public speaking.
- *Social class or celebrity intimidation:* Fear of contacting affluent or prominent prospects.
- *Role ambivalence:* Embarrassment about the perceived negative role of selling as a career.
- *Exploitation guilt:* Apprehension about being seen as exploitative and manipulative by family, relatives, and friends, so you avoid making sales calls on them.

There are several things you can do to overcome such concerns. Here are some suggestions:

- Listen carefully to the excuses other salespeople offer to rationalize their call reluctance so that you will learn to recognize your own similar rationalizations.
- Use supportive role playing and discussions with sales colleagues to overcome fear.
- Make some initial prospect contacts with a partner for support, then make calls on prospects without partner support.
- Review and reenact recent sales calls with sales colleagues to critique your performance and monitor signs of progress.
- Shift your focus from individual prospect personalities to sales objectives by setting the objectives down in writing before you make a sales call.
- Rehearse sales calls with sales colleagues to reinforce positive behaviors.[7]

A quick review of Chapter 8 will also help you discover ways to handle initial sales call reluctance. And bear in mind that even the top professionals get a little nervous about important initial sales calls. Try to think of it this way: Your nervousness shows that you really care about your prospect and your selling "performance." In fact, perhaps you should worry if you are *never* nervous before an important initial sales call!

APPROACHING THE PROSPECT

Although a letter, a telephone call, or a brief cold call is often perfectly acceptable for arranging an initial sales call, most professional selling situations absolutely require that the actual approach be a well-planned, face-to-face meeting with the prospect. Despite all that we have said about the usefulness of computer and telecommunications technologies, most prospects are still most impressed—and best persuaded—by an in-person visit by a salesperson. And the old saying that

---

[7]Paul Frichtl, "Fear of Phoning," *Industrial Distribution,* January 1986, p. 65.

Interactions during the first few minutes between the salesperson and prospect create an impression that may be difficult to change.

APPROACH The first face-to-face contact with the prospect.

"you never get a second chance to make a first impression" suggests how important the **approach,** that first face-to-face contact with the prospect, can be.

When we meet new people, we tend to size them up or categorize them in some way. We think things like: "Boy, this guy is pushy" or "She really seems bright and nice." Clothes and accessories (glasses, briefcase, umbrella, jewelry, or pen), general grooming, facial expressions, body postures, voice tones and inflections, and choice of words all send messages. Interactions during the first few minutes between the salesperson and prospect create an impression that may be difficult to change. Roger Ailes, political media adviser to Presidents Bush and Reagan, claims that people start to make up their minds about others within *seven seconds* after meeting them, triggering a chain of emotional reactions ranging from reassurance to fear.[8] Leonard Zunin, author of *Contact: The First Four Minutes,* claims that during the first four minutes after meeting a salesperson, the prospect decides whether or not to buy.[9] Thus, we need to do all we can to make sure that the prospect's first impression of us is a positive one.

Depending upon the selling situation, several strategies can be effectively used to approach the prospect. Table 11-3 outlines ten of the most effective approach strategies. We'll briefly discuss each of them.

Self-Introduction Approach

A warm smile and a firm handshake are important at the beginning and end of the sales call. In the introduction, sales reps should greet prospects by name and give

[8]Roger Ailes with Jon Kraushar, *You Are the Message* (Homewood, Ill.: Dow Jones–Irwin, 1988), p. 2.
[9]Leonard Zunin, *Contact: The First Four Minutes* (New York: Nash Publishing, Ballantine Books, 1972), p. 109.

TABLE 11-3   Strategies for Approaching Prospects

■ Self-introduction	Smoothly and professionally greet prospect.
■ Mutual acquaintance or reference	Mention the names of satisfied customers who are respected by the prospect.
■ Customer benefit	Offer the customer benefit immediately.
■ Compliment or praise	Subtly and sincerely compliment the prospect.
■ Survey	Ask permission to obtain information about whether the prospect might need your product.
■ Free gift or sample	Offer a free gift, sample, or luncheon invitation.
■ Question	Get the prospect involved in two-way communication early by asking an appropriate question.
■ Product or ingredient	Show the customer the product or a sample or model of it.
■ Product demonstration	Begin demonstrating the product upon first meeting the prospect.
■ Dramatic act	Do something dramatic to get the prospect's attention.

their own name and company. For example: "Good morning, Mr. Stevens, I'm Marie Potts from Quaker Oaks here for our ten o'clock appointment." Most sales reps present their business card at this point, but some prefer to wait until the close of the interview for emphasis. One highly successful salesperson used a unique and somewhat questionable introductory approach to call on CEO prospects, as described in the next Selling in Action box.

Mutual Acquaintance or Reference Approach

Mentioning the names of several satisfied customers who are respected by the prospect (even if they are competitors) can be a very compelling approach. For example: "Your colleague George Bidwell at Monsanto has just switched to our process, and so we now serve four of the top five chemical companies in the area." Testimonial letters from satisfied customers can be especially valuable when selling goods or services where the investment or social risk is high, such as when the customer is considering the purchase of a computerized information system, investment services, or expensive jewelry. Salespeople must avoid mere name-dropping because prospects often do contact the people you mention before buying. So be sure that the people behind the names you drop will verify your testimonial.

Customer Benefit Approach

Because all prospects, whether individuals or organizations, seek to solve problems or obtain benefits from their purchases, it is easy to understand why many successful sales approaches begin with a strong statement about immediate customer benefits. Some examples of the customer benefit approach are the following statements:

■ You can save 20 percent or more on your fleet automobile expenses by using our leasing plan.

■ Our new, high-speed mainframe computer can cut your MIS costs by up to 30 percent.

Selling In Action

Delivering the Mail

Chief executive officers are generally viewed as awesome figures by most salespeople, but W. Patrick Hughes doesn't believe it. "Top people in corporate America are pretty much like everybody else," he says. "They're always interested in listening to someone with creative ideas if the approach is nonthreatening."

Early in his career when he sold tax shelters in $50,000 lots for the Boston firm of Cheverie & Company, Hughes decided that CEOs would be among his best prospects. "I was so new I didn't know how things should be done," he says, "so I didn't get caught up in the write-a-letter or make-a-phone-call routine." Instead, he made cold calls on prospects at their offices in his Connecticut territory, trying his best not to look like a salesperson.

"I have a letter of introduction for Mr. Smith," he'd tell the receptionist, naming the CEO as he showed her an envelope containing a handwritten letter on linen stationery. Noticing that he carried neither sample case nor sales kit, the receptionist would usually promptly call the boss's secretary.

Hughes feels that the success of the technique depended on his ability to differentiate himself in the mind of the CEO's secretary. Therefore, he made it a point not to sit with other salespeople while awaiting her arrival in the reception area. He stood apart and, when she appeared, presented her with the letter saying that he'd be happy to call or phone at Mr. Smith's convenience. Because she assumed that he was not a salesperson, the secretary's guard was usually down and she would take the letter back to her boss.

Even though the letter itself was nothing more than the usual sales letter, Hughes nearly always got in to see the CEO, often on the same call. "I think I succeeded because the CEOs were curious," says Hughes, now an account executive with Employee Benefit Plan Administration, Inc., of Hampton, New Hampshire. "They'd never seen anyone use this approach before." Hughes named his special technique "Delivering the Mail."

Source: Martin Everett, "Selling to the CEO," *Sales & Marketing Management,* November 1988, p. 61.

■ Independent research companies have judged our compact Baby Bull bulldozer to be the best value on the market for construction firms with an annual sales volume under $50 million.

■ By converting your insurance policy to our new family plan, you will have $50,000 more coverage at the same price you're paying now.

Compliment or Praise Approach

If done subtly, a sincerely delivered compliment can be a positive approach to a prospect and can set a pleasant atmosphere for the interview. Most people are eager for positive feedback or praise. Most prospects, too, enjoy praise, so long as the salesperson is not patronizing. An indirect compliment is often more effective than a direct one, which may be dismissed as empty flattery. Some statements exemplifying the compliment approach are:

- I can't help but ask you about that beautiful antique clock you have on your wall. Would you tell me something about it?
- Your secretary is really efficient and thoughtful. She called me at 8 o'clock this morning to let me know that you would have to change our appointment to 3 P.M.
- Congratulations on your company's recent award as one of Pittsburgh's top ten corporate "good citizens." That's an honor that any company would like to win.

Survey Approach

Whether over the telephone or face-to-face, the survey approach is widely used by salespeople selling stocks and bonds, insurance, security systems, computerized information services, or any product where a potential need cannot be established without obtaining basic information about the prospect. Simply asking the prospect's permission to ask a few survey questions is usually an inoffensive and nonthreatening way to begin a sales call. For example: "Mr. Peters, may I ask you a few questions about your information needs? Your answers will help us determine whether you can substantially benefit by subscribing to one of our electronic information services." After receiving a "yes" answer, the salesperson can probe further to learn the exact nature and intensity of the prospect's needs. If the prospect should say "No, I'm too busy now," the salesperson can suggest calling back later that day or the next at a more convenient time. For example: "Would after 4 P.M. today or before 9 A.M. tomorrow be better for you?" A follow-up phone call at the agreed time will more often than not be successful in obtaining the prospect's responses to the survey questions.

If you were going to use a compliment or praise approach with the prospect who occupies this office, how would you formulate your compliment?

Free Gift or Sample Approach

Door-to-door salespeople discovered long ago that a sample of the product or a small gift, such as a key chain, can help establish goodwill and gain entry to a prospect's home. Similarly, professional salespeople today can offer a luncheon invitation, a free seminar, trial use of a product, or a limited sample of services (like estate planning or investment advice) as a means of approaching organizational and especially promising consumer prospects. Salespeople must avoid violating legal and ethical guidelines in using this approach, however.

Question Approach

Asking questions is a good way to get prospects involved in two-way communication. Prospects may disclose valuable information (such as their level of interest in your product) when they respond to your questions. One type of question helps qualify prospects. For example: "If I could show you how your organization can increase profits by ten percent or more by using our new desktop publishing software, would you be willing to give me a half hour of your time?" Such a question commands the prospect's thoughtful consideration, separates the "lookers" from the "buyers," and moves the salesperson along the path to an early sales close if the subsequent sales presentation meets prospect expectations. Most salespeople avoid asking questions that prospects are likely to answer negatively. The classic "May I help you?," which many retail sales clerks use mechanically, makes it all too easy for the prospect to brush the salesperson aside with a "No, thanks, I'm just looking" response.

Product or Ingredient Approach

Most sales reps like to carry a sample, model, or picture of the product on sales calls. This approach allows prospects to immediately see what you are selling and often creates prospect curiosity, which permits a smooth transition into the sales presentation and demonstration. A cutaway cross section of a new type of heavy-duty hydraulic pump or a miniature model of a large machine tool can significantly enhance the impact of your first contact with potential customers.

Product Demonstration Approach

Demonstrating the product upon first approaching the prospect can be an excellent way to show the benefits being offered and get immediate prospect involvement. For example, Melitta, Inc., a German-based coffee and coffee products distributor, outfitted a van as a traveling salesroom to introduce the Melitta coffee-maker system in New York and Philadelphia area supermarkets. After driving the van to the headquarters of wholesale and retail chains, Melitta salespeople went inside to invite everyone from purchasing agents to top management to come out to the van for a cup of fresh coffee and pastry. "We were able to talk to the buyers in a relaxed atmosphere, free from telephone interruptions, with all the facilities we needed for demonstration," asserts Melitta's national sales manager. "Frequently six or seven top chain executives would visit the van, rather

Should other approaches fail, the sales rep can turn to a dramatic or attention-getting strategy.

than the one or two we would have been able to see during ordinary office calls. They stayed longer too—and they bought."[10]

Dramatic Approach

Should other approaches fail, the sales rep can turn to a dramatic or attention-getting strategy. Some sales reps have placed $10 on the prospect's desk and announced, "If I can't show you in the next twenty minutes how our product will do everything I claim it will, you can keep the ten dollars." Dramatic approaches may range from mere cuteness to impressive presentations to utter outlandishness. Giving a prospect a teddy bear—with your business card attached, of course—can be a charming way of introducing yourself or following up with a prospect. I even knew one sales rep who dressed up as Superman in order to win a large order for office supplies.

A word of warning about dramatic approaches: Know thy prospect. Some prospects might think you are being too familiar or pushy or be offended by a display of blatant showmanship.

Which Approach Is Best?

No single approach will work with every prospect. The choice depends on the customer category and the personality of the individual being approached. Salespeople may need to try different approaches on successive occasions when earlier approaches have not proved successful in winning the prospect's attention and interest in the sales presentation. Even such apparently minor aspects of the

[10]*Progressive Grocer*, October 1973, p. 13.

approach as the initial greeting of the prospect or the use of a business card can often make the difference between a successful and an unsuccessful approach.

GREETING THE PROSPECT

The very first part of the approach, the greeting itself, can set the tone for the entire interview and often affect the long-term relationship. You should practice appropriate facial expressions and body positions. Your handshake and manner of presenting your business card also should be practiced because they are part of the physical greeting that accompanies your verbal greeting.

Facial Expression

Nearly all of us like to see a pleasant, smiling face, even when we're not in a very good mood ourselves. Salespeople should practice the art of warmly smiling with their eyes as well as their mouths while simultaneously greeting prospects. As simple as this sounds, we all know people who smile only with their mouths while their eyes remain cold or dull. Although nothing is said, many people notice this lack of harmony between the mouth and eyes. Coordinating and holding the smile while making the verbal greeting is something you should practice in front of a mirror. When you are ready, try it out on a friend who will give you an honest appraisal and helpful advice on how to make your greeting sincere and warm. The best salespeople always try to assume the most positive things about the people they are going to meet. Many of us, of course, seem to assume the worst. Stir up genuinely positive feelings for the prospect, and your smile and eyes will project enthusiasm and a warm, gracious disposition.

The greeting itself can set the tone for the entire sales interview and often affect the long-term relationship.

Body Posture

Salespeople are usually advised to maintain comfortable, erect posture in greeting prospects in order to project a positive attitude. In general, this is appropriate advice. In some cases, however, it might be better for the salesperson to bend slightly at the waist or gently bow or nod the head when greeting and shaking hands with the prospect because a "stiff" posture might imply feelings of superiority. Also, when a salesperson is much taller than a prospect, it is impolite to maintain an erect posture that forces the prospect to look and reach too far upward for the greeting. Courtesy, politeness, and consideration for others will aid your common sense in determining the appropriate body posture for greeting a prospect.

Shaking Hands

We often judge others and are judged by them by the way we shake hands. Some top salespeople will tell you that it's best to let the prospect decide whether or not to shake hands. A friendly extended hand can be a very positive way to begin

not to shake hands. A friendly extended hand can be a very positive way to begin a sales call, but it can also turn off some reserved people, especially on cold calls. Use your common sense to size up the situation. If a prospect is seated behind his desk when you put out your hand, you're forcing him to stand up. This may not be a good way to begin a sales interview. In social settings, good etiquette formerly required the person in the superior position to decide whether or not to shake hands, and men were generally taught to let women initiate handshakes. Today, however, most communication does not take place between people who have definite superior-inferior relationships, and many businesswomen are impatient with the idea that only they can initiate a handshake. Salespeople should not force a handshake on a prospect, but they should be ready to extend a hand whenever the situation warrants it. A handshake sends a silent message about the salesperson, as the following classic handshake styles illustrate.

- ■ *Seal-the-Deal:* Firm and warm with smiling eye contact, it communicates "trust me" and says you are confident and have nothing to hide.
- ■ *The Fish:* Extending a limp hand to someone is like handing him or her a fish. You are not showing warmth because you are not grasping the prospect's hand, and you are sending a negative message about your self-confidence.
- ■ *Three-Fingered Claw:* Thrust out only two or three stiff fingers and you're telling prospects how distasteful you find them and that your handshake is strictly perfunctory.
- ■ *Bone Crusher:* Some salespeople, thinking that a powerful handshake sends a very positive, confident message, literally crush the prospect's hand. This handshake will probably turn off most prospects because it makes them think you're trying to dominate them.
- ■ *The Pumper:* A few salespeople pump the hand of the prospect almost as if they're drawing water up from a well. People don't want their hand pumped, and will wonder about your long-run sensitivity to their needs if you are so boorish up front.
- ■ *The Death Grip:* Some salespeople keep shaking hands for an interminable length of time and seem unwilling to let go. A handshake is a greeting, not an embrace. And any salesperson who hangs on too long to the hand of a member of the opposite sex is inadvertently sending a sexual message.
- ■ *The Dish Rag:* Salespeople who are nervous about meeting a prospect or customer may present a sweaty hand for shaking and reveal their nervousness. Even when you don't feel nervous, it's a smart practice to take a few seconds to dry your hands on a handkerchief before going in to see the prospect.

Handshake Guidelines

In extending your hand for a handshake, go in with your thumb up and out, so the other person can get his or her hand in. Make sure the "web" between your thumb and forefinger firmly touches the other person's "web." Always shake hands from the elbow, not the shoulder or wrist.[11]

Presenting Your Business Card

Usually, you should present your business card shortly after shaking hands with a prospect because this will help the prospect to keep your name and company in mind as you talk. It's a good idea to present a business card each time you call on a prospect until you're sure that he or she knows your name and your company.

---

[11]"Management Digest (Special Advertising Section)," *Newsweek,* November 27, 1989, p. 3.

Because prospects see many salespeople only once or twice a year, it is a little presumptuous, and sometimes embarrassing, to take for granted that prospects will remember you from one sales call to the next. When a sales supervisor or manager is traveling your territory with you, presenting your business card to each prospect will help prevent you from being embarrassed in front of your boss. In some cultures such as Japan, exchanging business cards and carefully examining them is a fundamental rule of business politeness and mutual respect.

BUYERS EXPECT PROFESSIONALISM

In today's intensely competitive and professional global buying and selling environments, "seat-of-the-pants" or "ad lib" approaches to making sales calls on prospects and customers seldom work. Increasingly sophisticated consumers and highly trained professional buyers expect professionalism from any salesperson who expects to win their business. No salesperson can be sloppy in preapproach planning and expect to win solid commitments from the prospect in the approach and initial sales call. The highest rewards and career success will be earned by those who prepare thoroughly for each sales call and carry out a well-planned and rehearsed approach strategy.

SUMMARY Professional salespeople carefully plan every sales call and establish specific objectives for achievement. The level of planning varies with the complexity of the situation and the importance of the customer's purchase decision. "Seeding" and sales promotion are effective ways to prepare a prospect for the sales call. Demographic and psychographic information about consumer or organizational prospects can be obtained from various internal and external sources. Selling the prospect on the appointment is a preliminary step that can help ensure a favorable reception for the sales call. Approach strategies need to be matched with the type of prospect and the selling situation, and thoroughly rehearsed before carrying them out. Even the salesperson's initial greeting during the approach can be critical in determining whether or not rapport is established with a prospect.

CHAPTER REVIEW QUESTIONS

1. Name five reasons for planning sales calls.
2. What are the six steps to preapproach success?
3. Define seeding and sales promotion and briefly explain why, when, and how each technique is used.
4. Name and describe in as much detail as you can three basic techniques for selling the sales appointment.
5. What are two valuable sources of consumer prospect information?

6. What are some electronic sources for information about organizational prospects?

7. With whom, when, and how would you use SPIN?

8. Describe the prenotification phone call approach to obtaining the initial sales appointment.

9. Which two important concepts might help you choose an appropriate sales presentation strategy?

10. List five kinds of sales stage fright. What would you do to overcome these fears?

11. Name as many different approach strategies as you can and briefly describe each.

TOPICS FOR THOUGHT AND CLASS DISCUSSION

1. Do you feel that credit bureaus are an acceptable source of information about consumers or an invasion of people's right to privacy?

2. Comment on the following statement: "Always take the information you've collected about an organizational prospect with a grain of salt."

3. What strategy would you use to arrange a sales appointment for each of the following situations:
    a. Selling a corporate jet to Donald Trump.
    b. Selling lighting fixtures to the hospital administrator of a large city hospital.
    c. Selling the arrangements committee of the American Marketing Association on choosing your resort hotel for the AMA's annual summer educators' conference three years from now.

4. You have a salesperson friend who fears calling prospects on the phone to arrange sales appointments. You'd like to help him or her overcome this fear. What's your advice?

5. Choose an approach strategy for each of the following prospect personality types:
    a. Driver
    b. Analytical
    c. Amiable
    d. Expressive

6. You've tried many different approaches with an organizational prospect who seems nice enough but just isn't impressed with you. Finally, you decide to risk a dramatic approach. Describe some dramatic approaches you might use.

PROJECTS FOR PERSONAL GROWTH

1. With a classmate, demonstrate each of the types of handshakes listed below. Describe your feelings toward each other as you perform each handshake.
    a. Seal-the-Deal
    b. The Fish
    c. Three-Fingered Claw
    d. Bone Crusher
    e. The Pumper
    f. The Death Grip
    g. The Dish Rag

2. Search your school or local library for a market research study conducted by a commercial research organization such as A. C. Nielsen, SAMI, or Donnelly. Prepare a report that discusses: (a) the purpose of the study, (b) the target market for the study, (c) how the information was obtained, and (d) the major findings of the study. If you

are unable to find such a study, ask your business reference librarian for assistance.

3. Develop an organizational prospect profile on a local company. You might start by requesting an annual report or other descriptive materials from the company's public relations office. After deciding what you are going to sell to the company, locate as many sources of information as you can about the company and include what you learn in your prospect profile. [*Note:* Practice cold calling by contacting representatives within the company itself, but be sure to indicate that you are a student working on this project!]

KEY TERMS

Preapproach The approach planning stage of the selling process.

Seeding Prospect-focused activities, such as mailing pertinent news articles, carried out several weeks or months before a sales call.

Prenotification A technique using an in-person cold call, a mailing, or a telephone call to send a strong signal to the prospect that the salesperson would like to schedule a sales call appointment.

AIDA Attention, interest, desire, and action: a well-known "canned" or "formulaic" selling approach that is also an effective method for selling the sales appointment.

Initial sales call reluctance A kind of sales stage fright that renders many salespeople reluctant to make the initial sales call.

Approach The first face-to-face contact with the prospect.

Case 11-1

MAKING INITIAL SALES CALLS

By Paul F. Christ, Delaware Valley College

John Gibbons smiles as he drives past the college library. He remembers the many long nights he spent there cramming for tests and finishing reports. But all that is finally over and now he has his first job. It feels good. Since his graduation eight months ago, he has been a sales representative for Electronic Business Communications Company (EBCC), and his old college town is part of his territory. John is driving by the campus on his way to the east side of town, where a number of industrial parks and business campuses have sprouted over the last five years. He believes this area of town holds great sales potential, and he tells his passenger, Matt Block, that he is eager to "press the flesh and sell some EBCC machines."

Matt Block has been a sales manager for ten

years and is respected and liked by his sales reps. One of the reasons his people like him is his management style. He rarely tells his reps how to run their territories unless they are in trouble or ask for his advice.

Matt hired John and likes his enthusiasm, but over the last few months he has become concerned with John's performance. His sales are not rising as quickly as those of other new EBCC salespeople. Matt understands that new reps often have problems, but experience has taught him that new reps should begin to show substantial signs of improvement by their sixth month in their sales territories. Because John is still finding it difficult to make sales in his eighth month, Matt is going along on his calls today to try to find out why.

Matt: Where are we headed?

John: We're going over to the east side of town. That's where the growth seems to be happening. Several new businesses have moved in and a few big companies have started branch offices there.

Matt: What kind of businesses?

John: I'm not really sure. I just remember when I was in college here, my business professors kept talking about this section of town being a booming area, so I thought we should make sure that EBCC is in on the ground floor.
[They enter the east side of town and quickly come upon an industrial park.]

John: Look over there, Matt. Marshall Company. I think I've heard of that company before. Don't they sell insurance or some type of financial service?

Matt: I really don't know. Can't say that I've heard of them.

John: Well, if they do, they sure can use some EBCC machines.
[John pulls the car into the parking lot and both men get out. John carries a briefcase containing his selling aids. They enter the building and approach the receptionist.]

Receptionist: Good morning. May I help you?

John: Yes, we're here to see the person who handles the ordering of electronic office equipment.

Receptionist: I'm not sure who that is. Do you know the name?

John: No, I don't. Do you think you could call someone to find out who it is?

Receptionist: *(Looking annoyed)* Let me see.
[The receptionist picks up the phone and dials a number. After explaining to the person on the other end of the line what John wants, she waits a moment, thanks the person, and hangs up.]

Receptionist: You want to go to Personnel. Go down the hallway and make the first

right. Then it's the first office on the right.

John: Okay, thanks.
[When John and Matt reach the Personnel Office, they come to the desk of Margaret Page, the front desk secretary.]

Margaret: Yes, sir. What can I do for you?

John: *(Handing his business card to her.)* I would like to see the person who orders your office equipment, please.

Margaret: Do you have an appointment?

John: No, I didn't know that one was required.

Margaret: Mr. Ford sees sales representatives only by appointment.

John: Well, could you just tell him that two representatives from EBCC are here.

Margaret: *(Sounding miffed)* I'm sorry but he is busy now. In fact, his schedule is booked tight all day.

John: All right, would you tell him that we dropped by, and that I'll try another time. Thank you.
[John and Matt leave the building and head to the car. As they get in the car, John turns to Matt.]

John: Well, no luck on the first one. You know, that has happened to me a lot lately. I've been having bad luck getting in to see buyers. Do you have any advice that might help me?

Questions

1. What do you think are John's major problems as a salesperson?

2. Outline a strategy for John in making initial sales call appointments so that he isn't turned away so often.

3. What approach might John use in first meeting and then winning over "gatekeepers" like receptionists and secretaries?

4. What kind of training program do you think EBCC has for new salespeople? What would you suggest that all new EBCC sales trainees be taught in the training program?

Case 11-2

APPROACHING PROSPECTS TO SELL A NEW PRODUCT

By James T. Strong, University of Akron

Don Miller recently took a sales position with Midwest Carpet Distributors selling a new line of area rugs. Midwest Carpet is very excited about the Nedecon line of area rugs because it will give retailers of furniture and floor coverings the opportunity to enter the area rug business with virtually no inventory. This is thought to be a very important selling point because even though both types of retailers have opportunities to sell rugs, they are often reluctant to do so because inventory costs are so high. This is especially true for furniture stores. Many of them shun the rug business because of the high inventory costs and slow turnover. While the profit margins are excellent on rugs, most furniture stores need to keep most of their inventory dollars in furniture and related stock.

The Nedecon line has a number of innovations. For example, the patented computer injection dying system allows the creation of intricate patterns using tufted carpet production technology at very moderate costs compared to the competition's machine-woven rugs. A Nedecon 6-by-9-foot rug retails for $699, while a machine-woven rug sells for twice that amount. Nedecon has decided to sell the rugs through independent carpet distributors, like Midwest Carpet, who stock the rugs and provide second-day delivery to retailers. To become a Nedecon rug dealer, a retailer simply has to buy three rugs (one of each size) and pay $50 for a unique display.

The display is truly eye-catching. It has 2-by-2-foot swatches of all the patterns in the line. Each swatch represents one-quarter of the pattern of the rug. The top of the display is a flat 2-by-2-foot square with perpendicular 8-foot mirrors on two of its sides. By fitting the swatch against the mirrors on the top of the display and looking into the mirrors, one can see the full repeat of the pattern. Consumers can also view the rugs in a professional-looking pattern book attached to the display. Armed with this stunning display and the promise of second-day delivery, retailers can enter the rug business without making a significant inventory commitment.

Don is very excited about the new line and he has already started to telephone accounts in the Toledo area that he feels would be good prospects. One of the first accounts he calls is a moderately high-end furniture store, Thrush's Interiors. The conversation goes like this:

"Hello, this is Don Miller from Midwest Carpets. May I talk to someone about the possibility of Thrush's taking on an area rug line?"

"We don't sell area rugs," answers a nasal voice.

"I see. Well, I have a very beautiful line of area rugs that requires no inventory on your part and guarantees second-day delivery and substantial profit for you." [*For 20 seconds there is dead silence.*]

"Ah, would you be interested in such a line?" stammers Don.

"We don't handle area rugs, please hold," replies the voice. [*After about two minutes, the hold button clicks off and the same voice says: "Thrush Interiors."*]

"Hello, yes, well, if your firm did consider buying rugs, which of your buyers would have responsibility for the purchase?"

"I have no idea," says the voice. "We don't handle rugs."

"Yes, you've made that clear. Would you be so kind as to ask one of your buyers who would have responsibility for rugs?" asks an increasingly frustrated Don.

"Hold please," the voice hisses. After what seems like ten minutes, the voice returns. "Mr. Hestvik said that we don't handle rugs and have no plans to take on a rug line. He said no buyer is assigned to area rugs."

"I see. Thank you," replies Don softly.

Don is really disappointed by the outcome of his phone call. Thrush's would be a perfect account for the Nedecon rug line. If only he could get to talk to the right person!

Don spends the remaining part of the week trying to set up appointments to show the rug line. He is finding it very difficult to get appointments with buyers. When telephoning, he frequently can't get past the receptionist or secretary to speak with a buyer. This is especially frustrating because Don prides himself on being a professional salesperson and believes that scheduling appointments with buyers is time-efficient and demonstrates the salesperson's professionalism. But getting appointments is proving to be far more difficult than he anticipated.

Now it is a week later, and Don is in the neighborhood of the Thrush store. He decides to drop in to see if he was right about Thrush Interiors being an ideal account for the area rugs. He walks in and begins browsing around the store. As he envisions how a Nedecon area rug would look in each display, there is no doubt in his mind that this account would be a natural for the Nedecon rug line. One of Thrush's salespeople walks over, introduces himself, and asks what rooms Don is decorating.

"Oh, I'm not decorating any rooms. My name is Don Miller. I'm with Midwest Floors, and we've got a great new line of area rugs that I was thinking would be a natural for Thrush's. What's really neat about them is that dealers don't need to stock the line because we guarantee second-day delivery. Here, take a look at these patterns." Don hands the pattern book to the salesman.

The salesman looks at the pattern book and after a minute asks, "What's the retail for these rugs?"

"Four hundred and ninety-nine dollars for the four-by-sixes, and eight hundred and ninety-nine for the nine-by-twelves. The rugs are made from tufted carpet using a computerized injection dying technology that creates a product almost as good as a machine-woven rug at half the price," Don explains quickly.

"Hey, that's not bad! Maria, look at these rugs. We could sell these. I've tried to tell our head buyer, Sam Hestvik, to stock area rugs, but he always says he doesn't have any available inventory dollars, and doesn't need another slow-moving line."

"Well, the pictures look nice, Marty, but I wonder what the goods look like," replies Maria, another Thrush salesperson.

"Wait here two minutes, and I'll bring you some samples," says Don as he hustles out to his station wagon. He knows that these two can't buy the line, but after such a long, relatively unsuccessful week, he needs some positive feedback. Anyway, he is interested in whether they think the line is worthwhile.

"Here's a four-by-six and a six-by-nine," says Don as he spreads two rugs out on the floor and begins brushing the pile.

The two Thrush salespeople start to examine the rugs carefully. At one point, Don thinks they are going to rip the rugs up in their intense inspection. They ask a number of questions, which Don feels he answers to their satisfaction, and they seem to be listening as he describes the Nedecon area rug program.

"This would be perfect for us, Maria—no inventory, fifty-six patterns, second-day delivery, reasonable prices, an attractive product. What a great add-on item!" exclaims Marty.

"You're right. Now, how can we convince Hestvik to take it on?" asks Maria.

"He's always interested in add-on sales. He'll go for this. What's he doing now?" asked Marty.

"I think he's working on the inventory."

"Don, let me take your samples in to show him. I'll be right back." Marty hurries into the back offices. Don can't believe his good fortune. One of the salespeople is actually going to sell the line for him! He can't help feeling that he should have gone along to explain the program, but Marty was so impulsive that he disappeared before Don could even suggest it. After five minutes, Marty comes back looking upset.

"That stupid clown. He told me that I should stick to selling and he'll do the buying. I think he's jealous of my interior design degree, so he hates to accept any of my suggestions. I'd be a much better buyer than that no-taste accountant. As usual, he brought up those vases I suggested he buy two years ago that didn't sell very well. He never even looked at the rugs. Sorry, pal, I guess I didn't help you any."

"Marty, you never should have gone in there while he was working on his precious inventory figures," scolds Maria, "You know how grouchy he gets when he learns how much we have in stock."

"That's the irony of it. This program doesn't require any inventory, but Hestvik thinks 'new line—more inventory.' The guy's got a closed mind that won't listen to new ideas."

Don thanks his two new friends, gives them the pattern books that Marty requested he leave, and leaves the store with the strong feeling that selling this line is going to be tougher than he thought.

Questions

1. What do you think of Don Miller's general approach to selling the new line of area rugs? What could he do differently to obtain appointments with buyers?

2. Critique Don's performance in trying to sell the area rugs to Thrush's. What were some positive things that he did? What mistakes did he make? How would you have handled this account?

3. What might Don do now to try to sell the area rugs to Thrush's?

4. What strategies would you advise Don to use in (a) trying to schedule appointments with retail buyers, (b) preparing for the sales call, and (c) approaching prospects for the first time?

Chapter 12

Sales Presentation and Demonstration

*Ours is the country where, in order to sell your product,
you don't so much point out its merits as you first work like
hell to sell yourself.*

LOUIS KRONENBERGER
Company Manners (1954)

"EVEN though my father was a professional salesperson, I didn't realize I wanted to become a salesperson until I took a college summer job as a computer programmer," says Susan Fu, a sales representative with Hewlett-Packard in Baltimore, Maryland. "I was working on a computer science degree and thought I wanted a technical career, but computer programming just doesn't provide many opportunities to meet and work with other people. The following summer, I became a sales assistant with a major computer company and decided to keep this position full time during school breaks and 20 hours per week during the school year for 14 months. This job showed me what sales was all about. I was able to accompany the company's sales representatives on sales calls. I liked the freedom they were given about how to approach their work. I admired how they handled so much responsibility and wished for the same opportunity to be an account team leader. And the best part was that they were out meeting with all kinds of people during the day, rather than sitting in an office with only a computer to talk to!"

With these thoughts in mind, Susan decided to take several business courses in her final year at the University of Maryland. One lecture in a course that year would come to hold special importance for her. She explains: "In a marketing class I took, I remember the lecture about professional selling. Like many people, I thought you had to be a smooth talker and quick on your feet to be a salesperson. But my professor stressed that the best salespeople are first and foremost

Profile

Susan Fu

excellent listeners who are sincerely interested in helping the customer fill a need or solve a problem. That sounded like something I could do well, so, after graduating in 1983 with a B.S. in Computer Science and a minor in Business, I interviewed with several firms for technical sales positions and decided to go with Hewlett-Packard as a staff sales representative."

We quickly learned from Susan that she hardly has a "typical" day or sales call. "Variety is another positive aspect of my job," says Susan. "On any one day, I may be on face-to-face customer calls all day, or hosting customers for a demo at our sales office, attending a trade show to generate leads, or prospecting by phone." In fact, because a typical sale of her products averages about $500,000, there can be a lot of time between sales for Susan. "I may go several months without making a significant sale. To keep myself focused on getting in front of customers, I set interim goals, such as making at least 24 sales calls each month, with half of these on new contacts, and at least two on executives. This way, if I've achieved these objectives without making a sale, I can feel good about this accomplishment and know that I'm spending my time correctly and that a sale will eventually happen because I'm doing the right things."

Besides the considerable financial rewards that Susan enjoys as a successful Hewlett-Packard sales rep, the company makes sure that there's plenty of positive reinforcement in other forms, too. "When a sale has been made and the order brought to the office," says Susan, "we ring a bell for each $50,000 worth of sales so that the entire office knows instantly that an order has been brought in. There are monthly district and quarterly area sales meetings where sales are recognized and profiled, and quarterly awards dinners—spouses invited! ■

SALES PRESENTATION AND DEMONSTRATION: THE PIVOTAL EXCHANGE

We tend to think of a "presentation" as a situation in which there is always a passive person or group of people to whom something is being shown or dis-

The Wheel of Professional Personal Selling

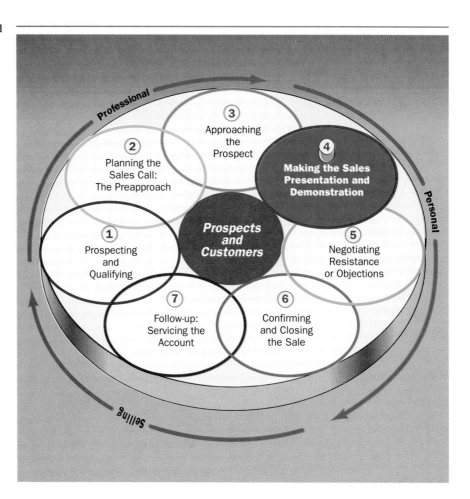

played. However, successful salespeople think of the sales presentation and demonstration as the pivotal exchange between seller and buyer in the sequence of exchanges that make up the selling process. When planning their sales presentation and demonstration strategies, the best salespeople "make room" for buyers' descriptions of problems, needs, ideas, and questions and actively solicit their participation at every phase of the presentation. This approach to personal selling is best exemplified in the *consultative problem-solving strategy,* which will be the major perspective of our discussions in this chapter and the remainder of the book (although we will discuss several other sales presentation strategies as well).

The First Sales Call and the Sales Presentation

In Chapter 11, we discussed planning and preparing for your first sales call with a new prospect. Once you have established initial contact with a prospect, however, when does the "sales call" end and the "sales presentation" begin? The answer to this question depends on the industry in which you're selling and the selling situation itself. If you're a paper company representative trying to dislodge a competitor and the buyer, who may have seen ten other reps that day, gives you exactly five minutes of his or her time, you would be wise to minimize the usual ice-breaking conversation and get right to your presentation—or offer to come back another day. But if you represent a large computer technology company and are trying to convince a prospect corporation that it needs a multimillion-dollar mainframe computer installation, you will no doubt make several sales calls just to gather information from various people within the organization before you feel ready to make a sales presentation to a key decision maker or decision-making committee.

PLANNING THE SALES PRESENTATION

An active, participatory exchange during a sales presentation may become routine once you have established a good relationship with your buyer. But how do you plan for that first, big presentation with a new prospect so that you're not the only one doing the talking? You might start by thinking of sales presentation planning in terms of five basic stages: information gathering, identifying prospect needs, preparing and presenting the sales proposal, confirming the relationship and the sale, and assuring customer satisfaction. Let's take a look at each of these stages.

Information Gathering

Traditional salespeople usually spend only a few perfunctory minutes in small talk after greeting the prospect. Taking for granted that the prospect undoubtedly needs the product, they then launch into a generic, off-the-shelf sales presentation. Today's sophisticated buyers, readily seeing through the self-serving orientation of such salespeople, quickly put up defenses against the sales spiel. Sales-

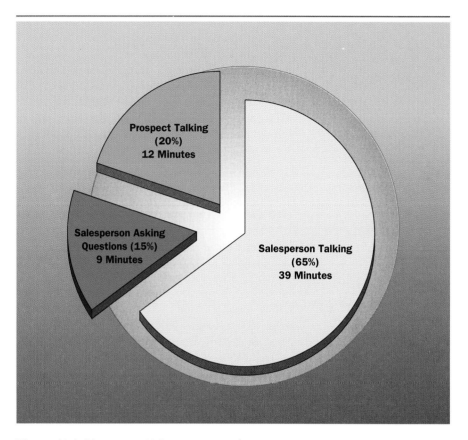

Figure 12-1 Time Spent Talking During a 60-Minute Sales Presentation

people who are obviously concentrating on their own needs instead of the prospect's will seldom succeed in the short run, and probably never in the long run.

Even if you are well prepared, you will walk into most presentations with at least two disadvantages: (1) missing information, and (2) information based on assumptions or opinions. Small talk can be used to gather or verify some of this information while simultaneously sizing up the prospect: What kind of person is this? What kind of mood is he or she in? What communication style should be used? What persuasive appeals might work best? Too much small talk, however, can be detrimental to the sales process. In a recent survey of 432 buyers of business products, 49 percent of the respondents listed "too talkative" as the major fault of salespeople, and 87 percent said salespeople do not ask the right questions about the buyer's needs. "Really listens" topped the list of qualities that buyers found most impressive in good salespeople.[1] Some observers claim that the typical salesperson talks almost 80 percent of the time during a sales presentation, leaving the prospect only about 12 minutes each hour to talk,[2] as illustrated in Figure 12-1. Obviously, the goal of an excellent salesperson would be to trade his or her 39-minute "wedge" of talk time for the 12-minute wedge owned by the prospect in this figure.

[1]*Business Marketing,* December 1989, p. 17.
[2]Estimates from Robert B. Miller and Stephen E. Heiman, *Conceptual Selling* (New York: Warner Books, 1987), p. 65.

Professional salespeople understand that the first step in the sales presentation is to gather all the relevant information they can about prospects and their perceived problems. First, they make sure they're talking to decision makers so neither party's time is wasted. Next, they ask probing questions (review the examples in Chapter 7) to encourage prospects to provide information on perceived problems, objectives, financial situation, needs, and personal feelings. Like a doctor's patients, prospects sometimes know they have a problem, but can only describe its symptoms. In such cases, salespeople may need to play the role of Sherlock Holmes to discover the underlying problems.

Identifying the Prospect's Problems and Needs

Using a consultative, problem-solving approach, the professional salesperson tries to uncover the prospect's perceived problems and needs through skillful questioning and *reactive* listening (discussed in Chapter 7). Note that the emphasis is always on the prospect's perceptions of his or her needs, not the salesperson's. It doesn't matter much what the salesperson thinks he's selling; what really matters is what the prospect thinks she's buying. People and companies buy for their own unique rational and emotional reasons. Until the salesperson uncovers those unique reasons, a sale will seldom take place. Today's professional salespeople spend more time defining client problems and needs than on any other activity in the selling process.

Preparing and Presenting the Sales Proposal

A traditional salesperson makes a standard product-oriented presentation and sales proposal to all prospects, regardless of their individual needs. By contrast, the modern professional salesperson custom-tailors the sales presentation and demonstration to the client's specific business situation, needs, and individual communication style. Wilson Learning Corporation studied the communication styles of 9,857 chemical managers (using the four communication styles discussed in Chapter 7) and found that 41 percent were *analyticals,* 24 percent *drivers,* 19 percent *amiables,* and 15 percent *expressives.*[3] Each sales presentation should match the particular buyer's unique combination of organizational and personal characteristics. Salespeople often must adjust their sales presentation to some particularly challenging prospects, as shown in Figure 12-2.

Whether presenting to consumers or professional buyers, the salesperson should concentrate on the expected benefits and how the prospect can best use the product to achieve those benefits. For sales presentations to business resellers such as distributors, wholesalers, or retailers, the salesperson must also include a marketing strategy showing how to *resell* the product to the customers of these middlemen. Finally, the salesperson must sell the prospect on the value of the product's benefits relative to its price, and the value added in buying this brand from this seller. Both consumers and professional buyers want to maximize the value received for their dollars, so they compare the bundle of product benefits offered by competitive products. **Value added** refers to the extra ben-

VALUE ADDED The extra benefits, from the prospect's perspective, one seller's product offerings have over those of competitors.

[3]As reported in Joel R. Evans and Barry Berman, *Marketing,* 4th ed. (New York: Macmillan, 1990), p. 253.

Today's sales professionals carefully plan and prepare the sales presentation and demonstration to the client's specific business situation, needs, and individual communication style.

efits, from the prospect's perspective, that one seller's product offerings have over those of competitors. Additional value can come from special product features, the brand's reputation for quality, product guarantees, or the seller's unique customer service. For example, Acoustic Imaging Technologies Corporation in Tempe, Arizona, has added value to its diagnostic ultrasound equipment by providing free an automatic one-year warranty extension from the date of any breakdown. Competitors offer only the standard one-year warranty.[4]

Confirming the Relationship and the Sale

In traditional sales negotiations, most of the salesperson's time is spent trying to overcome buyer resistance and attempting to close the sale by prevailing over the "stubborn" customer. Salespeople using this approach see prospects as adversaries or challengers to be hustled into early purchase commitments. Professional salespeople, on the other hand, see their prospects as *business partners,* and try to cultivate a relationship with them based on trust, mutual interests, and cooperation. Only when they fully understand the prospect's needs and believe that they have the best product to satisfy those needs do they attempt to close the sale.

Assuring Customer Satisfaction

Traditional salespeople tend to neglect customer service. Immediately after the sale, their interest, contact, and relationship with the customer fall off rapidly. That is why they have to work at rebuilding rapport with the customer months

[4]*INC.,* October 1989, p. 130.

Skeptical Sid and Sally

Make a very conservative sales presentation. Avoid puffery, stay with the facts. Understate a little, especially in areas where the prospect is very knowledgeable. Provide testimonials and proof of performance, and use demonstrations.

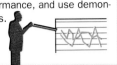

Silent Sam and Sue

To get Silent Sam or Sue to talk, ask questions and be more personal than usual. Get them to tell you about some of their interests, problems, and successes.

Argumentative Arnie and Alice

Do not be drawn into verbal combat with people who like to argue or contradict your statements. Keep your composure and maintain a pleasant countenance while you let them release their emotions and make their points. If you are patient and non-combative, you will usually get the chance to make your presentation.

Paula and Pete Procrastinator

Summarize benefits that will be lost if they don't act quickly. Reassure them that they have the authority and the ability to make decisions. Provide some incentive to act now to help them overcome their indecision.

INCENTIVES:
★ *ACT TODAY-AND YOU WILL RECEIVE*
★ *NEVER PUT OFF NOW WHAT YOU CA*

Gwendolyn and Garfield Grouch

Ask questions to get at any underlying problems or hidden agenda. Try to get them to tell their story.

Edith Ego and Ollie Opinionated

Listen attentively to whatever they say, agree with their views, cater to their wishes, and flatter their egos.

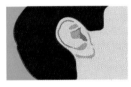

Irma and Irwin Impulsive

Speed up the sales presentation, omit unneeded details, and hit the highpoints. Try to close early if the situation seems right.

Mary and Melvin Methodical

Slow down the sales presentation to adjust your tempo to theirs Provide additional explanations for each key point and include many details.

Teresa and Tim Timid or Carol and Corey Cautious

Talk at a gentle, comfortable, deliberate pace. Use a simple, straightforward, logical presentation. Reassure them on each key point.

Tom and Tina Talkative

Don't allow their continuous "small talk" to permanently derail your sales presentation. Listen politely, but try to get back on track as quickly as possible by saying something like: "By the way, that reminds me that our product has . . ." Then try to wrap up the sales presentation as quickly as you can.

Charlene and Charlie Chip-on-the-Shoulder

Don't argue or become defensive with them. Remain calm, sincere, and friendly. Agree with them as much as you can. Try to show respect for them.

Bick and Betty Busy

For people who seem to have little time, you will need to open with the major customer benefit to generate their interest and perhaps gain more of their time.

FIGURE 12-2 Prospect Categories and Strategy
Source: Adapted from Rolph E. Anderson, Joseph F. Hair, and Alan J. Bush, *Professional Sales Management* (New York: McGraw-Hill, 1988), p. 596.

later, when they make another sales call. Professional salespeople make a commitment to provide full service and assistance to the buyer before, during, and after the sale. They understand that fully satisfying current customers generates repeat sales, referrals to other prospects, and increased sales as customer needs grow.[5]

ADAPTIVE VERSUS CANNED SALES PRESENTATIONS

ADAPTIVE SELLING Any selling method or technique that stresses the adaptation of each sales presentation and demonstration to accommodate each individual prospect.

CANNED SELLING Any highly structured or patterned selling approach.

The opportunity to customize or adapt each presentation to individual prospects differentiates personal selling from every other promotional tool. **Adaptive selling** is the fruit of this opportunity. It stresses the unique advantage skilled salespeople have in being able to adjust their selling behavior to the particular prospect and selling situation.[6] Still, some sales managers, in an effort to improve efficiency while controlling the accuracy and ethics of the sales message, have found structured or **canned selling** to be best for some types of prospects, selling situations, and salespeople.

Salespeople sometimes think of canned and adaptive sales presentations as polar extremes. Believing that the role of the professional salesperson is diminished as the sales presentation takes on more structure, some salespeople protest that "anybody can read a script or play a videocassette." Most salespeople prefer to have wide latitude in deciding what to say and show prospects. When 850 manufacturers' agents were asked to select the factor that was most important in motivating them to do their best work, 86 percent said "being allowed to do the job the way they think it should be done, with minimum supervision and control."[7]

Nevertheless, the best sales presentations often blend the canned and adaptive approaches. In his book *Ed McMahon's Superselling,* Johnny Carson's sidekick, who has sold everything from vegetable slicers and fountain pens on Atlantic City's boardwalk to pots and pans door-to-door to countless products on television, says:

> I believe that perfecting your presentation is probably the most important work you can do now to advance your sales career. . . . I learned my routines so thoroughly I could do them in my sleep. I rehearsed my entire sales interview down to each lifted eyebrow and dropped tone. In selling situations after that I could let my mouth run smoothly with minimal attention and use my mind for studying the prospects and planning my next move. Until you can do the same, you're making yourself work under a tremendous handicap. There is only one way you can free your mind to give a professional, order-winning performance: You have to know your lines. That includes not just your basic presentation but the permutations and combinations as well. Without even thinking, you have to be able to adapt your presentations to the buyer and the circumstances under which you're selling. Ques-

Using adaptive selling techniques, skilled salespeople can adjust their sales presentations to each particular prospect and buying situation.

[5]Tony Alessandra and Jim Cathcart, "Non-Manipulative Selling," *Industrial Distribution,* June 1985, p. 49.

[6]Barton Weitz, Harish Sujan, and Mita Sujan, "Knowledge, Motivation, and Adaptive Behavior: A Framework for Improving Selling Effectiveness," *Journal of Marketing,* October 1986, pp. 174–191.

[7]Dick Berry and Ken Abrahansen, "Three Types of Salesmen to Understand and Motivate," *Industrial Marketing Management,* July 1981, pp. 207–218.

tions such as the following should be running through your mind constantly as you work to fit what you say to suit the person you're trying to persuade:

How is this prospect reacting?

Should I speed up or slow down?

Should I get more technical or should I skip the heavy data?

What will get this [prospect] excited about my product?

What's my best close?

Why isn't this [prospect] smiling?[8]

While the debate between the advocates of canned and adaptive sales presentations continues, actual sales presentations are increasingly making use of video- and audiocassettes, slides, transparencies, flip charts, and computer-developed graphics. Many salespeople have found that these tools help them to present introductory and overview information efficiently and effectively, while allowing them to closely observe the prospect's reaction in order to better adapt later parts of the sales presentation to the prospect.

Multimedia or high-tech sales presentations risk coming across as too slick to some prospects. While a highly programmed multimedia presentation may help a salesperson be viewed as a skilled professional by decision makers in a consumer products company, this same presentation may look like orchestrated hucksterism to a group of conservative engineering managers at a public utility. It is essential for the salesperson to know the normal communication method and style of each prospect before developing a sales presentation strategy.

SALES PRESENTATION STRATEGIES

In preparing effective sales presentations to achieve specific objectives, you can use several alternative presentation strategies. As summarized in Table 12-1, these include the stimulus-response, formula, need satisfaction, depth selling, selling to a buyer group, team selling, and the consultative problem-solving approach. All of these strategies can be used alone or in various combinations. Let's briefly discuss each of these seven basic sales presentation strategies.

Stimulus-Response

Stimulus-response strategies call for presenting stimuli (selling points) in such a way as to elicit favorable responses from prospects while leading them toward the sales close. In order to obtain a series of "yes" responses from the prospect while demonstrating the product, the sales rep may ask leading questions like: "Don't you hate to see your plant scrap barrels filled up at the end of each day with products that don't meet specifications and have to be thrown away?" "Wouldn't you like to turn out perfect products every time by using our computerized metal-working lathes in your plant?" This sales presentation technique can be very effective for novice salespeople talking to relatively naive prospects (in fact, it is widely used for training new salespeople), but it may come across as phony and robotlike if rigidly followed. Salespeople who deal with sophisticated

[8]Ed McMahon, *Ed McMahon's Superselling* (Englewood Cliffs, N.J.: Prentice Hall, 1989), pp. 22–26.

TABLE 12-1   Sales Presentation Strategies

STRATEGY	APPROACH	ADVANTAGE OR DISADVANTAGE
Stimulus Response	Salesperson asks a series of positive leading questions.	Prospect gets in the habit of saying "yes" and may respond positively to the close. Can appear manipulative to more sophisticated prospects.
Formula	Salesperson leads the prospect through the mental states of buying (attention, interest, desire, and action).	Prospect is led to purchase action one step at a time, and the prospect participates in the interview. May come across as too mechanical and rehearsed to win prospect's trust and confidence.
Need Satisfaction	Salesperson tries to find dominant buying needs; causes prospect to see the need through questions or image-producing words.	Salesperson listens and responds to the prospect while "leading" the prospect to buy; the salesperson learns dominant buyer needs and motivations. Salesperson must not overlook latent needs of prospect that are not articulated.
Depth Selling	Salesperson employs a combination of several sales presentation methods.	A customized mix of the best elements of all of the strategies that can realize most of their advantages. Depth selling requires exceptional salesperson skill and experience.
Selling to a Buyer Group	Salesperson makes the sales presentation to a group of decision makers from different areas, e.g., purchasing, engineering, finance, and production.	Allows the salesperson to reach all buying center decision makers simultaneously. Difficulty sometimes in satisfying the collective needs of the group plus individual member needs.
Team Selling	Salesperson sells all the features while avoiding intragroup conflicts and promoting harmony. Salesperson must identify and cater to the needs of each interest group.	Team selling involves counterparts from both the buyer and seller organizations interacting and cooperating to find solutions to problems. Salesperson serves as coordinator of the buyer-seller team interactions.
Consultative Problem Solving	Salesperson carefully listens and questions to fully understand the prospect's problems and specific needs, then recommends the best alternative solutions.	By working together to understand and solve customer problems, prospect and salesperson create a trustful, consultative relationship and focus on "win-win" outcome.

buyers should employ the stimulus-response approach only if it can be smoothly incorporated into the product demonstration.

Formula

Formula sales presentation strategies tend to emphasize product features rather than prospect needs, but they do have the advantage of encouraging prospect involvement. *AIDA* is the name of the most commonly used formula. As we briefly discussed in Chapter 11, AIDA tries to move prospects toward a purchase decision by sequential progression through four mental states: *attention, interest, desire,* and *action.* The salesperson must capture the prospect's undivided attention, then arouse the prospect's interest by describing benefits and pointing out advantages, stimulate the prospect's desire for the benefits by offering proof, and finally motivate the prospect to take purchase action.

Need Satisfaction

Need satisfaction strategies avoid talking about the product or service until the sales representative has discovered the prospect's dominant needs or wants. Through skillful questioning, the salesperson encourages prospects to reveal their psychographic makeup (attitudes, interests, opinions, personality, and lifestyle) and needs. Need-satisfaction strategy requires the salesperson to be a patient, perceptive listener and observer of body language in order to fully understand what the prospect is saying and feeling. This approach is most appropriate when the potential purchase involves a significant economic and psychological commitment on the prospect's part. Some dominant needs are latent rather than manifest, and may not be articulated because of embarrassment or guilt. Thus the salesperson has to be able to read between the lines as the prospect describes his or her needs.

Depth Selling

Depth selling is a strategic mix of several sales presentation strategies. For example, a sales representative might start with an overall formula strategy (AIDA) while using probing need-satisfaction questions to discover buying motives, then turn to stimulus-response questions to get the prospect thinking positively about the product, and finally move to the consultative problem-solving strategy to suggest alternative solutions and win the prospect's confidence. It requires a very talented, perceptive, and flexible salesperson to effectively employ the depth-selling presentation strategy.

Selling to a Buyer Group

When the sales rep is dealing with several members of a purchasing committee or a group of people influential in a buying decision, group-selling strategies are necessary. Because each member of the buying team may be interested in a different product characteristic, the salesperson must appeal to the individual buying criteria of each member as well as to group motives. For example, engineers may emphasize structural strength, production people may stress quality and timely delivery, and purchasing agents may focus on price and postpurchase service.

One popular format for group presentations follows this sequence: *prospect problem, product, benefits, evidence, summary,* and *action.* Here's what a basic presentation using this format might look like:

BASIC GROUP PRESENTATION

Problem: Good morning, ladies and gentlemen. I'm delighted to be at Elf Toy Company this morning and to have this chance to talk with you—and to bring you some good news. First, based on my discussions with many of you, it is my understanding that the poor adhesive quality of the glue you're currently using has been a major source of customer complaints and merchandise returns to your retailers. Two of your newest toys are being recalled at a cost of several hundred thousand dollars because the glue is simply not holding. Is that essentially correct? *[Additional discussion of the problem may take place here as members of the prospect group clarify the specific nature of their collective and individual needs. Information gathered at this point can help the salesperson make some adjustments in the focus of the sales presentation.]*

Product: Well, I'm delighted to report that our new product, Fantastic Glue, is the answer to your problem. Fantastic Glue is a revolutionary new adhesive recently developed and tested at our research laboratories, and it will be available next month. I've got a sample of it right here, in the bright blue tube on the table. After four years of intense effort, our research scientists developed this unbelievable product that more than doubles the holding properties of any other industrial-strength glue on the market—and what's more, it sets up twice as fast.

Benefits: Fantastic Glue will completely solve your product adhesion problems, raise customer satisfaction, and enhance your company's reputation for quality products. Your customer complaint department people may become as lonely as the Maytag repairman. At the same time, your company's annual profits will jump by several thousand dollars, not only from increased sales, but because Fantastic Glue's fast-setting properties will make your glueing operations nearly twice as efficient,

saving you hundreds of hours of employee time and labor. Equally important, you may even see an improvement in morale on the production line because your employees will notice the higher-quality product resulting from the use of our adhesive, and they will also appreciate the fact that it dries quickly and gives off no harmful fumes as it dries.

Evidence: Our packaging and shipping department has been using Fantastic Glue for the past three months now, and everybody gives it rave reviews. I know from my personal experience that Fantastic Glue is terrific. I've taken samples home to repair some broken toys and appliances. My husband and kids think I'm brilliant now that I can repair about anything that gets broken. Let me prove it to you. Here's one of the "broken" toys that was returned by one of your unhappy customers. I'll just brush on a little Fantastic Glue, and in one minute it'll be ready to be repackaged and shipped out. *[After doing the demonstration]* Now, isn't that truly fantastic!

Summary: Well, there you have it. You've seen the incredible qualities and benefits yourself. Fantastic Glue will immediately solve your adhesive problems, stop the customer complaints about broken toys, enhance your company's reputation for quality, improve production-line morale, and dramatically improve your company's profits by making your glueing operations more time- and cost-efficient.

Action: I've got some more good news for you. As a special incentive for new buyers to try Fantastic Glue, we're offering a 20 percent discount with a double-your-money-back guarantee. In fact, if you order today, I'll even personally guarantee that Fantastic Glue will be delivered to you by this Thursday so you can start solving those glueing problems as soon as possible. How many gallons do you think you'll need?

Team Selling

INFLUENTIALS People in the buyer organization who strongly influence or actually help make the buying decision.

As organizational buying functions become more centralized and buying committees more expert, team-selling strategies become increasingly important. Team selling is a response to the growing buyer insistence that sellers spend less time pitching products to them and more time helping them solve their problems. Research shows that the average industrial salesperson successfully contacts only three out of every ten buying **influentials**—those people in an organization who strongly influence or actually help make the buying decision—for

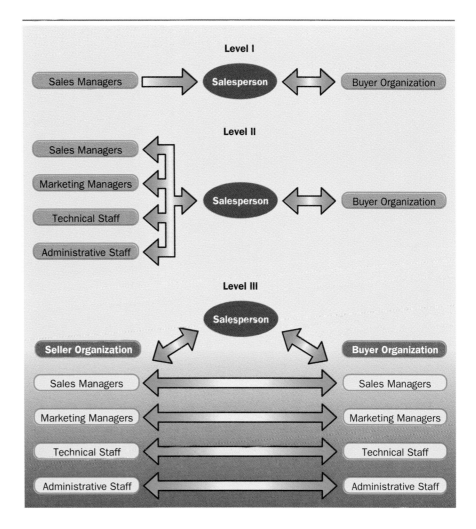

FIGURE 12-3 The Three Levels of Team Selling

reasons that oftentimes are inherent in the buying organization's system.[9] With a team-selling approach, the chances of reaching most members of the buying center are significantly increased.

The Three Levels of Team Selling

Depending on the organization, the customer, and the sales situation, the exact nature of team selling can vary widely. Team selling usually takes place at one of three distinct levels, as illustrated in Figure 12-3.

■ At the first level, team selling simply means that the field salesperson is supported closely by the sales manager, the district manager, and perhaps the national sales manager.

---

[9]"The 'Short Reach' of Salespeople," *Sales & Marketing Management,* July 2, 1984, pp. 24–26.

■ At a second level, the salesperson's field efforts are closely integrated with the customer-oriented efforts of other departments in his or her company. The salesperson serves as a coordinator of all the company's activities that affect the customer organization and constantly asks the question: Where can I find the best resources to help solve a specific customer need or problem?

■ At the third and highest level, all of the seller team members, including sales, marketing, technical, and administrative staff, work directly with their counterparts in the buyer organization. From the presidents of the two companies on down, there are open lines of communication, interaction, and cooperation between matched counterparts in the seller and buyer organizations. While the salesperson acts as the team coordinator and main contact person for both the buyer and the seller teams, counterparts from the buyer and seller teams are allowed to interact directly with each other.

Preparing for Team Selling

In preparing for a team sales presentation, members of the sales team pool their ideas on what they think will be the most important prospect problems and needs to address during the sales presentation. Team members must agree on a primary sales objective and give the team leader (usually the salesperson) authority to shift to a secondary or backup objective if necessary. Finally, they should decide what basic role or area of expertise each will handle in terms of asking and answering questions.

Steelcase, Inc., an office furniture manufacturer based in Grand Rapids, Michigan, provides a complete headquarters support staff for its national network of franchised dealers (customers) as well as for its salespeople. Steelcase's manager of sales training program development says: "Many of our sales are quite large—furnishing an entire new office building, for example. Some of our customers are multinational corporations. Servicing them requires the involvement of dozens of people, both inside and outside of our organization, in order to sell and then install a project for them."[10] A typical Steelcase prospect organization includes at least three buying influentials: an *economic buyer* (the purchasing agent), an *aesthetic buyer* (the designer or space planner), and a *functional buyer* (the facility manager). Steelcase requires sales and headquarters support staff specialists in each of the three areas to work with their dealer counterparts. Further illustration of the Steelcase approach to team selling is provided in the next Company Highlight.

Consultative Problem Solving

The most frequently recommended and most successful sales presentation strategy for today's professional salespeople is *consultative problem solving.* A consultative problem-solving sales presentation focuses on the prospect's problems, not the seller's products. It emphasizes the partnership of buyer and seller and stresses "win-win" outcomes in negotiations, which is why most salespeople and customers see it as the best sales presentation method. Consultative problem solving is a completely nonmanipulative approach that involves creative ques-

[10]Jim Rapp, "Team Selling Is Changing the Sales Trainer's Role," A Special Report from *Training,* May 1989, pp. 6–10.

Company Highlight

Introducing a New Product by Team Selling

Before introducing a beautifully designed and engineered new line of office chairs, Steelcase, Inc.'s management was concerned that advertisements in a catalog or trade magazine wouldn't sufficiently convey the line's uniqueness to its national network of franchised dealers or to prospective ultimate customers—purchasers of office equipment at various business organizations. To convince prospective customers to visit a Steelcase dealer showroom for a demonstration, sales presentations were made to selected individuals within each customer organization. Steelcase's sales strategy consisted of two objectives. The first objective was to train dealer salespeople to sell demonstration appointments to prospects. The second objective was to train dealer salespeople to then sell the chairs' benefits to prospects during the appointment. Two half-day training programs were developed by Steelcase's sales training development department. Delivered at each dealer's location, the first half-day

covered making appointments by phone. Programs were presented in the morning so that salespeople could spend the afternoon on the phone making appointments. Once appointments were made, the second half-day session focused on helping dealer salespeople conduct face-to-face sales presentations and demonstrations.

After the training, a dealer rep and a Steelcase rep went to each appointment together, working as a team to "sell" the prospect on a showroom demonstration. And they continued working as a team during the actual showroom sales presentation and demonstration. Results of the team approach were outstanding. The new chair line got off to one of the fastest starts in the company's history.

Source: Adapted from Jim Rapp, "Team Selling Is Changing the Sales Trainer's Role," A Special Report from *Training*, May 1989, pp. 6–10.

tioning and reactive listening in open, two-way communication with customers. Although professional salespeople use consultative problem solving with customers of all types, it is most effective for sellers of complex technical products who seek to establish long-run relationships of trust, confidence, and respect with their customers.

In applying consultative problem-solving strategies, salespeople must make full use of their listening and questioning skills to understand the prospect's problems and discover precise needs. Several face-to-face meetings, telephone calls, in-depth research, and the help of backup technical specialists may be required to prepare a final written proposal that accurately analyzes the prospect's problems and recommends alternative solutions. Contrasted with traditional canned formula presentations, dramatic product demonstrations, or splashy multimedia shows, the consultative problem-solving approach is an effective, straightforward, and uncomplicated selling strategy, as described to the author by one young salesperson in the next Selling in Action box.

Selling in Action

A Consultative Problem-Solving Sales Presentation

I used to think that not having a dazzling sales presentation style worked against me, but no more. Recently, I earned my biggest commission ever, and it was the easiest sales presentation I ever made. Four competing salespeople and I were scheduled to make a sales presentation to a local manufacturer. I'd been up against these four sales reps before, and I knew each of them would make a multimedia, show-biz–type presentation to try to get the business. Recognizing that I didn't have a high-tech sales presentation or the kind of flair to beat them at their game, I decided not to compete in their game at all. Instead, I spent my time trying to learn as much as I could about the prospect's problems. First I went to the library and read about the prospect in various sources that the reference librarian helped me find. Then I talked to several noncompeting salespeople who had done business with the company. Next I got a personal plant tour, arranged by one of the plant supervisors, to see how the prospect's assembly line operates. During the tour, I asked my supervisor friend and the employees I met along the way a bunch of questions. And I wrote down in my little notebook any question that didn't get answered to my satisfaction.

On the day of the sales presentation, I didn't take in any audio-visual aids at all, just my notebook of questions and a couple of pens. After saying hello and shaking hands with the four people (from purchasing, engineering, production, and finance) who were going to hear my presentation, I opened up by asking a question. "I understand you have some problems at your Philadelphia assembly plant. Do you mind giving me your perspectives on the problems?" They each took turns talking. As soon as they all had said everything they wanted in response to that question, I asked another question. And it kept going like that. I'd ask a question and they'd answer it, often providing a lot of interesting information that I wouldn't have known to ask about. After a while, we were talking back and forth like members of the same team working toward the same goals—and come to think of it, we were!

They probably talked 90 percent of the time, which was fine with me because I was taking notes and getting the information I needed. At the end of three hours, I summarized what I thought had been said, and they helped me clarify a few points. Then I said: "I'm confident that we can provide the right products and service to solve your problems, and I'll send you a written proposal within a week." Two weeks after receiving the proposal, one of them called to say that my company had won the contract. They didn't even quibble over price, just told me to move ahead on the contract as fast as possible.

Later, after I got to know the four people who heard my sales presentation quite well, one of them told me that my presentation was the only one that asked for their perspectives on their company's problems. All the other sales reps took up the entire time doing an elaborate "dog-and-pony" show centered on the products they had to sell. As one of the manufacturer's people put it: "They were trying to sell products, you were trying to help us solve our problems."

SALES PRESENTATIONS TO ORGANIZATIONAL PROSPECTS

BUSINESS STRATEGY In sales presentations to organizational prospects, the salesperson's explanation of how the product can profitably be used by the prospect. Also called a "business plan."

When making sales presentations to consumers, the salesperson focuses on illustrating the benefits to be obtained from personal use of the product. But sales presentations to organizational prospects and customers must include a **business strategy** (also called a "business plan") explaining how the product can profitably be resold or used to make other products. Organizational customers must be convinced of the soundness of the overall business strategy before they will buy the product. Because of the importance of purchasing decisions to their success, large organizational customers often ask salespeople to make presentations to a group, including people from purchasing, accounting, production, engineering, marketing, and finance. Before making a sales presentation to a group, the salesperson must answer three basic questions to ensure that the presentation is appropriately tailored for the audience. Then the salesperson must keep in mind seven guidelines for making effective sales presentations to prospect groups, as outlined in Table 12-2.

Alignment of the Sales Presentation

Generally, the more precisely a sales presentation's content and communication style are aligned or matched with the characteristics, desired benefits, and communication style of the audience, the more effective the presentation will be.

Who Is the Prospect Audience?
Top salespeople always identify and confirm their audience before delivering their sales presentations. Some salespeople have been known to make sales

Because of the importance of purchasing decisions to their success, large organizational customers often ask salespeople to make presentations to a group.

TABLE 12-2   Sales Presentation Alignment and Guidelines for Prospect Groups

Alignment of the Sales Presentation	
■ Who is the audience?	■ How do they prefer to communicate?
■ What benefits are they seeking?	
Sales Presentation Guidelines	
■ Begin with an audience-focused statement of purpose.	■ Encourage personal interaction and participation.
■ Translate the product into customer benefits.	■ Show your commitment to customer service.
■ Energize the sales presentation and demonstration.	■ Ask for specific action.
	■ Critique the sales presentation.

presentations focused on highly technical aspects of a product, only to learn later that there were no engineers or technicians in the audience—just marketing and finance people. Unless they know the characteristics and frames of reference of their prospects, even the best sales presenters are unable to communicate persuasively. The audience should be identified before the sales presentation is prepared, and then confirmed at the start of the presentation. Probably the most straightforward way to confirm the audience is to ask a direct question like: "It's my understanding that everyone in the room is an engineer. Is that correct?"

What Benefits Are the Prospects Seeking?
Depending on their type of business or nonprofit activities and the macroenvironment, organizational prospects may have unique problems and needs at different stages in their life cycle. In general, however, the sales presentation should take as its perspective the carrying out of the primary functions of the organization. For example, a sales presentation to retailers and wholesalers needs to explain how they can profitably resell the product, while a sales presentation to industrial firms needs to focus on how the product will improve profitability in producing and marketing other products.

How Do the Prospects Prefer to Communicate?
Find out ahead of time how members of the prospect group communicate with one another so you can prepare and rehearse your sales presentation appropriately. Several questions need to be answered: What special jargon and gestures do the prospects use? How do they normally dress—business suits, sports coats, or blue collars? What beliefs and attitudes underlie their business relationships and decisions? What do they recognize as achievements and why? Do they prefer a formal style or a more relaxed style? How is space (proxemics) handled? Do they favor transparencies, slides, videotapes, printed material, or verbal communication? Do they prefer open, give-and-take discussions?

Group Sales Presentation Guidelines

After aligning the sales presentation content and communication style with the audience, professional salespeople generally follow some basic presentation guidelines.

Begin with an Audience-Focused Statement of Purpose

Many traditional salespeople outline their sales presentations according to the points they want to make to prospects. But the most effective presentations focus on what the audience wants to hear. The opening-purpose statement should clarify the presentation goals and approach. For example:

> Our purpose today is to show you how Roberts Company can help you solve your product quality problems. Our approach will be to demonstrate how we solved similar problems in other industries and companies by presenting four different scenarios. Finally, we have these four goals for this presentation: (1) to illustrate our understanding of your problem, (2) to demonstrate the benefits provided by our new punch press, (3) to show how it will pay for itself within the first year of use, and (4) to explain how we will maintain and service the equipment to ensure that it remains in top working order.

Translate the Product into Prospect Benefits

Prospects are interested in benefits or solutions for their problems, not necessarily the benefits the salesperson thinks he or she is selling. All the pizazzy features and advantages of the product or service will have little impact unless you can hit the prospects' "hot buttons" of desired benefits. The best salespeople realize that they are selling **expected outcomes**—the results the prospect expects from the product, not the results the salesperson *thinks* the prospect expects. If the salesperson hasn't been able to pinpoint earlier the major benefits sought by prospects, sometimes the product demonstration will make it obvious which benefits are most valued by prospects.

EXPECTED OUTCOMES The results the prospect expects from the product, *not* the results the salesperson thinks should be expected.

Energize the Sales Presentation to Make It Memorable

A sad tie can spoil the appearance of a suit, but **SAD TIE** is an acronym that can be a memory aid to salespeople planning how to spice up a sales presentation to buying center members, as summarized in the next vignette.

SAD TIE A memory-aid acronym standing for Statistics, Analogies, Demonstrations, Testimonials, Incidents, and Exhibits—one or all of which the salesperson may use to spice up a sales presentation.

Encourage Interaction and Participation

Nothing develops a relationship faster or better than interpersonal give-and-take discussions. Salespeople can learn more about prospect needs and perceptions through direct discussions than from any market research technique. Some salespeople try to get prospects involved at various points during and after the sales presentation by simply asking: "Are there any questions?" Unfortunately, this nonspecific approach seldom stimulates much response from the audience and does little to strengthen the buyer-seller communication. A better way to obtain prospect participation after completing part of the sales presentation is for the salesperson to ask specific questions such as: "Can you tell me how the system I've shown you might help you in your work?" or "Now, would one large, central workstation or a group of smaller ones best meet your needs?" If no one volunteers to answer even specific questions like these, the salesperson can direct the question in a nonthreatening way to a particular member of the buying group.

While facilitating interaction with and among prospects, you should always avoid being caught in the middle of arguments or conflicts that break out between members of the prospect audience. Refrain from taking sides or making

SAD TIE

Statistics: Business audiences are particularly receptive to the use of a few statistics because they use them to make their own sales pitches to their bosses. Too many numbers, however, can be confusing, so show just enough to make key points. It's best to also show the numbers in a pictorial form such as a pie chart or bar chart.

Analogies, Similes, and Metaphors: Innovative use of analogies, similes, and metaphors can bring special life to sales presentations. Most salespeople will tell you that analogies are an effective way to win people over to your way of thinking. *Analogies* enable prospects to better visualize something complex by relating it to something different but familiar and easier to understand. For instance, talking about a billion dollars is rather vague until you tell people how many miles that many dollars would stretch if laid end to end, or how many $100,000 homes you could buy with it. *Similes* are direct comparisons using the words *like* or *as*. For example: "Our cellular car phone makes you feel like a CEO" or "Ford Taurus. Think of it as the official pace car of the Fortune 500." *Metaphors* imply comparisons between otherwise dissimilar things without using *like* or *as*, often creating a dramatic visual image. For example: "Robust long life almost seems to be something bred into the Mercedes-Benz genes." "Let Cadet software fight your business battles for you!"

Demonstrations: Use actual product demonstrations or simulations to bring benefits to life for the prospect and create a memorable impression. Nothing is more impressive to prospects than seeing, feeling, touching, tasting, or smelling the product benefits. Some salespeople are so confident of their products that they believe "If they try it, they'll buy it."

Testimonials: Support your position with expert testimony. People will be more easily persuaded if you provide testimonial support from a source that the prospect respects. The product testimonial doesn't have to be a direct one, but can be implied: "Did you notice that Phil Donahue uses one of our cordless microphones on his morning television show?" "Do you know that President Bush uses this same model of fishing rod when he goes fly-casting?"

Incidents: Describing an unusual but relevant incident brings a point home and usually makes a lasting impression. For example, if you're selling a new hearing aid, you could relate a specific experience your grandfather had with an early model.

Exhibits: An exhibit is a selling prop that can take many forms. It can be a display at a trade show, the flipchart you're using as you talk, or a model of the product. The purpose of an exhibit is to help the prospect actually *see* (or visualize) your product's features and benefits. Using the hearing aid example again, you could show a display of different devices used by the hard-of-hearing over the years, ranging from the large trumpetlike instruments of yesteryear to today's barely visible miniaturized versions.

judgmental statements while trying to steer the discussion back to the sales presentation agenda.

Show Your Commitment to Customer Service

Most people like people who like them, so it's important to show prospects and customers that you care about them and will be there for them after the sale. Explain your professional selling philosophy to them. Let them know that you want a permanent relationship or partnership with them and that their success is your success. Tell them that you want them to be lifetime customers, not one-time customers, so you are committed to customer satisfaction and service.

Ask for Specific Action

Just as in sales presentations to individual buyers, it is important and necessary for salespeople to seek some kind of commitment from a group of buyers. Although you should try trial closes to win a sale whenever appropriate, you must also be prepared to seek other specific prospect action. Every sales call should include several possible secondary objectives in case a purchase commitment cannot be obtained. Perhaps the prospects can be persuaded to try a small amount of the product on a trial basis or agree to schedule an appointment for another sales presentation to a larger buying committee. By accomplishing at least one or more of their secondary objectives, salespeople learn to view nearly every sales call as a partial success that furthers the prospect-seller relationship and moves closer to future mutually satisfying sales negotiations.

Critique the Sales Presentation

After every group sales presentation, salespeople can prepare for the next one by critiquing the one just finished. If other members of the seller organization attended the sales presentation, they can help the salesperson by offering their insights. For maximum benefit, debriefings should be made both orally and in writing in a positive climate that encourages candor and learning. Feedback and corrective action stimulate learning and lead to improved performance in subsequent sales presentations.[11]

GENERAL GUIDELINES FOR EFFECTIVE SALES PRESENTATIONS

To achieve effective interpersonal communication with consumer or organizational prospects, all salespeople should observe several general guidelines. The ones we will briefly discuss are set forth in Table 12-3 for quick reference.

Look Like a Successful Salesperson

An important part of any sales presentation is the salesperson's personal appearance. Many companies use consultants to conduct seminars for their salespeople on personal grooming, the selection of clothing and accessories, and the use of body language. A few salespeople have been successful despite dressing in bizarre ways, but most professional salespeople make sure that their appearance helps them make sales. What's the best way to dress? The answer, of course,

---

[11]David Severson, "When a Sales Pitch Won't Do," *Training and Development Journal,* June 1985, p. 44–50.

TABLE 12-3   General Guidelines for Effective Sales Presentations

- Look like a successful salesperson.
- Develop rapport early.
- Adjust to the customer's communication style.
- Present the strongest customer benefits and selling points first.
- Establish credibility.
- Involve the customer fully.
- Make the presentation fun.
- Arouse as many of the customer's five senses as possible.
- Combine factual and emotional appeals.
- Look for and use responsive behaviors.
- Help prospects draw the right conclusions.

DRESSING FOR SALES PRESENTATION SUCCESS

Goal: To convey feelings of trust, reliability, confidence, and professionalism to prospects.

Clothes: Wear conservatively cut clothes in muted or neutral colors that make little obvious impression but subliminally speak of power, confidence, and success. Avoid bright hues, intricate patterns, and anything that's trendy or showy. Dark blue is nearly always safe.

Shoes: The effect of the most beautiful business clothes will be quickly diminished by the sight of a pair of unsightly shoes.

Makeup: Saleswomen should wear only moderate makeup unless they represent a cosmetics company and are showing off a new line. If your makeup says: "I'd rather be partying than doing business," getting serious attention from a prospect will be an uphill battle.

Jewelry: Neither salesmen nor saleswomen should wear ostentatious or noisy jewelry that may suggest a preoccupation with appearance.

Briefcase: Choose a conservative, unobtrusive briefcase in dark brown or cordovan. A flat zipper case is a good choice because it makes you look organized and like someone who deals only with important matters. When the case starts to show wear, get a new one.

Business Cards: Choose simple, dignified business cards without gaudy logos or emblems. Always carry them in a special metal or leather business card case to keep them from becoming dirty or dog-eared.

Pens and Pencils: Never ask a customer to sign a $20,000 order with a 50-cent-ballpoint pen. Carry a fine pen and pencil set and always keep them handy so you don't have to fumble to find them.

SOURCE: David Severson, "When a Sales Pitch Won't Do," *Training and Development Journal,* June 1985, pp. 18–19.

---

depends on the prospect, the selling situation, and the product, but the following vignette provides some general advice.

Develop Rapport Early

Call the prospect by name, give quiet, sincere compliments, and be careful about expressing opinions. Perhaps the simplest way to establish rapport is to mention the prospect's name wherever this is appropriate. In the words of television talk show host Dick Cavett: "It's magical. If you can develop the habit of remembering and using the other person's name, you almost don't have to worry about anything else in conversation."[12] Use an appropriate form of address (Mr., Ms., Dr.) until a first-name relationship is established. Ask "How are you this morning, Dr. Clark?" instead of just "How are you this morning?" Be careful not to use the prospect's name too frequently. This may make you seem insincere. In using compliments, it is critical that the salesperson not appear insincere or obsequious. An understated compliment is usually better than one that's too strong. While greeting the prospect, discreetly observe the prospect's office. Is the view from the window especially nice? What kinds of pictures, awards, or degrees are on the walls? Genuine compliments can be made about any number of things, such as an achievement of the prospect or his family, a helpful secretary, new office furniture, an impressive piece of high-tech equipment, the view from the prospect's office, or an attractive flower plant or sculpture. Finally, salespeople should be careful about expressing strong opinions. Some prospects are fiercely

---

[12]Dick Cavett, "The Art of Conversation," *The American Express,* August 1981, pp. 1–4.

loyal to a local sports team, political party, or public figure, and may become angry if the expressed view differs from theirs.

Adjust to the Customer's Communication Style

Try to make the sales presentation in the style that best communicates with the customer. Use words, symbols, gestures, body language, and examples that relate to the prospect's experience and working environment. You may want to review Chapter 7 at this time for specific ideas on communicating with customers.

Present the Strongest Customer Benefits and Selling Points First

First points and last points are most likely to be heard and recalled. Remember that prospects are interested in what the product will do for them. When making presentations to business prospects, you sharply increase your chances for a sale if you offer personal benefits to the buyer as well as to his or her company. Tying personal and company benefits together in sales presentations has proved to be an effective strategy for Compaction Technologies of Portland, Oregon. Salespeople are told to show how much money Compaction's hazardous-waste trash compactor will save a company over the course of a year. More than half of Compaction's prospects give bonuses to employees who suggest ways to cut costs, so purchasing agents who buy the compactor often use Compaction's figures on cost savings to justify earning a personal bonus.[13]

Establish Credibility

People buy from people they trust, so it is essential to establish your honesty and credibility with prospects. By readily admitting obvious weaknesses in the product, everything else you say becomes more believable. Products like Volkswagen automobiles, Avis car rental, and Listerine mouthwash have shown how readily admitting an obvious shortcoming can increase credibility. Listerine did well with the slogan: "The taste you hate twice a day." Most people were already aware of Listerine's unpleasant taste, but openly advertising this fact was an unusual marketing strategy in that it shifted consumers' attention away from the product's medicinal taste and enhanced their belief in its germ-killing benefits.

Involve the Prospect Fully

Encourage specific responses. These will indicate whether or not prospects are understanding the sales presentation and demonstration. For instance, ask individual prospects whether they can fully hear or see a demonstration. While presenting a product's features and benefits, ask what features or benefits the prospect finds most appealing. In sales presentations and product demonstrations,

---

[13]*INC.,* November 1989, p. 150.

salespeople can facilitate the learning process for prospects by using four learning principles:

- *Participation:* Prospects who actively participate in the sales presentation and demonstration retain more information and tend to develop more favorable attitudes toward the product.
- *Association:* Prospects remember new information better if they can connect it to their personal knowledge, past experiences, and frames of reference.
- *Transfer:* Prospects who see the product being used in situations similar to their own can better visualize the benefits they will derive from the product.
- *Insight:* Product demonstrations bring together the facts and figures from the sales presentations into something tangible that often leads to special insights that favorably impress the prospect.[14]

Make the Sales Presentation Fun

Try to express technical ideas in creative ways by painting word pictures. Even technocrats appreciate the imaginative use of words to describe their areas. In the 1980s, creative terms like *corporate raider, hostile takeover, greenmail, white knight, shark repellant,* and *poison pill* brought life and greater understanding to what could otherwise be very complex and dull financial market descriptions.

Don't be afraid to use a little lighthearted humor in the sales presentation to help establish rapport. Gentle humor can be an effective way to get prospects to relax and open up to you. Salespeople skilled at using humor know that people buy from someone they trust, tend to trust someone they like, and usually like someone who makes them laugh. In using humor, however, salespeople must be careful to follow some basic rules:

- *Don't put people down.* Clever put-downs are likely to backfire and make people nervous about being around you. Gentle humor aimed at no group or person except perhaps yourself is safest.
- *Don't tell ethnic jokes.* They are nearly always offensive to someone, and the prospect will think you lack sensitivity. It's best to play it safe by not even using a dialect or accent in telling a joke unless you're very talented and sure you won't offend anyone by using the dialect or accent.
- *Don't make puns.* Even the best ones tend to sound silly and childish, detracting from your professionalism.
- *Don't tell dirty jokes.* Jokes that are raunchy or even risqué tend to offend some people, and will lower their opinion of you.

Arouse as Many of the Prospect's Five Senses as Possible

Use the actual product or a mock-up of it in the sales presentation. If the prospect can see, hear, feel, smell, and taste the product, it will make a much greater impression and remain with the prospect longer. Because many prospects are used to seeing professional-looking reports and computer graphics in their jobs

---

[14]Anthony Alessandra, James Cathcart, and Phillip Wexler, *Selling by Objectives* (Englewood Cliffs, N.J.: Prentice Hall, 1988), p. 206.

TABLE 12-4 Visual Aids

VISUAL AID	ADVANTAGES	DISADVANTAGES
Flipcharts	Flexible, informal, encourage group interaction.	Hard to see by some people in large groups.
Chalkboards	Informal, spontaneous.	Can be messy, cause screeching noises, hard to see by large groups.
Overhead Transparency Projectors	Can be seen by large group, allow lights to be kept on, inexpensive.	Require that equipment be checked out ahead of time, light is dim.
Slides	Professional appearance, good for large audiences, inexpensive to make.	Inflexible, must turn out lights for best effects, slides "become" the presenter, mechanical.
Proposals and Handouts	Prospects don't have to worry about taking notes, shows thorough preparation.	Distracting if given out before the presentation, can be ineffective unless tailored to prospect.
Videotapes	Entertaining, exciting, shows professional effort.	Can be impersonal and too slick, very expensive, video "becomes" the presenter, can be ineffective unless tailored to prospects.
Product Demonstrations	Allow prospects to gain first-hand experience with product.	If the product doesn't work right, the prospect may get turned off; need backup product to avoid this pitfall.

or on television, expectations for audio-visual aids are high, especially among younger prospects, who have grown up with color television, computers, videotapes, stereo music, and full-color magazines and textbooks. Brightly colored bar graphs and pie charts that convert rows of numbers into visual displays help convey an impression of professionalism while increasing prospect interest and understanding of the sales presentation. Remember to make the sales presentation as *visible* as possible because people learn 1 percent through taste, 1.5 percent through touch, 3.5 percent through smell, 11 percent through hearing, and 83 percent through sight. And they retain 10 percent of what they read, 20 percent of what they hear, 20 percent of what they see, and 50 percent of what they see and hear.[15] Table 12-4 lists the advantages and disadvantages of the visual aids most often used in sales presentations.

Combine Factual and Emotional Appeals

Prospects need factual appeals to *justify* switching to a new brand, but they need emotional appeals to *want* to switch. Before making an emotion-based purchase decision, most prospects want to be able to defend their purchase choice with a rational reason. Silver-tongued retail salespeople have often enticed customers to make an emotional decision to buy an expensive product, like a camera, by giving them a rationale like this:

> Think how glad your grown children will be someday when you show these beautiful pictures of them as toddlers. You owe it to your family to get the best camera you can buy to capture and preserve their childhood for them.

[15]Charles C. Wanous, "21 Ways to Finesse a Group Presentation," *Business Marketing*, October 1983, p. 130.

In selling to an industrial customer, a sales representative for an aircraft manufacturer might say something like this to a corporate CEO:

> What's one of the biggest wastes of executive time? Commercial airline travel, where your valuable time is continually being wasted by take-off and landing delays, check-in lines, and waiting for luggage! With your own corporate aircraft, you and your top executives can save hundreds of hours a year of your valuable time. What could benefit your company more? And the privacy and personal convenience afforded by a company airplane will enable you and your executives to work in flight, freshen up, and arrive on time for your important meetings.

Simple *suggestion* is a very powerful selling tool. You can help prospects visualize how it might feel to own the product and enjoy its benefits by a suggestion like this: "Just imagine how impressed your client will be when you turn out beautiful reports like these with the new Olympia desktop publishing system." You can convey the idea of urgency by a suggestion such as: "Don't you think you'd better double the size of your usual order before the price increases?" You can plant a seed of doubt about the competitor's product without directly disparaging it by a suggestion like: "Don't you think your office staff will prefer a laser printer with a proven durability record that can print six pages a minute over an unproven one that can print only four pages a minute and costs almost as much?" Instead of bluntly telling prospects and customers what they should buy, you can soften the approach by making a direct suggestion like: "Based on the experiences of other companies about your size, I'd suggest you buy the heavy-duty photocopier."

Fear can be another valuable tool in sales presentations. Life insurance salespeople frequently use fear to set up a scenario of the devastating economic effect on the family if the breadwinners should die unexpectedly, or the economic damage to a corporation if it should face a huge product liability lawsuit. In most cases, however, mild fear appeals are more effective than strong ones in persuading an individual to buy or do something. People tend to reject or blot out strong fear appeals if they can postpone purchase action. A few years ago, the National Highway Safety Commission tried to encourage automobile drivers to fasten their seatbelts by running television advertisements showing the ghastly specter of death hovering over a terrible highway accident. Subsequent research found this fear appeal was too strong for people to want to remember, so they erased it from their memories. Later advertising switched to a more acceptable approach that emphasized fastening a seat belt around someone you love.

Look for and Use Responsive Behaviors

RESPONSIVE BEHAVIORS Positive verbal and nonverbal feedback from the prospect.

During the sales presentation and demonstration, observe whether the prospect's behavior is responsive or unresponsive. Starting with the opening greeting, **responsive behaviors** include a friendly handshake, buoyant facial expressions and body language, uninhibited sharing of personal feelings, no apparent concern for time, considerable small talk and storytelling, little emphasis on facts and figures, physical proximity, and positive nonverbal feedback. If the prospect seems unresponsive, the salesperson should try to shift the presentation approach or propose coming back at another time.

Is everyone in this buyer group exhibiting "responsive behavior"? How can you tell? What would you do if you were the sales rep making the presentation to this group?

Help Prospects Draw the Right Conclusions

Prospects will not necessarily reach the conclusions you want them to. Conclude the sales presentation and demonstration by giving a summary and interpretation of the facts. While it may sound repetitive, some top presenters follow this advice: "First, tell prospects what you're going to say and show. Then say and show it. Finally, tell them what you said and showed." This approach pulls together the major points of the sales presentation and sets up prospects to follow a course of action they themselves suggested.

What Would You Do?

You are 25 minutes into a planned 40-minute sales presentation on a new specialty chemical to three engineers in a conference room of a large soap manufacturer. During your presentation, you have paused four times to ask if there are any questions, and each time all three engineers have nodded their heads "no." The room is very warm, and you are concerned that you are talking too much and losing your small audience's attention. To revive them, you are thinking about pausing to tell a very funny and relevant, although somewhat risqué, joke, but you are not sure how the three conservative-looking engineers will react.

WRITTEN PRESENTATIONS

Whether used at the time of the verbal sales presentation or mailed as a follow-up after the sales call, a written presentation can be very effective in winning sales. Erisco, Inc., a $15 million New York City company that sells software packages for benefit and health claims programs, uses written presentations to back up its oral sales presentations. Written presentations force salespeople to be very specific about prospect needs and ensure that they do their homework. Putting the sales presentation in writing also enables the prospect to share information with other key decision makers in the company. Typed presentations, usually from 10 to 20 pages long, allow the salesperson to reinforce the material presented orally and to bring in more material, such as detailed financial analyses that cannot be adequately covered in a verbal presentation.

Carefully study the tips for writing effective sales presentations outlined in Table 12-5 and discussed in the following paragraphs.

Tailor Each Written Sales Presentation to the Specific Customer

Let your personality and your desire for a positive relationship come through. Use words and comments and cite incidents that make the prospect know that you're talking directly to him or her. Avoid sending obvious form letters prepared by the home office.

Make the Opening Paragraph of the Presentation Sparkle

The opening paragraph of your proposal is like the headline of a newspaper column or an advertisement. It's most important because its job is to grab attention and motivate the prospective reader. Innovation, creativity, and drama ought to be guidelines in writing this opening paragraph.

Sequence Benefits in the Most Effective Order

To grab the prospect's attention and maintain his or her interest, present major benefits at the beginning and then summarize them at the end. Combine rational and emotional appeals so that the prospect has both a *rationale* and the *desire* to buy your product.

TABLE 12-5 Tips for Written Sales Presentations

■ Tailor each sales presentation to the specific customer.	■ Use a lively and logical format.
■ Make the opening paragraph sparkle.	■ Never disparage competitors.
■ Sequence benefits in the most effective order.	■ Ask for action.
■ Be positive and upbeat.	■ Personalize the proposal with a handwritten note.
■ Use a natural, conversational writing style.	■ Double-check and proofread everything.

Be Positive and Upbeat

Present statements in a positive rather than a negative way. For example, say: "Over 75 percent of our customers express total satisfaction with this exciting new product," instead of: "Only 25 percent of our customers express less than total satisfaction with this exciting new product." Use robust, active verbs and avoid passive indirect phrases. For example, say: "Driving this revolutionary new automobile will convince you that it's the best," instead of: "If you were to drive this revolutionary automobile, you would be convinced that it's the best." Minimize use of tentative words like *maybe, promising, perchance, tentatively, hopeful, perhaps, likely, apt,* and *possible.* Instead of saying: "We hope you will not be disappointed," say: "We're positive that you will be pleased." Use simple, unpretentious words such as *use, gather, meet, talk, happen,* and *begin* instead of *utilize, assemble, convene, converse, transpire,* and *commence.* Remember a favorite rule of many writers: *Less (words) is more.*

Use a Natural, Conversational Style in Writing

A stilted writing style will make the proposal seem contrived, distant, and legalistic. Some prospects do have a very formal communication style themselves, but they are the exception in today's business environment. You should always be careful about overusing a certain word or phrase, and try to include a lively variety in sentence form and length. To test your writing style, read the material aloud to hear how it sounds. Better yet, read it to colleagues to see how it sounds to them.

Use a Lively and Logical Format

Many people become discouraged and lose interest when they see nothing but a continuous flow of words on a page. As a student, how many times have you read a couple of pages of your textbook, then counted how many pages you have left to read? Obviously, in such situations, you are not enjoying your reading. Paragraph headings, charts, graphs, tables, and pictures break up the monotony by giving readers a chance to pause and refresh themselves before continuing to read. They can also help clarify material, add interest, and guide prospects through the narrative.

Never Disparage Competitors

It will only reflect negatively on you, your company, and your products if you belittle competitors. Most salespeople avoid mentioning competitors unless making a beneficial but objective comparison or in response to prospects' questions about competitors.

Ask for Action

Like an in-person sales presentation, a written sales presentation should seek some kind of commitment from the prospect. To schedule a follow-up, in-person sales call, for instance, you could close the letter with a graciously assertive postscript (P.S.) like: "I'll call you Thursday around 10:00 A.M. to get your reaction to the sales proposal and to answer any questions you may have." If possible, however, it is best to try to encourage the prospect to respond to you. For example, you might give the prospect two or three alternative sales proposals covering different product quality, order quantities, prices, and payment plans and include a questionnaire or checklist in the sales letter for the prospect to complete and return. A postage-paid envelope might facilitate the prospect's timely response, but be a little careful about this. Postage-paid cards and envelopes are often used by magazines and sweepstakes houses, and some organizational prospects might think it somehow inappropriate or cheapening to initiate a large-scale buying negotiation by giving them a break on a 25-cent envelope!

Personalize the Proposal with a Handwritten Note

Humanize and personalize your sales letter by including a friendly note in your own handwriting. Even salespeople who don't normally use written presentations should at least write polite follow-up letters to customers after each sales visit to thank them and perhaps review what was covered and agreed to. Because so few salespeople write them, gracious follow-up letters or cards can give salespeople the edge that differentiates them from competitors in opening new accounts or in nuturing relationships with prospects and customers.

FROM THE DESK OF JONATHAN DEVIENNE

Dear Ms. Abraham,

Just a note to thank you for taking the time to speak with me yesterday.

I am delighted that I was able to show you several Hass Electronics products that might help streamline production at Jones & Kirsch Manufacturing.

Although we do have a lunch appointment for next Thursday, I would like to urge you to call me at (405) 365-9472 if you need any other information about my company or products in the meantime.

Best Regards,

Jonathan Devienne

Double-Check and Proofread Everything

When you are trying to win the prospect's confidence, you must pay attention to details—names, addresses, prices, and delivery dates. And make sure that you spell the prospect's name correctly! As I know from my own experience with my first name, *Rolph,* many people have unusual spellings of their first or last names. So unless you double-check the spelling of the prospect's name or company, you may inadvertently send a message that says you aren't very precise in business dealings. This might not hurt sales for a landscaper, but it could lose clients for a public relations firm or advertising agency whose business is "wordsmithing." When you've completed a first draft, put the sales presentation aside for an hour or a day, then review it with a fresh eye. Writers often think they have said something when they haven't actually put it down on paper. Don't be lazy or embarrassed about rewriting the proposal several times. Ernest Hemingway is said to have rewritten every line of his novels at least 20 times. Finally, ask another person to edit your final draft. Even professional writers need editors.[16]

INNOVATIONS IN BUSINESS-TO-BUSINESS SALES PRESENTATIONS

As the costs of personal selling continue to climb, companies are seeking more efficient and effective ways of reaching prospects and making sales presentations. Several options, with different impacts and costs, are evolving. These include national account management, demonstration centers, industrial stores, telemarketing, and mobile sales centers.

National Account Management

NATIONAL ACCOUNT MANAGEMENT Any complete selling system that centralizes and coordinates a company's selling efforts, especially as these are directed at large, centralized buyer accounts.

In response to an organizational buying environment that is becoming increasingly centralized, large seller companies are turning more and more to national account management. Also called "key account management," **national account management** is any complete selling system that centralizes and coordinates a company's selling efforts, especially as these are directed at large, centralized buyer accounts. Westinghouse, AT&T, Union Carbide, Olin, Digital Equipment, Dow Chemical, and Pitney Bowes are among the growing number of companies that have structured their sales force to serve large key accounts. Pitney Bowes' U.S. Business System Division, a producer of mailing, shipping, and copying products, assigns 3,650 salespeople to cover its one million business market customers, as follows:

- ■ 50 national account managers serve its 400 largest customers.
- ■ 100 major account managers call on 1,500 major customers who have centralized procurement.

[16]Based in part on Carol Rose Carey, "Putting Your Pitch in Writing," *INC.,* March 1983, pp. 113–114; and Ed McMahon, *Ed McMahon's Superselling* (Englewood Cliffs, N.J.: Prentice Hall, 1989), pp. 38–39.

■ 3,500 area sales representatives cover all of its other existing and potential customers (approximately one million).

The primary objective of national account management programs is to increase profits from large, complex accounts by becoming their preferred or sole supplier. To accomplish this, a supplier must establish organizational interrelationships across multiple levels, functions, and operating units in both the buying and selling organization. In some industrial firms, the national account manager (NAM) has line authority over a large, dispersed sales and support team. In other firms, the NAM is a single salesperson who sells to and coordinates support for one or two large customers.

International Key Accounts

National or key account management is growing overseas, too, as large retail chains have centralized their purchasing power. In the United Kingdom, ICI Paints has nine national account managers responsible for selling over £100 million worth of Dulux paints to 33 retail reseller customers each year. At Brooke Bond Foods, 24 account managers bring in more than 80 percent of a business worth £360 million. At Birds Eye Wall's, the story is similar—20 national account managers handle between 60 and 70 percent of the turnover. With so much business going through the hands of so few, sellers must carefully select and train national account managers because company success literally depends on them.

Demonstration Centers

Many companies build specially designed demonstration centers where organizational customers can evaluate complex industrial equipment (such as machine tools, telecommunications equipment, and computers) and salespeople can tailor product demonstrations for prospects and customers. Many companies encourage their outside salespeople to "sell a visit" to their demonstration centers, then use inside salespeople to close the sale at the demonstration center. Both outside and inside salespeople earn commissions from the sale.

Industrial Stores

Some companies, usually manufacturers of office equipment, have actually set up retail stores to attract small-business customers whom salespeople simply don't have time to call on. A few years ago, IBM decided that it was unprofitable for its salespeople (called "marketing representatives") to make sales calls on small businesses and consumers whose purchase potential was less than $25,000. For these small buyers, IBM set up retail stores in large cities where customers could come in to see the equipment, hear a sales presentation, and view a live demonstration. Unfortunately, even this industrial store approach turned out to be unprofitable for IBM, so it eventually abandoned the stores to allow major retailers like Sears to handle small buyers.

Telemarketing

Companies that sell to organizations have learned a great deal about telemarketing from companies that sell to consumers. A few years ago, a telemarketer at General Electric received a phone call about an electricity cogeneration system. After qualifying the inquiry, he passed the information along to the company sales engineers. The result? A $100 million sale. Another telemarketer at W. A. H. Taylor, a $7 million industrial distributor in Allentown, Pennsylvania, opened an account with the U.S. Navy. Two years later, without the help of an outside sales-person, the telemarketer received a $134,000 order.[17]

Mobile Sales Centers

In 1982, the U.S. electric utility industry did not buy a single turbine generator for any of its power plants, jeopardizing the very survival of Westinghouse's Orlando, Florida–based Power Generation Commercial Division. To survive, the division refocused its efforts from new unit sales to servicing and modernizing existing turbine engines. A $100 million marketing program, including advertising, direct mail, meetings, and product literature, was launched. In addition, a sales center on wheels was built. This mobile sales center was a tractor trailer with its own diesel generator for electricity, a 17 by 23 foot conference room, and the latest audio-visual equipment. By taking the division's technology to potential customers, the mobile sales center was so successful in marketing the company's new business operations that it opened up several multimillion-dollar negotiations with new and old customers.[18]

More recently, Marriott has begun a program that invites corporate travel executives to step aboard a 48 by 8 foot truck containing a re-creation of a typical room at Marriott "Courtyard," the company's moderately-priced hotel chain. The truck will visit 22 cities in 1990-1991. About six weeks after each stop, a new Courtyard hotel opens in the area.[19]

SELLING THE LONG-TERM RELATIONSHIP

Whether selling to organizations or consumers, *selling the long-term relationship* is proving to be a successful strategy. Don Pokorni, who earns a six-figure income selling commercial and industrial real estate in southern California, explains his sales philosophy this way:

> Most people in my field concentrate on listing properties or selling them. I work the other side of the street, concentrating on human relationships. I meet execu-

[17]Bill Kelley, "Is There Anything That Can't Be Sold by Phone?" *Sales & Marketing Management,* April 1989, pp. 60–64.

[18]Mary Kae Marinac, "Taking a Marketing Program on the Road," *Business Marketing,* October 1986, p. 112.

[19]Rahul Jacob, "Mountain Goes to Mohammed," *Fortune,* July 2, 1990, p. 16.

tives who might not have a current need; I get to know them, their business and their requirements very well. Then, when they have a need, I am the obvious choice to call, since I am able to fill their needs quickly and to their exact specifications. This approach takes more time, but it leads to the best deals and to the most lasting business relationships.[20]

As many industries seek to improve quality and reduce costs, the trend toward closer supplier relationships, longer-term contracts, and fewer suppliers is spreading. At Digital Equipment Corporation (DEC), supplier contracts now average 18 to 36 months, and DEC's goal is product life contracts. At Chevrolet, three-year contracts are already being made, and five-year pacts are being considered.

What these trends tell selling organizations is that selling the long-term relationship is not just another strategy; it is fast becoming the *only* strategy.

SUMMARY

As the pivotal exchange between buyers and sellers, the sales presentation should be based on a carefully developed strategy. Most professional salespeople use the consultative problem-solving strategy, which requires full use of their listening and questioning skills to understand the prospect's problems and needs. Consultative problem solving emphasizes the partnership of buyer and seller, and stresses "win-win" outcomes in negotiations. Whether presenting to an individual or a group, salespeople can improve the effectiveness of their sales presentations by following some basic guidelines for dress, communication style, types of appeals, and presentation format. Finally, as personal selling costs rise, various alternatives in business-to-business sales presentations are evolving, including national account management, demonstration centers, industrial stores, telemarketing, and mobile sales centers.

CHAPTER REVIEW QUESTIONS

1. Why are the sales presentation and demonstration so important in the professional personal selling process?

2. What are the basic steps in planning the sales presentation?

3. In a typical one-hour sales presentation, how is the "talking time" usually divided between the prospect and the salesperson?

4. Explain the difference between adaptive and canned sales presentations.

5. List and briefly describe the seven basic sales presentation strategies. Which one is generally considered best for professional salespeople? Why?

6. What is the consultative problem-solving sales presentation strategy? Give an example of a selling situation where this strategy would be especially appropriate.

7. Why are (a) clothing and accessories and (b) the use of humor important considerations in developing an effective sales presentation?

8. Describe and give an example of each of the following aids for sales presentations: (a) analogies, (b) similes, and (c) metaphors.

[20]Ibid., p. 43.

9. In making presentations to groups, what does the acronym SAD TIE mean?

10. Give some basic guidelines for written sales presentations.

11. What is national account management and how does it work?

TOPICS FOR THOUGHT AND CLASS DISCUSSION

1. Why do you think the consultative problem-solving sales presentation is the most popular strategy with professional salespeople? What are the benefits of this strategy to the prospect or customer?

2. Why do you think most salespeople talk four times as much as the prospect in the typical sales presentation (as shown in Figure 12-1)?

3. Using Figure 12-2, name at least five special prospect categories and describe an appropriate strategy for a sales presentation to each.

4. Do you think an oral or a written sales presentation is more effective for business-to-business selling? Why?

5. Over the next ten years, do you think national account managers will become less or more important in business-to-business selling? Why?

6. Are sales presentations and demonstrations more important for tangible products or for intangible services? Why?

7. In business-to-business selling, which *three* of the following options do you think will prove most beneficial to personal selling over the next 20 years: national account management, demonstration centers, industrial stores, telemarketing, mobile sales centers? How and why?

PROJECTS FOR PERSONAL GROWTH

1. Contact two sales representatives and ask them to identify five information-gathering questions that they most frequently ask prospects.

2. Research the following industries and report on the methods and approaches each uses to sell its products:
   a. Airplane manufacturers
   b. Large mainframe computer manufacturers
   c. Manufacturers of telephone systems

3. Contact three professional sales reps (one who sells to manufacturers, one who sells to resellers, and one who sells to consumers) and ask them how they prepare for a sales presentation and demonstration. Prepare a report on each type of salesperson, including information on such things as preparation methods, dress style, and demonstration techniques.

4. Go to a library and research the subject of "remembering people's names." Report on several suggestions given by different authors to help remember people's (=prospects' and customers') names when you first meet them.

5. With a classmate, take turns playing the role of a publishing company sales rep trying to sell a new textbook to a college professor who might be nicknamed "Skeptical Sid." Then prepare a *written* presentation directed toward the teacher of your personal selling class. Depending on how creative or cooperative your professor is, you may want to ask him or her to play one of the prospect stereotypes presented in Figure 12-2.

6. Assume you are a sales representative for a manufacturer of automatic fire sprinkler systems for commercial buildings. Outline sales presentations using each of the seven basic strategies. For each strategy, create and then describe the individual or group of prospects to whom you're presenting.

KEY TERMS

Value added The extra benefits, from the prospect's perspective, one seller's product offerings have over those of competitors.

Adaptive selling Any selling method or technique that stresses the adaptation of each sales presentation and demonstration to accommodate each individual prospect.

Canned selling Any highly structured or patterned selling approach.

Influentials People in the buyer organization who strongly influence or actually help make the buying decision.

Business strategy In sales presentations to organizational prospects, the salesperson's explanation of how the product can profitably be used by the prospect. Also called a "business plan."

Expected outcomes The results the prospect expects from the product, *not* the results the salesperson thinks should be expected.

SAD TIE A memory-aid acronym standing for Statistics, Analogies, Demonstrations, Testimonials, Incidents, and Exhibits—one or all of which the salesperson may use to spice up a sales presentation.

Responsive behaviors Positive verbal and nonverbal feedback from the prospect.

National account management Any complete selling system that centralizes and coordinates a company's selling efforts, especially as these are directed at large, centralized buyer accounts.

Case 12-1

ANALYZING THE SALES PRESENTATION

By Paul F. Christ, Delaware Valley College

Ron Essinger, a sales representative for Allied Container Company, is sitting in front of the desk of Wil Levers, the head purchasing agent for Streamline Office Equipment Company. Just after Ron finished his 20-minute sales presentation, Mr. Levers's secretary buzzed him for an important phone call. Picking up the phone, Mr. Levers spun his chair around so that his back was to Ron, and he is now deeply engaged in conversation with the person on the other end. While Mr. Levers is talking on the phone, Ron reflects on his sales presentation, and wonders if there is anything else he can do to convince Mr. Levers to purchase his line of shipping containers.

Streamline Office Equipment Company would be a big account to land. Prior to making the sales

call, Ron carefully developed and rehearsed a sales presentation strategy based on his research on Streamline and on information obtained from noncompeting salespeople about Mr. Levers, considered an *analytical* type of personality who is interested only in the lowest price.

Now Ron mulls over how he just covered the five basic objectives of his sales presentation and what he should do when Mr. Levers hangs up the phone. Here are Ron's thoughts on each objective:

1. *Build rapport:* Initially, Mr. Levers acted very low-key and analytical, just as I was told he would. But I got his interest by asking him several nonthreatening questions about his son, who I know is a football player at the University of Missouri. My gentle

probing questions put him in the right frame of mind to respond to my questions and even prompted him to ask a few of his own later.

2. *Uncover problems and perceived needs:* At first, when I asked him to describe some of his major packaging problems, he claimed Streamline didn't have any special packaging problems. I told him how amazing that was and thanked goodness that all my other customers have a lot of packaging problems, or I'd be standing in a bread line somewhere. Hearing that, he laughed, loosened up a little, and admitted that his company occasionally experienced some "minor" problems when Streamline equipment got damaged in customers' warehouses. Mr. Levers elaborated: "Usually the damage is caused by forklift trucks cutting through our heavy-duty cardboard boxes and puncturing our equipment. Although we're really not responsible for damage in the customer's warehouse, our company philosophy is that 'the customer is always right,' so we allow them to return any damaged equipment still in the packing box. Guess it would help if our packing boxes were made of tougher material, but we get a great price on the heavy-duty cardboard boxes."

3. *Learn how satisfied Streamline is with its current supplier:* When I asked how satisfied Streamline is with its current supplier, Mr. Levers said everybody in the company seemed "satisfied," except perhaps the quality control manager who handles customer complaints about equipment. Although he didn't say so, I think Streamline's major supplier is Mega Container because I saw some Mega cardboard box flats outside the warehouse near where I parked my car. Mr. Levers didn't seem interested in even talking about buying our metal containers, even though I told him they would eliminate any problems of equipment damage in shipping or storage, and the price was only about 15 percent higher than for heavy-duty cardboard containers. Anyway, I've already put our product brochure for the metal containers on his desk.

When I asked him if he would consider changing suppliers if we could offer him a lower price for the same-quality product he was buying now, he replied that he would have to see the total sales proposal, not just the price. I'll have to get back to him with a written sales proposal. Maybe I should prepare four different sales proposals, one for each quality of container we sell. That's a lot of work. Bob and Jennifer in Marketing might be free to give me a hand with them.

4. *Demonstrate that Allied Container has the right products to solve Streamline's problems and satisfy its needs:* I gave him several information brochures about our products and carefully pointed out the features and benefits of our four major packaging products. I also stressed that Allied takes great pride in its reputation for customer service and keeping customers satisfied. I told him that our prices are competitive with any supplier in the industry, but—darn it!—I couldn't find our latest price list sheet. I must have left it on the prospect's desk at my first sales call. Oh well, I'll send Mr. Levers our new price sheet when I mail him the written sales proposals next week.

5. *Convince Mr. Levers that he can trust me and Allied Container Company* to deliver quality products at fair prices backed up by excellent service. I showed him a list of other companies we sell to and he seemed impressed. I told him that I will personally service his account once a month and that I always carry a beeper that will allow him to reach me in any emergency.

When I mentioned that our company was spending a lot of money on research to develop new environmentally safe packaging products, I must have hit his "hot button" because his eyes really lit up and he asked several questions about what we were doing. He said that he was chairing a committee on environmental issues for the Purchasing Agent Association and that the PAA was holding a regional conference in three months on the topic of environmental packaging. Mr. Levers is going to present a paper at the conference, and Streamline's vice president of marketing will be a major speaker at the conference. I asked if our company could help him at this meeting, and he gave me some suggestions that I'll follow up on with some of our R&D people.

Maybe I should ask him whether he knows about the union strike that began at Mega yesterday. Of course, I don't want to come off like I'm knocking a competitor.

Just as Ron is mulling over his last thought, Mr. Levers finishes his phone call, spins his chair around to face him, and says: "Now, where were we?"

Questions

1. What should Ron say and do now? How do you think Mr. Levers will react? Why?

2. What do you think about Ron's sales presentation? What could he have done better?

3. What advice would you give Ron for capitalizing on the interest Mr. Levers showed in environmental packaging?

Case 12-2

WHAT MAKES HIM SO SUCCESSFUL?

By Lisa L. Houde, Drexel University

Fiona Sawicki is a new sales representative for Crisham Pharmaceuticals. After graduating near the top of her class with a degree in biology from an Ivy League university, Fiona had interviewed with several companies for a job in research and development before taking a couple of interviews in technical sales—mainly as a lark because her college roommate had challenged her to do it. Surprisingly, the two sales interviews convinced Fiona to switch directions and start her business career in professional selling with Crisham.

After completing an intensive one-month training program, which concentrated mainly on product knowledge but included some training in basic selling techniques, Fiona was assigned to a territory that consisted largely of small private medical practices and hospitals. Fiona did well in training and felt she learned a great deal about the company's products and the proper "steps" in selling. But her first month was disappointingly slow, even though she faithfully followed the same selling steps she had learned in the training program. After Fiona's second slow month, her sales manager suggested that she spend a day traveling with one of the company's rising star sales reps, Dan Clover. Fiona was a little perturbed to be asked to tag along behind another sales rep who had only about a year's more selling experience. And Dan was only 22 years old—her age! She felt she could learn more from a real veteran rep. Fiona also knew that Dan didn't even have a technical degree. Nevertheless, she felt she had to comply with her sales manager's request.

The two young sales representatives meet for breakfast at 7:00 A.M. on Monday of the following week. Dan suggests that Fiona just observe the calls they are going on and hold her comments until the end of the day, when they will sit down together to critique the entire day. The first call is at 8:00 A.M. at a large center-city drugstore pharmacy run by a father-and-son team. As they get out of the car, Fiona is surprised to see Dan remove his suitcoat and roll up his shirtsleeves. She is about to remark that she really doesn't think it's appropriate to be so casual (after all, they are representing a respected company with an image to uphold), but, remembering Dan's re-

quest to watch the day's progression with an open mind, Fiona resists the temptation to say anything.

As they enter the store and head back to the pharmacy department, Fiona notices that neither pharmacist has a white lab coat on and their sleeves are rolled up. Dan and the senior pharmacist head back to his office with Fiona tagging behind. They chat casually about fishing while Fiona stands by silently but impatiently waiting for them to get down to business. "What a waste of time," Fiona thinks to herself as the two men talk on and on about fishing. "Dan probably hasn't memorized the sales presentation that we were taught, so he's trying to sidetrack the conversation to keep from being embarrassed in front of me." While they talk, Fiona glances around the office at all the nature scenes on the walls. Many show the father and son pharmacists, each with a rod and reel wading in mountain streams up to their hips. Fiona feels they are very tranquil scenes, but somewhat monotonous. Even the magazines on the coffee table look alike: *Field and Stream, Wildlife, Hunting and Fishing,* and *Backpacking.* "Boy, I'd hate to be stuck a long time in this room," Fiona thinks. Finally, the two stop chatting and Dan mentions the new drug they should have been discussing the entire time. Dan speaks briefly about the benefits of the new drug and leaves some information. Fiona is dumbfounded. They have been here for 25 minutes and Dan has only talked about their company's products for 5 minutes. And even more amazing, as they are leaving, the senior pharmacist says: "I'll give the new drug a try, Dan, to see how it works. I'll call you with my order by the end of next week."

Their next call is with Dr. Stanley Hafer at a large city hospital on the north side of the city. Fiona notices that Dan rolls down his sleeves and replaces his jacket before entering the hospital. After signing in at the security desk, they are escorted to the doctor's office by the doctor's nurse, Ruth Blair. Fiona is surprised to hear Dan's conversation with the nurse. He speaks to her about Crisham's new product, asks her opinion on some of the company's other products, and even leaves a sample and some product brochures with her. Fiona can't believe that Dan is wasting all this time and energy on the nurse when everyone knows that it is the doctors who make all the decisions. After Dan has spent about 15 minutes with the nurse (while Fiona tries not to act upset), they go in to see Dr. Hafer. They have only a few minutes with the doctor, who is expected in surgery shortly. Fiona is surprised that the doctor asks only a couple of questions about the drug before excusing himself and heading out the door. As he leaves, Dr. Hafer calls back: "Leave your product brochures and a sample with my nurse, Mrs. Blair."

On the way out of the medical office, Dan stops to say good-bye to Mrs. Blair, and Fiona is interested to hear her say: "I'm sure the doctor will give your new drug a try. Why don't you call me next week to check on how we like it?"

The third call of the day is in the same hospital, just down the hall. As they enter the room, Dan greets the nurse by her first name, Sandra. Fiona can't believe how informal Dan is acting with Sandra—telling her jokes and asking about her son's Little League games. Fiona thinks to herself: "How could this guy be one of the company's rising young stars? He wastes time on each call, and he doesn't stick to the selling steps that we were taught in the training program. Matter of fact, he seems to change his style and approach on each call. He isn't consistent or professional!"

The last call of the morning is at Dr. Beverly Pruett's office. After announcing themselves at the receptionist's desk, Dan and Fiona wait quietly in the reception room for about 15 minutes before the nurse asks them to come in. Dan's behavior finally seems to be appropriate because he doesn't say anything other than a polite hello to the nurse. As they enter the doctor's office, Fiona notices that Dan's whole attitude has changed from that exhibited in the previous sales calls. He waits for the doctor to sit before seating himself. He goes through the entire presentation (just the way they were trained to in class). The doctor stops Dan and asks him several difficult questions. Fiona is impressed with Dan's direct, no-nonsense answers. But she is also surprised that Dan doesn't take the opportunity to expand on certain points and bring up other products. Fiona knows that the appointment is supposed to last only 20 minutes, but what harm would it do to take a little extra time? Fiona is startled to realize that Dan has neatly condensed into 20 minutes a presentation that normally takes her 45 minutes. When all points have been covered, Dan concludes the presentation by graciously but directly asking for the order. It is interesting to observe the doctor glance at her watch, think over the information for a few long seconds, then agree to place an order for the new product.

By the end of the day, Fiona is really confused. Dan doesn't use the same selling technique twice. Sometimes he calls the prospect by his or her first name, sometimes not. Sometimes he goes through the entire presentation, sometimes just parts. In certain offices, he seems to spend more time talking about other subjects than the company's products. After certain calls, he comes right out and asks for the order, but after others, he simply thanks the doctor for his or her time. He doesn't seem to be following a prepared script, yet each call seems to get results. Fiona is really unsure what, if anything, she has learned from watching Dan. Perhaps it will be sorted out when they critique the day together now as they head for a nearby coffee shop.

Questions

1. What do you think Dan will tell Fiona about his selling philosophy and use of different sales presentation strategies?

2. Describe in one or two sentences the most important lesson you think Fiona should have learned on her day in the field with Dan.

3. What advice would you offer Fiona to help her sell more successfully in her sales territory?

Chapter 13

Negotiating Sales Resistance and Objections

He who findeth fault meaneth to buy.

THOMAS FULLER, M.D.
Gnomologia (1732)

"I studied liberal arts in college, namely economics and organizational behavior. I did have one marketing class. I'd have to say that, in retrospect, my psychology classes were the most pertinent to what I now do for a living. Selling is all about understanding people and how they think. When you know that, you can better understand how they'll act and what will cause them to buy," says Christine Sanders, a Chicago-based Major Account Representative for the Copy Products Division of Eastman Kodak Company. Like many salespeople who had active academic and social lives while in college, Christine maintains that her extracurricular activities—not her studies—really led her to pursue a sales career.

As a co-chairperson of Northwestern University's Dance Marathon, an annual campus-wide event that raises $100,000 for charity, Christine got her first exciting taste of selling: "My partner and I were in charge of soliciting prizes for the event. We raised a record $30,000 worth of prizes by cold-calling Evanston and Chicago hotels, restaurants, and businesses. I found myself energized by the challenge of persuading organizations to work with us, and I loved the interaction with so many different types of people."

Building upon this early, significant selling experience, as well as on her goal-oriented personality and an intensive nine-week Kodak sales training course, Christine has evolved into a highly skilled, knowledgeable salesperson with a polished, sensitive sales approach. She offers this advice to new salespeople: "The key to a salesperson's success is to know what selling style works best for that individual. My selling style, for example, could be called a 'relationship selling' approach. I strongly believe that 'people buy from people'; consequently, the better I know the person I'm selling to—and the better they know me—the more successful I will be. Trying to copy another successful salesperson's style is rarely effective because chances are it will feel unnatural to another individual. Customers will quickly sense a salesperson's uneasiness. You have to know yourself and apply who you are to every aspect of selling. I'm always amazed to see how many different sales approaches work."

Christine also stresses the importance of viewing customer resistance and objections as a natural, useful part of the selling process. "I've come to realize that objections are your best source of feedback from a prospect or customer because these objections can lead you straight to the buyer's perceived areas of need," she says. Trial closes seem to work best for her in getting to the bottom of sales resistance. Explains Christine: "Trial closes are a must in every selling cycle. If you never trial close a customer, how do you really know where you stand in terms of closing the sale and what the customer's objections may be to your product or company? Basically, you can't lose. If the customer is ready to sign, you've gotten the order. If the customer isn't ready to sign yet, he or she will probably voice some objections, which are actually signals that you are still in the running." Like her whole selling style, Christine's style of handling sales resistance is simple, sincere, and direct. "I want my customers to know that they can trust me and feel comfortable with me because I honestly try to look out for their interests and their companies' best interests when I make my recommendations." ■

Profile

Christine M. Sanders

After reading this chapter, you should understand:

- ☐ The various types of buyer resistance and objections
- ☐ The importance of win-win negotation outcomes
- ☐ Techniques for negotiating resistance and objections
- ☐ The unique aspects of international sales negotiations
- ☐ Business etiquette in other cultures

OBJECTIONS: THE SALESPERSON'S BEST FRIENDS

"Without sales resistance, I wouldn't have a job" is a comment often made by successful salespeople. They understand that if prospects put up no resistance to buying, then the first seller who reached them would make the sale and trained salespeople wouldn't be needed at all. Most professional salespeople appreciate that a certain amount of prospect resistance shows involvement and can be healthy in negotiations between buyers and sellers. Some salespeople even call objections "their best friends" or "rungs on the ladder of selling success" because serious negotiations seldom begin until the prospect's objections surface.

WHAT ARE BUYER RESISTANCE AND OBJECTIONS?

OBJECTION Anything that the prospect or customer says or does that impedes the sales negotiations.

Most buyer resistance consists of objections. An **objection** is anything that the prospect or customer says or does that impedes the sales negotiations. Buyer objections can be both a challenge and an opportunity. Some novice salespeople let initial prospect objections discourage them so much that they all but lose the sale at that point. In reality, however, there is a greater chance for a sale when prospects raise objections. One study found that salespeople had a 10 percent higher success rate when buyers raised objections than when they seemed to have none.[1]

Signs of Interest

Prospect objections are usually positive signs of interest and involvement in the sales presentation. Objections are often indirect ways for prospects to say that they want to know more. Prospects may be saying: "Persuade me or give me more evidence so that I can convince my boss that I've made the right decision." Professional buyers sometimes purposely make negative statements about some aspect of a product in order to elicit more information from the salesperson that they can use later to defend their purchase decisions.

[1]John Franco, "Skills, Coaching, and the Three Questions Sales Managers Ask Most," *Business Marketing*, December 1984, p. 97.

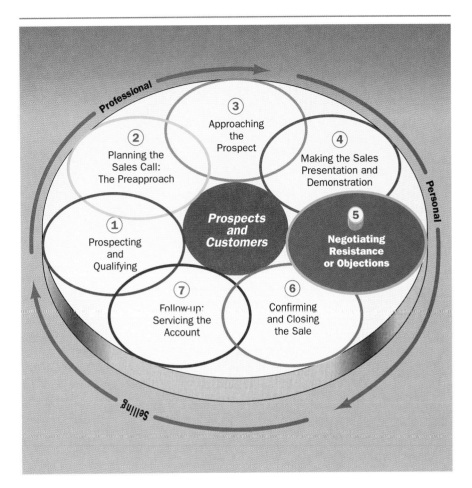

The Wheel of Professional Personal Selling

Nonverbal Resistance

Prospect or customer resistance is part of nearly every negotiation. It doesn't even have to be active. Sometimes a prospect shows resistance by remaining silent or through body language such as shaking his or her head, frowning, glancing at the time frequently, playing with a watch or some desk accessory, reading the mail while the salesperson talks, yawning or exhaling a big breath, or just looking bored, puzzled, or expressionless. When salespeople spot this passive kind of resistance, they must find some way to perk up the presentation and secure the prospect's attention, interest, and involvement. A direct way to accomplish this is to ask the prospect some open-ended questions, such as: What problems are your company's managers most concerned about?

Vague Forms of Resistance

Even the best-prepared, most professional selling negotiations occasionally suffer from misunderstandings or miscommunications that create subtle forms of buyer resistance that are difficult to uncover and eliminate. For example, you may notice during your negotiations that the buyer is showing a hesitancy or caution that is inhibiting your interaction. There are many possible reasons for this. Perhaps the buyer feels somewhat distrustful of you because he or she has noticed that a couple of comments you made in your sales presentation contradicted your company's product literature. Few buyers will come right out and question your integrity, so the best advice to follow when you're up against a vague wall of resistance is *tread carefully*. Use gentle, nudging questions and phrases to try to uncover the reason for the resistance. Here are some examples:

■ "You seem a little uncomfortable with something. Is there anything I've missed or that you'd like me to try to clarify?"
■ "You look like you've got a gently nagging question . . . ?"
■ "You seem a little puzzled by something. Is there any other information I can get for you?"

Types of Objections

VALID OBJECTIONS
Sincere concerns that the prospect needs answered before he or she will be willing to buy.

INVALID OBJECTIONS
Delaying or stalling actions or hidden reasons for not buying.

Objections may be either valid or invalid. **Valid objections** are sincere concerns that the prospect needs answered before he or she will be willing to make the commitment to buy. Once these valid objections are identified, they can be dealt with in a variety of ways that we'll discuss below. **Invalid objections** are delaying or stalling actions or hidden reasons for not buying. Obvious delaying or stalling objections can be recognized by such statements as: "I've got to prepare for a meeting in ten minutes, so I don't have time to talk now," or "Around here, all decisions are shared, so just leave your product literature for us to look over and we'll get back to you if we're interested." The hidden reasons for not buying

Hidden reasons for not buying are often difficult for the prospect to reveal.

that such objections mask are often too personal or embarrassing for the prospect to reveal, which is why they remain unspoken. Some examples:

- "I'm not going to buy from you because I always buy from my old friend Charlie."
- "Your company is too small and unknown for me to be able to justify buying from you to my boss."
- "I don't like your style. You act and sound insincere and patronizing to me."

Uncovering hidden reasons like these is very difficult because the prospect is unlikely to ever admit them to the salesperson. Sometimes the salesperson can learn the prospect's hidden reasons for not buying by cultivating a relationship with a receptionist, secretary, or other employee in the office who knows why the prospect isn't receptive. However, this can be a long-term process that may not be worth the effort, because even when hidden reasons are identified, they may still be major obstacles to the sale.

Uncovering the Prospect's Key Objection

KEY OBJECTION The customer's most important objection.

Determining the customer's most important or **key objection** is one of the salesperson's most difficult and intriguing tasks. Although buyer resistance almost always consists of more than one objection, there is usually one objection that acts like a "keystone" in the buyer's "arch of resistance," as depicted in Figure 13-1. Here the key(stone) objection is the product's styling, though the buyer is also objecting to the price, delivery terms, service contract terms, and lack of accessories. If the sales rep confronting this particular arch of resistance

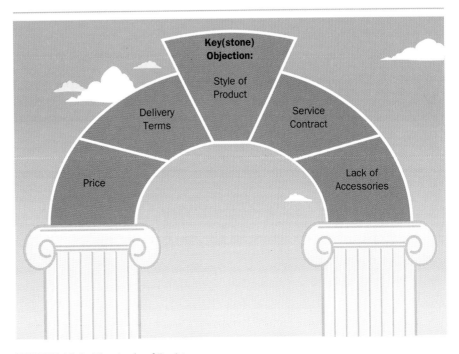

FIGURE 13-1 The Arch of Resistance

can show the buyer an acceptable product style and thus knock out the keystone objection, there's a good possibility that the other objections that make up the arch of resistance will fall quickly thereafter.

How can you uncover a prospect's key objection? One subtle way to start is to engage the prospect in informal conversation before moving into the sales presentation. Encourage the prospect to reveal his or her personal concerns by asking probing questions like:

- "Are there any special benefits you're looking for?"
- "What are your major concerns in purchasing and installing the new equipment?"
- "Are you leaning toward any special kind of equipment or particular features?"

Your successful identification and resolution of the buyer's key objection will give you a powerful opportunity to resolve many or all of the other objections in short order. This is especially true if the key objection is taken care of quickly. In this case, your next statement to the buyer should be: "I'm glad we were able to resolve that problem. Now I'm confident that we'll be able to iron out these other sticking points without much difficulty." A word to the wise, however: Don't be overconfident. It takes a skilled salesperson to identify, "nail down," and resolve the key objection without allowing another, lesser objection to become the new key objection. If the negotiations threaten to take this turn, you might try reminding the buyer that you thought the problem just resolved was the biggest one and that this or that other objection was relatively minor. Otherwise, resign yourself quickly (and as happily as possible) to starting back at square one.

NEGOTIATING RESISTANCE

NEGOTIATION Mutual discussion and arrangement of the terms of a transaction or agreement.

In dealing with prospect or customer objections, the operative word is "negotiation." Several dictionaries define **negotiation** as "mutual discussion and arrangement of the terms of a transaction or agreement." This definition implies mutual understanding and satisfaction between the negotiating parties. In professional personal selling, negotiation does not mean manipulating or outfoxing an opponent in a contest where there is a clear winner and loser. Instead, it means that buyers and sellers work together to reach mutually satisfying agreements and solve problems of shared interest. Thus, both the buyer and the seller come out of the negotiation as winners.

Negotiating Objectives and Strategies

Buyers use negotiations to achieve various objectives, including lower price, higher quality, special services, and concessions on delivery or payment. The best way to negotiate with prospects is to show them a plan that presents the buyer-seller relationship as a creative problem-solving partnership. There are several basic strategies for moving a customer away from a resistance to a problem-solving mentality:

- Focus on issues where you and the prospect have the most agreement. Leave the areas of widest disagreement until last. Reaching amicable agreements on several easier issues sets up a pattern for win-win negotiation and shows the salesperson's interest in working with the customer.

- ■ Take a relatively firm negotiating position initially so that when you compromise, the prospect will feel that he or she negotiated a bargain. This approach also helps you find the lowest combination of price and terms acceptable to the buyer.

- ■ Try to avoid making the first concession except on a minor point. Studies show that the side that makes the first concession usually gets the worst end of the agreement, and that negotiation losers tend to give away too much in each concession.[2]

- ■ Keep track of the issues resolved during the discussions. Use frequent recaps to confirm the progress being made.

- ■ Concentrate on problem-solving approaches that satisfy the needs of both the buyer and the seller.

- ■ Agree to a solution only after it is certain to work for both parties.

- ■ Begin negotiations with your highest expectations in price and terms. Concessions from that point on should be in small increments and in return for something from the other party. A salesperson should carefully consider the relative value of any potential concession from the prospect's perspective.

- ■ Do not allow yourself to be emotionally blackmailed. Remain calm at all times, recognizing that some prospects and customers will use contrived emotion (such as anger) to obtain concessions in negotiations.

Negotiation Outcomes

Every sales negotiation has four possible outcomes. Only one of these four outcomes, *win-win,* will further the business relationship and set the stage for future sales agreements. Figure 13-2 contains a matrix depicting the four sales negotiation outcomes. Let's briefly discuss each of them.

Seller Win–Buyer Win Agreements

WIN-WIN NEGOTIATIONS The kind of negotiation in which both parties feel satisfied with the outcome—the only kind of negotiation that professional salespeople seek!

When both parties feel satisfied with the outcome, you have the basis for a continuing mutually beneficial relationship. **Win-win negotiations** are the only kind that lead to long-run success for salespeople and the only kind that professional salespeople seek. Even in automobile sales, a field that receives more than its share of criticism, Joe Girard, the self-professed "greatest salesperson in the world," stresses that you should never take advantage of a customer. He declares:

> Sixty-five percent of my customers are repeats. That's because I treat them the way they want to be treated. I take care of them because if I treat them right, they'll bring in more customers. . . . Quote a reasonable price, regardless of the customer's savvy. Sooner or later, the customer is going to find out whether or not he got a fair price, so if you want repeat business and a good reputation, treat all customers fairly.[3]

Seller Win–Buyer Lose Agreements

When the salesperson feels good about the agreement but the buyer is dissatisfied, the business relationship is in trouble. A buyer who feels taken advantage of

---

[2]Homer B. Smith, "How to Concede—Strategically," *Sales & Marketing Management,* May 1988, p. 79.
[3]*Philadelphia Inquirer,* July 3 and 4, 1978, p. 12-A, and *US,* January 10, 1978, p. 49.

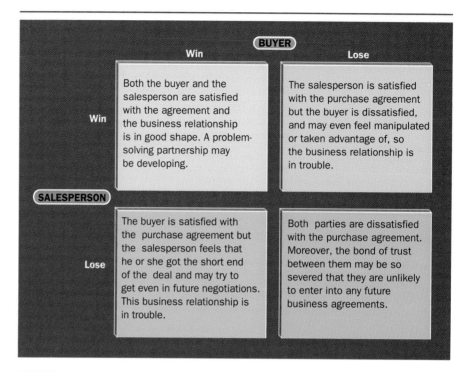

FIGURE 13-2 Sales Negotiation Outcomes

may refuse to have anything more to do with the salesperson or the company he or she represents. Some buyers also feel vindictive and may seek to destroy the salesperson's relationships with other prospects and customers.

Seller Lose–Buyer Win Agreements

Sometimes salespeople offer an extraordinarily low price on a temporary basis in order to win an order from a new customer, reasoning that they'll be able to make up the profit loss on future orders. Unfortunately, an unusually low price or other one-time concession can create expectations on the part of the buyer for similar "super-deals" in the future. And the customer may be angry if they aren't continued. Automobile manufacturers and dealers fell into this trap in the 1980s by offering cash rebates and low interest, or even no-interest, loans on new cars in order to stimulate sales and compete with foreign competition. Whenever they returned to normal pricing strategies, customers were reluctant to buy because they perceived that they were no longer getting a good deal.

Occasionally, a prospect or customer who knows that a salesperson wants his or her business badly will pressure for a "seller lose–buyer win" agreement, thinking erroneously that it will create a long-run advantage. In reality, however, the buyer only temporarily wins the upper hand by squeezing the seller. Sellers can't stay in business by losing on each agreement, so they will find a way to make up the loss from the buyer, perhaps by cutting corners on quality or service.

Seller Lose–Buyer Lose Agreements

An agreement that results in a loss for either the buyer or the seller usually leads to a deteriorating "lose-lose" situation and the eventual end of the relationship.

What Would You Do?

You are negotiating price with a new buyer for a large company that moved into your territory during the last three months. Your strategy is always to start off sales negotiations with a high price so that you have plenty of room to make price concessions as you and the buyer go back and forth over price and terms. You are stunned when this buyer agrees to your opening price quote for a sizable order. You made two sales of about the same quantity last week at a price nearly 20 percent lower. Your commission will be doubled if you make the sale at this high price, but you know that the buyer will be paying too much.

Occasionally, lose-lose agreements can be sustained for a while if both parties somehow believe that they are winning. For example, a shortsighted buyer may force a salesperson eager for new business to accept an unprofitable agreement. In order to make the agreement profitable, however, the salesperson may put the buyer's purchase on a low priority for delivery, neglect to inform him about special discounts, and generally ignore his service pleas. Gradually, both buyer and seller will see this relationship as a lose-lose situation and the buyer will look elsewhere.

In negotiating sales agreements, what it all boils down to is this: *Both buyers and sellers are best off in the long run when they conscientiously strive to reach agreements that are win-win for both.*

Dissatisfaction and Dissonance

A salesperson should not take it for granted that the buyer is satisfied with the deal, even when the salesperson knows that it was a fair one. A recent study conducted by the White House Office of Consumer Affairs found that 96 percent of dissatisfied customers never complain directly to the seller, although 91 percent will never buy from that seller again. And the average unhappy customer will tell another nine people about the perceived raw deal.[4] So it is wise always to ask buyers whether or not they're satisfied with the agreement, and if not, why not. Everything possible should then be done to bring about satisfaction for that customer, to avoid allowing negative publicity to reach the other nine prospects.

POSTPURCHASE DISSONANCE Any concern on the buyer's part that he or she did not do well in the sales transaction.

After the purchase, not only outright buyer dissatisfaction but the mere concern on the part of the buyer that he or she did not do well in the transaction may lead to the anxiety and worry that is called **postpurchase dissonance.** Buyer dissonance is caused by the feeling that another buyer may have gotten a better deal by driving a harder bargain, or that the seller may have cut corners on some

[4]As reported in Robert B. Miller and Stephen E. Heiman, *Conceptual Selling* (New York: Warner Books, 1987), p. 165.

Salespeople can express through their communication styles their win-win frame of mind.

aspect of the contract that wasn't spelled out very clearly. Professional salespeople make it a practice to telephone or visit the customer after successfully negotiating a contract to reassure the buyer about the agreement and the salesperson's desire to further the long-run relationship.

Conveying the Win-Win Attitude

Not only must salespeople negotiate with a win-win attitude, they must convey their sincere belief in fair and mutually satisfying agreements to prospects and customers. They can do this by asking prospects and customers need-clarifying questions, encouraging them to enter into negotiations as full and equal partners, and reassuring them that the focus of the negotiations is on solving their problems, not selling the salesperson's products.

It is also important for salespeople to express through their communication styles that they are operating from a win-win frame of mind. Sometimes speaking too rapidly, too loudly, or too glibly conveys the impression that the salesperson is trying to push something on the prospect. This is why, as we discussed in Chapter 7, it's essential for successful negotiations that salespeople match their communication styles to those of their prospects and communicate with them on an *adult-to-adult* basis.

PLANNING FOR OBJECTIONS

One of the best ways to minimize objections is to learn what the prospect's objections are *before* you begin the sales presentation, and then adapt the sales presentation to cover these points. By doing this, you'll be in a better position to control the negotiations, and thus greatly improve your chances of making the sale. If you can successfully anticipate a prospect's objections, you can prepare evidence, testimonials, and demonstrations for the sales presentation and subsequent negotiations to effectively soften or preempt them. To carry out this strategy, several preliminary steps are necessary. They are discussed in the following paragraphs.

Keep a Running File of the Most Typical Objections

Develop a master list of the prospect objections that come up in your experience and that of other salespeople, and classify them according to type, such as product, price, delivery, installation, service, or company. Include brief descriptions of successful and unsuccessful ways of dealing with each objection.

Determine Whether the Objections Are Valid

As mentioned before, some objections are merely defense mechanisms used by the prospect to stall or slow down the sales process in order to gain some time to think about the purchase. Valid objections, on the other hand, are those concerns that won't go away and will prevent the sale from taking place unless the salesperson can satisfactorily defuse them.

Sell the Prospects on the Benefits

By emphasizing the bundle of benefits that the prospect will derive from the product, the salesperson can overwhelm many objections and push them into the background. Salespeople must remember to cover the intangible benefits as well as the tangible ones. Brand image, expertise and experience in the area, state-of-the-art technology, timely delivery, flexible credit terms, prompt installation, training assistance, and outstanding postpurchase service may be more important to customers than quality or price differences among competing products.

GUIDELINES FOR NEGOTIATING OBJECTIONS

There are several general rules that can help salespeople successfully negotiate prospect and customer objections, as outlined in Table 13-1 and discussed in the following paragraphs.

Don't Be Defensive

Learn to welcome objections because they represent the prospect feedback and involvement that salespeople need to begin closing a sale. In voicing an objection, the prospect is not attacking you or your product, but merely seeking more information.

TABLE 13-1   General Rules for Negotiating Objections

■ Don't be defensive.	■ Don't overanswer.
■ Make sure you understand the objection.	■ Don't be drawn into squabbles.
■ Don't disparage the prospect's objection.	■ Don't fake an answer.
■ Never argue with a prospect.	■ Confirm your answers but don't question
■ Try to lead the prospect to answer his or her own objection.	them.

Make Sure You Understand the Objection

Too many salespeople jump on an objection before the prospect even completes the thought. Interrupting a prospect in midsentence will cause him or her to feel pressured and to move to the defensive. By answering too quickly before you fully hear and understand the objection, you may inadvertently respond to an objection the prospect hasn't thought of—and thereby set up another hurdle you will have to overcome. Always pause for a moment and reflect on exactly what the prospect has said before you attempt to answer the objection.

Don't Disparage the Prospect's Objection

Never allow the prospect to lose face in a negotiation. Treat any objection as an intelligent, rational one so that the prospect's ego is not deflated. A prospect who loses face is usually a lost customer.

Never Argue with a Prospect

Never respond to an objection by saying "no." Begin by appearing to agree. However, don't use the word "but." The "Yes, but . . ." opening is just another way of saying "no." You can't win sales by winning intellectual or rational debates with prospects. You may win the argument on points, but you'll lose the sale.

Try to Lead the Prospect to Answer His or Her Own Objection

By asking leading questions, the salesperson can often enable the prospect to answer the objection raised. Without showing any impatience, sarcasm, or condescension, politely ask the prospect or customer to elaborate on the objection.

Observe how the salesperson in the following dialogue gently leads the prospect past initial objections to the purchase commitment.

> **Prospect:** I don't think these filing cabinets will look right in our contemporary new office. They're too old-fashioned-looking.
>
> **Salesperson:** I think I know what you're saying. What is it that you think makes them look that way to you?
>
> **Prospect:** I think it's the design. Although I guess there aren't too many options in designing a filing cabinet, are there?

Salesperson: You're right. Filing cabinets are usually designed to make maximum use of limited office space. Maybe it's some particular feature, like the handles, that makes them look a little old-fashioned?

Prospect: Yeah, I think that's it. The handles are too bulky looking.

Salesperson: I could probably have those handles changed to something a little more contemporary if you'd like. Looking around now, I'm just realizing how many filing cabinets you have in this office. Some of them are positioned so cleverly and decorated so nicely that you barely notice they're filing cabinets. With all the records your people keep, filing cabinets in here must get a real workout every day. Guess they have to be extra strong.

Prospect: Yes, you know we keep the entire company's records in this office, so we're opening and closing file cabinet drawers all day long. Our file cabinets have to be tough. Hmmmm, the more I think about it, no one really notices filing cabinets after a while. They sort of blend in with the rest of the office, and we can turn them around so that the handles don't show much. I think we'd better stay with traditional file cabinets that have strong handles.

Salesperson: I think you're right. With all the work done in this office, you want filing cabinets that are as strong as possible. And I'll bet your office staff will come up with a lot of ways to make the cabinets fit in beautifully with the rest of the office.

Prospect: You got that right! Within a week, my people will have plants and pictures covering every file cabinet in here. Like you, a lot of people won't even notice how many filing cabinets there are.

Salesperson: Since you're going to need them by the end of the month, I'll go ahead and reserve six new cabinets for you now, if that's okay with you?

Prospect: Good, let's do it!

Another technique for leading the prospect to answer his or her own objection is to "put the shoe (objection) on the other foot." Consider the following conversation:

Prospect (Mr. Zisk): Look, we're not interested in buying any forklift trucks from ACE Equipment. The last ones we bought ten years ago all developed transmission problems within the first year, and we had to get rid of them. So don't waste your time or mine by trying to make a sales pitch. Just don't let the door slam behind you as you go out.

Salesperson: Mr. Zisk, I know how you feel because I heard all about those disastrous transmission problems with the 1981 models when I took this job last year. It really shook up our company. If you were CEO of ACE, what would you have done about the problem?

Prospect: Well, I'd have brought in a brand-new team of engineers to completely redesign all those defective transmissions. That's what I would have done!

Salesperson: Well, Mr. Zisk, you're right on, because that's exactly what our CEO did. We completely redesigned our transmissions, so that now they're rated the best in the industry. The March issue of *Popular Mechanics* called the new ACE transmissions an engineering breakthrough. We're so confident of their quality and durability now that we're offering a twenty-four-month guarantee on every transmission. If an ACE transmission breaks down dur-

> ing the first two years, it's replaced free of charge. It's our no-risk offer to customers who will give us the chance to redeem ourselves.
>
> **Prospect:** Okay, let's hear your proposal. We do plan to buy some new forklifts this quarter.

Instead of trying to defend his company, the salesperson in this dialogue deflected the objection back to the prospect by asking him to assume the role of the ACE Equipment CEO in solving the problem. Then he told the prospect that his advice matched what the CEO actually did, flattering the prospect's ego and softening him up for a sales presentation.

Don't Overanswer

Some salespeople attach too much significance to an objection and try to destroy it in their response. Just answer the objection—don't try to bury it under an avalanche of information. Prospects and customers don't buy because of the salesperson's ability to demolish objections. They buy because they want the benefits from the product. After answering the objection, quickly return to a positive benefit.

Two of the most common mistakes in handling objections are belaboring a single point and rebutting every point a buyer makes. Salespeople who do either of these things are sending the message that they don't think the buyer is very bright. Even if the buyer *is* slow-witted and occasionally wrong, the salesperson must avoid letting him or her feel put down!

Don't Be Drawn into Squabbles

Some objections may simply be unanswerable, either because of the product's limitations or the prospect's personality. No product has all the advantages or can solve everyone's problems. And some prospects will refuse to be convinced no matter how completely the salesperson answers each of their objections. It is counterproductive to spar with such people. Once you've answered an objection as well as you can, go on to another point by saying something like: "I understand your concern, Mr. Fitzgerald. I've given you all the information I have at this time, but I'll get back to you later when I learn more. Now, I'd like to tell you about another benefit that I think you'll be pleased to hear about."

Don't Fake an Answer

If you don't know how to answer an objection, don't try to concoct some seemingly plausible answer. You may jeopardize your long-run credibility with the prospect if it turns out that you're wrong. No prospect expects you to know everything. In fact, many will appreciate you more if you're not a "know-it-all." When you don't know the answer, just tell the prospect that you don't know but that you'll find out and report back as soon as you can.

Confirm Your Answers but Don't Question Them

After answering an objection, it's a good practice to confirm your answer to make sure the prospect was listening or understood you correctly. Say something like: "That's the answer to your problem, isn't it?" or "With that objection covered, we're ready to talk about some more benefits, aren't we?" These types of rhetorical questions are okay since they don't really call for an answer. However, salespeople should avoid making comments like "Have I completely answered your question?" or "I've clarified that point fully, haven't I?" Such questions and the use of definitive adverbs like "completely," "fully," or "entirely" sound arrogant and imply that your brilliant response has prevailed over the prospect's objection. Just to save face, prospects are likely to raise another issue or objection.

PRICE RESISTANCE

PERCEIVED VALUE The value of a product as seen (perceived) by the prospect.

Prospect resistance to price is probably the most common and most difficult objection for most salespeople to deal with, and classic methods for doing so are presented in the following vignette. However, if people bought merely on the basis of price, there would eventually be only one seller left in each product category—the one with the lowest price. Most buyers, in fact, are more concerned about *relative* value for their money than about *absolute* price. Usually, a price objection means that the salesperson has not convinced the buyer of the value of the product in terms of its price. Professional salespeople seldom try to sell on the basis of price; instead, they sell *value*. The prospect determines value—or more accurately, **perceived value**—by mentally dividing perceived benefits by the price, as in this equation:

$$\text{Perceived Value} = \frac{\text{Perceived Benefits}}{\text{Price}}$$

CLASSIC METHODS FOR HANDLING PRICE RESISTANCE

Price resistance can often be handled in one of the following ways:

■ Break the price down into smaller installments over time.
  Example: "It's only 50¢ a day, less than the cost of a cup of coffee at a convenience store."

■ Make price-value comparisons with competitive products.
  Example: "In this magnificent Lexus LS-400, you get all the features of the BMW for $6,000 less."

■ Emphasize its "one-of-a-kind" uniqueness.

  Example: "Sharp's FO-330 fax machine is the only fax available that gives you all these high-tech, high-performance features at this low price."

■ Work down from higher-priced product alternatives to a level that the prospect finds acceptable.
  Example: "You can buy the premier model at $6,300, the champion at $5,400, or the challenger model for $4,200. Which one do you think will best fit your needs?"

The salesperson's essential job, therefore, is to convince the prospect that the value of the perceived benefits to the prospect significantly exceed the product's price.

Value Analysis and Industrial Buyers

When dealing with price resistance, all organizational sales representatives can learn a great deal from their colleagues involved in industrial selling. You saw in Chapter 6 how industrial buyers use strategies like *supplier reduction* and *cost-based procurement* to obtain the highest-quality products at the lowest possible prices. In order to deal specifically with price resistance, the industrial sales representative is always prepared to provide the industrial buyer with a value analysis. Sometimes called "value engineering" or "value assurance," **value analysis** shows how the salesperson's product is the best value for the buyer's (organization's) money. It is usually a printed document that assesses a product's cost as compared to its value and is often presented as part of the sales proposal. Most industrial salespeople spend much of their time trying to provide alternative—better, cheaper, more efficient—products for their customers, and this often involves replacing a competing product. A value analysis is absolutely essential for such competitive situations. There are three basic approaches to the preparation and presentation of a value analysis: (1) unit cost, (2) product cost versus value, and (3) return on investment. Let's briefly examine each of these approaches.

VALUE ANALYSIS Usually a printed document that shows how a product is the best value for the money.

Unit Cost
A value analysis using the unit cost approach simply breaks the costs of the product down into smaller units. If you can show that your product's price per unit is lower than the competing product's price per unit, and that you offer the same or better quality, you will probably make the sale. For example, a large baking company might need a particular kind of detachable bolt that workers use to secure its large bread-cooling trays to stationary racks. These bolts are frequently replaced for safety. Currently, the buyer purchases packages of ten bolts from your competitor for $120, or at $12 per unit. You know that you can beat the competitor's price by selling in larger packages, so you write her a simple value analysis showing how she can obtain packages of 50 high-quality bolts for $500, or $10 per unit, 75 bolts for $630, or $8.40 per unit, and 100 bolts for $700, or $7 per unit.

Product Cost versus Value
For a broader portrait of a product's true value, you could prepare a value analysis that reveals the product's costs over time. Returning to the example above, your competitor is also selling the large bakery a special switch for dough mixers in its central baking facility for $55 per unit. You offer the customer a similar switch for $100. You know that the customer must replace your competitor's switch every three months and you can prove that your switch will last three times as long. Furthermore, you know that the customer uses twelve of these switches in the baking facility at one time. Your value analysis of this situation for an 18-month period might look like this chart:

Total Price: Competitor Switches—12 × $55 = $660		Your Switches— 12 × $100 = $1,200
0 months	$660	$1,200
3 months	$660	—
6 months	$660	—
9 months	$660	$1,200
12 months	$660	—
15 months	$660	—
18 months	$660	$1,200
Total Cost/18 months:	$4,620	$3,600
Total Customer Savings with Your Switches ———→		$1,020

Return on Investment

Finally, all industrial buyers are interested in what percentage of "return on investment" they can expect from the purchase of a particular product. **Return on investment,** abbreviated as ROI, refers to the amount of money expected from an investment over and above the original investment. Because it produces measurable results that can be spoken of in terms of a percentage return, many companies view an industrial purchase as an "investment."

For example, you are now trying to sell the baking company from the examples above a computer inventory and ordering system. After discussions with the buyer(s), foremen, and workers, you and the baking company agree that computerization would save the company at least $5,000 per month in hourly wages paid to workers in charge of the inventory and ordering systems. The monthly cost of your equipment is $4,000, including full customer technical assistance and repair and replacement service. Now you can prepare a simple table to reveal the customer's potential ROI for this arrangement:

Value of Hourly Wages Saved	$5,000 per month
Cost of Equipment	−$4,000 per month
Customer's Cost Savings	$1,000 per month

Return on Investment ($5,000 ÷ $4,000) = 125 percent per month

If your company provides you with ready-made estimates and tables, make sure that you understand them thoroughly before presenting them to the buyer. Whatever value analysis approach you decide to use, you should always encourage customers to make the cost computations themselves, so that they fully accept the results of the analysis.

Whether or not they are engaged in industrial selling specifically, all consultative salespeople should carry out their own value analysis programs on their own products and actively participate with those of their customer organizations. You should be aware that many organizations regularly perform value analysis studies on the products they buy and sell to discover ways to provide their own customers with the same basic product at a lower price, or a better product at the same price. Make time to hone your value analysis skills and make sure your customers know that they are getting true value for their money with your product.

TECHNIQUES FOR NEGOTIATING OBJECTIONS

Prospects may bring up objections for many different reasons. Sometimes a prospect will use an objection as a stalling device or a means to escape gracefully from the sales negotiations. When prospects say they want to think it over or can't afford to buy now, they may be merely trying to cope with their purchase anxiety by delaying a decision. Unless the salesperson can calm the prospect's anxieties by emphasizing benefits to be derived at minimal risk, the sale may be lost. Various methods have been developed and tested to handle prospect objections,[5] as outlined in Table 13-2.

Let's discuss and illustrate the different strategies for negotiating resistance or dealing with objections under five categories: put off, switch focus, offset, denial, and provide proof.

Put-Off Strategies

One type of strategy for handling a prospect's objections might be called "put off" because it requires the salesperson to delay dealing with them.

I'm Coming to That
Although most objections should be answered as soon as they are raised, some should be put off until near the end of the presentation because a premature answer may turn off prospects. "What's the price?" is a question that should be answered later in the sales presentation, after product benefits have been fully discussed. The salesperson can delay giving an exact answer to this question by saying: "I think you'll be pleased by the value you'll receive for your dollars. But, if you don't mind, I'll return to price in just a few minutes because there are three product-service options I need to lay out for your consideration."

Pass Off
Salespeople cannot avoid all objections or criticism of their products. Sometimes the best response to a prospect's objection is to smile and say nothing. For example, a prospect comment like: "My two little kids will probably take this answer phone apart within the first hour unless I hide it under the bed." Here the prospect has stated a problem that he or she can best deal with, unless the salesperson knows some specific way to protect the machine from the prying hands of little children.

Switch Focus Strategies

A second set of strategies for negotiating prospect objections relies on the salesperson's ability to switch the prospect's focus through various tactics.

---

[5]For further explanation of techniques for handling buyer objections, see Alan J. Dubinsky, "A Factor Analytic Study of the Personal Selling Process," *Journal of Personal Selling & Sales Management,* Fall/Winter 1980–81, p. 30.

TABLE 13-2   Techniques for Handling Buyer Objections

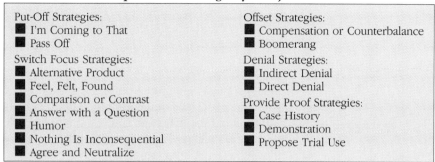

Put-Off Strategies:
- I'm Coming to That
- Pass Off

Switch Focus Strategies:
- Alternative Product
- Feel, Felt, Found
- Comparison or Contrast
- Answer with a Question
- Humor
- Nothing Is Inconsequential
- Agree and Neutralize

Offset Strategies:
- Compensation or Counterbalance
- Boomerang

Denial Strategies:
- Indirect Denial
- Direct Denial

Provide Proof Strategies:
- Case History
- Demonstration
- Propose Trial Use

Alternative Product

Most times the salesperson will have more than one product alternative or model to sell. Each product will have its advantages and disadvantages compared to the others. When an objection is raised about a feature of one product, the salesperson can switch the prospect's focus to another product that doesn't have that objectionable feature.

Feel, Felt, Found

A very versatile technique that enables the salesperson to agree with the prospect's objection, confirm that it's a normal reaction to the product, and then disconfirm the objection over the longer run is called "feel, felt, found." For example, a business prospect may comment: "This computerized lighting system is too complex for me to operate. I'm not a very intuitively mechanical person." In response, the salesperson can say: "I know how you *feel* because I'm not very mechanical myself. In fact, many of my customers *felt* the same way when they first saw all the gauges and buttons on this computerized model, but they soon *found* out that they need to use only three buttons to do everything most people want. The other twelve buttons are just for fine-tuning the three main operations. You'll be amazed how comfortable you'll be with all the buttons in a few weeks, and you'll be happy to have the extra options for the subtle lighting effects and flexibility they provide."

Comparison or Contrast

By comparing the product with another acceptable or unacceptable alternative, salespeople can often dissolve prospect resistance. For instance, a favorable comparison with other alternatives might be made when a business prospect objects to the high price of a computerized credit information service by the salesperson's saying: "A report from a traditional credit bureau costs ten dollars or more per name and may take days to receive, but our on-line service enables you to instantly obtain a complete credit report on any of over four million people in the Delaware Valley area for less than ten cents per name."

Answer with a Question

This is a versatile technique that separates valid objections from invalid ones or allows the salesperson to zero in on the specific reason for buyer resistance. If a potential client says: "I don't think your company has enough expertise or experience in accounting to audit a company the size of ours," the client representative for the accounting firm might reply: "Why do you think we don't have sufficient expertise or experience?" This response forces the prospect away from the generalized resistance to a more specific objection that the rep can more readily deal with.

Humor

Telling a humorous story to ease the tension and defuse an objection can be an effective approach if done skillfully. Not every salesperson can tell a funny story well, but for those who can, humor is a valuable tool. For example, if the prospect says the price is too high, the salesperson might tell a story similar to the one in the vignette on the opposite page.

Nothing Is Inconsequential

Seemingly unimportant comments made under the prospect's breath should not be ignored by salespeople unless no response is the best alternative. For example, a quietly uttered comment like "I don't care much for the color" may seem inconsequential, but the salesperson should not let it pass just because it isn't forcefully stated. The objection may be very important, though the prospect may be reluctant to express it strongly because to do so might seem "silly." In this case, the salesperson might shift the focus by saying: "I didn't care much for the color at first either because I felt it was too drab, but I discovered that it's a very easy color to live with day in and day out."

Agree and Neutralize

For many objections, the salesperson can state some level of agreement, then go on to neutralize the objection. For example, a prospect may say to a salesperson for a contracting firm: "Your firm estimates that it will take nearly twice as long and cost twenty-five percent more to complete this office building than any of your competitors." The salesperson can say: "Yes, you're right. That's because our completion estimates are accurate and our cost projections include the highest-quality materials and the work of skilled professionals. If we build it, you'll never have to tell your commercial tenants about any delays in their move-in

A humorous anecdote can often provide a quick antidote for tension and even sales resistance during the sales interview.

SOQ NOP

The senior regional sales manager from John Deere was wearing an odd tie tack. It was in the shape of a cross. The vertical letters spelled out DEERE, the horizontal SOQ NOP. When asked what the letters stood for, his reply was: "Sell on quality, not on price." He added, "It's my toughest job, in down markets, to make my own people realize that the objective is to sell the benefits, not just resort to price [as the only selling leverage]. I tell them a story. I was going after a sale [for Deere] some years ago. It came down to two final contenders. The fellow making the buy called me in to give me one last chance. His message in a nutshell: 'You're just too high on the price side. No hard feelings, and we hope we can do business with you again in the future.' I was about to walk out the door, unhappy to say the least.

Then I had an inspiration. I turned and said: 'Those are nice-looking boots you've got on.' He was a bit surprised, but said: 'Thanks,' and he went on to talk for a minute or so about those fine boots, what was unique about the leather, why they were practical as well as fine quality. I said to him at the end of his description: 'How come you buy those boots and not just a pair off the shelf in an Army-Navy store?' It must have taken 20 seconds for the grin to spread all the way across his face. 'The sale is yours,' he said, and he got up and came around his desk and gave me a hearty handshake.

Source: Tom Peters and Nancy Austin, *A Passion for Excellence* (New York: Random House, 1985), p. 51.

---

date. And you won't be getting complaints from tenants about the quality of the materials or the work. We do it right the first time. Our way does take a little more time and money initially, but it will save you time and money in the long run."

Offset Strategies

A third set of strategies for dealing with objections uses the technique of offsetting the objection with a benefit.

Compensation or Counterbalance

Counter an objection that cannot be denied by citing an even more important buying benefit. An industrial distributor may complain to a manufacturer's rep: "I'm not sure I want to stock your new Hercules portable industrial vacuum cleaner. What are my customers going to say when they learn that it can only be used for fifteen minutes before it has to be recharged, while the competitive brand, Powerman, can be used for thirty minutes before recharging?" In reply, the salesperson can point out: "You can tell them that's correct, but the competitor's portable vacuum is nearly twice as large and weighs over twice as much as ours, so it's more difficult to carry around a plant floor and harder to stow away. Our studies show that only eight percent of industrial users run a vacuum cleaner for more than fifteen minutes at a time. We decided to make our Hercules comfortable for plant employees to use by keeping it lightweight, while covering over ninety percent of their usage times. I think we made the right trade-off, don't you?"

Boomerang

Turn the objection into a reason for buying, but be careful to avoid making the prospect look simple-minded for raising the objection. In selling anything that has a safety concern associated with it, the boomerang method is a good technique in response to various objections, such as price, design, weight, or size. For instance, a Fortune 500 company CEO who wants to buy a corporate airplane for top executive use might say: "Your aircraft costs fifty thousand dollars more than your competitor's." In response, the salesperson can say: "Yes, and there are obvious reasons for that: construction quality and safety features. Do you and your top executives want to fly in an airplane built by the lowest bidder?"

Denial Strategies

A fourth category of techniques for dealing with prospect objections calls for denying the objection, either indirectly or directly.

Indirect Denial

Using the indirect denial approach, the salesperson agrees with the prospect's objection, but then follows up with a disclaimer. For example, a prospect for a truck manufacturer might say: "I can't take a chance on buying from you because your truck tires have a reputation for poor quality." Using this indirect denial method, the salesperson can answer: "You're absolutely right. We did have a quality control problem in some of our older plants about seven years ago. But now we have state-of-the-art manufacturing equipment and modern quality control procedures in all our plants. For the past three years, our truck tire quality has consistently been among the best in the business, as rated by several independent research laboratories. We've regained nearly all our old customers, and we're anxious to win back your business, too. Let me show you what we have to offer."

Direct Denial

Occasionally, prospects or customers will relate some incorrect information to a salesperson as a reason for not buying. Many rumors, both true and false, tend to circulate about companies or industries, and some can hurt sales badly. In past years, for example, silly rumors have circulated about McDonald's using worms in their hamburgers and about Procter & Gamble's corporate trademark symbolizing a satanic cult. Today a common rumor about a company is that of impending bankruptcy. When a salesperson is confronted with such a rumor, it's usually best to tackle it head-on: "Yes, I've heard that rumor myself, and I can assure you that there's absolutely no truth to it. Our annual report shows our latest accounting audit. A well-known accounting firm gives us a complete bill of health. Would you like me to have a copy sent to you?"

Negative publicity about a salesperson's company or products can make sales calls particularly challenging. Consider the problems of Wang salespeople

Provide Proof Strategies

The fifth category of responses to objections involves providing proof of the qualities of the product by citing a case history, giving a demonstration, or letting the prospect use the product on a trial basis.

Company Highlight

When Bad Publicity Struck at Wang

After Wang Laboratories, Inc., reported a staggering $424.3 million loss and replaced its president, two Boston sales representatives sent customers a letter saying: "We fully expect that you will soon be reading stories in the press reporting the "Amazing Comeback at Wang." Like Audi salespeople when the car was tainted by charges of sudden acceleration, or Exxon dealers in the wake of the *Valdez* oil spill, Wang's salespeople were trying to cope with bad publicity about their company. Salespeople representing troubled companies are in a tough situation: They must respond to prospects' and customers' questions honestly, yet not cause alarm. If they attempt to sugarcoat the situation, they may jeopardize their credibility with prospects and customers over the long run.

Wang's customers are mostly data processing managers who want to be sure that they are buying from stable companies that will be around to solve future problems and upgrade their computer systems. A former Wang sales manager in Indianapolis, who used to earn up to $150,000 a year, believes that his office had all but closed on a $1.5 million image system to pharmaceutical maker Eli Lilly & Company when the story about Wang's finances hit the newspapers. Lilly executives quickly decided that they couldn't take a chance on Wang's survival.

For professional buyers, the selection of an undependable supplier is a career-risking decision, claims the supervisor in the admissions office at Boston University. The university was planning to install a $250,000 system to computerize student applications, and Wang was a major contender for the contract before the publicity about the company's financial condition. Wang was dropped from consideration after the story of its losses broke because the university couldn't be sure that Wang wouldn't be in Chapter 11 bankruptcy within a few months.

After Wang reported huge losses, the first priority for the company's sales force was to make sure that it held on to existing customers. Wang's marketing department quickly provided the sales force with answers to likely prospect questions such as: "How could you not have known you were going to lose $424.3 million?" and "Is Wang still a viable company?"

"It's very important that we exude confidence, even though within the family we know there's a lot of hard work ahead," said Richard Miller, the Lowell, Massachusetts, computer concern's new president, in a video message to salespeople. He also warned the salespeople about negativism. "Our customers watch us for the hidden message," he said. "Look a customer right in the eye and say: 'I'm glad to be at Wang.'"

Source: William M. Bulkeley, "Tough Pitch: Marketing on the Defense," *The Wall Street Journal,* October 18, 1989, p. B1.

Case History

Tell the experience of another satisfied customer. Although the story can be presented in various lengths or dramatizations, the bottom line will be how satisfied other customers are with your company's product. For instance: "Mack Turkey Farms has seen their average bird's weight increase by nearly a pound since they started using our K240 turkey feed last year."

Demonstration

All good salespeople know the advantages and disadvantages of their products versus those of competitors. A demonstration dramatizing these major advantages to the prospect is one of the best ways to overcome various objections. However, salespeople should carefully avoid unfair or deceptive product demonstrations that are merely "surrogate indicators" of a product's benefits.

Propose Trial Use

A good way to deal with many potential objections simultaneously is to propose that the buyer use the product on a trial basis for a short period. Objections to joining book or record clubs and to buying magazine subscriptions, financial newsletters, newspapers, or automobiles are often resolved through free trial use of the product. Even people's fears of new technology have been conquered by trial use of products. A few years ago, Apple Macintosh computer dealers were urging people: "Take a Macintosh out for a test drive. See for yourselves how user-friendly a computer can be." This no-risk trial allowed many people to vanquish their fears of computers before making a commitment to buy.

INTERNATIONAL NEGOTIATIONS

Nearly every American company is interested in increasing international sales. But this is little more than wishful thinking until the company's sales representatives find foreign customers, build trustful relationships with them, and bring

Selling in Action

Creative Handling of an Objection

Duane Mason sells pleasure boats made by several manufacturers to retailers throughout the Midwest. Over 6 feet tall and weighing about 325 pounds, Mr. Mason is an imposing figure. Last year he grossed $400,000 on $8 million in sales. After paying overhead that included $100,000 for entertaining customers, he cleared about $200,000 and was named Manufacturer's Representative of the Year by *Boat and Motor Dealer* magazine.

Like many top salespeople, Mason is creative in dealing with buyer objections. "I walked into one dealer and tried to sell pontoon boats," he remembers. The dealer wasn't buying. "He said that in two years no one had ever come in and asked for a pontoon boat. I said: 'Well, I bet no one has come in for a haircut, either. But I've got a barber pole in my trunk, and I bet if you put it out, within two weeks someone will come in here and ask for a trim.'" Mason sold him a trailerload of four pontoon boats on the spot and has sold him plenty more since.

On the road about two-thirds of the time, Mason covers around 75,000 miles annually. He is constantly dreaming up promotional schemes to help his dealers—and thus himself—sell more, like the time he brought along a man in a gorilla suit to a trade show. Mason's theme: "People go ape about Charger boats."

Source: Fortune, October 26, 1987, p. 134.

the global sales concept to reality. With intensifying global competition, salespeople in the 1990s and beyond will play a major role in helping the United States remain economically strong.

From foreign perspectives, American salespeople usually seem to negotiate with a "winner-take-all" attitude. This attitude sees negotiation as a contest where the objective is to outwit the other side. Europeans, by contrast, always appear to take a win-win approach in negotiations that focus on cooperation and mutual benefits. This is not because they are more principled or generous, but because they understand that such an arrangement is in their own long-run best interests. Foreign negotiators generally believe that a healthy relationship is characterized by trust and shared interests, not by a complex legal contract. Because they place more importance on thoroughly understanding the other negotiators and their perspectives, they like to spend time socializing before transacting business. Socializing provides insights that facilitate the negotiations and improve the relationship.[6]

Concessions

Timing and willingness to make concessions vary greatly from country to country. Soviets and Eastern Europeans are tough negotiators because they are slow to make concessions. They realize that any concession they could make now can also be made next week. In contrast, Americans tend to make concessions quickly when negotiations aren't moving along quickly. Cultures also differ in the importance that negotiators attach to being likable and their desire to create goodwill with their opponent. Soviet and Eastern European negotiators, for instance, do not seem to care about their "popularity" with Westerners, so it is much easier for them to be rigid, inscrutable, and unwilling to reciprocate when the other side makes a concession.

American salespeople negotiating in Japan frequently have been so frustrated by the pace of negotiations that they've made expensive concessions long before the Japanese are even ready to negotiate. Japanese and Middle Eastern negotiators generally build in a great deal of maneuvering room between their opening stance and their planned final position. Initial extreme negotiation stances are part of a strategy that ensures that they will have plenty of room later to make concessions that will not hurt them. Negotiators in other cultures, such as Latin Americans, assume their opponents are overreaching, and that every opening offer or asking price is highly negotiable.

Know Your Negotiating Partner

In foreign negotiations, salespeople must be aware of local customers' traditions, customs, habits, and sensibilities. More than courtesy, this is a matter of practicality to avoid misunderstandings, enhance mutual respect, and increase the chances for success in the negotiations. In some European countries, personal selling must be accomplished unobtrusively because industrial buyers do not like to be seen in public with sales reps. When approaching customers in foreign

[6]Samfrits Le Poole, "Negotiating with Clint Eastwood in Brussels," *Management Review,* October 1989, pp. 58–60.

countries, salespeople must be able to learn and adapt to unfamiliar behavioral rules. Consider the following vignette about appropriate behavior in Japan.

Resistance and Objections

Some caveats and guidelines for negotiating resistance and objections in international settings are discussed in the following paragraphs.

Don't Be in a Hurry

American salespeople usually want to get down to business, believing that "time is money." U.S. sales representatives must fight the temptation to push right to the point and try to close the sale. Asian and South American cultures find our standard American directness offensive.

Understand Time

Salespeople who hope to negotiate business deals in developing nations may need to adjust their attitude toward time. Business appointments are flexible to people in most developing countries. If something comes up that's more important, like a festival or a wedding, then business gets postponed. In Latin countries, it is called the *mañana* (tomorrow) syndrome. In Spain, people move at a leisurely pace. Most offices and shops close for siesta (1:30 to 4:30 P.M.), and restaurants do not usually reopen until after 9 P.M. or get into full swing until 11. However, attitudes toward time may vary within a given country. In São Paulo, Brazil, the pace is much like that of a large city in the United States, while in Rio de Janeiro, business discussions do not begin until considerable socializing and a feeling of *simpatico* (warm empathy and deep understanding) have been established. People in developing countries have a habit of "looping" their conversations with foreigners. They may begin a conversation by talking about the last

---

SELLING IN JAPAN

Sales calls are not taken lightly in Japan. A salesperson should never make a cold call on a Japanese prospect without a formal introduction. If a sales rep doesn't know anyone who can make the introduction, he or she should contact the U.S. office of the Japanese company, call a U.S. federal or state government representative in Tokyo, or hire a consultant.

Relationships in Japan are based largely on trust. Insisting on a written contract will leave a negative impression with most Japanese businesspeople. Be content with sealing the initial deal with a handshake and leave signing a written contract to another meeting. Do not try to ingratiate yourself during a business meeting by using humor. Even though Japanese businesspeople may joke before or after a business meeting, and later in a social setting, their business meetings are always strictly business. Always accept after-hours social invitations but never bring your spouse because the Japanese business executives will not bring theirs. At dinner, wait for the toast before you drink and always keep your neighbor's glass full. Let the Japanese host pick the subjects of conversation. Do not brag about yourself or members of your family during conversation because Japanese etiquette is to be humble, even about your children. To sell successfully in Japan, you must adapt and earn the trust of your Japanese hosts.

Source: "The Delicate Art of Doing Business in Japan," *Business Week*, October 2, 1989, p. 120.

time they saw you or some other chitchat, then move into substantive issues concerning the business at hand—only to switch back abruptly to some social topic.

Continue Gathering Information

Even a well-prepared salesperson doesn't have all the facts before negotiations begin. There is always missing information and "soft" information based on assumptions, opinions, or rumors. Therefore, it is important to use small talk during socializing and the negotiations themselves to obtain valuable information about your foreign prospects and what issues they perceive as most important. Inexperienced salespeople tend to think that small talk at the beginning of negotiations is merely a perfunctory routine, not something truly useful.

Be Comfortable with Silence

Salespeople who try to fill any negotiating vacuum with talk may be making a serious mistake. Japanese, Chinese, and Korean businesspeople use silence as a bargaining weapon when negotiating with Americans. Since most Americans are uncomfortable with long periods of silence, they will often jump in and lower the price, just to get the conversation going again.[7]

Never Be Confrontational or Argumentative

Seldom is anything gained in negotiations by losing your cool or attacking the other party. This is just as true in a foreign country as it is at home. Such behavior makes it clear to the other side that you consider the negotiations a contest, not a shared partnership. Even if you are simply acting belligerent in order to gain a concession, it will be offensive to most foreign negotiators and will seldom contribute to furthering the relationship. To repeat: Always negotiate with a *buyer win–seller win* attitude, and convey that feeling to foreign buyers.

Thoroughly Prepare Before Any Negotiations

Learn about the foreign buyers' culture, religion, ethical standards, and social customs. Most American salespeople are already at a language disadvantage in dealing with foreign prospects and may have to work through an interpreter. They cannot afford to neglect their homework in learning about their foreign prospects. Knowledge is power in any negotiation, but especially in international negotiations.

BUSINESS ETIQUETTE IN OTHER CULTURES

American salespeople need to learn as much as they can about basic cultural etiquette when negotiating in different countries. Avoiding a mistake in business etiquette can often mean the difference between successful and unsuccessful negotiations. Let's discuss some of the basic issues in international business etiquette.

---

[7]*INC.*, January 1990, p. 106.

Business Cards

Japanese businesspeople follow a ritual in exchanging business cards. The salesperson's business card should always be given to the most important person first. When the salesperson is given a card in return, he or she must never merely give it a cursory glance and stuff it in a pocket, as many Americans routinely do. Such behavior is seen as insulting. Japanese always study the person's business card during an introduction, carefully noting company affiliation and rank. In France, business cards are exchanged at the end of the meeting, not at the beginning, and their cards are about four times the size of the American business card.

Eye Contact

Cultural differences even determine what's acceptable with regard to eye contact. Contrary to American culture, constant eye contact is considered impolite in many cultures. After Barbara Walters interviewed Colonel Muammar el-Quaddafi in Libya in the spring of 1989 for the television news program *20/20,* she said: "He wouldn't look me in the eye. I found it disconcerting that he kept looking all over the room but rarely at me." In America, when people won't look us in the eye, we think they are untrustworthy. However, in Arab cultures, for a male to avoid eye contact with a female is actually a compliment. For a man to look at a woman straight on, and continuously, would be considered almost as serious as a physical assault. In Asian cultures, it's not proper to look a superior in the eye too often. A bowed head is a signal of deference to an authority figure.

First Names

Instant use of first names is considered disrespectful in France, England, and Japan. First names are used only among family members and intimate friends. In the United Kingdom, office mates for 30 years may still call each other by their

For Japanese businesspeople, exchanging business cards is a very important, formal part of an introduction.

last names and use "sir" in addressing one another. The British keep engagement calendars and frown upon spur-of-the-moment invitations. Business is conducted in the office, while lunch, dinner, and weekends are for socializing.

The Chinese are very sensitive to status and title. Never rely on "Mr." to take the place of a person's proper title, such as "Committee Member," "General," "Factory Manager," or "Bureau Chief."

In Italy, university graduates have titles and you're expected to use them— *dottore* for liberal arts, *avvocato* for law, *ingegnere* for technical fields, and *professore* for both professors and most medical doctors. Don't expect Italians to remember your name on first introduction.

What Does "Yes" Mean?

In Latin and Asian cultures, the word "yes" has many meanings. Businesspeople of neither culture consider it polite to say "no." "Yes" may mean "yes," "maybe," or "no," depending on context, tone, and nonverbal factors. Assuming a deal was concluded when a Spanish or Japanese negotiator said "yes," more than one American salesperson has happily caught the next plane home, only to be embarrassed later upon learning that no deal had been struck.

Beware the Smiling Handshake

In some German-speaking countries, salespeople should avoid smiling when shaking hands with prospects because the combination may be seen as too affectionate. Yet, in another part of the world, the Chinese often show regard for a member of their own sex by publicly holding hands or by some other physical contact, whereas the opposite sexes rarely make any public show of affection.

Watch Your Body Language

We saw in Chapter 7 how important nonverbal communication is in every selling situation. American body language often causes trouble in international negotiations. Putting your feet up on your desk so that the soles can be seen is insulting to an Arab. Even crossing your legs is less respectful than keeping both feet on the floor. Slouching in your chair or not standing up when people of higher rank or age enter or leave the room is also discourteous. And make sure that you are aware of proper seating arrangements in a meeting room or a restaurant. In Germany, men walk and sit to the left of all women and men of senior business rank. Men rise when a woman leaves or returns to the table. If you have doubts about where you should sit, wait for someone to tell you where to sit.

What Holiday Is It?

Holidays vary around the world, and American salespeople abroad should buy a local calendar, not an American one, to efficiently plan their activities. International political differences can make even traditional festivities offensive to your hosts. Americans at the London office of an international communications firm happily decorated their office with shamrocks and St. Patrick figures on March 17th, never giving a thought to the antipathy between the English and the Irish.

In August, nearly everyone in Europe is on holiday trips that are usually planned about a year in advance. Salespeople traveling abroad during this period must make their reservations early to avoid disappointment. Americans who brag "I haven't had time for a vacation in two years" will not be well regarded by Europeans, who value quality of life very highly. Vacations are also one of the best "small talk" subjects to discuss when meeting Europeans for the first time.

Don't Call Them "Foreigners"!

American salespeople must be careful about using the word "foreigner" in another country. Remember: You are the foreigner there! It's best to use a neutral term like "host country national." Be careful not to refer to developing nations as "third world countries" or call the homes "huts," the clothes "costumes," and the people "natives." Such expressions will make you appear insensitive and ignorant.

A Way of Life

Corruption and bribery are commonplace in some developing nations. Such practices don't carry the negative connotation they do in the United States; they are simply a way of life. It is illegal for American firms to offer or give bribes to foreign companies. But what about a gift given as a goodwill gesture or an inducement to do future business? What is the difference between a "commission," a tip, and a bribe? Realize that in some situations you might have to explain quietly to your foreign prospects that you are bound by certain U.S. laws and practices.

Face-to-Face

Any significant business transaction in a developing country takes place face-to-face. Letters, telexes, faxes, and even telephone calls often go unanswered. If you want to get something done, you almost always have to do it in person. Human interaction and relationships are more important than business schedules.

Modesty

A businessperson from a developing country might assume an attitude of self-effacement in social and business situations. In some cultures, an individual does not want to seem to rise too high above others, for fear of leveling mechanisms such as accusations of practicing witchcraft or of trying to be superior. Even in an advanced country like Japan, people still say: "The nail that sticks up gets hammered down."

COMPANY EXPERIENCES IN INTERNATIONAL SALES

American companies and salespeople have mixed track records in international selling. Those who have thoroughly studied their host country generally have success, while those who haven't often fail or make several mistakes before succeeding.

Radio Shack is one of the leading sellers of consumer electronic items in the United States, but the company made many mistakes when it went international. In Belgium, Tandy failed to have a government tax stamp on its store window signs. In Germany, Tandy discovered that it was breaking laws by giving away flashlights, a common sales promotion device in the United States. In Holland, Tandy missed the Christmas shopping crowds, learning the hard way that sales promotions aimed at December 25 were too late because the Dutch give their presents on December 6, St. Nicholas Day.

Avon did poorly when it first attempted to market its personal-care products in Japan the way it did everywhere else, using a large number of women selling door-to-door. Avon found that most Japanese women were too reserved to call on strangers, so the company allowed the timid ones to sell to acquaintances instead. Avon also started an advertising campaign that was low-key and poetic. In the 10 years that followed, Avon's sales grew annually at a rate of over 25 percent.

SUMMARY

Without sales resistance, there would be little need for salespeople. Prospect objections are usually positive signs of interest and involvement in the sales presentation. Uncovering and negotiating the prospect's key objection is one of the salesperson's most important and challenging tasks. Several objectives and strategies are available to salespeople in negotiating prospect resistance. Concession strategies are especially important. In every sales negotiation, there are four possible outcomes, but only one, *win-win*, will further the buyer-seller relationship and encourage future negotiations. Anticipating objections and preempting them in the sales presentation is one of the best ways to minimize objections. The most common objection is to price, which means that the salesperson has not convinced the prospect of the *value* of the product. Perceived value can be determined by the ratio of the prospect's perceived benefits to the product's price. Techniques for negotiating prospect objections can be divided into five basic categories. Successful international selling requires thorough knowledge of business etiquette and negotiating styles in different cultures.

CHAPTER REVIEW QUESTIONS

1. What is meant by buyer resistance and objections?

2. Distinguish between valid and invalid objections.

3. Describe at least ten concession strategies.

4. Name and explain the four possible outcomes in any business negotiation.

5. What steps are involved in planning for prospect objections?

6. Give several guidelines for negotiating objections.

7. What is meant by the term "perceived value"? How is "perceived value" determined?

8. What are the three basic approaches to the preparation and presentation of a value analysis and how does each approach work?

9. What are the basic techniques in each of the five categories for handling buyer objections?

10. Describe several caveats and guidelines for negotiating resistance and objections in international markets.

11. Outline some rules of business etiquette in other cultures.

TOPICS FOR THOUGHT AND CLASS DISCUSSION

1. Why are objections sometimes called the salesperson's "best friends"? Wouldn't it be better for salespeople if prospects didn't have any objections to buying their products?

2. Why is the concept of the buyer's "arch of resistance" and the "keystone objection" (Figure 13-1) valuable to salespeople?

3. Why is the term "negotiation" appropriate for describing how the salesperson should handle prospect resistance and objections?

4. Describe some ways that a salesperson could change the prospect's "perceived value" for a product.

5. Compare the sales negotiating approach of the typical American salesperson with that of the typical Japanese salesperson.

6. Discuss some of the ways that business etiquette in some cultures differs from that in the United States—for example, with regard to business cards, eye contact, use of first names, the meaning of "yes," accepting gifts, saying "thanks," posture, and physical distance.

PROJECTS FOR PERSONAL GROWTH

1. Go to the *Business Periodicals Index* or do a computer search to find five articles on *business negotiation*. Read them and prepare a list of guidelines from each article. Then compare and contrast the five lists of guidelines to eliminate any redundancies. Finally, look at your total list to see if there are any inconsistencies. In class, compare the list you developed with those developed by classmates given the same assignment.

2. Ask four professional salespeople about their philosophies and strategies in negotiating prospect resistance and objections. Judge from your discussions whether they believe in "win-win" or "win-lose" outcomes in negotiating with prospects. Explain your reasons for making this judgment about each salesperson.

3. Ask three professional salespeople who sell to different customer categories what their favorite techniques are for handling buyer resistance and objections. Do the negotiating techniques differ with the customer type? If so, explain why.

KEY TERMS

Objection Anything that the prospect or customer says or does that impedes the sales negotiations.

Valid objections Sincere concerns that the prospect needs answered before he or she will be willing to buy.

Invalid objections Delaying or stalling actions or hidden reasons for not buying.

Key objection The customer's most important objection.

Negotiation Mutual discussion and arrangement of the terms of a transaction or agreement.

Win-win negotiations The kind of negotiation in which both parties feel satisfied with the outcome—the only kind of negotiation that professional salespeople seek!

Postpurchase dissonance Any concern on the buyer's part that he or she did not do well in the sales transaction.

Perceived value The value of a product as seen (perceived) by the prospect.

Value analysis Usually a printed document that shows how a product is the best value for the money.

Return on investment (ROI) Refers to the amount of money expected from an investment over and above the original investment.

Case 13-1

NEGOTIATING PRICE

By James T. Strong, University of Akron

Chuck Johnson and his sales manager, Tom Barnhart, have been trying to sell DuraFlor residential sheet vinyl to Bargain City Stores for many years. Johnson and Barnhart work for McGranahan Distributing Company of Toledo. McGranahan's handles the DuraFlor line of resilient flooring products, which includes both flooring tile and sheet vinyl. In the resilient flooring market, the six competing major manufacturers all use "traditional" marketing channels of independent distributors, who sell to retailers, who, in turn, sell to the general public or contractors.

Bargain City operates a chain of 65 discount stores throughout Ohio, Michigan, and Indiana, with headquarters in Toledo, Ohio. The firm concentrates on secondary markets, and while they stock all the major product lines of other mass merchandisers, they have an excellent do-it-yourself building materials department. Don Schramm is the chief buyer for this department, and his strategy is to buy good value at the low end of the market to sell in Bargain City outlets. It is commonly known throughout the industry that Bargain City buyers always want good product quality at the lowest possible prices, with low price being their top priority.

The product that Johnson and Barnhart are attempting to sell to Mr. Schramm is a low-end line of 12-foot sheet vinyl flooring called Imperial Accent. This line has 12 different patterns and 56 stock-keeping units. McGranahan's sold the Imperial Accent line to Schramm seven years ago, and the sales volume was $250,000. Now, with Bargain City's expansion, Johnson estimates the first-year order volume should be over $500,000. Johnson lost the business when another distributor offered Schramm a 15 percent discount on a similar product made by Congolese Manufacturing. At the time DuraFlor was unwilling to meet the competitor's lower price because it felt that its superior brand awareness increased retailer inventory turnover and justified a higher price.

DuraFlor controls over 60 percent of the entire resilient flooring market, but only 30 percent of the low-end 12-foot sheet flooring market. The low-end market is a fiercely competitive one because the manufacturing process, called *rotogravure*, is so common that no manufacturer has a competitive cost advantage. The process allows virtually any picture to be made into a pattern. Thus, top sellers can be copied by competitors, and it is difficult to maintain styling advantages. Because of this, DuraFlor has tended to neglect this market.

Recently, Chuck heard that the distributor who has been supplying 12-foot sheet vinyl to Bargain City is having financial problems and is not able to keep its customers' stores stocked. On the chance that Bargain City might be looking for a new supplier, Tom called Mr. Schramm and was delighted to hear him confirm a sales call appointment with him and Chuck.

Chuck and Tom have decided to ask the DuraFlor district manager, Ron Harris, to participate in the sales presentation to Bargain City because his firm will untimately have to lower the price to McGranahan Distributing if McGranahan's is to win the business from Bargain City. McGranahan's current profit margin is 24 percent on the DuraFlor product.

In the precall strategy meeting, Johnson, Barnhart, and Harris decide to stress the improved styling and other product features of Imperial Accent and the benefits it offers to Bargain City in terms of inventory turnover because of its high brand awareness with the store's customers. The three of them agree that they will have to do some "paper-and-pencil" selling by demonstrating in specific numbers how profitable the DuraFlor line would be for Bargain City. They also agree that Johnson and Barnhart will finish the sales call with a review of the inventory monitoring, prompt delivery, and sales support that McGranahan's can provide.

After waiting in the lobby of Bargain City's large headquarters building for 35 minutes, the three men, Johnson, Barnhart, and Harris, are led by a receptionist to Mr. Schramm's office. Schramm's assistant buyer, Sixto Torres, is also there and, seeing the three of them march in, comments: "Oh boy, they're bringing in the big guns today. We're in for a real dog-and-pony show, boss." Everybody laughs, and greetings are exchanged all around.

Then Tom Barnhart says: "We appreciate the opportunity to review the merits of the Imperial Accent line with you today, Don. I'm sure by the conclusion of our meeting that you'll agree that it offers an attractive profit opportunity for Bargain City."

"I'll be the judge of that," snaps Schramm, peering menacingly over his bifocals while leaning forward in his chair.

"Here are the twelve patterns in the Imperial Accent line," says Chuck Johnson, as he lays the patterns before Schramm and Torres. "As you can see, DuraFlor has restyled the line with five new patterns, including geometric designs, floral, and the always-popular brick patterns. We've also brightened the color palette in the line because market research has shown us that low-end buyers prefer brighter colors."

"What do you think of this pattern, Sixto?" asks Harris, holding up a bright red, rather garish 36-by-36-inch sample.

"It's really ugly," replies Torres. "I wouldn't have it in my house. But who cares what I think about the pattern—how does it sell?"

"It's brand new and we don't have any data on it yet," answers Harris.

Barnhart jumps in. "Don, Sixto, here's a list of the top twenty-five sellers nationwide, by color and by pattern. We suggest you begin by stocking all the patterns to see how they sell in your different markets. We'll ship new inventory promptly to any of your stores as needed."

Schramm leans forward. "Mm, so we won't have to stock anything in our warehouse? How quickly will you be able to fill our orders?"

"That's right, Don, we'll handle all the inventory concerns and my salespeople will regularly call on all of your stores to make sure the twelve-inch roll racks are stocked," says Barnhart.

Harris chimes in: "The Imperial Accent line is really coming on strong lately, Don." Holding up a sample of the new embossing, he continues: "Our improved rotogravure process allows us to emboss the product now, enabling it to hide subfloor irregularities better than any product on the market. We're also using new 'hi-fidelity' inks that give these brighter colors."

Schramm puts his glasses on and folds his arms as his assistant picks up one of the samples and compares it to a sample of the Congolese product they are now carrying. "This doesn't look any different from the Congolese product," says Torres. "How many mills is the wear layer on your product?"

"Eight," says Harris.

"Congolese has a ten-mill wear layer," replies Torres.

"That's because they pump it up with air. We don't do that. Our research shows this product is the most durable in its product class." Harris is tired of competitors making claims that imply greater durability, while what they're doing is literally blowing hot air into the product. DuraFlor has always been very conservative in its product claims, perhaps too conservative.

Harris continues talking, interrupting Barnhart, who is trying to get the discussion back to what McGranahan's can do for Bargain City. "Don, look at this profit opportunity," says Harris, handing a sheet of paper to Schramm. "If you buy Accent from McGranahan's at two dollars and five cents per square yard and sell it for three ninety-nine, you'll make almost forty-nine percent gross margin. Now with sixty-some stores, eight rolls per store, and seven turns a year, with the average roll being, say, one hundred square yards, that's a profit of $369,000. I know it will take a while to get the Congolese off your racks, but these are the kind of profit dollars you could be generating in a year or two." Harris smiles and looks at Schramm.

Schramm crosses his arms again and stares at the sheet Harris has put on his desk. He rubs his eyes and grimaces slightly. "Well, for one thing, Ron, if I were to pay two dollars and five cents per square yard for this product, Sixto would have my job the next day. It's nice of you to try and help me run my department, but if I made a forty-nine percent margin on this product, it wouldn't exactly be a bargain for the customer, now would it?"

"I think Ron was just trying to point out the profit potential, Don. Obviously, you'll be changing the numbers to fit Bargain City's marketing strategy," offers Johnson. "And remember that two percent of all your purchases will accumulate in a fifty-fifty co-op advertising fund."

"We're only paying a dollar eighty-two per square yard for the Congolese product. Can you meet that price?" asks Schramm.

"We'll sure try," quickly responds Barnhart. "What about it, Ron, can we get there?"

"I don't know for sure," says Harris to Schramm. "Let me talk to the product manager and get a price to Tom, and he'll give a price to you. If we can meet Congolese's price, will you give us the business, Don?"

"Maybe," Schramm replies. "Come back with your best price and we'll see. The products look similar to me, your styling has improved, and the co-op program is good, but I've got to look at what your competitors are offering before I make up my mind."

"Remember, Don, we'll carry all the inventory, service your stores so the managers won't have to remember to order, and deliver the products right off our own truck so you won't take any risk of damage during delivery. And the cost of all this is in the price of the goods. You'll never get a bill for delivery charges. What have you got to lose? How about giving us a shot at the sheet goods business?" pleads Johnson.

"We'll see," says Schramm.

Later that week Harris calls Barnhart with a wholesale cost that would yield McGranahan's a price of $1.90 per square yard with a normal margin. Barnhart calls Johnson into his office and asks if he will be willing to take a 2 percent commission instead of 3 percent in order to help bridge the 8-cent gap. Thinking that it is critical to meet the competitor's price of $1.82 in order to win the business, Johnson agrees to take the cut in his commissions. Barnhart calls Schramm with the price of $1.82 per square yard, reviews all the benefits of the Imperial Accent line and the services provided by McGranahan's, and asks for the order. Schramm says he will let him know in a few days, after he gets all the prices from other suppliers.

When Schramm calls back three days later, he says McGranahan's can have the business if they will take another nickel off their price. Apparently, the Congolese distributor has lowered the price to keep from losing the business. Barnhart really doesn't have a nickel to give. He has already cut the price to the bone, and another nickel off will reduce McGranahan's gross margin to 17 percent, not a very attractive deal considering all the services they will be providing. Barnhart thinks for a few minutes, then calls Johnson in to discuss the new terms that Bargain City is requesting.

Questions

1. Should McGranahan's lower the price to Bargain City by another 5 cents? Should Johnson agree to take an even lower commission to win the order?

2. What types of closing techniques did Johnson, Barnhart, and Harris use? By being more persistent, do you think the three-member sales team could have won the order during the sales call on Bargain City's buyers, Schramm and Torres?

3. Do you think it was a good idea to bring Ron Harris, the district manager of DuraFlor, along to help make the sales presentation to Bargain City? Why or why not?

4. How successful do you think Johnson, Barnhart, and Harris were in negotiating price resistance during the sales call? How well did they do in negotiating concessions? What, if anything, should they have done differently?

5. What would you advise Chuck Johnson and Tom Barnhart to say in responding to Mr. Schramm's request for another nickel cut in price to win the Bargain City business?

Case 13-2

LEARNING TO HANDLE PROSPECT OBJECTIONS

Rachel Glassman sips her morning coffee as she waits for the last trainee to return from the morning break. Rachel, who holds the position of regional sales training manager for a multinational machine tool company, is in the middle of a long and intense day of sales training for recently hired salespeople. Today the training is concentrating on negotiating customer resistance and objections. From past experience, she knows that this part of the company's five-week training program is one of the most difficult for new representatives to master. Over the years, Rachel has tried many approaches to help trainees learn negotiation strategies and tactics. One of the best approaches, she feels, is to combine video simulations with role-playing sessions, for two reasons. First, former trainees who used the videos claim that the simulations are very close to what they later experienced in real sales situations. This testimonial on the part of former trainees makes current trainees more responsive, since they understand that what they are viewing will be of value to them once they are assigned to a sales territory. Second, by using role plays immediately following the viewing of the videotapes, the sales trainees are able to practice and reinforce the negotiation strategies and techniques they just learned.

Today Rachel is presenting six simulated selling situations in which a sales representative deals with customer resistance or objections. In the first three segments, which were viewed before the morning break, the videos followed a representative through a sales presentation and showed how to handle various types of customer objections. The last three segments, which Rachel will present after the break, are again vignettes of sales presentations where the salesperson encounters various types of customer resistance and objections. In these videotapes, however, at the point when the objection is raised, the tape stops and the trainees are asked to recommend a strategy or technique to deal with the situation. When all sales trainees have made a recommendation, the simulation is restarted and the viewer observes how the representative actually handled the customer's objection.

The essence of these three videotaped situations, along with brief summaries of the responses of the three sales trainees, follow.

Situation #1. An American sales representative is just concluding a sales presentation to four Japanese businesspeople from a large petroleum refinery by presenting a chart showing the price of the product (a hydraulic lift carrier for lifting fully loaded 55-gallon steel drums) for various order quantities. After finishing, the sales rep sits down opposite the four businesspeople and says: "Would you like to place an order for one hunderd at this month's special low price of eight hundred and ninety-nine dollars each?" All four of the Japanese executives nod their heads and say "yes" but say nothing else. After two more minutes of silence, the sales rep looks at his wristwatch and begins to fidget in his seat.

Bob: It's obvious that the Japanese business executives are unhappy with the price, so the sales rep should quote a lower price.

Pete: I'd just sit there silently until one of the Japanese executives spoke. They're just using their silence as a negotiating strategy.

Alison: I think that the sales rep ought to ask the Japanese businesspeople if they have any questions. They may be looking for more information that will give them reasons to buy. I would talk about product quality and customer service as this point.

Situation #2. A salesperson is just completing a sales presentation on a Power Spray water broom to Cecil Jergens, a purchasing agent for National Industrial Equipment. The sales rep's concluding statement is: "As you have seen, Mr. Jergens, the water broom enables workers to simultaneously wash away and sweep up tough dirt and grime from factory or plant floors in minutes. At the price of $34.95 each, it's a tremendous bargain, and I'm sure that each one of your plant managers will want several."

"Yes, the water broom looks like a useful product," responds Mr. Jergens, "but your price is nearly three times the price of our heavy-duty industrial brooms, which do a good clean-up job. I don't see the value in paying three times as much for a product that does the same job."

Bob: Mr. Jergens seems to have some hidden agenda. I think he's probably buying the industrial brooms from a friend of his who he has dealt with for years. I don't think there's much of a chance for a sale here.

Pete: Mr. Jergens still isn't convinced of the benefits of the water broom relative to its price. I think the sales rep has to restate the benefits of the water broom in terms of worker time saved, cleanliness of the plant floors in ridding them of ground-in oil and grease as well as dirt, and improved worker morale. The sales rep ought to point out that the water broom's benefits relative to its price are actually much greater than the traditional industrial broom's benefits compared to its price. So, Mr. Jergens will get more value for his dollars by buying the water broom.

Alison: At three times the price of the industrial brooms, perhaps the price of the water brooms is too high. I'm sure the sales rep has some room to negotiate on price, so I'd recommend offering the water broom at a lower price—say twenty-three ninety-five—to see how Mr. Jergens responds.

Situation #3. After making the sales representation and demonstration, a sales representative for Tool Storage Cabinet, Inc., asks the purchasing agent for Tebbets Machining Company this question: "May I go ahead and order five of these welded steel tool chests for your plant, Mr. O'Connor, so your machinists can soon have the peace of mind that comes from knowing that their valuable tools are secure?"

"Well, I know the machinists want more secure tool chests," replies Mr. O'Connor, "but I don't think they're going to like the combination locks on the doors. They're used to using keys, and it's going to slow them down a lot to have to remember and work the combinations each time they want to open the doors of their tool chests."

Bob: The engineers who designed those tool chests weren't very customer oriented. They should have known that the machinists would want access by keys instead of a combination lock. I'd go back to headquarters and tell them that we need to redesign the locking device on our tool storage chests.

Pete: I'd try to turn this apparent disadvantage into an advantage. I think the sales rep could correctly say that the locks were purposely designed with combination locks for some well-thought-out reasons. First, keys get mislaid, lost, or stolen, and anyone with the key can use it to get into the tool chest. Combinations are not likely to get lost or stolen. Second, if a key is left at home, the machinist has to return home to get the key, but a combination is carried around in one's head. Third, when there is a turnover in the plant, a new machinist can securely use the former employee's tool chest by merely changing the combination, rather than having to rework the entire locking device for a new key. Fourth, key locks can be picked open by talented thieves, but few thieves can open combination locks. By pointing out these advantages of the combination lock, I think the sales rep can overcome the prospect's objection.

Alison: I'd tell Mr. O'Connor that I bet some of the machinists will prefer the combination lock to the key lock tool chests, and that I'd appreciate him taking a little poll to find out. Then I'd tell him that we can provide both types of locking devices, depending on what the machinists want. If I found out later that our company didn't offer anything but the combination lock, I'd call Mr. O'Connor back and tell him that I'm sorry but I was mistaken about us selling the key-lock type. Then I'd ask for an order for the combination-lock tool chests, assuming that some of the machinists will prefer them.

Questions

1. Look at each of the three situations one at a time. In your opinion, which of the sales trainees seems to be on the best track toward handling the objection in each situation? How do you think the prospect will respond to the approach of the other two sales reps in each case?

2. Which one of these sales reps would you prefer to be assigned to a territory where you were the sales manager? Why?

3. What do you think of the process of setting up a situation via a videotape, stopping the tape to let sales trainees explain how they would deal with the situation, then showing how the sales rep actually dealt with the situation?

Chapter 14

Confirming and Closing the Sale

Take my factories and my money, but leave me my salesmen and I'll be back where I am today in two years.

ANDREW CARNEGIE

Profile

"EARN the right to ask for their business." This statement sums up Sal DeMarco's ideas about closing the sale. Sal, an Advisory Marketing Representative for ROLM Company in Los Angeles, stresses three main stages that he works through with every customer en route to the close: (1) survey of requirements (thorough interviews of department heads, other appropriate personnel, and the customer's customers to assess the customer's needs); (2) proposal (discussions and workshops to develop various levels of implementation for the proposed product); and (3) closing statement: "I would like to have your business so that we can start working toward the goals we have described."

Sal has an unusual background, which he believes has helped him immensely in his sales career. When he arrived at Rensselaer Polytechnic Institute, he wanted to be a nuclear engineer. Soon, however, he realized that with his people-oriented personality, he would not be happy in a laboratory, so he decided to major in business. The dynamic world of sales and marketing seemed to be a natural career goal for a person who put himself through college by playing drums in several fine rock and jazz groups. After graduation, Sal gained some valuable business experience in a marketing staff position and, later, a field sales position with a major U.S. company. His strong, growing interest in computers and telecommunications convinced him to interview with IBM, where he was hired as a sales representative for the ROLM Division. In 1989, ROLM Company was established as a telecommunications marketing and service organization jointly owned by IBM and Siemens, the well-known German electronics concern.

Sal DeMarco

Though Sal has many exciting success stories, he always seems to feel especially proud of his *latest* sale. His most recent sale involved a vice-president of a California-based natural vitamin company. Sal says: "She was responsible for moving the company's entire headquarters facility, including a large amount of aging telecommunications equipment. I saw an opportunity to assess what her new needs might be and possibly sell her some new equipment." Sal prepared for the interview by carefully researching and compiling a list of ten solid reasons why the customer should invest in his products. Sal continues: "This move was a big hassle and I knew they would take the easy way out and move the old equipment. But I also knew that this vice-president figured it was going to cost almost as much to move the old equipment as it was to buy new. When I arrived at her office, she simply asked me to give her my three best reasons why she should buy from me. I specifically avoided a complicated discussion of the cost advantage and concentrated on (1) redesigning her telecommunications system to meet current goals, (2) reliability, and (3) new technology to meet future goals. After a ten-minute discussion, she asked me to bring the contracts in." The sale was worth over $200,000.

Sal has two pieces of advice for college students thinking about a personal selling career. "First, find a company that has the same standards that you have and that sells a product you truly believe in. And second, be patient with yourself. My motto, based on my sales experience at ROLM, is: *Success Through Partnership.* Good, solid relationships may take months or years to grow—but sales will definitely follow!"

After reading this chapter, you should understand:

☐ When to attempt a trial close

☐ Why some salespeople fail to close

☐ 20 basic closing techniques

☐ The principles of persuasion in closing

☐ How to deal with rejection

A common saying in show business is: "It's easier to get on than it is to get off." This is also true in sales. The close is the "final curtain." It's the time when you take your bow and accept applause for giving a great performance. Closing is the make-or-break point in selling. It's that moment of truth when having a little extra knowledge or skill can mean the difference between winning or losing a commission. Only one question really matters at this point: Can I close this buyer?[1]

CLOSING IS CONFIRMING THE SALE

CLOSE The stage in the selling process where the salesperson tries to obtain an agreement from the prospect to purchase the product.

The stage in the selling process where you try to obtain an agreement from the prospect to purchase the product is called the **close.** Some scholars and practitioners prefer to use the term "confirming sales" instead of "closing sales." In their view, *closing* incorrectly implies the end of the selling process, when, in reality, much hard work must follow the sale to win repeat business.

Another sore point is the overemphasis often given the close in the total selling process. Entire books have been written on so-called power closes. Many of the closing techniques advocated in popular trade books, and by some sales trainers, smack of manipulation and trickery. They imply that the importance of the sales close justifies dubious means to achieve it. But a close at an ethical cost is not worthwhile and will eventually backfire on the salesperson.

CLOSING IS PART OF THE ONGOING SELLING PROCESS

Instead of viewing it as the end or the pinnacle of the selling process, professional salespeople understand the close as one more integral part of the ongoing selling process and the buyer-seller relationship. No matter how clever your closing strategies, you aren't likely to make the sale unless you have done a good job at each stage of the selling process leading up to this point. At the same time, no matter how brilliantly you have performed in the preceding stages of the

[1]Ed McMahon, *Ed McMahon's Superselling* (New York: Prentice Hall Press, 1989), pp. 113–114.

448

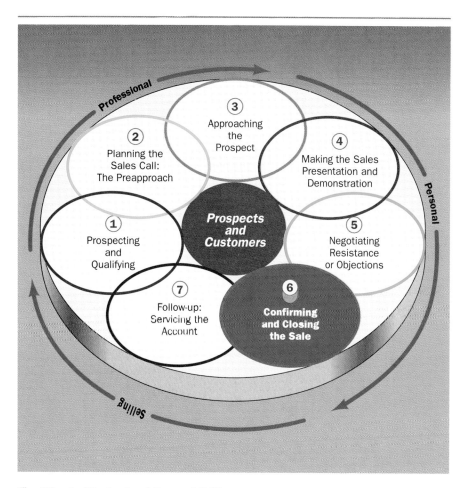

The Wheel of Professional Personal Selling

selling process, you can still lose the sale if you don't use the right closing strategy and tactics. A successful close confirms the win-win agreement reached with a buyer and ensures the continuation of the buyer-seller relationship. Because it is convenient and widely accepted, we will use the term "closing the sale." Keep in mind, however, that the close is not the end, but merely a continuation of the selling process.

Trying to Close: The Trial Close

TRIAL CLOSE Any well-placed attempt to close the sale, which can be used early and often throughout the selling process.

Professional salespeople are prepared to close anywhere, anytime, because they know their ABC's—Always Be Closing.[2] They use the **trial close**—any well-placed attempt to close the sale—early and often throughout the selling process. Some salespeople refer to the trial close as a "miniclose," but when handled properly, a small trial close can quickly become *the* big close. Let's say that a

[2]Joseph P. Vaccaro, "Best Salespeople Know Their ABC's (Always Be Closing)," *Marketing News*, March 28, 1988, p. 10.

salesperson has thoroughly discussed product features, advantages, and benefits with the prospect, who seems very interested in the product. The salesperson might then ask: "May I tell our warehouse personnel to reserve a hundred units for you?" or "Would next week be a convenient time for you to take shipment?" If the prospect says "yes" to either question, the sale is confirmed and the trial close has been successful. But if the buyer isn't ready to place the order, the salesperson can simply resume the sales presentation and patiently wait until the buyer again seems prepared to place the order—either during the same presentation or during a later sales call. Salespeople should continue with their sales presentation when they encounter such caution signs as:

- A trial close that fails to get a positive response from the prospect.
- An interruption that disrupts the prospect's frame of mind.
- Another objection or request for more information.

Trial Closing Cues

With a little practice and experience, you will learn to look and listen for cues that indicate it's time for a trial close. Positive verbal cues occur when the prospect asks specific questions about the product or says something positive about it, or when the salesperson does a good job answering a particular objection. Nonverbal signals that indicate an appropriate time for a trial close occur when the prospect begins showing substantial interest in the product and what the salesperson is saying, or when the salesperson finishes the sales presentation and demonstration. The verbal and nonverbal closing cues summarized in Table 14-1 should help you recognize trial close opportunities and time your trial closes effectively.

AVOIDING THE CLOSE

We can philosophize and theorize all we like about how professional selling should be done, but its main objective remains a constant: to close the sale. Unfortunately, some salespeople actually avoid the close for one reason or another.

Experienced Salespeople

Even after two or three years of selling, many salespeople are still not as effective as they could be when it comes to closing sales. Experienced salespeople sometimes inadvertently avoid the close because they are so wrapped up in their polished, well-rehearsed sales presentation that they don't want to close until they've gotten through all of it. Still other veteran sales reps become so complacent about selling techniques that have worked well in the past that they avoid trying new closing methods in new selling situations.

**TABLE 14-1   Verbal and Nonverbal Signals Indicating It's Time
for a Trial Close**

Verbal Cues

When the prospect asks . . .

- about product price, delivery, installation, or service;
- if there are any special discounts, deals, or special incentives to buy;
- a hypothetical question about buying: "If I do decide to buy . . .";
- who else has bought the product;
- what other customers think about the product;
- if a special feature is included or available;
- whether the product can accomplish a particular task;
- the salesperson for an opinion about one product version versus another;
- what method of payment is acceptable.

When the prospect says . . .

- something positive about the product;
- that he or she has always wanted some particular product feature.

When the salesperson . . .

- successfully answers one of the prospect's objections;
- asks if the prospect has any more questions and receives a "no" answer or silence.

Nonverbal Cues

When the prospect . . .

- begins closely studying and handling the product;
- tests or tries out the product;
- seems pleased by the product's performance or by some feature of the product;
- looks more relaxed;
- becomes more friendly;
- increases eye contact with the salesperson;
- looks over the order form or picks up the pen the salesperson has handed him or her;
- nods head in agreement or leans toward the salesperson;
- begins to listen more attentively to the salesperson;
- lends the salesperson a pen;
- unconsciously reaches for his or her checkbook or wallet (consumer prospects).

When the salesperson . . .

- finishes the sales presentation;
- completes a successful product demonstration;
- hands the order form and a pen to the prospect.

The best salespeople are sensitive to every opportunity to close and are always shaping their closes to fit the individual prospect and selling situation. This often means trying new closes, or at least old closes with new twists—both of which not only improve closing effectiveness but also help keep the selling job interesting and exciting.

If you harbor guilt feelings about asking people to make a purchase commitment, then you are probably just thinking negatively about the role of selling.

New Salespeople

There are three basic reasons why new salespeople avoid the close: (1) lack of confidence in themselves, their product, or their company; (2) guilt about asking people to part with their money; and (3) a general fear of failure that causes them to postpone the attempt to close as long as possible.

Lack of confidence is common in new salespeople thrust into selling situations with what they feel is inadequate training. One way to overcome this lack of confidence is to talk with other salespeople, both those who are new and dealing with the same confidence problem themselves, and sympathetic veterans who can tell you stories about their own shaky confidence during their first few months in sales. Most sales managers understand this common problem and can help by providing encouragement, information on confidence-building books and exercises, and perhaps additional training.

If you harbor guilt feelings about asking people to make a purchase commitment, then you are probably just thinking negatively about the role of selling. Professional salespeople realize that they are helping people solve their problems and that they are performing a vital and important societal function. People don't buy unless they have a need for your product and believe they are getting value for their money. A closed sale is thus a confirmation of your useful and important role in the buyer's life and livelihood.

Some salespeople consider the close so terribly important and dramatic that, ironically, they can never find just the right moment to make the close! Procrastination will provide you with temporary comfort if you are fearful of facing that critical decision point when all your previous work in the selling process may come to naught. Fear of failure can be overcome by recognizing that few products are ever sold on the first sales call. Only about 6 percent of all sales are made after one sales call, 9 percent by two calls, and just 34 percent after three calls. On average, 4.3 calls are needed to close most business-to-business sales, although the number varies by industry. In the food industry, only 2.6 calls are needed, but in business services, 5.6 calls are required.[3] Failure to close on a particular call seldom means that the sale is irretrievably lost. There will be other opportunities. The best salespeople and achievers in nearly all areas share one winning attitude: Never give up.

The next vignette contains an inspiring story about a salesperson who was so patient and persevering that when the close came, it actually took him by surprise.

LETTING THE CUSTOMER CLOSE THE SALE

Salespeople who strongly advocate win-win selling sometimes advise turning the tables on traditional selling by *letting the customer close the sale.* Most sales can't be closed anyway until the prospect is ready to buy. By that time, the prospect is probably as anxious to move ahead as the salesperson is. In fact, when the proposed sales agreement is obviously a win-win situation, many customers will

---

[3]"Sales Tactics Take on a New Look as Corporations Rethink Strategy," *The Wall Street Journal,* April 28, 1988, p. 1; John A. Byrne, "Motivating Willy Loman," *Forbes,* January 30, 1984, p. 91.

PERSEVERANCE PAYS OFF

One salesperson who refused to give up was John Riordan, a sales rep several years ago for Olivetti Underwood. He was assigned a territory that included a large federal government installation in Columbus, Ohio. Although this installation used about 5,000 typewriters, IBM seemed to have a lock on the business because Charley, the head purchasing agent, preferred that brand. Lower prices or better deals on competitive brands made no difference to him.

On his initial call, John was told by Charley that the installation bought only IBM typewriters and that he would be wasting his time trying to sell any other brand. Refusing to give up, John cultivated a relationship with Charley's young assistant, Bob. He made it a point to call on the installation at least once a month, when he would teach Bob all about typewriters. After about ten months, John got a call from Bob asking him to stop by the following morning. Arriving early, John was told by Bob that Charley had taken early retirement and that he, Bob, was now the head purchasing agent. Before John could even congratulate him on his promotion, Bob asked whether the Olivetti Underwood machines met all gov-

ernment specifications. After checking to make sure that they did, John was delighted to hear Bob say: "Okay, what's the 50-machine price?" John personally installed each one of those 50 machines and instructed the typists. He also arranged for the company service manager to meet with his counterpart at the installation to set up a two-day course for the installation's repair technicians and a spare parts inventory system. Finding that everything ran smoothly for three months, Bob placed another order for 150 machines! Those 200 machines enabled John to make 225 percent of his annual quota and were largely responsible for a key promotion in his career.

Later Bob told John that his refusal to give up and his willingness to share information with him without any apparent return was the reason he put in the first order for 50 machines. John's thorough follow-up on those machines and the support provided by the company's service department earned the second order for 150 machines. Reciprocity and perseverance were the two key ingredients in John's success.

actually trial-close the salesperson by asking questions like "How soon can I get the product?" or "What credit terms do you offer?"

In many situations, letting the customer close for you makes good sense. Think about it: You have carefully prepared, rehearsed, and delivered all or a good part of your sales presentation to a person you previously qualified as a very likely buyer of your product, and you have just finished negotiating this person's most pressing objections. At this moment, it is in the prospect's best interest to close the win-win, problem-solving agreement quickly in order to receive the desired benefits as soon as possible. As one salesperson puts it: "My hit ratio is a lot better on major sales when I let the customer close than it was when I tried to trial-close him every sentence or two."[4]

FAB, KAI, and PAS Salespeople

Some sales managers view their successful salespeople as one of three basic types: FAB, KAI, or PAS. Salespeople who overwhelm prospects by presenting product features and benefits one after another, while simultaneously trying to close, are FAB (features, advantages, and benefits) salespeople. Salespeople who slowly and subtly lead prospects toward the sale by providing a steady stream of

[4]Mack Hannan, "Let the Customer Close for You," *Sales & Marketing Management,* August 1986, pp. 68–70.

At ROLM, we encourage our most valuable employees to look into other professions.

And they look pretty hard. Into Insurance, Banking, Healthcare, or whatever your field happens to be. Because, along with knowing the telecommunications business, we require our reps to have a knowledge of yours. Only then can they help design a telecommunications system to meet your specific needs.

Our people stay involved in your profession long after your voice and data facilities are combined into one integrated system. Because a system can't help your business run more effectively

until each of your employees knows how to use it. We'll recommend specific applications designed to improve productivity. PhoneMail® for instance. The voice messaging system that not only eliminates missed and garbled messages, but also records, stores, routes, or even ties messages to a computer. And Automatic Call Distribution that functions as a communications manager to expedite and route your customers' calls to available agents as efficiently as possible.

It takes some extra time and effort, not to mention a lot of investigation, to learn a new profession. But at ROLM,® that's the only way we work. Because we know the best way to mind our business is to make sure we're minding yours.

For more information, call ROLM at 1-800-624-8999 extension 235, or contact your authorized ROLM Business Partner.

We ask better questions. You get better answers.

® ROLM and PhoneMail are registered trademarks of ROLM Systems. © 1990 ROLM Company

Based on what you see in this ad, do you think ROLM company encourages its salespeople to be PAS salespeople? Why?

useful information are KAI (knowledge and information) salespeople. KAI salespeople will give prospects advance notice about an upcoming price change one week, an insightful article on the industry the next week, early warning about a potential product shortage, and perhaps a luncheon invitation to report on a new product that will soon be available. Eventually, the prospects see what they want and buy. The third type are PAS (problems and solutions) salespeople. They don't really try to close customers. Instead, they work with prospects to identify and solve their problems and create opportunities to lower costs, increase productivity, and improve profits. For PAS salespeople, the sales close or purchase decision is simply the mutually beneficial agreement that buyer and seller reach together.[5]

The PAS Attitude

Most professional salespeople know that in today's highly competitive business environment, they will seldom be the first or the last salesperson a buyer meets. Organizational buyers, in particular, are usually visited by several salespeople offering a wide choice of appropriate goods and services. Literally letting the customer close the sale may not be a practical technique in very competitive selling situations. Still, the attitude behind this technique—which we will call the **PAS attitude**—should not be discounted. The salesperson with the PAS attitude is actually three salespeople in one: He or she must thoroughly know the features, advantages, and benefits of the product (the FAB salesperson) and gather the knowledge and information needed to serve the customer best (the KAI salesperson) in order to work toward the primary and overriding goal of discovering and solving the customer's problems (the PAS salesperson).

Experienced PAS salespeople are not hesitant to ask for the order because they know they have done everything possible to show the customer a way to solve his or her problems. At each "closing moment" in your own professional selling career, you can double-check for the presence of the PAS attitude by asking yourself some key questions:

■ Have I really addressed the needs of this unique customer and effectively dealt with the customer's objections?

■ Am I really thinking primarily of this customer's best interests?

■ Can I honestly say that the sales agreement I'm about to close will be a mutually beneficial one?

[5]Ibid.

PAS (problems and solutions) ATTITUDE A selling approach that seeks to work with prospects to identify and solve their problems and create opportunities to lower costs, increase productivity, and improve profits.

PAS salespeople work with prospects to identify and solve their problems and create opportunities for them to lower costs, increase productivity, and improve profits.

Company Highlight

How Amdahl Competes with IBM

Amdahl Corporation sells mainframe computers in direct competition with IBM, and its salespeople are encouraged to approach prospects who are already committed to IBM products. When they call on these prospects, they give them a coffee mug with Amdahl's name boldly displayed on the side and tell them to leave it on their desk the next time an IBM salesperson comes around and they'll get a million-dollar discount. Customers tell Amdahl that, sure enough, when IBM salespeople see the coffee mug, their eyes bulge—and IBM usually offers them a large price discount soon afterward.

How does this technique help Amdahl close sales? Well, once the prospect sees how a mere coffee mug with the Amdahl name on it gets them lower prices from IBM, they start thinking how much more effective it would be if the IBM salesperson saw an actual Amdahl product on the floor. "Once we've sold one Amdahl system, even a small one," claims a marketing manager, "the next sale is twenty times easier."

Source: Eric Olsen, "Breaking the Sales Barrier," *Success,* May 1990, p. 49.

If you answer "yes" to each of these questions, then you have the PAS attitude and will no doubt be furthering the long-run buyer-seller relationship by your sales close.

BUYERS' NEGOTIATING STYLES

You must be prepared to close buyers who have a variety of negotiating styles.[6]

Some buyers are *hard bargainers* who keep several suppliers competing fiercely against one another to win their business. These buyers negotiate aggressively to win every possible concession from the salesperson. They tend to see negotiations as a contest and will pull out every weapon in order to win. In dealing with hard bargainers, you must guard against being pressured into an unprofitable, one-shot agreement because hard bargainers will readily switch to a new supplier who offers better terms next time.

Facilitators try to work efficiently and cooperatively with salespeople to reach a mutually acceptable agreement. They understand that win-win arrangements are to each party's advantage. Facilitators are a joy to work with.

---

[6]This section is adapted from Alan J. Dubinsky and Thomas N. Ingram, "A Classification of Industrial Buyers: Implications for Sales Training," *Journal of Personal Selling and Sales Management,* Fall–Winter 1981–82, pp. 46–51.

Straight shooters exhibit honesty and integrity throughout negotiations and do not try to pressure the salesperson into making concessions. You must avoid the temptation to take advantage of straight shooters because these buyers will be good long-term customers if you treat them fairly.

Socializers enjoy the camaraderie of interpersonal relationships and dislike being rushed through the sales presentation and close. If you stay relaxed and informal in your sales presentations and spend some time in friendly chit-chat, you will usually be very successful in closing the sale with these buyers.

Persuaders make their own sales presentations about the reputation and quality of their company. Sometimes they are simply trying to tell you (especially if you represent a better-known company) that their company deserves respect, too. Other times they are interested in convincing you that their company is very successful and that treating them well in purchasing agreements might well lead to a profitable long-term relationship. Be patient and let persuaders tell their stories. Show respect for them and their companies, and express appreciation for their business.

Finally, *considerate buyers* empathize with salespeople and try to work with them to reach mutually acceptable agreements. Considerate buyers understand that every successful partnership involves give-and-take, so they take a very reasonable approach to negotiations. In fact, these buyers are often so considerate that they will accept product substitutes or even compromises in the purchase agreement. Never take advantage of their good nature and flexibility. Considerate buyers are almost always excellent long-run customers.

Obviously, some buyers will be harder to work with and more difficult to close than others, but your challenge as a professional salesperson is to work out *win-win* agreements with all buyers, regardless of their personalities and negotiating styles.

PRINCIPLES OF PERSUASION IN CLOSING

In developing closing strategies for various buyer negotiating styles and buying situations, you will benefit from a basic understanding of the principles of persuasion, seven of which are outlined in Table 14-2. Let's briefly discuss each of these principles.

Consistency

Experienced buyers are usually quite consistent in their thoughts and behavior and, consequently, in their decision making. It therefore stands to reason that if you can achieve a series of positive agreements with the buyer on individual product benefits during the sales presentations, the stage will be set for a close that is merely a continuation of this pattern of positive responses. For example, a commercial insurance agent who asks for agreement from a company insurance officer on various reasons for buying corporate insurance—to ensure the survival of the company against disasters, to protect shareholder value, to protect corporate officers from lawsuits—is building to the close using the consistency principle of persuasion. By winning a "yes" from the prospect on each advantage,

TABLE 14-2   Basic Principles of Persuasion

Consistency Principle. Prospects and customers like to be logical and consistent in their thought and behavior. Several "yes" answers during the sales presentation will probably lead to a "yes" answer at the close.
Commitment Principle. Prepurchase efforts by prospects to learn about a product tend to increase their commitment to buying the product.
Reciprocity Principle. In most cultures, when one person does someone a favor, the second person feels obligated to return the favor. Oftentimes the reciprocated favor is more valuable than the original one.
Validation Principle. Prospects are more likely to purchase a product when they learn that people and companies similar to themselves and their companies have already purchased it.
Authority Principle. Prospects are more likely to buy from salespeople and companies they perceive as being experts in their field.
Scarcity Principle. When a product becomes scarce, it is often perceived as more valuable and desirable. The likelihood of persuading a prospect to buy increases when the prospect anticipates an unfavorable change in the product's status (availability, quality, or price).
Friendship Principle. Prospects are more easily persuaded by salespeople they like. This could be seen as an offshoot of the consistency principle because it would be inconsistent behavior to refuse to buy from a friend!

Source: Dr. James T. Strong, assistant professor of marketing at the University of Akron, provided the insights for this list of the principles of persuasion.

the salesperson makes it harder for the prospect to say "no" to buying a policy, because a refusal would be inconsistent with the prospect's earlier agreements.

Commitment

Another principle of persuasion is commitment. Each time a prospect agrees to meet with you—to participate in a product demonstration, to read the product literature, to visit the supplier's plant, or to have lunch with you—that prospect is making a commitment of time and effort to the eventual purchase of the product. A retailer who makes a special trip to a manufacturer's warehouse sale has made a strong commitment or investment of time and effort that is consistent with buying. The more effort the retailer expends to get to the manufacturer's warehouse, the greater the commitment effect and the higher the likelihood of buying.

Reciprocity

As we saw in Chapter 3, reciprocity is a common practice between companies, even if it is in some cases legally questionable. It is a simple fact of life that most people tend to feel obligated to return favors. If you do something nice or helpful for a buyer, that buyer will generally try to return the favor in some way, often by buying your product. And because in many organizations a single buyer is responsible for hundreds of thousands of dollars' worth of purchase decisions, your return on several small favors to that individual can be substantial. For instance, a computer salesperson who provides "mouse" pads and glare-reducing monitor screens for a prospect's office computers free of charge may help the prospect's buyer look good, and this may set the stage for that buyer to press his or her superiors to place their order for 30 new laser printers with the salesperson.

Validation

Consumers and organizations alike monitor the appropriateness of purchase decisions by considering the opinions and purchase behaviors of similar individuals and companies. Such validation takes the risk of embarrassment or managerial disapproval out of the purchase decision at hand. You can help prospective buyers validate their purchase decisions by pointing out that a respected individual or company already uses your product. In organizational buying situations, where there is often a group of decision makers, you might be able to bring a little peer pressure to bear on reluctant members of the group by asking for the advocacy of one or two key members who are friendly and sympathetic to your proposal.

How do you think this Xerox sales representative could use the authority principle of persuasion to close a sale?

Authority

One step beyond the validation principle is the authority principle of persuasion, which is based on the idea that buyers are more likely to purchase from salespeople and companies that are perceived as experts in their field. The "validation" for buying a product is the salesperson's or seller company's excellent reputation alone. "Nobody ever got fired for buying from IBM," goes a saying from the days when IBM was the undisputed leader in business computing. This saying points up the fact that buyers are less likely to be blamed for making a mistake if they purchase from organizations that are perceived as experts. Even if you don't work for a famous company, you can know your product, its applications, and the market so thoroughly that you successfully compete with sales reps from big-name companies.

Scarcity

SCARCITY PRINCIPLE If a product is in short supply, it is often perceived as more valuable and desirable than one that is plentiful.

If a product is in short supply, it is often perceived as more valuable and desirable than one that is plentiful. Of all the principles of persuasion mentioned here, the **scarcity principle** is probably the most limited because an honest salesperson will indicate to a buyer that a product is in short supply only when it really is. (How many instances of a "one-of-a-kind" deal or "limited time only" offer can you think of when the deal was far from unique and the offer was repeated again and again?) Nevertheless, a manufacturer sometimes underestimates the demand for a product, and inventory, shipping, and distribution problems often threaten to make a product scarce. Such situations can provide a real opportunity for the salesperson.

For example, a sales rep for a paper manufacturer might say to the buyer for a magazine publisher: "Because this Super Z quality paper requires a special liquid in its drying process that is hard to get right now, current Super Z stocks are going fast and may take several months to replenish. Some of my customers are taking no chances and have already ordered a six-month supply."

Friendship

At the heart of the persuasive principle of friendship lies the simple fact that people will more readily buy from people they like.

A Warning about Friendship

One of the goals of the selling process as a whole is to develop a solid, friendly relationship with the prospect. This is common sense. If you cannot honestly say that you are on friendly terms with a prospect by the time you are ready to try to close, then you may not be ready to make the close. Unfortunately, some sales-people tend to rely too much on their friendship with the prospect, and this can lead to big problems. For example, you might feel guilty about asking your friend (the prospect) for the sale, or perhaps your friend will buy from someone else because he or she knows that you, as a friend, will "understand."

Any one or various combinations of the seven principles of persuasion can be effective when used within the overall framework of a closing strategy. A wide range of basic closing strategies have been developed over the years, and the salesperson can tailor each to fit a particular prospect and his or her own personal selling style. In the next few pages, we will briefly discuss some of the most popular closing strategies.

CLOSING STRATEGIES

Table 14-3 provides a reference tool for the 20 effective closing strategies we will now discuss. This is not a comprehensive list, but it does introduce you to a reasonably extensive repertoire of useful ideas for closing sales. Some of these ideas will not be appropriate for your selling style or for the selling situations you typically find yourself in. However, take care not to limit yourself to learning and consistently using just one or two different strategies. The more strategies you know and experiment with, the greater your chances for closing the sale with a vast array of different buyers.

Stimulus-Response Close

By steering prospects through a series of questions to which they almost certainly have to answer "yes," you can build a pattern of positive responses that make it easier for the prospect to make the purchase commitment. Here are two examples of appropriate questions: "You would like an energy-efficient air conditioning system, wouldn't you?" "These are the benefits you're seeking, aren't they?" Inexperienced salespeople are often taught this approach to closing because it can be readily learned and has proved effective in many selling situations. However, because the stimulus-response closing approach is rather mechanical and

TABLE 14-3 20 Closing Strategies

TECHNIQUE	EXPLANATION
Stimulus-Response Close	Use a sequence of leading questions to make it easier for the prospect to say "yes" when finally asked for the order.
Assumptive Close	Assume that the purchase decision has already been made so that the prospect feels compelled to buy.
Minor Points Close	Secure favorable decisions on several minor points leading to eventual purchase of the product.
Choice Close	Offer the prospect alternative products from which to choose.
Standing Room Only (SRO) Close	Suggest that the opportunity to buy is brief because demand is great and the product is in short supply.
Special Deal Close	Offer a special incentive to encourage the prospect to buy now.
Success Story Close	Tell a story about a customer with a similar problem who solved it by buying the product.
Testimonial Close	Provide written or verbal testimonies supporting the product from satisfied customers. Especially effective are endorsements from people who are well known or respected by the prospect.
Impending Event Close	Warn the prospect about some upcoming event that makes it more advantageous to buy now.
Summary Close	Summarize the advantages and disadvantages of buying the product before asking for the order.
Counterbalance Close	Offset an objection that cannot be denied by balancing it with an important buying benefit.
Contingent Close	Get the prospect to agree to buy if the salesperson can demonstrate the benefits promised.
Turnover Close	Turn the prospect over to another salesperson with a fresh approach or better chance to make the sale.
Boomerang Close	Turn an objection around so that it becomes a reason for buying.
Ask-for-the-Order Close	Ask for the order directly or indirectly.
Order Form Close	While asking the prospect a series of questions, start filling out basic information on the contract or order blank.
Puppy Dog Close	Let the prospect take the product home for a while and, as with a puppy, an emotional attachment may develop, leading to purchase.
Pretend-to-Leave Close	Start to walk away, then "remember" another benefit or special offer after the prospect has relaxed his or her sales defenses.
No Risk Close	Agree to take the product back and refund the customer's money if the product doesn't prove satisfactory.
Lost Sale Close	When the sale seems lost, apologize for not being able to satisfy the customer and ask what it would have taken to get him or her to buy, then offer that.

requires little participation by prospects, sophisticated buyers may find it condescending and insulting.

Assumptive Close

If the prospect shows a strong interest in your product, you can try to close the sale by expressing the assumption that he or she will purchase the product. This can be done both verbally and nonverbally. You might show verbal assumption by asking questions like these: "Should I alert our credit department to activate an account for you?" and "Will you just verify your shipping address to make sure that the product is delivered precisely where you want it?" The quickest way to express your nonverbal assumption of a close is to hand the prospect a pen and your purchase agreement.

Minor Points Close

The quickest way to express your nonverbal assumption of a close is to hand the prospect a pen and your purchase agreement.

You can close the prospect on a series of minor decisions, and then move incrementally to larger decisions until the sale is closed. Unlike the stimulus-response close, where your goal is essentially to construct a simple pattern of several positive responses to yes-or-no questions, the minor points close requires you to construct something that is more like a road map or portfolio of specific information about the prospect's needs. For example, you might start by asking: "Which color do you like best?" or "Do you prefer the stationary or the portable model?" and progress to questions like: "Are you interested in our installment payment plan?" or "Would monthly or bimonthly invoicing be best for you?"

Choice Close

By asking prospects which of two or more alternative products they prefer, you do not give them the opportunity to say "no." Questions that can help you set up the choice close include: "Which of these chairs do you think would be most appropriate for your office staff, the commodore or the executive model?" and "Will you want the standard five-year or the lifetime service plan?"

Standing Room Only (SRO) Close

By showing or implying that a lot of other people are interested in buying the product, you can put psychological pressure on the prospect to buy now. Although salespeople may be honestly describing the nature of the competition for a high-demand product, the SRO close has sometimes been associated with questionable ethics. For example, some real estate salespeople have been known to deliberately schedule overlapping appointments with potential buyers. Seeing so many other buyers interested in the property can pressure prospects to make a quick decision to buy. In another situation, a salesperson might tell a buyer: "Companies have been snatching up these new car phones the minute they lay their eyes on them. If you think your field supervisors will want them, I'd suggest you place your order now for the twenty, so I can put a hold on them until Tuesday. That should give your people enough time to make up their minds, shouldn't it?" For most organizational selling situations, the SRO close is probably inappropriate or even unethical, unless you can honestly state—and show—that the product really is in great demand.

Special Deal Close

When the prospect hesitates to make the purchase commitment despite your best efforts to close, a special deal may provide the incentive to buy now. Try declaring: "If you'll agree to sign the contract, I'll call my boss to see if I can get approval to let you delay your first payment until January" or "If you buy today, I'll include the one-year service contract for free."

PRICE DISCOUNT
Reduction off the standard list price for various reasons.

Offering a **price discount** is a common way to close sales. Salespeople are often authorized to offer prospects and customers reductions off the standard list price for various reasons, including paying within a certain period of time, buying a large quantity, buying out of season, cooperating in promotional campaigns, and serving a designated function or role in the channel of distribution. Reminding prospects and customers of a price discount can often tip the balance toward closing the sale. The next vignette discusses how price discounts work.

Success Story Close

Relating a story about how one of your other customers solved a similar problem with the product can reassure a prospect about buying now. You might say something like this:

> You know Elizabeth Rakowski, the purchasing agent for Superior Plumbing Supplies in Pebbleville? Well, Elizabeth was having a hard time getting packaging mate-

---

PRICE DISCOUNTS

■ *Cash discounts* are an incentive for buyers to pay the invoice within a specified time period. To illustrate, 2/10, net 30, are typical terms offered to most organizational buyers. If the customer pays within 10 days, 2 percent is taken off the total bill. No discount is given if the customer pays after the 10th day, and the entire amount is due within 30 days.

■ *Quantity discounts* allow the buyer a lower price for purchasing in multiple units or above a certain dollar amount.

—*Noncumulative discounts* (one-time): "I can let you have one for $530 or two for $950."

—*Cumulative discounts* (summary of annual purchases): "We offer 4 percent discount on total sales over $5,000, and for sales over $10,000, we offer a 5 percent discount."

■ *Trade discounts* are given to middlemen (retailers, wholesalers, and distributors) for performing various functions for the manufacturer such as break bulk, storage, financing, and transportation: "Wholesalers receive 40 percent off the list price, and retailers receive 32 percent off."

■ *Seasonal discounts* are price reductions given to buyers who buy products out of season: "We're offering a 15 percent discount on all bathing suits ordered before March 15th."

■ *Promotional allowances* are concessions in price given to customers who participate in a promotional campaign or sales support program: "We'll give you $2,000 on each order of 100 to help offset your local newspaper advertising costs on behalf of our new line of cameras."

rials that would hold up in shipping some of Superior's heavier plumbing parts to customers. She tried every conceivable type of box offered by every packaging materials and container company you can name. When I heard about her problem, I told her that I'd give her 10 of our new reinforced Tough Guy brand containers to test by shipping Superior's most troublesome products to California and back. If our Tough Guys didn't hold up, I promised to pay the shipping charges. But if they did hold up, I wanted an order for 5,000 units! Well, when our Tough Guys came back looking almost brand new and the plumbing parts didn't have a mark on them, Elizabeth called me all excited and insisted on an order for 10,000 units. If you want to listen to a true believer in our Tough Guy containers, just give Elizabeth a call.

Testimonial Close

Sometimes you can close a sale by showing your prospect letters from satisfied customers or—better yet—from well-known and widely respected people who are satisfied customers. Endorsements by prominent executives or celebrities of both consumer and industrial products will often encourage prospects to buy because they trust the judgment and integrity of the endorser. It's best if you can obtain these endorsements in writing and have copies of them made on fine-quality paper. Even if you manage to close the sale without these testimonials, it's a good idea to use them as leave-behinds to reassure the buyer of the wisdom of his or her purchase decision.

Impending Event Close

When you can give early warning about an event that will alter, say, the product's price or availability, the prospect will readily see that it is more advantageous to buy now. Salespeople who give their customers timely information that helps them buy wisely and efficiently gain their customers' trust and gratitude. On the other hand, nothing irritates customers more than not being alerted to upcoming price increases or product shortages or finding out too late that they were sold a product just before it went on sale.

Summary Close

Also called the "T-account" or "Ben Franklin close" because of this Founding Father's rational approach to making decisions, a summary close uses a simple analysis in the form of a T-graph to show the advantages and disadvantages of buying the product. It's usually best for the salesperson to assist but to let the prospect actually prepare the T-account so that it becomes the prospect's analysis, not the salesperson's. Seeing that the product's benefits far outweigh its costs usually leads the prospect to the purchase decision. Figure 14-1 provides an example of the summary or T-account analysis for considering the purchase of a Macintosh laptop computer.

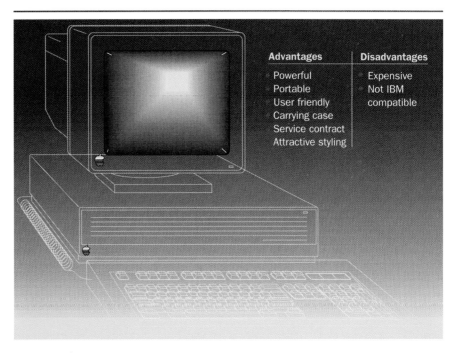

FIGURE 14-1 Macintosh Computer T-Account Analysis

Counterbalance Close

Prospects who raise a legitimate objection to buying the product can often be closed on that point of resistance if you can counterbalance their objection with a significant benefit. The prospect may object:

> Your company's automatic conveyor belt system is just too expensive for our warehouse operations. We'll just stay with our manual system.

To counterbalance this, you might reply:

> Mr. Greenhaus, you said you were planning to add another person to your warehouse crew. How much will you pay that new employee in wages and benefits—$14,000 or $16,000? Well, our equipment costs only $9,800 fully installed, and you'll increase warehouse productivity so much that you won't need to hire another person. You'll save at least $4,000 the first year, and more thereafter because our equipment won't demand a raise. I don't see how you can go wrong with it, do you?

Contingent Close

CONTINGENT CLOSE
Convincing a prospect to agree to buy by showing that the product will do what the salesperson says it will do.

Convincing the prospect to agree to buy if you can show that the product will do what you have said it will do is called a **contingent close.** For example, you could ask: "If I can show you how our equipment can help your company cut inventory costs by twenty percent, will you buy?" By setting up this contingency,

Prospects who raise a legitimate objection to buying the product can often be closed on that point of resistance if you can counterbalance their objection with a significant benefit.

you have essentially closed the sale if you can substantiate your claims about the product.

Turnover Close

In team-selling situations, when the prospect is not responding to the sales-closing techniques of one salesperson, it's often a good strategy to turn the prospect over to another salesperson with a different closing strategy. In using this turnover close, the first salesperson may play the all-business, unyielding negotiator, while the second salesperson or manager is friendly and flexible. To make this switch in salespeople, the first salesperson might say: "I've got to run to a meeting now, but Neil Stacey—who's as knowledgeable as I am about desktop publishing systems—will give you more information and answer any questions you might have."

Experienced field sales reps usually know well in advance of an attempted close whether or not their relationship with a prospect is a good one. If for one reason or another it is not, they often bring a sales manager or colleague to the next sales appointment to handle the closing of the sale.

Boomerang Close

BOOMERANG CLOSE
Turning a prospect's objection or point of resistance around so that it becomes a reason for buying.

In the **boomerang close,** the salesperson turns a prospect's objection or point of resistance around so that it becomes a reason for buying. For instance, an automobile dealership prospect might remark:

> I like the looks and modern style of this automatic garage door, but it's so slow that it takes twice as long to open and close as our other garage doors. I'm afraid that our mechanics and customers will lose patience with its slowness.

You might truthfully counter:

> Yes, this new model opens and closes at about half the speed of the older models. I'm sure you know how dangerous these heavy commercial garage doors are and, like most managers, you can probably tell some tragic stories about people being hit by them. Based on studies of these accidents over the past five years, we found that cutting the garage door speed in half would probably reduce the number of accidents by 75 percent. Garage managers where they're using this new door say that it takes only a few days to adjust to its pace, and there hasn't been an accident reported yet. I think you'll find that the added safety more than compensates for its slower operation.

Ask-for-the-Order Close

An effective but sometimes overlooked close is to simply ask for the order in a graciously assertive way. For example:

> Let me use my laptop computer to order the product for you now so we can start solving your company's production-line problems as early as next week.

Order Form Close

As a variation of the assumptive close, you can use verbal and nonverbal signals to gently pressure the prospect into buying. By asking the prospect a series of basic questions (spelling of his or her name, address, and telephone number) while writing this information on the contract, the salesperson leads the prospect

Selling in Action

Turning a Complaint into a Sales Close

An advertising salesperson was making a sales call on one of his current customers without having read the latest issue of the magazine in which he was selling advertising space. The president of the firm approached the salesperson as he entered and lividly pointed to a scathing editorial reference to his company in the magazine. "Did you see this?" he sputtered. "All morning I've been getting calls from my best customers, and you want me to buy advertising space!"

Instead of acting defensively, the salesperson replied: "The fact that your best customers have called clearly shows that our publication reaches the people you want to reach. Rather than a six-time contract, we should talk about a contract for twelve."

The salesperson's quick thinking resulted in a successful boomerang close on a new contract for 12 advertisements.

Source: Sales & Marketing Management, September 1989, p. 104.

toward the close. After the basic information is filled in, the salesperson hands the order form and a pen to the prospect and, in a friendly way, says something like: "Okay, I've filled out the order form with your requirements. Check it over and just sign on the dotted line there."

Order Form Preparation

This is a good time to mention one of the major pitfalls of working with that essential piece of sales paperwork, the order form. One of the most likely times to lose a sale during the closing stage is when the salesperson is doing calculations on sales agreement forms. Many new salespeople lose their first two or three sales because they literally can't fill out the order form fast enough. As the salesperson is slowly completing the form, the buyer has time to reconsider the purchase or to think of more objections. Therefore, it's important to practice filling out the necessary paperwork for a sale until you can do it almost reflexively while continuing to reassure the customer.

Puppy Dog Close

Who can resist a puppy dog? People who take a puppy into their home for a few days usually become so attached to it that they keep it. Similarly, when you let prospects try out a product at home or in the office for a few days or weeks, they usually form an attachment that makes it difficult for them to return the product. Although this closing strategy works most effectively with expensive consumer products such as automobiles, stereo components, and yes, pure-bred puppies, organizational salespeople may also find appropriate opportunities for using it. For example, an aircraft manufacturer's sales rep who has arranged for two or three trial uses of a corporate helicopter might visit the prospect's buying team and say: "Well, your colleagues seem pretty pleased with our 'copter's performance. May I take that as a sign that you'd like to own the aircraft?"

Pretend-to-Leave Close

In retail selling, when a prospect does not respond after several trial closes, the salesperson can excuse him or herself to wait on some other customers or to do another task. As the salesperson starts to walk away, many prospects will let down their guard and even feel disappointed to see the salesperson leaving them. At that moment, the salesperson can suddenly turn around and come back to tell the prospect about one final benefit or incentive to buy that he or she "forgot" to mention. Catching the prospect off-guard like this with another benefit often leads to a successful close.

Because of the highly competitive nature of most organizational selling situations, business-to-business sales reps should be very careful about using the pretend-to-leave close. Some buyers might feel that you are playing games with them or simply take your intended departure as a sign of your indifference.

No Risk Close

Prospects differ widely in the degree of risk they perceive in various purchase decisions. Some professional buyers are especially fearful about making a mistake that will cost their company a lot of money. One common way to alleviate the fear of making a purchase mistake is to offer prospects a money-back guarantee if they are not fully satisfied with the product. A variation on this close is to let the prospect try the product on a free-trial or small-sample basis for a period of time. Small trial-sized packages of products, promotional coupons, and money-back guarantees are all methods to close sales by taking some of the risk out of buying.

Lost Sale Close

Even when it appears you have lost the sale, you have still another chance to close. At this point, you can apologize to prospects for not being able to satisfy them, then ask what it would have taken to make the sale. Thinking the salesperson has admitted defeat and merely wants to improve his or her skills by humbly asking for help, many prospects readily reveal their *real* objection at this point or what it would *really* have taken to get them to buy. With this information, you can now deal with the real objection and offer whatever the customer says he or she wanted to close the deal.

INTEGRATING PERSUASION PRINCIPLES AND CLOSING STRATEGIES

Each of the 21 closing strategies we have discussed obviously relates to one or more of the seven persuasion principles we discussed previously. The stimulus-response closing strategy, for example, is based on the consistency principle of persuasion. You are setting up a series of questions that call for almost automatic "yes" responses and lead the prospect along a *consistent* thought route all the way through the close. Table 14-4 illustrates one way to relate the closing strategies to appropriate persuasion principles, but it doesn't represent the only way. Set up your own table and relate the persuasion principles to the closing strategies the way *you* think they fit together. For example, in your opinion, does a puppy dog close more clearly relate to the commitment principle or to the friendship principle?

SILENCE CAN BE GOLDEN IN CLOSING

According to sales trainer J. Douglas Edwards: "Whenever you ask a closing question, shut up. The first person to speak loses." It is important to not speak after asking a closing question because, using a tennis metaphor, you have just hit the ball into the prospect's court and the pressure is on the prospect to hit it back by answering your closing question and committing to the purchase. If you speak first after the closing question, the ball automatically bounces back into your court.

TABLE 14-4   Integrating Persuasion Principles and Closing Strategies

PERSUASION PRINCIPLES	CLOSING STRATEGIES
■ Consistency	Stimulus-Response
	Assumptive
	Minor Points
■ Commitment	Choice
	Summary
	Counterbalance
	Contingent
	Boomerang
	Trial
	Ask for the Order
	Lost Sale
	Order Form
■ Reciprocity	Special Deal
	No Risk
■ Social Validation	Success Story
	Testimonial
■ Authority	Success Story
	Testimonial
■ Scarcity	Standing Room Only
	Impending Event
	Pretend to Leave
■ Friendship	Puppy Dog
	Turnover

Now, it may sound easy to remain silent for a few seconds, but this seems to be one of the hardest things for salespeople to do. Assume that you ask this closing question: "Well, Mr. Thurstone, which model do you like best—the Mohawk or the Eagle?" If you remain silent, Mr. Thurstone is pressured to commit himself to one of the models, and probably the purchase. But if you speak first, Mr. Thurstone doesn't have to answer. Even if Mr. Thurstone vacillates for

What Would You Do?

You are a sales engineer for industrial chemicals working for Du Pont Corporation located in Wilmington, Delaware. You arrive at a potential customer's plant in Trenton, New Jersey, just in time for an appointment with a purchasing agent that was scheduled three weeks ago. You have prepared and practiced a brilliant one-hour sales presentation focusing on specific benefits that you think will overwhelm the agent and stimulate him to immediately buy $100,000 worth of chemicals from you. As soon as you walk into his office, the purchasing agent says: "I'm sorry but I only have fifteen minutes to spend with you today. I've looked over your product brochures and I'm impressed. I've decided to place a twenty-five-thousand-dollar order with you."

several minutes, you should resist the temptation to break the silence. The salesperson who breaks the silence by saying something like: "Oh well, we can return to that decision later" is letting Mr. Thurstone off the hook and must work to set up another closing opportunity. Remaining silent for whatever time it takes for the prospect to answer the closing question will put gold in your pockets.

QUESTIONABLE CLOSING TECHNIQUES

Besides the ones we've discussed, there are other closing techniques suggested in books and in sales seminars by well-known practitioners and sales trainers. Some of these techniques, however, are ethically questionable and imply that "salesperson win–customer lose" sales negotiations are acceptable. A common characteristic of such techniques is that they use manipulation or trickery to dupe the prospect into making some sort of purchase commitment. Let's look at two examples of questionable closes: (1) the erroneous conclusion and (2) the porcupine close.

Erroneous Conclusion

Although it looks like a technique that only the Three Stooges or Groucho Marx would be comfortable with, manipulative salespeople occasionally use the *erroneous conclusion close* with some success. By discovering almost any morsel of information having to do with the prospect's purchase considerations, the salesperson "hooks" the prospect into making a buying commitment—of sorts—by first pretending to have misunderstood the morsel of information and then acting as if the prospect had originally intended that to be the only important factor in his or her purchase decision. For example, in talking to a married couple looking over some carpet in a large department store, the salesperson may overhear the wife say to her husband: "John, even if we found a carpet we liked, it would have to be delivered on Thursday, my day off." Later, after showing the couple several carpets, the salesperson says: "Remember, we have free home delivery on any carpet you buy. Friday is your day off, isn't it?" When the woman corrects the salesperson by responding: "No, Thursday is my day off," the salesperson says: "Oh, that's right. Let me write that on my order pad before I forget it. Now, you like this beige carpet. Good choice! How many yards can I put you down for?" Surprisingly, once that little bit of information has been written on the order pad, some people feel almost committed to buy.

Porcupine

A closing technique that looks even more like a trap than the erroneous conclusion, and has just as little regard for the prospect's needs and wants, is the *porcupine close*. When a prospect asks a question about a product feature, the salesperson immediately turns the question around and asks whether he or she wants a product with that feature. If the answer is "yes," then the prospect has fallen into a verbal trap and is stuck (hence the reference to the "porcupine"). For example, a woman looking at pianos in a large music store might ask the salesperson: "Do you have a Baldwin upright piano in a dark walnut color?" The salesperson immediately turns the prospect's question into a closing question: "Do you want a Baldwin upright piano with a dark walnut color?" The prospect will, of course, confirm her earlier question, and when the salesperson shows a dark walnut Baldwin piano to her, she realizes that she has basically agreed to buy it. In this simpleminded close, the salesperson is always careful to restate the prospect's question or comment in such a way that the prospect's "yes" answer is automatic. Rephrasing the question to "If we have the Baldwin upright piano in a dark walnut color, will you buy it?" shifts the emphasis from the desired color to whether she'll buy and will probably yield a "no" or at best a "maybe" answer.

Today's professional salespeople do not feel comfortable using closing techniques that attempt to entrap prospects and do not want to include them in their repertoire. Closes like the erroneous conclusion and porcupine are good examples of the worst techniques used by yesterday's manipulative salespeople. The vast majority of today's increasingly sophisticated prospects and customers will quickly see through such manipulative closes and will refuse to buy from salespeople who use them.

CLOSING MISTAKES

Many sales are lost because the salesperson makes simple mistakes. Every salesperson has made most types of mistakes at least once, but top professionals learn the fundamentals of closing sales and make fewer mistakes than less successful salespeople. Some of the most common mistakes that hamper the closing of a sale are outlined in Table 14-5.

HOW DO YOU HANDLE SALES REJECTION?

If you simply cannot close the sale, you should not feel discouraged or personally rejected. Not even the very best salesperson makes a sale every time. In fact, the sales hit ratio can be very low, depending on the product, competition, and prospects. In his book *How to Master the Art of Selling,* Tom Hopkins argues that salespeople have to develop positive attitudes toward sales rejection.[7] Instead of failure, rejection should be viewed as:

- A learning experience that will enable you to do better next time.
- Helpful feedback that will spur you to develop more creative closing approaches.
- An opportunity to develop a sense of humor and begin to lose your fear of future rejection.
- The motivation to spend more time practicing selling skills and improving performance.

[7]Tom Hopkins, *How to Master the Art of Selling* (New York: Warner Books, 1982), pp. 87–93.

TABLE 14-5   Closing Mistakes

■ **Talking past closing signals:** Salespeople can become so enamored of their own sales presentations and demonstrations that they talk past several prospect closing signals.

■ **Failure to recognize prospect buying signals:** Salespeople sometimes fail to hear and see closing signals while they are making their sales presentations and demonstrations.

■ **Projecting a lack of confidence:** Salespeople who don't believe in themselves, their products, and their companies will display a lack of confidence that will be picked up and mirrored back by prospects, who then will not buy.

■ **Reluctance to attempt trial closes on early calls:** Every sales call is an opportunity to close the sale. Salespeople who make no attempt to close until the third or fourth call will often miss closing opportunities, and may lose many sales to more assertive salespeople.

■ **Inflexibility in using closing techniques:** Some salespeople have success with one closing technique, then fall into the habit of relying on it almost exclusively. No one closing technique is appropriate for all customers, or with any one customer at all times. Professional salespeople learn to use an array of closing techniques as the selling situation requires.

■ **Giving up too soon:** Persistence is an essential quality of the successful salesperson. A recent Sales and Marketing Executives study found that less than 20 percent of sales were made after four sales calls, but over 80 percent of sales are made by the fifth call.*

■ **Lingering too long after the close:** Generally, after a sale has been closed, the salesperson should make a polite but speedy exit. Lingering too long afterward can endanger a sale because the prospect may think of new objections or rehash old ones.

■ **Failure to practice closing skills:** Like all professionals, whether doctors, lawyers, entertainers, public speakers, or baseball players, salespeople will find their skills growing rusty unless they devote considerable time to practicing and improving them. Salespeople who practice using the appropriate closing skills for each individual sales call develop a significant advantage over salespeople who don't practice.

■ **Lack of alternative closing strategies:** For every selling situation, the salesperson should plan alternative closing strategies in case the preferred ones don't seem to be working.

■ **Failure to understand the need to close:** Only the most naive salesperson fails to understand that the close is an essential stage in the selling process. An outstanding sales presentation is seldom enough to get the prospect to buy. Unless the salesperson skillfully uses trial closes, many sales will never be accomplished.

Source: Reported in The Competitive Advantage, sample issue, 1989, p. 6.

■ Just a part of the selling game you must accept in order to continue to play and win.

No One Wins All the Time

In challenging activities like closing sales, your average doesn't have to be very high to achieve great success. Let's use a baseball analogy. Ty Cobb stole 94 bases in 144 attempts during his best year, for a success rate of two out of every three. Another ballplayer, Max Carey, had a 94 percent success rate one year when he stole 51 bases out of 54 tries. If Carey had kept up that ratio, he would have far surpassed Cobb's long-time record. But Carey didn't try often enough. The dif-

DEALING WITH REJECTION

■ *Never equate your worth as a human being with your success or failure as a salesperson:* It's how honestly and fairly you treat other people that should determine your opinion of yourself over the long run.

■ *Separate your ego from the sale:* If the prospect doesn't buy, assume that he or she simply feels that the product doesn't fit his or her needs or offer the best value for the money—at least at this time.

■ *Don't automatically assume that you or your selling skills are the problem:* Some prospects are very difficult persons, and others may just be having a bad day.

■ *Call on another prospect:* When one prospect rejects your product, simply look in your file for another promising prospect. The more prospects you have, the more confident you'll feel.

■ *Positively anticipate rejection and it will not overwhelm you:* Expect it, but don't create it. Think in advance what your response to rejection will be.

■ *Remember that there are many more rejections than successes in nearly all types of selling:* According to the law of averages, each rejection increases the chances of success on the next sales call.

■ *Recognize the possibility that not buying may be the only decision the prospect can make at this time because of timing, shared decision making, or budget constraints:* Many prospects will not feel comfortable revealing these reasons to you since they reflect negatively on their own power.

Source: Adapted from Tom Reilly, "Salespeople: Develop the Means to Handle Rejection," *Personal Selling Power,* July–August 1987, p. 15.

ference in the level of fame between Cobb and Carey points out that it's not the number of times you *fail,* it's the number of times you *try* that usually determines outstanding success.[8]

One enterprising salesperson even figured out *how many times he needed to fail* in order to make $67,500 in commissions for the year. "All I have to do," he told his sales manager, "is make 2,444 telephone calls or about 10 per day." Here's the way he figured it. "My average sale earns me about $900 in commissions, and it usually takes me 2.5 sales calls to make one sale. On average, I must make 13 phone calls to get one appointment with a prospect, so I need 33 phone calls to get 2.5 appointments and one sale. To earn $67,500 in commissions, I have to close 75 sales, which means I need to obtain 188 appointments from 2,444 phone calls. In other words, I need 32 people to say 'No' to me before getting that 'yes' leading to a sale."[9]

IMMEDIATE POSTSALE ACTIVITIES

As mentioned at the beginning of this chapter, the close of a sale is not the ending but the confirmation of a buyer-seller relationship. Salespeople must continue to work hard to ensure that customers receive continued postpurchase service and satisfaction. However, during the immediate postsale period, there are some critical activities for salespeople:

[8]Ibid., pp. 92–93.
[9]Based in part on an analysis presented in Warren Greshes, "Don't Count Your Blessings, Count Your Rejections," *Sales & Marketing Management,* October 1989, p. 103.

WHAT DO YOU DO WHEN
THE PROSPECT DOESN'T BUY?

■ *Don't burn any bridges:* Never show disappointment, frustration, anger, or any other negative emotion to the prospect. Future opportunities to sell the prospect are more likely to come your way if you maintain a positive attitude.

■ *Analyze lost sales:* Review the selling process from start to finish to see what might have gone wrong or been improved upon. Be as objective as possible so that you benefit from this postmortem.

■ *Help the prospect shop the competition:* If the prospect wants to look at competitive products before buying, you can help him or her do so by outlining on an index card or sheet the specific criteria for comparing the quality and overall performance of products in the category. Specifics on your product should already be entered on the card.

■ *Call back with new information or appeals:* Keep the relationship alive by providing the prospect with relevant new information such as interesting articles on the industry, new-product introductions, special deals, and upcoming price changes.

■ *Schedule another sales appointment:* Arrange another sales appointment whenever you have a new sales proposal or product you think the prospect might be interested in.

■ *Never give up:* As long as a prospect needs your product category, don't give up on making the sale. Organizational and operational changes can quickly alter buying criteria. Many long-term relationships and profitable sales arrangements have come after years of prospect refusals to buy.

■ Call or write within a few days to *thank* customers for their orders, to reassure them about their purchases to relieve any postpurchase dissonance (see Chapter 5), and to let them know that you are there to help them with any problems. Solving little problems for customers can substantially increase their satisfaction and help further the long-run buyer-seller relationship. After a sale, some salespeople make it a practice to send customers a little thank-you gift. Appropriate items might be candy, wine, flowers, fruit baskets, clever toys, and tickets to the theater or a sports event.

■ Check on your customers' orders to make sure that they will be delivered on time. If there is going to be a delay in a delivery, warn the customer. Even though it won't be good news, customers will appreciate receiving this advance notice because it will allow them to make the appropriate adjustments in their operations.

■ Contact the credit and billing department to confirm that they have the correct information on your customers' orders before sending out invoices. Few things irritate customers more than receiving and having to straighten out erroneous bills.

■ Try to be there when the product is delivered to the customer. Helping the customer set the product up and get it in working order will do wonders for furthering that long-run relationship.

■ Promptly update your records after a sale so you'll be prepared for the next sales call on that customer. Include the latest sale, personnel or organizational changes, new problems and needs, purchase plans, and any other relevant developments.

KEEPING THE CUSTOMER SOLD

After closing a sales agreement, professional salespeople celebrate their success only a short time because they understand that "keeping the customer sold" can be as challenging and time-consuming as winning the order in the first place.

One of the most important things for you to do immediately after a sale is to contact the credit and billing department to confirm that they have the correct information about your customer's order *before* they send out the invoice.

Some salespeople have made the analogy that keeping a customer is like trying to keep a lover who is continually being pursued and romanced by others from straying. You can't take the lover or the customer for granted. You must work at trying to please them, to make sure that they are satisfied with the current relationship, and to do everything you can to improve upon it so that they are not tempted to leave you for a competitor. Even when the buyer-seller relationship matures into a "partnership" or "marriage," the professional salesperson does not let up on the tender loving care but rather continues to treat the customer like a new lover instead of an old spouse. Remember: Winning new customers is much harder and less profitable than keeping your old customers.

SUMMARY

The sales close is an integral part of the ongoing personal selling process. A successful close is confirmation of the sale and the furtherance of the buyer-seller relationship. Salespeople should be prepared to use a trial close at any propitious time during the selling process. There are numerous verbal and nonverbal cues that can alert salespeople that it's time for a trial close. Some salespeople fail to close because of insufficient confidence, feelings of guilt, or a fear of failure. It usually takes four calls to successfully close most sales, so persistence pays off.

Salespeople must learn to close buyers with various negotiating styles, ranging from hard bargainers to considerate buyers. Several basic principles of persuasion can be effectively applied within the framework of different closing strategies. Questionable or unethical closes are those that try to trick or dupe the customer in some way. These manipulative approaches are ill-advised and likely to backfire on the salespeople who use them. No one is successful at sales all the time, so salespeople must learn to deal with rejection. There are several immediate postsale activities that salespeople need to carry out if they are to satisfy customers and develop a positive long-run buyer-seller relationship.

CHAPTER REVIEW QUESTIONS

1. What is meant by a "trial close"?
2. When should salespeople try to close?
3. What verbal and nonverbal cues from the prospect indicate that it's time for a trial close?
4. What are some of the reasons that some salespeople don't even attempt to close?
5. What is the PAS attitude in personal selling?
6. Describe the six basic negotiating styles of buyers.
7. What are seven principles of persuasion?
8. Describe at least 12 of the 20 basic closing strategies.
9. Name ten closing mistakes.
10. List some ways for a salesperson to deal with rejection.
11. What should the salesperson do when the prospect doesn't buy?
12. Describe the immediate postsale activities of a successful salesperson.

TOPICS FOR THOUGHT AND CLASS DISCUSSION

1. Which do you think is a more appropriate term for stage 6 in the personal selling process: (a) closing the sale or (b) confirming the sale? Why?
2. What would you say to a salesperson friend who must overcome confidence, guilt, and fear-of-failure problems before attempting to close sales?
3. Which of the 21 closing strategies provided in Table 14-3 do you think you would prefer to use in your professional personal selling career? Why?
4. Why do you think *silence* can be so effective after attempting a trial close?
5. What would you do if a prospect didn't buy from you—both right after the sales call and several days or weeks later?
6. Assume you have just made a substantial sale. What steps would you take to further the buyer-seller relationship?
7. What is meant by the term "rejection"? Why are most of us so afraid of it? How do you personally cope with various types of rejection in your life?

PROJECTS FOR PERSONAL GROWTH

1. Ask three business-to-business salespeople to explain their favorite closing strategies. Give each strategy a name. How many of them are discussed in this chapter? In your opinion, are any of the closes used by the salespeople questionable or unethical? Why?

2. Ask the three salespeople what percentage of their prospects and customers fall into each of the six buyer negotiating styles: hard bargainers, facilitators, straight shooters, socializers, persuaders, and considerate buyers. Are there any other styles that they would add to this list? Which of the different buyer negotiating styles do they prefer to sell to? Why?

3. Share stories with other members of your class about how each of you has recently used one or more of the seven basic principles of persuasion to negotiate something. Do any of your classmates have a favorite persuasion technique that they rely on most often?

4. Survey five people in different occupations about how they deal with rejection. Would these methods also apply to personal selling? Explain how.

KEY TERMS

Close   The stage in the selling process where the salesperson tries to obtain an agreement from the prospect to purchase the product.

Trial close   Any well-placed attempt to close the sale, which can be used early and often throughout the selling process.

PAS (problems and solutions) **attitude**   A selling approach that seeks to work with prospects to identify and solve their problems and create opportunities to lower costs, increase productivity, and improve profits.

Scarcity principle   If a product is in short supply, it is often perceived as more valuable and desirable than one that is plentiful.

Price discount   Reduction off the standard list price for various reasons.

Contingent close   Convincing a prospect to agree to buy by showing that the product will do what the salesperson says it will do.

Boomerang close   Turning a prospect's objection or point of resistance around so that it becomes a reason for buying.

Case 14-1

LOOKING FOR AN OPPORTUNITY TO CLOSE THE SALE

After working at Choi Company for four years as a supervisor in the shipping department, Fred Liska was recently asked if he would like to be considered for a position on the sales force. Although he's been taking college courses at night for two years, it will be several years before he earns his degree, so Fred jumped at the chance to become a sales representative for the company.

Mr. Choi, who started the company after emigrating from South Korea 15 years ago, has always taken a special interest in Fred. He personally recommended him for sales because he thinks his personality and conscientiousness make him an ideal salesman. Although there is no formal training program for new salespeople at Choi Company, Fred was given the opportunity to "learn how to sell" first-hand by spending three weeks traveling on sales calls with Pete Hayes, one of Choi Company's senior sales reps. Pete told Fred to "just follow me around, and watch and listen. If you have any questions, save them until after each sales call." Pete seemed to know all the people on his sales calls by their first names, and he spent as much time socializing as selling. Not once during the three weeks did he complete a full sales presentation, and he often failed to discuss some product features and benefits. Nevertheless, Fred had to admit that Pete got quite a few orders during the three weeks, though it looked to him as if Pete was mainly taking orders instead of doing creative selling. Nearly every time that Pete asked for an order, he got one—oftentimes even before he was halfway through a sales presentation. "Well," Fred thought to himself, "Choi does make the best instrument carts in the industry, so maybe they sell themselves." Fred mentally rehearsed what he knew about Choi carts. They are made of sturdy welded steel with rubber-padded, nonconductive, nonslip surfaces and a heavy bottom shelf that helps protect against tipping or falling. Each cart has two swivel and two rigid rubber wheels for easy mobility while carrying up to 1,300 pounds of equipment or instruments. Attractively finished in gray enamel, the carts contain a utility drawer that can hold tools, supplies, and other small items. The price is $395.90 per cart, or $3,459 for a quantity of ten.

On the first Monday after completing his three weeks of field training, Fred nervously approaches his first sales call. The prospect is Deborah Connors, purchasing agent for Scientific Laboratories—a Chicago-based firm specializing in conducting laboratory analyses for medical doctors. After introducing himself and handing Ms. Connors his business card, Fred begins his sales presentation. Since nothing is more impressive than seeing the instrument cart as it is being described, Fred has wheeled one right into Ms. Connor's office. As he is explaining some of the features, advantages, and benefits of the Choi instrument cart, Fred notices Ms. Connors moving the cart back and forth and feeling its surface. She pulls out the cart's drawer and smiles when she sees the neat little compartment trays inside. At this point, she interrupts Fred's presentation to say: "If we do decide to buy, how long will it take to have delivery?" Fred answers: "Two weeks," and continues with his sales presentation, showing several pictures of the cart being used at various types of companies.

Studying the pictures, Ms. Connors asks: "Will the Choi cart really carry thirteen hundred pounds? It doesn't look that strong." Fred replies: "One of our largest customers, Metropolitan Hospital, regularly carries equipment weighing over fifteen hundred pounds on the carts without any problems." Fred thinks to himself: "If she doesn't quit interrupting, I'll never get through my sales presentation," but he doesn't let any irritation show and smoothly continues with the presentation and demonstration. At this point, Fred pulls out the special drawer with compartment trays and mentions that Choi is the only cart available with this feature. Ms. Connors smiles and remarks: "Yes, I think putting those compartment trays inside the drawer is a really clever idea. I don't know how many times I've needed a test tube, some tape, or a pair of scissors when I'm carting laboratory samples and instruments from one room to another. We could keep basic supplies in those little drawers and save a lot of time and extra steps." Fred nods his head and continues to point out other features of the cart. He smiles to himself, thinking: "I'm almost done with my sales presentation. Nothing much left to talk about except the price."

Just then, Ms. Connors's secretary interrupts to say that Henry Bauman, the vice president of operations, needs to see her right away in his office. Ms. Connors excuses herself and says: "Ask my secretary to schedule another appointment with me, Fred. I know what this meeting with Mr. Bauman is about, and it's going to take the rest of my time today. Thanks for coming in."

Fred feels deflated. "Boy," he thinks, "what lousy timing. In two more minutes, I would have finished my sales presentation and started my close. I'm sure she would have placed an order when I asked for it." Dejectedly, he picks up his sales presentation materials, places them on the cart, and pushes it out to Ms. Connors's secretary's desk to schedule another appointment.

Questions

1. Do you believe Ms. Connors would have placed an order when Fred completed his sales close? Why?

2. What do you think of Fred's sales presentation?

3. Could Fred have tried a trial close before Ms. Connors left for the other meeting? When?

4. What advice would you give Fred for future sales calls?

Case 14-2

USING PERSUASION PRINCIPLES AND CLOSING STRATEGIES

Peggy Markley is a sales rep for Versatile Office Equipment (VOE), selling the Assurance brand of portable photocopiers, facsimiles, word processors, and dictation machines. Peggy is a genuinely friendly person whom everybody seems to like because she makes it so obvious that she likes people. She has a smile and a friendly word for nearly everybody she encounters on a sales call. Although not striking in physical appearance, her beautiful personality makes people take special notice of her. Once she has made a sales call, she seldom has to reintroduce herself to anyone. In each of her five years as a sales rep for VOE, Peggy has surpassed her annual quota, earning her membership in the company's High Flyers Club. Her record for keeping customers is unmatched by any other VOE sales rep.

Stories about her attention to customers are often used in training seminars for new salespeople. One of the favorites told about her is the time she was making a sales presentation in a prospect's office when they were interrupted by a phone call from the hospital saying that the man's pregnant wife had just gone into labor and would soon be delivering a baby. Because the prospect had taken public transportation to work, Peggy insisted on driving him to the hospital so he didn't lose any time getting there. They arrived just in time for the man to see his first baby being born. Well, his wife was so grateful that Peggy became a family friend who was frequently invited to dinner. Peggy also won a very profitable account. Surprisingly, none of the other customers whose appointments she had to cancel that day were upset with her when they heard the story. In fact, all of them readily rescheduled their appointments.

Peggy seems to routinely do thoughtful things for her prospects and customers—whether it's bringing in hot cider and doughnuts on a wintry day in January, dropping off mail for them at the post office on her way to another appointment, or lending them her copy of a great book that she has just finished reading. Many of her customers say: "Peggy's more like a friend than a salesperson."

But Peggy Markley is not just a nice person. She's a top-notch sales professional, and her sales presentations and demonstrations are considered as good as anybody's. She stresses product quality, delivery, and customer service instead of price, point-ing out that paying a little higher price for the best gives the greatest value in the long run. One of her typical strategies in dealing with price objections is to compliment a customer on her or his clothes or accessories; for example: "Your briefcase is so handsome and professional looking, I'm sure you didn't buy it because it was the lowest-priced one. You bought it because it was the best value for your money, right? Well, the same principle applies here—you'll get more value for your dollars by buying Assurance products. No other company comes close to matching our product quality, prompt delivery, return privileges, money-back guarantees, and customer service at this competitive price." To reinforce her statements, Peggy always carries around a notebook of testimonial letters from satisfied customers and a list of prominent companies that are currently using Assurance products. Frequently, she brings a technical expert from Versatile's engineering, operations, or design departments along with her on a sales call to help analyze a customer's unique problems and suggest a solution. Extremely conscientious about warning her customers about upcoming price changes or product shortages, she frequently offers to set aside inventory for them at the current price for delivery later.

Recently, Peggy has been asked to spend two weeks in Versatile's Training and Development (T&D) department to help prepare a comprehensive sales training program for newly hired salespeople. The new Director of T&D, Frank Sherry, who was hired from the staff of the local university, quickly heard about Peggy's unique sales abilities and decided to ask her to help develop the new sales training program. After talking to Peggy, he was surprised to learn that she had never gone through any formal sales training herself. She had shifted into sales from the Customer Relations department when the company issued a general call for new salespeople from in-house staff. About five years ago, after spending two weeks learning about the company's products and a week traveling with a senior sales rep, she was given her own territory and told by her sales manager to just "go sell 'em." As Peggy told Mr. Sherry: "I don't think I could teach anybody to sell the way I do. The things I do are just natural extensions of my personality. I care about people and I try to make them feel important. I've never tried to analyze what I do."

Frank Sherry knows that Peggy is well-liked and respected by everyone in the company and that her association with his new training program will give it credibility. He also feels that she has some unique selling concepts and approaches that he and his staff can draw on and convert into meaningful formats to teach others. He tells Peggy he doesn't expect her to try to design a training program herself, but would like her to just sit down with him and other members of the T&D staff and describe what she does during a typical working day, concentrating especially on her interactions with prospects and customers. Peggy agrees to do this.

Questions

1. Do you think Peggy uses any particular persuasion principles or selling strategies that might be taught to others, or is her success largely attributable to her unique personality?

2. Assume that you are Frank Sherry and that you are trying to develop a teachable model or system to train others how to do what Peggy seems to do almost instinctually. Based on the limited information provided, identify and give examples of the specific principles of persuasion and closing strategies that Peggy applies in her personal selling activities.

3. Should new salespeople be taught to sell like Peggy Markley, or should each sales trainee be allowed to develop his or her own personal style, closing strategies, and persuasive techniques? Why? Outline a sales training module for new sales trainees that integrates the basic persuasion principles with different closing strategies.

Chapter 15

Following Up: Providing Customer Service

Quality service is an investment in future sales.

WARREN BLANDING, Customer Service Institute

Profile

Karen Morrell

KAREN Morrell began her sales career with Colgate-Palmolive Company just two short days after she walked across the stage to receive her B.A. degree from Clemson University in May 1986. Her interest in consumer product sales, however, started long before her college days even began.

In high school, Karen worked in a local drugstore in upstate New York. She found herself handling the responsibilities of ordering products, greeting customers and handling their requests, and selling the services of the store. When she wasn't working, Karen was busy playing soccer, cheerleading, and running track, all of which, she says, helped her decide on a career in sales: "I love competition, whether it's on the playing field or off, and sales has the extra attraction of working with people."

These days, Karen is earning quite a reputation at Colgate for being a tough competitor as well as for extremely effective customer follow-up and service. In fact, when Karen was asked what the favorite part of her job is, she replied: "I love to return to an account after a successful sale, knowing that they're as pleased with the sell-through of the product as I was by being able to make the sale. When my accounts have any problems, they know they can count on me to take care of them. It's that simple—and that hard! The surest way to achieve success in selling is to provide your accounts with good follow-up and continued service."

Karen went on to tell us about one of her first realizations of the importance of customer service: "It was an account in my first territory in Memphis, Tennessee. I wasn't sure how to develop the account into one that would prove successful for Colgate. It was especially difficult because I was the new kid on the block. But after a few months, the account was so in tune to Colgate that they began turning to me for promotional ideas." Apparently, Karen had performed some of the best customer service the account had ever witnessed—and was hardly aware that she was doing such a great job. "My buyer saw me returning with eagerness to show him how he could profit from the sale of my products. He quickly realized that I sincerely wanted to work with him to promote Colgate product and improve the flow of customers into his stores."

Now based in Jacksonville, Florida, Karen is faced with the challenge of a chain account-dominated market. She maintains that her success in this new environment is due mostly to her enthusiastic customer service. Although Karen has taken on the added responsibility of training new Colgate salespeople, she seems a little reluctant to move too quickly into a sales management position, away from day-to-day field selling. "There really is nothing better than the feel of making a sale. I've been selling for four years now, and I can't live without it." No wonder she was recently inducted into Colgate's Hall of Fame! ■

After reading this chapter, you should understand:

- Why it's so important to keep customers
- The concept of customer service
- Customer service expectations, perceptions, and satisfaction
- Customer service strategies
- Retail store customer service

FOLLOW-UP AND CUSTOMER AND PROSPECT SERVICE

FOLLOW-UP Customer service provided not only after the sale is closed but throughout the selling process.

In most textbooks on personal selling, the final chapter on the selling process is devoted to "follow-up" or "service after the sale." This is potentially misleading for those trying to learn about how sales are made today. The fact is that **follow-up** service is provided not just after the sale is closed, but throughout the selling process. The most successful salespeople know that if they make an effort to service a valuable prospect like an old customer, chances are that prospect will appreciate the special attention and sooner or later become a valuable customer. Excellent customer (or *prospect*) service should be a significant part of your vision for success in selling. Let's discuss follow-up and customer service as you need to practice them during the selling process as a whole, and then turn our attention to specific postsale activities.

What Is Customer Service?

CUSTOMER SERVICE A concept that has five basic dimensions: reliability, tangibles, responsiveness, assurance, and empathy.

Customer service is a somewhat elusive concept that is defined uniquely by each different customer group. However, based on a number of studies on service quality, five basic dimensions of service have been identified:

- *Reliability:* The ability to perform the desired service dependably, accurately, and consistently.
- *Tangibles:* The physical facilities, equipment, and appearance of sales and service people.
- *Responsiveness:* The willingness to provide prompt service and help to prospects and customers.
- *Assurance:* Employees' knowledge, courtesy, and ability to convey trust and confidence.
- *Empathy:* The provision of caring, individualized attention to prospects and customers.[1]

RELIABILITY The ability to perform the desired service dependably, accurately, and consistently; the single most important component of customer service.

Salesperson **reliability** is the single most important factor with about half of all customers surveyed.[2] Customers must have confidence that the expected ser-

[1] Leonard L. Berry, A. Parasuraman, and Valarie A. Zeithaml, "The Service-Quality Puzzle," *Business Horizons,* September–October 1988, pp. 35–43.
[2] Ibid., p. 18.

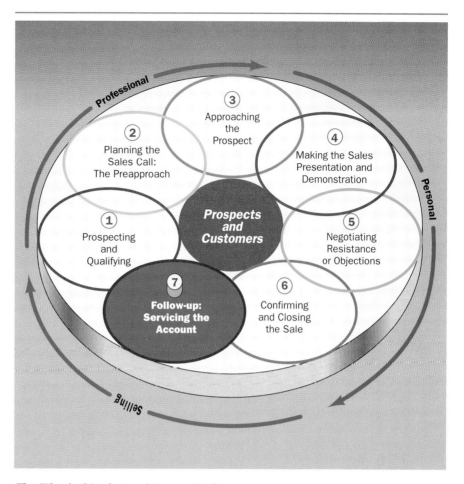

The Wheel of Professional Personal Selling

vice will be delivered accurately, consistently, and dependably. Note the order in which Canadian buyers of industrial equipment ranked 13 service elements, as shown in Table 15-1.

SERVICE CREATES SALES

Professional salespeople realize that while it's the *promise* of great service that persuades prospects to buy the first time, it's the *performance* of great service that persuades them to become repeat customers. The Cambridge, Massachu-

TABLE 15-1 Perceived Importance of Different Services

1. Meet quoted delivery date	**8.** Replacement guarantee
2. Prompt quote	**9.** Wide range of products
3. Technical problem solving	**10.** Pattern design
4. Discounts from list price	**11.** Credit facilities
5. After-sales service	**12.** Test facilities
6. Sales representation	**13.** Machining facilities
7. Ease of contact	

Professional salespeople realize that it's the promise of great service that persuades prospects to buy the first time, but it's the performance of great service that persuades them to become repeat customers.

setts–based Strategic Planning Institute, through its PIMS (Profit Impact of Market Strategy) program, analyzed the performance of 2,600 companies over 15 years. Its studies show that the companies customers perceive as having the highest quality come out on top on almost every measure of success—sales, market share, asset turnover, return on investment. *Customer service* is one of the most powerful ways to shape that perceived quality.[3]

Satisfied customers tend to be loyal and provide the stable sales base that is essential to long-term profitability. A pattern of one-time buyers is a warning signal that customer expectations are not being met. The PIMS database reveals that companies rated high on customer service charge 9 percent more on average for their products and grow twice as fast as companies rated poorly.[4]

Because of superior service, Weyerhaeuser Company's wood products division is able to charge a healthy premium even for its commodity-grade two-by-fours. Weyerhaeuser developed a computer system for retail home centers and lumberyards that allows homeowners to custom-design decks and other home-building projects. Premier Industrial Corporation, a distributor of industrial parts in Los Angeles, charges up to 50 percent more than competitors for every one of the 250,000 items it sells and earned nearly 28 percent on sales of about $600 million in 1989. How is Premier able to command such premium prices? Again, superb customer service is the answer. For example, when a Caterpillar tractor plant in Decatur, Illinois, called Premier to get a replacement for a $10 electrical relay that had stopped an entire production line, a Premier sales representative found the part and rushed it to the airport for a flight to St. Louis, where another Premier sales rep picked it up and took it to Decatur. By 10:30 that night, the Caterpillar production line was running again.[5] The message is clear: *Customers are willing to pay for good service.*

Training Salespeople in Customer Service

The best companies train, retrain, and motivate their salespeople to provide solid customer service. Shared Medical Systems, the nation's largest seller of computerized services to health-care organizations, requires all its salespeople to take three weeks of sales and customer service training each year. And service quality is often an integral part of the reward system for sales and service people, as illustrated in the following vignette.

PRODUCT QUALITY The perceived performance of the tangible product in satisfying customer expectations.

SERVICE QUALITY All the activities supporting the sale, from the initial contact through the postsale servicing, that meet or exceed customer expectations and enhance the value of a product.

PRODUCT AND SERVICE QUALITY

Quality consists of two components: product and service. **Product quality** is the perceived performance of the tangible product in satisfying customer expectations. It is concerned with whether a product performs as promised. **Service quality** includes all the activities that support the sale, from the initial contact

[3]Ibid.
[4]Eric R. Blume, "Customer Service: Giving Companies the Competitive Edge," *Training & Development Journal,* September 1988, p. 25.
[5]*Business Week,* March 12, 1990, p. 88.

CUSTOMER SERVICE PAYS

Many of the 7,000 U.S. hospitals are adding guest relations programs to train and motivate physicians, nurses, and other employees in patient hospitality. Radford Community Hospital is one of several hospitals providing special incentives for quality service performance. For its Guaranteed Services program, Radford set up a fund of $10,000, from which it pays patients who have a justified complaint ranging from cold food to long waits in the emergency room. Any money not paid out of the fund at the end of the year is divided among the hospi-

tal's employees. So if there are 100 employees and no patients have collected for a complaint by the end of the year, each employee gets a $100 bonus. In the first six months after implementing the Guaranteed Services program, the hospital had to pay out only $300 to patients.

SOURCE: Philip Kotler, *Marketing Management: Analysis, Planning, Implementation, and Control* (Englewood Cliffs, N.J.: Prentice Hall, 1988), p. 482.

---

through the postsale servicing, that meet or exceed customer expectations and enhance the value of a product. It can include product information, technical assistance, financing, order processing, delivery, installation, maintenance and repair, parts availability, and attitudes of service personnel as perceived by prospects and customers.

Perceived Service Quality and Customer Satisfaction

PERCEIVED SERVICE QUALITY The quality of service that individual customers believe they deserve and expect to receive.

In most competitive industries, product quality is eventually matched by other producers, so the real competition boils down to service quality and, beyond this, to perceived service quality. Federal Express defines service as "all actions and reactions that customers perceive they have purchased."[6] Most companies have *general* customer service policies, but **perceived service quality** refers to the quality of service that *individual* customers believe they deserve and expect to receive. Salespeople, as the single most important part of the company's prospect and customer service program, must be sensitive to each individual prospect's and customer's service demands and expectations.

When it comes to perceived service quality, salespeople have four basic kinds of prospects and customers to deal with, each pulling them in a different direction, as shown in Figure 15-1. Every customer is either "good" (profitable, cooperative) or "bad" (not very profitable or cooperative) and demands either "lots of service" or "little service."

How do you service these four different types of customers? Here's some advice:

- *Good Customer/Lots of Service:* Working extra hard to please this customer should be a joy for you. If it is not, then you must start to change your attitude immediately. Refer to Chapter 8 of this book for help.
- *Bad Customer/Lots of Service:* You may eventually have to speak with your sales manager about this customer, but look to yourself first: Are you providing the wrong

[6]Christopher H. Lovelock, *Managing Services: Marketing, Operations, and Human Resources* (Englewood Cliffs, N.J.: Prentice Hall, 1988), pp. 263–264.

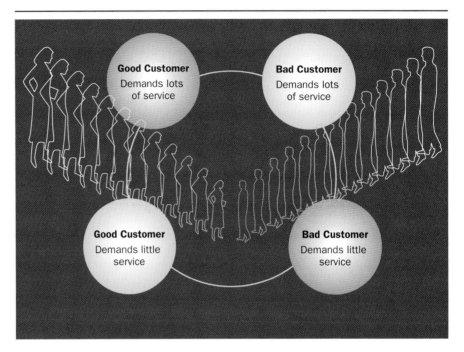

Figure 15-1 The Four Basic Directions of Customer Service

kinds of service to the wrong people in the organization? If the customer was once "good" and then turned "bad" (stopped buying or paying bills), find out why. You may be able to save the situation.

■ *Good Customer/Little Service:* Nothing wrong with this situation, right? Wrong! Are you constantly monitoring the service situation with this customer, making sure that the appropriate people in the organization are getting the products and services they need? Beware of your own complacency.

■ *Bad Customer/Little Service:* Once again, you should look to yourself first. Is the customer "bad" because you haven't been providing appropriate services to the appropriate people? Speak with your sales manager about this potentially salvageable situation, too.

Rising customer service expectations and a decreasing tolerance for poor service are expected to have the greatest impact on salespeople's effectiveness in the years ahead.[7] Technical Assistance Research Programs Institute (TARP) found that, on average, one out of every four customers is dissatisfied enough with customer service to switch suppliers. Over 90 percent of these unhappy customers will never again buy from that company, and will tell at least nine other people about their negative experience.[8] In a recent Gallup Organization survey of senior management executives at 615 companies, "service quality" ranked at the top of the list of business concerns.[9]

---

[7]*Training & Development Journal*, September 1989, p. 11; Kate Bertrand, "In Service, Perception Counts," *Business Marketing*, April 1989, pp. 32–36.

[8]Joan C. Szabo, "Service = Survival," *Nation's Business*, March 1989, pp. 16–21.

[9]John Humble, "Five Ways to Win the Service War," *Management Review*, March 1989, pp. 43–45.

For many unsatisfactory purchases, customers simply do not bother to complain, especially when the purchase was not expensive. They just buy elsewhere next time.

Customers have certain overall expectations for service quality that are influenced by their past experience, personal needs, advertising, and word-of-mouth information. *Customer satisfaction is assured when the customer's expectations for perceived service quality are exceeded.* But if there is a gap between what they expect and what they perceive they are getting, customers will be disappointed in the quality of the service.[10]

Customers Who Don't Complain

As you may have guessed from our discussion of the two customer types who are getting very little service, you cannot afford to assume that no complaints means customers are satisfied. Only 1 out of 27 customers who are dissatisfied will actually file a complaint.[11] For many unsatisfactory purchases, customers simply do not bother to complain, especially when the purchase was not expensive. They just buy elsewhere next time. That is why measuring customer satisfaction with service performance is essential. Even if your company regularly measures overall customer satisfaction, you should verify your own customers' level of satisfaction with your products and services. Just as poor service by competitors creates an opportunity for you, poor service by you creates an opportunity for your competitors.

SEGMENTING CUSTOMER SERVICE MARKETS

New salespeople quickly learn that service strategy is a balancing act. If you provide too little or the wrong kind of service, customers will switch to other sellers. But if you provide too much service, costs may increase to the point

[10]Rolph E. Anderson, "Consumer Dissatisfaction: The Effect of Disconfirmed Expectations on Perceived Product Performance," *Journal of Marketing Research*, February 1973, pp. 14–15.
[11]Ibid.

CUSTOMER SERVICE SEGMENTATION
A strategy for grouping customers with similar service expectations into service segments and then developing a service plan for each segment.

where sales to the customer become unprofitable. Simply providing extraordinary service to all customers won't ensure profits. For example, Service Supply Corporation of Indianapolis, the "House of a Million Screws," provides superior service to all its customers, but its profits remain below industry averages.

Customer service segmentation is a strategy for grouping customers with similar service expectations into service segments and then developing a service plan for each segment, which allows the seller company to service large numbers of customers profitably. Note that while general market segmentation (as discussed in Chapters 5 and 6) focuses on what people and organizations *need*, customer service segmentation focuses on what they *expect*. To segment customers effectively, seller companies research how their customers value different kinds and levels of services, then estimate the costs and benefits of providing the desired services.

Sharing Service Requirements

Some customers are able and willing to perform some services for themselves in return for lower prices or more convenience. Consumers who shop at self-service stores, use automatic teller machines, or bag their own groceries, and industrial buyers who order parts and supplies through computers linked directly to their suppliers, are sharing the service load with suppliers. Other customers, such as those who shop at exclusive clothing boutiques on Rodeo Drive in Beverly Hills, expect and are willing to pay for private shopping appointments, advice from a fashion consultant, and unlimited alterations. Segmentation of customers by their service expectations, the value they place on different services, and their willingness to perform certain services themselves can help salespeople estimate the cost of serving them.

Ranking Customer Value

The most successful seller companies devote massive human and financial resources to support their salespeople's efforts to meet and exceed customer service expectations. There will be times, however, when customers' demands for service will exceed your company's capacity to provide it. In fact, studies have shown that service quality drops off sharply when demand exceeds *75 percent* of capacity.[12] This is why it is necessary for salespeople to be able to rank their customers according to overall value. When customer service demands exceed capacity, salespeople should give their best customers first priority and cut back on service to less valued customers. Resourceful salespeople are prepared for such contingencies and may be able to offer temporarily slighted customers some special treatment, such as an immediate or future price discount or more favorable credit terms.

[12]William H. Davidow and Bro Uttal, "Service Companies: Focus or Falter," *Harvard Business Review*, July–August 1989, p. 79.

RISING DEMAND FOR SERVICE

The rising expectations of consumers and organizations for quality products are being matched by their rising expectations for quality service. Buyers are more and more reluctant to take risks on service quality when they make their purchase decisions. In addition to fundamental product quality, therefore, sellers must be able to prove that the services that come with the product are of the highest quality.

Services, whether provided as part of the price of a product or offered as optional service contracts, are becoming an increasingly important part of the bundle of product benefits. Most large consumer appliances, for example, are sold with limited warranties and optional service contracts covering different periods of time. And IBM's maintenance division now offers organizational customers help in designing and building data centers, planning computer networks, and even running entire computer departments. IBM customers alone spend some $100 billion yearly on such tasks. Another computer company, DEC, recently helped Boeing Company design a factory computer network. In 1993, it is estimated, the computer industry's total service revenues, including maintenance, network design, and training, will reach $67 billion, while computer hardware sales will fall to $46 billion.

Some sellers are using rental programs to reduce their customers' risks in making purchases. Ft. Worth, Texas–based Tandy Corporation, the mother company of Radio Shack stores, has a "try and buy" program that lets government agencies and large companies rent laptop computers for six months to evaluate them. Other well-known resellers, such as Businessland, Inc., and ComputerLand Corporation, also have rental programs and provide on-location microcomputer support and service to Fortune 500 customers.

Quality service is especially important for salespeople who represent small businesses. Because small businesses must often charge higher prices than larger competitors, providing superior service is a relatively inexpensive way for their salespeople to differentiate their products and remain price and value competitive in the eyes of customers. Norrell Temporary Services, based in Atlanta, has exceeded the average growth in its industry over the last five years by not charging clients for their cleaning service if they are dissatisfied in any way—even if the problem doesn't show up for several weeks.

Responding to Rising Service Competition

The United States has become a service-based economy. Services account for 71 percent of U.S. employment and 75 percent of output. Internally generated services provide more than 80 percent of the value added in most manufacturing processes. Worldwide and domestic competition in services is increasing rapidly. Japanese-owned companies in America are moving aggressively into banking, financial services, entertainment, restaurants, hotels, and many other retailing operations. The Japanese cultural emphasis on providing individual services courteously and deferentially will make them formidable competitors in any

Company Highlight

Service-Oriented Wholesaler

Bergen Brunswig Drug Company, located in Orange, California, is a drug wholesaler selling to 9,500 hospitals, regional drug chains, and independent drugstores nationwide. Its salespeople are called "consultants" to emphasize the service focus of their jobs. Bergen Brunswig's 235 salespeople offer customers a number of computer programs to speed ordering and delivery. A comprehensive training program, with hands-on experience in all departments of the company as well as in pharmacies, ensures that Bergen Brunswig's salespeople will be able to implement any service program the company chooses to offer. Space Management, a merchandising program based on product sales data, aids retailers in getting the right products in the right place at the right time; for a monthly fee, Bergen Brunswig advises customers on product and shelf arrangement. Compu-Phase is a computer system for processing prescriptions, storing patient information, and updating prices. The Good Neighbor Pharmacy advertising program gives retailers the advertising benefits enjoyed by chains without sacrificing their local identity. Beyond order entry, shelf management, and inventory control systems, Bergen Brunswig offers financial management programs. Largely because of its service orientation, Bergen Brunswig's sales force was recently ranked first by customers in *Sales & Marketing Management*'s annual Best Sales Force Survey.

Source: "Bergen Brunswig Locks in Sales with Service," *Sales & Marketing Management,* June 1987, p. 48; "Bergen Brunswig Writes a Winning Prescription," *Sales & Marketing Management,* January 17, 1983, pp. 38-39.

industry, so U.S. companies have their work cut out for them. Some American firms, like Bergen Brunswig Drug Company, have initiated several innovative computer programs to improve service to customers.

FOLLOW-UP: MAKING AND KEEPING CUSTOMERS

The American Management Association reports that 65 percent of the average company's sales come from its present, satisfied customers. As Table 15-2 shows, it's more than twice as expensive to win a new account as it is to increase sales from an existing account, yet neglect after the sale is the most common failing of most companies.[13] Companies also spend an average of 53 percent more on travel and entertainment for new accounts.[14]

[13]Thomas P. Reilly, "Sales Force Plays Critical Role in Value-Added Marketing," *Marketing News,* June 5, 1989, p. 8.
[14]*Sales & Marketing Management,* January 1990, p. 38.

TABLE 15-2   Cost Comparison Between Obtaining a New Account and Keeping an Existing Account

TYPE OF ACCOUNT	NUMBER OF CALLS NEEDED TO CLOSE	COST OF A SALES CALL	TOTAL COST OF A SALE
New	7	$239	$1,673
Existing	3	$239	717
Difference	4	0	$ 956

Customer Follow-up Strategies

In order to maximize customer satisfaction after a sale, salespeople should consider the following basic service strategies.

Express Appreciation for the Customer's Business

Salespeople should be conscientious about showing genuine appreciation for their customer's business. You can show appreciation in many ways, from merely saying "thank you" in a sincere, enthusiastic way (in person, by telephone, or in a handwritten note) to sending the customer a useful gift, such as an address book or small calculator, with the seller's logo.

Make Sure Products Are Delivered and Installed on Time

Whenever possible, the salesperson ought to be on hand when the customer's order is delivered. By being there, the salesperson shows that he or she cares about pleasing the customer and that any potential problems will be promptly resolved. An additional benefit is that the salesperson learns to see this important aspect of service from the customer's viewpoint.

Whenever possible, the salesperson should be on hand when the customer's order is delivered.

Selling in Action

Salesperson . . . and Serviceperson

Richard Angarita, a sales rep for Rainin Instrument Company, a supplier of laboratory instruments in Woburn, Massachusetts, sold over 100 systems in 18 months, at prices up to $30,000, in a territory where the previous sales rep had sold only two instruments in two years. Considered a sales consultant by customers, Mr. Angarita is thoroughly familiar with the products he sells because he is both the territory's salesperson and a highly trained service technician. He sells, installs, repairs, and trains customers how to use his company's products. Expert at explaining product features and benefits, he quickly gains the trust of his customers by providing quality service promptly. If he doesn't think the equipment will meet the customer's expectations, he won't sell it to them. After all, he's the service technician who will have to resolve any later problems or complaints.

Source: "Sales/Marketing Genius of the Month," *Sales & Marketing Digest,* March 1989.

Assist Customers with Credit Arrangements

It is often frustrating for customers to deal with company credit personnel. A salesperson who has already made it a point to establish and maintain a good relationship with the credit department can serve as an effective go-between, facilitating the credit-granting process and insulating the customer from potential problems.

Help Customers with Warranty or Service Contracts

When customers need repair service or to return a defective product, it's best for the salesperson to serve as the liaison with company service people. Not only will customers appreciate your saving them time and effort, but you will get to know your company's customer service people.

Represent Customers in Solving Their Problems with Your Company

Customers don't know the seller company's organization, policies, procedures, or personnel, so the best salespeople serve as their customers' advocates within the company, whether in handling product repairs, exchanges, returns, or complaints. Having one contact person whom they can count on to take care of problems can be a tremendous relief to customers. Let your customers know that you want them to call you whenever they have a problem and that you will strongly represent their interests in any dispute with your company. Learning who's who in providing customer service within your company and developing a positive personal relationship with them ahead of time should help you avoid many bureaucratic problems in obtaining service for your customers.

Keep Customers Informed

Customers want to know ahead of time about possible product shortages, price changes, upcoming sales, new products, and any other information that may affect them or their business operations. They will quickly lose trust in and respect for salespeople who allow them to be surprised by things that adversely affect them or their businesses.

Ask Customers About Their Level of Satisfaction

As we have learned, the absence of complaints does not indicate that a customer is satisfied. It is part of the professional salesperson's job to find out how satisfied customers are and what services they feel should be performed better. Even when they work for a company that surveys overall customer satisfaction periodically, salespeople can obtain product-specific, detailed feedback, while showing genuine concern for customers, by asking them about their level of satisfaction with products and supporting services. Sometimes the salesperson will discover that a competitor's product and service are unsatisfactory—which creates an opportunity to replace that competitor's product.

Think of Prospects and Customers as Individuals.

The best salespeople do not view their customers as abstract or impersonal "companies" or "accounts," but rather as individuals. Get to know as many employees as possible in your customers' organizations, not just the purchasing agents and managers. Whenever possible, see how and by whom your products and services are used among production, office, and maintenance personnel. **Selling by walking around** the customer's organization to meet people, understand their jobs, and develop personal relationships at all working levels is a service-oriented strategy used successfully by many top salespeople. Dean Witter, the brokerage firm, probably expresses the customer service concept best: "We measure success one investor [customer] at a time."

<td>SELLING BY WALKING AROUND Going around the customer's organization to meet people, understand their jobs, and develop personal relationships at all working levels in order to find out the customer's service needs and how to satisfy them.</td>

Ask Customers How Else You Might Help Them

Salespeople should regularly ask their customers what other services they would like or what problems they'd like solved. Until late 1987, Du Pont Company sold only adhesives to the shoe industry. It was only after a Du Pont salesperson asked Reebok International how Du Pont could help further that Du Pont came up with the idea of inserting flexible plastic tubes into the soles of Reebok's new ERS athletic footwear lines. The tubes gave the shoes a more lively, bouncy feel, and the success of the ERS lines helped Reebok's net earnings increase 27 percent in 1989—which made Reebok an even more loyal customer of Du Pont.[15]

Routine Actions and Behaviors Affecting the Postsale Relationship

In addition to, or as a subcategory of, customer follow-up strategies immediately after a sale, there are many actions and behaviors you should strive to learn and employ to further influence your new customer's favorable postsale perceptions

[15]*Business Week,* March 12, 1990, pp. 90–91.

What Would You Do?

In reviewing your territory's annual sales report provided by your sales manager, you notice that one of your steady customers, World Floors and Walls, a large paint and wallpaper wholesaler, did not buy any painting or wallpaper supplies from your company during the last six months. Normally, this wholesaler places two big orders annually, one in each half of the year. You called on World twice during the past six months to see how things were going and to leave some new-product information brochures. Your main contact person has always been one of three senior buyers, Lorraine Grady, whom you've known for four years. When you took her and a colleague to lunch during your last visit to World's headquar-

ters offices, Lorraine was very cordial and did not mention any problems. You didn't make any sort of sales presentation on either of your recent visits because World has a direct computer hookup with your company's order-processing department, and the usual practice has always been merely to replenish basic stock. You also recall that, over coffee, the junior colleague made a joking remark about how companies "like yours" were doing "anything" to move product, "even *bribing* the junior buyers!" Now you contact World and find out that Lorraine has taken a three-month maternity leave and that one of the other senior buyers, whom you know casually, has been promoted to director of purchasing.

of you and your organization. These actions and behaviors, as summarized in Table 15-3, are part of every professional salesperson's routine interactions with his or her customers. Review the table briefly. Most of the positive entries should look like simple common sense to you by now.

TABLE 15-3   Salesperson Postsale Actions and Behaviors

POSITIVE ACTIONS AND BEHAVIORS	CORRESPONDING NEGATIVE ACTIONS AND BEHAVIORS
Initiate positive phone calls.	Make only callbacks.
Make recommendations.	Make justifications.
Use candid language.	Use accommodative language.
Use the telephone.	Use correspondence.
Show appreciation.	Wait for misunderstandings.
Make service suggestions.	Wait for service requests.
Use "we" problem-solving language.	Use "owe us" legal language.
Anticipate problems.	Respond only to problems.
Use jargon or concise language.	Use long-winded communications.
Air personality problems.	Hide personality problems.
Talk of "our future together."	Talk about making good on the past.
Routinize responses.	Use fire drill/emergency responses.
Accept responsibility.	Shift blame.
Plan the future.	Rehash the past.

Source: Reprinted by permission of *Harvard Business Review.* An exhibit from "After the Sale Is Over," by Theodore Levitt (September–October 1983). Copyright 1983 by the President and Fellows of Harvard College; all rights reserved.

Building Customer Relationships Through Service

Service-oriented salespeople can do a number of things to add value to their product offerings and to further the buyer-seller relationship. First, they can urge their companies to simplify ordering procedures for customers by instituting on-line computer entry or fax-order entry. Second, they can find ways to help the customer become operational quickly and efficiently. This includes arranging for special packaging or coding on boxes or just-in-time (JIT) delivery; helping the customer receive, handle, store, or transfer products; and training the customer's staff to use the new products. Beyond this, the salesperson can assist customers in producing, marketing, and distributing products to their own customers. Other possible services are minimizing downtime by securing replacement parts quickly and obtaining swift resolution of customer complaints.[16] Even periodically sending customers thoughtful little reminders such as pens, calendars, notepads, and other advertising specialties with the company logo on them, or cards for special occasions such as birthdays, wedding anniversaries, and holiday greetings, can give the salesperson a perceived service edge on competitors.

How Do You Spell SERVICE?

S = Satisfaction . . . make sure that customers are satisfied.

E = Expectations . . . fulfill customer expectations for service.

R = Responsiveness . . . solve customer problems promptly.

V = Value . . . make sure customers perceive that the service benefits they receive exceed the price they pay.

I = Initiative . . . seek ways to provide extra services to customers.

C = Concern . . . show customers that you care about them.

E = Enthusiasm . . . provide customer services eagerly and with a smile.

HANDLING CUSTOMER COMPLAINTS

Sellers seldom welcome customer complaints, but the professional salesperson recognizes them as opportunities to improve relationships with customers. A recent TARP study showed that up to 70 percent of customers who complain will buy from the seller again if their complaint is resolved satisfactorily, and over 95 percent will buy again if their complaints are resolved promptly.[17] Several basic rules for dealing with customer complaints are given in the following paragraphs.

[16]Thomas P. Reilly, "Sales Force Plays Critical Role in Value-Added Marketing," *Marketing News,* June 5, 1989, p. 8.
[17]Ibid., p. 21.

Nothing is ever gained by making a customer angry, and there is no surer way to do so than to argue with the customer's version of a complaint.

Anticipate

Try to anticipate customer complaints and resolve them before the customer expresses them. Salespeople who spot or become aware of potential problems with their products should alert customers immediately.

Listen

Listen closely and patiently to the customers' complaints without interrupting. Whenever a customer complains, show a sincere desire to help by carefully hearing out the full version of the complaint.

Don't Belittle

As we have learned, very few customers actually complain, and those few who do are seldom unreasonable when the problem is understood from their perspective. Customer complaints are a valuable source of information that can help to improve the quality of your product and service. Never belittle a customer's complaint. Remember, it is the customer who defines quality service, not you or your company.

Encourage

Do not try to keep customers from venting their emotions. Instead, encourage them to talk and fully express their feelings. Customers may have stored up their feelings of frustration for several hours, days, or weeks. After expressing these feelings, they often become much more reasonable and willing to compromise in resolving their problems.

Don't Argue

Never argue with customers or take their complaints personally. Nothing is gained by making a customer angry, and there is no surer way to do that than to dispute the customer's version of the complaint. As a salesperson, you will not usually be the target of the complaint unless you unwisely add to the customer's frustrations by reacting defensively. Remember, your job is to try to resolve the problem to the satisfaction of the customer. J.C. Penney's motto, "The Customer Is Always Right," should never be forgotten in handling complaints.

Record the Facts

Write down the facts as the customer perceives them. If the customer is making the complaint over the telephone, let him or her know that you are carefully recording the facts without passing judgment. Your professionalism will reassure the customer and encourage him or her to state the facts more objectively.

Understand

Let customers know that you understand their complaint. Verbally repeat complaints as you record them to reassure customers that you are hearing their complaints accurately. Ask nonthreatening and nonjudgmental questions to clarify their various points and to let them know that they are communicating successfully.

Empathize

Try to see the problem from the customer's viewpoint. Top sales and service people have the ability to empathize with customers and view any problem from their perspective.

Don't Excuse

Neither make excuses for service problems nor criticize service personnel. Customers are not interested in excuses or criticisms of your co-workers. They want their problems solved promptly and satisfactorily. Excuses and putdowns of co-workers will only create a negative image of you and your company.

Resolve the Problem

Try to solve each problem quickly and fairly even if that means the sale will become unprofitable. Remember, unresolved complaints have a ripple effect. It's far better to solve a customer's complaint at a small loss than to allow the ripple effect from that unhappy customer to create potentially large losses.

Reassure

Reassure customers that their problems will be solved promptly. When you cannot resolve the complaint on the spot, tell the customer that you will do so as quickly as possible. Give the customer the telephone numbers of appropriate people to call to check up on the progress of the solution—or, better yet, call the customer back within a short time to report on your own progress in resolving the complaint.

Thank the Customer

Thank customers for voicing the complaint. Welcome them as people who care enough to try to help you improve your product and service. In most organizational situations, a customer complaint is a sign of the buyer's trust in the salesperson to get the problem resolved. Fearing hassles or embarrassment, most organizational customers save themselves the trouble of complaining by simply switching to another supplier. One study estimated that 50 dissatisfied customers

---

CUSTOMERS AT THE TOP

In his book *At America's Service*, Karl Albrecht says: "Firms that embrace a customer-service philosophy see their organization as an inverted pyramid. Who's on top? Customers, of course. Every facet of the company is dedicated to supporting them and ensuring that their needs, expectations, and problems are dealt with satisfactorily. Next come supervisors, middle managers, and, finally—at the bottom—senior executives. This organization scheme, when implemented successfully, makes each level of management support the next, and everybody supports the customer."

Source: Reported in Joan C. Szabo, "Service = Survival," *Nation's Business*, March 1989, p. 19.

---

will simply stop buying the product for every dissatisfied person who complains.[18]

Follow Up

Even after you think that a customer's complaint has been resolved, make sure by following up—preferably in person, but at least by telephone or in writing. Few customers are persistent enough to complain a second or third time if their complaints go unresolved. Instead, they will write you and your company off as incompetent or uncaring and buy from a competitor.

Keep a Record

It is important to maintain records on all customer complaints and their outcomes so that, through analysis, you can spot patterns of problems with certain types of products or customer groups and take corrective action.

CLOSING WITH THE CUSTOMER SERVICE TEAM

Although you are usually the one to ask for the prospect's business, you never close alone. In Chapter 4, we saw how important it is for salespeople engaged in organizational selling to work smoothly and effectively with marketing and other in-house teams in order to gain their support in cultivating the best possible relationships with customers. If you have done your job properly, by the time you ask for the prospect's business, you will already know all of the postsale details—product availability and delivery schedules, whether or not the customer will be able to get a credit approval, and so on. Immediately before you close the sale, however, you should once again check with your colleagues and friends on the (1) customer credit, (2) order-processing, and (3) delivery teams to iron out any potential difficulties. Let's quickly review the role that these three teams play in the selling situation.

---

[18]"Don't Complain About Complaints," *Sales & Marketing Management*, September 13, 1982, p. 158.

Credit Team

For most salespeople, the most important individual on the credit team is the *credit manager,* whom we briefly met in Chapter 9. There are two natural sources of conflict between salespeople and credit managers. The first is essentially geographical. Credit management is a centralized function in most companies, whereas selling occurs out of decentralized, regional offices. The second and much more potent source of conflict is role-related. Salespeople are expected to be their customers' advocates for credit approvals, while credit managers are expected to protect the company from entering into sales agreements with customers who won't be able to make their payments. Table 15-4 lists the most common complaints salespeople and credit managers have about each other.

The best salespeople actively search for ways to minimize the effects of these sources of conflict. Many companies actually encourage their credit managers to spend a week or two each year working in the field with their salespeople. Other companies schedule joint training meetings where salespeople and credit managers can exchange ideas and even roles—in role-playing exercises. Still other companies simply require their salespeople to collect long-overdue accounts,

TABLE 15-4 Gripes and Groans Between Credit and Sales

Credit's Gripes About Salespeople:

- Salespeople often overcommit the company.
- Salespeople approve payment delays for customers without even notifying Credit.
- Salespeople will do almost anything to avoid the refusal of credit to a customer, including going around Credit to appeal to upper management for support.
- Salespeople often argue for the profit "potential" of marginal prospects, and thereby compromise the credit manager and jeopardize the company's profits.
- Salespeople sometimes write up huge orders for normally low-to-moderate-volume customers without getting a financial update or even considering that one might be needed.
- Salespeople promise special credit services that simply cannot be performed.
- Salespeople won't even admit the possibility of customer nonpayment: To them, every customer is "as good as gold."

Salespeople's Groans About the Credit Department:

- Credit doesn't explain what it needs to evaluate prospects and customers. Sales is excluded from the policy and process.
- Excessive demands on prospective customers weaken the potential for sales.
- Sales often has to "patch up" relationships with customers after their contacts with Credit.
- Credit operates in a corporate ivory tower and doesn't understand the difficulties of working in the field.
- Credit is too quick to condemn a customer who's past due and won't negotiate to save the account. It is too short-run oriented.
- Credit doesn't notify sales in time that a customer is past due or that the account has been referred for third-party collection.
- Sales isn't notified when a customer's credit is being reevaluated.

Source: Nathaniel Gilbert, "The Missing Link in Sales and Marketing: Credit Management," *Management Review,* June 1989, pp. 24–30.

If you want excellent relationships with your order processing and product delivery teams, you will take time to tell managers and workers the "story" of a successful sale and thank them for their hard work in supporting the sale.

which quickly gives the salesperson an understanding of the credit manager's problems.

Order-Processing and Product Delivery Teams

The goal in designing a physical distribution system is to develop minimum cost systems for a range of customer service levels, then provide the service level that generates the highest profits, or sales minus distribution costs. The order-processing and product delivery teams must learn to appreciate that the full range of their policies, procedures, and activities affects customer perceptions of service, including credit rules, complaint procedures, minimum order sizes, order cycles, inventory returns, stockouts, and promised deliveries. Salespeople, in turn, must carefully check customer order forms to minimize misunderstandings and keep customer service people informed about any unique customer requirements.

It is an unfortunate fact of American business that the people responsible for order processing and product delivery often miss out on the excitement of cultivating a new customer and increasing business with an old one. If you want excellent relationships with these important teams, you will take the time to tell managers and workers the "story" of a successful sale and thank them for their hard work in supporting that sale. This will give them not only a sense of the excitement surrounding your closed sale, but also some specific ideas about that particular customer's order-processing and delivery expectations. In time, it will have the added benefit of making your customers especially memorable to people whom you may occasionally have to call upon for rush deliveries, special delivery terms, and the like. When salespeople show that they care about their customers, the feeling usually becomes contagious and is picked up by the order-processing and transportation staff.

As in the credit area, order-processing and product delivery managers can be helped to develop a customer orientation by participating with salespeople in training meetings that include interactive role playing. Good relationships between salespeople and personnel in the departments of traffic and transportation, inventory control, warehousing and packaging, and sales order service will help avoid customer complaints like those reproduced in Table 15-5.

KEEPING UP WITH RISING CUSTOMER SERVICE EXPECTATIONS

In order to provide quality service, salespeople and their backup customer service teams must stay close to customers and their evolving expectations. Staying close to customers means keeping several basic concepts constantly in mind.

Only Customers Can Define Customer Satisfaction

Continually soliciting customer feedback is the best way to determine what customer service is and should be. Carlson Systems, an Omaha-based distributor of

TABLE 15-5 Typical Customer Service Complaints

Traffic and Transportation:	Problem with containers in packaging plants
Damaged merchandise	Special-promotion merchandise not specified in
Carrier does not meet standard transit time	delivery
Merchandise delivered prior to date promised	Warehouse release form errors
Carrier fails to follow customer routing	Shipping incorrect types and quantities of
Carrier does not comply with specific instructions	merchandise
Carrier neglects notification of bad order care	Papers not mailed promptly to headquarters
Errors on the bill of lading	Field warehouse deliveries of damaged merchandise
Condition or type of rolling equipment not	**Sales Order Service:**
satisfactory	Delayed shipments
Inventory Control:	Invoice errors
Stockouts	Sales coding errors
Contaminated products received	Brokerage errors
Product identification errors	Special instructions ignored
Poor merchandise shipped	No notification of late shipments
Warehousing and Packaging:	Name and address errors
Merchandise delivered late	

Source: Adapted from Charles A. Taft, *Management of Physical Distribution and Transportation,* 7th ed. (Homewood, Ill.: Richard D. Irwin, 1984), p. 252.

fasteners and packaging products, asks its customers to fill out regular "report cards" rating the company from poor to excellent on such services as handling back orders and invoice errors.[19]

Frontline People Are Most Aware of Customer Service Problems and Opportunities

Usually, it's policies, systems, and procedures, not employee motivation, that stand in the way of better customer service. When salespeople and other frontline people are asked for suggestions on how to better serve customers, they respond with numerous practical ideas. An example of a retailer that understands the importance of the customer relationship is presented in the next Company Highlight.

Everyone Serves a Customer

Salespeople have customers, receptionists have customers, traffic managers have customers, custodians have customers—everybody in the organization has internal customers to serve, and all directly or indirectly serve the organization's external customers. Serving internal customers well leads to the kind of synergy that creates success for the entire organization in satisfying external customers.

[19]*Business Week,* January 8, 1990, pp. 33, 86.

BETTER SERVICE THROUGH PARTNERSHIP

As the demand for quality service rises, many manufacturers are forming partnerships with just a few of their resellers—wholesalers, distributors, and retailers. Partnerships between manufacturers and middlemen bring cost savings through larger purchase volumes, reduced competition, and predictable markets. In addition, the usual adversarial role is replaced by one built on trust and cooperation.

To facilitate service delivery, many buyers and sellers have interconnected their computer systems. De-signs, Inc., a Brookline, Massachusetts, retail chain, has linked its computers directly to Levi Strauss Company. Now Levi Strauss knows which of its products is selling fastest because sales data are transmitted directly from the point of sale to the manufacturer's computers. Sharing data enables Levi Strauss to anticipate and make timely delivery of needed products to Designs.

SOURCE: *Business Week*, January 8, 1990, pp. 33, 86.

Customer Service Is a Partnership with the Customer

The salespeople and companies that most consistently provide the highest-quality customer service are those that have developed a partnership with their customers, as described in the vignette above.

CUSTOMER SERVICE RETAIL STYLE

Professional field salespeople can learn a great deal from their colleagues in retail selling. Although most retail selling does not reflect the complexities of, say, organizational selling, retail salespeople do use many techniques that field salespeople could usefully apply. Review the following retail sales techniques and see if you can think of ways to incorporate some of them into your own selling, closing, and customer service practices.[20]

Focus on the customer:

- Put the customer ahead of all other duties.
- Listen without interrupting.
- Make eye contact.
- Smile and use a pleasant tone of voice.

Provide efficient service:

- Get to the next customer quickly.
- Keep small talk to a minimum.
- Keep waiting lines short.

Enhance self-esteem:

- Recognize the customer's presence immediately.
- Use the customer's name.

[20]"Selling Today," *Training and Development Journal*, March 1988, pp. 38–41.

■ Treat the customer as an adult.
■ Compliment the customer when appropriate.

Several retailer resellers have differentiated themselves from their competitors by offering superior customer service. Before establishing their customer service policies, however, each retailer must determine what services its target customers want and are willing to pay for. At Nordstrom, customer service means giving a mostly upscale clientele special care and consideration. At Wal Mart Stores, it simply means ensuring that supplies of low-priced merchandise are adequate and that checkout lines are kept short.

Customer service and follow-up are two of the most powerful ways for sellers to differentiate themselves. In today's selling environment, providing service is no longer merely an extra thrown in with a product's other, lesser features. Providing service is fast becoming the single most important benefit offered as an integral part of the product.

Company Highlight

Personal Service at Nordstrom Department Stores

Nordstrom, Inc., a family-owned chain of department stores with annual sales of about $2 billion, continues to expand while other department stores are losing market share to discount stores, catalog sales, and specialty shops. Largely because of its extraordinary personal service to customers, Nordstrom's sales per square foot are twice the industry average. Believing that it is easier to train people with no selling experience than to correct the bad habits of experienced retail salespeople, Nordstrom generally hires people who have had no previous selling experience. Its 20,000 nonunion salespeople receive up to 10 percent commission on sales and earn nearly twice the national average for all retail salespeople. Nordstrom's salespeople maintain personal notebooks on customers' sizes and fashion preferences, write daily thank you notes, and call customers to suggest a shirt or blouse to go with a recent suit purchase. In some stores, a tuxedoed bootblack will shine shopper's shoes

while a pianist plays soft background music. Fresh flowers fill the dressing rooms with delightful fragrances. Salespeople frequently stay after hours to help customers choose and wrap gifts. Nordstrom will take back any item, even without a receipt, cash checks, and make clothing alterations the same day. Nordstrom stores sell 150 percent more than industry average and spend little on advertising because their customers keep coming back for the service.

Source: Compiled from several sources, including: *Wall Street Journal,* February 20, 1990, pp. A1, A16; Eric R. Blume, "Customer Service: Giving Companies the Competitive Edge," *Training & Development Journal,* September 1988, p. 25; William H. Davidow and Bro Uttal, "Service Companies: Focus or Falter," *Harvard Business Review,* July–August 1989, p. 84; Anthony Ramirex, "Department Stores Shape Up," *Fortune,* September 1, 1986, pp. 50–52; Steve Weiner, "Caught in a Cross-Fire, Brand-Apparel Makers Design Their Defenses," *Wall Street Journal,* January 24, 1984, pp. 1, 17; Isadore Barmash, "Private Label: Flux," *Stores,* April 1987, pp. 17–23.

SUMMARY   Nearly two-thirds of the average company's sales come from its present satisfied customers. Winning a new account is twice as expensive as increasing sales with an existing account. Customers' satisfaction and their perceptions of the quality of a company and its products are largely determined by the service they receive. Customer service has five dimensions, the most important of which is reliability. Service quality is determined by customer perceptions, not what the seller thinks. The absence of customer complaints doesn't necessarily mean that customers are satisfied, because only about 1 out of 27 dissatisfied customers will actually complain. The rest will just start buying from another supplier. Customer service strategy calls for segmenting the customers to be served, then identifying those segments whose service expectations can be profitably met. Customer complaints should be recognized as opportunities to improve customer relationships. Salespeople need the help of the company's customer service team and internal staff to satisfy their customers' service expectations. Salespeople and their companies who provide the highest-quality service usually form partnerlike relationships with their customers. A few retail store chains have trained their salespeople to differentiate their offerings by providing superior customer service. Customer service expectations and standards will continue to rise, and it will be up to America's salespeople to sell and coordinate this customer service.

CHAPTER REVIEW QUESTIONS

1. What most influences customer perceptions of a company's overall quality?
2. Name and define the five dimensions of customer service. Which of these dimensions is perceived as most important by customers?
3. What proportion of dissatisfied customers will actually complain?
4. How do you define customer dissatisfaction?
5. What is the number-one reason customers switch to competitors?
6. Name some basic customer follow-up strategies.
7. List some positive and negative actions that can affect postpurchase relationships with customers.
8. Why should customer service markets be segmented?
9. About what percent of customers who complain will buy from the seller again if their complaint is solved satisfactorily?
10. What percent of customers who complain will buy again from the seller if their complaints are resolved promptly?
11. Name three complaints salespeople have about credit managers and three that credit managers have about salespeople.
12. Name five commonly used retail sales techniques.

TOPICS FOR THOUGHT AND CLASS DISCUSSION

1. What is your personal definition of customer service and what do you think are the most important dimensions of customer service?
2. How do you think customer service expectations are changing?
3. Why do only a very low percentage of dissatisfied customers ever complain?
4. Explain why it's important to segment customer service markets.
5. Have you ever made a formal complaint about a product? Why? Was your complaint answered? How?

6. As a new salesperson, how would you go about gaining the cooperation of the company's customer service team in solving your customers' problems?

7. Explain this statement: "Everyone serves a customer, either an internal one or an external one."

8. How does forming a buyer-seller partnership affect customer service?

9. Why do you think there is such disparity among retail store chains in terms of customer service?

PROJECTS FOR PERSONAL GROWTH

1. (a) Ask four of your classmates to brainstorm with you about what commercial and nonprofit organizations consistently provide the best customer service. Try to come up with three examples of each category, then take turns explaining the reasons for each selection. (b) Ask each of your four classmates to select two organizations that usually provide the worst customer service. Take turns explaining why.

As each of your classmates gives his or her explanations, write down the key points. After everyone has finished, identify the key criteria your classmates mentioned that cause organizations to be perceived as providing the *best* and the *worst* customer service.

2. In your college library, find two articles about how companies measure business customer satisfaction, and two articles on measuring consumer satisfaction. From the perspective of the customer (business and consumer), critique the methods described for handling customer complaints. As part of your critique, consider the channels of communication open to customers (both business and consumer) for providing feedback to sellers. Finally, outline an ideal system for obtaining regular feedback on customer satisfaction and promptly resolving customer complaints.

3. Select two area companies and contact the customer service manager for each by telephone or letter. Ask the following questions: (a) How does your company define customer service? (b) Who's responsible for customer service? (c) How do you measure your customers' level of satisfaction with your products and services? (d) What is your general process for handling customer complaints? After obtaining this information, write your own critique of the way the two companies are dealing with these critical concerns for retention of customers.

KEY-TERMS

Follow-up Customer service provided not only after the sale is closed but throughout the selling process.

Customer service A concept that has five basic dimensions: reliability, tangibles, responsiveness, assurance, and empathy.

Reliability The ability to perform the desired service dependably, accurately, and consistently; the single most important component of customer service.

Product quality The perceived performance of the tangible product in satisfying customer expectations.

Service quality All the activities supporting the sale, from the initial contact through the postsale servicing, that meet or exceed customer expectations and enhance the value of a product.

Perceived service quality The quality of service individual customers believe they deserve and expect to receive.

Customer service segmentation A strategy for grouping customers with similar service expectations into service segments and then developing a service plan for each segment.

Selling by walking around Going around the customer's organization to meet people, understand their jobs, and develop personal relationships at all working levels in order to find out the customer's service needs and how to satisfy them.

Case 15–1

HANDLING CUSTOMER SERVICE PROBLEMS

By Lisa Houde, Drexel University

Rob Azar is pretty excited. Actually, he is thrilled. He has just closed a good order with an account that had stopped buying from his company. Most of the other sales reps said it couldn't be done, but Rob knew he could do it. After all, they didn't call him the "Slammer" for nothing.

On the first of the year, Rob was promoted to account representative at Master Mailers, Inc., the mailing equipment manufacturer he works for. Although he has been with Master Mailers only about three years, he has quickly moved up through the ranks. In fact, in his three years with the company, he has been promoted at the end of each year. Interestingly, Rob always experiences very high sales at the beginning of a year, but his sales slowly taper off toward the end of the year. This has never really concerned him because he knows that numbers are the bottom line, and he always surpasses his sales quotas. Besides, after he "blows" through a territory, he is always promoted out of it, so the end-year dropoff isn't a problem for him.

Rob has been in his new assignment for only three months, and as usual, he is going like gangbusters. He has a center-city hospital assignment that contains both users and nonusers of his company's mailing equipment. While his old territory was made up of many smaller accounts, his new territory consists of larger accounts that have much more potential. As a result, he has to spend more time with these accounts, getting to know them and understanding their needs.

On this particular day, Rob is pretty pleased with himself. He has just closed a substantial order with one of his higher-potential accounts. Union Hospital is currently a limited user, buying only 20 percent of their mailing equipment from Master Mailers. Rob really went after this account, knowing there is a lot more business to be had there. The head of the purchasing department, Marilyn Krane, has been with the hospital for years. During the sales call, she told Rob about her reluctance to buy from him because the hospital experienced several customer service problems with Master Mailers in the past. Rob, who is known for his exceptional ability to negotiate prospect resistance and objections, was

able to convince Ms. Krane to give his company another chance by assuring her that he will be personally responsible for the account in all ways, and that Union Hospital can count on him to take care of any problems they might have at any time with his company or its products. In reality, Rob has a whole team of people behind him to service the account, and if anything does go wrong, he feels he can just direct Ms. Krane to one of them.

After Rob brings all the paperwork back to the office and receives hearty congratulations from his district sales manager, Roger Stone, he gives the order to Joan Newman, the district office administrative assistant, to process.

The following Friday, Rob learns that the mailing machine that Union Hospital ordered is in short supply. Although the usual product delivery time is five to ten working days, delivery time for this particular model has been pushed back to three to four weeks. When Rob finds out about the delay, he runs to his manager, telling him that he needs his help in getting a unit in five days for the hospital order. Mr. Stone is very upset with Rob because it is standard practice for all salespeople to check on product availability before they guarantee a delivery date. Nevertheless, he immediately calls the company's vice president of manufacturing. The vice president tells Mr. Stone that there is no way delivery on that particular model can be speeded up because there are higher production priorities. Hearing this, Mr. Stone tells Rob he has no option but to call the account promptly and let them know about the delay in delivery.

Rob is not eager to call Ms. Krane because he knows she will be upset and he is afraid she will cancel the order. Since it is already Friday afternoon, he decides to wait until Monday to call the account, hoping that in the meantime he'll think of something.

Rob has several sales calls to make on Monday, and before he knows it, the day is over and he still hasn't called Ms. Krane. On Tuesday morning, he receives a phone message from Ms. Krane asking for confirmation of the scheduled delivery date. Rob waits until he knows she will be out to lunch before returning her call. For the next two days, he deliberately plays telephone tag with Ms. Krane. Finally, on Thursday, Rob knows he has to let her know that the new mailing machine is not going to be delivered that Friday. Ms. Krane is very upset when Rob tells her the bad news, but he calms her down by assuring her it will be only one more week before delivery, and that he will bring her a "loaner" machine on Friday morning, which he does.

The next week passes and still the new equipment has not been delivered to Union Hospital. A very upset Ms. Krane leaves another message for Rob asking about the promised delivery, but Rob doesn't bother to return her call. He rationalizes that the hospital has the "free" use of a loaner machine, so there isn't any big problem.

When the equipment is finally delivered the following week, Rob calls to make sure that it is working to the hospital's satisfaction. Ms. Krane seems calmer, but not all that happy. Rob figures he'll wait a couple of weeks for things to settle down, and then take her out to a four-star restaurant for lunch to smooth things over.

About two weeks later, before Rob has had a chance to invite Ms. Krane for lunch, she calls to ask his help in straightening out a billing problem. Rob suggests they discuss it over lunch the following day. At lunch, he takes notes on the problem. It seems that Master Mailer has billed the hospital for a feature that the new mailing machine does not have. Rob explains that this is not a serious problem and promises to take care of it. He takes the erroneous invoice and says he will call Ms. Krane within two days to let her know the problem has been resolved. But things get so busy for Rob over the next two days that he never does take care of the billing problem. In fact, it slips his mind until he receives another phone message from Ms. Krane asking whether the hospital's bill has been corrected. When he calls Ms. Krane back, he assures her that he is working on the problem and that it will be resolved shortly. As soon as Rob gets back to his office that day, he makes a point of giving the problem invoice to Joan Newman to handle. After all, he reasons, he is a sales rep, not a credit rep.

About a month later, Rob receives an urgent phone call from Ms. Krane. It seems that Master Mailers' credit department has notified Union Hospital that all its future purchases will be on a C.O.D. basis because the hospital has failed to pay its last invoice. Ms. Krane is furious, saying Union Hospital does not do business this way. After Rob apologizes, he promises that he will get the matter resolved that day.

Rob immediately returns to the office, and in about four hours he has the situation settled. Mr. Stone, who has heard about the problem from his secretary, asks Rob why credit has so mismanaged the Union Hospital account. Reluctant to explain the whole embarrassing set of circumstances, Rob puts Mr. Stone off by saying: "You know credit's philosophy: 'The customer is always wrong.' But I got it straightened out, boss. Got to run now to another sales appointment. Talk to you later." Rob calls Ms. Krane the following morning to let her know that everything is fine and that the hospital's account is completely straightened out.

Over the next two months, Rob is extremely busy chasing down new sales. Since he hasn't heard from Ms. Krane, he assumes things are going well with the Union Hospital account. Actually, he doesn't feel that comfortable calling Ms. Krane with the delivery and billing problems so fresh in her mind. By the middle of the third month, Rob calls Ms. Krane to set up another sales call, figuring that by this time, all the past problems have been put to rest and he can safely approach her for additional orders.

When Rob arrives at the hospital, he is surprised to see one of his biggest competitor's mailing machines in an office. He pokes his head into the office and comments to the women using it: "That looks like a new machine, is it?" The woman replies: "Yes, it is. We just got this machine this week and four others just like it. It's a great little machine. I really love it." Rob feels his stomach sink as he thinks about losing out on a sale of five brand new units. Boy, could he have used those commissions! He approaches Ms. Krane's office with a growing sense of discouragement about winning a larger share of Union Hospital's business.

Questions

1. Do you think that Rob is customer service oriented? Why or why not?

2. What customer service mistakes did Rob make in handling the Union Hospital account? What should he have done differently?

3. What should Rob have done after making his initial sale to Union Hospital?

4. What advice would you give Rob now in his efforts to win a higher share of business from Union Hospital?

Case 15–2

DEFECTIVE PRODUCT CRISIS

After graduating from the City College of New York, where he majored in political science and was a third-team All-American basketball player (who almost made it to the NBA!), Darren Jones took a sales position in his home state of New York with Olympia Sports Company. Olympia is one of the country's largest manufacturers of sporting equipment, and sells to wholesalers, retail stores, and large high schools and colleges. Although it faces considerable competition from better-known companies like Wilson and Spaulding, Olympia enjoys a good reputation for the quality of its products.

Darren, nicknamed "Dr. D" by his teammates and college basketball fans, loves sports and feels that selling athletic equipment is the ideal job for him. He is especially happy with his territory because it covers New York, New Jersey, and Pennsylvania—all states where he is well known for his basketball ability. Darren's customers like him because of his outgoing personality and his incredible knowledge of college and pro sports. Most customers flash a big smile and say something like: "Always good to see Dr. D!" when they see Darren coming.

Darren seems to be on target for meeting his sales quota in his second year of selling. It was primarily his regional fame and easygoing personality that helped him meet his quota in his first year. His normal sales presentation goes something like this: After introducing himself (and usually gaining immediate recognition as Dr. D) and his company, Darren hands the prospect several product brochures. Then he talks about sports until the prospect turns to business with a question like: "So, Darren, what's Olympia offering these days?" Because he is always careful to find out beforehand exactly what the prospect is interested in, Darren almost always has a specific piece of product information or even a sample product to show the prospect right away. Surprisingly, most customers don't seem to need much more than that before Darren closes another sale.

Recently, Darren was upset to learn that two of his retail customers have made major equipment purchases from another, smaller supplier. Darren knows the competing salesperson who "stole" these accounts. Reggie McArthur is a short, slight man of about the same age as Darren. Darren recalls that once last year he arrived at a customer's office just as Reggie was dashing out of it. When he entered the customer's office, Darren was confronted with the sight of several competing product brochures and sample products placed in a careful arrangement on the customer's desk. After making two or three mildly disparaging remarks about the brochures and sample products, which the customer laughed off, saying: "Be nice now, Dr. D, that guy's got to make a living, too," Darren talked sports for a little while and left the office with a small order for some knee pads.

Darren chuckles as he thinks about Reggie, whom he has come to regard as a "wimp." "The guy is always trying to make up for his inadequacies by acting like a flunky ball-boy for his customers," thinks Darren, "writing cute thank-you notes after every sale, actually delivering equipment for customers (he looked like he was breaking his poor little back last month when I saw him delivering that backboard!), and always doing errand work like hand-delivering credit paperwork and asking customers to fill out surveys." Darren can't understand how anybody can act in such a self-demeaning way with customers. Doesn't Reggie's company have personnel to do all that minor stuff?

In addition to the loss of these two accounts, Darren's sales manager recently warned him that Olympia has received several complaints about faulty bolts in weight-lifting benches and basketball backboard mounts. Apparently, bolts on several of Olympia's midrange models are literally snapping into two pieces after only a couple of months' use. So far, nobody in Darren's territory has made a complaint, except for the high-school basketball coach who told him a couple of months ago that the top two bolts of a new backboard had popped when one of his players made a slam dunk. The coach was somewhat concerned because many of his better players have always "abused" the equipment this way without breaking any bolts. Darren paid to have two new bolts installed and then made a half-dozen picture-perfect slams himself to test them out, to the great glee of the coach and his team.

Now, about a week after the sales manager's warning, Olympia's CEO has circulated an urgent memorandum to the sales staff about the faulty bolts problem. The CEO is requesting all salespeople to quietly inform customers who purchased certain models of bench and backboard that they should refrain from using the equipment until replacement bolts are sent to them. The salespeople are also being asked to check each customer's equipment within one week of shipment of the new bolts.

Darren is irritated by this memo because it seems to him that management is making a big deal out of a small problem. "Well," he thinks, "I'll let my customers know they're getting new bolts, but I don't have time to check up on every customer afterwards."

Two weeks later, while Darren is watching a pro basketball game on TV, he receives a telephone call from his sales manager. At first not recognizing his manager's voice because it sounds so "down-in-the-mouth," Darren learns that a female senior at one of his high-school accounts broke her arm yesterday when an Olympia weight-lifting bench collapsed under her and a 50-pound free weight glanced off her arm. After relaying this message, Darren's manager asks: "Did you make sure they changed the bolts in that bench?" Darren admits that he didn't check, to which his boss snarls in reply: "This could have been a lot worse, but as it is, we're probably facing a lawsuit. You'd better come into the office tomorrow morning at around eight thirty to discuss the situation with the regional sales manager. I'll see if we can get one of our lawyers over here, too. We've got a real problem on our hands."

After gulping out an "Okay," Darren hangs up the phone and slumps in his chair to think, the sounds and images from the TV basketball game all at once becoming a confusing blur.

Questions

1. When faulty equipment is sold to customers, is it the salesperson's problem or that of the company's manufacturing and quality control departments?

2. What do you think of Darren's response to his CEO's memo? How would you have responded? Do you think the memo was adequate? What evidence did Darren have that the faulty bolts could be any more than a "small problem"?

3. What can Darren and his district and regional sales managers do at this point? What would you do if you were Darren? Do you feel that notification of the problem should absolve Olympia and Darren from blame? Why or why not?

4. From the information provided in this case about Darren's sales presentation and customer service methods and his relationships with his competitors and with personnel in his own company, what can you infer is wrong with Darren's overall attitude toward his selling activities? Outline a plan for him to improve himself in these areas.

Chapter 16

Managing Your Time and Your Territory

Today's professional salespeople must operate like field marketing managers for their territories.

Profile

Sam Waicberg

S AM Waicberg, now a Marketing Representative for NYNEX Company, clearly remembers the beginning of his sales career. It was his senior year in college, and the second year of his work-study program, when he was able to get a work-study job as a marketing support assistant with a major computer company. This position placed him very close to field selling and marketing activities. Then one day, Sam says, "The office marketing manager and I attended a trade show. We were standing in our company's booth when a prospect walked in and started asking me questions about our products. I had carefully studied our product brochures and prepared a little 'cheat sheet' of product info before the show, so I was able to answer all of his questions. The marketing manager was so impressed that she brought over to me every customer who came into the booth that day to let me explain our products." The marketing reps who operated out of Sam's office quickly recognized his expertise with product information and began to take Sam along with them on sales calls. "In many cases, I was actually selling for them," says Sam, "and I got fed up doing all this work and seeing them get the commissions!" By the time he was ready to graduate, Sam's phone was ringing off the hook with sales job offers.

Like more and more organizational sales reps, Sam deals with one major account and a handful of smaller accounts. Sam emphasizes the fact that managing a national account is sometimes more challenging than managing a territory with many smaller accounts. He explains: "Within the account, each location, each subsidiary, and each division has its own separate projects and standards and, at times, acts like its own separate company. All the products I sell and the support I give to each of these separate entities must simultaneously meet both the requirements of that particular entity as well as the requirements of the parent company—and this can be a real challenge! But I'm also responsible for overseeing the performance of other NYNEX representatives who service the account in other parts of the United States and the world."

With all of this responsibility, it's no wonder that Sam is extremely sensitive about how he spends his time. "In sales, you learn efficiency and management skills very quickly. Eventually, if you really work at it, you become so skilled and disciplined that you can set priorities, make major decisions, put projects together, and even organize major events at the drop of a hat. You also learn to be objective-targeted and goal-oriented. Sales is based on performance, and I keep my performance at its highest level by constantly setting priorities, objectives, and goals for myself. I spend most of my time at my major account's headquarters, interacting with the main decision makers and with employees who actually use the equipment I sell (the end-users). I've found it a very useful management technique to keep a record of the people I meet with each day and which of their problems I've been able to solve. This record-keeping allows me to develop profiles of individuals and entire departments and divisions within the account, and these profiles form the basis of my future suggestions for improving the account's efficiency through the use of my products." ■

After reading this chapter, you should understand:

- Why salespeople must be concerned about efficiency as well as effectiveness in allocating their time
- Salespeople as field marketing managers
- How to use ROTI to manage the territory
- Methods for developing efficient routing of sales calls
- How to manage stress

SELF-MANAGEMENT

Unlike performance in most jobs, which is usually judged subjectively by a boss, performance in professional selling is fairly easily measured and depends mainly on salespeople's own abilities and how well they manage their territories. Few jobs demand more self-management than professional selling. Self-management, in which boss and worker are the same person, is probably more difficult than management of other people, in which feedback from various sources can keep workers on track and motivated. As their own managers, salespeople are the ones who must decide what to do, and how and when to do it. They set the daily performance standards for themselves. They decide whether to be hard-driving or complaisant, to be customer service oriented or indifferent, to use modern technology or not, and, in the long run, whether to succeed or fail.

Effectiveness and Efficiency

EFFECTIVENESS Results-oriented focus on achieving selling goals.

EFFICIENCY Cost-oriented focus on making the best possible use of the salesperson's time and efforts.

Successful salespeople understand that their success depends not only on their effectiveness, but on their efficiency too. **Effectiveness** is *results-oriented* and focuses on achieving selling goals, while **efficiency** is *cost-oriented* and focuses on making the best possible use of the salesperson's time and efforts. Together, the two equal success:

$$E_1 \text{ (Effectiveness)} + E_2 \text{ (Efficiency)} = S_1 \text{ (Sales Success)}$$

How Salespeople Spend Their Time

A recent study of nearly 10,000 sales representatives showed that 33 percent of their time is spent in face-to-face selling, 20 percent in travel, 16 percent in phone selling, 16 percent in account service and coordination, 10 percent in administration, and 5 percent at internal company meetings (see Figure 16-1).

The 33 percent figure for face-to-face selling may not seem impressive, but this is a higher percentage than other studies have found. In fact, previous studies have shown that the average salesperson spends only about two hours daily or

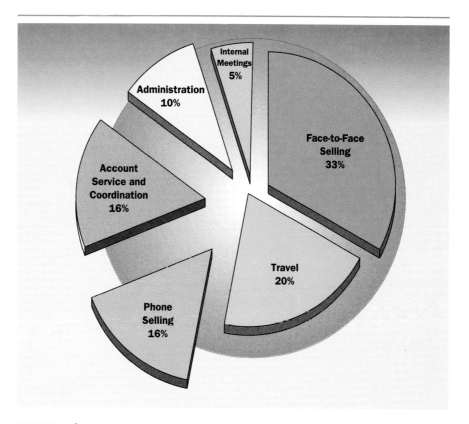

FIGURE 16-1 How Salespeople Spend Their Time
Source: Sales & Marketing Management, January 1990, p. 39.

ten hours a week in face-to-face selling.[1] Perhaps growing professionalism among salespeople and increased use of the latest telecommunication tools have contributed to greater face-to-face selling time.

Whether salespeople spend a quarter or a third of their time in face-to-face selling can have a tremendous impact on their sales effectiveness and efficiency. If we assume that the typical salesperson works 40 hours per week and takes a two-week annual vacation, that leaves just 500 hours a year (40 × 50 × .25 = 500) for face-to-face selling for salespeople who devote 25 percent of their time to this activity. Those salespeople whose efficiency allows them to devote 33 percent of their time to face-to-face selling spend 660 hours a year (40 × 50 × .333 = 660), or 160 hours more, on achieving selling goals. Table 16-1 shows, given each of these assumptions, how much an hour of the salesperson's time is worth at different earning levels. For someone earning $50,000 a year, each hour of selling time costs $100 if only 25 percent of working time is spent in face-to-face selling, but that cost drops to $76 an hour if selling time is increased to 33 percent. Obviously, then, increased efficiency yields a substantial payoff for a salesperson.

[1]"How Salespeople Spend Their Time," McGraw-Hill Laboratory for Advertising Performance, in *Sales & Marketing Management,* July 1986, p. 29.

The most successful sales-people are the most pre-pared to make maximum use of their limited face-to-face selling time with prospects.

Time Use in Different Fields

Salespeople who sell to other businesses are involved in a variety of activities. How much time a salesperson spends on such activities as face-to-face selling, selling by telephone, traveling and paperwork, and service calls varies with the industry, as shown in Table 16-2. Salespeople in the chemical industry spend an average of 34 percent of their time on face-to-face selling and 11 percent on service calls, whereas salespeople in the instruments industry spend only 16 percent of their time on face-to-face selling, but the same 11 percent on service calls.

The most successful salespeople are those who are most prepared to make maximum use of their limited face-to-face selling time with prospects. A study

TABLE 16-1 What an Hour of a Salesperson's Selling Time Is Worth

	APPROXIMATE WORTH OF AN HOUR	
EARNINGS	*Salespeople Who Spend 25% of Time on Face-to-Face Selling (500 hrs./yr.)*	*Salespeople Who Spend 33% of Time on Face-to-Face Selling (660 hrs./yr.)*
$ 20,000	$ 40	$ 30
30,000	60	45
40,000	80	61
50,000	100	76
60,000	120	91
70,000	140	106
80,000	160	121
90,000	180	136
100,000	200	152

TABLE 16-2 How Salespeople in Different Fields Spend Their Sales Day

SIC # AND INDUSTRY	AVERAGE LENGTH OF DAY	FACE-TO-FACE SELLING	SELLING BY PHONE	TRAVELING AND WAITING	PAPERWORK AND SALES MEETINGS	SERVICE CALLS	OTHER
SIC #28 Chemicals and allied products	544 min.	34%	13%	30%	12%	11%	0%
SIC #30 Rubber and plastic products	561 min.	23%	10%	40%	18%	8%	1%
SIC #34 Fabricated metal products	523 min.	26%	14%	24%	25%	7%	4%
SIC #35 Machinery, except electrical	533 min.	27%	16%	29%	20%	6%	2%
SIC #36 Electrical and electronic equipment	516 min.	18%	26%	15%	30%	9%	2%
SIC #38 Instruments and related products	521 min.	16%	27%	19%	23%	11%	4%
SIC #50 Wholesale trade, durable goods	569 min.	27%	18%	27%	16%	11%	1%
Overall average	529 min.	25%	17%	25%	22%	8%	3%

Source: Based on "Involvement of Salespeople in Different Daily Activities Varies by Industry," Report 7023.3, *Laboratory of Advertising Performance* (New York: McGraw-Hill Research, 1987).

conducted by the Forum Corporation identified several characteristics that distinguish high-performing salespeople from average performers. High-performing salespeople were found to:

■ Possess excellent product knowledge, knowledge of competitors, and face-to-face selling skills.

■ Be virtual clearinghouses of information, advisers, relationship builders, problem solvers, customer advocates, and deal makers.

■ Exercise the influence skills needed to work with both internal staff and customers. Because salespeople generally have no subordinates, they must work through others over whom they have little or no direct control. Influencing others to change their priorities and interrupt their schedules is a major part of the job.

■ Recognize that the skills required to service an account are different from those required to make a sale. Therefore, high-performance salespeople do not abdicate responsibility for installation, implementation, and service to technical support staff, and they continue to maintain a close postsale client relationship that their customers find valuable.[2]

[2]"Survey Identifies Traits of High-Performing Sales Reps," *Marketing News,* September 16, 1983, p. 14.

TABLE 16-3   Activities of Salespeople

BASIC ACTIVITIES	EXAMPLES OF TASKS INVOLVED
Selling process	Search out leads, prepare sales presentations, make sales calls, negotiate resistance.
Working with orders	Process orders, expedite orders, handle shipping problems.
Servicing the product	Test equipment, provide training, supervise installation.
Managing information	Disseminate information to and gather information from customers, provide feedback to superiors.
Servicing the account	Monitor inventory, set up point-of-purchase displays, stock shelves.
Conferences/meetings	Attend sales meetings, set up and staff exhibits at trade shows.
Training/recruiting	Recruit new sales reps, train new sales reps.
Entertaining customers	Take clients to dinner, golfing, stage plays.
Out-of-town traveling	Travel overnight to sales appointments.
Working with distributors	Establish and maintain relationships with distributors, extend credit, collect past-due accounts.

Source: Adapted from William C. Moncrief, "Selling Activity and Sales Position Taxonomies for Industrial Salesforces," *Journal of Marketing Research*, August 1986, pp. 261–270.

Activities of Salespeople

According to a study of nearly 1,400 salespeople from 15 manufacturing industries, salespeople carry out the ten basic activities listed in Table 16-3. These activities vary in importance according to the industry, the prospects or customers, the products, and the situation. It is up to each salesperson to determine what relative weight to assign to each of these activities in a given market environment and to prioritize his or her time accordingly.

SALESPEOPLE AS FIELD MARKETING MANAGERS

In many companies, the modern professional selling job has evolved into that of field marketing manager for a sales territory. Today's salespeople have more responsibilities than ever before and must fill many roles. They are largely their own bosses in their sales territories, but must work with groups of people over whom they have little control and who often impose conflicting demands and expectations on them. As *field marketing managers,* salespeople research the needs of their prospects and customers, analyze evolving markets to spot opportunities for new products and new customers, forecast sales for their territories, continually study buyer behavior to stay in touch with changing market segments, devise marketing strategies to help customers improve their profitability, and use central information systems to keep themselves and their customers informed. In contrast to sales or marketing managers, however, salespeople are responsible for managing only their own activities, not those of other people in a sales force or marketing department. Table 16-4 summarizes the many management and marketing activities of today's professional salesperson.

TABLE 16-4   Professional Salesperson's Management and Marketing Activities

MANAGEMENT ACTIVITIES	
Problem analysis	Analyze customer problems that can be solved by the salesperson's products or services.
Setting objectives	Establish sales volume and market-share levels needed in a territory to ensure a strong competitive position.
Financial analysis	Evaluate the impact of a customer's purchase on that customer's personal or business financial health.
Supervision and coordination	Work with others in the salesperson's own firm to answer questions, supply information to prospects, provide customer service; coordinate efforts of a company selling team.
Training	Educate buyers in the proper and productive use of products sold by the salesperson.
Controlling	Review personal time allocations to various prospects, customers, and other tasks to determine how to become more productive.
MARKETING ACTIVITIES	
Research	Investigate prospect and customer needs and recommend product changes or new product ideas.
Market analysis	Determine the size and needs of various market segments; continually search for new market opportunities.
Sales forecasting	Predict sales volume for different customer groups and individual accounts to help allocate selling time.
Buyer behavior	Study the buying process to become more effective in adjusting to different motivational and behavioral needs of prospects and buyers.
Marketing strategy	Understand the overall marketing strategy of customers in order to assess the impact of purchases on their inventory, distribution, product development, pricing, sales, and profits.
Information systems	Use computers and other telecommunications technology to supply and access data needed in competitive efforts of the salesperson and the buyer or seller company.

Source: Adapted from Thomas R. Wotruba and Edwin K. Simpson, *Sales Management: Text and Cases* (Boston: PWS-Kent Publishing Co., 1989), p. 48

Return on Time Invested

ROTI (RETURN ON TIME INVESTED) The designated return divided by the hours spent achieving it.

ROTI, or **return on time invested,** is a financial concept that can help salespeople spend their time more profitably with prospects and customers. *Return* can be measured in various ways, such as dollar sales to a customer, profits on a certain product category, or new customers won. ROTI is the designated return divided by the hours spent achieving it. For example, if a salesperson spends 60 hours in preparing a sales call, making a sales presentation, and providing service to a customer who orders $90,000 worth of products, that salesperson's ROTI is $90,000 divided by 60 or $1,500. Another salesperson who invests 30 hours of time to make a sale of $25,000 has an ROTI of $833.

In order to know their ROTI for different activities, customers, and products, salespeople need to keep accurate hourly records. Although this may sound like tedious record keeping, it takes only a few minutes a day to record this information, and ROTI calculations do help salespeople manage their time more effectively and efficiently. Simple *sales call plan and results sheets,* like the one depicted in Figure 16-2, can be completed each week and filed in folders or put on a computer for later analysis.

Sales Growth and ROTI

To increase sales, the salesperson has four alternatives: (1) market penetration,

SALES CALL PLAN AND RESULTS							

Year _____
Month _____

Salesperson: _____   Planned Days: _____   Days of Month: _____

Territory: _____   Actual Days: _____   Days of Month: _____

PLANNED CALLS		TOTAL COMPLETED CALLS	

Sales Calls _____

Presentations _____

Demonstrations _____

Customer Service _____

Telephone Calls _____

Sales Calls _____

Presentations _____

Demonstrations _____

Customer Service _____

Telephone Calls _____

CUSTOMER COVERAGE PLANNED

"A" Account Calls _____

"B" Account Calls _____

"C" Account Calls _____

"A" Completions _____

"B" Completions _____

"C" Completions _____

PROSPECTS AND CUSTOMERS

Company	Persons Contacted	Customer Category	Location City/State	Travel Time / Miles	Call Purpose	Time Spent on Call	Call Results

FIGURE 16-2 Sales Call Plan and Results Sheet

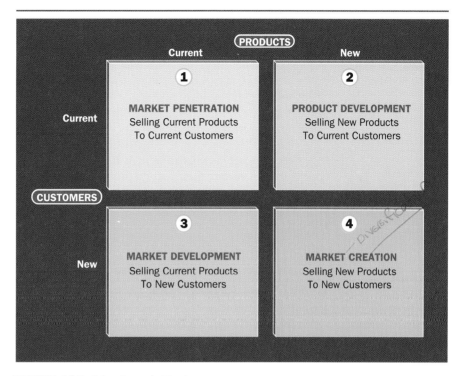

FIGURE 16-3 Sales Growth Matrix

(2) market development, (3) product development, and (4) market creation (see Figure 16-3).

MARKET PENETRATION
A sales growth strategy that calls for salespeople to sell larger quantities of their current products to current customers.

Market penetration is a sales growth strategy that calls for salespeople to sell larger quantities of their current products to current customers. As customers prosper and grow, they usually buy larger quantities of products, and it is up to the salespeople serving these customers to make sure that the increased quantities are purchased from their companies. Superior customer service and regular sales calls to ask for larger orders are necessary for a market penetration strategy to succeed.

MARKET DEVELOPMENT
A sales growth strategy that calls for salespeople to sell current products to new customers.

Market development, selling current products to new customers, is an essential activity for any salesperson in order to replace customers who switch to another supplier, leave the area, or go out of business. Skillful prospecting and qualifying is the key to achieving a high ROTI with new customers because considerable time must be spent building a buyer-seller relationship of trust before making a sale. A low ROTI in market development suggests the need to do a better job in prospecting and qualifying. Headquarters telemarketing teams can often handle the prospecting for the salesperson and categorize customers on how soon they are interested in buying the product—say, within two weeks, a month, three months, six months, or a year.

PRODUCT DEVELOPMENT
A sales growth strategy that calls for salespeople to sell new products to current customers.

A third way to increase sales is by selling new products to current customers, or product development. As the company employees closest to customers and their needs, salespeople are often the source of new-product ideas. In introducing a new product, the most efficient use of selling time will generally be to call on current customers who are known to need the new product's benefits. Because salespeople already have working relationships with these customers, they don't have to go through the slow process of introducing themselves and their companies and establishing credibility before making the sales presentation for the new product.

MARKET CREATION
A sales growth strategy that calls for salespeople to sell new products to new customers.

Finally, sales growth can come through **market creation,** a strategy in which the salesperson tries to sell new products to new customers. This is usually the most difficult type of selling and will likely have the lowest short-run ROTI, though the long-run payoff can be substantial, depending on the size of the market created. *Creation* might seem like a strong word for finding new customers for new products, but many salespeople can testify how difficult it often is to convince new customers to buy new products, especially when they're not dissatisfied with their current products. A customer's need for a new industrial or consumer product can lie dormant or unrecognized until stimulated by an innovative professional salesperson.

SETTING PRIORITIES

Setting priorities is essential. Salespeople who don't set priorities often work on relatively minor tasks first because they are the easiest to complete and thus provide a feeling of accomplishment. Priorities should relate to specific objectives to be accomplished over a certain time period, such as a year, a quarter, a month, or a week. Once selling objectives have been determined, they should be ordered according to their importance and a date should be assigned for the completion of each one. Top-performing salespeople always set priorities in their work, for they recognize the truth of the three axioms discussed in the following paragraphs.

Parkinson's Law
Work tends to expand to fill the time allotted for its completion. For example, if a salesperson has eight hours to write a sales proposal, it will probably take that much time to complete the task. But if the salesperson has only four hours, he or she will somehow manage to complete the proposal within that time frame.

Concentration Principle

CONCENTRATION PRINCIPLE Most sales, costs, and profits come from a relatively small proportion of customers and products; also known as the "80-20 rule."

Often called the "80-20 rule," the **concentration principle** says that most of a salesperson's sales, costs, and profits come from a relatively small proportion of customers and products. An illustration: Avon sells its cosmetic products in over 50 countries, but only 8 countries account for 86 percent of the company's sales and 90 percent of its profits. Avon has also found that about 20 percent of its sales reps account for over half of its sales.[3] Another example: USV Pharmaceutical Company increased its sales 250 percent over four years by eliminating sales calls on 330,000 small accounts in order to concentrate on 70,000 major ones.[4]

[3]Paul Markovits, "Direct Selling Is Alive and Well," *Sales & Marketing Management,* August 1988, pp. 76–79.
[4]Robert F. Vizza and T. E. Chambers, *Time and Territorial Management for the Salesman* (New York: The Sales Executives Club of New York, 1971), p. 97.

Iceberg Principle

Like an iceberg, which shows only 10 percent of its mass above the water, many sales problems remain largely hidden beneath the surface of overall positive sales totals. In many companies, sales, costs, and profitability analyses by territory, product, customer, and salesperson are prepared for the sales manager. Salespeople should not hesitate to ask their sales managers for those detailed analyses that are relevant to their territories. If this information is unavailable, they should develop their own analyses of products and customers within their territories.

Performance Measures

All salespeople want to know how well they're doing. Instead of reliance on one performance measure such as sales volume, a balance of several quantitative and qualitative standards is better because performance in one area can conflict with performance in another. For instance, a salesperson who emphasizes keeping sales and service expenses low may find sales revenue adversely affected.

Quantitative measures, like dollar or unit sales volume or net profit by product or customer, affect sales or expenses directly, and can usually be measured objectively.

Qualitative measures, such as the salesperson's product knowledge, customer relationships, or ethical behavior, have a more indirect and longer-run impact on sales and expenses, and thus must be evaluated on a more subjective basis. From the perspective of prospects and customers, qualitative measures of salesperson performance are probably even more important than quantitative ones. For instance, according to a survey of 432 corporate buyers, the most valued salespeople are those who:

Salespeople who don't set priorities will often work on relatively minor tasks first because they are the easiest to complete and provide an immediate sense of accomplishment.

- Really listen (mentioned by 28 percent of buyers).
- Answer questions well (mentioned by 25 percent of buyers).
- Don't waste the customer's time (mentioned by 19 percent of buyers).
- Have good presentation skills (mentioned by 18 percent of buyers).[5]

Another way to look at sales activities is as efforts and results. *Sales efforts* include such selling activities as the number of sales calls made on potential new accounts, and such nonselling activities as the number of service calls, displays set up, collections made, and customer complaints handled. *Sales results* include such outcomes as the number of orders obtained, average dollar amount of the orders, percent of quota achieved, and gross margins by product or customer type. Quantitative measures of a salesperson's selling efforts and selling results are shown in Table 16-5.

Sales Quotas

Derived from sales forecasts, sales quotas are performance objectives and motivation incentives for salespeople. They are usually stated in terms of dollar or unit volume, and sales managers rely heavily on them as standards for appraising the performance of individual salespeople. To spur themselves on to greater performance, some top-performing salespeople establish even higher quotas for themselves than those assigned by their sales manager. If their company does not

[5]*The Wall Street Journal,* March 22, 1990, p. B1.

TABLE 16-5 Quantitative Measures for Salesperson Performance

PERSONAL SELLING EFFORTS	PERSONAL SELLING RESULTS
Sales Calls: ■ Number on current customers ■ Number on new prospects ■ Number of sales presentations ■ Number of sales demonstrations ■ Selling time vs. nonselling time ■ Call frequency ratio per customer type *Selling Expenses:* ■ As percent of sales volume ■ As percent of sales quota ■ Average per sales call ■ By customer type ■ By product category ■ Direct-selling expense ratios ■ Indirect-selling expense ratios *Customer Service:* ■ Number of service calls ■ Number of customer complaints ■ Percent of sales (units/dollars) returned ■ Delivery cost per unit sold ■ Displays set up ■ Average time spent per call	*Orders:* ■ Number of orders obtained ■ Number of orders canceled by customers ■ Average order size (dollars or units) ■ Batting average (orders ÷ sales calls) *Sales Volume:* ■ Dollar sales ■ Unit sales ■ Percent of sales quota obtained ■ Sales by customer category ■ Sales by product type ■ Market share *Margins:* ■ Gross margin for territory ■ Net profit for territory ■ Gross margin by customer and product ■ Net profit by customer and product *Customer Accounts:* ■ Number of new accounts ■ Number of lost accounts ■ Number of overdue accounts ■ Dollar amount of accounts receivable ■ Collections from accounts receivable ■ Percent of accounts sold

assign them specific quotas, salespeople should establish their own goals or quotas for various performance measures in their territories.

There are four types of quotas that salespeople ought to consider: (1) *sales volume quotas,* such as dollar or unit sales; (2) *financial quotas,* such as gross margin, net profit, or expenses; (3) *activity quotas,* such as the number of sales calls made or the number of dealer training sessions given; and (4) *combination quotas,* which include both financial and activity goals. It is important to have activity quotas as well as financial quotas because meeting activity quotas can continue to motivate salespeople who are not achieving their financial quotas.

Customer Reviews of Performance

More and more customers are conducting annual reviews of the performance of their suppliers. Salespeople should ask for an annual evaluation of their performance by customers and participate in this review process at a special meeting. Obtaining feedback from customers is one of the most effective ways to keep from losing touch with customers. A survey of 432 buyers at small and large companies by Communispond, a New York City–based management consulting firm, found that the major reason customers switch suppliers is that they were offered a better deal by a new supplier, and the second most important reason is that "the sales rep got out of touch."[6]

ACCOUNT AND TERRITORY MANAGEMENT

SALES TERRITORY
A control unit that contains customer accounts.

The primary reason for establishing sales territories is to facilitate the planning and control of the selling function by enhancing market coverage, keeping selling costs low, strengthening customer relations, and coordinating selling with other marketing functions. As selling costs escalate, territory management is becoming increasingly important. A **sales territory** is a control unit that contains customer accounts. Most salespeople are assigned a geographical control unit such as a state, county, ZIP code area, city, or township because they are the basis of a great deal of government census data and other market information. Territories can also be assigned according to other market factors like buying habits and patterns of trade flow.

Once the geographical control unit has been established, customers and prospects in the territory are analyzed on the basis of their sales potential. First, the salesperson should identify prospects and accounts by name. Many sources containing this information are available. Computerized Yellow Pages are one of the most effective for identifying customers quickly. The Instant Yellow Pages Service contains a database of over 6 million U.S. businesses by name, mailing address, and phone number. Salespeople can also use company records of past sales; trade directories; professional association membership lists; directories of corporations; mailing lists of trade books and periodicals; chambers of commerce; federal, state, and local governments; and personal observation. After potential accounts are identified, the next step is to estimate the total sales potential for all acounts in each geographical control unit. The third step is to classify the accounts according to their annual buying potential. Those with the highest sales potential can be assigned to category A, and receive the largest share of the salesperson's time; average potential accounts can be classified as B's; accounts with less than a certain sales potential can be put into category C. Based on this analysis, the salesperson can decide which accounts to make sales calls on and which ones to contact by telephone or direct mail.

As illustrated in Figure 16-4, the concentration principle is usually clearly seen after customers have been ranked by sales potential. Here customers in category A (20 percent) account for 70 percent of the sales volume, those in category B (25 percent) for 23 percent of sales, and those in category C (55 percent) for only 7 percent of sales.

An increasing number of companies are using *computer programs* to assist their salespeople in account analysis, planning, and control. Orion Research is an example of a company that has established a computer program to help its salespeople use their time more efficiently and effectively.

Many organizations still do not use computerized mathematical models to help their salespeople because these models are so complex. In addition, not

[6]*Sales & Marketing Management,* February 1990, p. 10.

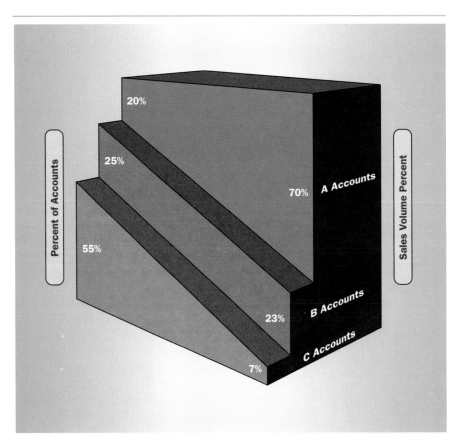

FIGURE 16-4 Ranking Customers According to the Concentration Principle

Company Highlight

Helping Salespeople at Orion Research

Orion Research, a Cambridge, Massachusetts, marketer of instrumentation equipment, uses a computerized inquiry-handling system called the Comprehensive Computerized Marketing System. From over 150 pieces of company literature, the CCMS selects the most appropriate ones for each prospect, and helps the sales force manage their time and territories so that they focus on prospects and customers that have the highest profit potential. CCMS continues to monitor sell-ing efforts until the order is either won or lost, and builds a continuous database for periodic analytical reports. Six months after implementing the CCMS, Orion Research's sales jumped 31 percent, with no increase in the size of the sales force.

Source: Thayer C. Taylor, "Giving Sales Leads a Leading Edge," *Sales & Marketing Management,* September 14, 1981, pp. 35–37.

every sales call can be accurately programmed because of the diverse variables that affect success and failure. A *portfolio analysis approach* that provides an alternative to the analytical rigor of the mathematical models is presented in Figure 16-5. In this approach, the sales call strategy is based on the account's attractiveness. Segment 1 represents what most companies call a *key account.* Segment 2 would be considered a *potential customer* or *prospect.* Segment 3 is a *stable account,* and Segment 4 represents a *weak account.* While this sales call portfolio analysis approach is logical and easy for salespeople to use, it is limited by the fact that all accounts are divided into only four segments.

ROUTING

TERRITORIAL ROUTING
Devising a travel plan or pattern to use when making sales calls.

Territorial routing is devising a travel plan or pattern to use when making sales calls. In most companies, individual salespeople still route themselves because they know their territories and their customers best.

Routing systems may be complex, but a basic pattern can be made simply by finding the accounts on the map and then deciding the optimal order for visiting

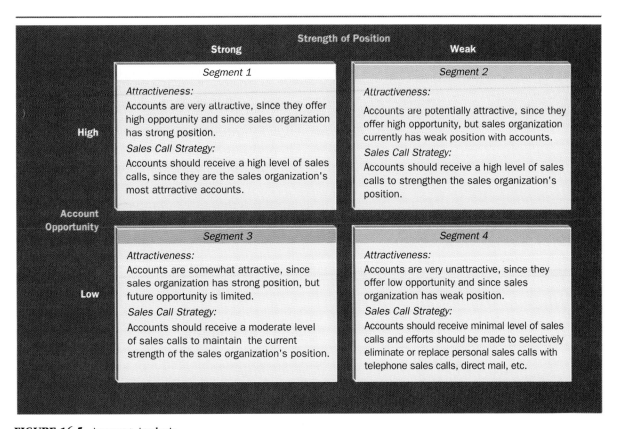

FIGURE 16-5 Account Analysis
Source: Raymond W. LaForge, Clifford E. Young, and B. Curtis Hamm, "Increasing Sales Call Productivity Through Improved Sales Call Allocation Strategies," *Journal of Personal Selling & Sales Management,* November 1983, p. 54.

each and the fastest route to take. Before developing a routing plan, the salesperson must determine the number of calls to be made each day, the call frequency for each class of customer, the distance to each account, and the method of transportation. With this information, the salesperson can locate present and potential customers on a map of the territory. In the past, accounts were often identified on a map by marking their location with felt-tip pens or by using different-colored round-headed pins for each account category. Today salespeople can just feed the information into a computer, and the computer will draw a routing plan in minutes. The objective in developing a routing path is to minimize backtracking and crisscrossing, thereby enabling the salesperson to use time in the most efficient manner.

Routing patterns are commonly straight or circular. With a *straight-line route*, the salesperson starts at the office and makes calls in one direction until he or she reaches the end of the territory. *Circular patterns* start at the office and move in a circle of stops until the salesperson ends up back at the office. Two less common and more complex route patterns are the cloverleaf and the hopscotch. A *cloverleaf route* is used when there are concentrations of accounts in specific parts of the territory. It is similar to a circular pattern, but rather than covering an entire territory, it circles only part of a territory. The next trip is an adjacent circle, and the pattern continues until the entire territory is covered. With *hopscotch patterns*, the salesperson starts at the farthest point from the office and hops back and forth, calling on accounts on either side of a straight line back to the office. For speed, the salesperson may fly to the outer limits of his or her territory, then drive back, calling on customers. On the next trip, the salesperson would go in another direction in the territory. Hopscotch and cloverleaf patterns are shown in Figure 16-6.

In the outer-ring approach to routing, shown in Figure 16-7, the salesperson first draws an outer ring around the customers to be called upon, then connects those customers inside the ring to the outer-ring route, using angles that are as obtuse as possible. The following general principles underlie this outer-ring approach to routing:

■ Customers in close proximity to one another should be visited in direct succession.

■ Sales calls should be made along the way so that there are no sharp angles in the route.

■ The same route should not be used to and from a customer, since retracing steps is the most acute angle of all.

■ Routes already traveled should not be crossed.

■ Daily travel routes should be as circular as possible.[7]

Using Computer Programs in Routing

Numerous computer-based interactive models have been successfully applied to sales force routing and territory management.[8] One, called the *nearest-city model*, can start from any given geographic point and select the shortest, least-cost

[7]Jan Wage, *The Successful Sales Presentation: Psychology and Technique* (London: Leviathan House, 1974), p. 83.

[8]For a review of various routing models, see Wade Ferguson, "A New Method for Routing Salespersons," *Industrial Marketing Management*, April 1980, pp. 171–178.

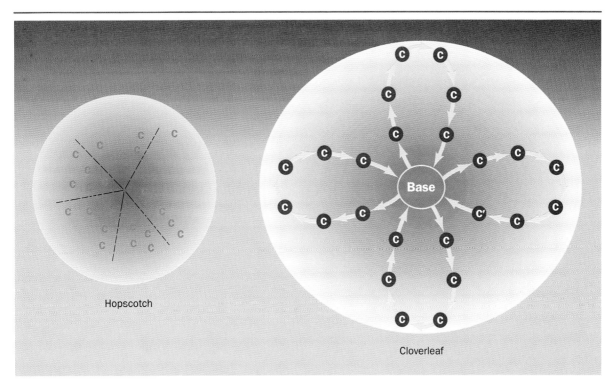

FIGURE 16-6 Hopscotch and Cloverleaf Routing Patterns

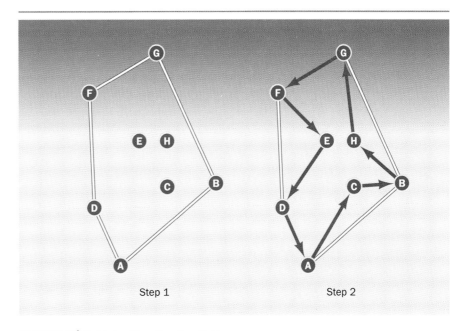

FIGURE 16-7 Outer-Ring Routing Pattern

distance between accounts. Nearly all computer routing models require input from salespeople on each customer's sales potential, call lengths, profit contribution, and estimated share penetration. Based on this information, the computer models realign sales territories into more manageable account groupings and route sales reps in terms of call frequencies, travel time, and length of call.

Reconfirming Appointments

Shortly before planning their daily territorial travel routes, whether these be computer-aided or something less sophisticated, sales reps should always confirm each of their appointments in order to minimize traveling and waiting time or the possibility that the prospect will not be available. On the actual day of the scheduled sales calls, it is a good idea to reconfirm each appointment to make sure a prospect isn't absent from work or at an unexpected meeting. Salespeople who have car phones can reconfirm an appointment while en route to the prospect's office.

WORKING SMARTER

In a recent survey, over 70 percent of senior-level training and development practitioners said that salespeople will need more highly developed skills by 1992.[9] In order to increase their efficiency, salespeople will also need to learn to work smarter by using the latest telecommunications equipment and avoiding time traps.

Using the Latest Technology

Salespeople can increase their selling effectiveness and efficiency by making use of the latest technologies. Battery-powered laptop computers, which can be used almost anywhere, are especially valuable to salespeople for keeping track of a wide variety of information on all their products and for providing customers with the latest-status information on their orders.

The experiences of diverse companies attest to the value of laptop computers to both salespeople and customers. To help in managing territories, completing paperwork, and gaining more face-to-face selling time, the pharmaceuticals division of Ciba-Geigy Corporation, located in Summit, New Jersey, equipped their 800 salespeople and 100 sales managers with laptop computers. Now Ciba-Geigy salespeople can obtain information about and for their 200,000 physician customers in a few seconds. Administrative tasks are taking about 20 percent less time, and reports are more accurate. Ciba-Geigy has estimated that every 1 percent boost in a rep's effectiveness increases revenue by $6.7 million per year.

At Shell Chemical Company, an automation system provides numerous benefits to the salespeople and their customers, as explained in the next Company Highlight.

[9]*Training & Development Journal,* September 1988, p. 11.

Company Highlight

Electronic Tool Kits at Shell Chemical Company

Shell Chemical Company uses a laptop computer–based tool kit of integrated software applications that improve the effectiveness and productivity of its field sales personnel. Shell Chemical's Sales Force Automation System allows salespeople to better prepare for sales calls by accessing timely date without relying on clerical staff. Some of its specific functions are:

Electronic mail: Enables sales reps to send and receive messages via an autodial phone.

Daily sales information: Lets sales reps receive reports of sales activities for their customers and products that are updated daily. Also allows salespeople to better manage their day-to-day expenditures and receive reimbursement more quickly.

Account management modules: Permits sales reps to obtain account information such as phone numbers, addresses, recent purchases, and prices.

Administrative reports: Enables salespeople to automate regular reports such as expense statements, letters for direct mail, graphics software packages for preparing charts and graphs, appointment calendars, and to-do lists.

Source: The Conference Board's Management Briefing: Marketing, April–May 1989, pp. 4–5.

Time Management

Training magazine's Industry Report estimates that almost two-thirds of U.S. organizations with more than 100 employees provide time-management training.

Paperwork

One of the most dreaded and time-consuming tasks of salespeople is handling paperwork. Like all other sales-related activities, paperwork ought to be scheduled on the salesperson's daily or weekly planning calendar. Digital Equipment Corporation puts onto audiotapes the 200 to 700 pages of memos, newsletters, brochures, reports, announcements, and other sales-related materials sent to salespeople each week. The tapes are recorded according to topics, so salespeople can choose exactly what they want to hear. Use of the tapes is voluntary, but so far, 68 percent of DEC's salespeople have elected to receive their paperwork on tape.[10]

Customer Service

Another time-consuming but important activity is providing customer service. Although it is hard to predict *what* customers will want *which* services *when*, salespeople need to recognize that customer service is a regular part of their job and should be scheduled like any other activity. Bro Uttal, co-author of *Total*

Paperwork is a dreaded and time-consuming chore for many salespeople.

[10]*Sales & Marketing Management,* February 1990, p. 32.

Customer Service—The Ultimate Weapon (Harper & Row, 1989), gives these suggestions for focusing customer service activities:

- Segment customers according to the costs and the potential profits in providing them with superior service.
- Remember that all customer contacts, whether through telephone operators, receptionists, secretaries, delivery and repair personnel, or customer service people, shape the perceptions of the salesperson's company's service. Salespeople should try to encourage all these customer-contact people to treat prospects and customers well.
- Continually stress the importance of customer service to people in the company. Salespeople should reinforce this attitude by their own actions.
- Design and use measures of service effectiveness, such as the percentage of on-time deliveries, the length of time it takes to repair a product, and the level of customer satisfaction.[11]

Excuses about Time

Some salespeople are chronically late, disorganized, and generally inefficient in using their time. Often the problem is the individual's attitude toward time and the tendency to make excuses for using it inefficiently. The most common excuses salespeople use are discussed in the following paragraphs.

I don't have sufficient time. There is always enough time to accomplish essential tasks. A salesperson who feels that he or she has insufficient time can usually overcome the problem by learning how to prioritze daily activities. Some tasks can be postponed or delayed indefinitely.

There are too many demands on my time. Learning how to say "no" is probably the most important timesaving technique a salesperson can learn. Salespeople who allow others to preempt their priorities are letting those other people control their time. Whenever someone places an unexpected demand on the salesperson's time, the salesperson should ask if this unplanned activity is more important than what he or she had planned to do with this time. If it isn't, the salesperson should give a courteous but brief explanation of why he or she cannot comply with the request.

I can do it better myself. Some salespeople have such a need for control and perfection that they waste a lot of their time doing unimportant tasks they could readily delegate to others. If someone else can do minor tasks well enough, the salesperson gains more time to spend on important projects. President Eisenhower once remarked that one of the most difficult adjustments for managers is learning to sign off on letters or accept completed work they aren't entirely pleased with.

If only I had more time each day. Everyone has the same 24 hours each day, but some people learn how to use those hours more efficiently. Working too many hours every day produces mental and physical fatigue, which can be counterproductive to overall performance. The professional salesperson learns to work smarter instead of harder.

---

[11]Ibid.

Selling in Action

Working Smarter

Harvey Cook sells $1.5 million worth of insurance policies each month, working only on Mondays and Tuesdays. Metropolitan Life's top salesperson says: "I don't have good weeks, and I don't have bad weeks. I'm so consistent I'm boring." A devout Mormon who spends most of his free time with his family, Cook makes most of his sales in his hometown of Mesa, Arizona. "So many salesmen feel they have to go anywhere to chase a sale," says Cook. "But I don't leave town. Traveling time could be selling time." Cook also tries to avoid working at night. He conducts about 75 percent of his business during the day. "I find out where I can meet with a client, or when his day off is, or when he has his vacation. I try to make it convenient." Now a millionaire, Cook makes calls in his silver Mercedes sports car. His wife loves flying, so on Thursdays he frequently takes her up in his Turbo Charge Cessna. Cook says: "I may look relaxed, but I'm a wild man on a Monday."

Source: "Superstars of Selling," *Success*, November 1984, p. 38.

I don't have time to plan. The old saying "Ask a busy person if you want something done" illustrates the importance of planning the use of one's time. People who achieve a lot have learned how to manage their time by skillful planning.

I can't find time to work on big projects. Because many complex projects cannot be finished quickly, people tend to let them slide until they can find large blocks of time to work on them. Professional salespeople use the *Swiss cheese approach* on big projects: They punch little holes in the project by doing small parts of it whenever they can. Better yet, they schedule at least an hour every day to work on major projects so that they do not procrastinate and get into a panic situation when the deadline draws near.

I can't prevent unexpected problems that disrupt my plans. Whenever the unexpected occurs, professional salespeople ask themselves this question: Is this more important than what I had planned to do at this time? If it isn't, they don't do it.

If only I could work faster. Most people make mistakes when they hurry, and there is never enough time to do everything. Setting priorities is the key. Professional salespeople do high-priority tasks and ignore low-priority ones.

It's better to do small tasks first. This is the exact opposite of what the best time managers do. The best salespeople create the habit of doing their most important tasks early in the day—before minor tasks crowd them out.

Falling into Time Traps

Many salespeople hurt their efficiency by falling into daily traps that waste their time. The most successful salespeople learn how to avoid time traps so that they get the most out of each hour and each day. Some of the most common time traps are listed in the following box.

Plan Each Day

Every salesperson can benefit from preparing a daily "To Do" list of projects and tasks that are prioritized into A, B, and C categories of importance. All the A priorities should be worked on first, until no more can be done on them. Then the B tasks should be tackled, and finally, C tasks. The A items are likely to be complex or long-term projects, so it is best to use the Swiss cheese approach to punch little holes in them at every opportunity because they are the top priority. For example, if one of a salesperson's A tasks is preparing a sales proposal for a large client, the salesperson should take every opportunity to work on that report during the day, if only by looking up a reference in the library or doing a few calculations. Most salespeople find that by doing a small piece of a major project every day they will complete it before they know it.

Steps to Manage Time More Efficiently

Although numerous guidelines have been suggested by time-management experts, most seem to agree on the following steps:

Each weekday afternoon, write down the schedule for the next day.

Committing their schedule to writing forces salespeople to think carefully about their plan. It helps them set realistic deadlines and motivates them to accomplish the plan. Many salespeople use a daily schedule sheet like the one pictured in Figure 16-8.

THE BOX OF TIME TRAPS

- Calling on unqualified or unprofitable prospects.
- Insufficiently planning each day's activities.
- Making poor territorial routing and travel plans.
- Making too many cold calls.
- Taking long lunch hours and too many coffee breaks.
- Making poor use of waiting time between appointments.
- Spending too much time entertaining prospects and customers.
- Not using modern telecommunications equipment like a car phone, beeper, facsimile machine, and laptop computer.
- Doing tasks that could be delegated to a staff person or to automated equipment.

- Failing to prioritize work.
- Procrastinating on major projects or contacting high-potential prospects, resulting in redundant preparation and paperwork.
- Inefficiently handling paperwork and keeping disorganized records.
- Failing to break up huge, long-range goals into small, currently manageable tasks.
- Ending workdays early, especially on Friday afternoons.
- Failing to insulate oneself from interruptions on sales calls or while doing paperwork.
- Conducting unnecessary meetings, visits, and phone calls.

DAILY SCHEDULE	DATE _____
HOURS	Appointments/Activities
8:00	
9:00	
10:00	
11:00	
12:00	
1:00	
2:00	
3:00	
4:00	
5:00	
Evening Hours	

FIGURE 16-8 Daily Schedule Sheet

On Friday afternoon, plan the schedule for the following week. By the middle of Friday afternoon, the salesperson has a good idea of what he or she has accomplished—or failed to accomplish—that week. The pressure has eased, so it is possible to think clearly. This is the ideal time to decide what needs to be accomplished the following week. This tactic allows salespeople to mentally rehearse their schedule over the weekend so that they will have a psychological head start Monday morning. When they arrive at the office, they can hit the ground running.

Concentrate on high priorities. Salespeople must learn to work on high-priority projects first, even when only a little can be accomplished on the project that day, before they switch to lower-priority tasks. Each day salespeople should pick one important task and concentrate on getting it done.

Spend time as if it were money. Salespeople who regard their time as a precious asset learn to use it more productively.

What Would You Do?

Your district manager calls you Wednesday evening and says he wants to work with you over the next two days as you make each of your sales calls. Last week you scheduled four two-hour sales calls on both Thursday and Friday of this week, so your appointment book is filled. However, two of these accounts, one on each day, are notorious for canceling out at the last minute. You are fearful that this will happen while your boss is working with you, and you are trying to decide how to avoid two hours of idle time each day in case of last-minute cancellations.

Stop procrastinating. This step involves changing a "do-it-later" habit into a "do-it-now" habit. As we noted earlier, some salespeople delay working on large projects until they can find large blocks of time, and this approach often causes them to leave their most important projects until the last minute, when they are forced to finish them quickly and poorly.

Schedule some personal time every day. The best way for salespeople to obtain personal time is to schedule it in their daily appointment book so that it's protected from intrusions. This is the time to listen to music, read a book, talk with friends and family, or go for a long walk. Personal time is not a luxury or something to postpone until it can be fitted into the schedule. It's a requirement for maintaining a healthy balance and control in every salesperson's life.

Good intentions are not enough. As the old saying goes: The road to hell is paved with good intentions. Salespeople prone to procrastination must stop talking about how they're going to manage their time better and start doing it now.[12]

MANAGEMENT OF STRESS

A recent Gallup Poll study commissioned by the New York Business Group on Health found that 25 percent of the work force suffers from anxiety disorders or stress-related illness, with about 13 percent suffering from depression. In terms of days lost on the job, the study estimated that each affected employee loses about 16 workdays a year because of stress, anxiety, or depression, which costs about $8,000 in terms of worker's compensation.[13]

[12]Thomas J. Quirk, "The Art of Time Management," *Training*, January 1989, pp. 59–61.
[13]*The Wall Street Journal*, October 20, 1989, p. B2E.

The first step for reducing stress is learning to recognize its symptoms.

Stress is not all bad. Some stress is necessary and desirable for excellent performance. Salespeople shouldn't try to eliminate stress, but to manage it. In modern life, we all face stress-producing hassles, helplessness, and hurriedness.

Hassles

Hassles are the irritating and frustrating little annoyances that happen to us every day. They include traffic jams, being cut off by another driver, inability to find a parking spot, erroneous bills, rising gasoline prices, bad weather, poor restaurant service, excessive noise, pollution, demands of children, and petty arguments. While individual hassles may be small, their cumulative effect can sometimes be crushing. When someone is feeling especially hassled, one more small irritant can be the final straw that causes that person to blow up.

It's important not to overreact to daily hassles but to keep in mind how unimportant they are over the longer run. Keeping a cool head and even looking for the humor in daily hassles can help prevent them from building up to the exploding point. Whenever you feel especially hassled, escape to a quiet place (even if only to your parked car or the quiet corner of a room) to relax, close your eyes, and think pleasant thoughts for several minutes. Then, after you feel relaxed and rested, you can start fresh on the rest of the day's activities.

Helplessness

Many people in today's society feel helpless. Our growing dependence on other people, bureaucratic organizations, and machines to function in our daily lives leaves many of us feeling vulnerable. When people believe they have little influence or control over their lives, stress is the usual result. Power, on the other hand, is very therapeutic, especially the power to influence those aspects of life that are stress-producing.

Salespeople may occasionally feel helpless in dealing with customers because they may slip into erroneously thinking that their job is to sell products to people instead of helping people to buy what they need. There is no power struggle between buyer and seller when salespeople view their job as helping others. Instead, there is a mutual spirit of trust and cooperation that leads to negotiating win-win agreements. Few jobs offer the control and freedom that professional selling does. The lifestyle, income, and job control of the salesperson are envied by many.

Hurriedness

Many of us are continually racing the clock to get things done by a deadline. Type-A salespeople feel constant time urgency or hurriedness in almost all aspects of their lives. They are restless people who tend to equate idle time with wasted time. Type A people are hard workers, very decisive, and used to doing several things at the same time. They usually move, walk, and eat rapidly, and feel impatient at the pace of events. They frequently schedule too many tasks in too short a time frame, so they seem chronically harried.

Salespeople who feel hurried much of the time need to learn to schedule and prioritize their time better. Those who overschedule their time are either poor planners or have a deliberate need to feel they are working as hard as possible. This type of person should keep in mind that it is not the total number of tasks accomplished that counts, but the few important results.

One important way to deal with a hurried lifestyle is exercise. Exercise has many benefits: It's a form of relaxation, a method of improving cardiovascular fitness, and a means for controlling body weight. Perhaps, however, its most undervalued effect is that it dissipates anxiety and aggressive energy.

Burnout

When stress continues for a long time without successful management, it can lead to burnout. Burnout has three basic components: physical, emotional, and mental exhaustion.

Physical exhaustion is characterized by low energy, chronic fatigue, and weakness. People undergoing burnout tend to be accident prone, susceptible to illnesses such as nagging colds, attacks of virus or flu, frequent headaches, nausea, muscle tension, back pains, and psychosomatic complaints. They also frequently experience changes in eating habits—either eating too much or eating too little.

Emotional exhaustion, the second component of burnout, primarily involves feelings of helplessness, hopelessness, and entrapment. In extreme cases, these feelings can lead to deep depression, emotional breakdown, or even serious thoughts of suicide. People who burn out feel that they need all the emotional energy they can muster merely to keep going through the motions of daily life. Salespeople who reach this stage usually stop caring about their goals and even other people, including family and friends.

Mental exhaustion, the third component of burnout, is manifested by the development of negative attitudes toward oneself, one's work, and even life itself. Feelings of disillusionment spill over to affect the person's attitudes toward family and friends as well. People who burn out often show coldness and hostility toward others.

How to Reduce Stress and Avoid Burnout

One of the most important things in reducing stress is to learn to identify oncoming states of stress so that you can take corrective action. Some people know that stress is building up when they start getting headaches, insomnia, heart palpitations, irritability, or "blowups." When you see stress building up, take steps to simplify your life.

- *Simplify, simplify, simplify.* Cut back on your schedule of activities.
- *Don't take job or school pressures home with you.*
- *Don't keep your schedule loaded up.* Schedule time for relaxation and for dealing with unanticipated stressful situations.
- *Stay healthy.* Develop a preventive approach to maintaining your health. Get regular sleep, maintain a balanced diet, exercise daily, stop smoking, and use alcohol only in moderation.
- *Space out potential stressful situations.*
- *Arrange for privacy and quiet time for yourself.*
- *Put things in perspective.* Don't let insignificant events bother you.
- *Establish support systems* among your family, friends, and colleagues.
- *Don't procrastinate.* Stressful situations get worse the longer you tolerate them.
- *Make decisions based on your needs rather than on the expectations of others.*
- *Take conscious control of your life.*

SUMMARY Professional salespeople are usually efficient and effective managers of their territories. Operating much like field marketing managers, they try to maximize their return on time invested (ROTI) in achieving sales growth—whether by market penetration, market development, product development, or market creation. They understand the various quantitative and qualitative measures of performance and conduct annual reviews of their performance with their individual customers. They use the most efficient account analysis and routing plans, sometimes developed by computers. They are excellent time managers who learn ways to work smarter, avoiding the classic time traps that plague lesser salespeople. Despite their high-pressure jobs, they learn to manage stress and avoid burnout.

CHAPTER REVIEW QUESTIONS

1. Define and distinguish between the terms *effectiveness* and *efficiency.*
2. How do salespeople actually spend their time?
3. What are the basic activities of salespeople?

4. Identify the major *management* and *marketing* activities of salespeople.
5. Describe the concept of return on time invested (ROTI).
6. What are the four ways that salespeople can increase sales in their territories?
7. Name at least ten quantitative measures of salesperson performance.
8. Give some guidelines for better time management.
9. What is meant by the terms *stress* and *burnout*?
10. How can salespeople manage stress and avoid burnout?

TOPICS FOR THOUGHT AND CLASS DISCUSSION

1. Is stress always negative or does it have a positive side? Explain.
2. Why are salespeople described as operating like field marketing managers? Do you think this is an accurate representation of the typical field salesperson? Explain.
3. What are the time traps that plague the management of your time? How do you try to avoid these traps?
4. What techniques do you use to plan, organize, and prioritize your daily activities? Do you use the Swiss cheese approach for large or complex projects? Give an example if you do.
5. What causes the most stress in your life and how do you manage this stress?

PROJECTS FOR PERSONAL GROWTH

1. Contact three salespeople and ask them how they plan, organize, and prioritize their daily activities. Evaluate their approaches in terms of ROTI.
2. Classify four of your student friends on the basis of your perceptions of their effectiveness and efficiency. Then ask each of them these two questions: (a) What are the *time traps* that are most responsible for wasting your time each day? (b) What techniques do you use to plan, organize, and prioritize your daily activities? Compare your friends' answers with your prior classification of them. Any surprises?
3. For the coming week, write down how you spend each hour of the seven days. At the end of the week, compute approximately how much of your time was used productively and how much was wasted. Draw up a plan for better managing your time and use it throughout the next week. Ask yourself at the end of this second week if you obtained more productive time. If you did, what made the difference?
4. Go the library and find three articles on managing a sales territory. Summarize them and report what you learned to your classmates.

KEY TERMS

Effectiveness Results-oriented focus on achieving selling goals.

Efficiency Cost-oriented focus on making the best possible use of the salesperson's time and efforts.

ROTI (return on time invested) The designated return divided by the hours spent achieving it.

Market penetration A sales growth strategy that calls for salespeople to sell larger quantities of their current products to current customers.

Market development A sales growth strategy that calls for salespeople to sell current products to new customers.

Product development A sales growth strategy that calls for salespeople to sell new products to current customers.

Market creation A sales growth strategy that calls for salespeople to sell new products to new customers.

Concentration principle Most sales, costs, and profits come from a relatively small proportion of customers and products; also known as the "80-20 rule."

Sales territory A control unit that contains customer accounts.

Territorial routing Devising a travel plan or pattern to use when making sales calls.

Case 16-1

PEARSON MACHINE TOOLS: TIME AND TERRITORY MANAGEMENT

Diane Mulholland and her husband, Mark Roberts, have shared a gloriously long weekend of sunbathing, swimming, waterskiing, and even a little gambling in Atlantic City, New Jersey. While driving back to New York City late Sunday evening, Diane thinks about how fortunate she is, at age 26, to have a handsome, fun-loving husband and a great job that gives her a lot of independence.

Diane accepted her job with Pearson Machine Tools after graduating from the State University of New York with a degree in marketing. Her first year with Pearson was spent in training, which consisted essentially of learning about machine tools and different customer needs. With a guaranteed salary of $28,500 for the first year and no sales pressure, Diane enjoyed the training, even though she didn't take some of it too seriously—especially the brief session on account and territory management. After all, she thought, training programs always give the theoretical approach to doing things, while the real work is different.

Only a month ago Diane was assigned to her own territory, and tomorrow she is due to begin her first long field trip. Arriving home late from her weekend, she feels relaxed, but also tired, and falls asleep without setting her alarm clock for 6:30 A.M.—as she had planned to in order to catch a 7:45 A.M. flight to Boston. Diane learned about the "hopscotch" routing pattern in a college course on personal selling, and she is going to use this technique on her week-long field trip. With the hopscotch routing pattern, she will fly to the most distant point of her territory, then rent a car and make sales calls along the route home.

Although she missed her 7:45 A.M. flight to Boston, Diane catches another flight about an hour later. Arriving in Boston around 10:00 A.M., she rents a car at the airport, checks into a convenient motel, and telephones the four accounts she plans to call on that day. Getting a busy signal on each of her first three calls, Diane decides to drive over to the first customer's office, since it is only 20 minutes away. On the drive over, she realizes that she probably should have set up precise appointments for each of her customers before leaving on this trip, but she sent out postcards last week informing them that she would be calling on them sometime this week.

11:00 A.M.: Upon announcing her business purpose to the receptionist at her first account's office, Diane is shocked to learn that the purchasing agent, Burt Haywood, suffered a mild heart attack two days ago and is still in the hospital. As yet, no one has been assigned to handle Mr. Haywood's work. After expressing her sympathy and good wishes for Mr. Haywood's quick recovery, Diane decides to go to lunch because it would be nearly noon before she could make it across midday traffic to her second account.

11:30 A.M.: Since she is on an expense account, Diane picks out one of the better restaurants nearby, where she has a 15-minute wait for a table. After being seated, she orders a cocktail and the restaurant's special broiled lobster lunch. Although expensive, it is delicious. Diane is now in a better frame of mind.

1:15 P.M.: Arriving at Simpson Electronics Company, Diane finds three other salespeople in the reception area waiting to see Robin Wolfe, the purchasing manager. Taking a seat, she chats pleasantly with Mr. Wolfe's secretary, then begins reading the latest copy of *Newsweek* she has in her briefcase. Diane always takes magazines with her on sales calls to help make the waiting time go faster. She winces, however, when she sees that two of the other sales reps are reading machine tool trade journals they brought with them.

1:45 P.M.: Mr. Wolfe's secretary ushers Diane into Mr. Wolfe's office, where the two exchange introductions and light conversation.

Mr. Wolfe: Well, I didn't expect to see you today, Ms. Mulrony.

Diane: Mulholland, Mr. Wolfe. But please call me Diane.

Mr. Wolfe: Oh, ah, sorry, ah, Diane. Well, folks are always spelling my last name without an *e.* I knew a Bob Mulholland in Pittsburgh—played French horn with the symphony out there, I think. Any relation?

Diane: I don't think so, but there sure are plenty of us Mulhollands around!

Mr. Wolfe: Wolfes, too! Now, what can I do for you today?

About two weeks ago, Diane spoke on the telephone with Mr. Wolfe's secretary about his needs. She asks him directly whether he is ready to replace the old punch press his secretary mentioned. To her dismay, Diane learns that Mr. Wolfe has already bought a new machine from one of Pearson's biggest competitors, who offered him a 15 percent discount on the machine.

Diane *(Greatly disappointed):* We've got a twenty percent discount special on our best model punch press all this month. And it's the same one I talked about with your secretary.

Mr. Wolfe: Oh, I'm sorry, Diane, but I guess my secretary didn't make herself clear to me about her conversation with you. I didn't get any promotional literature from you, so I didn't know any details, anyway. The foundry foreman certainly likes Pearson equipment best. But you know, with all the business we've given Pearson over the years, Diane, I'd think you'd want to keep me better informed about upcoming deals.

Diane: I was going to mail the promotional pieces out last week, but since I was coming down to see you this Monday, I didn't think it would be necessary.

2:30 P.M.: Really upset about missing out on a $25,000 order, Diane consoles herself with a candy bar and a Coke before calling her last two accounts for the day. On the first call, she learns that Louise St. Germain—the head buyer at Crown Laboratories—started her vacation today and won't be back for two weeks. Someone is filling in for her, but that person doesn't have authority to buy equipment—only supplies and maintenance items.

2:45 P.M.: Telephoning her last account for the day, Diane is relieved to hear that Ken Endicott is in and will see her as soon as she gets there. Since it's only a five-minute drive, Diane takes a short coffee break first.

3:15 P.M.: Diane and Mr. Endicott have just exchanged friendly greetings when Mr. Endicott's secretary buzzes him. Mr. Frey, the vice president of purchasing, wants to see him immediately. Apologizing for the interruption, Mr. Endicott leaves but tells Diane to relax because he will probably be back within a half hour. Again, Diane takes out her magazine to read.

4:00 P.M.: Mr. Endicott returns and tells Diane that he has an emergency project to do for Mr. Frey but that he will be glad to see Diane early tomorrow morning. Although Diane has another customer scheduled for tomorrow morning, she says that will be fine and waves good-bye.

4:10 P.M.: Leaving Mr. Endicott's office, Diane feels down because it hasn't been a good day. It is already past 4:00 P.M., so she decides against trying to reach any more customers today. Instead, she drives back to her motel for a phone call to Mark and a quick nap before dinner. Tomorrow has to be a better day!

Questions

1. How would you evaluate Diane Mulholland as a manager of her time and territory? Give some specific examples to support your evaluation.
2. What would you recommend to help Diane improve her effectiveness and efficiency?
3. Outline the information that the Pearson training program should have included in order to prepare Diane for managing her territory.

Case 16-2

COPING WITH PRESSURES

It is another typical morning for Jim Rosenthal. His two young children, 3-year-old David and 5-year-old Edith, are yelling and screaming at each other and resisting their mother's attempts to get them to take their baths. It is always a hassle in the morning because Jim and Mary both go out to work. Jim is a sales representative for Cranson Industrial Scales, and Mary is a loan officer with First Regional Bank of St. Louis. Jim takes the kids to nursery school each morning at 7:30, and Mary picks them up before 6:00 each night. Jim loves his family dearly, but he is usually relieved to drop the kids off at nursery school and head out on sales calls. Alone in his car, he can find the peace and quiet (if traffic conditions aren't too bad) he needs to focus his attention on his sales calls for the day.

This morning Jim is sitting at the kitchen table gulping down a cup of black coffee and trying to complete some paperwork that the district sales manager has been bugging him about for over a week. Things haven't been going too well lately. Jim hasn't made a sale in a week, and his annual sales quota is beginning to seem unreachable. Jim calls on over 200 accounts in his geographically small territory, selling various types of Cranson industrial scales and measuring devices for automatically weighing products and packages on assembly lines. Around 6 percent of his accounts purchase over $25,000 worth of products from him a year, and account for nearly 75 percent of his total sales. Over half of his accounts buy less than $500, making up around 5 percent of his sales. The rest of his accounts tend to fall into the $2,000–$5,000 purchase range, accounting for about 20 percent of his sales. Of course, his figures aren't exact because accounts sometimes phone in orders directly to headquarters. But Jim gets credit for those sales, too.

Jim makes it a practice to call on each of his smaller accounts at least three times a year and his larger accounts eight to ten times annually. Also, because they are conveniently located on his way to or from other accounts, Jim calls on several small accounts as often as eight times a year. He believes it would be foolish to neglect these accounts just because of their size—they might quickly grow into large accounts. He has been surprised to discover that some of his biggest accounts don't seem to require as many sales calls or as much service as some of his smaller accounts. Some of the big accounts order almost routinely at certain times of the year, and Jim always makes a point of calling on them around that time. Several small accounts, however, demand a lot of customer service—even calling Jim two or three times a month about various problems that he spends a lot of time correcting, either in person or by phone through the Cranson headquarters field support staff. Although he never says so, Jim sometimes thinks that certain of these small accounts are more trouble than they are worth. But his commitment to customer service keeps him responding to their requests.

Jim can't figure it out. Five years ago, when he had half as many accounts, he had little trouble making his annual sales quota. But in the last few years, as his customer list doubled, Jim seems to have less time and is finding it harder to make his quota. This is especially frustrating because he feels that he is working "smarter" than ever. He has even devised his own routing pattern (shown in Figure 16-1A) by printing a shadow capital G on a map of his territory at the location of each of his 13 giant accounts (those buying over $25,000 of Cranson products yearly), a capital C at the location of each of about 50 of his medium-size customers (those buying over $2,000 worth of Cranson products yearly), and a small c for over 120 small customers who buy less than $2,000 each year. He traced a circle around his territory and drew 12 radius lines (each about 25 miles long) in different directions from his home to the outer edge of his territory to create 12 zones.

Jim always takes time on Friday morning to schedule appointments by phone with customers in a particular zone for the following week. Then, starting each Monday, he works his way out and back home each day of the week, making sales calls within that zone. He schedules appointments with the largest accounts in the zone first, then schedules the smaller accounts in between sales calls on the large accounts. Because some zones have many accounts and a lot of customer service needs, Jim frequently finds it necessary to work the same zone two straight weeks or more to cover them all.

Jim has heard about maximizing a salesperson's return on time invested (ROTI) in sales training courses, but feels it is too much work to maintain records on sales by the time invested in them. He

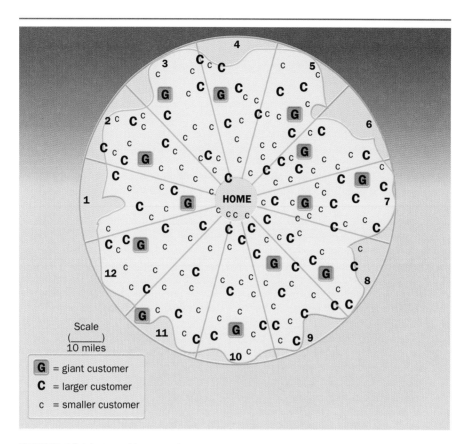

FIGURE 16-1A Jim's Territorial Routing Zones

isn't even convinced that ROTI is a good indicator of proper time use because a few of his current low-activity accounts have been known to suddenly place a large order with him. Since Jim was careful to keep the relationship going for years despite low sales, he was one of the first sales reps these customers thought of when they decided to switch suppliers.

Jim normally schedules at least an hour on a sales call with his giant accounts, about 30 to 45 minutes with large accounts, and 20 minutes or so with the smallest customers. Of course, the actual time he spends with each prospect or customer varies substantially, depending on the customer's schedule, his or her frame of mind, type of problems, and need for information.

Lately, Jim has felt frustrated because of traffic jams and a lack of convenient parking in his highly congested territory. He was 30 to 45 minutes late for three appointments last week, and two of his customers said they'd have to reschedule because they didn't have any additional time to spare him when he

arrived late. Jim often thinks about getting a car phone so he can at least let customers know when he is going to be late and perhaps reschedule the appointment over the phone, but he's not sure a car phone would relieve the pressure that's been building up on him for the last few months.

With all the extra sales calls he is making in an effort to get back on track toward his sales quota, doing all the paperwork that headquarters requires, and coping with the kids at night while he and his wife try to keep up with the numerous household chores, Jim feels tired at home and seldom has time while working for lunch or even a coffee break. Usually, he buys a can of soda and a hot dog for lunch at a convenience store and gobbles them down in his car on the way to his next sales call. Lately, he has noticed himself becoming increasingly irritable with his wife and kids at night, and it bothers him that he is obviously bringing the pressures of his job home with him. Unless sales pick up fast, Jim isn't sure that he will be able to take his annual two-week vacation with his family. Perhaps, he thinks, he can work every other day during his vacation to try to get back on track toward his annual sales quota. Right now, it would help if he could just get a good night's sleep instead of tossing and turning for several hours, worrying about his quota and the next day's schedule!

Questions

1. Do you think that Jim is working smarter or just harder? What do you think about Jim's sales call allocation and routing plan for his accounts? Can you suggest any improvements?

2. How well do you think Jim invests his time? What might he do differently?

3. What advice would you give Jim about achieving his annual sales quota?

4. What would you suggest to Jim to help him deal with the stress in his life?

Chapter 17

Managing the Sales Force

Take good care of your customers and your employees, and everything else will fall into place.—Communications Satellite Corporation's sales management philosophy

PETER and Rinaldo Pierangeli know perhaps somewhat better than many other businesspeople exactly what it's like to watch a business grow and modernize. They grew up with their family's company, a plumbing and industrial hardware supply reseller and wholesaler called Pierangeli Group, Inc. The brothers share the responsibilities of National Sales Manager and National Marketing Manager. The company, which is based just outside of Philadelphia, stocks over 30,000 products that they buy directly from manufacturers and, after repackaging, sell to end-users. We found it helpful to talk with the Pierangeli brothers because their company is structured in such a way that it has allowed them to gain a perspective of both direct-to-consumer and organizational selling. Pierangeli Group's Hardware Division concentrates on retail and wholesale consumer sales, while the Institution-Commercial Division employs 60 sales representatives who sell to apartment complexes, industrial plants, schools and universities, military bases, and hotels in territories across the United States. We asked the Pierangellis to discuss how they manage their salespeople and what their sales managers do.

"Right now, the most important thing our regional sales managers do is hire and train people for our territories. In the last few years, and largely because of our rapid growth and changing business practices, our turnover rate for salespeople has been about 25 percent per year," says Pete. "After hiring a new salesperson, the sales manager works with him or her for two weeks solidly, then every other week solidly for a total of 13 weeks. Then we bring the new person into headquarters for one week and show him or her every aspect of our business. After that, the salesperson works individually, with, of course, the appropriate sales manager's supervision."

Profile

Peter and Rinaldo Pierangeli

When we remarked that 60 people is not a very large number of salespeople for such ambitious (national) coverage, Peter and Rinaldo explained that recent computer and telecommunications improvements have made it possible for Pierangeli Group not only to stay on top of existing accounts, but also to predict potential business. "We recently outfitted all of our salespeople with hand-held computers for placing orders and relaying messages to headquarters. Sales managers, headquarters staff, and customers keep in touch with the salespeople through these computers as well as through pagers and voice mail. Meanwhile, because we're shifting our field sales emphasis to specific accounts within certain markets, we are developing a telemarketing division to support our field sales and customer service efforts. And because fast delivery is so crucial in our industry, we have set up warehouse and office facilities in several locations across the country. This allows our salespeople to guarantee two-day delivery and allows us as a company to compete with large mail-order houses that don't offer their customers face-to-face service." ■

□ How sales managers spend their time

□ The eclectic role of the professional sales manager

□ Why sales managers need to be marketing-oriented

□ The specific duties and responsibilities of sales managers

PROMOTION FROM SALESPERSON TO SALES MANAGER

Superior performance in field selling for a few years can earn a salesperson promotion to sales manager. Ironically, the very qualities, skills, and attitudes that enable someone to be an outstanding salesperson can sometimes be counter-productive in the sales manager's job. New sales managers must learn and apply administrative skills such as planning, organizing, directing, motivating, analyz-ing, and controlling. Beyond this, a sales manager must use sophisticated inter-personal skills in serving as the connecting link between the sales force and headquarters management.

Depending on the nature of the organization and the attitude of top man-agement toward the sales function, the sales manager's duties can vary along a long continuum. In some companies, the sales manager is little more than a supervisor of the sales force, a kind of "supersalesperson" who shows the others how to do it. In other companies, the sales manager is responsible for forecast-ing, planning, budgeting, and territorial profit. And in some progressive compa-nies, the sales manager is a marketing manager in every way but position title. Sales managers at different hierarchical levels may have several different position titles and responsibilities, as shown in Table 17-1.

From Buddy to Boss

A common problem facing salespeople who are promoted to sales manager is going from "one of the gang" to "the boss." After sharing complaints, personal ambitions, and private weaknesses with other sales reps for years, it is awkward for a new sales manager to suddenly have authority over his or her friends. To avoid this situation, some companies have a policy of transferring new sales managers to districts where they have no previous social relationships.

Whether they stay or move to another district, all new sales managers need training before taking on their new responsibilities. Unfortunately, few compa-nies provide sufficient training for those making the switch from sales rep to sales manager. Thus, new sales managers often seem to confirm the *Peter principle:* In a hierarchy, every employee tends to rise to his or her level of incompetence.[1] The major reasons for their inadequacy are (1) illogical selection criteria for promotion to sales management, (2) inadequate sales management training, (3)

[1]Laurence J. Peter and Raymond Hull, *The Peter Principle: Why Things Always Go Wrong* (New York: William Morrow & Co., 1969).

548

TABLE 17-1   Titles and Responsibilities of Sales Managers

Top-Level Sales Executives
Vice President of Sales: Top sales executive who reports to the company CEO or senior vice president of marketing. The vice president of sales is involved in strategy planning for the company and is directly responsible for developing sales strategy. In companies that do not have a vice president of marketing, the vice president of sales is responsible for all marketing activities.
National Sales Manager: The link between overall marketing strategy and the line sales managers who are responsible for carrying out sales plans in their respective regions. Involved in both strategic and tactical planning, the national sales manager is responsible for communicating top-level decisions on sales operations to regional sales managers and for providing overall direction to the sales force.
Middle-Level Line Sales Managers
Regional, Division, and Zone Sales Managers: These managers are responsible for sales activities in successively smaller subdivisions of the company's sales organization. Zone sales managers report to division sales managers, who report to regional sales managers.
First-Level Sales Managers
District, Branch, and Field Sales Managers: First-level line sales managers with successively smaller territorial responsibilities who handle the day-to-day activities of their salespeople and sales staffs.
Sales Supervisor: An experienced salesperson who supervises a few salespeople in a given sales branch or field territory.
Key Salesperson Responsibilities
National Account Manager (NAM), Key Account Executive (KAE): These are examples of the titles given to top-performing salespeople who are responsible for selling to a few major customers, such as large national chains like Toys 'R Us, WalMart, Sears, and K Mart.
Salespeople
Marketing Representative, Territory Manager, Account Representative, Account Manager, Sales Representative, Sales Engineer: These are only a few of the titles used for salespeople in different consumer and industrial firms.
Sales Staff
Assistant to the Sales Manager, Sales Analyst, Sales Training Manager: These titles are representative of the many staff positions that support the functions of sales management. Staff people work at every level in the sales organization, from corporate headquarters to the smallest branch office. Many have very impressive titles, such as *corporate vice president of sales* or *assistant national sales manager*, yet have no line sales management authority. Sales staff personnel assist in performing a variety of related functions at different levels in the sales organization; for example: sales planning, sales promotion, sales recruiting, sales training, and sales analysis.

lack of a marketing orientation in handling sales operations, and (4) insufficient blending of sales and marketing activities.[2] When their organizations fail to give them sufficient help to successfully make the transition from salesperson to sales manager, new sales managers must take it upon themselves to learn how to function effectively in their diverse new roles.

DOER OR MANAGER?

Some sales organizations suffer because the sales manager remains too involved in "doing" instead of "managing." As Figure 17-1 shows, sales managers spend at least 29 percent of their time in personal selling, either face-to-face or by phone. They spend 15 percent of their time traveling, and another 17 percent on account service and coordination. Only 24 percent of their time is spent on administration, with another 14 percent on internal meetings.

DOING Time spent by managers on activities that subordinates can do.

MANAGING Time devoted to determining how to accomplish work through other people.

Time spent on activities that subordinates can do is **doing.** For example, when sales managers make sales calls on their own, they are "doing" because this is work that their salespeople can perform. Time devoted to determining how to accomplish work through other people is **managing.** Sales managers who make sales calls with the salespeople to observe, analyze, and coach them in improving their presentations are performing management duties.

Many sales managers spend too much time in the field because they feel most comfortable using the same skills that earned them promotion to sales manager. And many do not understand their new managerial responsibility for profit through effective and efficient use of human, material, and financial resources. The difference between a skillful sales manager and a mere "doer" can make a substantial impact on the success of sales force efforts.

ECLECTIC ROLE OF THE PROFESSIONAL SALES MANAGER

Just as the old stereotype of the salesperson is disappearing, so is the old stereotype of the sales manager. As Rosenbloom and Anderson put it:

> Perhaps there was a time when the sales manager had to be the "kingfish salesman," a master salesperson in charge of the sales force. It was the sales manager's job to "get the sales force going and to keep it going" to meet the sales goals of the company, and who could do that better than someone who knew what it took to achieve sales objectives and who could serve as a role model for other members of the sales force? Implicit in this view of the sales manager's job is the belief that the job is a very narrow one, requiring only good selling skills and perhaps some ability to impart these particular skills to the rank and file. . . . But times have changed. A far more intense and complex competitive environment, sophisticated products and

---

[2]Rolph E. Anderson and Bert Rosenbloom, "Eclectic Sales Management: Strategic Response to Trends in the Eighties," *Journal of Personal Selling and Sales Management,* November 1982, pp. 41–46.

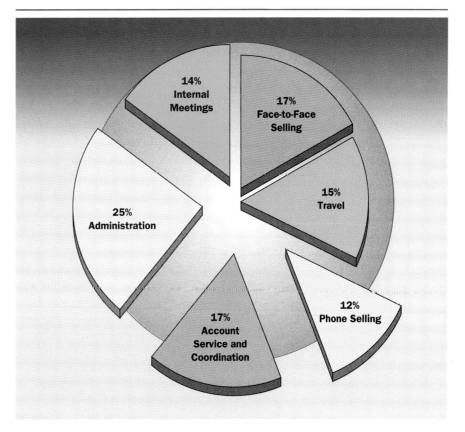

FIGURE 17-1 How Sales Managers Spend Their Time
Source: Sales & Marketing Management, January 1990, p. 39.

services, professional buyers, and purchase decisions shared by several layers of management and technical experts have profoundly altered the nature of the sales manager's job. It is no longer enough for sales managers to be "super salespeople." Now they must be "super marketers."[3]

Today's sales managers must carry out most of the functions of marketing managers as well as those pertaining specifically to sales management. In their role as sales managers, they plan, direct, and control the personal selling activities—including recruiting, selecting, equipping, organizing, assigning, routing, supervising, compensating, motivating, and evaluating salespeople. Beyond these duties, sales managers must be sales forecasters, budget managers, market analysts, strategic planners, students of buyer behavior, opportunity managers, intelligence gatherers, scarce-product allocators, accounts receivable collectors, cost and profit analysts, leaders, and master communicators in serving as the linchpin between the sales force and the company's marketing organization. Few, if any, jobs in a company are more important than the sales manager's because sales is

---

[3]Bert Rosenbloom and Rolph E. Anderson, "The Sales Manager: Tomorrow's Super Marketer," *Business Horizons,* March–April 1984, p. 50.

the only activity that directly generates income—all other activities support this revenue-producing function. Unless its products can be profitably sold, an organization will not survive.

Marketing-Oriented Sales Managers

Companies are looking for more versatile sales managers these days. Strong financial capability, as well as sound marketing experience, is sought. To improve sales and marketing coordination, General Foods' division sales managers report directly to a national sales manager, but they also have a dotted-line relationship with the head of a marketing division. This dual reporting arrangement helps keep division managers more closely informed about how their particular product lines are being marketed and sold. Without profit information and accountability, sales managers may focus on generating sales volume even when big volume is less profitable than smaller, more specialized sales. Companies that require the sales manager to personally sell to and handle several large accounts are evidencing a sales-volume orientation.

Today's most successful sales managers have a broad marketing-oriented perspective on their jobs. They think in terms of profit planning, long-run trends, threats, opportunities, market segments, and information systems. By contrast, sales managers who have a narrow "selling concept" of their jobs tend to think in terms of sales volume, short-run tactics, individual accounts, and field work instead of market analysis. Table 17-2 contrasts the marketing-oriented and the selling-oriented sales manager.

TABLE 17-2   Selling-Oriented versus Marketing-Oriented Sales Managers

SELLING-ORIENTED SALES MANAGERS FOCUS ON:	MARKETING-ORIENTED SALES MANAGERS FOCUS ON:
Sales Volume: Increasing current sales to meet volume quotas. Usually not very knowledgeable about precise profit differences among customer or product categories.	*Profit Planning:* Planning marketing mixes to satisfy customer segments in order to achieve market share and profit objectives. Know the profitability of each market segment (customer, product, territory, salesperson).
Short Run: Committed to today's products, markets, customers, and sales tactics.	*Long run:* Continually analyzing opportunities for profitable new products, markets, and strategies to assure long-run growth.
Individual Customers: Satisfying each customer without recognizing the potential for efficiencies in serving similar customer groupings.	*Market Segments:* Developing strategies to satisfy customer categories and types more effectively and efficiently.
Field Work: Prefer to spend large amount of time personally selling to customers instead of planning, directing, and controlling overall sales force efforts.	*Information Systems:* Continually analyzing markets, plans, results, and controls to improve efforts toward organizational goals and objectives.

Source: Adapted from Philip Kotler, "From Sales Obsession to Marketing Effectiveness," *Harvard Business Review*, November–December 1977, pp. 67–75.

DEVELOPING MANAGERIAL ABILITIES

Sales force performance is seldom any better than the quality of sales management. Without the right recruiting and hiring strategy, organizational structure, goals, training, compensation plan, motivational tools, leadership, and evaluation methods, no sales force can achieve and sustain excellence. The value of sales managers to their companies can be substantially enhanced by providing them with broad management training first, then training across functional lines. Some companies regularly bring sales managers into headquarters for cross-training in finance, operations, and marketing. General management and functional area training not only enables them to do a better job in managing the sales force, it also helps prepare them for promotion to higher management levels.

Interpersonal Effectiveness

Successful sales managers usually rate very high on an overall human quality that may be called "interpersonal effectiveness."[4] They know (1) what stages of training and development each salesperson is in and how to help the individual reach full potential, (2) how to use rules and regulations to accomplish essential tasks, (3) how to operate within a strategic planning framework to reach goals and objectives, and (4) how to identify problems, analyze alternatives, make decisions, and motivate people to implement those decisions.

[4]*MBA Executive,* November–December 1978, p. 23.

Successful sales managers usually rate very high on interpersonal effectiveness.

Androgynous Sales Managers

Corporate values in the American culture are shifting from the *vertical values* of rugged individualism, autonomy, dominance, and independence to the *horizontal values* of interdependence, mutuality, networking, and coalition building. It is a transformation from a predominantly masculine value system to an androgynous one that blends so-called masculine and feminine values.[5] Sales managers in the 1990s and beyond will be required to bring the personal goals of increasingly diverse salespeople and customers into harmony with those of the organization. In the past, organizational norms generally rewarded managers who were largely task-oriented, competitive, decisive, unemotional, tough, and logical problem solvers. But this concept of management is giving way to a more sensitive style that emphasizes understanding people and helping them to achieve their personal goals along with those of their organization. Future sales managers will accomplish organizational goals by building close, trusting, familylike relationships with salespeople, support staff, and customers from diverse backgrounds and frames of reference. Those who will be most successful in increasing sales productivity, maintaining high morale, and satisfying customers will exhibit humanistic behavior that is largely free of sex, race, age, or cultural stereotyping. General Electric has successfully implemented a unique development program for sales managers, as described in the next Company Highlight box.

SPECIFIC DUTIES AND RESPONSIBILITIES OF SALES MANAGERS

Professional sales managers must plan, organize, direct, and control the individual and collective efforts of the sales force to effectively and efficiently achieve organizational goals and objectives. More specifically, they must do all the tasks outlined in Figure 17-2. Although we deal with each of the sales manager's responsibilities sequentially, some may be performed simultaneously or in some other order than that shown. Sales management duties must be accomplished within the larger framework of company goals and objectives and marketing strategies. And they must be accomplished while continually monitoring the macroenvironment (technological, competitive, economic, legal, cultural, ethical) and working with the company's *stakeholders* (employees, suppliers, financial community, media, stockholders, special interest groups, government, and the general public).

In the pages to follow, we will discuss each of the sales manager's duties and responsibilities.

Analyze the Situation

Before a sales manager can develop plans or set goals, he or she must first know the current situation and where the sales organization seems headed if no

---

[5]Alice G. Sargent and Ronald J. Stupak, "Managing in the '90s: The Androgynous Manager," *Training & Development Journal,* December 1989, pp. 29–35.

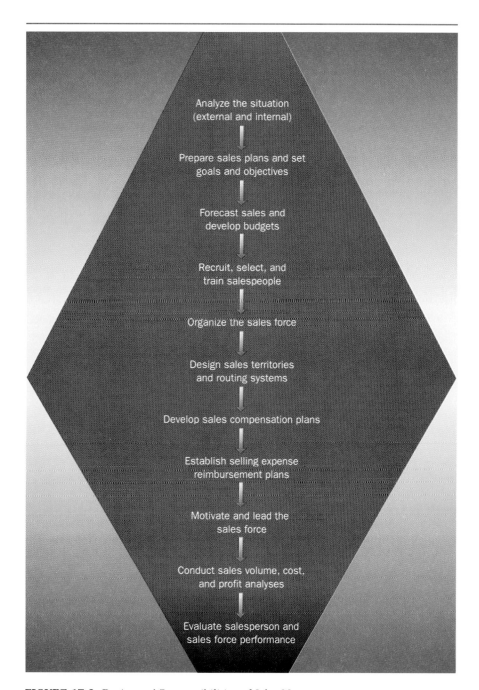

FIGURE 17-2 Duties and Responsibilities of Sales Managers

changes are made. A thorough situation analysis will include the following variables:

- *Market characteristics and trends:* Number and types of potential buyers, developing trends and growth patterns, demographic and psychographic profiles, buying patterns, and service expectations.

Company Highlight

Developing Sales Managers at General Electric

Each time sales managers at General Electric are scheduled for training, they are evaluated by the salespeople who report to them as well as by their peer sales managers. The questionnaire that the sales manager's peers and subordinates fill out asks about the manager's skills and effectiveness across a wide range of managerial and technical areas. Sales managers receive three kinds of feedback: (1) individual results outlining strengths and weaknesses in such areas as delegation, interpersonal relationships, and leadership; (2) performance comparisons with other sales managers in that training class; and (3) performance comparisons (based on GE's database of questionnaires covering many years) with other sales managers at the same stage in their careers.

On the first day of training, each sales manager is given individual counseling on ways to improve his or her performance, and a personalized plan is worked out to address specific areas of weaknesses. These evaluations are done solely for managerial development purposes. They are not part of the company's formal performance evaluation program, so results are never sent to the sales manager's boss. Many sales managers continue to track their personal progress by voluntarily repeating the evaluation process periodically. According to General Electric's manager of corporate management development, most sales managers "love" the feedback from their salespeople and peers as long as they know the results stay outside the chain of command.

Source: Jack Carew, "When Salespeople Evaluate Their Managers," *Sales & Marketing Management,* March 1989, p. 26.

- ■ *Benefits and relative values offered:* What benefits and overall value are offered by each of the company's products and services from the perspectives of prospects and customers?
- ■ *Pricing mix:* What are the organization's current pricing strategies, policies, credit approval procedures, and payment terms for customers?
- ■ *Promotional mix:* How effective is the company's present promotional mix (personal selling, advertising, sales promotion, and publicity programs) vis-à-vis the competition?
- ■ *Distribution systems:* How efficient are the company's storage and transportation facilities, channels of distribution, and intensity of distribution?
- ■ *Competition's strengths and weaknesses:* Who are the company's competitors and what are their strengths and weaknesses in terms of products, prices, brands, market shares, advertising, sales promotion, and selling efforts?
- ■ *Sales, cost, and profit data by market segments:* Which products, markets, territories, and salespeople account for what percent of sales, costs, and profit? It might be helpful to consider sales in the district or region over the last 2–4 years in order to get a clearer picture of sales trends before you arrived.

Prepare Sales Plans and Set Goals and Objectives

The critical function of sales managers is planning because it creates the framework for all other managerial decision making. Studies have consistently shown that effective managers plan more than less effective managers.[6]

Sales Planning

A sales plan provides several benefits. It gives direction and focus to selling efforts, improves cooperation and coordination, and bolsters morale when the entire sales organization actively participates in the process. Planning also helps establish a basis for control. It sets up individual and team standards by which sales force performance can be measured and deviations identified in time to take corrective actions. Finally, planning increases the sales organization's flexibility in responding to unexpected developments in the market.

Planning is a continuous process because as soon as the first version of a plan is written, something has probably changed in the marketing environment—perhaps a competitor's advertising campaign or pricing strategy—that may call for altering the plan. **Planning** is making decisions now to bring about a desired future. Planning seeks to make the future more manageable by anticipating possible events, then outlining present action to deal with those events while working toward organizational goals. It allows sales managers to be *pro*active rather than *re*active. Before developing a sales plan, sales managers ought to think through the sequence of questions outlined in Table 17-3.

Setting Goals and Objectives

Sales managers are responsible for setting performance standards for the sales force. **Sales goals** give the sales force broad long-run direction and general purpose, while **sales objectives** are specific targets to be achieved within a designated time period. A goal of the sales force may be to become recognized as providing the best customer service in the industry, whereas a sales objective may be to increase sales by 15 percent during the coming quarter.

Over 40 percent of Fortune 500 companies use the management-by-objectives (MBO) approach to set performance standards for their salespeople. Under

PLANNING Making decisions now to bring about a desired future.

SALES GOALS Performance standards that give the sales force broad long-run direction and general purpose.

SALES OBJECTIVES Specific targets to be achieved within a designated time period.

[6]For example, see Lyndon E. Dawson, Jr., Timothy Paul Cronan, and Harold B. Teer, Jr., "Sales Force Planning, Implementation, and Control Using Artificial Intelligence," in *Proceedings: Southern Marketing Association,* edited by Robert S. Franz, Robert M. Hopkins, and Alfred G. Toma (LaFayette: University of Southwestern Louisiana, 1979), pp. 398–401; and Ian H. Wilson, William R. George, and Paul J. Solomon, "Strategic Planning for Marketers," *Business Horizons,* December 1978, pp. 65–73.

TABLE 17-3 An Overview of the Planning Process

■ Diagnosis:	Where are we now?
■ Prognosis:	Where do we seem to be headed if no changes are made?
■ Objectives:	Where should we be headed?
■ Strategy:	What is the best way to get there?
■ Tactics:	What specific tasks need to be done by whom and when?
■ Control:	What performance measures must be monitored continuously in order to know how we're doing?

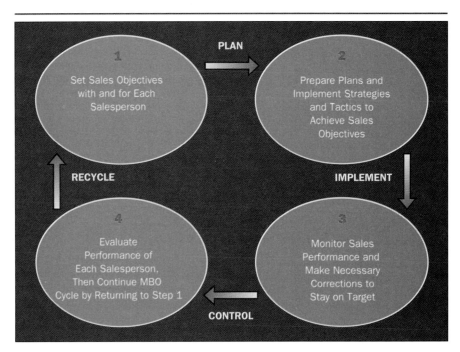

FIGURE 17-3 The MBO Process

the MBO process, there are four basic steps the sales manager follows in setting sales objectives *with* and *for* salespeople, as shown in Figure 17-3.

Forecast Sales and Develop Budgets

From the giant manufacturing corporation to the small "mom-and-pop" retail store, sales forecasts are the cornerstones of all operational planning and budgeting. In a manufacturing firm, the sales forecast helps determine production schedules, purchase quantities, inventory levels, promotional expenditures, material and labor inputs, product outputs, and profits. Too high a sales forecast can result in a large inventory of unsold goods, plant shutdowns, and layoffs. On the other hand, too low a sales forecast can mean out-of-stocks, lost sales, and customers who switch to other suppliers and are lost permanently.

SALES FORECAST The company's best estimate of dollar or unit sales that it will achieve during a given period under a proposed marketing plan.

SALES QUOTA A specific sales goal assigned to a salesperson, sales region, or other subdivision of the seller organization.

Sales Forecasting Concepts

Sales managers are concerned with five distinct concepts in attempting to estimate demand and forecast sales. *Market capacity* is the number of units of a product that would be taken by a market during a given period if the product were free. *Market potential* is the highest possible expected industry sales of a product over a given period in a specified market. *Sales potential* is an estimate of the company's maximum share of total market potential. The **sales forecast** is the company's best estimate of dollar or unit sales that it will achieve during a given period under a proposed marketing plan. Finally, the **sales quota** is a specific sales goal assigned to a salesperson, sales region, or other subdivision of the seller organization. A sales quota is a motivational goal that is usually tied to incentive compensation for salespeople.

Sales Forecasting Techniques

Many companies use several quantitative and nonquantitative methods to develop sales projections before settling on a particular sales forecast.

Nonquantitative techniques. Nonquantitative forecasting techniques rely primarily on judgment or opinion. Because they are subjective, these techniques are often called "guesstimates" or "forecasts by intuition," but they are widely used and are often superior to the most sophisticated quantitative methods. Nonquantitative techniques can be subdivided into judgment methods and counting methods. *Judgment methods* consist of the jury of executive opinion, the Delphi method, and the sales force composite. *Counting methods* include the survey of customer's buying intentions and test marketing. The jury of executive opinion and sales force composite methods are the most commonly used forecasting techniques.

Quantitative techniques. Quantitative forecasting techniques can be divided into time series methods and causal methods. Under *time series methods* are decomposition, moving averages, and exponential smoothing. *Causal methods* include correlation and regression analysis, econometric models, and input/output models.

Before deciding on any forecasting method, sales managers should evaluate it in terms of its costs, needed resources, accuracy, weaknesses, data required, time to develop, and major uses.

Prepare the Sales Budget

SALES BUDGET The financial plan of expenditures needed to accomplish the sales forecast and achieve other organizational goals and objectives.

To implement any plan, funding is needed, so preparation of the sales budget is a critical part of the sales planning process. A **sales budget** is the financial plan of expenditures needed to accomplish the sales forecast and achieve other organizational goals and objectives. Sales budgets serve three primary purposes: (1) profit planning, (2) coordinating the marketing mix, and (3) controlling selling activities. Most sales organizations have specific budget procedures, formats, worksheets, and timetables for developing sales budgets. Sales managers can use a quarterly sales budget form and budget control chart, as pictured in Figure 17-4, to monitor budget variances throughout the year so they can take timely corrective action when discrepancies appear.

Recruit, Select, and Train Salespeople

Recruitment, selection, and training of salespeople are probably the most important activities of the sales manager because the quality of the sales force will have the greatest impact on the organization's sales success. In recent years, these activities have become even more important. One reason is that the cost of recruiting, selecting, and training salespeople has increased dramatically. Another is that Equal Employment Opportunity (EEO) legislation has made hiring and firing decisions more complex than ever. Because of the critical importance of these activities to the organization's success, sales managers need an effective system for recruiting, selecting, and training salespeople.

Line items	January			February			March		
	Budget	Actual	Variance	Budget	Actual	Variance	Budget	Actual	Variance
Sales									
Expenses Salaries									
Commissions									
Bonuses									
Social Security									
Medical insurance									
Retirement									
Travel Lodging									
Food									
Entertainment									
Office expenses Mail									
Telephone									
Photocopying									
Promotion Samples									
Catalogs									
Price lists									
Selling aids									
Premiums									
Awards									
Advertising									

FIGURE 17-4 Quantitiy Sales Budget and Control Chart

Recruitment

Recruiting is finding potential salesperson applicants, telling them about the company, and getting them to apply for a sales position. In many sales organizations, recruiting is a continuous process to replace salespeople who leave. One survey reported that 28 percent of all responding firms had an annual turnover rate in their sales force of over 20 percent, and another 38 percent had a turnover rate of between 11 and 20 percent.[7] A recent Dartnell Corporation study of 6,102 firms found that the sales force turnover rate varied widely by industry. In building materials, it was 12 percent; in chemicals, 13 percent; in petroleum products, 23 percent; and in general machinery, 24 percent.[8]

High turnover rates multiply recruiting and training costs because such expenditures can never be recouped when people quit and new people must constantly be hired and trained. The average cost of training a salesperson is approximately $11,600 in consumer products, $22,200 in industrial products, and $14,500 in service industries.[9] A vice president with New England Mutual Life

[7]Arthur Bragg, "Recruiting and Hiring Without Surprises," *Sales & Marketing Management 1981 Portfolio*, 1980, p. 66.
[8]"Turnover Rates by Industry," *Sales & Marketing Management*, February 20, 1984, p. 67.
[9]*Sales & Marketing Management*, February 20, 1989, p. 23.

Insurance estimates that the loss of one salesperson because of poor recruiting and selection can cost a company $75,000—even more when the effort and expense of selecting, training, developing, and managing are figured in.[10] Thus, a major goal of sales managers is to reduce the turnover rate in their sales forces. To recruit applicants who have high potential to be successful in a specific selling job, sales managers should follow these steps:

1. *Analyze the work* to be done in the sales position because each sales job is different, depending on the mix of products, customers, and objectives.

2. *Prepare a detailed job description* so there is no doubt about what the job involves.

3. *Decide what qualifications are desired* to do the job well.

4. *Select the best means for attracting a pool of qualified applicants.* Sales managers do not want to waste their time or that of applicants by attracting people who are not qualified, so it is important to use the best recruiting sources. Frequently used sources are intracompany announcements, advertisements, competitors, colleges, and employment agencies.

Selection

After the recruiting process has provided the sales manager with a pool of applicants from which to choose, the *selection process* involves choosing which candidates best meet the qualifications and have the greatest aptitude for the sales job. Some companies have constructed a profile of desirable salesperson characteristics by measuring the characteristics of high-performing members of their present sales force. Applicants are then compared to this profile. Such "success profiles," however, have been found to be weak predictors of superior performance in selling. Proper sales training appears to be more helpful than any innate qualities in producing good salespeople.

Numerous selection tools and techniques are available to help sales managers in the selection process, including initial screening interviews, application forms, in-depth interviews, reference checks, physical examinations, and tests. None of these selection tools should be used alone because each collects different information. Generally, the more tools used, the higher the probability of selecting successful salespeople. Recent studies have shown that ability tests have a higher prediction validity of actual on-the-job performance than any other variable—they are more than four times as accurate as the personal interview. Still, ability tests are only able to select successful salespeople about half the time,[11] as shown in Figure 17-5.

Selection tools and techniques can usually eliminate the most unqualified and identify the most qualified recruits, but most candidates fall somewhere between these extreme groups. Thus, selection tools can only assist sales managers in exercising their own good judgment in deciding whom to hire.

Training

A survey of several hundred sales managers revealed that "inadequacy in *sales training*" is one of their most critical problems.[12] In the past, sales trainees were

[10]James W. Kerley and David W. Merrill, "New England Life Takes Steps to Insure Its Future," *Sales & Marketing Management,* August 12, 1985, p. 74.

[11]Richard Kern, "IQ Tests for Salesmen Make a Comeback," *Sales & Marketing Management,* April 1988, p. 44.

[12]*Sales & Marketing Management,* October 15, 1979, p. 182.

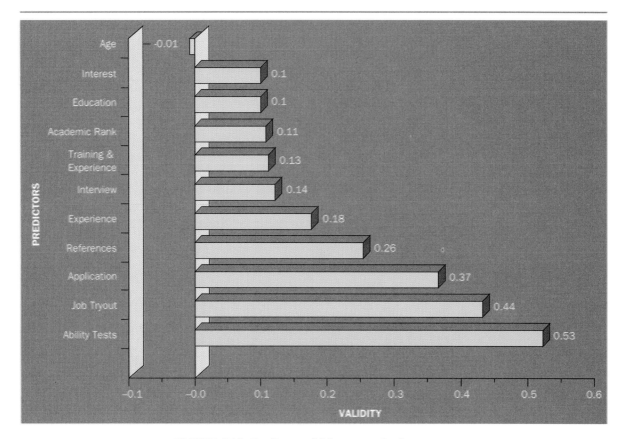

FIGURE 17-5 Predictors of Salesperson Performance

often subjected to the "sink or swim" method of training: Immediately after being hired, they were sent into a sales territory to learn from experience—or fail and fall away. Another popular sales training approach of the past, which is still widely used today, is the "buddy system," in which the sales trainee is assigned to a senior sales rep and told to learn by observation and imitation. Too often, this type of training leads to wasteful recruiting and selection efforts, poor sales force morale, bad selling habits, high turnover rates, and poor customer relations—all of which adversely affect company profits.

Proper sales training appears to be more helpful than any innate qualities in producing superior salespeople. Dow Chemical's training program for its industrial sales reps lasts from 25 to 30 weeks, and IBM generally puts its new sales reps through two years of training.

The overall objective of sales training is to develop salespeople who can achieve the organization's goals. Specific benefits of training programs are increased role clarity for salespeople, faster development, improved morale, higher job satisfaction, better customer relations, lower turnover, increased sales, and higher company profits. In the best sales training programs, sales trainees are taught to *serve* prospects and customers as trusted consultants and problem solvers. In the worst sales training programs, sales trainees are taught manipulative techniques to *push* products on prospects and customers.

Sales managers should keep in mind that proper sales training appears to be more important than innate sales ability for success in selling.

Organize the Sales Force

The purpose of sales force organization is to facilitate the achievement of sales goals and objectives by arranging activities efficiently, coordinating efforts, ensuring prompt response to market needs, and keeping channels of communication open with customers, employees, and concerned stakeholders. As we learned in Chapter 9, sales organizations have traditionally been organized into five types: geographic, product, functional, market, or some combination of the four.

Geographic sales organizations are the most common, but they are most often used in combination with product, functional, or market structures. Geographic sales organizations are most appropriate when customers are widely dispersed and customers in similar industries are located near one another. A *product* organization is best when product complexities and differences are great and new-product introductions are frequent. *Functional* organizations are best when activities, such as sales training, require special expertise. *Market*-oriented sales organizations are best when customer needs and products purchased vary greatly from one industry to another and it is important to avoid confusion and duplication of effort in serving customers.

Combinations of the four basic types of sales organizations are preferred when products are unique and complex, customer needs and products purchased vary widely, and customers are dispersed but grouped by industry type or product needs. Larger companies like General Foods, Du Pont, and NCR are most likely to use combination sales organizations.

Sales Force Size

In developing a sales organization, the size of the sales force is an important consideration. Three widely used methods for determining sales force size are equalized work load, incremental productivity, and sales potential.

Equalized work load. With the work load approach, each salesperson is assigned a group of customers that demand about the same total sales time and effort.

Incremental productivity. Based on the theory of marginal analysis, the incremental productivity method advocates increasing the size of the sales force until the profit generated from the last salesperson hired just equals the cost of employing that salesperson. In economic terms, hire new salespeople until *marginal revenue equals marginal costs.*

Sales potential. With this approach, the sales manager estimates what the average sales rep will achieve in terms of annual sales volume. This figure is then divided into the company's total sales forecast for the year to determine how many salespeople will be required. In equation form, these relationships are:

$$N = \frac{S}{P} \times (1 + T)$$

where N = number of salespeople needed
S = annual sales forecast for the company
P = estimated sales productivity of the average salesperson
T = estimated percentage of annual sales force turnover

To illustrate, assume that the company sales forecast is $20 million, annual sales volume productivity per salesperson is $800,000, and the expected annual rate of sales force turnover is 20 percent. Thus:

$$N = \frac{\$20,000,000}{800,000} \times 1.20 = 30$$

Adjustments may be needed in both sales force size and structure in response to changes in competitive strategies or other developments in the marketing environment. Sales managers will also need to decide whether to substitute independent manufacturing agents or inside telemarketing salespeople for some or even all members of the direct sales force.

Design Sales Territories and Routing Systems

A *sales territory* is a market segment or group of present and potential customers who share some common characteristics relevant to purchasing behavior. Territories should be assigned on the basis of sales potential, which, in turn, will decide individual *sales quotas* for salespeople. The primary reason for establishing sales territories is to guide the efforts of the sales force and to control their selling activities. But sales managers typically have more specific reasons for establishing territories, such as enhancing market coverage, keeping selling costs at a minimum, strengthening customer relations, controlling and evaluating individual salespeople, and coordinating personal selling with other marketing functions.

The starting point in establishing sales territories is the selection of a geographical control unit. Traditionally, political boundaries, such as states, counties, ZIP code areas, cities, metropolitan areas, and trading areas, have been used because so much government census data and other market information are broken out by these units. As people continue to move to the suburbs and exurbs, political units are giving away to metropolitan statistical areas (MSAs). MSAs are boundaries that include a central city as well as its surrounding suburban area and satellite cities. The U.S. Office of Management and Budget has defined a metropolitan statistical area as an area that contains a city of at least 50,000 people and a total population of at least 100,000 (75,000 in New England). A primary metropolitan statistical area (PMSA) includes a population of one million or more, and a consolidated metropolitan statistical area (CMSA) contains two or more PSMAs.

After sales territories have been determined, management may design a formal pattern or *routing* for sales representatives to follow in calling on customers, although some sales managers prefer to have salespeople assume responsibility for scheduling and routing themselves. In either case, a predetermined plan should be carried out. Few salespeople make optimal use of their most precious resource—time. Thus, one of the most important jobs of sales managers is to train their salespeople in techniques for better managing their time and territory, as we discussed in Chapter 16.

Develop Sales Compensation Plans

Sales compensation plans are the "steering wheels" that enable sales managers to guide the activities of salespeople. To illustrate, an electrical equipment manufacturer with one sales force serving several divisions found that its sales reps devoted most of their sales time to the "big ticket" items in only a few divisions. After implementing a bonus plan that rewarded salespeople who met at least 70 percent of the quota for all product lines, a better-balanced product mix was achieved.

In most companies, sales force compensation is about 79 percent of total direct-selling costs. Travel and entertainment expenses account for about 11 percent, and automobile expenditures for about 10 percent. Compensation mixes vary widely across industries, companies, and types of sales tasks. Depending upon the selling situation, any of the five basic methods of financial compensation compared in Table 17-4 may be appropriate.

Increasing demands on salespeople to perform customer service and other nonselling activities are stimulating reappraisals of basic compensation plans. Sales managers want a plan that gives them maximum control over how salespeople allocate their time. They prefer a plan that offers a balance between selling costs and sales results. Finally, sales managers want a plan that is simple to administer, easily understood by salespeople, and sufficiently flexible to ensure timely adjustment to changing market conditions. From the perspective of salespeople, the compensation plan should offer income regularly, rewards for superior performance, and fairness—in terms of their experience and ability, the pay of co-workers and competitors' sales reps, and the cost of living.[13]

Ideally, compensation plans are designed to achieve organizational objectives, such as greater market share, higher profit margins, successful introduction

[13]For other perspectives on sales compensation plans, see Alan J. Dubinsky and Eric N. Berkowitz, "The Frequency of Monetary Compensation for Salesmen," *Industrial Marketing Management,* January 1979, pp. 12–23; William Strahle and Rosann L. Spiro, "Linking Market Share Strategies to Salesforce Objectives, Activities, and Compensation Policies," *Journal of Personal Selling and Sales Management,* August 1986, pp. 11–18.

TABLE 17-4 Comparison of Sales Force Compensation Methods

METHOD AND % OF COMPANIES USING	ADVANTAGES	DISADVANTAGES	PREFERRED SITUATIONS OR TIMES FOR USE
Straight salary (4.7%): Fixed amount of money paid regularly, usually weekly or monthly	Provides financial security to salespeople. Helps develop sense of loyalty to company. Gives higher degree of control over sales activities. Simple to administer.	No financial incentive for extra selling efforts. May increase selling costs because salaries go up even when no sales are made. May overpay the least productive and underpay the most productive salespeople.	Team selling situation; new sales trainees; long negotiating periods; missionary selling; introducing new products or opening up new territories.
Commissions only (3.5%): Set amount or percentage on each unit or dollar sale	Income directly tied to productivity. No ceiling on potential earnings. Costs proportional to sales. Salespeople have maximum work freedom. Poor performers will quit. Income based on accomplishments, not subjective evaluations by sales manager.	May emphasize sales volume instead of profitable sales. Salespeople develop little loyalty to company. Turnover increases when economy is weak as marginal salespeople quit. Customer service activities are neglected. Sales manager has limited control over salespeople.	Companies with little capital can keep sales costs proportional to sales. Often used for part-time salespeople or manufacturers' reps. For companies with little interest in service or long-term customer relationships.
Salary and bonus (45.9%): Fixed amount of pay plus lump sum bonus payment if objectives are achieved, or *Salary and commissions* (45.9%): Fixed amount of pay plus set amount or percentage on each unit or dollar sale	Provides the greatest flexibility and control over salespeople because all desirable sales activities are rewarded. Gives salespeople an assured income plus incentive. Allows frequent, immediate reinforcement of desired sales behavior. Allows team selling efforts to be rewarded.	Can be complex and misunderstood by salespeople. May be expensive to administer. May not achieve management objectives if not carefully conceived.	Best for established companies that want salespeople to perform all the selling and customer service activities.

Source: Based on data provided in "Survey of Selling Costs," *Sales & Marketing Management*, February 16, 1987, p. 57.

of new products, more new accounts, and lower selling costs. But over 50 percent of companies admit having difficulty adjusting their compensation plans to organizational objectives.[14] One survey showed that nearly half the companies surveyed revise their sales compensation plans annually, even though their corporate goals and objectives stay the same for several years.

[14]*Marketing News,* November 1986, p. 1.

Establish Selling Expense Reimbursement Plans

Most professional sales representatives need an expense account to travel, stay overnight on the road, and entertain customers. Instead of being viewed as expenses, these selling expenditures can be considered investments that will yield future dividends. Over the past decade, the cost of supporting a field sales force has jumped 84 percent. Meals ($178), lodging ($489), and automobile expenses ($216) for one field salesperson now total over $883 weekly. The average cost of a sales call is nearly $225 for industrial, $196 for consumer, and $166 for service markets.[15]

Most companies reimburse their salespeople for expenditures on meals, lodging, automobiles, phone calls, entertainment, and laundry while traveling to call on prospects and customers. Because salespeople usually put out their own money for these daily expenses, it is important to their morale and personal budgets that they receive reimbursement quickly. Three basic expense reimbursement plans are widely used: unlimited, limited, and combination.

Unlimited Reimbursement Plans

These are the most popular reimbursement plans because they repay salespeople for all necessary selling and travel expenses. The drawback for the company is that unlimited plans tempt some salespeople to be extravagant and others to pad their expense accounts. Unlimited reimbursement also makes forecasts of selling costs more difficult.

Limited Reimbursement Plans

These plans restrict expense repayment to a total dollar amount per week or month, or to a certain dollar limit per item (e.g., motel room, daily meals, cents per mile traveled). Limited payment plans tend to reduce expense account padding and allow expenses to be estimated more accurately. One of their disadvantages, however, is that they can make salespeople so expense conscious that they avoid expenditures that could win sales and increase profits. Another disadvantage of limited reimbursement plans is that they tempt salespeople to juggle their reporting of expenditures from one time period to another in order to avoid going over expense ceilings. A third disadvantage is that they require frequent revision of expense ceilings during inflationary periods as well as different ceilings for different areas of the country because of variations in the cost of living.

Combination Reimbursement Plans

Combination plans establish limits on some items, such as food and lodging, but not on others, such as transportation. One variation of the combination plan relates expenses to sales. For example, the salesperson may be reimbursed for expenses up to 5 percent of net sales or be awarded a bonus for keeping expenses below 5 percent of net sales. Probably the greatest advantage of this approach is that it makes sure that expenses do not get out of line in relation to sales. Its major disadvantage is that it diverts some of the sales rep's attention from obtaining profitable sales to worrying about expense ratios.

---

[15]*Sales & Marketing Management,* February 26, 1990, p. 15.

What Would You Do?

One of your top salespersons submits expense reimbursement requests each week that are about 50 percent higher than those of your other salespeople. This salesperson covers the Manhattan area of New York City, where costs are higher than in other cities, though not by 50 percent. You don't want to anger this talented salesperson, who brings in about 25 percent more sales volume and profits than your average salesperson, but you feel you have to do something.

Motivate and Lead the Sales Force

Effective motivation of salespeople is one of the most powerful means for increasing sales force performance, yet estimates are that nearly 85 percent of the work force is weakly motivated.[16] Sales managers have generally had to develop their own approaches to motivating the sales force, based on a mixture of intuition, folklore, tradition, and personal experiences.[17] Most studies on sales force motivation have assumed that (1) financial rewards are the most important motivators of sales efforts, and (2) proper design of the compensation package is the best approach to motivating salespeople.[18] However, sales forces tend to include diverse personality types who are motivated by nonfinancial as well as financial incentives. A classic study by Darmon found five types of salesperson attitudes and responses to financial incentives:

1. *Creatures of habit:* Try to maintain their standard of living by earning a predetermined amount of money.
2. *Goal-oriented:* Prefer recognition as achievers by peers and by superiors; earnings serve mainly to "keep score."
3. *Satisfiers:* Perform just well enough to keep their jobs.
4. *Trade-offers:* Allocate their time according to a personally determined ratio of work and leisure that is not influenced by opportunities for increased earnings.
5. *Money-oriented:* Seek to maximize their earnings. These people may sacrifice family relationships, personal pleasures, and even health to increase their income.[19]

Theories of Motivation

One of the oldest of all approaches to motivating people is instilling fear. When Julius Caesar's troops didn't meet his expectations, he lined them up and executed every tenth man. Although fear may still be effective in short-run emer-

[16]*Business Week,* June 9, 1980, p. 52.

[17]Orville C. Walker, Jr., Gilbert A. Churchill, Jr., and Neil M. Ford, "Motivation and Performance in Industrial Selling: Present Knowledge and Needed Research," *Journal of Marketing Research,* May 1977, pp. 156–168.

[18]Nick DiBari, "Straight Talk," *Sales & Marketing Management,* October 1984, p. 48.

[19]René Y. Darmon, "Salesmen's Response to Financial Incentives: An Empirical Study," *Journal of Marketing Research,* November 1974, pp. 418–426.

Sales managers must continually strive to keep the sales force highly motivated.

gency situations, today's salespeople are generally well educated, mobile, and independent, so fear is not a practical long-run motivator. Some modern approaches to motivation are the motivator-hygiene theory, expectancy theory, and inequity theory.

Motivator-hygiene factors. Herzberg's research found two types of factors associated with worker satisfaction or dissatisfaction.[20] Sources of satisfaction are called *motivators* because they are necessary to stimulate individuals to superior efforts and performance. Motivators relate to the content of the job itself, and include responsibility, achievement, recognition, and opportunities for growth and advancement. Sources of dissatisfaction are called *hygiene factors* because they are necessary to keep employee performance from dropping or becoming unhealthy. Hygiene factors relate to the work environment, and include salary, company policies and administration, supervision, and working conditions.[21]

Maintaining a "hygienic" work environment does not motivate employees any more than water purification improves health. But just as water purification helps avoid ill health, a good work environment helps avoid dissatisfied employees and declines in productivity. In other words, hygiene factors cannot improve productivity, but their absence can cause it to decrease. To improve productivity, sales managers must maintain hygiene factors (pleasant work environment) while providing motivators (job enrichment) for the sales force.

Expectancy theory. Expectancy theory contends that salespeople can be motivated to work toward a goal when they expect their efforts will pay off. Each

[20]See Frederick Herzberg, Bernard Mausner, and Barbara Block Synderman, *The Motivation to Work,* 2nd ed. (New York: John Wiley & Sons, 1959).

[21]J. Sterling Livingston, "Pygmalion in Management," *Harvard Business Review,* July–August 1969, pp. 94–102; Rom J. Markin and Charles M. Lillis, "Sales Managers Get What They Expect," *Business Horizons,* June 1975, pp. 200–206.

person estimates, at least subjectively, the probability of success in a given undertaking and the value of the payoff. The amount of effort someone will exert on something depends on its "valence" or value to that person and the expectancy of accomplishing it. In equation form:

$$\text{Effort} = \text{Expectancy} \times \text{Valence}$$

where   Effort = the salesperson's motivation to perform

Expectancy = the degree to which the salesperson believes that certain performance levels will lead to certain outcomes (scaled from 0 to 1)

Valence = the value placed on each outcome (scaled −1 to +1, with extremes indicating strong displeasure or pleasure and 0 meaning indifference)

To illustrate, let's assume a sales manager who wants to increase sales of a new product asks all the salespeople to make three extra sales calls a week to introduce the product and offers a special $50 bonus for every sale. If the salespeople believe that the extra calls will likely result in more sales, their personal expectancy rating may be .6. The $50 bonus for selling each new product may be highly valued—say, .8 for valence. Then the likely increased effort would be .48 (.6 × .8). Sales managers can devise various incentive plans to maximize the product of expectancy and valence for their salespeople.

Inequity theory.   According to the inequity theory of motivation, people compare their relative work contributions and rewards with those of others in similar situations. Inequity is perceived when the individual feels either under- or overrewarded for his or her contribution relative to others. The stronger the feeling of inequity, the stronger the drive to reduce this tension. People respond in different ways to the perception of inequity. Salespeople who feel underpaid or underrewarded relative to others making similar contributions may decrease their selling efforts, while those who feel overpaid may increase their efforts. Some salespeople will reduce their inequity tensions by distorting their perceptions of their rewards and contributions versus those of others. Finally, some will deal with a perceived inequitable situation by quitting their job or changing their comparison group.

Experience to date indicates that few companywide performance improvement programs succeed for long. Employee motivation depends on so many diverse, individualized factors that blanket motivation approaches tend to be ineffective. On the other hand, attempts to motivate each individual separately are inefficient. The most practical approach for sales managers is to segment their salespeople into similar groups according to their motivation needs.

Leadership

LEADERSHIP The ability to convince salespeople that their work has a meaningful purpose and to inspire them to extraordinary achievements.

Traditionally, there have been two distinct approaches to the study of **leadership:** universalistic theories and contingency theories. In contrast to the *universalistic* approaches to leadership, which assume that there is "one best way" for managers to lead subordinates, *contingency* theories assume that successful leadership depends on various situational conditions such as the leader's power, the maturity and status of subordinates, and the job to be done.

Fiedler's work indicates that effective leadership depends on three situation variables:

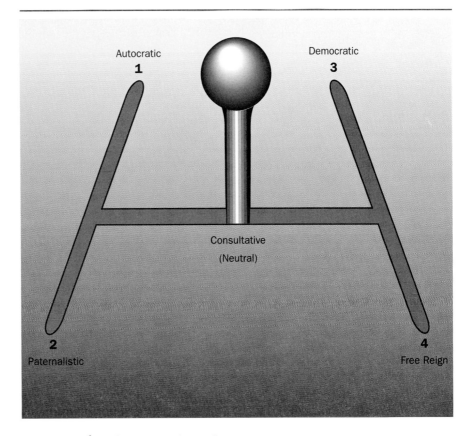

FIGURE 17-6 Shifting Leadership Styles

1. The quality of the leader's personal relationships with members of the group.
2. The formal power or authority provided by the leader's position.
3. The degree to which the group's task is structured.[22]

Leadership styles. Effective sales managers match their style to the maturity and duties of their sales force. A range of leadership styles from task-oriented to human relations–oriented can be successful as long as the style correctly matches the situation. Experienced salespeople, used to operating largely independently, may resent a sales manager who exercises tight supervision and control over their activities. Conversely, an inexperienced sales force used to close supervision may feel anxiety about the abilities of a sales manager who allows too much freedom of action. One way of visualizing leadership styles is as a "four-speed automobile gearshift," as shown in Figure 17-6.

A sales manager may need to shift leadership style as the composition and responsibilities of the sales force change. Using our analogy of the gearshift, the sales manager exercises strong pulling power in first (autocratic) and second (paternalistic) gear, with the sales force largely dependent on the sales manager

[22]Fred E. Fiedler, "The Leadership Game: Matching the Man to the Situation," *Organizational Dynamics,* Winter 1976, pp. 6–16.

for rewards and punishments. In neutral (consultative), the sales manager exerts little push or pull and allows the salespeople to influence management decisions. In third (democratic) and fourth (free reign) gear, the sales manager functions in a largely passive manner as salespeople operate quite independently.

Conduct Sales Volume, Cost, and Profit Analyses

Sales managers are charged with the responsibility for using their resources to accomplish that balance between sales volume and costs that will result in the highest long-run organizational profits. Some sales managers overstress selling activities and sales volume to the neglect of cost controls and profitability analysis. Although sales volume analysis is helpful in evaluating and controlling sales efforts, it says nothing about the profitability of these efforts. Remember, high sales volume does not ensure profits. Other sales managers focus on total profits, and are satisfied if these are acceptable. Because they fail to look at profits by major market segments, such as customers, products, territories, and salespeople, they continue to assign sales force resources and efforts arbitrarily or equally among territories, product lines, or customer classes.

To increase the effectiveness and efficiency of sales force efforts, sales managers need to pay attention to cost and profitability analyses by market segments so that they can direct resources to those areas with the highest dollar return. An example of this kind of sales analysis is provided in the next Selling in Action box.

Evaluate Salesperson and Sales Force Performance

Any meaningful system for evaluating salespeople requires job descriptions and mutually agreed upon performance standards. Standards for measurement of performance include (1) salesperson-to-salesperson comparisons, (2) current-to-past-performance comparisons, and (3) actual-to-expected-performance comparisons. For effective managerial control and evaluation, standards of performance must be established, actual performance must be compared to the predetermined standards, and appropriate corrective action must be taken to improve performance. Not to be overlooked in evaluating sales force performance are ethical guidelines and social responsibility standards. Nothing destroys the credibility and performance of salespeople faster than the perception by potential customers that they do not operate ethically or with a sense of social responsibility.

Key Performance Factors

Sales managers seldom have the time to closely monitor all aspects of sales force performance continually, so they select key performance factors to monitor instead. Most companies use a balance of several variables to control sales operations because reliance on a single index can be misleading or even dangerous. For instance, if a company were to overstress keeping service expenses low, customer satisfaction and sales volume might deteriorate.

Quantitative measures, like dollar sales volume or the number of new accounts obtained, tend to affect sales or expenses directly, and can be measured

Selling in Action

Sales Analysis by Computer

When he went to the annual sales meeting, Bob Ippolito, a district sales manager for Varian Associates' Varian Instrument Group, took a briefcase bulging with detailed computer analyses of sales volume for each model of lab equipment he sells, the activity of each account, what was selling where, and how each of these stacked up against the norm and against the expected—along with a strategy to make up the differential. Ippolito didn't have to stay up nights to prepare all this; he had help. Next to the reports in his briefcase was his secret weapon—a portable computer.

Ippolito is one of a growing number of marketing and sales executives taking advantage of the speed, flexibility, and targeting provided by a micro or personal computer (PC). In his order log, he enters basic sales information, including date, account name, order number, model number, and sales volume. At any moment, he can tell what and how much was sold. He can review individual account activity or profile the territory by product sold. This allows him to spot trends, such as an increase in number of orders or a shift in demand for products. "It's not just reporting," he says, "it helps my strategic planning."

Recently faced with assigning territories to two new salespeople, Ippolito tapped the order information already in his computer and generated reports of sales activity by ZIP code, by combinations of ZIP's, and by breakouts of the product mix. Because he could try many combinations "as quickly as you can talk about it," he easily determined well-balanced territory assignments. "From a management standpoint, that can affect a person's success or failure," he says.

Source: Lita M. Elvers, "Managing with the PC: Selling's Latest Secret Weapon," *Sales & Marketing Management*, December 3, 1984, p. 64.

objectively. *Qualitative measures*, such as the salesperson's product knowledge or relationship with customers, have a more indirect and longer-run impact on sales and expenses, and thus must be evaluated largely on a subjective basis. Both quantitative and qualitative measures are important to sales force success and should be part of the evaluation process.

PEMS

Every organization has some sort of *performance evaluation monitoring system (PEMS)*. In smaller companies, this system may be largely informal, relying on the firsthand observations of supervisors. As an organization grows, sales managers are less able to closely monitor each employee's daily activities, so they turn to a more formalized PEMS.

Performance appraisal systems should do three essential things:

- ■ Provide feedback to each salesperson on individual job performance.
- ■ Help salespeople modify or change their behavior to develop effective work habits.

■ Provide information to sales managers on which to make decisions on promotion, transfer, and compensation of salespeople.

There are three successive stages in an effective PEMS: performance planning, performance appraisal, and performance review.

Performance planning. This is probably the most important phase of the PEMS because it allows the salesperson to obtain the counsel of the sales manager in deciding three key questions: Where am I going? How will I get there? How will I be measured?

Performance appraisal. The appraisal phase of the PEMS consists of feedback, or mini-evaluations, given to salespeople by sales managers on each specific task, project, or goal accomplished. Sales managers should provide some form of recognition, praise, correction, or comment following every performance.

Performance review. This periodic summing up of the daily appraisals reviews where the salesperson is in his or her personal development. It should answer the question: How am I doing? and lead into the next performance planning stage.[23] Sales managers need to keep a permanent record of these performance reviews so that individual salespeople can track their progress and other sales and marketing managers can review that progress.

Evaluating Overall Sales Force Performance

The *sales audit* is a frequently used device to evaluate thoroughly and objectively an organization's sales organization, environmental opportunities and challenges, goals, objectives, policies, strategies, and results. A sales audit seeks to answer two critical questions: Are we doing things correctly? and (more important) Are we doing the correct things?

In conducting sales audits, there are two basic approaches: horizontal and vertical. The *horizontal sales audit* is more systems-oriented in that it is an examination of the entire sales force effort. By contrast, a *vertical audit* is an in-depth study of one major component of selling efforts, such as the compensation plan or the effectiveness and efficiency of sales force territorial assignments.

Although the vertical sales audit suggests that selling efforts can be analyzed in isolation from other marketing efforts, all elements of the marketing mix influence one another. Thus, the results from any vertical audit ought to be reexamined in relationship to other vertical audits. In the final analysis, all marketing efforts must be compatibly integrated to achieve the desired synergistic impact in the marketplace.

SUMMARY   When salespeople are promoted to sales manager, they must guard against the tendency to continue being "doers" instead of becoming managers. Professional sales managers have an eclectic role. They need to maintain a *marketing* as

[23]Ed Yager, "A Critique of Performance Appraisal Systems," *Personnel Journal,* February 1981, pp. 129–132.

opposed to a *selling* perspective in their jobs. Sales managers of the future will need an androgynous value system to manage salespeople from diverse cultures and backgrounds. Sales managers plan, lead, and control the personal selling activities of an organization. Although their specific duties and responsibilities vary across companies and industries, most sales managers must carry out a similar set of basic functions: (1) analyzing the situation; (2) preparing sales plans, goals, and objectives; (3) forecasting sales and developing budgets; (4) recruiting, selecting, and training salespeople; (5) organizing the sales force; (6) designing sales territories and routing systems; (7) developing sales compensation plans; (8) establishing selling expense reimbursement plans; (9) motivating and leading the sales force; (10) conducting sales volume, costs, and profit analyses by market segments; and (11) evaluating individual and collective sales force performance. While carrying out their responsibilities, sales managers must be proactive rather than merely reactive to a continually changing sales environment.

CHAPTER REVIEW QUESTIONS

1. Give the job titles and describe the duties of at least five different levels of sales managers in an organization.
2. Distinguish between a "doer" and a "manager."
3. How does the typical sales manager spend his or her time?
4. What are the differences between *marketing-oriented* and *selling-oriented* sales managers?
5. Define the concept of androgynous sales managers.
6. Explain the MBO (management-by-objectives) process.
7. Describe at least two quantitative and two qualitative forecasting techniques.
8. Describe three approaches for determining sales force size.
9. What are the different sales force compensation methods?
10. Name and describe five types of salespeople in terms of their attitudes toward work and financial incentives.
11. Identify the different leadership styles and describe the situation in which each is most appropriate.
12. What is PEMS?

TOPICS FOR THOUGHT AND CLASS DISCUSSION

1. What do you think it will be like to be a professional salesperson in the year 2010? Describe how you think the sales manager's job will have changed by then.
2. Why do you think many companies fail to recognize emerging opportunities in their own markets until long after competitors have captured major shares? How can a sales manager avoid such myopia?
3. What criteria would you use in selecting new salespeople? Why?
4. Do you think sales managers ought to be evaluated by their salespeople as well as by their peers (other sales managers)? What are some of the benefits and potential problems with such evaluations?

5. Assume that your company sales forecast is $60 million, annual sales volume productivity per salesperson is $1,200,000, and the expected annual rate of sales force turnover is 25 percent. How many salespeople are needed?

6. Assume that you are a new branch sales manager. How would you go about devising a strategy to motivate your field sales force of ten people, five of whom have been with the company ten years or more, two of whom are new to the company but experienced in sales, and three of whom are recent college graduates who have just finished the initial one-month sales training?

PROJECTS FOR PERSONAL GROWTH

1. Contact three sales managers in three different fields and ask them to describe their typical day to you. Then ask them what they consider to be their most important duties. Finally, ask them what managerial training their companies provided to prepare them for their sales management jobs.

2. Go to your library and read at least three articles published during the last two years on salesperson performance review and evaluation. Then contact two professional salespeople and ask them how they are evaluated. Do they have sales volume, activity, and financial quotas? Are they evaluated on any qualitative criteria? Do they have a chance to rebut the evaluation?

3. Write to the national sales managers of ten large companies and ask what process and specific criteria they use to evaluate salespeople. Compare responses across companies.

4. Write to five companies and ask them how they select new salespeople. What tests do candidates take? How many interviews does a candidate who is eventually hired undergo within the company? What percent of candidates are offered jobs?

KEY TERMS

Doing Time spent by managers on activities that subordinates can do.

Managing Time devoted to determining how to accomplish work through other people.

Planning Making decisions now to bring about a desired future.

Sales goals Performance standards that give the sales force broad long-run direction and general purpose.

Sales objectives Specific targets to be achieved within a designated time period.

Sales forecast The company's best estimate of dollar or unit sales that it will achieve during a given period under a proposed marketing plan.

Sales quota A specific sales goal assigned to a salesperson, sales region, or other subdivision of the seller organization.

Sales budget The financial plan of expenditures needed to accomplish the sales forecast and achieve other organizational goals and objectives.

Leadership The ability to convince salespeople that their work has a meaningful purpose and to inspire them to extraordinary achievements.

Case 17-1

ASSUMING THE DUTIES AND RESPONSIBILITIES OF SALES MANAGEMENT

Stepping out of his regional sales manager's office, Clark Ragsdale is "walking on a cloud" because he has just been promoted to branch sales manager in charge of seven other salespeople. Clark can't wait to tell his wife, Gloria, so he calls her as soon as he reaches his car phone to tell her the good news: "I begin the new job next week, so starting next Monday, I'll be home for dinner on time. And I won't be worrying now about making my sales volume quota because I get a good salary plus an attractive bonus just for helping my salespeople reach their quotas!" After the call, Clark basks in Gloria's heartwarming words of praise and congratulation for a little while before calling to confirm a lunch meeting with a customer. As he drives to the restaurant, Clark thinks about how great it is to be working with a growing company like Telecommunications Technology, Inc. (TTI), and selling products he really believes in (and appreciates the use of), like the company's best-selling Global brand cellular phones. The future looks bright!

Six months later, Clark is learning that sales management isn't as easy as it looked when he was a salesperson. He is somewhat overwhelmed by all his responsibilities and surprised that he has been given so little training for his new managerial duties. Within the last three weeks, two of the seven salespeople assigned to his branch have quit to take sales jobs with other companies. Clark doesn't think their leaving had anything to do with his leadership because both told him that they had been planning to leave for some time but had waited until the end of the quarter so they could collect their commissions. Part of the problem, they claimed, is that TTI pays solely on commissions. Both salespeople wanted to be able to provide better customer service to established accounts, even accounts that weren't yielding big orders. Also, both have little children at home and were concerned about what it would be like in a few years if they were still knocking themselves out in the field with no guarantee of monthly earnings. Clark knows from experience that it is really tough on one's family to try to budget when one doesn't know what one's earnings will be each month.

Clark is wondering whether some of the other salespeople reporting to him have similar worries and are also thinking about leaving. Most of them have mentioned the "inconvenience" of receiving commission only. All of them have families. Clark makes a mental note to review the company's sales compensation plan at his first opportunity. Perhaps it needs changing, but to Clark's knowledge, no other sales manager has said anything about that. In any case, his immediate problem is to fill the two vacant sales positions—and this is not proving as easy as he thought it would be.

After placing an advertisement in the local newspaper based on the standard ad that TTI uses to hire salespeople, Clark is surprised to receive over 100 letters and resumes. Many people do not meet the ad's clearly stated educational or experience requirements, and others have submitted such weak resumés or poor cover letters that they are eliminated, too. Ten applicants look excellent on paper, and Clark invites all of them in for testing and personal interviews. Reviewing the results of several tests that TTI asks job candidates to take, Clark sees that four people have scored much higher than the other candidates on the tests for intelligence, sales aptitude, personality, and vocational interest. He decides to invite those four back for in-depth interviews in the order of how well they scored on their tests.

Clark is dismayed by the results of the in-depth interviews with the two candidates who scored highest on the written tests. Both seem to lack the drive, enthusiasm, flexibility, and personality of the two lower-scoring candidates. In fact, the candidate who scored highest on the tests overall became quite defensive after failing to correctly answer a routine mathematical question during the "What Would You Do?" section of Clark's verbal interview: "A customer asks for a 30 percent discount on your price of $200. What would the price have to be for this customer?" Obviously embarrassed, the candidate claimed to be thrown off guard by such a "silly" question and unable to think for a few minutes. The other high scorer on the written tests couldn't explain adequately why she is interested in a sales career and didn't show a good understanding of what a professional salesperson does. Clark has always heard that test scores have a higher predictability for individual success in sales than personal interviews, but he is reluctant to go against his instincts. These people really won't do. He needs more time to think about all four candidates.

Clark is also concerned about how to motivate and lead his sales team. Except for the two new trainees he will hire soon, the salespeople in his branch have from six to ten years' experience in sales. In fact, three of them have more sales experience than Clark. Clark feels that he has to treat all the salespeople fairly and equitably, and that they have to perceive that he is doing so. He isn't sure what leadership style is most appropriate for his salespeople, however, and he is even less sure how to motivate the entire sales team.

"Boy, being a sales manager is no picnic," thinks Clark. "It seems to require far too much time and effort just to hire competent salespeople. And I haven't even begun to think about how to analyze different market segments for profitability, set up performance quotas, or establish a performance evaluation system for my current salespeople."

Questions

1. Do you think there is anything wrong with TTI's present compensation plan? Explain. What would you recommend?

2. Which of the four salespeople whom Clark invited back for in-depth interviews would you hire—the two who scored highest on the written tests, or the two who performed best in the interviews? Why? What other approaches might Clark consider to find the best candidates for the two sales positions?

3. How would you recommend that Clark go about deciding how to motivate his seven-person sales force? Do you think he should use similar motivational strategies and techniques for all members of his sales force? Explain.

4. What leadership style do you think will be most effective with the five current salespeople? What about the two new sales trainees? Should Clark change his leadership style from salesperson to salesperson, or use a consistent style with all members of his sales force?

Case 17-2

WHAT'S THE BEST EXPENSE REIMBURSEMENT PLAN?

Katya Marcus, middle western region sales manager for the Engine Housings division of Rocket Industries, one of the country's largest commercial aerospace propulsion technology companies, is going over last month's expense reports for her field sales representatives. Rocket's national sales manager, Diane Mullick, recently sent a memo to all the regional sales managers requesting that they carefully review all personal selling costs because the company is almost $400,000 over the forecasted budget for the year. Diane stated in her memo: "After reviewing your salespeople's expenses, I would appreciate your recommendations as to whether we should continue with our present policy of unlimited expense account reimbursement."

Katya has been caught off guard by Diane's memo. Frankly, she hasn't been paying much attentin to her region's sales budgets and expense

accounts this year because sales have been so outstanding, running nearly 20 percent over last year.

After reviewing the expense records of her two district managers and eight field sales reps, Katya finds that three sales reps have travel and entertainment (T&E) expenses 25 to 30 percent higher than average. That afternoon she calls all three of the high-spenders and tells them that she wants to see each of them tomorrow at 8:00 A.M. at the regional sales office in downtown Chicago. That evening, while going over the expense reports submitted by the three reps during the past year, Katya realizes that these three are among her top-producing salespeople. She begins to think about each of these reps, the jobs they do, and why they might spend more T&E money than other reps.

Jerry Derr: An energetic, take-charge young man in his late 20s, Jerry joined Rocket Industries after serving as a navy pilot for five years following graduation from college. Jerry always accepts any assignment, no matter how tough, without complaint. And his outrageous stories and sense of humor add a great deal to the sense of camaraderie and good morale of the sales force.

Beth Esler: After earning a master's degree in physics and teaching high school physics for five years, Beth took an executive job with Midwestern Airlines in customer relations. Following three years in that field, she decided to move into sales, and joined Rocket Industries two years ago. Beth has been selected to the President's Rocket Club for making 120 percent of quota in each of her two years with the company, and seems to have high potential for management. She is an extremely conscientious, sincere, and cooperative person who is well liked by her customers and the other Rocket salespeople.

Roberto Orlando: Born in the Dominican Republic, Roberto came to the United States with his parents as a teenager. A very talented musician, he often entertains his sales colleagues at the annual sales meeting Rocket Follies by playing mean piano and even meaner tenor sax solos. He has the kind of friendly, exuberant personality that makes him popular with everyone. Roberto loves baseball and often uses his T&E money to entertain customers at afternoon baseball games. He is more fun-loving and operates on a more unpredictable schedule than most of the other salespeople, but he always exceeds his sales goals.

It is a few minutes before 8:00 A.M. the next day, and the three salespeople are waiting in Katya Marcus's outer office when she comes in, greets them in a friendly way, and asks Roberto to come into her office first. Katya tells the other two salespeople to make themselves comfortable for about a half hour.

Interview with Roberto Orlando: Once inside her private office, Katya comes directly to the point and asks: "Roberto, why did you spend nearly thirty percent more in your territory this past six months than the average salesperson in our region?"

Roberto quickly responds: "Katya, the short answer is that my sales are nearly thirty percent higher than those of the average salesperson in our branch. You know as well as I do that you've got to spend money to make money. Many of my buyer groups are Hispanic-Americans, and they usually share my love for sports, so when I've got them near the closing point, I invite them to the ball park to put them in the right mood to clinch the deal. If you look at my T&E expenses, you'll see that I keep them at a fairly con-

sistent ratio to sales. I'm not spending wildly, I'm spending wisely. The company shouldn't be looking at expenses without also looking at revenues to see who's bringing in the highest profits."

Interview with Beth Esler: Again, Katya opens the conversation with a direct question: "Beth, I won't waste your time. I asked you in today to find out why your T&E expenses are running nearly twenty-five percent higher than those for the average salesperson in our region."

Beth think for a few seconds, then begins speaking very deliberately. "Katya, you know that I'm handling four of the largest accounts in our sales region, and that each of them demands a great deal of service. Unfortunately, they are located in separate corners of my territory, so I'm spending a lot of time and money traveling to each. You know that I'm not a spendthrift. If you check, you'll see that seventy-five percent of my T&E expenses go to these four accounts. I find that I need to spend a day or two with each whenever I make a sales or customer service call. Of course, they always expect me to treat them to lunch at an expensive restaurant. And if I'm staying overnight, three or four engineers and managers usually suggest going out to dinner to continue our problem solving, and I'm expected to pick up the check since I'm the one on the expense account. Katya, you know that we can't afford to lose any of these accounts, so we've got to give them tender loving care. Our competition has been knocking themselves out lately trying to steal away these 'biggies.'

"Personally, I think it might be a good idea for the national sales manager to ask the regional sales office to submit annual forecasts of T&E expenses, instead of headquarters deciding what T&E expenses should be without any input from us. They don't seem to appreciate what we're trying to accomplish out here in the field."

Interview with Jerry Derr: When Katya asks him why he is spending 28 percent more on T&E than the average salesperson in the branch, Jerry answers: "Katya, I'm running twenty percent ahead of my sales quota this year largely because I'm winning new accounts for us in my territory. My territory is filled with emerging high-tech companies that could become the next IBM, Xerox, or Apple Computer. The fastest and best way to get in on the ground floor with these new accounts is to wine and dine them so you become friends with the key decision makers. A little investment up front in entertainment may lead to a big sales and profit payoff later. And a few years down the road, who knows how great the payoff might be with some of these companies as our customers. Every day I hear people at these companies talk about technology breakthroughs they're working on that can revolutionize the telecommunications industry. Katya, we've got a potential gold mine here. We can't afford to blow it because a few bean counters at headquarters are more worried about current expenses than long-run revenue."

After listening to their explanations for their high T&E expenses, Katya realizes why these three are such good salespeople: They are really convincing. Katya ponders the alternatives to unlimited reimbursement plans. Limited reimbursement plans place a ceiling on what can be spent on a certain item, like meals or a room, or how much can be spent during a fixed period of time, like a day or a week. Another possibility is a combination reimbursement plan that combines aspects of the unlimited and limited plans. One interesting possibility is restricting reimbursement to a certain percent of sales—say, 5 percent. But that might cause the salespeople to start worrying about their ratios instead of going all-out to win profitable sales.

Questions

1. What do you think of each of the arguments used by the salespeople in defending their T&E expenses to Katya?

2. What do you think of Beth Esler's suggestion that the national sales manager ask the branch sales offices to submit annual forecasts of their T&E expenses? What are the pros and cons of using such forecasts?

3. What expense reimbursement plan would you suggest that Katya recommend to the national sales manager? How would you defend this recommendation?

Appendix A

Starting Your Professional Personal Selling Career

YOUR CAREER IN SALES

Your career choice will play a major role in determining your income, lifestyle, success, and personal happiness. For highly motivated men and women, a career beginning in professional personal selling offers exceptional benefits and advancement opportunities because job performance in sales is measured more objectively than in most fields. Some of the many benefits offered by a sales career are:

- High earnings potential.
- Job freedom and independence.
- Special perquisites like a company car, company credit card, club memberships, and incentives for superior performance.
- Opportunities to travel and entertain customers on an expense account.
- Continual job challenge and excitement.
- Tax deductions for home offices and other expenses not covered by the company.
- Opportunities to meet and interact with new and diverse people.
- Recognition within the company because top salespeople are the highly visible superstars who generate revenue for the organization.
- Fast-track opportunities for promotion all the way to the top of an organization.
- Jobs for diverse types of individuals with varied backgrounds to match up with diverse prospects and customers.
- High mobility because good salespeople are always in demand.
- Chance to contribute to a healthy, growing economy by solving people's problems and making a real difference in your company's "bottom line."
- Multiple career paths: professional selling, sales management, marketing management.

Career Path Options

There are three major career paths branching out from personal selling. You usually begin your sales career as a sales trainee for a few weeks or months. Then you become a sales representative with a territory to manage. After a few years in the field, you may be given an opportunity to make a career designation: either professional selling, sales management, or marketing management.

Professional Selling
If you choose the professional selling path, your first promotion after *sales representative* will be to *senior sales representative.* After several years in this job, you may be promoted to *master sales representative.* Top-performing master sales reps are often promoted to *national* or *key account sales representatives* with responsibility for selling to a few major customers like Du Pont, Procter & Gamble, and WalMart.

Sales Management
If you choose the sales management route, you'll probably advance through *sales representative, sales supervisor,* and *sales manager* at the branch, district, zone,

division, and regional levels. From this point, you may be promoted to *national sales manager* or even *vice president of sales.*

A close alternative to the sales management career path is the *sales management staff* route. Here you might serve as a *sales analyst, sales training manager,* or *assistant to the sales manager.* Staff people work at every organizational level, and may hold positions in sales planning, sales promotion, sales recruiting, sales analysis, or sales training. Although people in sales management staff positions have no line authority over the sales force, they may hold impressive titles such as *assistant national sales manager* and often switch over to top positions in line management.

Marketing Management

Following success in field sales, the salesperson might choose and be selected for the marketing management career path. This path often starts with promotion to *product* or *brand manager* for a product category such as Quaker Oats' Captain Crunch breakfast cereal or Pillsbury's Hungry Jack biscuits. Success in product management leads to promotion to *director of product management,* then *vice president of marketing* and maybe even *president and CEO.*

SOURCES OF SALES JOBS

Companies recruit salespeople through various internal and external sources. Among the most widely used *internal sources* are employee newsletters, bulletin board announcements, and employee referral programs, which may offer employees a "finder's fee" for recommending potential salespeople. Current salespeople and purchasing agents are especially good sources because they know what sales jobs demand and they hear about competitors' salespeople who are discontent and about to leave. Sometimes the company will make an announcement to all employees that they are looking for people interested in transferring into sales. If there aren't enough qualified or interested people among present employees, the company will use *external sources* such as newspaper advertisements, employment agencies, colleges and universities, career conferences or job fairs, and professional organizations. People interested in sales careers should make a habit of reading the daily *newspapers* covering the areas in which they would like to work. *The Wall Street Journal* is a good source of quality sales jobs across the nation and world. *Trade journals* offer information on specific types of sales jobs and often have an employment section. The *Ayer Directory of Publications* lists the trade journals for any industry that interests you. *Private employment agencies* can help find sales jobs, though some charge a fee of up to 20 percent of the applicant's first-year earnings. (For higher-caliber sales jobs, the fee is paid by the employer, not the job seeker.) Salesworld and Sales Consultants are nationwide employee agencies that specialize in finding quality salespeople.

College and university campuses are most likely to be used by large companies with sales trainee programs. Campus recruiters usually do not expect you to have sales experience. In fact, a lot of companies prefer college students who have not learned the bad selling habits that many experienced salespeople have picked up. Campus placement centers can help you set up interviews and pre-pare your resumé, and will provide facilities for meeting with company repre-sentatives. One of the most useful job-hunting booklets for graduating college students is the *College Placement Annual,* which has been published annually for decades. It lists the addresses and the persons to contact at numerous com-panies that are seeking students in different career fields, including sales. It often provides detailed information on the jobs, as well as guidance on writing a resumé and preparing for an interview.

Cooperative education programs, offered at universities like Drexel, North-eastern, and Cincinnati, obtain jobs for students in their chosen career field with one of several thousand participating companies. Students combine their course work with work in their career field of interest during two six-month co-op cycles. By working a year during the educational process, students learn what conditions are really like in their chosen career field and at the same time earn substantial money to help pay for tuition when they return to school. Students who perform well are usually offered jobs upon graduation by the company with whom they co-oped. *Sales internship programs,* offered by such companies as Procter & Gamble and Automatic Data Processing, are also gaining popularity. Although you can learn a lot in an intern program, you usually do not earn any money. *Job fairs* bring hundreds of employers and job seekers together in one location for mini-interviews and are good opportunities for students to circulate their resumés. One organizer of job fairs, Career Concepts, conducts job fairs in 11 cities and charges the participating companies a fee. *Professional associations,* such as the American Marketing Association and Sales and Marketing Executives International, encourage students to join and interact with members. Contacts made at the meetings of such associations oftentimes lead to sales jobs. The *Marketing News* is a biweekly newspaper for AMA members that reports on the marketing profession and describes job openings in a regular section called "The Marketplace."

You can learn about sales jobs from a variety of other sources, including employers, professors, friends, acquaintances, and relatives, so keep your resumé up-to-date and stay alert to all opportunities.

WHAT ARE COMPANIES LOOKING FOR IN NEW SALESPEOPLE?

Individual companies in different industries, large and small, look for diverse qualities in their sales recruits. At IBM, the personnel director notes: "We search for individuals who are intelligent, quick learners, problem solvers. We don't look for specific academic backgrounds. We've hired some music majors, because they have very logical minds."[1] Some companies like to hire college athletes because of their competitive drive and ability to work as members of a team. It seems that every company has its own idea about what makes a successful salesperson, so learn as much as you can about the type of person a particular company likes to hire before you go on an interview or even send your resumé and cover letter to that company. Clues about the type of sales candidates a

[1]William B. Mead, "The Life of a Salesman," *Money,* October 1980, pp. 117–124.

company seeks can often be found in annual reports and magazine articles about the company.

In general, successful sales candidates have the following characteristics:

Self-Motivation:
- Able to explain why they selected sales as a career path.
- Exhibit and communicate high energy levels, indicating the ability to work long and hard without discouragement.
- Have a track record of setting and achieving meaningful goals.
- Initiate action and influence events rather than being merely passive observers.
- Express thoughts and ideas clearly and directly.
- Organize thoughts logically.
- Ask insightful questions about the company.
- Listen attentively.

Interpersonal Skills:
- Interact comfortably in a friendly fashion with diverse types of people in different situations.
- Have the persuasive ability to win the confidence of others.
- Are flexible and adaptable to new situations.
- Handle rejection and disappointments without losing confidence or effectiveness.

Planning/Organizing Skills:
- Establish realistic short-run and long-run objectives.
- Prioritize tasks.
- Develop clear strategies to achieve objectives.
- Have the ability to make sound judgments and decisions based on facts.[2]

HOW WILL YOU BE SCREENED FOR A SALES JOB?

A great variety of selection tools, techniques, and procedures are used to select candidates for the sales force. Most companies use initial screening interviews, application forms, in-depth interviews, reference checks, physical examinations, and a number of tests. Application forms and job interviews tend to be most heavily used, and the majority of final hiring decisions are based on successful personal interviews—first a screening interview, then a final, in-depth interview with the sales manager to whom you will report.

Screening Interviews

The initial screening interview is the first hurdle that you will have to clear to be seriously considered for a sales job. To prepare for this initial screening, try to anticipate the questions you may be asked and mentally prepare your response to

---

[2]For more insights, see Timothy J. Trow, "The Secret to a Good Hire: Profiling," *Sales & Marketing Management,* May 1990, pp. 44–55.

TABLE A-1   Questions Often Asked in a Job Interview

- Why do you want to work for our company?
- What do you know about our company?
- Can you give me five reasons why we should hire you?
- What are your major strengths?
- What are your major weaknesses?
- What were your extracurricular activities in college?
- Where do you see yourself in five years? Ten years?
- How would your friends describe you? Are they right about you?
- What is your greatest accomplishment to date? Why?
- What is your greatest failure to date? Why?
- Why do you think you would be a good salesperson?
- Can you "sell" me something that's right here on my desk?
- What was your best subject in college? Why?
- How much do you expect to earn your first year in sales with us?
- How much do you think you'll earn in your third year? Fifth year?

each. See how you would answer the questions in Table A-1, which are typical of the questions that interviewers may ask.

Are You a Member of a Protected Group?

Women, African-Americans, Asian-Americans, Native Americans, and Spanish-surnamed people are protected under civil rights law, and any questions asked of these protected categories of people must not have the effect of limiting job opportunities for them. As illustrated in Table A-2, there are many questions that cannot legally be asked of a candidate in a job interview.

Because of employers' concerns about women becoming pregnant and taking maternity leave or having to be absent from work to care for a sick child, female applicants for sales jobs are especially likely to be asked illegal questions by interviewers. Some potential employers have been known to use sneaky means to get answers to illegal questions. For example, one sales manager admits that he usually takes female sales applicants out to a fine restaurant for dinner, then casually begins discussing his own family and how his responsibilities to

TABLE A-2   Questions Interviewers Cannot Legally Ask

SUBJECT	ILLEGAL QUESTIONS
Marital status	What is your marital status? Have you ever been divorced? Are you living with anyone? Do you plan to get married?
Children	Do you have children? Do you plan to have children or any more children? Who will take care of your children while you work?
Physical status	How much do you weigh? How tall are you?
Medical status	What is your medical history? How many days of work did you miss each year on your last job?
Military experience	What type of military discharge do you have? What branch of the military did you serve in?
Age	How old are you? (Interviewers are not even permitted to estimate your age and note it in their report.)
Home	Do you rent or own your home? Do you live in an apartment or a house? Do you have a mortgage?

them sometimes impinge on his work. In a relaxed atmosphere, this indirect approach usually causes people to open up and reveal all the information sought by the sales manager. Many women have lost job opportunities because they have talked too freely about the problems of raising children and having a career at the same time. Finally, some company interviewers will simply ask illegal questions that put women in a no-win situation. While you do not need to answer any question not related to job performance, if you refuse to answer the illegal inquiries, you risk alienating the interviewer and being turned down for the job for some contrived reason.

Rationalizing that interviewers who ask unlawful questions don't deserve to be answered truthfully, some women simply lie. A divorced mother of two children, one of whom is severely handicapped, says: "Even though I'm a very reliable worker, I knew if I told the truth, I wouldn't get the job, and I needed this job badly. So I said I wasn't married—which was true—and I had no intention of having children—which is sort of true because certainly I don't plan to have any more children. I got the job. I figured that my kids were none of their business, so it didn't matter what I told them. Once I was hired, what could they do?"[3]

Screening Tools and Tests

Selection tools and techniques are frequently used to spot very poor candidates and to identify highly qualified candidates. Most candidates, however, fall between these extremes, so the screening tools serve largely as supplements to managerial judgment in the selection process. Consultants who study salespeople, such as Boston-based McBer & Company and Charles River Consulting, can usually predict who will fail at selling, but cannot reliably predict which salesperson will do best. Nevertheless, you will probably be thoroughly analyzed, tested, and evaluated as a candidate for a sales job, especially for the larger companies.

Testing
Various tests are used by companies to increase the probability of selecting good salespeople, to reduce sales force turnover, and to increase sales productivity. Testing employees and job applicants had its heyday in the 1950s. Then companies gathered information on prospective workers through psychological profiles, employment histories, criminal records and personal data, and tests. Use of tests in the selection of salespeople was widespread until the late 1960s. Shifting values in the 1960s and 1970s brought about the federal Equal Employment Opportunity guidelines that restricted employers' use of tests unless they could show the tests were scientifically valid selection tools that didn't discriminate against specific racial or social groups. After passage of the 1964 Civil Rights Act, companies using pre-employment testing of applicants dropped from 83 percent to 25 percent because of complaints filed under Title VII of the act that tests were used to discriminate against minority groups.

Testing is not illegal if the questions and procedures used are relevant to job performance. Small and medium-sized companies are less likely to use testing because they lack the specialized experts and number of employees to substan-

[3]Arthur Eliot Berkeley, "Job Interviewers' Dirty Little Secret," *The Wall Street Journal,* March 20, 1989, p. A14.

tiate the validity of their tests. Although most sales managers rely more heavily on the personal interview than on any other tool in selecting new salespeople, you may be asked to take one or more of several basic types of tests: (1) intelligence, (2) knowledge, (3) vocational interest, (4) sales aptitude, (5) personality, (6) polygraph, (7) attitude and lifestyle, and (8) drug and AIDS tests.

Intelligence tests. Designed to measure the individual's ability to think and to be trained, intelligence tests include vocabulary, math, and logic questions. Interestingly, scoring very high on these tests may not get you the job. Some companies have found that people who score above a certain level tend to become bored on the job, while those who score below a certain level have difficulty doing the job. Intelligence tests help sort out these applicants and thereby reduce costly salesperson turnover. Some popular intelligence tests are the *Otis Self-Administering Test of Mental Ability, Thurstone Test of Mental Alertness, SRA Verbal,* and the *Wonderlic Personnel Test.*

Knowledge tests. These tests attempt to gauge how much an applicant knows about a certain market, product, service, or sales technique. Results can indicate what type and level of initial training program will be necessary.

Vocational interest tests. These tests attempt to measure how closely an applicant's interests match the interests of other people who have successfully performed the job. Interests are believed to be strong indicators of motivation, and a few firms have found relationships between interest test scores and selling success. The *Gordon Occupational Checklist, Kuder Occupational Interest Survey,* and *Strong-Campbell Interest Inventory* are examples of interest tests.

Sales aptitude tests. These tests measure an individual's innate or acquired social skills and sales ability. Numerous sales aptitude tests are available, including *Diagnostic Sales Intelligence Tests, Empathy Test, General Sales Aptitude Section of Aptitude Tests for Occupations,* and *Sales Aptitude Checklist.* All of IBM sales applicants take an Informational Processing Aptitude Test to determine if they have the ability to learn technical information.

Personality tests. These tests try to measure the behavioral attributes believed important to success in selling, such as assertiveness, initiative, and extroversion. Personality has many complex aspects, including values, social adjustment, emotional stability, temperament, and personal behavior patterns such as aggressiveness, persistence, and need for achievement. General Motors, American Cyanamid, J. C. Penney, and Westinghouse Electric use personality-assessment programs to evaluate and make promotion decisions on many current employees.

Yankee Companies, Inc., an oil-and-gas firm in Massachusetts, claims to have significantly cut its high turnover rate by using a personality-assessment test. Test takers are asked to review a list of phrases and adjectives, such as "life of the party," "sympathetic," and "aggressive," and then answer two questions: "Which of these adjectives describes how you think you are expected to act by others?" and "Which of these adjectives describes who you really are?"[4]

---

[4]"Can You Pass the Job Test?" *Newsweek,* May 5, 1986, pp. 46–53.

Personality Dynamics, Inc. (PDI), a management consulting and testing firm, believes that personality has more to do with successful selling than such factors as experience or training. PDI compares potential salespeople's answers on 179 questions like the following:

1. If the following activities paid the same compensation and carried equal status, which would you choose: (a) representing clients in court, (b) performing as a concert pianist, (c) commanding a ship, or (d) advising clients on electronic problems?
2. Among these statements, which best describes you? (a) I don't need to be the focus of attention at parties. (b) I have a better understanding of what politicians are up to than most of my associates. (c) I don't delay making decisions that are unpleasant.[5]

Personality tests are frequently given to sales applicants because many sales managers have a largely unsubstantiated belief that certain traits are important to the selling success and that they can be measured by a given test. Thus, a sales manager who thinks aggressiveness is important to sales success will select candidates who score high on the aggressiveness dimension. Various personality tests are available, including the *Adjective Checklist, Bernreuter Personality Inventory, Gordon Personal Profile, Survey of Interpersonal Values,* and the *Thurstone Temperament Schedule.*

Polygraph tests. Sometimes called the lie detector, the polygraph measures blood pressure, heartbeat, respiration, and skin response in response to questions as indicators of personal honesty. Because of concern about its validity, federal law now restricts the use of polygraph testing in all but a few situations (e.g., national security matters).

Attitude and lifestyle tests. These tests became popular in the late 1980s because of the emergence of drug abuse as a major problem in the workplace and legislation that restricted the use of polygraph tests. Their primary purpose is to assess honesty and spot drug abusers.

Drug and AIDS tests. The U.S. Chamber of Commerce estimates that drug and alcohol abuse among workers costs employers $60 billion a year in lost productivity, accidents, higher medical claims, increased absenteeism, and theft of company property to support the drug habit. Employers are increasingly likely to require job seekers and present employees to submit samples of urine or blood for analysis. The Labor Department reports that 4 million applicants and nearly 1 million workers were tested for drugs in 1988.[6] Workers are protected from surprise tests unless there is evidence of a problem or they hold jobs that pose high risks to public safety.

Because companies are afraid of wrongful discharge suits and liability for faulty products, drug tests and other types of testing are being increasingly used as a personnel management tool. A recent national survey revealed that over 50 percent of companies have adopted pre-employment drug testing programs and another 15 percent plan to do so within two years. Over one-third of companies surveyed have a targeted enforcement program with surveillance, search, and

[5]Richard Nelson, "Maybe It's Time to Take Another Look at Tests as a Sales Selection Tool?" *Journal of Personal Selling & Sales Management,* August 1987, pp. 33–38; and Sara Delano, "Improving the Odds for Hiring Success, *INC.,* June 1983.

[6]*U.S. News & World Report,* March 13, 1989, p. 52.

detection tactics to identify abusers and dealers. Estimates are that 4 to 10 percent of employees in any company have a substance-abuse problem serious enough to merit treatment, and costs for a 21-day detoxification program range from $4,000 to $14,000.[7]

Some corporations are also monitoring current employees as well as job applicants for AIDS. California has barred testing for the AIDS virus or antibody as a condition of employment, and lawsuits and union grievances are being filed to challenge such testing in the workplace.

Personal Interviews

Recruits who successfully pass screening interviews and testing go on to the most important and final hurdle in being hired—the in-depth personal interview. Table A–3 lists some of the negative factors that frequently cause candidates for sales jobs to be rejected.

SELLING YOURSELF TO A PROSPECTIVE EMPLOYER

Your personal services are the product, and you must convince prospective employers that they should buy your product over those of other potential candidates for the sales job. All the steps of the personal selling process apply: (1) prospecting for potential employers, (2) planning your approach, (3) approaching with your resumé and cover letter, (4) making your sales presentation and demonstrating your qualifications in a personal interview, (5) negotiating resistance or persuading the employer that you are the best candidate for the job, (6) confirming the agreement by enthusiastically asking for the job, and (7) following up by thanking the prospective employer for the interview and reinforcing a positive impression.

Prospecting for an Employer

After learning all about what you have to sell (your knowledge, skills, abilities, interests, motivations, and goals) and identifying the type of job you think you'd like, you might begin your personal selling process by looking at the *College Placement Annual* at your college placement office. This manual provides a variety of information about prospective employers and lists them according to the types of jobs they have available. Other sources of information about prospective employers include the annual *American Marketing Association* membership directory (company listings), the *Yellow Pages* of telephone books in cities where you'd like to live and work, and classified sections of *The Wall Street Journal* or city newspapers. Before contacting a particular company, look up its annual report and stock evaluation (in *Value Line, Standard & Poor's*, or various other sources) in your college library to learn as much as possible about the

---

[7]"Firms Debate Hard Line on Alcoholics," *The Wall Street Journal*, April 13, 1989, p. B1.

TABLE A-3 Possible Reasons for Rejecting Sales Candidates

■ Poor appearance	■ Failure to ask questions
■ Weak interpersonal skills	■ Cynical attitude
■ Lateness for interview with no excuse	■ Weak sense of humor
■ Poor application form or resumé	■ Low moral standards
■ Lack of goals or career plan	■ Radical views
■ Poor academic record	■ Intolerance or prejudice
■ No extracurricular activities	■ Evidence of wasted time
■ Inability to express self clearly	■ Poor personal hygiene
■ Insufficient enthusiasm	■ Laziness
■ Lack of confidence	■ Lack of ethics
■ Unreasonable expectations	■ Inability to accept criticism
■ Immaturity	■ Dislike of schoolwork
■ Tactlessness	■ Arrogant attitude
■ Discourteousness	■ Unhappy marriage
■ Criticism of past employers	■ Poor relationship with parents
■ Lack of vitality	■ Social ineptitude
■ Limp handshake	■ Overemphasis on money
■ Unhappy social life	■ Poor body language
■ Narrow interests	■ Failure to thank interviewers for their time
■ Evasiveness in answering questions	

company and its prospects for the future. You might also obtain a list of articles on the company from the *Business Periodicals Index* (BPI).

College Placement Office

At your college placement office, find out which companies are going to be interviewing on campus on what dates, then sign up for interviews with those companies that seem to best match your job skills and requirements. Usually, the college placement office has several books, pamphlets, or files that will give you leads on other prospective employers that may not be interviewing on campus that term. Although campus interviews are convenient, students seldom get a job without taking follow-up interviews with more senior managers at company headquarters. These headquarters interviews may take a full day or more and involve long-distance trips, so you will need to schedule your interviewing time carefully.

Job hunting can be expensive. Printing your resumé, typing cover letters, buying envelopes and stamps, making long-distance telephone calls, traveling, and a new suit or two will require a sizable outlay of money. Although most companies eventually reimburse you for all expenses incurred on a company visit, they seldom pay in advance. Reimbursement can take several weeks, so you may encounter some cash flow problems over the short run.

Employment Agencies

Although many employment agencies receive fees from employers for providing good job candidates, others charge job seekers (sometimes thousands of dollars or up to 20 percent of the first year's salary) for helping them find jobs. Make sure you fully understand the fee arrangement before signing up with an employment agency. Some employment agencies may not be worth your time and/or money because they use a programmed approach to helping you write your resume and cover letter and to prospect for potential employers. Potential employers have seen these "canned" formats and approaches so many times that your personal advertisement (your resumé and cover letter) will appear almost indistinguishable from others.

The Hidden Job Market

Nearly 90 percent of available jobs are never advertised and never reach employment agency files,[8] so creative resourcefulness often pays off in finding the best jobs. Consider every reasonable source for leads. Sometimes your professors, deans, or college administrators can give you names of contacts at companies looking for new graduates. Do not be reluctant to let other people know that you're looking for work. Classmates, friends, and business associates of your family can oftentimes be of help—if not directly, at least by serving as extra pairs of eyes and ears alert to job opportunities for you.

Planning Your Approach

After identifying potential employers looking for people with your abilities and interests, you need to prepare a *resumé* (or personal advertisement) for yourself. Your resumé should focus on your achievements to date, your educational background, your work experience, and your special abilities and interests. If you know what job you want (such as sales representative for a consumer products company), you may want to put your *job objective* near the top of your resumé. If you're not sure what job you want or want to send out the same resumé for several different jobs, then you can describe your job objective in your *cover letter.*

Some students make the mistake of merely listing their job responsibilities with different employers without indicating what they accomplished on the job. When looking for a job, students must remember that employers want people who have a *track record of achievement*. You must distinguish yourself from those who may have had the same assigned job responsibilities, but performed poorly. If you made a positive contribution on a job, say so on your resumé—in quantitative terms if you can. Examples: Reorganized office files to reduce staff searching time by nearly 20 percent; named Employee of the Month; received $500 reward for an innovative customer service suggestion; increased sales in my territory by 10 percent; received a 15 percent raise after three months on the job; promoted to assistant store manager after four months. If your work experience is minimal, consider a "skills" resumé that emphasizes your personal abilities such as organizing, programming, or leadership skills, but give supporting evidence whenever you can. Examples of various types of resumés and cover letters can be found in the *College Placement Annual* and in various other job-hunting publications that your college business reference librarian can direct you to. Figure A-1 is an example of a resumé, and Figure A-2 is an illustration of a cover letter.

There is no one correct format to use for a resumé. A little tasteful creativity can help differentiate your resumé from countless look-alikes. Most resumés of new college graduates are only one page long, but don't avoid going to a second page if you have something important to present. One student so blindly fol-

[8]Tom Jackson and Davidyne Mayless, *The Hidden Job Market* (New York: Quadrangle Books, New York Times Book Company, 1976), pp. 95–122.

Catherine James
4111 Sandy Drive
Ocean View, MD 21758
(301) 898-0000

Education

Earned B.A., with honor, in Marketing Management (June 1991). On Dean's List last three semesters.
Overall GPA = 3.4/4.0

Activities and Honors

Vice President, Beta Gamma Sigma (business administration honorary for top 10% of class); Treasurer,
Phi Omega Chi Sorority; varsity women's basketball team, 1989 – 91; advertising manager for the
Coyote Howls student newpaper. Selected to Who's Who Among American College Students, 1990 – 91.

Work Experience

Summer 1990 – Telemarketing Sales Supervisor, Gibson Kitchens, Inc. Supervised a telemarketing sales
team of seven people contacting homeowners about remodeling their kitchens. Increased sales 25% over
previous summer's record.

Summer 1989 – Assistant Sales Representative, Reynolds Whoesale Food Company. Traveled with sales
representative throughout northern Maryland territory. Set up displays, inventoried stocks, and restocked
store shelves. Received cash bonus when sales in our territory were highest in the company during June – August.

Summer 1988 – Field Salesperson, Carver Towels, Inc. Sold $18,400 worth of bathroom and kitchen
towels door-to-door in Baltimore, Maryland, area. Selected to Carver Achiever Club for meeting sales
quota three straight months.

Hobbies and Interests

Golf, tennis, jogging, and reading biographies.

FIGURE A-1 Partial Sample Resumé

lowed the one-page resumé rule that he left off his service as an army officer—a
fact that is usually viewed highly positively by prospective employers, especially if
it involved leadership responsibilities or valuable work experience.

In the cover letter, recognize that you must convince the prospective
employer to grant you an interview. Therefore, you must talk in terms of the
employer's interests, not just your own. You are answering the question: Why
should we hire you? You may need to send letters and resumés to a hundred or
more companies in order to obtain five to ten interviews, so do not be discouraged if you do not get replies from all companies or are told by many companies
that there are no job openings at present. You'll probably need only a few interviews and just one job offer to get your career started.

Review some of the publications and sources mentioned under the prospecting section above and ask your business reference librarian to show you

Catherine James
4111 Sandy Drive
Ocean View, MD 21758
(301) 898-0000

Ms. Elizabeth Burton
Sales Manager
Sampson Office Furniture Company
Philadelphia, PA 19106

Dear Ms. Burton:

For nearly thirty years, my father has been buying Sampson chairs, desks, and filing cabinets for his law office, so I know firsthand what high-quality products you sell. My career interest is in sales, and I would rather work for Sampson than any other company.

This June, I graduate from Northern Maryland State University with a B.A. in marketing management and I would like to apply for a job as a sales representative with your company. After successfully working in sales during all three of my summer jobs, I have learned that my interests and abilities are well suited for professional selling. My college course electives (Personal Selling, Sales Management, Public Speaking, Business Writing, and Public Relations) have been carefully selected with my career objective in mind. My extracurricular activities in sports and campus organizations have also helped prepare me for working with a variety of people and competitive challenges.

Will you grant me an interview so that I can show you that I'm someone you should hire for your sales team? I'll call you next Monday afternoon to arrange an appointment at your convenience.

Look forward to meeting you.

Sincerely,

Catherine James

Enclosure

FIGURE A-2 Sample Cover Letter

other sources where you can learn about the prospective employer so that you can tailor your cover letter. Remember, employers think in terms of their needs, not yours.

Making Your Approach

You can contact prospective employers by mail, telephone, or in person. A personal contact within the company who can arrange an interview for you will enable you to avoid competing head-on with the large number of other candidates looking for a job with the company.

Most students start their approach in the traditional way by mailing their resumé and cover letter to the recruiting department of the company. Unless your resumé matches a particular need at that time, it will probably be filed away for possible future reference or simply discarded. To try to get around the system, some students send their letter by express Mail or Mailgram, or address it to a key line executive (e.g.: Mr. Sanford Biers, Vice President of Marketing), with *personal* written on the envelope. They believe that bypassing the company's personnel office will increase the likelihood that their cover letter and resumé will be read by someone with authority to hire. A senior executive may forward your resumé without comment to personnel, where it might receive special attention because it came down from the top. (Who knows, maybe you're the boss's niece?) Some executives will like your chutzpah and tell personnel to schedule you for an interview, while others will resent your attempt to go outside normal channels and therefore reject you out of hand.

Making Your Sales Presentation

Your personal sales presentation takes place during the interview with the prospective employer's recruiting team. Try to make a positive impression on everyone you encounter in the company, even while waiting in the lobby for an interview. Sometimes managers ask their receptionists and secretaries for their opinions of applicants. Your friendliness, courtesy, professional demeanor, personal habits, even the magazines you choose to read while waiting, can be positives or negatives. It is less impressive to be seen reading a popular magazine like *People* or *Sports Illustrated* than something more professional such as *Business Week* or *The Wall Street Journal.*

During the interviews, do not merely respond to the interviewer's questions. Ask some sensible questions of your own to indicate that you are alert, energetic, and sincerely interested in the job. The personal interview is your opportunity to persuade the prospective employer that you should be hired. To use a show business analogy, you will be onstage for only a short time (during the personal interview), so try to present a positive (but honest) image of yourself.

Sometimes interviewers will ask you to *demonstrate* your communication abilities by writing a timed essay about your life or by selling something (such as a desk stapler) to them. Others may deliberately ask you off-the-wall or hostile questions to see how you respond. Interviewers at one Fortune 500 company routinely ask candidates for sales jobs simple math questions (What's 8% of 80?) to see whether they can think under stress. Keep cool and confident during any unorthodox interviewing approaches and you will come off well.

On aptitude and psychological tests, many experts say that it isn't very difficult to "cheat" if you are able to "play the role" and answer like the type of person that the company is looking to hire. Usually, the so-called safe approach in most personality and preference (interest) tests is to not take extreme positions on anything that is not clearly associated with the job you're applying for. However, it is probably in your long-run best interest to be honest in your responses so that you do not create unrealistic expectations that you will not be able to fulfill. It is just as important that you not create a false impression and begin your sales career with a company that isn't right for you as it is to secure employment in the first place.

Dealing with Resistance or Objections

Sometimes interviewers will bluntly ask: "Why should we hire you?" This requires you to think in terms of the employer's needs and to present your major "selling points" or customer benefits. Other interviewers may bring up reasons why you are not the ideal candidate. For example: (a) "We're really looking for someone with a little more experience." (b) "We'd like to get someone with a more technical educational background." (c) "We need someone to start work within two weeks." These kinds of statements are similar to *objections* or requests for additional information. In other words, the interviewer is saying: "Convince me that I shouldn't rule you out for this reason." To overcome such objections, you might respond to each along the following lines: (a) "I've had over a year's experience working with two different companies during my cooperative education jobs, and I've worked part-time with a third company all during college. I'm a fast learner and I've adapted well to each of the three companies, so I feel that my working experience is equivalent to that of someone who has three or four years' experience with the same company." (b) "Although I didn't choose to earn a technical undergraduate degree, I've taken several technical courses in college, including basic engineering courses, chemistry, physics, and two years of math, so I have a blend of a technical and a managerial education. I'm very confident that I can quickly learn whatever is necessary technically to do the job." (c) "Well, I do have one more term of school, so I couldn't start full-time work in two weeks, but perhaps we could work out an arrangement whereby I could work part-time during the evenings or on weekends until I graduate."

Good salespeople do not allow an objection to block a sale. Providing reasonable solutions or alternative perspectives often overcomes employer resistance and objections. At the least, it allows room for further negotiation toward a compromise solution.

Confirming the Agreement by Asking for the Job

Although it is not likely that a prospective employer will offer you a job on the spot during the job interview, you should nevertheless let the interviewer know that you definitely want the position and are confident that you will do an excellent job for the employer. You'll need to use your best judgment in deciding whether to use other closing techniques such as the *summary close* or the *standing-room-only* close. For example, with the summary close, you can summarize your strong points that match up with the company's needs, to reinforce in the interviewer's mind that you are right for the job. The standing-room-only close (where you let the prospective employer know that you have other job offers and will need to make a decision within a limited time) may be appropriate when you sense that the employer is very impressed with you and needs a little push to offer you the job now rather than interview more candidates. This puts the ball in the prospective employer's court to come up with a good offer quickly or risk losing you to another company.

In each of the stages of the personal selling process, you should be gathering feedback from the interviewer's body language and voice inflections or tone.

Following Up

Within a few days after any job interview, whether you want the job or not, business courtesy requires you to write thank-you letters to interviewers. In this thank-you letter, you can reinforce the positive impression you made in the interview and again express your strong interest in working for the company. If you don't hear from the company within a few weeks about the job, it may be appropriate to write another letter expressing your continuing interest in the job and asking for a decision so you can consider other options if necessary. As a possible reason for this follow-up letter, you might mention an additional personal achievement since the interview, more fully answer one of the interviewer's questions, or perhaps send a newspaper or magazine article of interest. A well-written, gracious follow-up letter gives you a chance to make a stronger impression on the interviewer, while at the same time exhibiting several positive personal qualities such as initiative, written communication skills, sensitivity to others' feelings, and awareness of business protocol.

YOUR EARLY SALES CAREER

Even though you may want to choose for your first job a company you will stay with throughout your working life, it is realistic to recognize that you will probably work for more than one company during your career. If you are not fully satisfied with your job or company during the first few years, remember that you are building experience and job knowledge that will increase your abilities and marketability for future job opportunities. Keep a positive outlook and do the best you can in all job assignments, and your chance for new opportunities will come. Do not be too discouraged by perceived mistakes that you may make in your career. Nearly every highly successful person has made, and continues to make, many mistakes. If you view these mistakes largely as *learning experiences*, they will not be so upsetting or damaging to your confidence. Have confidence that you can probably do whatever you make up your mind to do.

Best wishes for a successful and happy sales career!

Photo Credits

Chapter 1: page 2—Photofest; page 6—Courtesy Mrs. Otto Hagel; page 7—Courtesy Data General; page 14—Courtesy Hewlett-Packard Company; page 15—Courtesy Honeywell; page 16—top—Gregg Mancuso/Stock, Boston; bottom—Henley & Savage/The Stock Market; page 17—Jon Feingersh/The Stock Market.

Chapter 2: page 36—left—Andrew Popper/Picture Group; right—Chuck Nacke/Picture Group; page 37—Courtesy Radio Shack/Tandy Corporation; page 39—Kevin Horan/Picture Group; page 46—Sandy Clark/The Stock Market; page 47—Superstock; page 54—Michael Stuckey/Comstock; page 56—Comstock.

Chapter 3: page 70—Jonathan Kirn/Picture Group; page 73—Jose Fernandez/Woodfin Camp; page 74—Henley & Savage/The Stock Market; page 90—Griffiths/Magnum.

Chapter 4: page 101—Courtesy Oscar & Associates, Chicago; page 109—Courtesy Hewlett-Packard Company.

Chapter 5: page 125—Paul Fusco/Magnum; page 136—Roy Morsch/The Stock Market; page 138—Jeffry W. Myers/Stock, Boston; page 144—Peter Vadnai/The Stock Market.

Chapter 6: page 168—Henley & Savage/The Stock Market; page 170—Ted Horowitz/The Stock Market; page 177—Tom Tracy/The Stock Market; page 180—John M. Roberts/The Stock Market.

Chapter 7: page 204—Diana Walker/Gamma-Liaison; page 206—Steve Liss/Gamma-Liaison; page 222—The Stock Market; page 223—Superstock; page 224—Ed Bock/The Stock Market; page 225—Four By Five.

Chapter 8: page 241—Superstock; page 246—The Stock Market; page 253—R. Llewellyn/Superstock; page 259—clockwise from top left—Michael Furman/The Stock Market; Ed Bock/The Stock Market; Paul Barton/The Stock Market; Paul Steel/The Stock Market.

Chapter 9: page 273—A. McGee/FPG; page 283—Courtesy IBM; page 285—D. Luria/FPG.

Chapter 10: page 305—Comstock; page 309—Jim Pickerell/FPG; page 311—Chris Collins/The Stock Market; page 313—Roy Morsch/The Stock Market; page 320—Courtesy Fairchild Industries; page 323—Rhoda Sidney/Stock, Boston.

Chapter 11: page 340—Jim Pickerell/FPG; page 343—Michael Stuckey/Comstock; page 354—John T. Turner/FPG: page 357—Rion Rizzo/FPG; page 359—Edward L. Taylor/FPG; page 360—Tom McCarthy/The Stock Market.

Chapter 12: page 374—D. Luria/FPG Int.; page 376—Charles Feil/FPG Int.; page 385—Henley & Savage/The Stock Market; page 395—Cody/FPG.

Chapter 13: page 412—Superstock; page 418—Superstock; page 428—Howard Grey/Tony Stone Worldwide; page 436—Comstock.

Chapter 14: page 452—Andrew McKim/Masterfile; page 455—Superstock; page 459—Xerox; page 462—Four By Five; page 466—Four By Five; page 476—Sperry Corp.

Chapter 15: page 486—Walter Bibikow/The Image Bank; page 489—Superstock; page 493—Liane Enkelis/Stock, Boston; page 498—Superstock; page 502—Courtesy Hewlett-Packard Company.

Chapter 16: page 516—Henley & Savage/The Stock Market; page 523—Superstock; page 531—Jim Brown/The Stock Market; page 537—Rommel/Masterfile.

Chapter 17: page 553—Lou Jones/The Image Bank; page 563—McGee/FPG; page 569—Jeffry W. Myers/FPG.

Glossary

Absorption training A system for training salespeople in which learning materials are sent directly to the salesperson for self-study.

Adaptive selling Any selling method that stresses the adaptation of each sales presentation and demonstration to accommodate each individual prospect.

Advertising The promotion of products by an identified sponsor who purchases mass media time or space.

Affirmative action The collective attempt by public- and private-sector institutions and organizations to correct the effects of discrimination in the education or employment of women and minorities.

AIDA Attention, interest, desire, and action: a well-known "canned" selling approach that is also an effective method for selling the sales appointment.

Approach The first face-to-face contact with the prospect.

Assertiveness The degree to which a person attempts to control or dominate situations and direct the thoughts and actions of other people.

Assimilation-contrast theory Asserts that consumers have latitudes of acceptance and rejection for product performance. They will assimilate minor discrepancies but exaggerate major ones.

Assimilation theory Asserts that psychological tension arises when consumers perceive a disparity between their expectations of a product and its performance. They will resolve the tension by altering their perception of performance to better match their expectations.

Attitude A selling approach that seeks to work with prospects to identify and solve their problems and create opportunities to lower costs, increase productivity, and improve profits.

Augumented product The complete product package: the core product plus product characteristics plus supplemental benefits and services.

Baby boomers The huge generation born between 1946 and 1964.

Baby busters The much smaller generation born between 1964 and 1976.

Bandwagon A persuasive technique that encourages a prospect or customer to buy a product by implying that the product is extremely popular among other customers with similar needs and requirements.

Boomerang close Turning a prospect's objection or point of resistance around so that it becomes a reason for buying.

Business defamation Any action or utterance that slanders, libels, or disparages the product of a competitor, causing the competitor financial damage, lost customers, unemployment, or lost sales.

Business strategy In sales presentations to organizational prospects, the salesperson's explanation of how the product can profitably be used by the prospect. Also called a "business plan."

Buying center A group of buyer organization members responsible for making purchases.

Caller ID A new technology that identifies the caller's telephone number before the call is answered.

Canned selling Any highly structured or patterned selling approach.

Centers of influence Individuals or groups of people whose opinions, professional activities, and lifestyles are respected among people in the salesperson's target markets.

Close The stage in the selling process where the salesperson tries to obtain an agreement from the prospect to purchase the product.

Cold calling Approaching or telephoning a prospect without an appointment.

Collusion An illegal arrangement in which competing sellers agree to set prices, divide up markets or territories, or act to the detriment of a third competitor.

Communication A process in which information and understanding are conveyed in a two-way exchange between two or more people.

Communication style The way a person gets his or her message across to other people.

Concentration principle Most sales, costs, and profits come from a relatively small proportion of customers and products; also known as the "80-20 rule."

Consultative selling Selling through understanding and helping to solve customer problems.

Contingent close Convincing a prospect to agree to buy by showing that the product will do what the salesperson says it will do.

Cooling-off rule A rule imposed by the Federal Trade Commission that requires door-to-door salespeople to give their customers a written notice stating that a customer who makes a purchase of $25 or more may cancel the purchase within three days without loss.

Core product What the customer actually seeks in terms of a problem-solving benefit.

Cost-based procurement A buyer strategy that considers *cost* over the long run rather than only *price* in the short run.

Credit investigator Early-nineteenth-century investigator hired by manufacturers and wholesalers to collect overdue bills from customers and verify creditworthiness; often also sold goods.

Credit manager The person in the selling company who researches a customer's ability to pay and often makes the financing decision for customers who need to postpone or finance all or part of their payment.

Critical listening A type of concentrated listening in

which you attempt to analyze the ideas presented by the speaker and make critical judgments about the validity and quality of the information presented.

Cross-selling Situation in which a salesperson gets a referral to a customer from a colleague within the company.

Culture In an organization, a set of formal and informal values that establishes rules for dress, communicating, and behavior.

Customer service A concept that has five basic dimensions: reliability, tangibles, responsiveness, assurance, and empathy.

Customer service segmentation A strategy for grouping customers with similar service expectations into service segments and then developing a service plan for each segment.

Databased marketing techniques Using computers to compile and generate mailing lists and other information about prospective customers.

Demographics The readily identifiable characteristics of consumers, such as age, sex, occupation, and income.

Derived demand Demand that is created as a result of consumer demand; typical of industrial markets.

Dichotomous question A type of question used to set up a clear-cut "either-or" answer for prospects and customers.

Direct marketing Any nonstore selling to consumers, including door-to-door selling, direct mail, telemarketing, electronic mail, and selling via television, videodisc, and automatic vending.

Direct-marketing techniques Techniques for selling products directly to consumers in their homes, such as catalog marketing, automatic vending, television home-shopping channels, and electronic shopping services.

Discriminative listening A type of concentrated listening in which you listen to understand and remember. This is the type of listening most often used by salespeople.

Doing Time spent by managers on activities that subordinates can do.

Door - to - door canvassing Literally knocking on every door in a residential or commercial area to locate prospects.

Dual management Especially of nonprofit organizations, a management system in which both professional managers and specialists without managerial training run an organization, sometimes resulting in conflict.

Effectiveness Results-oriented focus on achieving selling goals.

Efficiency Cost-oriented focus on making the best possible use of the salesperson's time and efforts.

Endless chain A classic method of prospecting in which the salesperson simply asks recently satisfied customers for prospect referrals.

Entering goods Ingredients or components that become part of the finished product, such as raw materials and semimanufactured goods.

Ethics The moral code that governs individuals and societies in determining what is right and wrong.

Evaluative question A type of question used within the open-ended question format to stimulate prospects and customers to talk about their general or specific goals, problems, and needs.

Exhibit marketing Demonstration of a line of company products at a special show to which the trade and sometimes the general public are invited.

Expected outcomes The results the prospect expects from the product, *not* the results the salesperson thinks should be expected.

FAB selling approach A method of selling that first uncovers the customer's needs and wants, then presents the product's features, advantages, and benefits.

Facilitating goods Goods consumed while assisting in the ongoing production process, such as maintenance and repair items.

Follow-up Customer service provided not only after the sale is closed but throughout the selling process.

Foundation goods Goods that are used in the production process but do not become part of the finished product, such as fixed major equipment and office equipment.

Green River ordinances Widespread local ordinances first established in 1933 in Green River, Wyoming, that require nonresidents to obtain a license to sell goods and services directly to consumers in that vicinity.

Greeters and drummers Early-nineteenth-century salespeople hired by suppliers to meet and entertain retail merchants; worked on commission.

Hierarchy of needs Maslow's conceptual framework of motivation in which lower-level human needs (physiological, safety and security) must be satisfied before higher-level needs (belongingness and love, self-esteem, and self-actualization) become activated.

Industrial buyer Also called the purchasing agent; the buying expert for an organization.

Influentials People in the buyer organization who strongly influence or actually help make the buying decision.

Initial sales call reluctance A kind of sales stage fright that renders many salespeople reluctant to make the initial sales call.

Inside salespeople or telemarketers Salespeople who sell from the office by answering unsolicited inquiries and generating leads and prospects for the field sales force.

Interference In communication, anything that hinders or stops a communicative exchange. Interference may be external (like loud office equipment) or internal (like negative opinions about new products).

Invalid objections Delaying or stalling actions or hidden reasons for not buying.

Job rotation "Rotating" employees through various jobs in an organization in order to help them obtain a better understanding of the organization's products, personnel, and ways of doing business.

Key objection The customer's most important objection.

Kinesics Describes bodily gestures and movements with regard to what these gestures and movements communicate to other people.

Lead Anything that points to a potential buyer.

Leadership The ability to convince salespeople that their work has a meaningful purpose and to inspire them to extraordinary achievements.

Lifestyle The manifestation of myriad influences acting on people to form their self-concepts, perceptions, and attitudes toward life, as well as their goals as consumers.

Managing Time devoted to determining how to accomplish work through other people.

Manufacturers' agents Independent salespeople who specialize in certain markets and sell for several noncompeting manufacturers on a straight commission basis.

Market creation A sales growth strategy that calls for salespeople to sell new products to new customers.

Market development A sales growth strategy that calls for salespeople to sell current products to new customers.

Market penetration A sales growth strategy that calls for salespeople to sell larger quantities of their current products to current customers.

Marketing concept Business philosophy that holds that achieving organizational goals depends on determining the needs and wants of target markets and satisfying them more effectively than competitors.

Marketing information system (MIS) Any systematized, continuous process of gathering, analyzing, and distributing market information.

Micromarketing manager Another name for a sales representative who skillfully applies the latest professional personal selling principles and marketing techniques in his or her designated territory or market.

Motive bundling Increasing a consumer's desire to purchase a product or service by showing how one purchase will solve several problems simultaneously.

NAME An abbreviation for the process of qualifying a lead in terms of Need for the product, Authority to buy, Money to be able to buy, and overall Eligibility to buy.

National account management Any complete selling system that centralizes and coordinates a company's selling efforts, especially as these are directed at large, centralized buyer accounts.

Negative reinforcement Reinforcement that punishes a certain behavior and thus makes it unlikely that that behavior will be repeated.

Negotiation Mutual discussion and arrangement of the terms of a transaction or agreement.

Objection Anything that the prospect or customer says or does that impedes the sales negotiations.

PAS (problems and solutions) **attitude** A selling approach that seeks to work with prospects to identify and solve their problems and create opportunities to lower costs, increase productivity, and improve profits.

Perceived service quality The quality of service individual customers believe they deserve and expect to receive.

Perceived value The value of a product as seen (perceived) by the prospect.

Personal selling Interpersonal presentation of products to one or more prospective customers to develop or maintain mutually beneficial exchange relationships.

Persuasion As salespeople should understand it, persuasion is a carefully developed communication process built upon a firm foundation of mutual trust and benefit shared between buyer and seller.

Philosophy In an organization, a program or system of beliefs and attitudes passed down from the founder to successive managers.

Planning Making decisions now to bring about a desired future.

Policies Predetermined decisions for handling recurring situations efficiently and effectively.

Positive reinforcement Reinforcement that rewards a certain behavior and thus makes it likely that that behavior will be repeated.

Postpurchase dissonance Any concern on the buyer's part that he or she did not do well in the sales transaction.

Preapproach The approach planning stage of the selling process.

Prenotification A technique using an in-person cold call, a mailing, or a telephone call to send a strong signal to the prospect that the salesperson would like to schedule a sales call appointment.

Price discount Reduction off the standard list price for various reasons.

Price inelasticity of demand Demand that hardly changes with a small change in price; characteristic of industrial markets.

Probing question A type of question used to "dig" or "probe" for information when prospects and customers have difficulty articulating their precise needs.

Procedures Descriptions of the specific steps for accomplishing a task.

Product Anything that is offered to a market to satisfy customer needs and wants, including tangible products and intangible services.

Product development A sales growth strategy that calls for salespeople to sell new products to current customers.

Product quality The perceived performance of the tangible product in satisfying customer expectations.

Professional reseller manager A modern-day scientific- and information-oriented buyer for a reseller.

Promotion Typically, a one-way flow of persuasive information from a seller to a buyer; *informs* prospective buyers about the benefits of a product or service, *persuades* them to try it, and *reminds* them later of the benefits they enjoyed the last time they used it.

Prospect A lead that has been qualified as a definite potential buyer.

Proxemics Refers to the spatial relationships (positions) of people and objects.

Psychographic profile Depiction of a consumer's activities, interests, and opinions (AIOs) as measured in a survey questionnaire or personal interview.

Psychographics The activities, interests, opinions, and lifestyles of consumers.

Publicity Providing newsworthy releases of information to the mass media in order to achieve favorable communications and goodwill for an organization, a product, a service, or an idea.

Random-lead searching The generation of leads by randomly calling on households or businesses. Sometimes called "blind" searching.

Reciprocity A mutual exchange of benefits; in industrial buyer-seller relationships, an informal agreement between two or more organizations to exchange goods and services on a systematic and more or less exclusive basis.

Reference group The group to which a person looks for values, attitudes, and/or behavior.

Reliability The ability to perform the desired service dependably, accurately, and consistently; the single most important component of customer service.

Responsive behaviors Positive verbal and nonverbal feedback from the prospect.

Responsiveness The level of emotions, feelings, or sociability that a person openly displays.

ROTI (return on time invested) The designated return divided by the hours spent achieving it.

Return on investment (ROI) Refers to the amount of money expected from an investment over and above the original investment.

SAD TIE A memory-aid acronym standing for Statistics, Analogies, Demonstrations, Testimonials, Incidents, and Exhibits—one or all of which the salesperson may use to spice up a sales presentation.

Sales budget The financial plan of expenditures needed to accomplish the sales forecast and achieve other organizational goals and objectives.

Sales forecast The company's best estimate of dollar or unit sales that it will achieve during a given period under a proposed marketing plan.

Sales goals Performance standards that give the sales force broad long-run direction and general purpose.

Sales objectives Specific targets to be achieved within a designated time period.

Sales promotion A short-run incentive or inducement offered to prospective customers to stimulate sales or to enhance the distribution of a product.

Sales quota A specific sales goal assigned to a salesperson, sales region, or other subdivision of the seller organization.

Sales territory A control unit that contains customer accounts.

Scarcity principle If a product is in short supply, it is often perceived as more valuable and desirable than one that is plentiful.

Seeding Prospect-focused activities, such as mailing pertinent news articles, carried out several weeks or months before a sales call.

Selective comprehension The tendency to understand and interpret information so that it is consistent with what an individual already feels and believes.

Selective exposure The process by which a person filters information, disregarding data that are not important or of interest at the time.

Selective-lead searching The application of systematic strategies to generate leads from predetermined target markets.

Selective retention The tendency to retain in memory only that information that supports preconceived attitudes and beliefs.

Self-empowerment A term that describes the action of affirming yourself—an important daily activity for salespeople.

Self-image The combination of your own thoughts and feelings about yourself and how you believe other people think and feel about you.

Self-talk The technique of literally talking to yourself in order to help shape or reshape your attitudes and behavior.

Selling The use of persuasive communication to negotiate mutually beneficial agreements.

Selling by walking around Going around the customer's organization to meet people, understand their jobs, and develop personal relationships at all working levels in order to find out the customer's service needs and how to satisfy them.

Selling process The seven-stage process of professional personal selling, from prospecting and qualifying prospects to following up and servicing customers.

Service quality All the activities supporting the sale, from the initial contact through the postsale servicing, that meet or exceed customer expectations and enhance the value of a product.

SMIS The abbreviation for a sales management information system, which is any system that collects, sorts, and analyzes information for the development of sales strategies.

Social selling The use of personality and social skills to sell products.

Spotters People working in ordinary people-contact jobs who can help salespeople obtain leads. Sometimes also called "bird dogs."

Stakeholders An organization's publics, including employees, the media, special interest groups, suppliers, government agencies, legislators, the financial community, stockholders, and the general public.

Synthetic experience The technique of using imagined or simulated experiences, thoughts, and feelings in order to force yourself to act, think, or feel in a positive way.

Tangible product Combination of a core product and product characteristics.

Territorial routing Devising a travel plan or pattern to use when making sales calls.

Territory blitz An intensified version of door-to-door canvassing in which several salespeople join efforts to call on every household or organization in a given territory or area.

Tie-in Refers to an often illegal situation in which a seller requires a customer to purchase an unwanted product along with the desired product.

Trial close Any well-placed attempt to close the sale, which can be used early and often throughout the selling process.

Valid objections Sincere concerns that the prospect needs answered before he or she will be willing to buy.

Value added The extra benefits, from the prospect's perspective, one seller's product offerings have over those of competitors.

Value analysis Usually a printed document that shows how a product is the best value for the money.

Videoconferencing The use of video technology in such a way that people in various locations can simultaneously participate in a meeting or conference.

Videodisc An electronic shopping system that collects product information on a disk similar to an audio compact disc and allows merchants and consumers to "play back" this information in their stores and homes.

Videotex A two-way electronic home-shopping system that links consumers with the seller's computer data banks via cable or telephone lines.

Voice mail Various electronic methods of sending and receiving voice messages, ranging from a simple telephone answering machine to a complex, computer-driven "mailbox" message storage and retrieval system.

Win-win negotiations The kind of negotiation in which both parties feel satisfied with the outcome—the only kind of negotiation that professional salespeople seek!

Yankee peddler Colonial American salesman who picked up goods from English merchants and colonial manufacturers and transported them throughout the colonies for sale to settlers.

Name and Company Index

Subject Index